After the Fact

After the Fact

THE ART OF HISTORICAL DETECTION

FIFTH EDITION

James West Davidson

Mark Hamilton Lytle
Bard College

Boston   Burr Ridge, IL   Dubuque, IA   Madison, WI   New York
San Francisco   St. Louis   Bangkok   Bogotá   Caracas   Kuala Lumpur
Lisbon   London   Madrid   Mexico City   Milan   Montreal   New Delhi
Santiago   Seoul   Singapore   Sydney   Taipei   Toronto

Higher Education

After the Fact: The Art of Historical Detection
Published by McGraw-Hill, an imprint of The McGraw-Hill Companies, Inc., 1221 Avenue of the Americas, New York, NY, 10020. Copyright © 2005, 2000, 1992 by The McGraw-Hill Companies, Inc. All rights reserved. No part of this publication may be reproduced or distributed in any form or by any means, or stored in a database or retrieval system, without the prior written consent of The McGraw-Hill Companies, Inc., including, but not limited to, in any network or other electronic storage or transmission, or broadcast for distance learning.

This book is printed on acid-free paper.

4 5 6 7 8 9 0 DOC/DOC 0 9 8 7 6

ISBN: 978-0-07-281852-9
MHID: 0-07-281852-2   (Combined)

ISBN: 978-0-07-281853-6
MHID: 0-07-281853-0   (Volume I)

ISBN: 978-0-07-281854-3
MHID: 0-07-281854-9   (Volume II)

Publisher: *Lyn Uhl*
Sponsoring editor: *Steven Drummond*
Developmental editor: *Kristin Mellitt*
Marketing manager: *Katherine Bates*
Production editor: *Jennifer Chambliss*
Production supervisor: *Richard DeVitto*
Art director: *Jeanne M. Schreiber*
Art editors: *Cristin Yancey and Katherine McNab*
Designer manager: *Preston Thomas*
Interior designer: *Kathy Theis*
Cover designer: *Linda Robertson*
Photo research coordinator: *Alexandra Ambrose*
Photo researcher: *Photosearch, Inc.*
Senior supplements producer: *Angela Kao*
Compositor: *ElectraGraphics, Inc.*
Typeface: *10.5/12 Janson*
Printer and binder: *RR Donnelley-Crawfordsville*

Cover image credits:
Combined (nurse) : The J. Paul Getty Museum, Los Angeles, Accession number 84.XT.172.4. Courtesy of The J. Paul Getty Museum.
Volume I (chest) : © Pocumtuck Valley Memorial Association, Memorial Hall Museum, Deerfield MA.
Volume II (face) : © David J. & Janice L. Frent Collection/Corbis

Library of Congress Cataloging-in-Publication Data

Davidson, James West.
    After the fact : the art of historical detection / James West Davidson, Mark Hamilton Lytle.—5th ed.
       p. cm.
    Includes bibliographical references and index.
    ISBN 0-07-281852-2 (softcover)
    1. United States—Historiography—Textbooks. 2. United States—History—Textbooks. I. Lytle, Mark H. II. Title

E175.D38 2004
973—dc22   2004049955

www.mhhe.com

About the Authors

JAMES WEST DAVIDSON received his PhD from Yale University. A historian who has pursued a full-time writing career, he is the author of numerous books, among them *The Logic of Millennial Thought: Eighteenth-Century New England* and *Great Heart: The History of a Labrador Adventure* (with John Rugge). He has also collaborated with Mark Lytle (and other coauthors) on *Nation of Nations: A Narrative History of the American Republic* and is working presently on *"They Say": Ida Wells, Lynching and the Social Construction of Race*.

MARK H. LYTLE, who received his PhD from Yale University, is Professor of History and Environmental Studies and Chair of the American Studies Program at Bard College. His publications include *The Origins of the Iranian-American Alliance, 1941–1953* and *The Uncivil War: America in the Vietnam Era* (forthcoming). He is also at work on a narrative history of Rachel Carson. For the 2001–2002 and 2004–2005 academic years he held the Mary Ball Washington chair in American History at University College Dublin.

Contents

Preface

We began this book nearly a quarter century ago by asserting that history is not some inert body of knowledge "out there" in the past, but a continual act of construction whose end product is being reshaped and made anew every time someone ventures into the archives. Since the previous edition was issued, we have ventured there ourselves to provide two new chapters for *After the Fact.*

"Material Witness" (Chapter 4) looks at inert objects that cannot speak yet provide historians with a great deal of information. The material culture of the hearth and home in the early republic may seem, at first glance, merely rustic reminders of a quaint era. Yet a closer look indicates that these objects occupied a world in the midst of swift change, in which the home was coming to be viewed as a place of refinement and a domestic refuge in the midst of a burgeoning market economy.

"The Body in Question" (Chapter 17) examines evidence most of us glance at every morning in the mirror. Cultural historians have paid a great deal of attention in recent years to the human body—its display and the attitudes expressed toward it—as one significant touchstone of a culture's meaning. We begin with the diagnoses of what seems at first a narrow medical problem: young women who think they are not thin enough and young men who think they are not big enough. We then follow these cultural distortions in order to place the human body within a broader perspective, as a marker of cultural obsessions both in the late twentieth century and (in surprisingly similar circumstances) the late nineteenth.

Meantime, we owe thanks to those who helped with revisions to this edition. For reviews of this book and for comments on one or both of our new chapters, we would like to thank Jean H. Baker, Goucher College; Abel A. Bartley, University of Akron; Carol Berkin, Baruch College; Joseph E. Bisson, San Joaquin Delta College; Betty Brandon, University of South Alabama; Douglas W. Dodd, California State University–Bakersfield; Harriet E. Amos Doss, University of Alabama–Birmingham; Ted Hamilton, Columbia College; Craig Hendricks, Long Beach City College; Andrew Holman,

Bridgewater State University; Paul Knoll, University of Southern California; Karen Miller, Oakland University; Carl H. Moneyhon, University of Arkansas–Little Rock; Tom Noer, Carthage College; James H. O'Donnell III, Marietta College; John Putman, San Diego State University; Jerry Rodnitzky, University of Texas–Arlington; Eric Paul Roorda, Bellarmine University; Carolyn Sexton Roy, San Diego State University; Michael Schaller, University of Arizona; Paul S. Sutter, University of Georgia; Stephen Taylor, Macon State College; and Vincent Vinikas, University of Arkansas–Little Rock.

In addition, friends, colleagues, and kin offered their usual frank, unvarnished, and constructive advice: Michael Stoff, John Rugge, and Eleanor Davidson. Mark Lytle is particularly indebted to Professor Richard Gordon of Bard College for his guidance on the eating disorders explored in Chapter 17. Finally, as always we received staunch support from those at McGraw-Hill: our editorial team, Steve Drummond, Kristen Mellitt, and Lyn Uhl; and our production team, Alexandra Ambrose, Jennifer Chambliss, Rich DeVitto, Andrea McCarrick, Preston Thomas, and Cristin Yancey.

Introduction

This book began as an attempt to bring more life to the reading and learning of history. As practicing historians, we have been troubled by a growing disinterest in or even animosity toward the study of the past. How is it that when we and other historians have found so much that excites curiosity, other people find history irrelevant and boring? Perhaps, we thought, if lay readers and students understood better how historians go about their work—how they examine evidence, how they pose questions, and how they reach answers—history would engage them as it does us.

As often happens, it took a mundane event to focus and clarify our preoccupations. One day while working on another project, we went outside to watch a neighboring farmer cut down a large old hemlock that had become diseased. As his saw cut deeper into the tree, we joked that it had now bit into history as far back as the Depression. *"Depression?"* grunted our friend. "I thought you fellas were historians. I'm deep enough now so's Hoover wasn't even a gleam in his father's eye."

With the tree down, the three of us examined the stump. Our woodcutter surprised us with what he saw.

"Here's when my folks moved into this place," he said, pointing to a ring. "1922."

"How do you know without counting the rings?" we asked.

"Oh, *well*," he said, as if the answer were obvious. "Look at the core, here. The rings are all bunched up tight. I bet there's sixty or seventy—and all within a couple inches. Those came when the place was still forest. Then, you notice, the rings start getting fatter all of a sudden. That's when my dad cleared behind the house—in '22—and the tree started getting a lot more light. And look further out, here—see how the rings set together again for a couple years? That's from loopers."

"Loopers?" we asked cautiously.

"Sure—*loopers*. You know. The ones with only front legs and back." His hand imitated a looping, hopping crawl across the log. "Inchworms. They damn near killed the tree. That was sometime after the war—'49 or '50." As his fingers traced back and forth among the concentric circles, he spoke of other events from years gone by. Before we returned home, we had learned a good deal about past doings in the area.

Now it occurs to us that our neighbor had a pretty good knack for putting together history. The evidence of the past, like the tree rings, comes easily enough to hand. But we still need to be taught how to see it, read it, and explain it before it can be turned into a story. Even more to the point, the explanations and interpretations *behind* the story often turn out to be as interesting as the story itself. After all, the fascination in our neighbor's account came from the way he traced his tale out of those silent tree rings.

Unfortunately, most readers first encounter history in schoolbooks, and these omit the explanations and interpretations—the detective work, if you will. Textbooks, by their nature, seek to summarize knowledge. They have little space for looking at how that knowledge was gained. Yet the challenge of doing history, not just reading it, is what attracts so many historians. Couldn't some of that challenge be communicated in a concrete way? That was our first goal.

We also felt that the writing of history has suffered in recent years because some historians have been overly eager to convert their discipline into an unadulterated social science. Undeniably, history would lose much of its claim to contemporary relevance without the methods and theories it has borrowed from anthropology, psychology, political science, economics, sociology, and other fields. Indeed, such theories make an important contribution to these pages. Yet history is rooted in the narrative tradition. As much as it seeks to generalize from past events, as do the sciences, it also remains dedicated to capturing the uniqueness of a situation. When historians neglect the literary aspect of their discipline—when they forget that good history begins with a good story—they risk losing that wider audience that all great historians have addressed. They end up, sadly, talking to themselves.

Our second goal, then, was to discuss the methods of American historians in a way that would give proper due to both the humanistic and scientific sides of history. In taking this approach, we have tried to examine many of the methodologies that allow historians to unearth new evidence or to shed new light on old issues. At the same time, we selected topics that we felt were inherently interesting as stories.

Thus our book employs what might be called an apprentice approach to history rather than the synthetic approach of textbooks. A textbook strives to be comprehensive and broad. It presents its findings in as rational and programmatic a manner as possible. By contrast, apprentices learn through a much less formal process; they learn their profession from artisans who take their daily trade as it comes through the front door. A customer orders a pewter pot? Very well, the artisan proceeds to fashion the pot and in doing so shows the apprentice how to pour the mold. A client needs some engraving done? Then the apprentice receives a first lesson in etching. The apprentice method of teaching communicates a broad range of knowledge over the long run by focusing on specific situations.

So also this book. Our discussion of methods is set in the context of specific problems historians have encountered over the years. In piecing the individual stories together, we try to pause as an artisan might and point out problems of evidence, historical perspective, or logical inference. Sometimes we focus on problems that all historians must face, whatever their subjects. These problems include such matters as the selection of evidence, historical perspective, the analysis of a document, and the use of broader historical theory. In other cases, we explore problems that are not encountered by all historians but are characteristic of specific historical fields; these include the use of pictorial evidence, questions of psychohistory, problems encountered analyzing oral interviews, the value of decision-making models in political history, and so on. In each case, we have tried to provide the reader with a sense of vicarious participation—the savor of doing history as well as of reading it.

Given our approach, the ultimate success of this book can be best measured in functional terms—how well it works for the apprentices and artisans. We hope that the artisans, our fellow historians, will find the volume's implicit as well as explicit definitions of good history worth considering. In choosing our examples, we have naturally gravitated toward the work of those historians we most respect. At the same time we have drawn upon our own original research in many of the topics discussed; we hope those findings also may be of use to scholars.

As for the apprentices, we admit to being only modest proselytizers. We recognize that of all the people who read this book, only a few will go on to become professional historians. We do hope, however, that even casual readers will come to appreciate the complexity and excitement that go into the study of the past. History is not something that is simply brought out of the archives, dusted off, and displayed as "the way things really were." It is a painstaking construction, held together only with the help of assumptions, hypotheses, and inferences. Readers of history who push dutifully onward, unaware of all the backstage work, miss the essence of the discipline. They miss the opportunity to question and to judge their reading critically. Most of all, they miss the chance to learn how enjoyable it can be to go out and do a bit of digging themselves.

PROLOGUE

The Strange Death
of Silas Deane

The writing of history is one of the most familiar ways of organizing human knowledge. And yet, if familiarity has not always bred contempt, it has
at least encouraged a good deal of misunderstanding. All of us meet history
at a tender age when tales of the past easily blend with heroic myths of the
culture. In Golden Books, Abe Lincoln looms every bit as large as Paul Bun-
yan, while George Washington's cherry tree gets chopped down yearly with
almost as much ritual as St. Nick's Christmas tree goes up. Despite this long
familiarity, or perhaps because of it, most students absorb the required facts
about the past without any real conception of what history is. Even worse,
most think they do know what it is and never get around to discovering what
they missed.

"History is what happened in the past." That statement is the everyday
view of the matter. It supposes that historians must return to the past through
the surviving records and bring it back to the present to display as "what really happened." The everyday view recognizes that this task is often difficult.
But historians are said to succeed if they bring back the facts without distorting them or forcing a new perspective on them. In effect, historians are seen
as couriers between the past and present. Like all good messengers, they are
expected simply to deliver their information without adding to it.

This everyday view of history is profoundly misleading. In order to
demonstrate how it is misleading, we would like to examine in detail an
event that "happened in the past"—the death of Silas Deane. Deane does not
appear in most American history texts, and rightly so. He served as a distinctly second-rank diplomat for the United States during the years of the
American Revolution. Yet the story of Deane's death is an excellent example
of an event that cannot be understood merely by transporting it, courier-
like, to the present. In short, it illustrates the important difference between
"what happened in the past" and what history really is.

AN UNTIMELY DEATH

Silas Deane's career began with one of those rags-to-riches stories so much appreciated in American folklore. In fact, Deane might have made a lasting place for himself in the history texts, except that his career ended with an equally dramatic riches-to-rags story.

He began life as the son of a humble blacksmith in Groton, Connecticut. The blacksmith had aspirations for his boy and sent him to Yale College, where Silas was quick to take advantage of his opportunities. After studying law, Deane opened a practice near Hartford; he then continued his climb up the social ladder by marrying a well-to-do widow, whose inheritance included the business of her late husband, a merchant. Conveniently, Deane became a merchant. After his first wife died, he married the granddaughter of a former governor of Connecticut.

Not content to remain a prospering businessman, Deane entered politics. He served on Connecticut's Committee of Correspondence and later as a delegate to the first and second Continental Congresses, where he attracted the attention of prominent leaders, including Benjamin Franklin, Robert Morris, and John Jay. In 1776 Congress sent Deane to France as the first American to represent the united colonies abroad. His mission was to purchase badly needed military supplies for the Revolutionary cause. A few months later Benjamin Franklin and Arthur Lee joined him in an attempt to arrange a formal treaty of alliance with France. The American commissioners concluded the alliance in March 1778.

Deane worked hard to progress from the son of a blacksmith all the way to Minister Plenipotentiary from the United States to the Court of France. Most observers described him as ambitious: someone who thoroughly enjoyed fame, honor, and wealth. "You know his ambition—" wrote John Adams to one correspondent, "his desire of making a Fortune. . . . You also know his Art and Enterprise. Such Characters are often useful, altho always to be carefully watched and contracted, specially in such a government as ours." One man in particular suspected Deane enough to watch him: Arthur Lee, the third member of the American mission. Lee accused Deane of taking unfair advantage of his official position to make a private fortune—as much as £50,000, some said. Deane stoutly denied the accusations, and Congress engaged in a heated debate over his conduct. In 1778 it voted to recall its Minister Plenipotentiary, although none of the charges had been conclusively proved.

Deane embroiled himself in further controversy in 1781, having written friends to recommend that America sue for peace and patch up the quarrel with England. His letters were intercepted, and copies of them turned up in a New York Tory newspaper just after Cornwallis surrendered to Washington at Yorktown. For Deane, the timing could not have been worse. With American victory complete, anyone advocating that the United States rejoin Britain was considered as much a traitor as Benedict Arnold. So Deane suddenly found himself adrift. He could not return to America, for no one

"You know his ambition—his desire of making a Fortune. . . . You also know his Art and Enterprise. Such Characters are often useful, altho always to be carefully watched and contracted, specially in such a government as ours."—John Adams on Silas Deane. (Photo: Library of Congress)

would have him. Nor could he go to England without confirming his reputation as a traitor. And he could not stay in France, where he had injudiciously accused Louis XVI of aiding the Americans for purely selfish reasons. Rejected on all sides, Deane took refuge in Flanders.

The next few years of his life were spent unhappily. Without friends and with little money, he continued in Flanders until 1783, when the controversy had died down enough for him to move to England. There he lived in obscurity, took to drink, and wound up boarding at the house of an unsavory prostitute. The only friend who remained faithful to him was Edward Bancroft, another Connecticut Yankee who, as a boy, had been Deane's pupil and later his personal secretary during the Paris negotiations for the alliance.

Although Bancroft's position as a secretary seemed innocent enough, members of the Continental Congress knew that Bancroft was also acting as a spy for the Americans, using his connections in England to secure information about the British ministry's war plans. With the war concluded, Bancroft was back in London. Out of kindness, he provided Deane with living money from time to time.

Finally, Deane decided he could no longer live in London and in 1789 booked passage on a ship sailing for the United States. When Thomas Jefferson heard the news, he wrote his friend James Madison: "Silas Deane is coming over to finish his days in America, not having one *sou* to subsist on elsewhere. He is a wretched monument of the consequences of a departure from right."

The rest of the sad story could be gotten from the obituaries. Deane boarded the *Boston Packet* in mid-September, and it sailed out of London down the estuary of the Thames. A storm came up, however, and on September 19 the ship lost both its anchors and beat a course for safer shelter, where it could wait out the storm. On September 22, while walking the quarterdeck with the ship's captain, Deane suddenly "complain'd of a dizziness in his head, and an oppression at his stomach." The captain immediately put him to bed. Deane's condition worsened; twice he tried to say something, but no one was able to make out his words. A "drowsiness and insensibility continually incroached upon his faculties," and only four hours after the first signs of illness he breathed his last.

Such, in outline, was the rise and fall of the ambitious Silas Deane. The story itself seems pretty clear, although certainly people might interpret it in different ways. Thomas Jefferson thought Deane's unhappy career demonstrated "the consequences of a departure from right," whereas one English newspaper more sympathetically attributed his downfall to the mistake of "placing confidence in his [American] Compatriots, and doing them service before he had got his compensation, of which no well-bred Politician was before him ever guilty." Yet either way, the basic story remains the same—the same, that is, until the historian begins putting together a more complete account of Deane's life. Then some of the basic facts become clouded.

For example, a researcher familiar with the correspondence of Americans in Europe during 1789 would realize that a rumor had been making its way around London in the weeks following Deane's death. According to certain people, Deane had become depressed by his poverty, ill health, and low reputation, and consequently had committed suicide. John Cutting, a New England merchant and friend of Jefferson, wrote of the rumor that Deane "had predetermin'd to take a sufficient quantity of Laudanum [a form of opium] to ensure his dissolution" before the boat could sail for America. John Quincy Adams heard that "every probability" of the situation suggested Deane's death was "voluntary and self-administered." And Tom Paine, the famous pamphleteer, also reported the gossip: "Cutting told me he took poison."

At this point we face a substantial problem. Obviously, historians cannot rest content with the facts that come most easily to hand. They must search the odd corners of libraries and letter collections in order to put together a complete story. But how do historians know when their research is "complete"? How do they know to search one collection of letters rather than another? These questions point up the misconception at the heart of the everyday view of history. History is not "what happened in the past"; rather, it is *the act of selecting, analyzing, and writing about the past.* It is something that is done, that is constructed, rather than an inert body of data that lies scattered through the archives.

The distinction is important. It allows us to recognize the confusion in the question of whether a history of something is "complete." If history were merely "what happened in the past," there would never be a "complete" history of Silas Deane—or even a complete history of the last day of his life. The past holds an infinite number of facts about those last days, and they could never all be included in a historical account.

The truth is, no historian would *want* to include all the facts. Here, for example, is a list of items from the past that might form part of a history of Silas Deane. Which ones should be included?

> Deane is sent to Paris to help conclude a treaty of alliance.
> Arthur Lee accuses him of cheating his country to make a private profit.
> Deane writes letters that make him unpopular in America.
> He goes into exile and nearly starves.
> Helped out by a gentleman friend, he buys passage on a ship for America as his last chance to redeem himself.
> He takes ill and dies before the ship can leave; rumors suggest he may have committed suicide.

*   *   *

> Ben Franklin and Arthur Lee are members of the delegation to Paris.
> Edward Bancroft is Deane's private secretary and an American spy.
> Men who know Deane say he is talented but ambitious and ought to be watched.

*   *   *

> Before Deane leaves, he visits an American artist, John Trumbull.
> The *Boston Packet* is delayed for several days by a storm.
> On the last day of his life, Deane gets out of bed in the morning.
> He puts on his clothes and buckles his shoes.
> He eats breakfast.
> When he takes ill, he tries to speak twice.
> He is buried several days later.

Even this short list demonstrates the impossibility of including all the facts. For behind each one lie hundreds more. You might mention that Deane put on his clothes and ate breakfast, but consider also: What color were his clothes? When did he get up that morning? What did he have for breakfast? When did he leave the table? All these things "happened in the past," but only a comparatively small number of them can appear in a history of Silas Deane.

Readers may object that we are placing too much emphasis on this process of selection. Surely, a certain amount of good judgment will suggest which facts are important. Who needs to know what color Deane's clothes were or when he got up from the breakfast table?

Admittedly, this objection has some merit, as the list of facts about Deane demonstrates. The list is divided into three groups, roughly according to the way common sense might rank them in importance. The first group contains facts that every historian would be likely to include. The second group contains less important information, which could either be included or left out. (It might be useful, for instance, to know who Arthur Lee and Edward Bancroft were, but not essential.) The last group contains information that appears to be either too detailed or else unnecessary. Deane may have visited John Trumbull, but then he surely visited other people as well. Why include any of that? Knowing that the *Boston Packet* was delayed by a storm reveals little about Silas Deane. And readers will assume without being told that Deane rose in the morning, put on his clothes, and had breakfast.

But if common sense helps select evidence, it also produces a good deal of pedestrian history. The fact is, the straightforward account of Silas Deane we have just presented has actually managed to miss the most fascinating parts of the story.

Fortunately, one enterprising historian named Julian Boyd was not satisfied with the traditional account of the matter. He examined the known facts of Deane's career and put them together in ways that common sense had not suggested. Take, for example, two items on our list: (1) Deane was down on his luck and left in desperation for America; and (2) he visited John Trumbull. One fact is from the "important" items on the list and the other from items that seem incidental. How do they fit together?

To answer that we have to know the source of information about the visit to Trumbull's, which is the letter from John Cutting informing Jefferson of Deane's rumored suicide.

> A subscription had been made here chiefly by Americans to defray the expense of getting [Deane] out of this country. . . . Dr. Bancroft with great humanity and equal discretion undertook the management of the *man* and his *business*. Accordingly his passage was engaged, comfortable cloaths and stores for his voyage were laid in, and apparently without much reluctance he embarked. . . . I happen'd to see him a few days since at the lodging of Mr. Trumbull and thought I had never seen him look better.

We are now in a better position to see how our two items fit together. And as Julian Boyd has pointed out, they *don't* fit. According to the first, Deane was depressed, dejected, almost starving. According to the second, he had "never looked better." Alert historians begin to get nervous when they see contradictions like that, so they hunt around a little more. And Julian Boyd found, among the collection of papers published by the Connecticut and New York historical societies, that Deane had been writing letters of his own.

One went to his brother-in-law in America, who had agreed to help pay Deane's transportation over and to receive him when he arrived—something that nobody had been willing to do for years. Other letters reveal that Deane had plans for what he would do when he finally returned home. He had seen models in England of the new steam engines, which he hoped might operate gristmills in America. He had talked to friends about getting a canal built from Lake Champlain in New York to the St. Lawrence River in order to promote trade. As early as 1785 Deane had been at work drumming up support for his canal project. He had even laboriously calculated the cost of the canal's construction ("Suppose a labourer to dig and remove six feet deep and eight feet square in one day. . . . 2,933 days of labour will dig one mile in length, twenty feet wide and eight feet deep.") Obviously, Deane looked forward to a promising future.

Lastly, Deane appeared to believe that the controversy surrounding his French mission had finally abated. As he wrote an American friend,

> It is now almost ten years since I have solicited for an impartial inquiry [into the dispute over my conduct]. . . . that justice might be done to my fortune and my character. . . . You can sufficiently imagine, without my attempting to describe, what I must have suffered on every account during so long a period of anxiety and distress. I hope that it is now drawing to a close.

Other letters went to George Washington and John Jay, reiterating Deane's innocence.

All this information makes the two items on our list even more puzzling. If Deane was depressed and discouraged, why was he so enthusiastic about coming back to build canals and gristmills? If he really believed that his time of "anxiety and distress" was "drawing to a close," why did he commit suicide? Of course, Deane might have been subject to dramatic shifts in mood. Perhaps hope for the future alternated with despair about his chances for success. Perhaps a sudden fit of depression caused him to take his life.

But another piece of "unimportant" information, way down in the third group of our list, makes this hypothesis difficult to accept. After Deane's ship left London, it was delayed offshore for more than a week. Suppose Deane did decide to commit suicide by taking an overdose of laudanum. Where did he get the drug? Surely not by walking up to the ship's surgeon and asking for it. He must have purchased it in London, before he left. Yet he remained on shipboard for more than a week. If Deane bought the laudanum during a temporary "fit" of depression, why did he wait a week before taking it? And if his depression was not just a sudden fit, how do we explain the optimistic letters to America?

This close look at three apparently unrelated facts indicates that perhaps there's more to Deane's story than meets the eye. It would be well, then, to reserve judgment about our first reconstruction of Silas Deane's career and

try to find as much information about the man as possible—whether or not
it seems relevant at first. That means investigating not only Deane himself
but also his friends and associates, such as Ben Franklin, Arthur Lee, and Edward Bancroft. Since it is impossible in this prologue to look closely at all of
Deane's acquaintances, for purpose of example we will take only one: his
friend Bancroft.

SILAS DEANE'S FRIEND

Edward Bancroft was born in Westfield, Massachusetts, where his stepfather
presided over a respectable tavern, the Bunch of Grapes. Bancroft was a
clever fellow, and his father soon apprenticed him to a physician. Like many
boys before him, Edward did not fancy his position and so ran away to sea.
Unlike many boys, he managed to make the most of his situation. His ship
landed in Barbados, and there Bancroft signed on as the surgeon for a plantation in Suriname. The plantation owner, Paul Wentworth, liked the young
man and let him use his private library for study. In addition, Bancroft met
another doctor who taught him much about the area's exotic tropical plants
and animals. When Bancroft returned to New England in 1766 and continued on to London the following year, he knew enough about Suriname's
wildlife to publish a book entitled *An Essay on the Natural History of Guiana
in South America.* It was well received by knowledgeable scholars and among
other things, established that an electric eel's shock was caused by electricity, a fact not previously recognized.

A young American bright enough to publish a book at age twenty-five and to
experiment with electric eels attracted the attention of another electrical exper-
imenter then in London, Ben Franklin. Franklin befriended Bancroft and introduced him to many influential colleagues, not only learned philosophers but also
the politicians with whom Franklin worked as colonial agent for Pennsylvania.
A second trip to Suriname produced more research on plants used in making
color dyes, research so successful that Bancroft soon found himself elected to the
prestigious Royal Society of Medicine. At the same time, Franklin led Bancroft
into the political arena, both public and private. On the public side, Bancroft
published a favorable review of Thomas Jefferson's pamphlet *A Summary View
of the Rights of British America;* privately, he joined Franklin and other investors
in an attempt to gain a charter for land along the banks of the Ohio River.

Up to this point we have been able to sketch Bancroft's career without
once mentioning the name of Silas Deane. Common sense would suggest
that the information about Bancroft's early travels, his scientific studies, his
friends in Suriname, tell us little about Deane, and that the story ought to
begin with a certain letter Bancroft received from Deane in June 1776.
(Common sense is again wrong, but we must wait a little to discover why.)

The letter, which came to Bancroft in 1776, informed him that his old
friend Silas Deane was coming to France as a merchant engaged in private
business. Would Bancroft be interested in crossing over from England to
meet Deane at Calais to catch up on news for old time's sake? An invitation

like that would very likely have attracted Bancroft's curiosity. He did know Deane, who had been his teacher in 1758, but not very well. Why would Deane now write and suggest a meeting? Bancroft may have guessed the rest, or he may have known it from other contacts; in any case, he wrote his "old friend" that he would make all possible haste for Calais.

The truth of the matter, as we know, was that Deane had come to France to secure military supplies for the colonies. Franklin, who was back in Philadelphia, had suggested to Congress's Committee of Secret Correspondence that Deane contact Bancroft as a good source of information about British war plans. Bancroft could easily continue his friendship with English officials, because he did not have the reputation of being a hotheaded American patriot. So Deane met Bancroft at Calais in July, and the two concluded their arrangements. Bancroft would be Deane's "private secretary" when needed in Paris and a spy for the Americans when in England.

It turned out that Deane's arrangement worked well—perhaps a little too well. Legally, Deane was permitted to collect a commission on all the supplies he purchased for Congress, but he went beyond that. He and Bancroft used their official connections in France to conduct a highly profitable private trade of their own. Deane, for instance, sometimes sent ships from France without declaring whether they were loaded with private or public goods. Then if the ships arrived safely, he would declare that the cargo was private, his own. But if the English navy captured the goods on the high seas, he labeled it government merchandise and the public absorbed the loss.

Deane used Bancroft to take advantage of his official position in other ways. Both men speculated in the London insurance markets, which were the eighteenth-century equivalent of gambling parlors. Anyone who wished could take out "insurance" against a particular event that might happen in the future. An insurer, for example, might quote odds on the chances of France going to war with England within the year. The insured would pay whatever premium he wished, say £1,000, and if France did go to war and the odds had been five-to-one against it, the insured would receive £5,000. Wagers were made on almost any public event: which armies would win which battles, which politicians would fall from power, and even whether a particular lord would die before the year was out.

Obviously, someone who had access to inside information—someone who knew in advance, for instance, that France was going to war with England—could win a fortune. That was exactly what Bancroft and Deane decided to do. Deane was in charge of concluding the French alliance, and he knew that if he succeeded Britain would be forced to declare war on France. Bancroft hurried across to London as soon as the treaty had been concluded and took out the proper insurance before the news went public. The profits shared by the two men from this and similar ventures amounted to approximately £10,000. Like most gamblers, however, Deane also lost wagers. In the end, he netted little for his troubles.

Historians know these facts because they now have access to the papers of Deane, Bancroft, and others. Acquaintances of the two men lacked this advantage, but they suspected shady dealings anyway. Arthur Lee publicly accused Deane and Bancroft of playing the London insurance game. (Deane shot back that Lee was doing the same thing.) And the moralistic John Adams found Bancroft's conduct distasteful. Bancroft, according to Adams, was

> a meddler in stocks as well as reviews, and frequently went into the alley, and into the deepest and darkest retirements and recesses of the brokers and jobbers . . . and found amusement as well, perhaps, as profit, by listening to all the news and anecdotes, true or false, that were there whispered or more boldly pronounced. . . . This man had with him in France, a woman with whom he lives, and who by the French was called La Femme de Monsieur Bancroft. At tables he would season his foods with such enormous quantities of cayenne pepper which assisted by generous burgundy would set his tongue a running in the most licentious way both at table and after dinner.

Yet for all Bancroft's dubious habits, and for all the suspicions of men like Lee and Adams, there was one thing that almost no one at the time suspected, and that not even historians discovered until the records of certain British officials were opened to the public more than a century later. Edward Bancroft was a double agent.

At the end of July 1776, after he had arranged to be Deane's secretary, Bancroft returned to England and met with Paul Wentworth, his friend from Suriname, who was then working in London for Britain's intelligence organization. Immediately Wentworth realized how valuable Bancroft would be as a spy and introduced him to two secretaries of state. They in turn persuaded Bancroft to submit reports on the American negotiations in France. For his services, he received a lifetime pension of £200 a year—a figure the British were only too happy to pay for such good information. So quick was Bancroft's reporting that the secretaries of state knew about the American mission to France even before the United States Congress could confirm that Deane had arrived safely!

Eventually, Bancroft discovered that he could pass his information directly to the British ambassador at the French court. To do so, he wrote innocent letters on the subject of "gallantry" and signed them "B. Edwards." On the same paper would go another note written in invisible ink, to appear only when the letter was dipped in a special developer held by Lord Stormont, the British ambassador. Bancroft left his letters every Tuesday morning in a sealed bottle in a hole near the trunk of a tree on the south terrace of the Tuileries, the royal palace. Lord Stormont's secretary would put any return information near another tree on the same terrace. With this system in operation, Stormont could receive intelligence without having to wait for it to filter back from England.

Did any Americans suspect Bancroft of double-dealing? Arthur Lee once claimed he had evidence to charge Bancroft with treason, but he never produced it. In any case, Lee had a reputation for suspecting everybody of everything. Franklin, for his part, shared lodgings with Deane and Bancroft during their stays in Paris. He had reason to guess that someone close to the American mission was leaking secrets—especially when Lord Stormont and

The Tuileries, much as it appeared when Bancroft and Lord Stormont used the south terrace as a drop for their secret correspondence. The royal palace overlooks a magnificent formal garden that, as a modern observer has noted, "seems so large, so full of surprising hidden corners and unexpected stairways, that its strict ground plan—sixteen carefully spaced and shaped gardens of trees, separated by arrow-straight walks—is not immediately discernable."

the British newspapers made embarrassingly accurate accusations about French aid. The French wished to keep their assistance secret in order to avoid war with England as long as possible, but of course Franklin knew America would fare better with France fighting, so he did little to stop the leaks. "If I was sure," he remarked, "that my *valet de place* was a spy, as he probably is, I think I should not discharge him for that, if in other respects I liked him." So the French would tell Franklin he *really* ought to guard his papers more closely, and Franklin would say yes, yes, he really would have to do something about that; and the secrets continued to leak. Perhaps Franklin suspected Deane and Bancroft of playing the London insurance markets, but there is no evidence that he knew Bancroft was a double agent.

What about Deane, who was closer to Bancroft than anyone else? We have no proof that he shared the double agent's secret, but his alliance with Bancroft in other intrigues tells against him. Furthermore, one published leak pointed to a source so close to the American commissioners that Franklin began to investigate. As Julian Boyd has pointed out, Deane immediately directed suspicion toward a man he knew perfectly well was not a spy. We can only conclude he did so to help throw suspicion away from Bancroft. Very likely, if Bancroft was willing to help Deane play his games with the London insurers, Deane was willing to assist Bancroft in his game with British intelligence.

Of the two, Bancroft seems to have made out better. While Deane suffered reproach and exile for his conduct, Bancroft returned to England still respected by both the Americans and the British. Not that he had been without narrow escapes. Some of the British ministry (the king especially) did not trust him, and he once came close to being hanged for treason when his superiors rightly suspected that he had associated with John the Painter, an unbalanced fanatic who tried to set England's navy ablaze. But Bancroft left for Paris at the first opportunity, waited until the storm blew over, and returned to London at the end of the war with his lifetime pension raised to £1,000 a year. At the time of Deane's death, he was doing more of his scientific experiments, in hopes that Parliament would grant him a profitable monopoly on a new process for making dyes.

DEANE'S DEATH: A SECOND LOOK

So we finally arrive, the long way around, back where the story began: September 1789 and Deane's death. But now we have a much larger store of information out of which to construct a narrative. Since writing history involves the acts of analyzing and selecting, let us review the results of our investigation.

We know that Deane was indeed engaged in dubious private ventures, ventures Congress would have condemned as unethical. We also have reason to suspect that Deane knew Bancroft was a spy for the British. Combining that evidence with what we already know about Deane's death, we might theorize that Deane committed suicide because, underneath all his claims to innocence, he knew he was guilty as Congress charged. The additional evidence, in other words, reveals a possible new motive for Deane's suicide.

Yet this theory presents definite problems. In the first place, Deane never admitted any wrongdoing to anyone—not in all the letters he wrote, not in any of his surviving papers. That does not mean he was innocent, nor even that he believed himself innocent. But often it is easier for a person to lie to himself than to his friends. Perhaps Deane actually convinced himself that he was blameless, that he had a right to make a little extra money from his influential position, and that he did no more than anyone would in his situation. Certainly his personal papers point to that conclusion. And if Deane believed himself innocent—correctly or not—would he have any obvious motive for suicide? Furthermore, the theory does not explain the puzzle that started this investigation. If Deane felt guilty enough about his conduct to commit suicide, why did that guilt increase ten years after the fact? If he did feel suddenly guilty, why wait a week aboard ship before taking the fatal dose of laudanum? For that matter, why go up and chat with the captain when death was about to strike?

No, things still do not sit quite right, so we must question the theory. What proof do we have that Deane committed suicide? Rumors about London. Tom Paine heard it from Cutting, the merchant. And Cutting reports in his letter to Jefferson that Deane's suicide was "the suspicion of Dr. Bancroft." How do we know the circumstances of Deane's death? The captain made a report, but for some reason it was not preserved. The one account that did survive was written by Bancroft, at the request of a friend. Then there were the anonymous obituaries in the newspapers. Who wrote them? Very likely Bancroft composed at least one; certainly, he was known as Silas Deane's closest friend and would have been consulted by any interested parties. There are a lot of strings here, which, when pulled hard enough, all run back to the affable Dr. Bancroft. What do we know about *his* situation in 1789?

We know Bancroft is dependent on a pension of £1,000 a year, given him for his faithful service as a British spy. We know he is hoping Parliament will grant him a monopoly for making color dyes. Suddenly his old associate Deane, who has been leading a dissolute life in London, decides to return to America, vindicate himself to his former friends, and start a new life. Put yourself in Bancroft's place. Would you be just a little nervous about that idea? Here is a man down on his luck, now picking up and going to America to clear his reputation. What would Deane do to clear it? Tell everything he knew about his life in Paris? Submit his record books to Congress, as he had been asked to do so many years before? If Deane knew Bancroft was a double agent, would he say so? And if Deane's records mentioned the affair of John the Painter (as indeed they did), what would happen if knowledge of Bancroft's role in the plot reached England? Ten years earlier, Bancroft would have been hanged. True, the angry feelings of the war had faded, but even if he were spared death, would Parliament grant a monopoly on color dyes to a known traitor? Would Parliament continue the £1,000 pension? It was one thing to have Deane living in London, where Bancroft could watch him; it would be quite another to have him all the way across the Atlantic Ocean, ready to tell—who knows what?

Admit it: if you were Bancroft, wouldn't you be just a little nervous?

We are forced to consider, however reluctantly, that Deane was not expecting to die as he walked the deck of the *Boston Packet*. Yet if Bancroft did murder Deane, how? He was not aboard ship when death came and had not seen Deane for more than a week. That is a good alibi, but then, Bancroft was a clever man. We know (once again from the letters of John Cutting) that Bancroft was the person who "with great humanity and equal discretion undertook the management of the *man* and [the] *business*" of getting Deane ready to leave for America. Bancroft himself wrote Jefferson that he had

* As the Author has brought a confiderable quantity of this Poifon to *England*, any Gentleman,
whofe genius may incline him to profecute thefe
experiments, and whofe character will warrant us
to confide in his hands a preparation, capable of
perpetrating the moft fecret and fatal villainy, may
be fupplied with a fufficient quantity of the *Woorara*, by applying to Mr. *Becket*, in the *Strand*.

An excerpt from *An Essay on the Natural History of Guiana in South America* by Edward Bancroft (Library of Congress)

been visiting Deane often "to assist him with advice, medicins, and money for his subsistence." If Deane were a laudanum addict, as Bancroft hinted to Cutting, might not the good doctor who helped with "medicins" also have procured the laudanum? And having done that, might he not easily slip some other deadly chemical into the mixture, knowing full well that Deane would not use it until he was on shipboard and safely off to America? That conclusion is only conjecture. We have no direct evidence to suggest that this scenario is what really happened.

But we do know one other fact for sure; and in light of our latest theory, it is an interesting one. Undeniably, Edward Bancroft was an expert on poisons.

He did not advertise that knowledge, of course; few people in London at the time of Deane's death would have been likely to remember the fact. But twenty years earlier, the historian may recall, Bancroft wrote a book on the natural history of Guiana. At that time he not only investigated electric eels and color dyes, but also the poisons of the area, particularly curare (or "Woorara" as Bancroft called it). He investigated it so well, in fact, that when he returned to England he brought samples of curare with him, which (he announced in the book) he had deposited with the publishers so that any gentleman of "unimpeachable" character might use the samples for scientific study.

Furthermore, Bancroft seemed to be a remarkably good observer not only of the poisons, but also of those who used them. His book described in ample detail the natives' ability to prepare poisons that,

> given in the smallest quantities, produce a very slow but inevitable death, particularly a composition which resembles wheat-flour, which they sometimes use to revenge past injuries, that have been long neglected, and are thought forgotten. On these occasions they always feign an insensibility of the injury which they intend to revenge, and even repay it with services and acts of friendship, until they have destroyed all distrust and apprehension of danger in the destined victim of the vengeance. When this is effected, they meet at some festival, and engage him to drink with them, drinking first themselves to obviate suspicion, and afterwards secretly dropping the poison, ready concealed under their nails, which are usually long, into the drink.

Twenty years later Bancroft was busy at work with the color dyes he had brought back from Suriname. Had he, by any chance, also held onto any of those poisons?

Unless new evidence comes to light, we will probably never know for sure. Historians are generally forced to deal with probabilities, not certainties, and we leave you to draw your own conclusions about the death of Silas Deane.

What does seem certain is that whatever "really happened" to Deane two hundred years ago cannot be determined today without the active participation of the historian. Being courier to the past is not enough. For better or worse, historians inescapably leave an imprint as they go about their business: asking interesting questions about apparently dull facts, seeing connections between subjects that had not seemed related before, shifting and rearranging evidence until it assumes a coherent pattern. The past is not history, only the raw material of it. How those raw materials come to be fashioned and shaped is the central concern of this book.

Additional Reading

The historian responsible for the detective work exposing the possibility of foul play on the *Boston Packet* is Julian Boyd. He makes his case, in much greater detail than can be summarized here, in a series of three articles titled "Silas Deane: Death by a Kindly Teacher of Treason?" *William and Mary Quarterly*, 3d ser., 16 (1959): 165–187, 319–342, and 515–550. For additional background on Silas Deane, see the entry in the *Dictionary of American Biography* (New York, 1946). (The DAB, incidentally, is a good starting point for historians who seek biographical details of American figures. It provides short sketches as well as further bibliographical references.) For details on additional intrigue surrounding the American mission to France, see Samuel F. Bemis, "The British Secret Service and the French-American Alliance," *American Historical Review* 29 (1923–1924): 474–495.

Interested readers who wish to examine some of the primary documents in the case may do so easily enough. Much of Deane's correspondence is available in *The Deane Papers*, published as part of the New-York Historical Society's *Collections* 19–23 (New York, 1887–1891) and in *The Deane Papers: Correspondence between Silas Deane, His Brothers . . . 1771–1795*, Connecticut Historical Society *Collections* 23 (Hartford, CT, 1930). These volumes shed helpful light on Deane's state of mind during his London years. The London obituary notices are reprinted in the *American Mercury* (Hartford, CT, 28 December 1789), the *Gazette of the United States* (Philadelphia, PA, 12 December 1789), and other newspapers in New York and Boston. See also the *Gentleman's Magazine* of London 59, pt. 2 (September 1789): 866.

American colonial newspapers are available in many libraries on microprint, published by the Readex Microprint Corporation in conjunction with the American Antiquarian Society.

Edward Bancroft's role as double agent was not established conclusively until the private papers of William Eden (Lord Auckland) were made public in the 1890s. As director of the British Secret Service during the Revolution, Eden and his right-hand man, Paul Wentworth, were in close touch with Bancroft. The details of the Bancroft-Wentworth-Eden connection are spelled out in Paul L. Ford, *Edward Bancroft's Narrative of the Objects and Proceedings of Silas Deane* (Brooklyn, NY, 1891). Further information on Bancroft may be found in Sir Arthur S. MacNalty, "Edward Bancroft, M.D., F.R.S. and the War of American Independence," Royal Society of Medicine *Proceedings* 38 (1944): 7–15. The Historical Society of Pennsylvania, in Philadelphia, has a collection of Bancroft's papers. And further background may be gained, of course, from the good doctor's own writings, chief among them the lively *Essay on the Natural History of Guiana in South America* (London, 1769).

We have pointed out that no evidence in the historical record conclusively links Edward Bancroft with Silas Deane's death. In an eminently fair-minded manner, we left you to draw your own conclusions. Yet as the lesson of this chapter makes clear, every historical narrative is bound to select facts in shaping its story—including this narrative. Given our limitations of space, we chose to concentrate on the evidence and arguments that illuminated Boyd's hypothesis most forcibly. So we suspect that most readers, if left to draw their "own" conclusions, will tend to find Bancroft guilty as charged.

Boyd's case strikes us as impressive too, but it certainly can be questioned. How sound, for instance, is the hypothesis about Deane's depression (or lack of it)? Many people who have contemplated suicide, it could be argued, do so over an extended period of time, and their moods of depression may alternate with happier periods. Perhaps Deane toyed with the idea, put it away, then returned to it in the gloomy confines of the *Boston Packet*. If Deane were a laudanum addict and had a large quantity of the drug on hand, might he not easily take an overdose during a sudden return of severe depression? For that matter, if he were a careless addict, might he not have taken an *accidental* overdose?

In another area, William Stinchcombe has suggested that, contrary to Julian Boyd's suggestion, Deane did not face any really hopeful prospects for success in America. If Deane continued to be destitute and down on his luck when he departed for America, then the suicide theory again becomes more probable. Stinchcombe's article, "A Note on Silas Deane's Death," may be found in the *William and Mary Quarterly*, 3d ser., 32 (1975): 619–624.

We can also report with pleasure that the first edition of this book sparked an interesting counter to Boyd's thesis. Dr. Guido Gianfranceschi, a surgeon from Danbury, Connecticut, read our prologue in a course on historical methods he was taking at Western Connecticut State College. He points out that a check of the standard medical reference *Goodman and Gilman's Phar-*

macological Basis of Therapeutics, 6th ed., (New York, 1980) reveals that Deane was not likely done in by curare. Though quite toxic when entering the bloodstream, curare is "poorly and irregularly absorbed from the gastrointestinal tract. d-Tubocurarine is inactive after oral administration, unless huge doses are ingested; this fact was well known to the South American Indians, who ate with impunity the flesh of game killed with curare-poisoned arrows." (It was also known to Bancroft, who notes in his own work that, "when received by the alimentary passage," the poison "is subdued by the action of the digestive organs.")

Of course, curare was only one of many poisons Bancroft learned about from the natives of Guiana. "I have spent many days in a dangerous and almost fruitless endeavor to investigate the nature and quantities of these plants," he reported in 1769, "and by handling, smelling, tasting, etc. I have frequently found, at different times, almost all the several senses, and their organs either disordered or violently affected." Could it have been another one of those deadly substances that Deane ingested? Perhaps. Boyd makes no guess what the poison might have been. But while Bancroft indicated he had brought home snake specimens, curare is the only poison he specifically mentions having in London. Furthermore, Gianfranceschi points out that the symptoms of opium overdose are similar to those Deane is said to have experienced prior to his death. Finally, for a third opinion, consult D. K. Anderson and G. T. Anderson, "The Death of Silas Deane," *New England Quarterly* 62 (1984): 98–105. The Andersons surveyed several medical authorities and concluded that Deane may well have suffered from chronic tuberculosis and died from a stroke or some other acute attack.

Murder, suicide, stroke, or accidental overdose? We eagerly await new evidence that our readers may turn up.

Interactive Learning

The *Primary Source Investigator* CD-ROM that comes with this book provides sources to explore the case of the "strange death of Silas Deane," an American patriot wrongly accused of treason. Correspondence between Deane and his family members, his cohorts, and the Congress illustrate Deane's unending quest to exonerate himself from the accusations against him. Correspondence between his supporters and detractors provides a variety of perspectives on the ways in which Deane was perceived by those around him.

CHAPTER 1
Serving Time in Virginia

As has become clear, the historian's simple act of selection irrevocably separates "history" from "the past." The reconstruction of an event is clearly different from the event itself. Yet selection is only one in a series of interpretive acts that historians perform as they proceed about their business. Even during the preliminary stages of research, when the historian is still gathering information, interpretation and analysis are necessary. That is because the significance of any piece of evidence is seldom apparent at first glance. The historian quickly learns that the words *evidence* and *evident* rarely amount to the same thing.

For historians attempting to reconstruct an accurate picture of the first English settlements in Virginia, the difficulty of taking any document at face value becomes quickly apparent. The early Virginians were, by and large, an enterprising lot. They gave America its first representative assembly, gave England a new and fashionable vice (tobacco), and helped establish slavery as a labor system in North America. These actions raise perplexing and important questions for historians, and yet the answers to them cannot be found in the surviving source materials without a good deal of work.

The difficulty does not arise entirely from lack of information. Indeed, some Virginians were enterprising enough to write history as well as make it, not the least of them being Captain John Smith. Smith wrote an account of the young colony entitled *A Generall Historie of Virginia*, published in 1624. Much of his history is based on eyewitness, firsthand knowledge. At the vigorous age of twenty-seven, he joined the expedition to Virginia in 1606 sent by the Virginia Company of London and played a crucial role in directing the affairs of the inexperienced Jamestown colony.

Yet Smith's evidence cannot be accepted without making some basic interpretive judgments. Simplest and most obvious—is he telling the truth? If we are to believe his own accounts, the young captain led a remarkably swashbuckling life. Before joining the Virginia expedition, he had plunged as a soldier of fortune into a string of complicated intrigues in central

Europe. There he waged desperate and brave warfare on behalf of the Hungarian nobility before being taken prisoner by the Turks. Once a prisoner, he was made a slave to a young but "noble Gentlewoman" with the romantic name of Charatza Tragabigzanda. The smitten princess "tooke (as it seemed) much compassion" on Smith. But alas, he came under the control of her sadistic brother, who reviled and taunted the captain so much that Smith lost his temper one day in the granary and "beat out [his] braines with his threshing bat" and made a daring escape, reaching England in time to sign on with the Virginia Company's expedition.

In Virginia the adventures came nearly as thick and fast. While the colony's governing council quarreled at Jamestown, Smith went off on an exploring and food-gathering mission. He established the first European contact with many of the Indian tribes around Chesapeake Bay, succeeded in buying needed corn from them, and was captured by a party of Indians loyal to Powhatan, the principal chief in the Chesapeake region. With Smith facing execution, once again he managed to win the affections of a beautiful princess—this one, Powhatan's young daughter Pocahontas.

How much of this romantic adventure story do we believe? The tone of Captain Smith's narrative makes it reasonably apparent that he was not the sort of man to hide his light under a bushel. (In writing of his adventures, he compared himself implicitly with Julius Caesar, "who wrote his owne Commentaries, holding it no less honour to write, than fight.") Indeed, several nineteenth-century scholars, including Henry Adams, challenged Smith's account of his Indian rescue as mere embellishment. Adams pointed out that the Pocahontas story did not appear in Smith's earliest published descriptions of the Virginia colony. Only in 1624, when the *Generall Historie* was issued, did the public first read of the Indian maiden's timely devotion. Smith probably invented the story out of whole cloth, Adams argued, in order to enhance his reputation.

We can, of course, look for independent evidence that would corroborate Smith's claims, but in the case of the Pocahontas story, no independent records survive. Yet other historians have defended Smith, Philip Barbour prime among them. Barbour has checked Smith's tales against available records in both Hungary and England and found them generally accurate as to names, places, and dates. Smith claimed, for example, that he used an ingenious system of torch signals to coordinate a nighttime attack by his Hungarian friends, "Lord Ebersbaught" and "Baron Kisell." No other records mention Smith's role, but we do know such an attack was launched—and that it was led by two Hungarians named Sigismund Eibiswald and Jakob Khissl. Similarly, although the records show no princess named Charatza Tragabigzanda, that may have been Smith's fractured pronunciation of the Greek *koritsi* (girl) *Trapedzoûndos* (from Trebizond). Possibly, when he tried to discover the identity of his new mistress, someone merely replied that she was *koritsi Trapedzoûndos*—a "girl from Trebizond."

Yet even if we grant Smith the virtue of honesty, significant problems remain when using his account, problems common to all historical evidence.

To say that Smith is truthful is only to say that he reported events *as he saw them.* The qualification is not small. Like every observer, Smith viewed events from his own perspective. When he set out to describe the customs of the Chesapeake Indians, for instance, he did so as a seventeenth-century Englishman. Behind each observation he made stood a whole constellation of presuppositions, attitudes, and opinions that he took for granted without ever mentioning them. His descriptions were necessarily limited by the experience and education—or lack of it—that he brought with him.

The seriousness of these limitations becomes clearer if we take a hypothetical example of what might happen if Captain Smith were to set down a history, not of Indian tribal customs, but of a baseball game between the Boston Red Sox and the New York Yankees:

> Not long after, they tooke me to one of their great Counsells, where many of the generalitie were gathered in greater number than ever I had seen before. And they being assembled about a great field of open grass, a score of their greatest men ran out upon the field, adorned each in brightly hued jackets and breeches, with letters cunningly woven upon their Chestes, and wearinge uppon their heades caps of a deep navy blue, with billes, of a sort I know not what. One of their chiefs stood in the midst and would at his pleasure hurl a white ball at another chief, whose attire was of a different colour, and whether by chance or artyfice I know not the ball flew exceeding close to the man yet never injured him, but sometimes he would strike att it with a wooden club and so giveing it a hard blow would throw down his club and run away. Such actions proceeded in like manner at length too tedious to mention, but the generalitie waxed wroth, with greate groaning and shoutinge, and seemed withall much pleased.

Before concluding any more than that Smith would make a terrible writer for the *New York Post* (we don't even know if the Yankees won!), compare the description of the baseball game with the account by the real Smith of what happened to him after his capture. (Smith writes in the third person, referring to himself as "he" and "Captain Smith.")

> At last they brought him to Meronocomoco, where was Powhatan their Emperor. . . . Before a fire upon a seat like a bedsted, [Powhatan] sat covered with a great robe, made of Rarowcun skinnes, and all the tayles hanging by. On either hand did sit a young wench of 16 or 18 yeares, and along on each side the house, two rowes of men, and behind them as many women, with all their heads and shoulders painted red; many of their heads bedecked with the white down of Birds; but every one with something: and a great chayne of white beads about their necks. At his entrance before the King, all the people gave a great shout. The Queene of Appamatuck was appointed to bring him water to wash his hands, and another brought him a bunch of feathers, in stead of a Towell to dry them. Having feasted him after their best barbarous manner they could, a long consultation was held, but the conclusion was, two great stones were brought before Powhatan. Then as many as could layd hands on

The Country wee now call Virginia beginneth at Cape Henry distant from Roanoack 60 miles, where was S.r Walter Raleigh's plantation: and because the people differ very little from them of Powhatan in any thing, I have inserted those figures in this place because of the conveniency.

King Powhatan comands C. Smith to be slaine, his daughter Pokahontas beggs his life his thankfullnes and how he subieeted 39 of their kings, reade y historie

printed by Iames Reeve

"And being ready with their clubs, to beat out his braines, Pocahontas the Kings dearest daughter . . . got his head in her armes, and laid her owne upon his to save him from death." The tale has been passed down as a romantic rescue, but from Powhatan's point of view, was this event an adoption ceremony designed to cement a political alliance?

him, dragged him to them, and thereon laid his head, and being ready with their clubs, to beat out his braines, Pocahontas the Kings dearest daughter, when no intreaty could prevaile, got his head in her armes, and laid her owne upon his to save him from death: whereat the Emperour was contented he should live to make him hatchets, and her bells, beads, and copper.

If we had not first read the account of the baseball game, it would not be nearly as obvious just how little Smith has told us about what is going on here. Indeed, anyone who reads the *Generall Historie* or any of the captain's writings will be impressed by their freshness and the wealth of detail. But that is because we, like Smith, are unfamiliar with the rituals of the seventeenth-century Chesapeake Indians. Quite naturally—almost instinctively—we adopt Smith's point of view as our own. And that point of view diverts us from asking questions to which Smith does not have the answer. What, after all, is the reason the Indians painted their heads and shoulders red and wore white down on their heads? We know no more than we did about baseball players who were described as wearing bright outfits with letters woven upon their chests.

Even more to the point, consider the *form* of Smith's narrative as it has been passed down to us over the years. The good captain is about to die until he is suddenly rescued at the last moment by "the Kings dearest daughter." Does the story have a familiar ring? Indeed—there is at least half an echo of Smith's being pitied by Princess Tragabigzanda. Equally important, the story has become prominent in our folklore because the romantic traditions of the nineteenth century delighted in such tales: a pure and noble-born woman saves the life of a brave commoner. Smith tells a story that fits a narrative pattern we love to hear.

But what if we lay aside the narrative perspective of Smith's story and consider the same facts from the point of view of Powhatan? Powhatan was the leader of a confederacy of Algonquian Indians living around Chesapeake Bay. He was, in short, the most powerful person in the region. But his control over the lesser chiefs in the area varied. Some tribal groups resisted paying tribute to him; others at a greater distance showed no allegiance and were indeed rivals.

Into this situation stepped Smith, along with the strange new tribe of white people who had just arrived from across the salt water. In hindsight, we see the arrival of Europeans as a momentous event that changed North America radically. But from Powhatan's point of view, here was simply another new group of people—strange indeed, but human beings nonetheless—whom he would have to set into the balance of his own political equation. Should he treat the newcomers as allies or enemies? Some historians and anthropologists have suggested that Powhatan's behavior toward Smith was in fact a kind of ritualized adoption ceremony and that Smith's supposed execution was a kind of initiation rite in which the captain was being ritually humiliated and subordinated. Once Smith passed the test of bravery in the face of apparent death, Powhatan was willing to adopt him as a vassal. As Smith himself puts it, Powhatan decides his prisoner can make hatchets for him and bells and beads for Pocahontas.

Powhatan's later actions also suggest that he now considered Smith a chief, or *werowance*, over this new tribe of English allies. At the end of a ceremony two days later, the chief told Smith "now they were friends" and that Smith should go to Jamestown and send back "two great gunnes, and a gryndstone"—just as other Indian allies supplied Powhatan with tribute. In return, Powhatan would give Smith land and treat him "as his sonne."

This interpretation of Smith's capture and adoption must remain speculative, but it is responsible speculation, informed by historical and anthropological study of the ways of Algonquian Indians. And we would have been blind to the interpretation without having separated Smith's *useful* information from the narrative perspective in which it came to us.

It is easy enough to see how a point of view is embedded in the facts of an eloquent narration. But consider for a moment evidence recorded by one of the pedestrian clerks whose jottings constitute the great bulk of history's raw material. The following excerpts are taken from the records of Virginia's general assembly and the proclamations of the governor:

> We will and require you, Mr. Abraham Persey, Cape Marchant, from this daye forwarde to take notice, that . . . you are bounde to accepte of the Tobacco of the Colony, either for commodities or upon billes, at three shillings the beste and the second sorte at 18d the punde, and this shalbe your sufficient dischardge.

> Every man to sett two acres corn (Except Tradesmen following their trades) penalty forfeiture of corn & Tobacco & be a Slave a year to the Colony. No man to take hay to sweat Tobacco because it robs the poor beasts of their fodder and sweating Tobacco does it little good as found by Experience.

In contrast to Smith's descriptions, these excerpts present small bits of information dependent on a great deal of assumed knowledge. Whereas Smith attempted to describe the Indian ceremony in some detail because it was new to him, Virginia's general assembly knows all too much about tobacco prices and the planting of corn. Policy is stated without any explanation, just as the box score in the paper lists the single line, "Yankees 10, Red Sox 3." In each case the notations are so terse, the "narratives" so brief, that the novice historian is likely to assume they contain no point of view at all, only the bare facts. But the truth is, each statement has a definite point of view that can be summed up as simple questions: (1) Did the Yankees win and if so by how much? (2) Should the price of tobacco be three shillings or eighteen pence or how much? (3) What should colonists use hay for? And so on. These viewpoints are so obvious, they would not bear mentioning—except that, unconsciously, we are led to accept them as the only way to think about the facts. Because the obvious perspective often appears irrelevant, we tend to reject the information as not worth our attention.

But suppose a fact is stripped of its point of view—suppose we ask, in effect, a completely different question of it? Historians looking back on twentieth-century America would undoubtedly learn little from baseball box scores, but at least by comparing the standings of the 1950s with those of the 1970s, they would soon discover that the Giants of New York had become the Giants of San Francisco and that the Brooklyn Dodgers had moved to Los Angeles. If they knew a bit more about the economic implications of major league baseball franchises, they could infer a relative improvement in the economic and cultural status of the West Coast. Similarly, by refusing to accept the evidence of tobacco prices or corn planting at its face value, historians might make inferences about economic and cultural conditions in seventeenth-century Virginia.

In adopting a perspective different from any held by the historical participants, we are employing one of the most basic tactics of sociology. Sociologists have long recognized that every society functions, in part, through structures and devices that remain unperceived by its members. "To live in society means to exist under the domination of society's logic," notes sociologist Peter Berger. "Very often men act by this logic without knowing it. To discover this inner dynamic of society, therefore, the sociologist must frequently disregard the answers that the social actors themselves would give to his questions and look for explanations that are hidden from their own awareness."

Using that approach, historians have taken documents from colonial Virginia, stripped them of their original perspectives, and reconstructed a striking picture of Virginia society. Their research reveals that life in the young colony was more volatile, acquisitive, rowdy, raw—and deadly—than most traditional accounts have assumed. Between the high ideals of the colony's London investors and the disembarkation points along the Chesapeake, something went wrong. The society that was designed to be a productive and diversified settlement in the wilderness soon developed into a world in which the single-minded pursuit of one crop—tobacco—made life nasty, brutish, and short. And the colony that had hoped to pattern itself on the free and enlightened customs of England instead found itself establishing something that the government of England had never thought to introduce at home: the institution of human slavery.

A COLONY ON THE EDGE OF RUIN

None of the English colonial ventures found it easy to establish successful settlements along the Atlantic coast, but for the Virginia colony, the going was particularly rough. In the first ten years of the colony's existence, £75,000 had been invested to send around 2,000 settlers across the ocean to what Captain Smith described as a "fruitfull and delightsome land" where "heaven and earth never agreed better to frame a place for mans habitation." Yet at the end of that time, the attempt to colonize Virginia could be judged nothing less than an unqualified disaster.

Certainly, most members of the Virginia Company viewed it that way. In 1606 King James had granted a charter to a group of London merchants who became formally known as "The Treasurer and Company of Adventurers and Planters of the City of London for the First Colony in Virginia." The Virginia Company, as it was more commonly called, allowed merchants and gentlemen of quality to "adventure" money in a joint stock arrangement, pooling their resources to support an expedition to Virginia. The expedition would plant a colony and extract the riches of the new country, such as gold or iron, and also begin cultivating crops that would yield a high return, such as grapes for the production of wine or mulberry trees for the production of silk. King James, a silkworm buff, even donated some of his own specially bred worms. The proceeds would repay the company's expenses, the investors (or "adventurers") would reap handsome profits, the colonists themselves would prosper, and England would gain a strategic foothold in the Americas. So the theory went.

The reality ran rather differently. After four difficult months at sea, only 105 of the original 144 settlers reached Chesapeake Bay in April of 1607. The site chosen at Jamestown for a fort was swampy, its water unhealthy, and the Indians less than friendly. By the end of the first hot and humid summer, 46 more settlers had perished. When the first supply ship delivered 120 new recruits the following January, it found only 38 men still alive.

The company correctly blamed part of the failure on the colony's original system of government. A president led a council of 13 men, but in name only. Council members refused to take direction and continually bickered among themselves. In 1609 the company obtained a new charter providing for centralized control in a governor, but when it sent another 600 settlers across, the results were even worse. Because a hurricane scattered the fleet on its way over, only 400 settlers arrived, leaderless, in September of 1609. Captain Smith, the one old hand who had acted decisively to pull the colony together, was sent packing on the first ship home, and as winter approached, the bickering began anew.

Nobody, it seemed, had planted enough corn to last through the winter. Settlers preferred to barter, bully, or steal supplies from the Indians. And the Indians knew that the English depended on them—knew that they could starve out the newcomers simply by moving away. When several soldiers stole off to seek food from the natives, the other settlers discovered their comrades not long after, "slayne with their mowthes stopped full of Breade, being donn as it seemeth in Contempte and skorne thatt others might expect the Lyke when they shold come to seek for breade and reliefe amongst them."

As the winter wore on, the store of hogs, hens, goats, sheep, and horses were quickly consumed; the colonists then turned to "doggs Catts Ratts and myce." Those settlers who were healthy enough searched the woods for roots, nuts, and berries, while others resorted to boiling boot leather. Conditions became so desperate that one man "did kill his wife, powdered [i.e., salted] her, and had eaten part of her" before leaders discovered his villainy and had him executed. By May 1610, when Deputy Governor Thomas Gates and the rest of the original fleet limped in from Bermuda, only 60 settlers out of 500 had survived the winter, and these were "so Leane thatt they looked Lyke Anotamies Cryeing owtt we are starved We are starved."

Grim as such tales are, we have almost come to expect them in the first years of a new colony. The Virginia experiment broke new ground in a new land. Mistakes were inevitable. But as the years passed, the colonists seemed to have learned little. Ten years after the first landing, yet another governor, Samuel Argall, arrived to find Jamestown hardly more than a slum in the wildnerness: "but five or six houses [remaining standing], the Church downe, the Palizado's [stockade fence] broken, the Bridge in pieces, the Well of fresh water spoiled; the Storehouse they used for the Church; the marketplace and streets, and all other spare places planted with Tobacco." Of the 2,000 or so settlers sent since 1607, only 400 remained alive and only 200 of them, Argall complained, were either trained or fit enough to farm. Even

John Rolfe, a prominent settler who was usually willing to put as good a face on affairs as possible, could not help taking away with the left hand the praises he bestowed with the right. "Wee found the Colony (God be thanked) in good estate," he wrote home hopefully, "however in buildings, fortyfications, and of boats, much ruyned and greate want." All in all, it was not much of a progress report after ten years.

In England, Sir Edwin Sandys was one of the adventurers who watched with distress as the company's efforts came to naught. Sandys lacked the financial means of bigger investors such as Thomas Smith, who had often presided as the company's treasurer. But Sandys's limited resources were precisely the point. Smith and the other big investors considered the Virginia enterprise just one venture among many: the East India Company, trading in the Levant, and the Muscovy Company. If Virginia did not pay immediate dividends, they could afford to wait. Sandys and his followers, with less capital and less margin for error, pressed for immediate reform. By 1618 Smith had agreed to introduce significant changes into the colony's organization; the following year Sandys was elected treasurer of the company. With real power in his hands for the first time, he set out to reconstruct the failing colony from the bottom up.

BLUEPRINT FOR A VIRGINIA UTOPIA

Sandys knew that if his schemes for reform were to succeed, he would have to attract both new investors to the company and new settlers to the colony. Yet the Virginia Company was deeply in debt, and the colony was literally falling apart. In order to entice both settlers and investors, Sandys offered the only commodity the company possessed in abundance—land.

In the first years of the colony, Virginia land had remained company land. Settlers who worked it might own shares in the company, but even so, they did not profit directly from their labor, because all proceeds went into the treasury to be divided only if there were any profits. There never were. In 1617 the company formally changed its policy. Old Planters, those settlers who had arrived in Virginia before the spring of 1616, were each granted 100 acres of land. Freemen received their allotment immediately, while those settlers who were still company servants received their land when their terms of service expired.

Sandys lured new investors with the promise of property too. For every share they purchased, the company granted them 100 acres. More important, Sandys encouraged immigration to the colony by giving investors additional land if they would pay the ship passage of tenant laborers. For every new tenant imported to Virginia, the investor received 50 additional acres. Such land grants were known as "headrights" because the land was apportioned per each "head" imported. Of course, if Old Planters wished to invest in the company, they too would receive 100 acres plus additional 50-acre headrights for every tenant whose passage they paid. Such incentives, Sandys believed, would attract needed funds to the company while also promoting immigration.

And so private property came to Virginia. This tactic was the much-heralded event that every schoolchild is called upon to recite as the salvation of the colony. "When our people were fed out of the common store and labored jointly together, glad was he could slip away from his labour, or slumber over his taske," noted one settler. But "now for themselves they will doe in a day" what before they "would hardly take so much true paines in a weeke." It is important to understand, however, that the company still had its own common land and stock from which it hoped to profit. Thus a company shareholder had the prospect of making money in two ways: from any goods marketed by company servants working company lands, or directly from his newly granted private lands, also known as "particular plantations."

Sandys's administration provided still other openings for private investment. By 1616 the company had already granted certain merchants a four-year monopoly on providing supplies for the colony. The "magazine," as it was called, sent supply ships to Virginia, where its agent, a man known as the "cape merchant," sold the goods in return for produce. In 1620 the company removed the magazine's monopoly and allowed other investors to send over supply ships.

Sandys and his friends also worked to make the colony a more pleasant place to live. Instead of being governed by martial law, as the colony had since 1609, the company instructed the new governor, George Yeardly, to create an assembly with the power to make laws. The laws would be binding so long as the company later approved them. Inhabitants of the various company settlements and the particular plantations were to choose two members each as their burgesses, or representatives. When the assembly convened in 1619 it became the first representative body in the English colonies.

Historians have emphasized the significance of this first step in the evolution of American democracy, and significant it was. But the colony's settlers may have considered it equally important that the company had figured out a way to avoid saddling them with high taxes to pay for their government. Once again, the answer was land, which the company used to pay officials' salaries. Thus the governor received a parcel of 3,000 acres plus 100 tenants to work it, the treasurer of the colony received 1,500 acres and 50 tenants, and so on. Everybody won, or so it seemed. The officers got their salaries without having to "prey upon the people"; the settlers were relieved "of all taxes and public burthens as much as may be"; and the sharecropping tenants, after splitting the profits with company officials for seven years, got to keep the land they worked. If the company carried out its policy, John Rolfe observed enthusiastically, "then we may truly say in Virginia, we are the most happy people in the world."

In 1619, with the reforms in place and Sandys in the treasurer's seat, the company moved into high gear. New investors sent scores of tenants over to work the particular plantations; the company sent servants to tend officers' lands; and lotteries throughout England provided income to recruit iron-mongers, vine-tenders, and glassblowers for the New World. The records of the Virginia Company tell a story of immigration on a larger scale than ever before: more than 1,000 settlers in 1619, Sandys's first year, and equal numbers in the following three years. Historians who do a little searching and counting in company records will find that some 3,570 settlers were sent to join a population that stood, at the beginning of Sandys's program, around 700.

It would have been an impressive record, except that in 1622, three years later, the colony's population still totaled only about 700 people.

The figures are in the records; you can check the math yourself. What it amounts to is that in 1622, there are about 3,500 Virginians missing. No significant number returned to England; most, after all, could hardly afford passage over, let alone back. No significant number migrated to other colonies. We can account for the deaths of 347 colonists, slain in an Indian attack of 1622. But that leaves more than 3,000 settlers. There seems to be only one way to do the accounting: those immigrants died.

Who—or what—was responsible for the deaths of 3,000 Virginians? Something had gone terribly wrong with Sandys's plans. The magnitude of the failure was so great that the leaders of the company did not care to announce it openly. When the king got word of it, only after the company had virtually bankrupted itself in 1624, he revoked its charter. The historian who confronts the statistical outlines of this horror is forced to ask a few questions. Just what conditions would produce a death rate in the neighborhood of 75 to 80 percent? A figure that high is simply staggering. For comparison, the death rate during the first (and worst) year at the Pilgrims' Plymouth colony stayed a little below 50 percent, and during the severe plague epidemics that swept Britain in the fourteenth century, the death rate probably ranged from 20 to 45 or 50 percent.

Obvious answers suggest themselves. The colony could not sustain such an influx of new settlers, especially since Sandys, in his eagerness to increase the population, sent so many people unprepared. Immigrants often arrived with little or no food to tide them over until they could begin raising their own crops. Housing was inadequate; indeed, the records are full of letters from the company in London begging the colony's governors to build temporary "guest houses" for the newcomers, while the governors' letters in return begged the company to send more adequate provisions with their recruits.

Disease took its toll. Colonists had discovered early on that Virginia was an unhealthy place to live. For newcomers, the first summer proved particularly deadly, so much so that it was called the "seasoning time." Those who survived the first summer significantly raised their chances of prospering. But dangers remained year-round, especially for those weakened by the voyage or living on a poor diet. Contaminated wells most likely contributed to outbreaks of typhoid fever, and malaria claimed additional victims.

The obvious answers do much to explain the devastating death rate, but anomalies remain. Even granting the seriousness of typhoid and other diseases, why a death rate higher than the worst plague years? Virginia's population was made up of younger men primarily and lacked the older men and women who would have been most weakened by these conditions. Even healthy settlers, of course, may be affected by malnutrition and semistarvation, but that brings the problem right back to the question of why, after more than ten years, the Jamestown colony was not yet self-sufficient.

Self-sufficiency required that colonists raise their own food. And the principal food raised in the area was corn. So the historian asks a simple question: how much work did it take to grow corn? A quick look at the records confirms what might be suspected—that no Virginian in those first years bothered to leave behind a treatise on agriculture. But a closer search of letters and company records provides bits of data here and there. The Indians, Virginians discovered, spent only a few days out of the year tending corn, and they often produced surpluses that they traded to the Virginians. A minister in the colony reported that "in the idle hours of one week," he and three other men had planted enough corn to last for four months. Other estimates suggested that forty-eight hours' work would suffice to plant enough corn to last a whole year. Even allowing for exaggeration, it seems clear that comparatively little effort was needed to grow corn.

Yet if corn could be grown easily, and if it was needed to keep the colonists alive, what possible sense is the historian to make of the document we encountered earlier, Governor Argall's proclamation of 1618 requiring "Every man to sett two acres corn (Except Tradesmen following their trades)." That year is not the last time the law appears on the books. It was reentered in the 1620s and periodically up through the 1650s.

The situation is a puzzle: a law *requiring* Virginians to plant corn? The colony was continually running out of corn, people were starving, and planting and reaping took only a few weeks out of the year. Under these circumstances, the government had to *order* settlers to plant corn?

Yet the conclusion is backed up by other company records. Virginians had to be forced to grow corn. The reason becomes clearer if we reexamine Governor Argall's gloomy description of Jamestown when he stepped off the boat in 1617. The church is down, the palisades pulled apart, the bridge in pieces, the fresh water spoiled. Everything in the description indicates the colony is decrepit, falling apart, except for one paradoxical feature—the "weeds" in the street. The stockades and buildings may have languished from neglect, but it was not neglect that caused "the market-place and streets, and all other spare places" to be "planted with Tobacco." Unlike corn, tobacco required a great deal of attention to cultivate. It did not spring up in the streets by accident. Thus Governor Argall's description indicates that at the same time that settlers were willing to let the colony fall apart, they were energetically planting tobacco in all the "spare places" they could find.

Settlers had discovered as early as 1613 that tobacco was marketable, and they sent small quantities to England the following year. Soon shipments increased dramatically, from 2,500 pounds in 1616 to 18,839 pounds in 1617 and 49,518 pounds in 1618. Some English buyers thought that tobacco could be used as a medicine, but most purchased it simply for the pleasure

Virginia's early planters marketed their tobacco to the Dutch as well as the English. This painting on an early-seventeenth-century ceramic tile shows a Dutch smoker attempting the novel accomplishment of blowing smoke through his nose. The new habit of smoking, at once popular and fairly disreputable, led to a demand for Virginia tobacco in Europe that drove up prices and sent enterprising colonists scrambling for laborers to help raise the profitable crop.

of smoking it. Sandys and many other gentlemen looked upon the "noxious weed" as a vice and did everything to discourage its planting. There had been "often letters from the Counsell" in London, he complained, "sent lately to the Governour for restraint of that immoderate following of Tobacco and to cause the people to apply themselves to other and better commodities." But his entreaties, as well as the corn laws, met with little success. Tobacco was in Virginia to stay.

VIRGINIA BOOM COUNTRY

The Virginia records are full of statistics like the preceding tobacco export figures: number of pounds shipped, price of the "better sort" of tobacco for the year 1619, number of settlers arriving on the *Bona Nova*. These statistics are the sort of box-score evidence, recorded by pedestrian clerks for pedestrian reasons, that we noted earlier. Yet once the historian strips the facts of their pedestrian perspective and uses them for his or her own purposes, they begin to flesh out an astonishing picture of Virginia. Historian Edmund Morgan, in his own reconstruction of the situation, aptly labeled Virginia "the first American boom country."

For Virginia was indeed booming. The commodity in demand—tobacco—was not as glamorous as gold or silver, but the social dynamics operated in similar fashion. The lure of making a fortune created a volatile society where wealth changed hands quickly, where an unbalanced economy centered on one get-rich-quick commodity, and where the values of stability and human dignity counted for little.

The implications of this boom-country society become clearer if we ask the same basic questions about tobacco that we asked about corn. Given the fact that Virginians seemed to be growing tobacco, just how much could one person grow in a year? If tobacco was being grown for profit, could Virginians expect to get rich doing it?

Spanish tobacco grown in the West Indies fetched 18 shillings a pound on the English market. Even the highest-quality Virginia product was markedly inferior and sold for only 3 shillings. And that price fluctuated throughout the 1620s, dropping as low as 1 shilling. What that price range meant in terms of profits depended, naturally, on how much tobacco a planter could grow in a year. As with corn, the few available estimates are widely scattered. John Rolfe suggested 1,000 plants in one year. William Capps, another seasoned settler, estimated 2,000 and also noted that three of his boys, whose labor he equated with one and a half men, produced 3,000 plants. Fortunately, Capps also noted that 2,000 plants made up about 500 "weight" (or pounds) of tobacco, which allows us to convert numbers of plants into number of pounds.

By comparing these figures with other estimates, we can calculate roughly how much money a planter might have received for a crop. The chart below summarizes how many plants or pounds of tobacco one or more workers might have harvested in a year. The extrapolated numbers in parentheses show the number of pounds harvested per worker and the income such a harvest would yield if tobacco were selling at either 1 or 3 shillings a pound.

Tobacco Production and Income Estimates

| Number of Workers | One-Year Production | | | Income | |
	Number of Plants	Number of Lbs.	One Man Lbs./Yr.	1s	3s
1 (Rolfe)	1,000		(250)	£12	£37.5
1 (Capps)	2,000	500	(500)	25	75
3 boys (1½ men)	3,000		(500)	25	75
4 men		2,800	(700)	46.5	139.5
6–7 men		3,000–4,000	(540)	27	81

Source: Based on data presented in Edmund Morgan, *American Slavery, American Freedom* (New York, 1975).

These estimates indicate that the amount of tobacco one man could produce ranged from 250 to 700 pounds a year, an understandable variation given that some planters undoubtedly worked harder than others, that some years provided better growing weather, and that, as time passed, Virginians developed ways to turn out bigger crops. Even by John Rolfe's estimate, made fairly early and therefore somewhat low, a man selling 250 pounds at 1 shilling a pound would receive £12 sterling for the year. On the high side, the estimates show a gross of £140 sterling, given good prices. Indeed, one letter tells of a settler who made £200 sterling after the good harvest of 1619.

Such windfalls were rare, but considering that an average agricultural worker in England made from 30 to 50 shillings a year (less than £3), even the lower estimates look good.

The estimates look particularly good for another reason—namely, because they indicate what a planter might do working *alone*. In a society where servants, tenants, and apprentices were commonplace, Virginians quickly discovered that if they could get other people to work for them, handsome profits could be made.

Back to the basic questions. How did an Englishman get others to work for him? In effect, he simply hired them and made an agreement, a bond indicating what he would give in return for their service and for how long the agreement was to run. The terms varied from servant to servant but fell into several general classes. Most favorable, from the worker's point of view, was the position of tenant. A landowner had fields that needed working; the tenant agreed to work them for a certain period of time, usually from four to seven years. In return, the tenant kept half of what he produced. From the landowner's point of view, a servant served the purpose better, since he was paid only room and board, plus his passage from England. In return he gave his master everything he produced. Apprentices, usually called "Duty boys" in Virginia because the ship *Duty* brought many of them over, made up another class of workers. Apprentices served for seven years, then another seven as tenants. Again the master's cost was only transportation over and maintenance once in Virginia.

Little in the way of higher mathematics is required to discover that if it cost a master about £10 to £12 sterling to bring over a servant, and if that master obtained the labor of several such servants for seven years, or even for two or three, he stood to make a tidy fortune. In the good harvest of 1619 one master with six servants managed a profit of £1,000 sterling. That was unusual perhaps, but by no means impossible. And Sandys's headright policies unwittingly played into the hands of the fortune-makers: every servant imported meant another fifty acres of land that could be used for tobacco.

The opportunities were too much to resist. Virginians began bending every resource in the colony toward growing tobacco. The historian can now appreciate the significance of Governor Argall's proclamation (page 6) that no hay should be used to "sweat," or cure, tobacco: obviously, colonists were diverting hay from livestock that desperately needed it ("it robs the poor beasts of their fodder"), thus upsetting Virginia's economy. The scramble for profits extended even to the artisans whom Sandys sent over to diversify the colony's exports. The ironmongers deserted in short order, having "turned good honest Tobaccoemongers"; and of similar well-intentioned projects, the report came back to London that "nothinge is done in anie of them but all is vanished into smoke (that is to say into Tobaccoe)." The boom in Virginia was on.

Planters were not the only people trying to make a fortune. The settler who raised tobacco had to get it to market in Europe somehow, had to buy corn if he neglected to raise any himself, and looked to supply himself with as many of the comforts of life as could be had. Other men stood ready to deal with such planters, and they had a sharp eye to their own profit.

The company, of course, sought to provide supplies through the magazine run by the cape merchant, Abraham Peirsey. And if we now return to the Virginia assembly's order, quoted earlier, requiring Peirsey to accept 3 shillings per pound for the "better sort" of tobacco, we can begin to understand why the assembly was upset enough to pass the regulation. Peirsey was charging exorbitant prices for his supplies. He collected his fees in tobacco because there was virtually no currency in Virginia. Tobacco had become the economic medium of exchange. If Peirsey counted a pound of the better sort of tobacco as worth only 2 shillings instead of 3, that was as good as raising his prices by 50 percent. As it happened, Peirsey charged two or three times the prices set by the investors in London. Further, he compounded injury with insult by failing to reimburse the company for their supplies that he sold. Sandys and the other investors never saw a cent of the magazine's profits.

Another hunt through the records indicates what Peirsey was doing with his ill-gotten gain: he plowed it back into the most attractive investment of all, servants. We learn this not because Peirsey comes out and says so, but because the census of 1625 lists him as keeping thirty-nine servants, more than anyone else in the colony. At his death in 1628 he left behind "the best Estate that was ever yett knowen in Virginia." When the company finally broke the magazine's monopoly in 1620, other investors moved in. They soon discovered that they could make more money selling alcohol than the necessities of life. So the Virginia boom enriched the merchants of "rotten Wynes" as well as the planters of tobacco, and settlers went hungry, in part, because liquor fetched a better return than food.

Given these conditions in Virginia—given the basic social and economic structures deduced from the historical record—put yourself in the place of most tenants or servants. What would life be like for them under these conditions? What were their chances for success?

For servants, the prospect was bad indeed. First, they faced the fierce mortality rate. Chances were that they would not survive the first seasoning summer. Even if they did, their master was out to make a fortune by their labor. Being poor to begin with, they were in no position to protect themselves from abuse. In England the situation was different. Agricultural workers usually offered their services once a year at hiring fairs. Since their contracts lasted only a year, servants could switch to other employers if they became dissatisfied. But going to Virginia required the expense of a long voyage; masters would hire people only if they signed on for four to seven years. Once in Virginia, what could servants do if they became disillusioned? Go home? They had little enough money for the voyage over, and likely even less to get back.

Duty boys, the children, were least in a position to improve their lot. The orphans Sandys hoped to favor by taking them off the London streets faced a hard life in Virginia. They were additionally threatened by a law the Virginia labor barons put through the assembly declaring that an apprentice who committed a crime during his service had to begin his term all over again. What constituted a crime, of course, was left up to the governor's council. One Duty boy, Richard Hatch, appeared before the council because he had commented, in a private house, on the recent execution of a settler, one Richard Cornish, for sodomy. Hatch had remarked "that in his consyence he thought that the said Cornishe was put to death wrongfully." For this offense he was to be "whipt from the forte to the gallows and from thence be whipt back againe, and be sett uppon the Pillory and there to loose one of his eares." Although Hatch had nearly completed his term of service—to Governor George Yeardly, who also sat on the council—he was ordered to begin his term anew.

Tenants would seem to have been better off, but they too were subject to the demand for labor. If immigrants could pay their passage over but were unable to feed themselves upon arrival, they had little choice but to hire themselves out as servants. And if their masters died before their terms were up, there was virtually always another master ready to jump in and claim them, legally or not, either as personal servants or as company tenants due in payment of a salary. When George Sandys, Sir Edwin's brother, finished his term as colony treasurer, he dragged his tenants with him even though they had become freemen. "He maketh us serve him whether wee will or noe," complained one, "and how to helpe it we doe not knowe for hee beareth all the sway."

Even independent small planters faced the threat of servitude if their crops failed or if Indian attacks made owning a small, isolated plantation too dangerous. William Capps, the small planter who recorded one of the tobacco production estimates, described his own precarious situation vividly. His plantation threatened by Indians, Capps proposed that the governor's council outfit him with an expedition against the neighboring tribes. The council refused, and the indignant Capps angrily suggested what was going through the wealthy planters' minds. "Take away one of my men to join the expedition," he imagines them saying,

> there's 2000 Plantes gone, thates 500 waight of Tobacco, yea and what shall this man doe, runne after the Indians? soft, I have perhaps 10, perhaps 15, perhaps 20 men and am able to secure my owne Plantacion; how will they doe that are fewer? let them first be crusht alitle, and then perhaps they will themselves make up the Nomber for their owne safetie. Theis I doubt are the Cogitacions of some of our worthier men.

AND SLAVERY?

This reconstruction of Virginia society, from the Duty boy at the bottom to the richer planters at the top, indicates that all along the line labor had become a valuable and desperately sought commodity. Settlers who were not in a position to protect themselves found that the economy put constant pressure on them. Their status as freemen was always in danger of debasement: planters bought, sold, and traded servants without their consent and, on occasion even used them as stakes in gambling games. There had been

"About the last of August came in a dutch man of warre that sold us twenty Negars." So wrote John Smith in 1619. The illustration is by Howard Pyle, a nineteenth-century artist who prided himself on his research into costume and setting. Yet even here, Pyle's depiction of the first African Americans probably reflects illustrations he saw of the very different slave traffic of the eighteenth and nineteenth centuries. These early arrivals may have been sold as servants, not slaves. Court records indicate that in the 1640s at least some black slaves had been freed and were purchasing their own land.

"many complaints," acknowledged John Rolfe, "against the Governors, Captaines, and Officers in Virginia: for buying and selling men and boies," something that "was held in England a thing most intolerable." One Englishman put the indignity quite succinctly: "My Master Atkins hath sold me for £150 sterling like a damnd slave."

Indeed, quite a few of the ingredients of slavery are found in Virginia: the feverish economic boom that sparked a fierce demand for human labor; the mortality rate that encouraged survivors to become callous about human life; the servants who were being bought and sold, treated as property— treated, almost, as slaves. If we were looking in the abstract to construct a society in which social and economic pressures combined to encourage the development of human slavery, boom-country Virginia would seem to fit the model neatly. Yet the actual records do not quite confirm the hypothesis.

The earliest known record of Africans in Virginia is a muster roll of March 1619 (discovered only in the 1990s), which shows thirty-two Africans (fifteen men and seventeen women) "in the service of sev[er]all planters." But are these Africans working as servants or as slaves? The muster roll doesn't say. Historians have combed the sparse records of early Virginia, looking at court records, inventories, letters, wills, church records—anything that might shed light on the way blacks were treated. Precious little information is available—but what little there is has been studied intensively. What we find is that very few Africans come to Virginia in the colony's first half century. People of African descent made up no more than 5 percent of the population at any time during those years.

Furthermore, the status of Africans who did come to Virginia varied widely. Before 1660 some were held as slaves for life, but others worked as servants. Still others either were given their freedom or were able to purchase it. Even the names in the record supply a clue to the mixed status of these early African newcomers. In the eighteenth century, once slavery was well established, planters tried to control the naming process, giving their slaves diminutive names such as Jack or Sukey, or perhaps a classical Caesar or Hercules, bestowed in jest. But during Virginia's early years Africans tended to keep their full names—names that often reflected the complex cultural landscape of the African coast, where Europeans and Africans of many backgrounds mixed: Bashaw Farnando, John Graweere, Emanuel Driggus. Other Africans tried to assimilate into English life. The man who first appeared in the colony's records as only "Antonio a Negro" changed his name to Anthony Johnson. "Francisco a Negroe" eventually became the freeman Frank Payne.

Only during the 1660s did the Virginia assembly begin to pass legislation that separated blacks from whites, defining slavery, legally, as an institution. Black Virginians, in other words, lived with white Virginians for more than forty years before their status became fully and legally debased. The facts in the records force us to turn the initial question around. If the 1620s with its boom economy was such an appropriate time for slavery to have developed, why *didn't* it?

Here, the talents of historians are stretched to their limits. They can expect no obvious explanations from contemporaries such as John Rolfe, Captain Smith, or William Capps. The development of slavery was something that snuck up on Virginians. It was part of the society's "inner dynamic," as sociologists would say—hidden from the awareness of the social actors in the situation. Even the records left by the clerks are scant help. The best that can be done is intelligent conjecture, based on the kind of society that has been reconstructed.

Was it a matter of the simple availability of slaves? Perhaps. During the time that Virginia was experiencing its boom of the 1620s, West Indian islands like Barbados and St. Kitts were being settled. There, where the cultivation of sugar demanded even more intensive labor than tobacco did, the demand for slaves was extremely high, and slavery developed more rapidly. If traders sailing from Africa could carry only so many slaves, and if the market for them was better in Barbados than in Virginia, why sail all the way up to Chesapeake Bay? Slave traders may not have found the effort worth it. That is the conjecture of one historian, Richard Dunn. Other historians and economists have argued that Chesapeake planters preferred white servants but that during the 1670s the supply of servants from England began to decrease, sending prices higher. At the same time, an economic depression in the West Indies sent the price of slaves falling and sent slave dealers looking to sell more slaves along the Chesapeake.

Edmund Morgan has suggested another possibility, based on the continuing mortality rate in Virginia. Put yourself in the place of the planter searching for labor. You can buy either servants or slaves. Servants come cheaper than slaves, of course, but you get to work them for only seven years before they receive their freedom. Slaves are more expensive, but you get their labor for the rest of their lives, as well as the labor of any offspring. In the long run, the more expensive slave would have been the better buy. But in Virginia everyone is dying anyway. What are the chances that either servants or slaves are going to live for more than seven, five, even three years? The chances are not particularly good. Wouldn't it make more sense to pay less and buy servants on the assumption that whoever is bought may die shortly anyway?

It is an ingenious conjecture, but it must remain that. No plantation records or letters have been found indicating that planters actually thought that way. Available evidence does suggest that the high death rate in Virginia began to drop only in the 1650s. It makes sense that only then, when slaves became a profitable commodity, would laws come to be passed formally establishing their chattel status. Whatever the reasons may have been, Virginia remained until the 1680s and 1690s what historian Ira Berlin has termed a "society with slaves" rather than a full-fledged "slave society" whose economy and culture revolved around the institution of slavery based on race. During the boom of the 1620s slavery did not flourish markedly.

Sometime between 1629 and 1630 the economic bubble popped. The price of tobacco plummeted from 3 shillings to a penny a pound. Virginians tried desperately to prop it up again, either by limiting production or by simple edict, but they did not succeed. Planters still could make money, but the chance for a quick fortune had vanished—"into smoke," as Sandys or one of his disillusioned investors would no doubt have remarked. It is much to the credit of historians that the feverish world of the Chesapeake has not, like its cash crop, entirely vanished into smoke.

Additional Reading

The works of Captain John Smith make a delightful introduction to Virginia. Smith is one of those Elizabethans whose prose struts, bounces, jars, and jounces from one page to the next. Although caution is necessary in reading Smith, he has provided historians with excellent source material for early encounters between Europeans and native Americans. His writings are gathered in Philip L. Barbour, ed., *The Complete Works of Captain John Smith*, 3 vols. (Chapel Hill, 1986). A briefer sampling can be found in Karen Ordahl Kupperman, ed., *Captain John Smith: A Select Edition of His Writings* (Chapel Hill, 1988). Kupperman provides a good introduction to historians' treatments of Smith, as does J. A. Leo Lemay, *The American Dream of Captain John Smith* (Charlottesville, VA, 1991). Lemay is a strong defender of Smith, sometimes unnecessarily contentious, but worth reading. Henry Adams's attack on the Pocahontas story can be found in Charles Francis Adams, *Chapters of Erie and Other Essays* (Boston, 1871), while a modern defense of the captain's veracity is Philip L. Barbour, *The Three Worlds of Captain John Smith* (London, 1964). The most interesting recent discussions of white–Native American relations in early Virginia are by Frederick Fausz, including an essay in William W. Fitzhugh, ed., *Cultures in Contact: The Impact of European Contacts on Native American Cultural Institutions, A.D. 1000–1800* (Washington, DC, 1985), pp. 225–268, and "An 'Abundance of Blood Shed on Both Sides': England's First Indian War, 1609–1614," *Virginia Magazine of History and Biography* 98 (1990): 3–56.

The reconstruction of boom-country Virginia described in this chapter depends heavily on the research presented in Edmund S. Morgan, *American Slavery, American Freedom* (New York, 1975). Morgan's account combines a lucid and engaging prose style with the imaginative and thorough research that is a model for the discipline. His book makes an excellent starting place for those readers who wish to learn more about seventeenth-century Virginia. Morgan's book is only the high point, however, in a resurgence of interest by historians in the whole Chesapeake Bay region. Useful starting points for sorting out these materials are Thad W. Tate and David L. Ammerman, eds., *The Chesapeake in the Seventeenth Century: Essays on Anglo-American Society* (Chapel Hill, 1979), and Lois Green Carr et al., eds., *Colonial Chesapeake Society* (Chapel Hill, 1988). Darrett B. and Anita Rutman, *A Place in Time: Middlesex County, Virginia, 1650–1750* (New York, 1984) continues Virginia's social history, using the microcosmic techniques that we examine, for New England, in the next chapter.

Readers wishing to explore primary source material on early Virginia will probably find that contemporary narratives like Smith's provide the best introduction. Many are available in Philip L. Barbour, ed., *The Jamestown Voyages under the First Charter, 1606–1609*, 2 vols. (London, 1969), and in the older but more complete Alexander Brown, *The Genesis of the United States* (Boston, 1890). Additional details about the starving time of 1609–1610 can be found in George Percy, "A Trewe Relacyon of the Procedinges and

Occurentes of Moment . . ." in *Tyler's Quarterly Historical and Genealogical Magazine* 11 (1922): 260–282. Although the official records of the Virginia Company and the colony are dense and difficult to read, they provide vital evidence. Interested readers will most profit if they bring to their reading a definite idea of the sorts of facts and the specific questions they wish to answer. For the early years, see Alexander Brown's collection; the period from 1619–1624 is covered in Susan Kingsbury, ed., *The Records of the Virginia Company of London*, 4 vols. (Washington, DC, 1906–1935). For the later period, surviving records can be found in H. R. McIlwaine, ed., *Minutes of the Council and General Court of Colonial Virginia* (Richmond, VA, 1924), and William W. Hening, *The Statutes at Large: Being a Collection of All the Laws of Virginia* (Richmond, VA, 1809–1823).

The earliest Africans in Virginia have been studied intensively, though also inconclusively. The most recent assessment is Engel Sluiter, "New Light on the '20 and Odd Negroes' Arriving in Virginia, August 1619," *William and Mary Quarterly* 54 (1997): 395–398. The question of why slavery did not develop during the first tobacco boom is discussed in Morgan's *American Slavery, American Freedom*, as well as in David W. Galenson, *White Servitude in the Colonial Labor Market: An Economic Analysis* (Cambridge, 1981). Much of the new scholarship on the development of slavery in Virginia (and elsewhere in North America) can be found in the masterful synthesis of Ira Berlin, *Many Thousands Gone: The First Two Centuries of Slavery in North America* (Cambridge, MA, 1998). Yoked to the question of how and why slavery developed is the question of the role of racial prejudice. Winthrop Jordan explored the issue in *White over Black: American Attitudes toward the Negro, 1550–1812* (Chapel Hill, NC, 1968). For a more recent evaluation of the debate, see Alden T. Vaughan, "The Origins Debate: Slavery and Racism in Seventeenth Century Virginia," *Virginia Magazine of History and Biography* 97 (1989): 311–354. A broad synthesis of the rise of slavery along the Chesapeake is by Allan Kulikoff, *Tobacco and Slaves: The Development of Southern Cultures in the Chesapeake, 1680–1800* (Chapel Hill, NC, 1986). See also J. Douglas Deal, *Race and Class in Colonial Virginia: Indians, Englishmen, and Africans on the Eastern Shore of Virginia during the Seventeenth Century* (New York, 1993); T. H. Breen and Stephen Innes, *'Myne Own Ground:" Race and Freedom on Virginia's Eastern Shore, 1640–1676* (New York, 1980); and Richard S. Dunn, "Masters, Servants, and Slaves in the Colonial Chesapeake and the Caribbean," in David B. Quinn, ed., *Early Maryland in a Wider World* (Detroit, 1982).

Interactive Learning

The *Primary Source Investigator* sources explore what it was like to "serve time" in seventeenth-century Virginia. Images depicting Native American towns and early maps provide visual clues to the cultures and landscapes early colonists encountered. Letters recounting the introduction of the first African slaves, as well as inventory lists outlining the supplies that potential colonists needed to have with them when they arrived in Virginia, illuminate the harsh realities of colonialism. Other sources explore the important role of tobacco production in the colony.

CHAPTER 2

The Visible and Invisible Worlds of Salem

Historians, we have seen, are in the business of reconstruction. Seventeenth-century Virginia, with its world of slaves, indentured servants, and tobacco barons, had to be built anew, not just lifted intact from the record. It follows, then, that if historians are builders, they must decide at the outset the scale of their projects. How much ground should be covered? A year? Fifty years? Several centuries? How will the subject matter be defined or limited? The story of slavery's arrival in Virginia might be ranked as a moderately large topic. It spans some sixty years and involves thousands of immigrants and an entire colony. Furthermore, the topic is large as much because of its content as its reach over time and space. The genesis of slavery surely ranks as a central strand of the American experience. To understand it adequately requires more breadth of vision than, for instance, understanding the history of American hats during the same period. The lure of topics both broad and significant is undeniable, and there have always been historians willing to pull on their seven-league boots, following in the honorable tradition of Edward Gibbon's *Decline and Fall of the Roman Empire.*

The great equalizer of such grand plans is the twenty-four-hour day. Historians have only a limited amount of time, and the hours, they sadly discover, are not expandable. Obviously, the more years covered, the less time available to research the events in each. Conversely, the narrower the area of research, the more the historian can become immersed in a period's details. A keen mind working on an apparently small topic may uncover relationships and connections whose significance goes beyond the subject matter's original boundaries.

Salem Village in 1692 is such a microcosm—one familiar to most students of American history. That was the place and the time witchcraft came to New England with a vengeance, dominating the life of the village for ten months. Because the witchcraft episode exhibited well-defined boundaries in

24

both time and space, it shows well how an oft-told story may be transformed by the intensive research techniques of small-scale history. Traditionally, the outbreak at Salem has been viewed as an incident divorced from the cause-and-effect sequences of everyday village life. Even to label the events as an "outbreak" suggests that they are best viewed as an epidemic, alien to the community's normal functions. The "germs" of bewitchment break out suddenly and inexplicably—agents, presumably, of some invading disease.

Over the past decades, however, historians have studied the traumatic experiences of 1692 in great detail. In so doing they have created a more sophisticated model of the mental world behind the Salem outbreak. They have also suggested ways in which the witchcraft episode was tied to the everyday events of village life. The techniques of small-scale history, in other words, have provided a compelling psychological and social context for the events of 1692.

BEWITCHMENT AT SALEM VILLAGE

The baffling troubles experienced in Salem Village began during the winter of 1691–1692 in the home of the village's minister, Samuel Parris. There, Parris's nine-year-old daughter Betty and his niece Abigail Williams had taken strangely ill, claiming that they had been "bitten and pinched by invisible agents; their arms, necks, and backs turned this way and that way, and returned back again . . . beyond the power of any Epileptick Fits, or natural Disease to effect." Later traditions—not necessarily reliable—suggested that the afflictions came after a group of girls met to divine what sort of men their future husbands might be, a subject of natural enough interest. Lacking a crystal ball, they used the next available substitute, the white of a raw egg suspended in a glass of water. At some point during these conjurings, things went sour. One of the girls thought she detected "a specter in the likeness of a coffin" in the glass—hardly an auspicious omen. Soon Betty, the youngest of the girls, began complaining of pinching, prickling sensations, knifelike pains, and the feeling that she was being choked. In the weeks that followed, three more girls exhibited similar symptoms.

Whatever the cause of the young girls' symptoms, the Reverend Parris was at a loss to understand the afflictions, as were several doctors and ministers he brought in to observe the strange behaviors. When one doctor hinted at the possibility of witchcraft, a neighbor, Mary Sibley, suggested putting to use a bit of New England folklore to reveal whether there had been any sorcery. Sibley persuaded two slaves living in the Parris household, John Indian and his wife, Tituba, to bake a "witch cake" made of rye meal and urine given them by the girls. The cake was fed to a dog—the theory of bewitchment confirmed, presumably, if the dog suffered torments similar to those of the afflicted girls.

This experiment seems to have frightened the girls even more, for their symptoms worsened. Thoroughly alarmed by the symptoms, Parris and several other adults pressed the girls for the identity of the specters they believed were tormenting them. When the girls named three women, a formal complaint was issued, and on February 29 the suspects were arrested, for, indeed, seventeenth-century New Englanders conceived of witchcraft as a crime. If the girls were being tormented, it was necessary to punish whoever was responsible.

Two of the women arrested, Sarah Good and Sarah Osbourne, were already unpopular in the village. The third accused was Parris's Indian slave, Tituba. Tituba may have been purchased by Parris during a visit to the Caribbean and was perhaps originally from South America, Florida, or the Georgia Sea Islands. Under examination by village magistrates, Sarah Good angrily denied the accusations against her, suggesting instead that Sarah Osbourne was guilty. Osbourne denied the charges, but the dynamics of the hearings changed abruptly when Tituba confessed to being a witch. One account of the trials, published eight years later, reported that her admission came after an angry Reverend Parris had beaten Tituba. For whatever reason, she testified that four women and a man were causing the afflictions of the young women. Good and Osbourne were among them. "They hurt the children," Tituba reported. "And they lay all upon me and they tell me if I will not hurt the children, they will hurt me." The tale continued, complete with apparitions of black and red rats, a yellow dog with a head like a woman, "a thing all over hairy, all the face hairy," and midnight rides to witches' meetings where plans were being laid to attack Salem.

During New England's first seventy years, few witchcraft cases had come before the courts. Those that had were dispatched quickly, and calm soon returned. Salem proved different. In the first place, Tituba had described several other witches and a wizard, though she said she was unable to identify them. The villagers felt they could not rest so long as these agents remained at large. Furthermore, the young women continued to name names—and now not just community outcasts but a wide variety of villagers, some respectable church members. The new suspects joined Tituba, Sarah Good, and Sarah Osbourne in jail. By the end of April the hunt had led to no less a personage than the Reverend George Burroughs, a former minister of the village living in Maine. Constables marched to Maine, fetched him back, and threw him in jail.

If someone confessed to witchcraft, the matter of identification seemed simple enough. But if the accused refused to admit guilt, then the magistrates looked for corroborating proof. Physical evidence, such as voodoo dolls and pins found among the suspect's possessions, were considered incriminating. Furthermore, if the devil made a pact with someone, he supposedly required a physical mark of allegiance and thus created a "witch's tit" where either he or his familiar, a likeness in animal form, might suck. Prisoners in the Salem trials were often examined for any abnormal marks on their bodies.

Aside from physical signs, the magistrates considered evidence that a witch's malice might have led to suffering on the part of the victim. This kind of black magic—harm by occult means—was known as *maleficium*. Villager Sarah Gadge, for example, testified that two years earlier she had refused Sarah Good lodging for the night. According to Gadge, Good "fell to muttering and scolding extreamly and so told said Gadge if she would not let her in she should give her something . . . and the next morning after, to said Deponents best remembrance, one of the said Gadges Cowes Died in a Sudden terrible and Strange unusuall maner."

The magistrates also considered what they called "spectral evidence," at once the most damning and dangerous kind of proof. Spectral evidence involved the visions of specters—likenesses of the witches—that victims reported seeing during their torments. In an attempt to confirm the connection between malice and injury, the magistrates kept the afflicted women in the courtroom to observe their behavior while the accused were being examined. "Why doe you hurt these children?" asked John Hathorne, one of the magistrates, in a typical examination. "I doe not hurt them," replied Sarah Osbourne. The record continues: "The children abovenamed being all personally present accused her face to face which being don, they ware all hurt, afflicted and tortured very much: which being over and thay out of theire fitts thay sayd that said Sarah Osburne did then Come to them and hurt them."

The problem with spectral evidence was that it could not be corroborated by others. Only the victim saw the shape of the tormentor. Such testimony was normally controversial, for theologians in Europe as well as in New England believed that spectral evidence should be treated with caution. After all, what better way for the devil to spread confusion than by assuming the shape of an innocent person? In Salem, however, the magistrates considered spectral testimony as paramount. When they handed down indictments, almost all the charges referred only to the spectral torments exhibited by accusers during the pretrial hearings.

Throughout the spring of 1692 no trials of the accused had been held, for the simple reason that Massachusetts was without legal government. In 1684 the Crown had revoked the colony's original charter and set up a new and unpopular government known as the Dominion of New England. But in 1689 William of Orange forced King James to flee England, and New Englanders took that opportunity to overthrow the Dominion. In the ensuing confusion, court cases had been brought largely to a standstill. The new governor of Massachusetts, Sir William Phips, at last arrived in May 1692 with a royal charter and quickly established a special investigatory court of oyer and terminer ("to hear and determine") to deal with the witchcraft cases.

On June 2 the court heard its first case, that of a woman named Bridget Bishop. Even before the Salem outbreak Bishop had been suspected of witchcraft by a number of villagers. She was quickly convicted and, eight days later, hanged from a scaffold on a nearby rise. The site came to be known as Witch's Hill—with good reason, since on June 29 the court again met and convicted five more women. One of them, Rebecca Nurse, had been found innocent, but the court's chief justice disapproved the verdict and convinced the jurors to change their minds. On July 19 Nurse joined the other four women on the scaffold, staunch churchwoman that she was, pray-ing for the judges' souls as well as her own. Sarah Good remained defiant to the end. "I am no more a witch than you are a wizard," she told the attend-ing minister, "and if you take away my life, God will give you blood to drink."

Still the accusations continued; still the court sat. As the net was cast wider, more and more accused were forced to work out their response to the crisis. A few, most of them wealthy, went into hiding until the furor subsided. Giles Cory, a farmer whose wife, Martha, was executed as a witch, refused to "put himself on the country"—that is, submit to a trial by jury. The tradi-tional penalty for such a refusal was the *peine fort et dure*, in which the victim was placed between two boards and had heavy stones placed on him until he agreed to plead innocent or guilty. Although that punishment had been out-lawed in Massachusetts, the court nonetheless carried it out. Cory was slowly crushed to death, stubborn to the end. His last words were said to be, "More weight."

Some of the accused admitted guilt, the most satisfactory solution for the magistrates. Puritans could be a remarkably forgiving people. They were not interested in punishment for its own sake. If a lawbreaker gave evidence of sincere regret for his or her misdeeds, Puritan courts would often reduce or suspend the sentence. So it was in the witchcraft trials at Salem (unlike most trials in Europe, where confessing witches were executed). But the policy of forgiveness had unforeseen consequences. Those who were wrongly accused quickly realized that if they did not confess, they were likely to be hanged. If they did confess, they could escape death but would have to demonstrate their sincerity by providing details of their misdeeds and names of other par-ticipants. The temptation must have been great to confess and, in so doing, to implicate other innocent people.

Given such pressures, the web of accusations continued to grow. August produced six more trials and five hangings. Elizabeth Proctor, the wife of a tavern keeper, received a reprieve because she was pregnant, the court being unwilling to sacrifice the life of an innocent child. Her husband, John, was not spared. September saw another eight victims hanged. More than a hun-dred suspected witches remained in jail.

Pressure to stop the trials had been building, however. One member of the court, Nathaniel Saltonstall, resigned in protest after the first execution. More important, the ministers of the province were becoming uneasy. In public they had supported the trials, but privately they wrote letters caution-ing the magistrates. Finally in early October, Increase Mather, one of the most respected ministers in the colony, published a sermon signed by four-teen other pastors that strongly condemned the use of spectral evidence. Mather argued that to convict on the basis of a specter, which everyone agreed was the devil's creation, in effect took Satan at his own word. That, in Mather's view, risked disaster. "It were better that ten suspected witches should escape, than that one innocent person should be condemned," he concluded.

Mather's sermon convinced Governor Phips that the trials had gone too far. He forbade any more arrests and dismissed the court of oyer and terminer. The following January a new court met to dispose of the remaining cases, but this time almost all the defendants were acquitted. Phips immediately granted a reprieve to the three women who were convicted and in April released the remaining prisoners. Satan's controversy with Salem was finished.

That, in outline, is the witchcraft story as it has come down to us for so many years. Rightly or wrongly, the story has become an indelible part of American history. The startling fits of possession, the drama of the court examinations, the eloquent pleas of the innocent condemned—all make for a superb drama that casts into shadow the rest of Salem's more pedestrian history.

Indeed, the episode is unrepresentative. Witchcraft epidemics were not a serious problem in New England and were even less of a problem in other American colonies. Such persecutions were much more common in old England and Europe, where they had reached frightening proportions. The death of 20 people at Salem is sobering, but the magnitude of the event diminishes considerably alongside the estimate of 40,000 to 60,000 people executed for witchcraft in early modern Europe. Furthermore, it can be safely said that the witchcraft affair had no lasting effect on the political or religious history of America or even of Massachusetts.

Now, a curious thing has resulted from this illumination of a single, isolated episode. Again and again the story of Salem Village has been told, quite naturally, as a drama complete unto itself. The workaday history that preceded and followed the trials—the petty town bickerings, the arguments over land and ministers—all these elements were for many years largely passed over. Yet the disturbances at Salem did not occur in a vacuum. They may indeed have constituted an epidemic, but not the sort caused by some mysterious germ pool brought into the village over the rutted roads from Boston. So the historian's first task is to take the major strands of the witchcraft affair and see how they are woven into the larger fabric of New England society. Salem Village is small enough that virtually every one of its residents can be identified. We can find out who owned what land, the amount of taxes each resident paid, what sermons people listened to on Sundays. In so doing, a richer, far more intriguing picture of New England life begins to emerge.

THE INVISIBLE SALEM

Paradoxically, the most obvious facet of Salem life that the historian must recreate is also the most insubstantial: what ministers of the period would have called the "invisible world." Demons, familiars, witchcraft, and magic all shaped seventeenth-century New England. For most Salem Villagers, Satan was a living, supernatural being who might appear to people, bargain with them, even enter into agreements. The men and women who submitted to such devilish compacts were said to exchange their souls in return for special powers or favors: money and good fortune, perhaps, or the ability to revenge themselves on others.

Most often, ordinary folk viewed witchcraft as a simple matter of *maleficium:* Sarah Good, for example, being thought to have caused one of Sarah Gadge's cows to die after a hostile encounter. The process by which certain people in a community gained a reputation for wielding occult power was described well in 1587 by George Gifford, an English minister who was himself quite skeptical of the reality of witchcraft:

> Some woman doth fall out bitterly with her neighbour: there followeth some great hurt . . . There is a suspicion conceived. Within few years after, [the same woman] is in some jar [argument] with another. He is also plagued. This is noted of all. Great fame is spread of the matter. Mother W is a witch. She had bewitched Goodman B. Two hogs died strangely: or else he is taken lame.
>
> Well, Mother W doth begin to be very odious and terrible unto many. Her neighbours dare say nothing but yet in their hearts they wish she were hanged. Shortly after, another [person] falleth sick and doth pine; he can have no stomach unto his meat, nor he cannot sleep. The neighbours come to visit him. "Well neighbour," sayeth one, "do ye not suspect some naughty dealing: did ye never anger Mother W?" "Truly neighbour (sayeth he) I have not liked the woman a long time."

Such suspicions of witchcraft were widespread in the early modern world. Indeed, the belief in *maleficium* was only one part of a worldview filled with magic and wonders—magic that could be manipulated and pursued by someone with the proper knowledge. Fortune-tellers provided a window into the future; objects like horseshoes brought good luck; earthquakes and comets warned of God's judgments. People who possessed more than the usual store of supernatural knowledge were known as "cunning folk" who might be called upon in times of trouble to heal the illness of a sick villager, cast horoscopes for a merchant worried about a ship's upcoming voyage, or discover what sort of children a woman might bear.

The outlines of such beliefs are easily enough sketched, but they convey the emotions of witchcraft about as successfully as a recital of the Apostles' Creed conveys the fire of the Christian faith. It may seem a simple matter to imagine how a Salem Villager who believed in such wonders might have behaved, but people who hold beliefs foreign to our own do not always act the way that we think they should. Over the years, historians of the witchcraft controversy have faced the challenge of re-creating Salem's mental world.

One of the first people to review Salem's troubles was Thomas Hutchinson, who in 1750 published a history of New England's early days. Hutchinson did not believe in witchcraft; fewer and fewer educated people did as the eighteenth century progressed. Therefore he faced an obvious question, which centered on the motivations of the accusers. If the devil never actually covenanted with anyone, how were the accusers' actions to be explained? Some of Hutchinson's contemporaries argued that the bewitched were suffering from "bodily disorders which affected their imaginations." He disagreed: "A little attention must force conviction that the whole was a scene of fraud and imposture, begun by young girls, who at first perhaps thought of nothing more than being pitied and indulged, and continued by adult persons who were afraid of being accused themselves." Charles Upham, a minister who published a two-volume study of the episode in 1867, was equally hard on the young women. "There has seldom been better acting in a theatre than displayed in the presence of the astonished and horror-stricken rulers," he concluded tartly.

Indeed, the historical record does supply some evidence to suggest that the possessed were shamming. When Elizabeth Proctor was accused of being a witch, a friend of hers testified that he had seen one of the afflicted women cry out, "There's Goody Procter!"[1] But when people in the room challenged the woman's claim as evidently false, she backed off, saying only that "she did it for sport; they must have some sport."

A month and a half after the hearings had begun, one of the tormented young women, Mary Warren, stopped having her fits. She began to claim "that the afflicted persons did but dissemble"—that is, that they were shamming. Suddenly the other accusers began to declare that Mary's specter was afflicting them. Placed on the witness stand, Mary again fell into a fit "that she did neither see nor hear nor speak." The examination record continued:

> Afterwards she started up, and said I will speak and cryed out, Oh! I am sorry for it, I am sorry for it, and wringed her hands, and fell a little while into a fit again and then came to speak, but immediately her teeth were set, and then she fell into a violent fit and cryed out, oh Lord help me! Oh Good Lord Save me!
>
> And then afterward cryed again, I will tell I will tell and then fell into a dead fit againe.
>
> And afterwards cryed I will tell, they did, they did they did and then fell into a violent fit again.
>
> After a little recovery she cryed I will tell they brought me to it and then fell into a fit again which fits continueing she was ordered to be had out.

The scene is tantalizing. It appears as if Mary Warren is about to confess when pressure from the other girls forces her back to her former role as one of the afflicted. In the following weeks the magistrates questioned Mary repeatedly, with the result that her fits returned and she again joined in the accusations. Such evidence suggests that the girls may well have been acting.

Yet such a theory leaves certain points unexplained. If the girls were only acting, what are we to make of the many other witnesses who testified to deviltry? One villager, Richard Comans, reported seeing Bridget Bishop's specter in his bedroom. Bishop lay upon his breast, he reported, and "so oppressed" him that "he could not speak nor stur, noe not so much as to awake his wife" sleeping next to him. Comans and others who testified were not close friends of the girls; there appears no reason why they might be conspiring with each other. How does the historian explain their actions?

---

1. *Goody* was short for *Goodwife*, a term used for most married women. Husbands were addressed as *Goodman*. The terms *Mr.* and *Mrs.* were reserved for those of higher social standing.

Even some of the afflicted women's behavior is difficult to explain as conscious fraud. It is easy enough to imagine counterfeiting certain fits: whirling through the room crying "whish, whish"; being struck dumb. Yet other behavior was truly sobering: being pinched, pummeled, nearly choked to death; contortions so violent several grown men were required to restrain the victims. Even innocent victims of the accusations were astounded by such behavior. Rebecca Nurse on the witness stand could only look in astonishment at the "lamentable fits" she was accused of causing. "Do you think these [afflicted] suffer voluntary or involuntary?" asked John Hathorne. "I cannot tell what to think of it," replied Nurse hesitantly. Hathorne pressed others with similar results. What ails the girls, if not your torments? "I do not know." Do you think they are bewitched? "I cannot tell." What do you think does ail them? "There is more than ordinary."

More than ordinary. Historians may accept that possibility without necessarily supposing, with Hathorne, the presence of the preternatural. Psychiatric research has long established what we now take almost for granted: that people may act for reasons they themselves do not fully understand. Even more, that emotional problems may be the unconscious cause of apparently physical disorders. The rationalistic psychologies of Thomas Hutchinson and Charles Upham led them to reject any middle-ground explanations of motivation. The Salem women had not really been tormented by witches, Hutchinson and Upham reasoned; therefore they must have been acting voluntarily, consciously. But given the attitudes that accompanied a belief in devils and witches, it is possible to understand the Salem episode not as a game of fraud gone out of control, but as a study in abnormal psychology on a community-wide scale.

Scholars of the twentieth century have been more inclined to adopt this medical model as an explanation of Salem's troubles. Indeed, one of the first to make the suggestion was a pediatrician, Ernest Caulfield. The accused "were not impostors or pests or frauds," he wrote in 1943; "they were not cold-blooded malignant brats. They were sick children in the worst sort of mental distress—living in fear for their very lives and the welfare of their immortal souls." Certainly, the fear that gripped susceptible subjects must have been extraordinary. They imagined themselves pursued by agents of the devil, intent on torment or even murder, and locked doors provided no protection. Anthropologists who have examined witchcraft in other cultures note that bewitchment can be traumatic enough to lead to death. An Australian aborigine who discovers himself bewitched will

> stand aghast. . . . His cheeks blanch and his eyes become glassy. . . . He attempts to shriek but usually the sound chokes in his throat, and all that one might see is froth at his mouth. His body begins to tremble and the muscles twist involuntarily. He sways backwards and falls to the ground, and after a short time appears to be in a swoon; but soon after he writhes as if in mortal agony.

Afterward the victim refuses to eat, loses all interest in life, and dies. Although there were no documented cases of bewitchment death in Salem, the anthropological studies indicate the remarkable depth of reaction possible in a community that believes in its own magic.[2]

Historian Chadwick Hansen has compared the behavior of the bewitched with the neurotic syndrome that psychiatrists refer to as "conversion hysteria." A neurosis is a disorder of behavior that functions to avoid or deflect intolerable anxiety. Normally, an anxious person deals with an emotion through conscious action or thought. If the ordinary means of coping fail, however, the unconscious takes over. Hysterical patients will convert their mental worries into physical symptoms such as blindness, paralysis of various parts of the body, choking, fainting, or attacks of pain. These symptoms, it should be stressed, cannot be traced to organic causes. There is nothing wrong with the nervous system during an attack of paralysis, or with the optic nerve in a case of blindness. Physical disabilities are mentally induced. Such hysterical attacks often occur in patterns that bear striking resemblance to some of the Salem afflictions.

Pierre Janet, the French physician who wrote the classic *Major Symptoms of Hysteria* (1907), reported that a characteristic hysterical fit begins with a pain or strange sensation in some part of the body, often the lower abdomen. From there, he explained, it

> seems to ascend and to spread to other organs. For instance, it often spreads to the epigastrium [the region lying over the stomach], to the breasts, then to the throat. There it assumes rather an interesting form, which was for a very long time considered as quite characteristic of hysteria. The patient has the sensation of too big an object as it were, a ball rising in her throat and choking her.

Most of us have probably experienced a mild form of the last symptom—a proverbial "lump in the throat" that comes in times of stress. The hysteric's lump, or *globus hystericus*, is more extreme, as are the accompanying convulsions: "the head is agitated in one direction or another, the eyes closed, or open with an expression of terror, the mouth distorted."

Compare those symptoms with the ones experienced by Richard Comans, who (we have already seen) was struck down in bed by the weight of Bridget Bishop's specter and so frightened, "he could not speak nor stur"; or the fits of another tormented accuser, Elizabeth Brown, described during the Salem hearings:

> When [the witch's specter] did come it was as birds pecking her legs or pricking her with the motion of thayr wings and then it would rize up into her stamak with pricking pain as nayls and pins of which she did bitterly complayn and cry out like a women in travail and after that it would rise to her throat in a bunch like a pullets egg and then she would tern back her head and say witch you shant choak me.

2. The records hint that at least one bewitchment death may have occurred, however. Daniel Wilkins apparently believed that John Willard was a witch and meant him no good. Wilkins sickened, and some of the afflicted girls were summoned to his bedside, where they claimed that they saw Willard's specter afflicting him. The doctor would not touch the case, claiming it "preternatural." Shortly after, Wilkins died.

A hysterical convulsive attack of one of the patients in Salpêtrière Hospital during the nineteenth century. J. M. Charcot, the physician in charge of the clinic, spent much of his time studying the disorder. Note the crossed legs, similar to some of the Salem girls' fits.

The diagnosis of hysteria, or at least of unconscious psychological pressures of one sort or another, has gained ground over the past decades. Yet the issue of fraud cannot be put so easily to rest. Bernard Rosenthal, a scholar who has recently reexamined the Salem court records, argues that a close reading of the depositions suggests that fraud and hysteria were intermingled. What are we to make, for example, of the testimony given against Sarah Good and another accused, Lydia Dustin, regarding their "torments" of one Susannah Sheldon?

Susannah Sheldon being at the house of William Shaw she was tied her hands a cross in such a manner we were forced to cut the string before we could git her hand loose and when shee was out of her fit she told us it [was] Goody Dustin that did tye her hands after that manner, and 4 times shee hath been tyed in this manner in towe weeks time[.] The 2 first times shee sayth it was

Goode Dustin and the 2 last times it was Sarah Goode that did tye her. We fur-
der testifie that when ever shee doth but touch this string shee is presently bit.

It is one matter to have "fits" through terror but another to have wrists
tied four times by a specter who is then said to have bitten Sheldon if she
tried to untie them. Unless we believe in invisible specters, the only reasonable explanation would seem to be that Susannah Sheldon had a confederate
who tied her hands. Similarly Deodat Lawson, a minister who devoutly believed in witchcraft, reported in March 1692 that

> Some of the afflicted, as they were striving in their fits in open court, have (by
> invisible means) had their wrists bound fast together with a real cord, so as it
> could hardly be taken off without cutting. Some afflicted have been found with
> their arms tied, and hanged upon an hook, from whence others have been
> forced to take them down, that they might not expire in that posture.

The conclusion, argued Rosenthal, must be similar: "Whether the 'afflicted'
worked these shows out among themselves or had help from others cannot
be determined; but there is little doubt that such calculated action was deliberately conceived to perpetuate the fraud in which the afflicted were involved, and that theories of hysteria or hallucination cannot account for
people being bound, whether on the courtroom floor or on hooks." Such evidence suggests a complex set of behaviors in which both hysteria and fraud
played a part.

As for the behavior of those accused, what seems clear is the frightening
dynamic unleashed by the magistrates' decision to regard confession as worthy of pardon while viewing denials of witchcraft as a sign of guilt. Indeed,
the magistrates appeared not to want to take no for an answer. John Proctor
complained that when his son was examined, "because he would not confess
that he was Guilty, when he was Innocent, they tyed him Neck and Heels till
the Blood gushed out at his Nose, and would have kept him so 24 Hours, if
one more Merciful than the rest, had not taken pity on him." Once Bridget
Bishop was executed in June, the lesson was chilling and direct. Those who
confessed to witchcraft—like Tituba—avoided being hanged. Those who
maintained their innocence were headed for the gallows.

Sarah Churchill, a young woman of about seventeen, experienced these
pressures. She apparently succumbed to her fears and testified that she was
a witch. Soon, however, she had second thoughts, for she came crying and
wringing her hands to an older friend, Sarah Ingersoll. "I asked her what she
ailed?" reported Ingersoll.

> She answered she had undone herself. I asked her in what. She said in belying
> herself and others in saying she had set her hand to the devil's Book whereas
> she said she never did. I told her I believed she had set her hand to the book.
> She answered crying and said no no no, I naver, I naver did. I asked then what
> had made her say she did. She answered because they threatened her and told
> her they would put her into the dungeon and put her along with Mr. Bur-
> roughs, and thus several times she followed [me] on up and down telling me

that she had undone herself in belying herself and others. I asked her why she didn't tell the truth now. She told me because she had stood out so long in it that now she darst not. She said also that if she told Mr. Noyes [an investigating minister] but once that she had set her hand to the Book he would believe her, but if she told the truth and said she had not set her hand to the book a hundred times he would not believe her.

Thus psychological terrors sprang from more than one source. The frights of the invisible world, to be sure, led many villagers to fear for their lives and souls. But the refusal of the magistrates to accept the denials of the innocent led to equally terrifying pressures to belie oneself in order to escape execution. In a cataclysm involving hundreds of people in the community, either as accused witches, horrified onlookers, or active accusers, it is perhaps not surprising that individuals behaved in a wide variety of ways.

THE VISIBLE SALEM

It would be tempting, having explored the psychological dynamics of Salem, to suppose that the causes of the outbreak have been fairly well explained. There is the satisfaction of placing the symptoms of the modern hysteric side by side with those of the seventeenth-century bewitched and seeing them match, or of carefully reading the trial records to distinguish likely cases of fraud from those of hysteria. Yet by narrowing our inquiry to the motivations of the possessed, we have left other important facets of the Salem episode unexplored.

In the first place, the investigation thus far has dealt with the controversy on an individual rather than a social level. But step back for a moment. For whatever reasons, approximately 150 people in Salem and other towns found themselves accused. Why were those particular people singled out? Does any common bond explain why they, and not others, were accused? Only after we have examined their social identities can we answer that question.

Another indication that the social context of Salem Village needs to be examined is the nature of hysteria itself. Hysterics are notably suggestible, that is, sensitive to the influence of their environment. Scattered testimony in the records suggests that sometimes when the young women saw specters whom they could not identify, adults suggested names. "Was it Goody Cloyse? Was it Rebecca Nurse?" If true, such conditions confirm the need to move beyond strictly personal motivations to the social setting of the community.

In doing so, a logical first step would be to look for correlations, or characteristics common to groups that might explain their behavior. Are the accusers all church members and the accused nonchurch members? Are the accusers wealthy and respectable and the accused poor and disreputable? The historian assembles the data, shuffles them around, and looks for matchups.

Take the two social characteristics just mentioned, church membership and wealth. Historians can compile lists from the trial records of both the accusers and the accused. With those lists in hand, they can begin checking the church records to discover which people on each list were church members. Or they can search tax records to see whose tax rates were highest and thus which villagers were wealthiest. Land transactions were recorded, indicating which villagers owned the most land. Inventories of personal property were made when a member of the community died, so at least historians have some record of an individual's assets at death, if not in 1692. Other records may mention a trade or occupation, which will give a clue to relative wealth or social status.

If you made such calculations for the Salem region, you would quickly find yourself at a dead end, a spot altogether too familiar to practicing historians. True, the first few accused witches were not church members, but soon enough the faithful found themselves in jail along with nonchurch members. A similar case holds for wealth. Although Tituba, Sarah Good, and Sarah Osbourne were relatively poor, merchants and wealthy farmers were accused as the epidemic spread. The correlations fail to check.

This dead end was roughly the point that had been reached when two historians, Paul Boyer and Stephen Nissenbaum, were inspired to take literally the advice about going back to the drawing board. More than a hundred years earlier Charles Upham had made a detailed map of Salem for his own study of the witchcraft episode. Upham examined the old town records, paced the actual sites of old houses, and established to the best of his knowledge the residences of a large majority of Salem Villagers. Boyer and Nissenbaum took their list of accusers and accused and noted the location of each village resident. The results were striking, as can be seen from the map on page 38.

Of the fourteen accused witches in the village, twelve lived in the eastern section. Of the thirty-two adult villagers who testified against the accused, thirty lived in the western section. "In other words," concluded Boyer and Nissenbaum, "the alleged witches and those who accused them resided on opposite sides of the Village." Furthermore, of twenty-nine residents who publicly defended the accused in some way, twenty-four lived in the eastern half of the village. Often they were close neighbors of the accused. It is moments like these that make the historian want to behave, were it not for the staid air of research libraries, like Archimedes leaping from his fabled bathtub and shouting "Eureka!"

The discovery is only the beginning of the task. The geographic chart suggests a division, but it does not at all indicate what that division is, other than a general east-west split. So Boyer and Nissenbaum began to explore the history of the village itself, expanding their microcosm of 1692 backward in time. They investigated a social situation that historians had long recognized but had never associated with the Salem witch trials: Salem Village's uneasy relation to its social parent, Salem Town.

Salem Town's settlement followed the pattern of most coastal New England towns. Original settlers set up houses around a central location and carved their farmlands out of the surrounding countryside. As a settlement prospered, the land in its immediate vicinity came to be completely taken up. As houses were erected farther and farther away from the central meeting

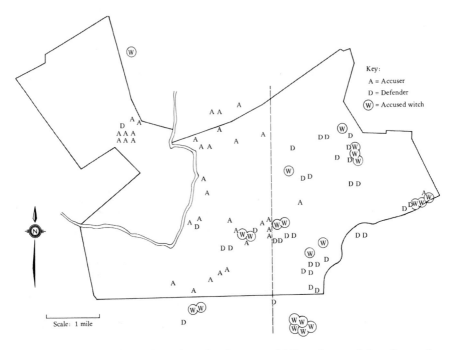

"The Geography of Witchcraft" (after Boyer and Nissenbaum, *Salem Possessed*, Harvard University Press, 1974)

house, outlying residents found it inconvenient to come to church or attend to other civic duties. In such cases, they sought recognition as a separate village, with their own church, their own taxes, and their own elected officials.

Here the trouble started. The settlers who lived toward the center of town were reluctant to let their outlying neighbors break away. Everyone paid taxes to support a minister for the town church, to maintain the roads, and to care for the poor. If a chunk of the village split off, revenue would be lost. Furthermore, outlying settlers would no longer share the common burdens, such as guarding the town at night. So the centrally located settlers usually resisted any movement for autonomy by their more distant neighbors. Such disputes were a regular feature of New England life.

Salem Town had followed this pattern. Its first settlers located on a peninsula extending into Massachusetts Bay, where they pursued a prosperous colonial trade. By 1668 four outlying areas had already become separate towns. Now the "Salem Farmers," living directly to the west, were petitioning for a similar settlement, and the "Townsmen" were resisting. In 1672 Massachusetts's legislature allowed Salem Village to build its own meeting house, but in other matters, the village remained dependent. Salem Town still collected village taxes, chose village constables, and arranged for village roads. The colony's records include petition after petition from villagers complaining about tax rates, patrol duties, boundary rulings.

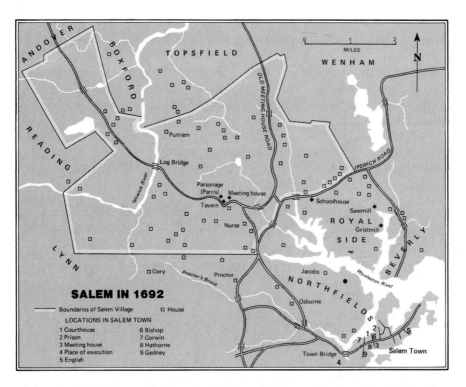

"Salem in 1692" (From *The Pursuit of Liberty: A History of the American People*, vol. 1, by R. Jackson Wilson, et al. Copyright 1966 by HarperCollins College Publishers. Reprinted by permission of Addison-Wesley Educational Publishers Inc.)

Here, then, is one east-west split—between the village and the town. But the line drawn on Boyer and Nissenbaum's map is *within* the village. What cause would the village have for division?

Many causes, the records indicate—chief among them the choice of a minister. When the village built its own meeting house, it chose James Bayley to be its pastor in 1673. Soon enough, however, some churchgoers began complaining. Bayley didn't attend regularly to his private prayers. Church members had not been fully consulted before his selection. After a flurry of petitions and counterpetitions, Bayley left in 1680, and George Burroughs was hired. Three years later Burroughs left in another dispute. He was succeeded by Deodat Lawson, who lasted through four more years of quarrels. Finally Samuel Parris occupied the pulpit after 1688. His term was equally stormy, and in 1696 his opponents finally succeeded in starving him out of the job by refusing to collect taxes to pay his salary.

The maneuverings that went on during the years of bickering seem bewilderingly complex. But Boyer and Nissenbaum recognized that the church records, as well as the petitions and counterpetitions, provided a key to local divisions. When the lists from the different quarrels were compared,

Boyer and Nissenbaum found that the same names were being grouped to-gether. The people who supported James Bayley usually supported George Burroughs and then opposed the second two ministers. Conversely, the sup-porters of Deodat Lawson and Samuel Parris had been the people who com-plained about Bayley and Burroughs. And—here is the link—the two lists from those disputes coincide closely with the divisions in 1692 between ac-cusers and accused.

Suddenly the Salem witch trials take on an entirely new appearance. In-stead of being a dramatic disruption that appears out of nowhere in a village kitchen and then disappears equally suddenly at the end of ten months, it be-comes an elaboration of a quarrel that has gone on for nearly twenty years!

What lay behind the divisions? One reading of the evidence suggests that the larger split between Salem Town and Salem Village was reflected in the village itself, with the villagers on the east retaining enough in common with the town to continue their affiliation and the westerners favoring complete separation. Boyer and Nissenbaum argue that the division also went beyond the simple geographical one to a difference in outlook and lifestyle. Salem Town was entering into its own as one of the major commercial centers of New England. It boasted a growing merchant class whose wealth would soon support the building of fine mansions. By contrast, the farmers in the western portion of Salem Village were tied more closely to traditional agrar-ian life: subsistence farming, spartan daily lives, a suspicion of the commer-cial habits of offering credit and making speculative investments. Worse, the Salem farmers found themselves increasingly hard-pressed. The land avail-able in the village was dwindling. What land there was proved less fertile than the broad plains on the eastern side of the village and along the north-ern flats of Salem Town.

Look, too, at the occupations of the accused witches and their defenders. Many lived along the Ipswich Road, a route that passed by the village rather than through it, a main thoroughfare for travelers and for commerce. The tradespeople who had set up shop there included a carpenter, sawmill oper-ator, shoemaker, and miller. And of course there were the taverns, mainstays of travelers, yet always slightly suspect to Puritans. The people along the Ipswich Road were not rich, most of them, but their commercial links were with Salem Town and with outsiders. They were small-scale entrepreneurs rather than farmers. Out of twenty-one villagers who lived along or near the road, only two signed petitions linking them with the western faction; thir-teen signed petitions linking them with the eastern faction. Tavern keeper John Proctor was hanged as a witch; his wife Elizabeth barely escaped with her life; and Joshua Rea, another tavern keeper on the road, signed a peti-tion defending Goody Nurse.

Boyer and Nissenbaum's reconstruction of village factions thus suggests an alternate way of looking at the Salem trials. Traditional accounts place Samuel Parris and his supporters as leaders of the village, terrorizing inno-cent villagers and controlling the trials. Certainly Parris's supporters had their day in 1692, but from the longer perspective they appear to have been fighting a losing battle. If Boyer and Nissenbaum are correct, the Salem trials were an indirect yet anguished protest of a group of villagers whose agrarian way of life was being threatened by the rising commercialism of Salem Town.

The brilliance of Boyer and Nissenbaum's research was to place the individual dramas of Salem into a larger social context. But their maps are not the only maps that can be drawn, nor their connections the only connections to be made. Boyer and Nissenbaum focused their attention on Salem Village. But as the witchcraft trials gained momentum, the fever spread to a few neighboring villages. In the summer of 1692, several of the possessed women of Salem were invited to Andover by concerned residents. The resulting round of accusations led to the arrest of nearly forty Andover villagers. A month later, a smaller outbreak centered in the fishing port of Gloucester, where six people were arrested. Several more of the accused from Salem had Gloucester ties. All these people were tried by the same court that dealt with the Salem cases.

Taking these additional episodes into account makes it more difficult to generalize about embattled farmers arrayed against a rising commercialism. Gloucester was a fishing port, while Andover, though it was just as agrarian as Salem Village, had no commercial "parent" the likes of Salem Town. But if rising commercialism was not the only, or primary, social factor influencing the Salem outbreak, what then?

Several historians, most recently Mary Beth Norton, have explored the connections between the trials and New England's Indian wars. Memories of King Philip's War of 1676 lingered in the region for many years, leaving inhabitants anxious and uneasy, especially along the frontier. Then came a new outbreak of violence in 1689, which the settlers referred to as "the second Indian war." In January 1692, just as the witchcraft controversy was getting started, word came from York, Maine, that Indians had massacred residents there. Indeed, a number of the accusers at the Salem trials experienced firsthand the horrors of the conflict. Mercy Lewis—one of the principal accusers—only two years earlier had seen her mother, father, sister, and brother murdered in an Indian attack.

Analyzing the chronology of the trials, Norton pointed out that the number of witchcraft accusations rose sharply only in April 1692. It was at this point that Abigail Hobbs was brought before the magistrates because of her reputation for being flippant about the spreading crisis. (She was "not afraid of anything," she supposedly boasted, because she had "Sold her selfe boddy & Soull to the old boy"—that is, to Satan.) During the late 1680s Hobbs had lived for some time along the Maine frontier. Under hostile questioning from the magistrates, she admitted that she had covenanted there with the devil—while "at Casko-bay." Having thus confessed, she quickly turned into an enthusiastic prosecution witness. Before her confession on April 17 only ten people had been charged with witchcraft. In the seven weeks that followed, the total jumped to sixty-eight. The spectral visions of Abigail Hobbs and Mercy Lewis led to the indictment of a number of folk from Maine, chief among them the Reverend George Burroughs, who seemed the ring-leader of the devilish conspiracy, in the eyes of many. The anxieties spawned by the frontier attacks, argued Norton, were what pushed the Salem hysteria beyond the bounds of the usual witchcraft trials of seventeenth-century New England.

In addition to the fear of Indian "devils," did the accusers perhaps fear religious demons? For years the colony's ruling Congregationalists had worried about the heresies spread by Quakers, members of the Society of Friends. In the 1650s and 1660s, Massachusetts Bay hanged four Quaker missionaries on the Boston Common. Other members of this Protestant sect had been whipped, thrown into prison, or driven from the colony. The Quaker belief that every person possessed his or her own divine inner light seemed to Congregationalists to suggest the blasphemous notion that God could speak directly to individuals. Even more disquieting, Friends caught up in their enthusiasm would "quake" when the holy spirit possessed them, behavior that seemed all too much like the fits of the Salem afflicted. "Diabolical Possession was the thing which did dispose and encline men unto Quakerism," warned Boston minister Cotton Mather, the son of Increase, in 1689.

By 1692, Congregationalists no longer had the power to persecute Quakers, for Massachusett's new charter guaranteed toleration to all Protestants. Yet many ordinary folk continued to harbor suspicions, and within Essex County, the largest concentration of Quakers lived in Salem. Aside from Salem, the next largest group lived in Gloucester. In Andover too, Quaker connections seemed to figure in the arrests. In most cases, hostility was directed not so much at the Quakers themselves as at Congregationalists who established social ties with them. Rebecca Nurse, who was pious and well respected in other ways, had taken an orphaned Quaker boy into her family. John and Elizabeth Proctor, the tavern keepers, counted a large number of Quakers among Elizabeth's family. Christine Heyrman, the historian who researched these connections, concluded that the western farmers of Salem may have worried less about how near they lived to commercial Salem than about "the even shorter physical distance separating the residences of the accused from Salem's Quaker enclave."

"WOMEN ALONE"

Whereas Boyer, Nissenbaum, and other historians have pursued correlations based on the social geography of witchcraft, another striking connection can be made. That connection is the link between witchcraft and gender.

By a large majority, the accused witches of Salem were women. Out of 178 accused who can be identified by name, more than 3 out of 4 were female. And it turns out that nearly half the accused men were husbands, sons, or other relatives of accused women. The gender gap widens further when witchcraft outside Salem is examined. Of 147 additional accused witches in seventeenth-century New England, 82 percent were women. In those cases that actually came to trial (41), 34 involved women and only 7 involved men. Of the women tried, 53 percent were convicted. Of the men, only 2 were convicted, or 29 percent. And of those people who were not only convicted but executed, women outnumbered men 15 to 2.

When historian Carol Karlsen examined the trial records in more detail, she found that the authorities tended to treat accused women differently from men. Magistrates and ministers often put pressure on women to confess their guilt. In New England cases (excluding Salem), when that pressure led a woman to confess a "familiarity with Satan," she was invariably executed, in accordance with the Biblical command, "Thou shalt not suffer a witch to live." But when men were accused, pressure was seldom applied to make them confess. In fact, confessions from men were not always accepted. In 1652 one John Broadstreet of Rowley admitted having familiarity with Satan. The court ordered him whipped and fined twenty shillings "for telling a lie." In 1674 Christopher Brown confessed to "discoursing with . . . the devil," but the court rejected his statement as being "inconsistent with truth." Hugh Crotia admitted that he had "signed the Devills book and then seald it with his bloud." A Hartford grand jury refused to indict him.

Such evidence suggests that, by and large, most seventeenth-century New Englanders expected women to be witches, whereas men who confessed were seldom believed. But why should women be singled out for such attention?

Part of the answer, Karlsen argues, lay in the cultural position of women. Like Martin Luther and other Reformation theologians, the Puritans exalted the role of motherhood over the chaste life of the convent; they saw women as partners and helpmates in marriage. Even so, Puritans retained a distinctly hierarchical conception of marriage. They viewed families as miniature commonwealths, with the husband as the ruler and his family as willing subjects. "A true wife accounts her subjection [as] her honor and freedom," noted Governor John Winthrop of Massachusetts.

A wife's unequal status was reflected legally as well: she was known in law as a *feme covert*—one whose identity was "covered" by that of her husband. As such, she had no right to buy or sell property, to sue or be sued, or to make contracts. Similarly, the patterns of inheritance in New England were male dominated. A husband might leave his widow property—indeed, the law required him to leave her at least a third of his estate. But she was to "have and enjoy" that property only "during term of her natural life." She could not waste or squander it, for it was passed on to the family's heirs at her death. Similarly, daughters might inherit property, but if they were already married, it belonged to the husband. If a young woman had not yet married, property usually seems to have been held for her, "for improvement," until she married.

Thus the only sort of woman who held any substantial economic power was a widow who had not remarried. Such a woman was known as a *feme sole*, or "woman alone." She did have the right to sue, to make contracts, and to

Older women—especially those who were reputed to have medical knowledge of herbs and potions—often came under suspicion of witchcraft both in England and in America. This English drawing of 1622 portrays the stereotypical willful older woman, a supposed witch by the name of Jennet Dibble. She was said to have been attended for forty years by a spirit in the shape of a great black cat called Gibb.

buy or sell property. Even when remarrying, a widow could sometimes protect her holdings by having her new husband sign a prenuptial contract, guaranteeing before marriage that the wife would keep certain property as her own. In male-dominated New England, these protections made the *feme sole* stand out as an anomaly—a woman alone who did not fit comfortably into the ordinary scheme of things.

Given that women in Puritan society were generally placed in subordinate roles, how does that fact help explain the preponderance of female witches? As it turns out, a significant number of accused witches were women who were *not* subordinate in some way. In refusing to conform to accepted stereotypes, they threatened the traditional order of society and were more likely to be accused of subverting it as witches.

A woman might stand out, for example, through a contentious, argumentative nature. If a woman's duty was to submit quietly to the rule of men and to glory in "subjection," then quite a few witches refused to conform to the accepted role. We have already seen how Sarah Good's "muttering and scolding extreamly" were perceived by Salem Villagers to have caused the death of cattle. Trial records are filled with similar accusations.

Often, more than short tempers were at stake. A remarkably high percentage of accused women were *femes sole* in an economic sense. Of the 124 witches whose inheritance patterns can be reconstructed from surviving records, as many as 71 (57 percent) lived or had lived in families with no male heirs. Another 14 accused witches were the daughters or granddaughters of witches who did not have brothers or sons to inherit their property. This figure is at least twice the number that would be expected, given the usual percentage of *femes sole* in the New England population. Furthermore, of the women executed at Salem, more than half had inherited or stood to inherit their own property. Such statistics suggest why witchcraft controversies so often centered on women.

TANGLED WEBS

The early modern world, including that of colonial New England, was uncertain, unpredictable, full of chance. Livestock, on which farm families depended, might die suddenly. The primitive knowledge of physicians proved all but useless in curing the ills of the poor and wealthy alike. Amidst so many unpredictable tragedies, witchcraft offered an explanation for misfortunes that otherwise might have seemed inexplicable. Witchcraft made the unpredictable predictable and the obscure sometimes all too terrifyingly clear.

Unlike diviners or witch doctors, historians have followed the example of the natural sciences in seeking testable, rational links between cause and effect. Yet the longing for a simple, coherent story remains strong. We all wish to see the confusing welter of events lock together with a clarity that leads us, like Archimedes, to cry Eureka—conversion hysteria! Or Eureka—the pressures of the new commercial economy! Or Eureka—*femes sole!*

Instead, the discipline of small-scale, local history forces humility. As historians sift the web of relationships surrounding the Salem outbreak, most have come to believe that its causes are multiple rather than singular. "Irreducible to any single source of social strain," concludes Christine Heyrman. No single "governing explanation," argues Bernard Rosenthal. The very fact that witchcraft outbreak did not recur elsewhere in New England suggests that the magnitude of Salem's calamity depended on an unusual combination of psychological and social factors.

Certainly, an agrarian faction in the village did not consciously devise the trials to punish their commercial rivals or Quaker-loving neighbors. Nor was the male Puritan patriarchy launching a deliberate war against women. But the invisible world of witchcraft did provide a framework that amplified village anxieties and focused them. As the accusations of a small circle of young women widened and as controversy engulfed the town, it was only natural that long-standing quarrels and prejudices were drawn into the debate. The interconnections between a people's religious beliefs, their habits of commerce, even their dream and fantasy lives, are intricate and fine, entwined with one another like the delicate root system of a growing plant. Historians who limit their examination to a small area of time and space are able, through persistent probing, to untangle the strands of emotions, motivations, and social structures that provided the context for those slow processions to the gallows on Witch's Hill.

Additional Reading

David Hall's *Worlds of Wonder, Days of Judgment* (New York, 1988) provides an excellent introduction to the way witchcraft fits into the larger belief systems of popular religion and magic. Hall also lays out historians' contrasting approaches to Salem in "Witchcraft and the Limits of Interpretation," *New England Quarterly* 58 (1985): 253–281. A review essay by John M. Murrin, "The Infernal Conspiracy of Indians and Grandmothers," *Reviews in American History* 31 (2003): 485–494, describes more recent studies, which include significant new material.

Some changes seem merely a matter of detail, such as the exact manner in which the outbreak began in Samuel Parris's kitchen. But details matter. Many accounts (including ours, in earlier editions) assumed that Tituba's knowledge of African magic sparked the baking of the witch cake and possibly even the original fortune-telling episode. Other historians have even assumed Tituba was African. In fact, that notion is a nineteenth-century addition, amplified over the years, as Chadwick Hansen shows in "The Metamorphosis of Tituba, or Why American Intellectuals Can't Tell an Indian Witch from a Negro," *New England Quarterly* 47 (1974): 3–12. Bernard Rosenthal, in *Salem Story: Reading the Witch Trials of 1692* (New York, 1993), makes it clear that a white New England neighbor, not Tituba, had the idea of baking a witch cake. See also Elaine G. Breslaw, *Tituba, Reluctant Witch of Salem: Devilish Indians and Puritan Fantasies* (New York, 1996), and Bernard Rosenthal, "Tituba's Story," *New England Quarterly* 71 (1998): 190–203. David C. Brown debunks other venerable myths in "The Case of Giles Corey," *Essex Institute Historical Collections* 121 (1985): 282–299.

Chadwick Hansen's *Witchcraft at Salem* (New York, 1969) presents the most detailed case for conversion hysteria among the accusers. But Rosenthal's *Salem Story* argues convincingly that conscious deception played some role, especially among the core accusers. Another theory has suggested that the accusers' fits can be explained by ergot, a fungus that sometimes grows on bread grains such as rye. See Mary A. K. Matossian, *Poisons of the Past* (New Haven, 1989), as well as Linnda R. Caporael, "Ergotism: The Satan Loosed in Salem?" in *Science* 192 (1976): 21–26. Yet another hypothesis, advanced in Louise Winn Carlson, *A Fever in Salem* (Chicago, 1999), suggests that the fits were caused by encephalitis, a bacterial or viral infection of the membranes surrounding the brain. To our mind, such medical theories are too narrowly monocausal (Eureka!) to hold up to close scrutiny. For a rebuttal to the ergot hypothesis, see Nicholas P. Spanos and Jack Gottlieb, "Ergotism and the Salem Village Witch Trials," *Science* 194 (1976): 1390–1394.

Paul Boyer and Stephen Nissenbaum apply the techniques of social history with lucidity and grace in *Salem Possessed: The Social Origins of Witchcraft* (Cambridge, MA, 1974). Other historians, however, have been skeptical about leaning too hard on rising commercialism as the outbreak's chief catalyst. For the contribution of anxiety over war and Indian raids, see the authoritative study by Mary Beth Norton, *In the Devil's Snare: The Salem Witchcraft Crisis of 1692* (New York, 2002); for Quaker connections, see Christine Leigh Heyrman, "Specters of Subversion, Societies of Friends" in David D. Hall et al., eds. *Saints and Revolutionaries: Essays on Early American History* (New York, 1984). Our discussion of gender and witchcraft relies on Carol Karlsen, *The Devil in the Shape of a Woman: Witchcraft in Colonial New England* (New York, 1987). Other approaches to the gender question can be found in John Putnam Demos, *Entertaining Satan: Witchcraft and the Culture of Early New England* (New York, 1982), and Elizabeth Reis, *Damned Women: Sinners and Witches in Puritan New England* (Ithaca, NY, 1997).

Other studies of witchcraft include Richard Godbeer, *The Devil's Dominion: Magic and Religion in Early New England* (New York, 1992). Godbeer has also written an insightful narrative of a different witchcraft trial (in Fairfield, Connecticut), which provides a useful counterexample to the Salem outbreak: *Escaping Salem: The Other Witch Hunt of 1692* (New York, 2004). See also Richard Weisman, *Witchcraft, Magic, and Religion in Seventeenth-Century Massachusetts* (Amherst, MA, 1984). Peter Charles Hoffer, *The Devil's Disciples: Makers of the Salem Witchcraft Trials* (Baltimore, 1996) provides useful legal background, though the author is often speculative. (He vividly describes Tituba's *African* years, for example, and her supposed Middle Passage voyage to the Caribbean.)

Comparison of the Salem trials with witchcraft in early modern Europe is useful. The place to begin is with Robin Briggs, *Witches and Neighbors* (New York, 1996). Briggs notes that although a belief in *maleficium* was widespread among the peasantry, it less often embodied grandiose satanic conspiracies. Older studies of English witchcraft worth consulting include Brian P. Levack, *The Witch-Hunt in Early Modern Europe*, 2d ed. (New York, 1995); Alan Macfarlane, *Witchcraft in Tudor and Stuart England* (New York, 1970); and Keith Thomas, *Religion and the Decline of Magic* (London, 1971).

The most fascinating primary sources are the records of pretrial examinations made by the Salem magistrates. These records can be found in *The Salem Witchcraft Papers: Verbatim Transcripts of the Legal Documents of the Salem Witchcraft Outbreak of 1692*, 3 vols. (New York, 1977). The collection sorts documents alphabetically, by the names of the accused witches. This arrangement is quite inconvenient in some ways, because many documents, obviously, refer to more than one of the accused. Bernard Rosenthal is preparing a new edition of the work that will be arranged chronologically, which when it appears should be definitive. George Lincoln Burr, ed., *Narratives of the Witchcraft Cases, 1648–1706* (New York, 1914; reissued 1968) is a convenient compendium of some contemporary accounts. Boyer and Nissenbaum have collected their own anthology of primary documents in *Witchcraft at Salem Village* (Belmont, CA, 1972), oriented more toward the social background of Salem.

Finally, parallels between the outbreak at Salem and modern controversies are worth pursuing. The question of whether repressed incidents of child abuse can be deduced through "recovered memory" are explored in a volume that makes explicit comparisons with the Salem witch trials. See Mark Pendergrast, *Victims of Memory: Sex Abuse Accusations and Shattered Lives*, 2d ed. (Hinesburg, VT, 1996), as well as Michael Shermer, *Why People Believe Weird Things: Pseudoscience, Superstition, and Other Confusions of Our Time* (New York, 1997). Also useful is Frederick Crews, "The Revenge of the Repressed," *New York Review of Books*, 17 November 1994 and 1 December 1994. Crews has collected these essays, along with responses by his critics, in *The Memory Wars: Freud's Legacy in Dispute* (New York, 1995). Elaine Showalter puts some of these controversies in the broader context of hysteria as it has been expressed over the years in *Hysteries* (New York, 1997).

Interactive Learning

The *Primary Source Investigator* sources explore the "visible and invisible worlds of Salem" during the infamous Salem witch trials. These documents include the original handwritten depositions of Anne Hutchinson and Mary Osgood, two women accused of witchcraft, as well as the examination of several men who were accused of witchcraft. Images depicting scenes of these examinations and of encounters with spirits visualize the deadly passions of the episode. Also included are letters between religious officials both supporting and denouncing the proceedings, as well as sermons that provide a glimpse into the "wondrous providences" that most of the English colonists saw around them.

CHAPTER 3
Declaring Independence

Good historians share with magicians a talent for elegant sleight of hand. In both professions, the manner of execution conceals much of the work that makes the performance possible. Like the magician's trapdoors, mirrors, and other hidden props, historians' primary sources are essential to their task. But the better that historians are at their craft, the more likely they will focus their readers' attention on the historical scene itself and not on the supporting documents.

Contrary to prevailing etiquette, we have gone out of our way to call attention to the problems of evidence to be solved before a historical narrative is presented in its polished form. As yet, however, we have not examined in detail the many operations to be performed on a single document. What at first seems a relatively simple job of collecting, examining, and cataloging may become remarkably complex, especially when the document in question is of major importance.

So let us narrow our focus even more than in the previous two chapters by concentrating not on a region (Virginia) or a village (Salem), but on one document. The document in question admittedly carries more import than most, yet it remains brief enough to be read in several minutes. It also has the merit of being one of the few primary sources that virtually every reader of this book already will have encountered: the Declaration of Independence.

The Declaration, of course, is one of the most celebrated documents in the nation's history. Drafted by Thomas Jefferson, adopted by the Second Continental Congress, published for the benefit of the world, memorialized in countless patriotic speeches, it is today displayed within the rotunda of the National Archives, carefully encased in a glass container filled with helium to prevent any long-term deterioration from oxygen. Every schoolchild knows that Congress declared the colonies' independence by issuing the document on July 4, 1776. Nearly everyone has seen the painting by John Trumbull that depicts members of Congress receiving the parchment for signing on that day.

Along with the Constitution and the Bill of Rights, the Declaration of Independence (*center*) is displayed within the rotunda of the National Archives. Since 1952, when the nuclear arms race was in full swing, these documents have been lowered every night into a 55-ton vault of reinforced concrete and steel, whose massive doors swing shut to protect them from the threat of atomic attack.

So the starting place is familiar enough. Yet there is a good deal to establish when unpacking the facts about such a seminal document. Under what circumstances did Jefferson write the Declaration? What people, events, or other documents influenced him? Only when such questions are answered in more detail does it become clear that quite a few of the "facts" enumerated in the previous paragraph are either misleading or incorrect. And the confusion begins in trying to answer the most elementary questions about the Declaration.

THE CREATION OF A TEXT

In May 1776 Thomas Jefferson traveled to Philadelphia, as befit a proper gentleman, in a coach-and-four with two attending slaves. He promptly took his place on the Virginia delegation to the Second Continental Congress.

Even a year after fighting had broken out at Lexington and Concord, Congress was still debating whether the quarrel with England could be patched up. Sentiment for independence ran high in many areas but by no means everywhere. The greatest reluctance lay in the middle colonies, particularly in Pennsylvania, where moderates such as John Dickinson still hoped for reconciliation.

Such cautious sentiments infuriated the more radical delegates, especially John and Samuel Adams of Massachusetts. The two Adamses had worked for independence from the opening days of Congress but found the going slow. America, complained John, was "a great, unwieldy body. It is like a large fleet sailing under convoy. The fleetest sailers must wait for the dullest and the slowest." Jefferson also favored independence, but he lacked the Adamses' taste for political infighting. While the men from Massachusetts pulled their strings in Congress, Jefferson only listened attentively and took notes. Thirty-three years old, he was the youngest delegate, and no doubt his age contributed to his diffidence. Privately, he conversed more easily with friends, sprawling casually in a chair with one shoulder cocked high, the other low, and his long legs extended. He got along well with the other delegates and performed his committee assignments dutifully.

The debate over independence seemed to sputter on fitfully until late May, when Jefferson's colleague Richard Henry Lee arrived from Williamsburg. Lee was under instructions from the Virginia convention to force Congress to act. On Friday, June 7, he rose in Congress and offered the following resolutions:

> That these United Colonies are, and of right ought to be, free and independent States, that they are absolved from all allegiance to the British crown, and that all political connection between them and the state of Great Britain is, and ought to be, totally dissolved.
>
> That it is expedient forthwith to take the most effectual measures for forming foreign alliances.
>
> That a plan of confederation be prepared and transmitted to the respective colonies for their consideration and approbation.

On Saturday and again on Monday, moderates and radicals earnestly debated the propositions. They knew that a declaration of independence would make the breach with England final. The secretary of the Congress, Charles Thomson, cautiously recorded in his minutes only that "certain resolutions" were "moved and discussed"—the certain resolutions, of course, being treasonous in the extreme.

Still, sentiment was running with the radicals. When delegate James Wilson of Pennsylvania announced that he felt ready to vote for independence, Congress set the wheels in motion by appointing a five-member committee "to prepare a Declaration to the effect of the said first resolution." The events that followed can be traced, in bare outline at least, in a modern edition of Secretary Thomson's minutes (*Journals of the Continental Congress: 1774–1789*). From it we learn that on June 11, 1776, Congress constituted

Jefferson, John Adams, Benjamin Franklin, Roger Sherman, and Robert Livingston as a "Committee of Five" responsible for drafting the declaration. Then for more than two weeks, Thomson's journal remains silent on the subject. Only on Friday, June 28, does it note that the committee "brought in a draught" of an independence declaration.

On Monday, July 1, Congress resolved itself into a "Committee of the Whole," in which it could freely debate the sensitive question without leaving any official record of debate or disagreement. (Thomson's minutes did not record the activities of committees.) On July 2 the Committee of the Whole went through the motions of "reporting back" to Congress (that is, to itself). The minutes note only that Richard Lee's resolution, then "being read" in formal session, "was agreed to."

Thus the official journal makes it clear that Congress voted for independence on July 2, not July 4, adopting Richard Henry Lee's original proposal of June 7. When John Adams wrote home on July 3 to his wife, Abigail, he enthusiastically predicted that July 2 would be remembered as "the most memorable Epoca in the History of America. I am apt to believe that it will be celebrated, by succeeding Generations, as the great anniversary Festival. . . . It ought to be solemnized with Pomp and Parade, with Shews, Games, Sports, Guns, Bells, Bonfires and Illuminations from one End of this Continent to the other from this Time forward forever more."

As it turned out, Adams picked the wrong date for the fireworks. Although Congress had officially broken the tie with England, the declaration *explaining* the action had not yet been approved. On July 3 and 4 Congress again met as a Committee of the Whole. Only then was the formal declaration reported back, accepted, and sent to the printer. Thomson's journal notes, "The foregoing declaration was, by order of Congress, engrossed, and signed by the following members. . . ." Here is the enactment familiar to everyone: the "engrossed" parchment (one written in large, neat letters) beginning with its bold "IN CONGRESS, JULY 4, 1776," and concluding with the president of the Continental Congress's signature, so flourishing that we still speak of putting our John Hancock to paper. Below that, the signatures of fifty-five other delegates appear more modestly inscribed.

If mention of the Declaration in Thomson's minutes concluded with the entry on July 4, schoolchildren might emerge with their memories reasonably intact. But later entries of the journal suggest that in all likelihood, the Declaration was not signed on July 4 after all, but on August 2. To muddy the waters further, not all the signers were in Philadelphia even on August 2. Some could not have signed the document until October or November.

So the upshot of the historian's preliminary investigation is that (1) Congress declared independence on the second of July, not the fourth; (2) most members officially signed the engrossed parchment only on the second of August; and (3) all the signers of the Declaration never met together in the same room at once, despite the appearances in John Trumbull's painting. In the matter of establishing the basic facts surrounding a document, historians are all too ready to agree with John Adams's bewildered search of his recol-

The Committee of Five—Adams, Sherman, Livingston, Jefferson, and Franklin—present their work to John Hancock, president of the Continental Congress, in a detail from *The Declaration of Independence* by John Trumbull. When Hancock finally put his elaborate signature to the engrossed copy, he is reported to have said, "There! John Bull can read my name without spectacles, and may now double his reward of £500 for my head."

lections: "What are we to think of history? When in less than 40 years, such diversities appear in the memories of living men who were witnesses."

Yet even with the basic facts in place, many important points remain to be answered about the Declaration's creation. Although Jefferson drafted it, what did the Committee of Five contribute? If the delegates made changes during the congressional debate on July 3 and 4, for what purpose? A historian will want to know which parts of the completed document were most controversial; surviving copies of earlier drafts could shed valuable light on these questions.

The search for accurate information about the Declaration's drafting began even while the protagonists were still living. Some forty years after the signing, both Jefferson and John Adams tried to set down the sequence of events. Adams recalled the affable and diplomatic Jefferson suggesting that Adams write the first draft. "I will not," replied Adams.

"You shall do it," persisted Jefferson.

"Oh no!"

"Why will you not do it? You ought to do it."

"I will not."

"Reasons enough." And Adams ticked them off. "Reason 1st. You are a Virginian and a Virginian ought to be at the head of this business. Reason 2nd. I am obnoxious, suspected and unpopular; you are very much otherwise. Reason 3rd. You can write ten times better than I can."

"Well," said Jefferson, "if you are decided, I will do as well as I can."

Jefferson, for his part, did not remember this bit of diplomatic shuttlecock. In a letter to James Madison in 1823 he asserted that

> the Committee of 5 met . . . [and] they unanimously pressed on myself alone to undertake the draught. I consented; I drew it; but before I reported it to the committee I communicated it separately to Dr. Franklin and Mr. Adams requesting their corrections; . . . and you have seen the original paper now in my hands, with the corrections of Dr. Franklin and Mr. Adams interlined in their own handwriting. Their alterations were two or three only, and merely verbal [that is, changes of phrasing, not substance].

So far, so good. Jefferson's "original paper"—which he endorsed on the document itself as the "original Rough draught"—is preserved in the Library of Congress. Indeed, the draft is even rougher than Jefferson suggested. As historian Carl Becker pointed out,

> the inquiring student, coming to it for the first time, would be astonished, perhaps disappointed, if he expected to find in it nothing more than the "original paper . . . with the corrections of Dr. Franklin and Mr. Adams interlined in their own handwriting." He would find, for example, on the first page alone nineteen corrections, additions or erasures besides those in the handwriting of Adams and Franklin. It would probably seem to him at first sight a bewildering document, with many phrases crossed out, numerous interlineations, and whole paragraphs enclosed in brackets.

These corrections make the rough draft more difficult to read, but in the end also more rewarding. For the fact is, Jefferson continued to record on this copy successive alterations of the Declaration, not only by Adams and Franklin, but by Congress in its debates of July 3 and 4.

Thus by careful comparison and reconstruction, we can accurately establish the sequence of changes made in one crucial document, from the time it was first drafted, through corrections in committee, to debate and further amendment in Congress, and finally on to the engrossed parchment familiar to history. The changes were not slight. In the end, Congress removed about a quarter of Jefferson's original language. Eighty-six alterations were made by one person or another, including Jefferson, over those fateful three weeks of 1776.

THE TACTICS OF INTERPRETATION

Having sketched the circumstances of the Declaration's composition, the historian must attempt the more complicated task of interpretation. And here, historians' paths are most likely to diverge—understandably so. To determine a document's historical significance requires placing it within the larger, more complex context of events. There is no single method for doing this, of course. If there were, historians would all agree on their reconstructions of the past, and history would be a good deal duller. On the other hand, historians do at least share certain analytical tactics that have consistently yielded profitable results.

What follows, then, is one set of tactical approaches to the Declaration. These approaches are by no means the only ways of making sense of the document. But they do suggest some range of the options historians normally call upon.

The document is read, first, to understand its surface content. This step may appear too obvious to bear mentioning, but not so. The fact is, most historians examine a document from a particular and potentially limiting viewpoint. A diplomatic historian, for instance, may approach the Declaration with an eye to the role it played in cementing a formal alliance with France. A historian of political theory might prefer to focus on the theoretical justifications of independence. Both perspectives are legitimate, but by beginning with such specific interests, historians risk prejudging the document. They are likely to notice only the kinds of evidence they are seeking.

So it makes sense to begin by temporarily putting aside any specific questions and approaching the Declaration as a willing, even uncritical reader. Ask only the most basic questions. How is the document organized? What are its major points, briefly summarized?

The Unanimous Declaration of the Thirteen United States of America.

When in the Course of human events, it becomes necessary for one people to dissolve the political bands, which have connected them with another, and to assume among the powers of the earth, the separate and equal station to which the Laws of Nature and of Nature's God entitle them, a decent respect to the opinions of mankind requires that they should declare the causes which impel them to the separation.—We hold these truths to be self-evident, that all men are created equal, that they are endowed by their Creator with certain unalienable Rights, that among these are Life, Liberty and the pursuit of Happiness.—That to secure these rights, Governments are instituted among Men, deriving their just powers from the consent of the governed,—That whenever any Form of Government becomes destructive of these ends, it is the Right of the People to alter or to abolish it, and to institute new Government, laying its foundation on such principles and organizing its powers in such form, as to them shall seem most likely to effect their Safety and Happiness. Prudence, indeed, will dictate that Governments long established should not be changed for light and transient causes; and accordingly all experience hath shewn, that mankind are more disposed to suffer, while evils are sufferable, than to right themselves by abolishing the forms to which they are accustomed. But when a long train of abuses and usurpations, pursuing invariably the same Object evinces a design to reduce them under absolute Despotism, it is their right, it is their duty, to throw off such Government, and to provide new Guards for their future security. Such has been the patient sufferance of these Colonies; and such is now the necessity which constrains them to alter their former Systems of Government. The history of the present King of Great Britain is a history of repeated injuries and usurpations, all having in direct object the establishment of an absolute Tyranny over these States. To prove this, let Facts be submitted to a candid world.—He has refused his Assent to Laws, the most wholesome and necessary for the public good.—He has forbidden his Governors to pass Laws of immediate and pressing importance, unless suspended in their operation till his Assent should be obtained; and when so suspended, he has utterly neglected to attend to them.—He has refused to pass other Laws for the accommodation of large districts of people, unless those people would relinquish the right of Representation in the Legislature, a right inestimable to them and formidable to tyrants only.—He has called together legislative bodies at places unusual, uncomfortable, and distant from the depository of their public Records, for the sole purpose of fatiguing them into compliance with his measures.—He has dissolved Representative Houses repeatedly, for opposing with manly firmness his invasions on the rights of the people.—He has refused for a long time, after such dissolutions, to cause others to be elected; whereby the Legislative powers, incapable of Annihilation, have returned to the People at large for their exercise; the State remaining in the meantime exposed to all the dangers of invasion from without, and convulsions within.—He has endeavoured to prevent the population of these States; for that purpose obstructing the Laws for Naturalization of Foreigners; refusing to pass others to encourage their migrations hither, and raising the conditions of new Appropriations of Lands.—He has obstructed the Administration of Justice, by refusing his Assent to Laws for establishing judiciary powers.—He has made judges dependent on his Will alone, for the tenure of their offices, and the amount and payment of their salaries.—He has erected a multitude of New Offices, and sent hither swarms of Officers to harass our people, and eat out their substance.—He has kept among us, in times of peace, Standing Armies without the Consent of our legislatures.—He has affected to render the Military independent of and superior to the Civil power.—He has combined with others to subject us to a jurisdiction foreign to our constitution, and unacknowledged by our laws; giving his Assent to their Acts of pretended Legislation.—For quartering large bodies of armed troops among us:—For protecting them, by a mock Trial, from punishment for any Murders which they should commit on the inhabitants of these States:—For cutting off our Trade with all parts of the world:—For imposing Taxes on us without our Consent:—For depriving us in many cases, of the benefits of Trial by Jury:—For transporting us beyond Seas to be tried for pretended offenses:—For abolishing the free System of English Laws in a neighboring Province, establishing therein an Arbitrary government, and enlarging its Boundaries so as to render it at once an example and fit instrument for introducing the same absolute rule into these Colonies:—For taking away our Charters, abolishing our most valuable Laws, and altering fundamentally the Forms of our Governments:—For suspending our own Legislatures, and declaring themselves invested with power to legislate for us in all cases whatsoever.—He has abdicated Government here, by declaring us out of his Protection and waging War against us.—He has plundered our seas, ravaged our Coasts, burnt our towns, and destroyed the lives of our people.—He is at this time transporting large Armies of foreign Mercenaries to compleat the works of death, desolation and tyranny, already begun with circumstances of Cruelty & perfidy scarcely paralleled in the most barbarous ages, and totally unworthy the Head of a civilized nation.—He has constrained our fellow Citizens taken Captive on the high Seas to bear Arms against their Country, to become the executioners of their friends and Brethren, or to fall themselves by their Hands.—He has excited domestic insurrections amongst us, and has endeavoured to bring on the inhabitants of our frontiers, the merciless Indian Savages, whose known rule of warfare, is an undistinguished destruction of all ages, sexes and conditions. In every state of these Oppressions We have Petitioned for Redress in the most humble terms: our repeated Petitions have been answered only by repeated injury. A Prince whose character is thus marked by every act which may define a Tyrant, is unfit to be the ruler of a free people. Nor have We been wanting in attentions to our Brittish brethren. We have warned them from time to time of attempts by their legislature to extend an unwarrantable jurisdiction over us. We have reminded them of the circumstances of our emigration and settlement here. We have appealed to their native justice and magnanimity, and we have conjured them by the ties of our common kindred to disavow these usurpations, which would inevitably interrupt our connections and correspondence. They too have been deaf to the voice of justice and of consanguinity. We must, therefore, acquiesce in the necessity, which denounces our Separation, and hold them, as we hold the rest of mankind, Enemies in War, in Peace Friends.

We, therefore, the Representatives of the United States of America, in General Congress, Assembled, appealing to the Supreme Judge of the world for the rectitude of our intentions do, in the Name, and by Authority of the good People of these Colonies, solemnly publish and declare, That these United Colonies are, and of Right ought to be Free and independent States; that they are Absolved from all Allegiance to the British Crown, and that all political connection between them and the State of Great Britain, is and ought to be totally dissolved: and that as Free and independent States, they have full Power to levy War, conclude Peace, contract Alliances, establish Commerce, and to do all other Acts and Things which independent States may of right do.—And for the support of this Declaration, with a firm reliance on the protection of divine Providence, we mutually pledge to each other our Lives, our Fortunes and our sacred Honor.

As befits a reasoned public document, the Declaration can be separated fairly easily into its component parts. The first sentence begins by informing the reader of the document's purpose. The colonies, having declared their independence from England, intend to announce "the causes which impel them to the separation."

The causes that follow, however, are not all of a piece. They break naturally into two sections: the first, a theoretical justification of revolution, and the second, a list of the specific grievances that justify this revolution. Because the first section deals in general, "self-evident" truths, it is the one most often remembered and quoted. "All men are created equal," "unalienable Rights," "Life, Liberty and the pursuit of Happiness," "consent of the governed"—these principles have relevance far beyond the circumstances of the colonies in the summer of 1776.

But the Declaration devotes far greater space to a list of British actions that Congress labeled "a long train of abuses and usurpations" designed to "reduce [Americans] under absolute Despotism." Because the Declaration concedes that revolution should never be undertaken lightly, the document proceeds to demonstrate that English rule has been not merely unwieldy and inconvenient, but so full of "repeated injuries" that "absolute Tyranny" is the result. What threatens Americans most, the Declaration proclaims, is not the individual measures, but the existence of a deliberate plot by the king to deprive a "free people" of their liberties.

The final section of the Declaration turns to the colonial response. Here the Declaration incorporates Richard Lee's resolution passed on July 2 and ends with the signers solemnly pledging their lives, fortunes, and sacred honor to support the new government.

Having begun with this straightforward reading, the historian is less likely to wrench out of context a particular passage, magnifying it at the expense of the rest of the document. Yet taken by itself, the reading of "surface content" may distort a document's import. Significance, after all, depends on the circumstances under which a document was created. Thus historians must always seek to place their evidence in context.

The context of a document may be established, in part, by asking what the document might have said but did not. When Jefferson retired to his second-floor lodgings on the outskirts of Philadelphia, placed a portable writing desk on his lap, and put pen to paper, he had many options open to him. Yet the modern reader, seeing only the final product, is tempted to view the document as the logical, even inevitable result of Jefferson's deliberations. Perhaps it was, but the historian needs to ask how it might have been otherwise. What might Jefferson and the Congress have declared but did not?

We can get a better sense of what Congress and Jefferson rejected by looking at a declaration made some ten years earlier by another intercolonial gathering, the Stamp Act Congress. Like Jefferson's, this declaration, protesting the Stamp Act as unjust, began by outlining general principles. In reading the first three resolves, note the difference between their premises and those of the Declaration.

I. That his Majesty's Subjects in these Colonies, owe the same Allegiance to the Crown of *Great-Britain*, that is owing from his Subjects born within the Realm, and all due Subordination to that August Body the Parliament of *Great-Britain.*

II. That his Majesty's Liege Subjects in these Colonies, are entitled to all the inherent Rights and Liberties of his Natural born Subjects, within the Kingdom of *Great-Britain.*

III. That it is inseparably essential to the Freedom of a People, and the undoubted Right of *Englishmen,* that no Taxes be imposed on them, but with their own Consent, given personally, or by their Representatives.

The rights emphasized by the Stamp Act Congress in 1765 differ significantly from those emphasized in 1776. The Stamp Act resolutions claim that colonials are entitled to "all the inherent Rights and Liberties" of "Subjects, within the Kingdom of *Great-Britain.*" They possess "the undoubted Right of *Englishmen.*" Nowhere in Jefferson's Declaration are the rights of Englishmen mentioned as justification for protesting the king's conduct. Instead, the Declaration magnifies what the Stamp Act only mentions in passing—natural rights inherent in the "Freedom of a People," whether they be English subjects or not.

The shift from English rights to natural rights resulted from the changed political situation. In 1765 Americans were seeking relief within the British imperial system. Logically, they cited rights they felt due them as British subjects. But in 1776 the Declaration was renouncing all ties with its parent nation. If the colonies were no longer a part of Great Britain, what good would it do to cite the rights of Englishmen? Thus the natural rights "endowed" all persons "by their Creator" took on paramount importance.

The Declaration makes another striking omission. Nowhere in the long list of grievances does it use another word that appears in the first resolve of the Stamp Act Congress—"Parliament." The omission is all the more surprising because the Revolutionary quarrel had its roots in the dispute over Parliament's right to tax and regulate the colonies. The Sugar Act, the Stamp Act, the Townshend duties, the Tea Act, the Coercive Acts, the Quebec Act—all place Parliament at the center of the dispute. The Declaration alludes to those legislative measures but always in the context of the king's actions, not Parliament's. Doing so admittedly required a bit of evasion: in laying out parliamentary abuses, Jefferson complained, rather indirectly, that the king had combined with "others"—namely Parliament—"to subject us to a jurisdiction foreign to our constitution, and unacknowledged by our laws; giving his Assent to their Acts of pretended Legislation."

Obviously, the omission came about for much the same reason that Jefferson excluded all mention of the "rights of Englishmen." At the Stamp Act Congress of 1765, virtually all Americans were willing to grant Parliament some jurisdiction over the colonies—not the right to lay taxes without American representation, certainly, but at least the right to regulate colonial trade. Thus Congress noted (in Resolve I) that Parliament deserved "all due Subordination."

By 1775 more radical colonials would not grant Parliament any authority over the colonies. They had come to recognize what an early pamphleteer had noted, that Americans could be "as effectually ruined by the powers of legislation as by those of taxation." The Boston Port Bill, which closed Boston harbor, was not a tax. Nor did it violate any traditional right. Yet the radicals argued, quite correctly, that Parliament could take away Americans' freedoms by such legislation.

Although many colonials had totally rejected all parliamentary authority in 1775, most had not yet advocated independence. How, then, were the colonies related to England if not through Parliament? The only link, radicals argued, was through the king. The colonies possessed their own sovereign legislatures, but they shared with all British subjects one monarch. Thus when the final break with England came, the Declaration carefully laid all blame at the king's feet. Even to recognize Parliament would be to tacitly admit that it had some legitimate connection with the colonies.

What the Declaration does *not* say, then, proves to be as important as what it did say. Historians can recognize the importance of such unstated premises by remembering that the actors in any drama possess more alternatives than the ones they finally choose.

A document may be understood by seeking to reconstruct the intellectual worlds behind its words. We have already seen, in the cases of Virginia and Salem, the extent to which history involves the task of reconstructing whole societies from fragmentary records. The same process applies to the intellectual worlds that lie behind a document.

The need to perform this reconstruction is often hidden, however, because the context of the English language has changed over the past two hundred years—and not simply in obvious ways. For example, what would Jefferson have made of the following excerpt out of a computer magazine?

> *Macworld's* Holiday Gift Guide. It's holiday shopping season again. *Macworld* advises you on the best ways to part with your paycheck. . . . It could be an audio CD, but it could also be a CD-ROM containing anything from an encyclopedia to a virtual planetarium to an art studio for the kids.

To begin with, terms like "audio CD" and "CD-ROM" would mystify Jefferson simply because they come from a totally unfamiliar world. Beyond the obvious, however, the excerpt contains words that might seem familiar but would be deceptively so, because their meaning has changed over time. Jefferson probably would have recognized "planetarium," though he might have preferred the more common eighteenth-century term *orrery*. He would recognize "virtual" as well. But a "virtual planetarium"? Today's notion of virtual reality would be lost to him unless he read a good deal more about the computer revolution.

Even more to the point, look at the innocuous phrase, "It's holiday shopping season again." The words would be completely familiar to Jefferson, but the world that surrounds them certainly would not. To understand the phrase, he would have to appreciate how much the Christmas holiday has evolved into a major commercial event, bearing scant resemblance to any eighteenth-century observance. (In John Adams's puritan New England, of course, even to celebrate Chrismas would have been frowned upon as a popish superstition.) Or to make an even subtler linguistic point: unlike a magazine article from the 1950s, this one from the 1990s never uses the word *Christmas*. The social reasons for this deliberate omission would undoubtedly have interested Jefferson, for it reflects a multicultural nation sensitive to the questions of equality and the separation of church and state. But unless he were aware of the ways in which American society had evolved, Jefferson would miss the implications hidden within language that to us seems reasonably straightforward.

By the same token, eighteenth-century documents may appear deceptively lucid to twentieth-century readers. When Jefferson wrote that all men were "endowed by their Creator with certain unalienable Rights," including "Life, Liberty and the pursuit of Happiness," the meaning seems clear. But as essayist and historian Garry Wills has insisted, "To understand any text remote from us in time, we must reassemble a world around that text. The preconceptions of the original audience, its tastes, its range of reference, must be recovered, so far as that is possible."

In terms of reassembling Jefferson's world, historians have most often followed Carl Becker in arguing that its center lay in the political philosophy of John Locke. Locke's *Second Treatise on Government* (1690) asserted that all governments were essentially a compact between individuals based on the principles of human nature. Locke speculated that if all the laws and customs that had grown up in human society over the years were stripped away, human beings would find themselves in "a state of perfect freedom to order their possessions and persons, as they think fit, within the bounds of the law of nature." But because some individuals inevitably violate the laws of nature—robbing or murdering or committing other crimes—people have always banded together to make a compact, agreeing to create governments that will order human society. And just as people come together to allow themselves to be governed, likewise they can overturn those governments wherein the ruler has become a tyrant who "may do to all his subjects whatever he pleases."

Jefferson's colleague Richard Henry Lee in later years commented that Jefferson, in writing the Declaration, had merely "copied from Locke's treatise on government." Yet as important as Locke was, his writings were only one facet of the Enlightenment tradition flourishing in the eighteenth century. Jefferson shared with many European philosophes the belief that the study of human affairs should be conducted as precisely as the study of the natural world had come to be. Just as Sir Isaac Newton in the 1680s had used mathematical equations to derive the laws of gravity, optics, and planetary motion, so the philosophes of Jefferson's day looked to quantify the study of the human psyche.

The results of such endeavors seem quaint today, but the philosophes took their work seriously. Garry Wills has argued that even more important to

Jefferson than Locke were the writings of Scottish Enlightenment thinkers, chief among them Francis Hutcheson. In 1725 Hutcheson attempted to quantify such elusive concepts as morality. The result was a string of equations in which qualities were abbreviated by letters (B = benevolence, A = ability, S = self-love, I = interest) and placed in their proper relations:

$$M = (B + S) \times A = BA + SA; \text{ and therefore } BA = M - SA = M - I, \text{ and } B = \frac{M - I}{A}$$

Jefferson possessed a similar passion for quantification. He repeatedly praised the American astronomer David Rittenhouse and his orrery, a mechanical model of the solar system whose gears replicated the relative motions of the earth, moon, and planets. Jefferson also applied classification and observation as a gentleman planter. If it were possible to discover the many relationships within the natural order, he reasoned, farmers might better plant and harvest to those rhythms. Even in the White House, Jefferson kept his eye on the Washington markets and recorded the seasons' first arrivals of thirty-seven different vegetables.

Wills argues that Jefferson conceived the "pursuit of Happiness" in equally precise terms. Francis Hutcheson had suggested that a person's actions be judged by how much happiness that person brought to other people. "That action is best," he argued, "which accomplishes the greatest happiness for the greatest number." According to Enlightenment science, because happiness could be quantified, a government's actions could be weighed in the balance scales to discover whether they hindered a citizen's right to pursue happiness as he or she saw fit. Thus for Jefferson the pursuit of happiness was not a phrase expressing the vague hope that all Americans should have the chance to live happily ever after. His language reflected the conviction that the science of government, like the science of agriculture or celestial mechanics, would gradually take its place in the advancing progress of humankind.

Historians' reconstructions of Jefferson's intellectual world, imaginative as they are, must remain speculative. We do not have Jefferson's direct testimony of what he was thinking, aside from a few recollections made decades after the event. When Garry Wills made his case for the importance of Scottish moral philosophy, he was forced to rely on circumstantial evidence, such as the presence of Francis Hutcheson's works in Jefferson's library or the topics Jefferson's professors lectured on during his college years—or even, more generally, what ideas and opinions were "in the air." Whether or not Wills's specific case stands up to examination, his method of research is one that historians commonly employ. By understanding the intellectual world from which a document arose, we come to understand the document itself.

ACTIONS SPEAK LOUDER?

More than a few historians, however, become uneasy about depending too heavily on a genealogy of ideas. To be sure, a historian can speak of theories as being "in the air" and of Jefferson, as it were, inhaling. But that approach may neglect the noisy and insistent world outside his Philadelphia lodgings. By June 1776 Congress was in the midst of waging a war as well as a revolution, and a hundred and one events demanded its daily attention. The morning that Richard Henry Lee submitted his motion for independence, delegates had to deal with troops being raised in South Carolina and complaints about the gunpowder manufactured by a certain Mr. Oswald of Eve's Mill. Over the following days they learned that the British fleet had sailed from Halifax, on its way to attack New York City. Events both large and small kept Jefferson and the other members of Congress from sitting down quietly for long to ponder over the creation of a single document.

Thus to understand the Declaration we must not only set it in the context of previous ideas, but also of contemporary events. "What was Jefferson thinking about on the eve of his authorship of the Declaration of Independence?" asked a recent biographer, Joseph Ellis. "The answer is indisputable. He was not thinking . . . about John Locke's theory of natural rights or Scottish commonsense philosophy. He was thinking about Virginia's new constitution." Throughout May and June, couriers brought news to Jefferson of doings in Williamsburg, the capital of his own "country," as he called it. There, on June 12, the Virginia convention adopted a preamble to its state constitution, written by George Mason. "All men are created equally free and independent and have certain inherent and natural rights," wrote Mason, ". . . among which are the enjoyment of life and liberty, with the means of acquiring and possessing property, and pursuing and obtaining happiness and safety."

These words reached Philadelphia little more than a week before Jefferson penned his immortal credo "that all men are created equal, that they are endowed by their Creator with certain unalienable Rights, that among these are Life, Liberty and the pursuit of Happiness." The point is not to expose Jefferson as a plagiarist, for he substantially improved Mason's version. Nor is it to deny that John Locke or Francis Hutcheson may have played a role in shaping Jefferson's (and Mason's) thinking. But seeing how closely Jefferson's language resembles George Mason's makes it clear how much Jefferson was affected by events around him.

Often enough, actions do speak louder than words. One way to put the Declaration in context is to compare it with the actions taken by other Americans during these same months. As historian Pauline Maier has noted, the Continental Congress was not the only body to issue a declaration of independence. She discovered at least ninety other resolutions to similar effect made between April and July of 1776. Some were issued by town meetings; others, by gatherings of militia or workers; still others, by grand juries or county conventions. These state and local declarations, argued Maier, "offer the best opportunity to hear the voice of the people . . . that we are likely to get."

Like Congress's Declaration, the local resolutions listed grievances that caused them to take up arms. Worrying less about theoretical consistency, these local declarations did not hesitate either to mention Parliament or to emphatically condemn it. Many pointed in particular to the Declaratory Act of 1766, in which Parliament asserted the right to make laws binding the colonies "IN ALL CASES WHATSOEVER," as one declaration stated in uppercase letters. It was Parliament that had no right to legislate whatsoever, colonials now countered.

Once this flat assertion was made, most local declarations did not bother to list a "long train of abuses." Instead, they focused on the outrages of the preceding year. New York's mechanics complained that the king "is deaf to our petitions," including Congress's Olive Branch Petition of July 1775. The war itself supplied many more grievances, beginning with the casualties at Lexington and Concord: "We hear their blood crying to us from the ground for vengeance," noted one Massachusetts town. Many resolutions condemned the "barbarous" act of hiring "foreign mercenaries" such as the German Hessians to prosecute the war for the king's "inhuman purposes."

In short, the local resolutions reflected the events around them even more strongly than the Declaration did. They underline the likelihood that sentiment for independence among most colonials did not really blossom until well after the fighting began. In that sense, the resolutions help us link the official Declaration more closely with the feelings of ordinary Americans.

Yet a problem remains. The proverb proclaims that actions speak louder than words, but all these declarations are still just words. The point of the aphorism is that we cannot always take words at face value—that often, actions are what reveal true feelings. We need not reject the Declaration's heartfelt sentiments in order to recognize that the Congress (or, for that matter, colonials themselves) may have had reasons for declaring independence that they did not enunciate fully, either in the Declaration or in local resolutions.

For example, consider the vexed topic of slavery, especially interesting in a document proclaiming that "all men are created equal." It has become commonplace to point out the contradiction between the Declaration's noble embrace of human liberties and the reality that many delegates to Congress, including Jefferson, were slave owners; or similarly, the inconsistency between a declaration of equality and the refusal to let women participate in the equal rights of citizenship.

Although such contradictions have attained the status of truisms, they deserve to be pointed out again and again. Indeed, much of American history can be seen as an effort to work out the full implications of the phrase "all men are created equal"—whether that history be the Civil War, wherein a vast and bloody carnage was required to bring an end to slavery, or the more peaceful Seneca Falls Convention, mounted in 1848 by women to proclaim their own Declaration of Sentiments supporting an equality of the sexes. The theme could be applied to the populist and progressive reform movements of the late nineteenth century, grappling as they did with the effect on equality of the monopoly powers of big business; or to the debates of the late twentieth century over civil rights and affirmative action. The implications of the Declaration have engaged the republic for more than two centuries and no doubt will continue to do so.

Granting the ironies of these unstated contradictions, it may still be worthwhile to return to the notion of actions and to examine the intriguing way in which slavery *does* appear in the Declaration. At first glance, the Declaration seems to say very little about slavery. In its long list of grievances, Congress merely notes that the king has "excited domestic insurrections amongst us"—in other words, encouraged slaves to revolt. The five words slip by so quickly we hardly notice them.

Slavery did not slip by so quickly in Jefferson's rough draft. His discussion of the institution appeared not as a grace note, but as the climax of his long list of grievances against the king:

> He has waged cruel war against human nature itself, violating its most sacred rights of life and liberty in the persons of a distant people who never offended him, captivating & carrying them into slavery in another hemisphere or to incur miserable death in their transportation thither. This piratical warfare, the opprobrium of *infidel* powers, is the warfare of the *Christian* king of Great Britain. Determined to keep open a market where *Men* should be bought & sold, he has prostituted his negative [used his veto power] for suppressing every legislative attempt to prohibit or to restrain this execrable commerce. And that this assemblage of horrors might want no fact of distinguishing die, he is now exciting those very people to rise in arms among us, and to purchase that liberty of which he has deprived them, by murdering the people on whom he also obtruded them: thus paying off former crimes committed against the *Liberties of* one people, with crimes which he urges them to commit against the *lives of* another.

The passage is in many ways both revealing and astonishing. It reveals, first, that Jefferson was very much aware of the contradiction between slavery and the Declaration's high sentiments. Not once but twice he speaks out. The enslavement of black Africans violates the "most sacred rights of life and liberty," he admits; and again, enslavement amounts to "crimes committed against the *Liberties of* one people." Yet in admitting the wrong, he blames the king for it! Jefferson based his charge on the fact that several times during the eighteenth century, Virginia's legislature passed a tariff designed to restrict the importation of slaves. It did so not so much from humanitarian motives (although these were occasionally mentioned) but because the colony's slave population was expanding rapidly. Importing too many Africans would lower the price of domestic slaves whom Virginia planters wanted to sell. The British administration, however, consistently disallowed such laws—and thus the king had "prostituted his negative" to prevent the slave trade from being restrained. For their part, white Georgians and South Carolinians were generally happy to see the trade continue, as were many New England merchants who made a profitable livelihood from it.

To accuse the king of enslaving black colonials was far-fetched enough, but Jefferson then turned around and hotly accused the king of *freeing* black colonials. In November 1775, the loyal Governor Dunmore of Virginia proclaimed that any slave who deserted his master to fight for the king would be freed. Dunmore's Proclamation, as it was called, outraged many white patriots. Hence Jefferson called King George to account for the vile "crime" of freeing slaves who remained loyal.

What the delegates in Congress thought of the passage does not survive. But their actions speak loudly. In the final draft, Jefferson's long passage has vanished. All that remains is the general accusation that the king has "excited domestic insurrections." It seems likely Congress simply rejected Jefferson's logic as being so tortuous that it could hardly withstand public scrutiny. The less said, the better.

DECLARING FOR FREEDOM

Saying less, however, is not the same as saying nothing. By not deleting the accusation regarding "domestic insurrections," Congress revealed that this particular issue remained a sensitive one. Indeed, other local declarations featured it prominently. Marylanders complained that slaves "were proclaimed free, enticed away, trained and armed against their lawful masters." Pennsylvanians objected that the British had incited "the negroes to imbrue their hands in the blood of their masters." North Carolina echoed the sentiment nearly word for word. The frequency of this complaint raises a question. Leave aside for a moment the issue of white attitudes toward slavery and liberty. How did the actions of *African Americans* affect the drafters of the Declaration?

On the face of it, the chance of answering that question seems far-fetched. The approximately 400,000 black slaves living in the colonies in 1776 could not leave a trail of resolutions or declarations behind them, for most were not allowed to. Yet the Declaration's complaint that Britain was stirring up American slaves brings to mind the similar laments of proslavery advocates in the 1850s and of segregationists during the 1950s and 1960s. Both repeatedly blamed "outside agitators" for encouraging southern blacks to assert their civil rights. In the eighteenth century, the phrase most commonly used was "instigated insurrection." "The newspapers were full of Publications calculated to excite the fears of the People—" wrote one indignant South Carolinian in 1775, "Massacres and Instigated Insurrections, were words in the mouth of every Child." And hardly children alone: South Carolina's First Provincial Congress voiced their own "dread of instigated insurrections." North Carolinians echoed the sentiment, warning that "there is much reason to fear, in these Times of general Tumult and Confusion, that the Slaves may be instigated, encouraged by our inveterate Enemies to an Insurrection."

But were the British "instigating" rebellion? Or were they taking advantage of African Americans' own determination to strike for freedom? As historian Sylvia Frey has pointed out, the incidence of flight, rebellion, or protest among enslaved African Americans increased significantly in the decade following the Stamp Act, despite the long odds that weighed against success. In 1765 the Sons of Liberty paraded around Charleston harbor shouting "Liberty! Liberty and stamp'd paper!" Soon after, black slaves organized a demonstration of their own, chanting "Liberty!" Planter Henry Laurens believed this action to be merely a "thoughtless imitation" of white colonials, but it frightened many South Carolinians.

With good reason. Look more closely at events in Virginia preceding Dunmore's Proclamation. Governer Dunmore in November 1775 offered freedom to able-bodied slaves who would serve the king. Six months earlier, anticipating the outbreak of hostilities, the governor had confiscated some of the colony's gunpowder to prevent it from falling into rebel hands. At that point, "some Negroes . . . had offered to join him and take up arms." What was Dunmore's reaction? He ordered the slaves "to go about their business" and "threatened them with his severest resentment, should they presume to renew their application." Patriot forces, on the other hand, demanded the return of the gunpowder and accused Dunmore of seizing it with the intention of "disarming the people, to weaken the means of opposing an insurrection of the slaves." At this charge Dunmore became "exceedingly exasperated" and threatened to "declare freedom to the slaves and reduce the City of Williamsburg to ashes."

In other words, the slaves, not Dunmore, made the first move in this particular game of chess! And far from greeting the slaves' offer with delight, Dunmore shunned it—until patriot fears about black insurrections made him consider the advantages that black military support might provide. Similarly, in 1773 and again in 1774 the loyal governor of Massachusetts, General Thomas Gage, was approached with five separate petitions from "a grate Number of [enslaved] Blacks" offering to fight for him if he would provide arms and set them free. "At present it is kept pretty quiet," Abigail Adams reassured her husband, John, who was off at the First Continental Congress.

By 1775 unrest among black slaves was common in many areas of the Carolinas and Georgia. South Carolina had taken on "rather the appearance of a garrison town," reported one observer, because the militia were patrolling the streets at night as well as during the day, "to guard against any hostile attempts that may be made by our domesticks." White fears were confirmed when a black harbor pilot, Thomas Jeremiah, was arrested, tried, hanged, and burned to death for plotting an insurrection that would enlist the help of the British navy. Jeremiah had told other blacks that "there was a great War coming soon" that "was come to help the poor Negroes." According to James Madison, a group of Virginia slaves "met together and chose a leader who was to conduct them when the English troops should arrive." The conspiracy was discovered and suppressed. Islands along the coast—Tybee Island and Sullivan's Island off South Carolina and Cockspur Island off Georgia—as well as English cruisers, attracted slaves striking for freedom. The slaves were not "inticed," reported one captain; they "came as freemen, and demanding protection." He could "have had near 500 who had offered."

The actions of these and other enslaved African Americans clearly affected the conduct of both British officials and colonial rebels. The British, who

---

RUN away from *Hampton,* on *Sunday* laft, a lufty Mulatto Fellow named ARGYLE, well known about the Country, has a Scar on one of his Wrifts, and has loft one or more of his fore Teeth; he is a very handy Fellow by Water, or about the Houfe, &c. loves Drink, and is very bold in his Cups, but daftardly when fober. Whether he will go for a Man of War's Man, or not, I cannot fay; but I will give 40s. to have him brought to me. He can read and write.
      NOVEMBER 2, 1775.   JACOB   WRAY.

RUN away from the Subfcriber, in *New Kent,* in the Year 1772, a fmall new New Negro Man named GEORGE, about 40 Years of Age, with a Nick in one Ear, and fome Marks with the Whip. He was about *Williamfburg* till laft Winter, but either went or was fent to Lord *Dunmore*'s Quarter in *Frederick* County, and there paffes for his Property. Whoever conveys him to me fhall have 5l. Reward.
            1 || JAMES · MOSS.

Masters whose slaves ran away commonly posted notices in newspapers offering rewards for their return. The advertisements often assumed that slaves had gone to join kin. But these advertisements from an issue of the *Virginia Gazette* in November 1775 indicate that slaveowners were frequently convinced that their male slaves might have gone to offer service to Lord Dunmore or to the British navy ("a Man of War's Man").

(like Dunmore) remained reluctant to encourage a full-scale rebellion, nevertheless saw that the mere possibility of insurrection might be used as an effective psychological threat. If South Carolinians did not stop opposing British policy, warned General Gage ominously, "it may happen that your Rice and Indigo will be brought to market by negroes instead of white People." For their part, southern white colonials worked energetically to suppress both the rebellions and all news of them. As two Georgia delegates to the Continental Congress informed John Adams, slave networks could carry news "several hundreds of miles in a week or fortnight." When Madison heard about the slave conspiracy in Virginia, he saw clearly the dangers of talking about the incident: "It is prudent such things should be concealed as well as suppressed," he warned a friend. Maryland's provisional government felt similarly about Governor Dunmore's proclamation in neighboring Virginia. It immediately outlawed all correspondence with Virginia, either by land or water. But word spread anyway. "The insolence of the Negroes in this county is come to such a height," reported one Eastern Shore Marylander, "that we are under a necessity of disarming them which we affected [sic] on Saturday last. We took about eighty guns, some bayonets, swords, etc."

Thus the actions of African Americans helped push the delegates in Congress toward their final decision for independence, even though the Declaration remained largely silent on the subject. By striking for liberty, slaves encouraged the British to use them as an element in their war against the Americans. As Lord North told the king in October 1775, British troops sent to Georgia and the Carolinas should expect to meet with success, especially because "we all know the perilous situation . . . [arising] from the great number of their negro slaves, and the small proportion of white inhabitants."

The Americans were pushed toward independence by this knowledge. Georgia delegates told John Adams that slaves in their region were simply waiting a chance to arise, and if "one thousand regular [British] troops should land in Georgia, and their commander be provided with arms and clothes enough, and proclaim freedom to all the negroes who would join his campaign, twenty thousand would join it from [Georgia and South Carolina] in a fortnight." James Madison, worrying about Lord Dunmore, confided that the possibility of a slave insurrection "is the only part in which this Colony is vulnerable; & if we should be subdued, we shall fall like Achilles by the hand of one that knows the secret." George Washington too perceived the threat. Dunmore must be crushed instantly, he warned in December 1775, "otherwise, like a snowball, in rolling, his army will get size." Although southern delegates at first attempted to pass legislation forbidding black Americans from serving in the Continental Army, Washington changed his mind and supported the idea, having come to believe that the outcome of the war might depend on "which side can arm the Negroes the faster." Until recently, few historians have appreciated the role African Americans played in shaping the context of independence.

Actions do speak louder than words—often enough. Still, the echoes of the Declaration's words and the persistent hold of its ideals have outlasted the often contradictory actions of its creators. Jefferson's entire life embodied those contradictions. More than any American president, save Lincoln, Jefferson contributed to the downfall of slavery. In addition to penning the Declaration's bold rhetoric, he pushed for the antislavery provision in the Northwest Ordinance of 1787, which served as a model for later efforts to stop slavery's expansion. Yet despite Jefferson's private criticisms of slavery, he continued to depend on the labor of enslaved African Americans throughout his life. Although he apparently maintained a sexual relationship with one of his slaves, Sally Hemings, upon his death he freed none, except five members of the Hemings family. Sally was not among them.

It lay with Abraham Lincoln to express most eloquently the notion that a document might transcend the contradictions of its creation. In 1857 Lincoln insisted that in proclaiming "all men are created equal," the founders of the nation

did not mean to assert the obvious untruth that all were then actually enjoying that equality. They meant to set up a standard maxim for free society, which should be familiar to all, and revered by all, constantly looked to, constantly labored for, and even though never perfectly attained, constantly approximated, and thereby constantly spreading and deepening its influence, and augmenting the happiness and value of life to all people of all colors everywhere.

"For the support of this Declaration," Jefferson concluded, "we mutually pledge to each other our Lives, our Fortunes and our sacred Honor." This sentiment was no idle rhetoric. Many delegates took the final step toward independence only with great reluctance. If the war was lost, they faced a hangman's noose. Even in victory, more than a few signers discovered that their fortunes had been devastated by the war. Yet it does no dishonor to the principles of the Revolution to recognize the flawed nature of Jefferson's attempt to reconcile slavery with liberty. Even less does it dishonor the Revolution to appreciate the role enslaved African Americans played in forcing the debates about independence. They too risked all in the actions—the unspoken declarations—that so many of them took to avail themselves of life, liberty, and the pursuit of happiness.

Additional Reading

The Declaration of Independence, surely one of the most scrutinized documents in American history, stands at the center of the American Revolution, surely one of the most scrutinized events in that history. Consequently, the interested reader has plenty of material upon which to draw.

For background on the Revolution, Edmund S. Morgan's *Birth of the Republic*, rev. ed. (Chicago, 1977) remains brief and lucid. More recent studies include Edward Countryman, *The American Revolution* (London, 1985), good on the social and economic background; and Robert Middlekauff, *The Glorious Cause* (New York, 1982), which treats military aspects more fully. For the Declaration itself, see Carl Becker's venerable yet still engaging *The Declaration of Independence: A Study in the History of Political Ideas* (New York, 1942). Garry Wills's wide-ranging contextual analysis of the Declaration can be found in *Inventing America: Jefferson's Declaration of Independence* (New York, 1978). Wills has been called to task for overstating his case by Ronald Hamowy in a classic cut-and-thrust maneuver entitled "Jefferson and the Scottish Enlightenment: A Critique of Garry Wills's *Inventing America*," *William and Mary Quarterly*, 3d ser., 36 (1979): 503–523. For a discussion of the local declarations of independence, see Pauline Maier, *American Scripture: Making the Declaration of Independence* (New York, 1997). Maier also examines how the Declaration outgrew its position of relative obscurity during the half century following the Revolution to become one of the "scriptural" texts of American history. In this light, Garry Wills's brilliant explication of another seminal document in American history is worth consulting: *Lincoln at Gettysburg: The Words that Remade America* (New York, 1992).

Readers wishing to do their own textual analysis will find Julian P. Boyd's *The Declaration of Independence: The Evolution of the Text* (Princeton, NJ, 1945) a good starting place. Worthington C. Ford, ed., *Journals of the Continental Congress: 1774–1789* (Washington, DC, 1904–1937) provides Charles Thomson's tantalizingly brief minutes. For a better sense of the delegates' concerns, see Edmund C. Burnett, ed., *Letters of Members of the Continental Congress* (Washington, DC, 1921–1936), and the much more inclusive edition of letters, Paul H. Smith, ed., *Letters of Delegates to Congress, 1774–1789* (Washington, DC, 1976–). A brilliant though somewhat eccentric analysis of the Declaration's text can be found in Jay Fliegelman, *Declaring Independence: Jefferson, Natural Language, and the Culture of Performance* (Stanford, CA, 1993). Fliegelman even finds meaning in the pauses and punctuation of the document.

As for Jefferson himself, the best brief starting place is Joseph J. Ellis, *American Sphinx: The Character of Thomas Jefferson* (New York, 1996). Ellis is perceptive about Jefferson's conflicting, often self-deceptive attitudes toward slavery and race. Although Ellis argued against the likelihood of Jefferson's having had an intimate and ongoing relationship with his slave Sally Hemings, he more recently reversed himself in light of evidence, based on a DNA analysis of Jefferson's descendants, that Jefferson fathered at least one child by Hemings; Annette Gordon-Reed, *Thomas Jefferson and Sally Hemings: An American Controversy* (Charlottesville, VA, 1997) lays out the debate. For the DNA findings, see the articles in *Nature 396* (5 November 1998): 13–14, and in the *New York Times*, 1 November 1998, A1.

Sylvia Frey's fine study, *Water from the Rock: Black Resistance in a Revolutionary Age* (Princeton, 1991), outlines the actions taken by African Americans during the Revolutionary years. See also Woody Holton, "Rebel against Rebel: Enslaved Virginians and the Coming of the American Revolution," *Virginia Magazine of History and Biography* 105 (1997): 157–192, and Peter H. Wood, "'Taking Care of Business' in South Carolina: Republicanism and the Slave Society," in Jeffrey J. Crow and Larry E. Tise, eds., *The Southern Experience in the American Revolution* (Chapel Hill, NC, 1978). For the relation of African American rebellion and the Declaration itself, see Sidney Kaplan, "The Domestic Insurrections of the Declaration of Independence," *Journal of Negro History* 61 (1976): 243–255.

Interactive Learning

The *Primary Source Investigator* sources explore the process of declaring independence from Great Britain. Included are the Olive Branch Petition, the Declaration of Sentiments, the first drafts of the Declaration of Independence, and the Articles of Confederation. In addition, there are ordinances concerning the Northwest Territory, early constitutions upon which the founders modeled the federal constitution, and correspondence between key members of the fledgling government. It is useful to examine the multiple drafts of the Declaration and the changes made in each version.

CHAPTER 4
Material Witness

Here's a mute witness, like many to be encountered in this chapter. It survives now in the collections of Memorial Hall Museum in Deerfield, Massachusetts. The Museum's best estimate is that the object was hammered together around 1820, somewhere in New England. It measures about 21 inches tall and 18 inches square. It would be seen around some, though not all, American houses during this era. Any guesses as to its use?

A crate, perhaps, for storage? If so, the material being stored would have to be bulky or it would fall out the rather large spaces between the slatting.

A contraption for holding wood by the fireplace? Not particularly practical, for the crate's shape would make it difficult to stack wood horizontally, and almost as awkward to do so vertically. Furthermore, the amount of firewood burned on a winter's day in New England would be far greater than what this crate could hold.

Also, look closely at the object. About halfway down on the back side is a horizontal piece of wood within the container that appears to be a small ledge. What could *that* be for?

In fact, the goods being "stored" in this container (for a container of sorts it is) were much more valuable to the occupants of the house than any firewood. Americans of the early nineteenth century would have recognized this contraption as a "baby tender," or "standing stool," used by parents to help toddlers stand but keep them from straying into mischief. The small ledge allowed the child to sit and rest. Tenders with wheels were also available, but the fancier versions actually possessed a certain disadvantage, because babies using them could propel themselves across the floor. This feature posed a significant danger in a house in which open fires for cooking or heating were regularly kept going. The records of Henniker, New Hampshire, make that clear. Between 1790 and 1830 seven children in that small town alone were scalded to death in accidents involving hot water, soups and stews, or hazards from similar housekeeping chores, such as boiling soap. Two other Henniker youngsters died falling into the fireplace during the same time period. And that total does not include lesser injuries, in which the children survived.

The baby tender was only one among hundreds of objects that played an intimate part in the everyday routines of Americans during the early republic, the period between the 1780s and the 1820s. A great many of those items are foreign to us today, despite the fact that versions of some have survived to the present. (Toddlers still careen around in wheeled "walkers," occasionally launching themselves into harm's way when parents forget to close gates at the top of stairs.) Like the changing context of the words examined in the previous chapter ("pursuit of happiness," for example), the context surrounding material objects has shifted as well. If historians are to understand the lives of past Americans both great and small, they need to breathe life not only into the abstract sentiments of the Declaration, but also the contours of the material environment—the stuff of everyday life.

Heat, one variable shaping those contours, is something we tend to take for granted in a fully industrialized society. We have just seen how the presence of open fires in houses necessitated the use of baby tenders. But keeping warm, particularly during the harsh New England winters, shaped the material environment in dozens of ways. Sarah Emery of Newburyport, Massachusetts, recalled that in the cold winter of 1820–1821, "china cups cracked on the tea table from the frost, before a rousing fire, the instant the hot tea touched them; and plates set to drain in the process of dishwashing froze together in front of the huge logs, ablaze in the wide kitchen fireplace." Most homes in the early republic had only one central fireplace, and the older the house, the larger and draftier it was likely to be. Seventeenth-century fireplaces were 2 or 3 yards wide—large enough to walk into—and their broad chimneys swept most of the heat straight up out of the house. In such breezy conditions, seating benches like the "kitchen settle" pictured here were designed to face the fire and shelter those sitting in them from the drafts. (Notice that the high back extends all the way to the floor to help keep the sitters' legs warm.)

If the main room was often drafty despite the presence of a fire, other rooms in the house were downright frigid. More than wind could whistle through the chinks of exterior walls and the cracks around windows. Abner Sanger's diary for December 19, 1793, noted laconically that he used his time "to clean out chambers [i.e., his rooms] of snow." Youngsters, who often slept in garrets, were not surprised to find light drifts along the floor and

rime from their breath frosting the tops of their blankets. Some folk moved their beds to the warmest room possible, in front of the main fireplace—but then they had to worry about stray sparks setting fire to their covers. Rooms abutting the chimney on the second floor or in the attic gained some secondary warmth and could be used for storing foods such as apples, squashes, onions, potatoes, carrots, and beets, all of which needed to be protected from freezing. When the thermometer really plummeted, however, "people's roots were frozen in the garret," as another diarist noted in 1788. Digging into the ground provided more reliable food storage; a "root cellar" penetrating deep enough beyond the frost line kept temperatures above freezing.

For those who could afford them, curtains draped on four-poster beds created a tent to conserve the warmer air generated by the bed's occupants. And children, siblings, husbands, and wives all doubled up to benefit from the shared body heat. Indeed, the practice was so common that sleeping alone seemed a bit odd. One young apprentice recorded several times in his diary the search for one or another nighttime companion: "I got Albert Field to sleep with me last night, & I must go and get somebody to sleep with me tonight for it is rather lonesome to lie alone." Many New Englanders also "banked" their houses, protecting the root cellar and first story by piling up insulation around the outside walls every autumn. They used leaves, tanbark, cornstalks, sand, or even "chip-dung."

Baby tenders, root cellars, and bed curtains are all items of everyday life that historians define as material culture. And those historians who make that field their specialty realize quickly how much the lives of Americans of this era were constrained, day in, day out, by circumstances far different from today's world. If it was a woman's task to spin wool, should she ask her husband or son to move the "great wheel" into a heated room? (Julia Smith of Glastonbury, Connecticut, did because she knew her fingers would not be nimble enough otherwise.) What sorts of trees supplied the most useful firewood, and when was the best time to lay in the year's supply? (For baking, coals from hickory or birch served well; and the winter snow cover facilitated hauling logs from the woodlot in a sleigh.)

Reconstructing the material culture of a people requires both hard work and imagination. Obviously, some information can be gleaned by examining objects discovered in attics or passed down by the descendants of those who first used them. The baby tender pictured at the opening of this chapter arrived at Memorial Hall Museum in 1960 with a tag identifying it as an "18th century primitive baby tender used in Mrs. Sheldon Howe's family for many years." But in examining the tender's 113 nails, the museum discovered that 100 of them were a type known as "cut nails," not commonly in use until after 1820. Thus the tender was more likely constructed in the early nineteenth century, which is only to say that the traditions handed down along with the objects are not always accurate. Scholars of material culture use a wide variety of written records and physical analysis to identify surviving objects and place them in their broader context.

We have already encountered some sources of evidence. Reconstructing the social world of Salem Village, historians drew upon household inventories taken upon the death of the house's owner. Such inventories provide room-by-room lists of the house's contents—not only major pieces of furniture, but often minor objects as well, whose value might be only a few pennies. Such inventories are not unfailingly reliable. When death was preceded by a long illness, some possessions might have already been passed on to other relatives. What else are we to make of a list including a fancy mirror and silver plates but no beds? However, by sampling enough estates, patterns emerge.

The bed curtains just mentioned, for example, were undeniably expensive. Did that limit their ownership solely to the rich? Historians have surveyed enough inventories to suggest that by the 1770s at least half the households in some towns used them. Although the cost may have been high, the warmth gained on cold nights apparently justified the expense. Other documentary records include family account books, which note daily expenses, extraordinary purchases, and even the number of cords of wood burned over time. More arcane records, such as fire insurance documents filed by prosperous homeowners, yield details about how many fireplaces were used at different times of the year. (Some rooms were shut up for the coldest months, it seems, because they were too much trouble and expense to heat.) And, of course, we have already quoted from diaries, which supply wonderfully concrete descriptions of everyday lives.

Yet some details elude us, as in the case of the fired clay object shown

here, dated around 1820. Any guesses as to its function? We should note immediately that its dimensions are too large to make it a cup for drinking. It was delicately referred to as a "chamber pot," used in an era when "privies" (outhouses) were often constructed at some distance from the house and inconvenient to reach, especially in the middle of the night or in winter. Historian Jane Nylander, whose study of material culture has illuminated many of the previously noted strategies for keeping warm, confessed herself at a loss for information when it came to chamber pots:

Chamber pots are listed in a few inventories, but they are conspicuously absent from many others. Considering the frequency with which they are excavated by historical archaeologists and the heavy reliance [by Americans of that day] on cathartics as medical remedies, it seems likely that the care of these useful vessels was an important daily chore. However, it is difficult to know the conventions associated with their use. . . . Abner Sanger's diary gives us two clues in this obscure area: on July 7, 1794, he purchased a "urine mug," and on November 19, 1778, he made a "shit house." Perhaps that was really the difference.

ROOM FOR IMPROVEMENT

It would be understandable, of course, if Sanger's descendants were not particularly eager to hand down his chamber pot as an heirloom. Indeed, the wonder is that so many chamber pots—and other objects—have survived the winnowing process that death inevitably brings. If you were to die suddenly, how many of your possessions would be saved and passed along? Valued photographs or letters, perhaps—but that old computer, whose processor is nearly worthless, with its obsolete floppy disks? The kitchen dish towels or the Pocahontas plastic tumbler from McDonald's, which somehow survived a purging? A lot of your own material culture would likely disappear into the landfill, not because your nearest and dearest are more ruthless than most relatives, but simply because there is scant room for these items in someone else's home, because the remnants are old and worn, or because their personal significance is lost on others.

Yet material objects that have disappeared in real life often survive in paintings or photographs, which also become visual archives for historians. A variety of material culture from the early republic can be seen in the paintings of John Lewis Krimmel, for example. Krimmel, a German immigrant who came to Philadelphia, was one of America's earliest painters of "genre scenes"—paintings of ordinary life rather than formal portraits of the well-to-do or grand paintings of historic events (such as John Trumbull's *Declaration of Independence;* see Chapter 3). Krimmel recorded the details of bustling parades and election-day crowds; indoors he painted weddings and tavern scenes. His paintings were full of everyday objects, including *Quilting Frolic,*

the painting shown on facing page, done around 1813. Krimmel depicts the end of a day on which a number of women have been working on the quilt at the left. A woman cuts the quilt free from its frame just as several other folk arrive to celebrate the project's completion. There will likely be some dancing, since a black fiddler is there to provide the music.

The room is filled with a veritable treasure trove for students of material culture. In examining the painting, we intend to follow the method of many preachers of the era, which was to present a text out of scripture and then "improve" (or explicate) its verses one by one. But before beginning, it may be useful for readers to try "improving" the painting themselves. Take a pencil and paper and jot down half a dozen items of material culture displayed in *Quilting Frolic*. Then consider how each might be used to illuminate the lives of the people pictured.

The likeliest place to begin, given the painting's title, is with the quilt itself, for quilting conjures up picturesque images of the young republic's simpler days. Sewing, after all, was women's work that young girls learned almost as soon as they could hold a needle. Harriet Kidder of Newark, New Jersey, recorded proudly in her diary that daughter Katy "has nearly completed her *quilt* . . . She has pieced every block—put them all together in long strips & assisted in sewing together these strips." A month later the Kidders celebrated that completion with a party, for it was Katy's fifth birthday. The age of five was a common marker of when a child might complete a quilt—at least when this particular diary was written, in 1847.

But the date is important, for by 1847 we are already well into the mid-nineteenth century, and it is a nostalgic misconception to envision quilting as an integral part of life during the colonial period, or even in 1820. Today, recycling is a virtue; we imagine stitching together a patchwork blanket as a thrifty way to reuse old scraps of cloth. Yet before the 1820s such quilting would have struck most Americans as sign of abundance, for it required patterned cloth, and such cloth was an imported luxury throughout nearly all of the eighteenth century. Most clothing was made of simple homespun. Paradoxically, the "rustic" practice of quilting was a by-product of the Industrial Revolution, which made low-cost patterned textiles readily available.

During the early years of the republic, quilts were simpler affairs, not made up of multiple pieces of cloth or decorative materials appliquéd to the cloth. A diary that mentioned a quilt in 1780 was more likely referring to a woman's petticoat, which was finished with the characteristic criss-cross stitch. The example shown here, from the later eighteenth century, was bright red and finished off with an elegant leaf and flower design that could have peeked through the fashionable open-front skirts of gowns of the period.

As for quilting a blanket, that was done by joining two large pieces of cloth that enclosed an insulating padding of carded wool or tow (fibers made from flax); the three layers were kept together by the crisscross stitch. The display side of the blanket was usually made of calamanco, a lustrous worsted wool, while the bottom was a simpler homespun. In Krimmel's scene, painted around 1813, the quilt appears to be of a single color and not made of piecework.

The social nature of the quilting frolic, however, was characteristic of both the colonial period and the nineteenth century. When work was arduous or lonely, as it was especially in sparsely populated rural areas, Americans continually looked for ways to gather and enjoy each other's company. New Englanders called the practice "changing works"—that is, one person helped another who would later return the favor in an exchange of work. We "spun and sang songs," recorded Ruth Henshaw in her diary in 1789, when her friend Sally came by for two days. When such get-togethers involved larger numbers of people and ended with a celebration they were called "frolics," and the completion of a quilt was only one of many excuses for such sociability. Esther Cooper, living on Long Island in the 1760s and 1770s, recorded going to "spinning frolics" on several occasions; her husband Simon proposed a wood-chopping frolic, for which the women "were very busie cooking for the work men," according to Esther.

So while Krimmel's quilt suggests one dimension of material culture, it is important to remember that quilting was by no means the only occupation that went on in rooms like this one. Historian Laurel Thatcher Ulrich tallied the references to work in the diary of Betty Foot, a Connecticut girl, from January through May 1775:

> Spinning appeared on twenty-three days, knitting on twenty-three, sewing fifteen, carding [wool] thirteen, and a cluster of other activities—quilting, hatcheling [separating flax fibers], spooling and quilling—on five. Betty mentioned her own weaving only once, on March 7, 1775, when "I stay'd at home & finish'd Molly's Worsted Stockings and fix'd two Gowns for Welch's Girls which came to 1s 6d [1 shilling, sixpence] and I wove while Nabby went to Milking." Her fifteen sewing entries included nine occasions on which she "fix'd" gowns for other people.

Krimmel's painting itself suggests that there was more than quilting going on every day in this room. The woman kneeling on the ground has her left arm resting on a sewing basket, and in the lower foreground at least two other similar work baskets can be seen.

Turning to another set of objects in the room, look at the cups and saucers on the tray carried by the young black servant (see the detail from the painting, page 81), and the plates and napkins on the tablecloth to the left. To modern eyes such objects seem unexceptional, yet they reveal much, particularly when we consider change over time. During the eighteenth century,

dining habits in the colonies were often primitive, especially in rural areas and among poorer folk. For example, a physician traveling in 1744 wrote about being offered a meal by a ferryman along the Susquehanna River

whom I found att vittles with his wife and family upon a homely dish of fish without any kind of sauce. They desired me to eat but I told them I had no stomach. They had no cloth upon the table, and their mess [i.e., food] was in a dirty, deep, wooden dish which they evacuated with their hands, cramming down skins, scales, and all. They used neither knife, fork, spoon, plate, or napkin because, I suppose, they had none to use.

Even in the late eighteenth century, dining could be primitive. At breakfast "my father and mother would eat out of one bason, myself and two sisters, out of the other," recalled Seth Sprague of Duxbury, Massachusetts. John Weeks of Salisbury, Vermont, remembered "the custom of setting the large six-quart dish in the centre of the table, while half a dozen or more children stood around it, each with a spoon, partaking of this homely but healthful repast of samp and milk." *Samp*, a Narragansett Indian term for cornmeal mush, was only one of many stews, soups, puddings, and porridges common at the time. Such fare was eaten easily enough out of an all-purpose dish known as a "porringer," a bowl that could be used to drink out of or to hold a semiliquid meal eaten with a spoon. Early porringers were often earthenware, like the one pictured here, im-

ported from England around 1690. After 1750, however, pewter and silver models became more common. In his autobiography, Benjamin Franklin recalled that his wife presented him with new dining ware, because she thought "*her* husband deserv'd a silver spoon and China bowl as well as any of his neighbors. This was the first appearance of [silver] plate and China in our house."

Given the dining habits prevailing at the beginning of the nineteenth century, Krimmel's portrayal of proper china cups and plates and napkins suggests that his Philadelphia frolickers prided themselves on their civilized fare. The tablecloth, too, is a mark of refinement. If you look closely you can see the fashionable fringe at its edges; by this date many American weavers were adding fringe to their homemade linen cloths. The painting is not detailed enough to show whether silverware is present. Although it almost certainly would have been used, we have no way of knowing whether the guests considered themselves polite enough to convey food to their mouths by using a fork rather than a knife, in the manner of the French and English. One manual of etiquette from the 1830s advised, "if you think as I do that Americans have as good a right to their own fashions . . . you may choose the convenience of feeding yourself with your right hand armed with a [knife's] steel blade; and provided you do it neatly and do not put in large mouthfuls, or close your lips tight over the blade, you ought not to be considered as eating ungenteely."

Another mark of refined dining, significant in its own right, is the cupboard at the left of Krimmel's painting. It displays china through its windows, so guests can admire the household's prosperity and good taste. The doors were unusual for 1813 in that they slid sideways rather than swinging out on hinges, an advantage in crowded quarters. Regardless of their date of manufacture, cupboards played a crucial role as a repository for family valuables—particularly valuables belonging to women. Like other precious possessions, cupboards themselves could be passed along in the family and treasured for their own sake.

One such heirloom, astonishing in its beauty, is the cupboard shown here belonging originally to Hannah Barnard of Hadley, Massachusetts.

Made sometime in the decade after 1710, its design reflected a local tradition among cabinetmakers in the Connecticut River region around Springfield. Cabinetmakers there both carved and painted designs on the wood, including the bright blue turned columns on the upper half of the Barnard cupboard. About 250 examples of these "Hadley chests" or similar items, created between 1680 and 1740, have survived. To have the owner's name painted in large letters was unusual, but out of 126 similar chests, at least 115 incorporated the owner's initials into the design. Other characteristic motifs include the two-petaled tulips joined to a single large leaf (seen to the inside of the letters of Hannah Barnard's name), the inverted hearts and diamonds below the tulips, the semicircles, and the twining vines flanking each side of the drawers.

In addition, the Hadley chests exhibit a revealing naming pattern. Barnard was Hannah's maiden name, though the chest was very probably made in anticipation of her marriage. Similarly, the great majority of initials displayed on other Hadley chests corresponded with maiden names, and only 6 bore the initials of both the wife and husband. In other words, the cabinets were associated with the woman of the household far more than with the man. As Laurel Ulrich has noted, the reason seems to be that such cabinets held goods that women traditionally owned—linens, damask napkins, embroidered samplers—passed down through the female line of a family, mother to daughter. We have already seen, in discussing the status of women during the colonial period, that the law treated men and women differently. That was the case in terms of inheritance. Traditionally "real" property—woodlands, fields, houses, barns, and other real estate—passed from one male to another. Because such property was not moveable, it could not travel from place to place.

By contrast, when a woman married, she moved from her own family to the home of her husband and took his name. Her possessions tended to be what the law referred to as "moveables"—property that could travel with her, including domestic animals and personal possessions such as a cupboard and its contents. As Ulrich observed, this division of property was not neutral. "In such a system, women themselves became 'movables,' changing their names and presumably their identities as they moved from one male-headed household to another." In 1813, when Krimmel painted *Quilting Frolic*, Hannah Barnard's cupboard was still being used by her descendants, a century after its manufacture. It left the family only when Hannah's great-granddaughter, Hannah Barnard Hastings Kellogg, was forced to part with it upon making the long trek to California. In an age of increasing mobility, even "moveables" had their limits.

Notice the broom lying on the floor at the lower right of *Quilting Frolic*. This broom is an advance over the coarser versions used in most homes in the 1780s. Older twig brooms could only banish leaves or clots of mud and dirt, leaving finer dust behind. Given those limitations, a careful housewife camouflaged the remaining dust by scattering a bit of clean white sand on the floor and brushing it into a pleasing herringbone pattern. "A white floor sprinkled with clean white sand . . . decorated a parlour genteely enough for any body," recalled one woman who grew up in Philadelphia near the turn of the century. Around 1800, however, some farmers began using the thinner stalks of sorghum grass (which came to be called "broomcorn") to manufacture a broom that swept up finer dust as well. This seems to be the variety used by Krimmel's quilters. By the 1830s millions had been sold.

In the right-hand corner of Krimmel's room stands a tall case clock, about 6 feet high—another reflection of the owner's good taste. In the first years of the republic, such a clock could be afforded only by the reasonably well-to-do. American clockmakers worked by hand, producing no more than about ten "movements" per year. The purchaser was expected to find a cabinet-maker to build a case for the movement. But by 1813 Eli Terry and other manufacturers had devised ways to turn out over a thousand movements a year, also significantly smaller and capable of fitting in cases only 20 inches high. The new clocks were cheaper too. Over the next decades they would be hawked far and wide by Yankee peddlers to Americans eager to add a bit of refinement to houses and even rude cabins.

As material culture, such clocks provided an ambiguous message about the world their owners occupied. The clock in Krimmel's painting was a mark of gentility as much or more than it was a precise timepiece. To be sure, urban Americans had some use for dividing the day into hours and minutes. Yet natural rhythms of light and dark often provided equally practical divisions of the day. Farmers knew quite well how far along the day had

come merely by looking out a window, and often they made fine distinctions. One Illinois farmer in the 1830s divided the hours before sunrise into no less than eight stages: long before day, just before day, just coming day, just about daylight, good light, before sunup, about sunup, and (finally) sunup. The faces of many clockworks reflected this affinity to the natural world; the one shown here gives not only the time but, above the clock face, a calculation of the moon's current phase. It was useful to know when a full moon was available, to provide better light for traveling or working at night. At the same time, the penetration of clocks into ordinary homes reflected an increased need to appear punctually either at work or at social events. A Massachusetts diarist in 1830 recorded having a fine time at a sleighing party: "They sing, going and returning, which sounds very prettily. Have some hot coffee, and return at half past nine." Krimmel's clock, then, was a part of the material environment that looked both backward to the genteel culture of the late eighteenth century and forward to an industrial era in which the hours of the day were more strictly regimented.

THE REFINING OF AMERICA

Thus far we have been dealing with material culture on a piecemeal basis: object by object, looking to tease out how each item shaped everyday life. But the case clock reminds us that with the passage of time, material culture is constantly changing. Quilting, we saw, meant something different in 1840 than it did in 1780. If material culture is constantly evolving, then a study of it may help chart the broader evolution of American society as well.

What longer-term trends are revealed by the objects in *Quilting Frolic?* Return to the painting's plates and napkins, and recall the physician's account of dinner with the ferryman's family, written some seventy-five years earlier. Contrasting the two ways of dining suggests that over time more refined habits of dining were coming into play. Yet that evolution is not a simple progression from the "barbarities" of 1744 to the "civilized" behavior of 1813. The physician himself was disgusted by the behavior of his hosts; he admitted to having "no stomach" for their meal. *Some* people in 1744 felt it uncouth to eat without silverware or napkins—and those folk, obviously, came from the higher ranks of society, like the physician, who could afford such refinements as silverware.

The spread of refinement, therefore, involved the diffusion of habits first practiced by social elites downward to Americans in the middle of the social spectrum—to a middle class that was itself becoming a distinctive part of American society during those years. Historian Richard Bushman has traced this process over several hundred years. The changes were gradual and usually appeared first in urban areas, where new cultural influences spread more easily. They appeared also where the process of industrialization took hold earlier, in New England and the Mid-Atlantic states, rather than in the South and the West—though those regions showed signs of change as well.

Genteel behavior was modeled after the manners of kings, queens, and the nobility. Over the centuries guides were published, known as "courtesy books," that instructed in the intricacies of proper conduct. *Rules of Civility*, a French publication of 1671 (also used in Britain), explained that those men and women with the highest social rank assumed the greatest places of honor, whether in a room (the space farthest from the door) or in a carriage (the back right seat) or in a bedroom (the bed itself). Behaviors of the smallest sort came under regulation: a servant of inferior rank was never to knock at the door of a nobleman—only to scratch! To be sure, such rules were extreme for eighteenth-century America, but George Washington, who always behaved with a high regard for civility, as a young man copied similar maxims out of another courtesy book: "In Company of those of Higher Quality than yourself Speak not ti[ll] you are ask'd a Question then Stand upright put of[f] your Hat and Answer in few words."

As these formulas made clear, genteel manners specified the proper relation to material objects such as doors, carriage seats, and beds. Hats were doffed to show respect—not only in Washington's day but in Krimmel's; note the guest in *Quilting Frolic* who is tipping his hat courteously. We have also seen how china, tablecloths, and clocks all served as markers of civility. One item missing in this array is a carpet—not surprising, for in 1813 such adornments were still relatively rare. In 1770 most Americans would have found it odd indeed to cover a room's wide plank flooring. *Rug* usually referred to a bed blanket, also called a "coverlid."

To modern eyes, a carpet would seem hardly to merit mention as an object toward which proper behavior must be paid. But in 1813 (and earlier) there were good reasons for not using carpets. Walking any distance out of doors coated shoes with mud or dirt that could easily deface fine rugs. Over time, dirt became less of an issue in urban areas with paved or cobblestone streets and sidewalks. In 1824 novelist Lydia Sigourney wrote a story based in part on a real experience, about a farmer mystified to see a rug on the parlor floor. Trying his level best to avoid getting it dirty, he worked his way around the edge of the room until blocked by a table. "I *must* tread on the kiverlid," he apologized; and when told that the carpet was meant to be walked on, replied, "I ha'nt been used to seeing kiverlids spread on the floor to walk on. We are glad to get 'em to kiver us up a' nights."

The trend toward refinement included more than the spread of genteel objects, for such ornaments were always being displayed within a larger setting. Thus we must examine not just the objects themselves but the space enclosing them, for space too was undergoing a steady evolution within the American home.

The earliest houses in British America were quite basic. Perhaps a third to a half or even more built during the seventeenth century featured a door that opened directly into the main room, known since medieval days as the "hall." Against one wall of this hall stood the large, drafty fireplace, which also doubled as a kitchen area. Later in the century houses were more likely to have two rooms on the first floor and another two on the second. On the first floor the additional room was known as the "parlor," but in effect it was the "best bedroom," where the mother and father slept and in which the most valuable furniture was kept, such as beds and dressers. Additional sleeping and storage space on the second floor was usually accessible by either a ladder or a stairway, the latter walled off to keep the heat in the main room from escaping upward. Windows were only about 2 feet square, also to keep heat in, which guaranteed dark and gloomy surroundings. Glass panes were preferred, but more than a few houses made do with oilcloth, which let through even less light.

Ordinary folk continued to use such houses during the eighteenth century, but those who could afford them increasingly built more spacious Georgian brick homes, which were coming into fashion in Britain. The main door no longer opened directly onto the central room, but onto an elegant hallway and staircase. No longer walled off and hidden, these stairs became part of the welcoming entryway. The main hall, which before had been a multifunctional space for eating, cooking, and sleeping, became more formal and finished, sometimes known as the "entertaining room." Walls were plastered and painted or wallpapered, instead of showing wood planking. The ceiling was finished too, no longer revealing the rafters and flooring of the room above. Corner moldings added refinement, and chair rails—molding at waist height—protected walls from being scratched by the elegant seats placed along a room's perimeter. More light brightened the rooms: sash windows ("the newest fashion" in 1710) allowed in more daylight than the old-fashioned casements, and the eighteenth-century gentry took advantage of the new cleaner-burning (though more expensive) spermaceti candles to light their homes in the evening.

Improvements in heating also reshaped rooms toward the end of the century. Benjamin Thomas, a Massachusetts man also known as Count Rumford, redesigned the traditional fireplace to make it smaller, less drafty, and more efficient. Benjamin Franklin's stove, inserted into a fireplace, also allowed more heat to radiate into the room. The smaller fireplaces were less convenient for cooking, but since the new houses had more space, the kitchen could be moved to a separate room at the back of the house, to the cellar, or, especially in the southern colonies, to an outbuilding behind the main house. (Krimmel's room features a smaller fireplace.)

Comfort, certainly, was part of the rationale behind the changes. But they were not merely about practicality. The newer architecture reflected the leisure that colonial elites enjoyed. (The traditional definition of a gentleman was that he did not need to work to support himself or his family.) The more money spent on furnishing the parlor—the most expensive room in the house—the less the parlor was involved with practical, everyday economic activities such as eating, spinning, cooking, or sleeping. Estate inventories tell the tale: as the eighteenth century progressed, fewer and fewer large houses listed beds located in the parlor room. Instead we find tea tables, chairs, and cupboards displaying the best china. And entertainment in the finest houses was not confined to the parlor; second-floor rooms might be outfitted for tea or even fine dining. That was one reason the open staircase and central hallway was so important. "The staircase must present itself boldly and freely to the sight," advised one British architectural authority, "otherwise all has a confused and poor aspect. It looks as if the house had no good upper floor." Historian William Thomas O'Dea has pointed out that the increase of candles used in sconces and candelabra was not "the result of utilitarian pressures for better lighting, but of the evolution of a way of life whose chief objects were entertainment and display."

Display indeed. Both O'Dea and Bushman have emphasized the theatrical quality of the newer architecture. Colonial elites saw themselves as leaders of their communities, and they felt obliged to present their leadership in highly visible ways. George Washington was painfully aware of being watched at all times, as the maxims he copied from his courtesy book demonstrated: "In the Presence of Others Sing not to yourself with a humming Noise, nor Drum with your fingers and Feet." Washington's visibility was peculiarly high, but all gentlefolk recognized that "in the Presence of Others," they must behave to a standard. "Wherever you are, imagine that you are observed," insisted a popular eighteenth-century ladies' handbook, "and that your Behaviour is attentively scanned by the rest of the Company all the while; and this will oblige you to observe yourself, and to be constantly on your Guard."

Given such attitudes, the houses of the elite were designed to display the elite and their possessions advantageously. Visitors traveled a path, which was often landscaped, toward an imposing mansion whose exterior walls were painted or constructed of brick, in marked contrast to most weather-beaten, unpainted houses. Ushered through a formal garden or courtyard, guests entered an impressive hallway and were led into rooms aglow with as many as a dozen candles, whose light was multiplied and reflected back by the silver plate, candlesticks, and trays. Mirrors on the wall and polished chairs and tables further magnified space and light. The activities that went on within these rooms were not so different from those enjoyed by ordinary folk—card playing, tea drinking, and dancing. It was the refinement that made the difference. The objects, the spaces, and the vistas all ennobled those who took their place on these stages.

THE MATERIAL IDENTITIES OF A MIDDLE CLASS

During the early republic the tastes of gentlemen and gentlewomen were increasingly adopted by Americans with less income and status. The process of refinement helped *create* a distinctive middle class, defined in part by the increase in urban living and in part by the habits of life its members adopted and the sorts of objects with which they surrounded themselves. Yet as Richard Bushman has pointed out, the process was not merely one of imitation. The notion of refinement itself was evolving because of who these middling sorts were and how their lives required them to live.

Unlike gentlemen, members of the middle classes were obliged to work. Tableware, china, carpets, and clocks were eagerly purchased, but those expenses required the generation of extra income. Some valued items, of course, could be manufactured at home, but often not as cheaply as they could be had in stores. The question was, where would the extra money be found? The census of 1810 provided one revealing answer, for it collected information on Americans' occupations and work habits. Both farm families and those living in cities and towns earned extra income through household manufacturing, producing textiles like the fringed tablecloth in Krimmel's painting or the new sorghum-grass brooms. Tench Coxe, who created a digest of the 1810 census shortly after it was completed, noted that cloth manufactured on small, home-based looms contributed "to the comfort and happiness" of the women who manufactured it and left men free "for the duties of the farm." With southern plantations producing ever more cotton since the invention (in 1793) of Eli Whitney's cotton gin, Coxe hoped that home manufacturing might increase and in the process "render every industrious female *an artizan*, whenever her household duties do not require her time."

Thus the quilting frame so prominent in Krimmel's painting was actually a sign of the conflicting forces of leisure and work. On the one hand, the room exhibited many signs of refinement and a desire to rise above the older, simpler ways of life. Yet work, not leisure, provided the rationale for the frolic, no matter how much fun was to be had once the quilt was finished. And what was true for Krimmel's one room was true for many other households, according to the census. Combining its data with information from town histories, probate wills, and deeds, historians have shown that nearly 90 percent of the households in Topsham, Maine—to take one example—were making cloth of some sort. Over half of these households had looms, and the cloth making went on in families whose male heads were tanners, shipwrights, joiners, and blacksmiths, among others. Both ordinary "yeomen" and even a few whom the census takers styled "gentlemen" found it profitable to manufacture clothing.

How the cloth was used varied from one house to the next. A good deal was created only for shirts, dresses, and trousers for the family. But other households were more ambitious. "My mother would change work with Zerniah's mother and other women, knitting and sewing for them while they would weave cotton and flax into cloth which we would get dressed into fustian [a strong fabric] at the mill for the boys and also for Father's summer working dress," recalled Mary Palmer Tyler. From this entry alone, it becomes clear that cloth making involved a patchwork of relationships, with the exchange of work between families and friends going on as of old—but now also with the presence of a "mill." In the early 1800s more and more mills were dotting the New England countryside. The census of 1810 listed over 600 carding mills, where wire-brush machines combed out wool or flax in preparation for spinning. Over 110 cotton-spinning factories sold thread to women who could weave it into cloth in their own homes. The women would then sell the cloth back to the factories. Thus home industry at first complemented the new factories, and the parlors of the middle class remained places where work mixed with leisure, and where spinning wheels and even looms crowded other furniture.

But with the coming of larger-scale factories like the Lowell mills, established in 1820, cheaper cloth could be turned out in quantity, making it more difficult for home manufacturers to compete. The decades following 1830 saw the separation of the workplace and the home into increasingly distinct spheres. The daughters of farmers began to take jobs in factories, rather than staying home to help mothers make cloth to be sold at market. As one New England minister noted, "The transition from mother-and-daughter power to water-and-steam power" produced "a complete revolution of domestic life." For middle-class families the home was becoming less a workplace and more a refuge from the workaday world beyond. Women were the moral guardians of this domestic domain, and working men retreated to it after the day's labor, expecting comfort and repose. By the mid-nineteenth century the "cult of domesticity," as historians have come to call it, was in full swing.

Historians can plot the material contours of these changes in the histories of individual houses, as they were remodeled and improved over the years. When Old Sturbridge Village moved the home of blacksmith Emerson Bixby from Barre, Massachusetts, to its museum grounds, it carefully studied Bixby's account books, the alterations of the house walls, and the layers of paint and wallpaper in order to document the process of refinement over time. In 1807 the dwelling was still primitive. Its somewhat uncharacteristic three-room configuration had a kitchen in the rear, with a parlor and sitting room in front. The parlor, also known as the "best room" (*br* on the plan) included a bed where the previous owners had slept. Although the front door opened directly onto that room, at least it could boast wallpaper on the upper half of the walls, as well as chair rails and wainscoting (a wood paneling) on the lower half, painted Prussian blue. Yet despite those refinements, the owners not only slept in the best room but ate there as well. The kitchen stairway was enclosed, following the old style, and a central chimney served the fireplace in each room. A small pantry was used for storage. In short, although a few eighteenth-century refinements had been introduced into the parlor, the house in 1807 functioned as had most simple seventeenth-century houses.

By the time Bixby finished a series of renovations around 1845, the size of the house and the functions of its rooms had changed (see the enlarged floor plan on pg. 90.) A few features remained as they were. There was no

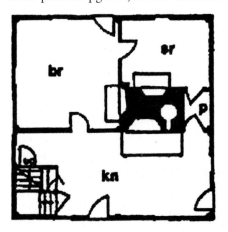

easy way to add a central stairway and a front entry hall, so access to the second floor remained through the kitchen. But the best room had become a full-fledged parlor; the door to the outside had been removed and was replaced by a window. A room (nr) was added on the first floor for Mr. and Mrs. Bixby, which allowed their bed to be moved from the parlor. And the interior walls were plastered throughout, and all the rooms were either wallpapered or painted a fashionable gray.

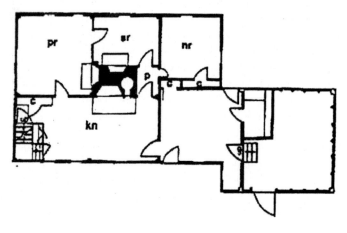

The exterior received attention as well. Bixby had the unpainted siding removed and new clapboard installed and painted white, a color that had come into fashion by the mid-1800s. (Eighteenth-century owners preferred a yellow or sand, or even russet or green, if brick was not used.) Also, the notion of a front lawn as an aesthetic element of a refined home came into play. We know this because archaeologists from Old Sturbridge excavated around the original site of the house. In the layers of the soil deposited before the 1840s, a good deal of refuse can be found: broken plates, ashes, and food scraps. Such garbage was simply thrown out through a convenient window, indicating no concern for the house's external appearance. After the 1840s, however, garbage was usually collected in designated spots at the rear. The backyard was improved too: a barn that stood close to the house had been torn down and a building for the animals was erected farther away, thereby increasing the separation between the polite space of the house and the work space behind.

We do not know for sure, but it would have made sense for the Bixbys to have added a fence around the yard, as many middle-class homes were doing. Contemporary architects were also recommending that shrubbery be used to decorate the house and soften its appearance. Again the contrast with the bolder display of eighteenth-century mansions is instructive: these new middle-class houses, envisioned as refuges, preferred to appear sheltered from the public bustle.

Given these changes in the home environment, look at one final engraving of a parlor (page 91), this one done about fifteen years after *Quilting Frolic*. Having analyzed the objects seen in Krimmel's painting, take a mo-

ment to catalog the material culture shown here. What differences do you notice, and how would you relate them to the social transformation that was under way?

In terms of objects, a number of items jump out. First, a pair related to size: the fireplace and the window. The former is much smaller, and the latter much larger than would have been seen a century earlier. A close look at the fire in the grate reveals that the flames are no longer fueled by wood but instead coal, which was increasingly used by urban residents. There is a carpet on the floor, which is conspicuously absent from *Quilting Frolic*. Other objects worth commenting on—we leave you the opportunity for a little research and speculation—are the clock over the mantel, the globe, the draperies, the footstools, the lamp in the window, and the vase in the right foreground.

Perhaps an even more interesting question revolves around the objects we do *not* see in the engraving. An inspector from Scotland Yard once famously inquired of Sherlock Holmes whether there was any clue crucial to determining the whereabouts of a missing racehorse. Attention must be paid to "the curious incident of the dog in the nighttime," Holmes replied. "The dog did nothing in the nighttime," protested the inspector. "That was the curious incident!" replied Holmes. In *Quilting Frolic* we see a plethora of objects related to the work activities of the people in the parlor: sewing baskets, a broom, a quilting frame, a grinder of some sort on the stool. All such items are conspicuously absent in the engraving from 1831. Work has been banished from the parlor. Furthermore, there is no cupboard full of dishes. Why not? What has replaced it?

Equally telling are the people portrayed in the engraving. Krimmel documents a boisterous social occasion, with thirteen people in the room. The scene in the engraving (titled *There Is No School Like the Family School*) has only three figures, an intimate family setting. Of course artists paint a wide variety of subjects, so the mere act of selection here results in a certain bias. Even so, this artist is clearly portraying an ideal in order to teach a moral lesson about the virtues of "the family school." Consider how this ideal contrasts with the view in Krimmel's painting. The family here is nuclear rather than extended: we see only a father, mother, and daughter. In Krimmel's painting, by contrast, a grandfather sits by the fire and perhaps three siblings are evident, as well as their mother, seated to the left of the fireplace. As the young republic became more urban and less agricultural, the average family size began to drop. On a farm, a large family made good economic sense, since boys could help fathers in the field, and daughters could assist mothers in sewing, spinning, weaving, and doing household chores. The growing urban middle class, on the other hand, recognized that an education was paramount to securing a good job and a comfortable home; and education was more expensive to provide for large families.

Finally, compare the notion of refinement revealed in the engraving of a middle-class family with the sort of refinement reflected in eighteenth-century architecture. For the well-to-do of the late eighteenth century, rooms made it possible for one to see and be seen in a public way, as the leaders of society. This notion of leadership could not extend to members of the much larger middle class of the 1830s. So while more folk enjoyed many of the consumer goods that had been available only to the upper classes fifty years earlier, the focus of that enjoyment was turned inward. Calvert Vaux, a leading architect of the 1850s, spoke for changing tastes when he referred to the parlor as "the general living-room of the family" that functioned quite differently from the traditional genteel parlor. The genteel parlor was kept immaculate, its door tightly shut,

> always ready for—what? For daily use? Oh, no; it is in every way too good for that. For weekly use? No, not even for that—but for *company* use; and thus the choice room, with the pretty view, is sacrificed, to keep up a conventional show of finery that pleases no one . . . All this is absurd. No room in any house, except, perhaps, in a very large mansion, ought to be set apart for company use only . . . certainly not the most agreeably situated apartment in the house, *which should be enjoyed daily.*

Of course, Vaux was protesting because even in his day many homeowners still preferred to keep the parlor "for company use only." Yet the logic of his reforming impulse gained converts over time, and a gradual transition continued. "The building of one moderately good house," commented a contemporary of Vaux's, ". . . will often occasion the introduction of a thousand commodities of a better taste into a rural community." That was certainly the case with Emerson Bixby. Virtually every existing house in his neighborhood had been remodeled in one way or another by the time his renovations got under way. Bixby was, in fact, a classic example of a fellow "keeping up with the Joneses."

DEFINING OURSELVES

In the end, the study of material culture insinuates itself into the smallest crannies of everyday life, as historians and archaeologists examine faded porringers, chip the paint off moldings, and grub about in the dirt to reconstruct even the garbage of a household. Yet material culture can lead as well to larger questions about our collective identities. There is an old German adage with an aggressively materialist bent: *Mann ist was Mann ißt* (one is what one eats). If we broaden the saying, there is much to be said for the notion that people construct their identities—that they become what they are—by the way they make use of the material culture all around them. The "middling sorts" of people in the early republic incorporated eighteenth-century notions of what gentlefolk ought to own and how they ought to behave. Yet their own notions of refinement took on a different form, in which refuge from work became more important than the social display of the eighteenth-century gentry.

Material culture thus helps us trace the young republic's first steps away from an agrarian society toward an urban and industrial nation. This is a long- and oft-told story, but the perspective of material culture provides a different angle of view. The traditional tale sets its gaze squarely on the rise of factories like the Lowell mills, as they began to turn out products on a large scale and supplant the old ways, thanks to such innovations as water- and steam-power and interchangeable parts. The shorthand we use to name this transformation is, of course, the Industrial Revolution.

Yet by focusing on the material interactions of ordinary folk, the perspective shifts. Industrial America was only in its infancy during the early republic. The first "manufactories" were not yet displacing work that was going on at home. Mothers and daughters still took their wool to a factory for carding, yet they spun and wove cloth at home to sell, often, at markets. While Emerson Bixby worked as a blacksmith in Barre, his wife Laura and her three daughters helped pay for their renovations by braiding straw for hats, as well as sewing shoe uppers that could be sold to shoe manufacturers. At the same time they received income from the sale of the farm's cheese and butter.

Thus even before factories came to dominate the American economy, ordinary folk were working harder in a host of different ways to earn additional income to buy goods that would refine their lives, give them more comfort, and allow them to enjoy some of the luxuries that the gentry possessed. Swap an old clay porringer for finer china, insisted Franklin's wife. Historians have begun to recognize the importance of this transformation, referring to a "consumer revolution" in eighteenth-century Britain and in America. To use the economists' metaphor of supply and demand, instead of talking about an industrial revolution that begins to *supply* a host of new goods to buyers, historians speak increasingly of an *industrious* revolution that began earlier in the eighteenth century, during which the *demand*—for everything from silverware to printed textiles to soap to glassware—led more and more people of the middling sort to work harder, and vary the sort of work that went on in the home, in order to produce and to purchase such coveted consumer goods. America's transformation during these early years has proved to be fascinatingly complex, and material culture has supplied a key to understanding how an emerging middle class evolved, as well as a market economy.

Yet the identities of material culture are not only collective and large scale, but also small and intensely personal. More than we realize, perhaps, the texture of our lives is built from the material world we have chosen or not chosen to incorporate: the feel of a familiar mug in our hand as we nurse hot coffee every morning, the comfort of a well-worn chair, the configuration of a "family room," the sheen of a pitcher passed down by a grandmother, even the cell phone in our pocket. Material culture is in constant flux. New items become integral to our way of living; old items grow less relevant, though often still cherished. How long does one hold onto a treasured set of china? Or a cupboard like Hannah Barnard's? We can all appreciate the material bond with the past expressed by Elizabeth Shackleton, an Englishwoman who in 1779 left the house she had lived in for many years because her son Thomas had taken possession of it upon marrying. Shackleton watched as son Tom went about improving the house, noting with regret the redecoration of "my poor, good, old yellow room. Transmogrified indeed into [an] elegance" that seemed a bit too fancy for her taste. But her sharp eye catalogued the alterations going on around her, as one generation gave way to the next:

> On this day I emptied all and everything belonging unto me out of my mahogany bookcase, bureau and drawers given unto me by my own tender, good, most affectionate parent. They were made and finished by Henry Chatburne on Saturday December the eighth one thousand seven hundred and fifty. I value them much but relinquish the valuable loan with great satisfaction to my own dear child Thomas Parker.

We *are* more than we eat, assuredly; more, even, than we build and make and buy. But close attention to such matters reveals how intimately material culture has shaped our lives, and the lives of those who came before us.

Additional Reading

The history of everyday lives has enjoyed a long popularity, even in the nineteenth century; hence many volumes are available describing the material contours of the young republic. The first chapter of Laurel Thatcher Ulrich's *The Age of Homespun: Objects and Stories in the Creation of an American Myth* (New York, 2001) gives an incisive overview of the mid- and late-nineteenth century's fascination with "olden times" in America. Jack Larkin's *The Reshaping of Everyday Life: 1790–1840* (New York, 1989) provides a useful modern overview, as well as an ample bibliography. (The book is one of the Everyday Life in America series, whose volumes cover other periods in American history, including Stephanie Grauman Wolf, *As Various as Their Land: The Everyday Lives of Eighteenth-Century Americans* [New York, 1993]). Jane C. Nylander, *Our Own Snug Fireside: Images of the New England Home, 1760–1860* (New York, 1993) is excellent and oriented more directly toward material culture. So is Barbara Clark Smith, *After the Revolution: The Smithsonian History of Everyday Life in the Eighteenth Century* (New York, 1985). Both are amply illustrated with paintings and photographs of contemporary objects. Thomas J. Schlereth, *Material Culture Studies in America: An Anthology* (Nashville, 1982) is another introduction.

The most accessible primary sources are diaries, some more helpful than others for studying material culture. Some writers are so fervently spiritual that little concrete is said about everyday objects; other diarists are merely terse. But a close reading of a good diary can reveal much. One example of such a reconstruction can be found in Laurel Thatcher Ulrich's *A Midwife's Tale: The Life of Martha Ballard, Based on Her Diary, 1785–1812* (New York, 1990). In fact, one interesting exercise might be to read first Ballard's diary, published in Charles Elventon Nash, *The History of Augusta: First Settlements and Early Days as a Town Including the Diary of Mrs. Martha Moore Ballard (1785–1812)* (Augusta, ME, 1904), and then go to Ulrich's book to see how she has supplemented and filled out this primary source using additional materials. A Web site focusing on Martha Ballard is also available at http://www.dohistory.org. Leads to other diaries can be found in Joyce D. Goodfriend, *The Published Diaries and Letters of American Women: An Annotated Bibliography* (Boston, 1987). A few starting points in this period, from among many, are Lois Stabler, ed., *Very Poor and of a Low Make: The Journal of Abner Sanger* (Portsmouth, NH, 1986); Frederick Tupper and Helen Tyler Brown, eds., *Grandmother Tyler's Book: The Recollections of Mary Palmer Tyler (Mrs. Royall Tyler), 1775–1866* (New York, 1925); and Sarah Emery, *Reminiscences of a Nonagenarian* (Newburyport, MA, 1879). Novels written during the period also provide arresting details, including Catherine Maria Sedgwick, *A New England Tale* (1822; reprinted New York, 2003); Sarah Josepha Buell Hale, *Northwood* (1827), and Lydia Maria Child, *Hobomok* (1824; reprinted, New Brunswick, NJ, 1986).

Although we spent a good deal of time "improving" *Quilting Frolic*, there are more than a few objects left unmentioned that would bear additional discussion. Our black-and-white reproduction of the painting makes it difficult to make out, but on the wall to the left of the chimney hangs a soldier's regalia, including cap and sword; and there are two pictures of ships over the mantle. Can you think of any reason for these items to appear, given the date of the painting? To the right of the chimney hangs a cage with a bright red bird. It occurred to us that Krimmel might have inserted the bird as a symbolic object. What arguments could be made one way or the other? A study of Krimmel's other paintings would be relevant to the case, as would the knowledge you now have of house-furnishing traditions of this era. (Would it also make a difference to know whether the red bird was a canary or a cardinal? Anneliese Harding, who has no doubt seen the original painting, asserts the latter.) And finally, over the door hang a musket and powder horn. Whether such arms were as common in America as once thought has been recently challenged in Michael Bellesiles's controversial *Arming America: The Origins of a National Gun Culture* (New York, 2000). For a sense of the hot debate swirling around that book, see the Forum, "Historians and Guns," *William and Mary Quarterly*, 3d ser., 59 (January 2002), 203–268. For more on Krimmel and his work, see Anneliese Harding, *John Lewis Krimmel* (Winterthur, DE, 1994), and Milo M. Naeve, *John Lewis Krimmel: An Artist in Federal America* (Newark, DE, 1987).

Several color reproductions of *Quilting Frolic* may be found on the Web (at this writing at least) by clicking on the "Images" tab at www.google.com and typing in "Quilting Frolic." Indeed, by image-searching terms like "porringer" or "chamber pot," one can become an instant virtual archaeologist, excavating a huge variety of material culture in a rather hit-or-miss way. We found the Web site of the Memorial Hall Museum of Old Deerfield (http://www.old-deerfield.org/museum.htm) especially helpful for material culture because its online archive makes available hundreds of objects that can be zoomed in on. Many of the objects shown in this chapter are from their collection. Old Sturbridge Village has less available online, but their virtual tour includes photos of both the exterior and the main bedroom of Emerson Bixby's house (http://www.osv.org/tour/bixby.htm). Finally, for an example of eighteenth-century elegance to contrast with nineteenth-century domesticity, see the virtual tour of Drayton Hall in Charleston, South Carolina. The Web site is still under construction, but the interior views allow zooming and are matched with floor plans (http://www.draytonhall.org).

Two books in particular do a superb job of placing material culture in a broader context: Richard L. Bushman, *The Refinement of America: Persons, Houses, Cities* (New York, 1992), and Laurel Thatcher Ulrich, *The Age of Homespun*, noted earlier. Both cover periods far broader than the early republic—all the better for revealing long-term trends. Although this essay had space to touch only briefly on the consumer revolution of the late eighteenth century, John Brewer and Roy Porter have gathered a collection of relevant essays on the transatlantic context in *Consumption and the World of Goods* (London, 1993). T. H. Breen, *The Marketplace of Revolution: How Consumer Politics Shaped Revolution* (New York, 2004) appeared too late to benefit this essay but no doubt contains useful material. For a discussion of the "industrious revolution" (rather technical and hard-going) see the article in Brewer and Porter's book by Jan de Vries, "Between Purchasing Power and the World of Goods," 85–132. For an early discussion of a "consumer revolution" in the eighteenth century, see Neil McKendrick, "Home Demand and Home Economic Growth," in McKendrick, ed., *Historical Perspectives: Studies in English Thought and Society in Honour of J. H. Plumb* (London, 1974). And for a discussion of the creation of a market economy in the United States, see Winifred Barr Rothenberg, *From Market-Places to a Market Economy: The Transformation of Rural Massachusetts* (Chicago, 1992), and Stuart M. Blumin, *The Emergence of the Middle Class: Social Experience in the American City, 1760–1900* (New York, 1989).

Interactive Learning

The *Primary Source Investigator* provides a number of sources, including several John Lewis Krimmel paintings revealing details of American everyday material culture, a mystery object to identify, and a number of colonial probate lists and estate inventories that provide a glimpse into the worldly possessions of Americans as they evolved throughout the colonial and early national periods. Other sources portray the changes in architectural style of American houses as their owners sought ever-higher levels of refinement.

CHAPTER 5
Jackson's Frontier— and Turner's

Ceremony, merriment, and ballyhoo came to Chicago in the summer of 1893, and predictably, the crowds swelled the fairgrounds to get a taste of it. Buffalo Bill's Wild West Show went through its usual broncobusting, war-whooping routines. Visitors gawked at a giant map of the United States fashioned entirely from pickles. Also on display were a huge telescope, destined for Yerkes Observatory; a long-distance telephone, connected with New York City; and a four-story high cross section of a new ocean liner. The amusement park—the "Midway Plaisance"—even boasted exotic exhibits in the living flesh. Irish peasants boiled potatoes over turf fires, Arabian veiled women and turbaned elders occupied their own village, while "Prince Pomiuk" of the Eskimos drove a dogsled through the warm summery dust.

The excuse for the fuss was Chicago's World's Columbian Exposition, held ostensibly to salute the 400th anniversary of Columbus's arrival in the Americas. More plausibly, the fair allowed proud Chicagoans to prove that they were more than hog butchers to the world and that they could out-exposition any metropolis on the globe. Given the total attendance of more than 12 million people over six months, the city made its case.

To further the exposition's reputation, several scholarly congresses were convened, including a World's Congress of Historians and Historical Students. And so on July 12, the curious tourist had the opportunity (or misfortune) of straying away from the booming cannibal drums of the Midway Plaisance and into the Art Institute, where five eager historians waited to present the fruits of their labors. On this hot evening, the papers were read back-to-back without relief, ranging from a discussion of "English Popular Uprisings in the Middle Ages" to "Early Lead Mining in Illinois and Wisconsin." The hardy souls who had not been driven off by the first four talks saw a young man in starched collar rise to present yet another thesis, this one titled "The Significance of the Frontier in American History."

The young man was Frederick Jackson Turner, a historian from the University of Wisconsin. Although none in the audience could have suspected it, his essay would spark four generations of scholarship and historical debate. The novelty of Turner's frontier thesis resulted not from his discovery of any previously unknown facts, but because he proposed a new theory, one that took old facts and placed them in an entirely different light.

THE SIGNIFICANCE OF THEORY

Turner's thesis is only one of many theoretical concepts that historians have used to bring order out of the chaotic past. Yet thus far, this book has avoided a direct discussion of the term *theory*. It is time to make amends, for theory is an essential part of the discipline of history, profoundly affecting the way historians go about their work. Indeed, if history is not merely "the past" itself, but instead a reconstruction of it, theory could be said to supply the blueprints needed to raise the ediface.

At one level, theory can be defined simply as hypothesis. In this sense, it is the analysis that explains a relationship between two or more facts. During the Salem witch trials, certain "afflicted" townspeople acted in violent but consistent ways. Before historians could conclude that these acts might constitute symptoms of neurotic behavior, they had to accept the concept of conversion hysteria as a valid theoretical explanation. Note that the Salem records do not provide this interpretation; theory is what supplies it.

In a broader sense, theory can be defined as a body of theorems presenting a systematic view of an entire subject. We use the term this way when speaking of the "theory of wave mechanics" or a "germ theory of disease." Often, small-scale theoretical constructs are a part of a larger theoretical framework. Conversion hysteria is only one of many behavioral syndromes classified as neuroses. In turn, the concept of neurosis is only one part of the larger body of theory accepted by modern psychology. Physicists, chemists, and other natural scientists often use mathematical formulas to summarize their general theories, but among social scientists and humanists, theorems become less mathematic and more elastic. Even so, when historians discuss a "theory of democracy" or a "theory of economic growth," they are applying a set of coherent principles to explain specific events.

Because historians study an event or period in its entirety, historical narrative usually incorporates many theories rather than just one. The historian of early Virginia will draw on theories of economic behavior (the development of joint stock companies as a means of capital formation), sociology (the rise of slavery as an institution of color), psychology (the causes of friction between white and black laboring classes), and so on. In this broadest sense, historical theory encompasses the entire range of a historian's training, from competence in statistics to opinions on politics and philosophies of human nature. It is derived from formal education, from reading, even from informal discussions with academic colleagues and friends.

Turner in 1893, the year he presented his thesis at the Columbian World Exposition; and the Johns Hopkins University seminar room for history students. At the head of the table is Professor Herbert Baxter Adams, who argued that American democratic institutions could be traced to British and European roots. Turner resented the lack of interest in the West at Hopkins. "Not a man I know here," he commented, "is either studying, or is hardly aware of the country behind the Alleghenies."

It follows that theory in this wider sense—"grand theory," as it might be called—plays a crucial role in historical reconstruction. While small-scale theory is called on to explain specific puzzles (why didn't slavery become entrenched in Virginia before 1660?), grand theory is usually part of a historian's mental baggage *before* he or she is immersed in a particular topic. Grand theory encourages historians to ask certain questions and not others. It tends to single out particular areas of investigation as worthy of testing and to dismiss other areas as either irrelevant or uninteresting. Thus, anyone who ventures into the field of history—the lay reader as well as the professional researcher—needs to be aware of how grand theory exerts its influence. Nowhere in American history is this influence better illustrated than in Frederick Jackson Turner's venerable frontier thesis.

Turner began his Chicago lecture with a simple yet startling fact he had found in the recently released census of 1890. "Up to and including 1880, the country had a frontier of settlement," the census reported, "but at present the unsettled area has been so broken into by isolated bodies of settlement that there can hardly be said to be a frontier line." Turner seized upon this "event"—the passing of the frontier—as a "great historic moment." The reason for its importance to him seemed clear: "Up to our own day, American history has been in a large degree the history of the colonization of the Great West. The existence of an area of free land, its continuous recession, and the advance of American settlement westward, explain American development."

Turner's broad assertion—a manifesto, really—challenged on several counts the prevailing historical wisdom. Scholars of Turner's day had approached their subject with an Atlantic Coast bias. They viewed the East, and especially New England, as the true bearer of American culture. Developments beyond the Appalachian range were either ignored or treated sketchily. Turner, who had grown up in the rural setting of Portage, Wisconsin and had taken his undergraduate degree at the University of Wisconsin, resented that attitude.

In addition, the reigning scholarship focused almost exclusively on political and constitutional developments. "History is past Politics and Politics present History" ran the slogan on the wall of the Johns Hopkins seminar room in which Turner had taken his PhD. In contrast, young Turner strongly believed that this narrow political perspective neglected the broader contours of social, cultural, and economic history. Historians who took the trouble to examine those areas, he felt, would discover that the unique physical and cultural conditions of the frontier, and not eastern cities, had shaped American character.

The frontier's effect on American character had been recognized in a casual way by earlier observers, but Turner attempted a more systematic analysis. In doing so, he drew on the scientific grand theory most prominent in his own day, Charles Darwin's theory of evolution. Whereas Darwin had proposed an explanation for evolution in the natural world, Turner suggested that America was an ideal laboratory for the study of cultural evolution. The American frontier, he argued, returned human beings to a primitive state of nature. With the trappings of civilization stripped away, the upward process of evolution was reenacted. Dramatically, Turner recreated the sequence for his audience:

> The wilderness masters the colonist. It finds him a European in dress, industries, tools, modes of travel, and thought. It takes him from the railroad car and puts him in the birch canoe. It strips off the garments of civilization and arrays him in the hunting shirt and the moccasin. It puts him in the log cabin of the Cherokee and Iroquois and runs an Indian palisade around him. Before long he has gone to planting Indian corn and plowing with a sharp stick; he shouts the war cry and takes the scalp in orthodox Indian fashion. In short, at the frontier the environment is at first too strong for the man. He must accept the conditions which it furnishes, or perish, and so he fits himself into the Indian clearings and follows the Indian trails. Little by little he transforms the wilderness, but the outcome is not the old Europe. . . . The fact is that here is a new product that is American.

Turner suggested that the evolution from frontier primitive to civilized town dweller occurred not just once but time and time again, as the frontier moved west. Each time, settlers shed a bit more of their European ways; each time, a more distinctively American culture emerged. That was why the perspective of eastern historians was so warped: they stubbornly traced American roots to English political institutions or, worse, the medieval organization of the Germanic town. "The true point of view in the history of this nation is not the Atlantic coast," Turner insisted, "it is the Great West."

From this general formulation of the frontier's effects, Turner deduced several specific traits that the recurring evolutionary process produced. Chief among them were nationalism, independence, and democracy.

Nationalism, Turner argued, arose as the frontier broke down the geographic and cultural identities of the Atlantic Coast: New England with its Yankees and the tidewater South with its aristocratic planters. The "mixing and amalgamation" of sections was most clearly demonstrated in the middle states, where both Yankees and southerners migrated over the mountains, where Germans and other northern Europeans joined the English in seeking land. There a new culture developed, possessing "a solidarity of its own with national tendencies. . . . Interstate migration went steadily on—a process of cross-fertilization of ideas and institutions." (Once again, note the Darwinian metaphor of "cross-fertilization.")

The frontier also promoted independence, according to Turner. The first English settlements had depended on the home country for their material goods, but as settlers pressed farther west, England found it difficult to extend that supply. Frontier towns became self-sufficient, and eastern merchants increasingly provided westerners with American rather than English products. The economic system became more American, more independent.

Most important, suggested Turner, the individualism of the frontier promoted democracy and democratic institutions. "Complex society is precipitated by the wilderness into a kind of primitive organization based on the family," Turner argued. "The tendency is anti-social. It produces antipathy to control, and particularly to any direct control." Thus westerners resented being taxed without being represented, whether by England and Parliament or by Carolina coastal planters. The frontier also broke down social distinctions that were so much a part of the East and Europe. Given the fluid society of the frontier, poor farmers or traders could and did become rich almost overnight. Social distinctions disappeared when placed against the greater necessity of simple survival.

Turner even argued that the West, with its vast supply of "free land," encouraged democracy in the East. The frontier acted as a safety valve, he suggested, draining off potential sources of discontent before they disrupted society. "Whenever social conditions tended to crystallize in the East, whenever capital tended to press upon labor or political restraints to impede the freedom of the mass, there was this gate of escape to the free conditions of the frontier. . . . Men would not accept inferior wages and a permanent position of social subordination when this promised land of freedom and equality was theirs for the taking."

The upshot of this leveling process was nothing less than a new American character. Turner waxed eloquent in his description of frontier traits:

> That coarseness and strength combined with acuteness and inquisitiveness; that practical, inventive turn of mind, quick to find expedients; that masterful grasp of material things, lacking in the artistic but powerful to effect great ends; that restless, nervous energy; that dominant individualism, working for

good and for evil, and withal that buoyancy and exuberance which comes with freedom—these are the traits of the frontier, or traits called out elsewhere because of the existence of the frontier.

What Turner offered his Chicago listeners was not only "the American, this new man," as Hector St. John de Crevecoeur had called him in 1778, but also a systematic explanation of how the new American had come to be.

It would be proper etiquette here to scold Turner's Chicago audience for failing to recognize a masterpiece when they were read one. But in some ways it is easier to explain his listeners' inattention than to account for the phenomenal acceptance of the frontier thesis by later historians. Undeniably, Turner's synthesis was fresh and creative. But as he himself admitted, the essay was a hypothesis in need of research and testing. Of this, Turner proved constitutionally incapable. Although he loved to burrow in the archives for days on end, he found writing to be an unbearable chore.

Consequently, Turner published only magazine articles in the influential *Atlantic Monthly* and other journals. But these articles, along with numerous lectures and a gaggle of enthusiastic students, proved sufficient to make Turner's reputation. Publishers flocked to Wisconsin seeking books by the celebrated historian. Turner, with hopelessly misplaced optimism, signed contracts with four publishers to produce eight separate manuscripts. None saw the light of day. The single book he completed (*The Rise of the West*, 1906) appeared only through the frantic efforts of editor Albert Bushnell Hart, who wheedled, cajoled, and threatened in order to obtain the desired results. "It ought to be carved on my tombstone," Hart later remarked, "that I was the only man in the world that secured what might be classed an adequate volume from Turner."

Why Turner's remarkable success? Certainly not because of his detailed research, which remained unpublished. Success was due to the attraction of his grand theory. Later critics have taken Turner to task for imprecision and vagueness, but these defects are compensated by an eloquence and magnificence of scale. "The United States lies like a huge page in the history of society," Turner would declaim, and then proceed to lay out history with a continental sweep. The lure of his hypothesis for historians was much like the lure of a unified field theory for natural scientists—a set of equations, as physicist Freeman Dyson has remarked, that would "account for everything that happens in nature . . . a unifying principle that would either explain everything or explain nothing." In similar (though less galactic) fashion, Turner's theory captured historians' imaginations. "The existence of an area of free land, its continuous recession, and the advance of American settlement westward, explain American development." That proposal is about as all-encompassing as a historian could desire!

The theory seemed encompassing, too, in its methods. The techniques of social science in historical research are so familiar today that we forget the novelty and brilliance of Turner's insistence on unifying the tools of research. Go beyond politics, he argued; relate geography, climate, economics, and social factors to the political story. Not only did he propose this unification, Turner also provided a key focus—the frontier—as the laboratory in which these variables could be studied. The fresh breeze of Turner's theory succeeded in overturning the traditional approaches of eastern historians.

By the time Turner died in 1932, a tide of reaction had set in. Some critics pointed out that the frontier thesis severely minimized the democratic and cultural contributions of the English heritage. Others attacked Turner's vague definition of the "frontier." (Was it a geographical place? A type of population, such as trappers, herders, and pioneers? Or a process wherein European traits were stripped off and American ones formed?) Other critics disputed the notion of the frontier as a "safety valve" for the East. Few European immigrants actually settled on the frontier; if anything, population statistics showed more farmers moving to the cities.

For our own purposes, however, it would be misleading to focus on these battles. Whether or not Turner was right, his theory dramatically influenced the investigations of other historians. To understand how, we need to take Turner's general propositions and look at the way he and others applied them to a specific topic.

An ideal subject for this task is the man whose name Turner himself shared—Andrew Jackson.[1] Jackson is one of those figures in history who, like Captain John Smith, seems always to be strutting about the stage just a bit larger than life. Furthermore, Jackson's wanderings took him straight into the most central themes of American history. Old Hickory, as his troops nicknamed him, led land-hungry pioneers into the southeastern United States, displacing Native Americans from lands east of the Mississippi, expelling the Spanish from Florida, and repelling the British from New Orleans. As president, he launched the war against the "monster" Bank of the United States, placing himself at the center of the perennial American debate over the role of economic power in a democracy. Above all, he came to be seen as the political champion of the common people. Here is a man whose career makes it impossible to avoid the large questions that grand theory will suggest.

How, then, did Turner's frontier hypothesis shape historians' perception of Jackson? What features of his career did it encourage them to examine?

JACKSON: A FRONTIER DEMOCRAT (TARNISHED)

For Frederick Turner, Andrew Jackson was not merely "one of the favorites of the West," he was "the West itself." By that rhetorical proclamation Turner meant that Jackson's whole life followed precisely the pattern of frontier evolution wherein eastern culture was stripped bare and replaced by the "contentious, nationalistic democracy of the interior."

1. The sharing of names is more than coincidence. Frederick Jackson Turner's father, Andrew Jackson Turner, was born in 1832 and named in honor of President Jackson, reelected that year.

Jackson's Scotch-Irish parents had joined the stream of eighteenth-century immigrants who landed in Pennsylvania, pushed westward until they bumped up against the Appalachians, and then filtered southwest into the Carolina backcountry. This was the process of "mixing and amalgamation" that Turner outlined in his essay. Turner had also shown how the frontier stripped away higher social organizations, leaving only the family as a sustaining bond. Andrew Jackson was denied even that society. His father died before Jackson's birth; his only two brothers and his mother died during the Revolution. At the age of seventeen, Andrew left Waxhaw, his boyhood home, never to return again. In effect, he was a man without a family—but not, as Turner saw it, a man without a backcountry.

Jackson first moved to the town of Salisbury, North Carolina, reading law by day and, with the help of high-spirited young friends, raising hell by night. Brawling in barrooms, sporting with young ladies, moving outhouses in the hours well past midnight—such activities gave Jackson a reputation as "the most roaring, game-cocking, horse-racing, card-playing, mischievous fellow that ever lived in Salisbury," according to one resident.

In 1788 the footloose Jackson grabbed the opportunity to become public prosecutor for the western district of North Carolina, a region that then stretched all the way to the Mississippi. There, in the frontier lands that now constitute Tennessee, Jackson hoped to make his reputation. Once settled in Nashville, he handled between a quarter and a half of all court cases in his home county during the first few years of his arrival. And he dispensed justice with the kind of "coarseness and strength" Turner associated with the frontier personality. When one enraged defendant stepped on prosecutor Jackson's toe to indicate his displeasure, Jackson calmly coldcocked the offender with a stick of wood. On another occasion, after Jackson had been appointed superior court judge in the newly created state of Tennessee, he stalked off the bench to summon a defendant before the court when no one else dared, including the sheriff and posse. The man in question, one Russell Bean, had threatened to shoot the "first skunk that came within ten feet," but when Jackson came roaring out of the courthouse, Bean pulled in his horns. "I looked him in the eye, and I saw shoot," said Bean, "and there wasn't shoot in nary other eye in the crowd; and so I says to myself, says I, hoss, it's about time to sing small, and so I did."

All in all, Jackson seemed a perfect fit for frontier democrat. Turner described in characteristic terms Jackson's election to the House of Representatives in 1796:

> The appearance of this frontiersman on the floor of Congress was an omen full of significance. He reached Philadelphia at the close of Washington's administration, having ridden on horseback nearly eight hundred miles to his destination. Gallatin (himself a western Pennsylvanian) afterwards graphically described Jackson, as he entered the halls of Congress, as "a tall, lank, uncouth-looking personage, with long locks of hair hanging over his face, and a cue down his back tied in an eelskin; his dress singular, his manners and deportment those of a rough backwoods-

Jackson the frontiersman: Russell Bean surrenders to Justice Jackson, as depicted in an 1817 biography. Wrote Turner, "If Henry Clay was one of the favorites of the West, Andrew Jackson was the West itself . . . the very personification of the contentious, nationalistic democracy of the interior."

man." Jefferson afterwards testified to Webster: "His passions are terrible. When I was President of the Senate, he was a Senator, and he could never speak, on account of the rashness of his feelings. I have seen him attempt it repeatedly, and as often choke with rage." At length the frontier, in the person of its leader, had found a place in the government. This six-foot backwoodsman, angular, lantern-jawed, and thin, with blue eyes that blazed on occasion; this choleric, impetuous, Scotch-Irish leader of men; this expert duellist and ready fighter; this embodiment of the contentious, vehement, personal west, was in politics to stay.

This was Turner at his rhetorical best, marshaling all the striking personal details that supported his theory. But he was not writing a full-length biography and so confined his discussion of Jackson mostly to a few paragraphs of detail.

One of Turner's graduate students went further. Thomas Perkins Abernethy studied at Harvard during the period when the university had lured Turner east from his home ground at the University of Wisconsin. Abernethy believed that to test the frontier thesis, it ought to be examined on a local level, in more detail. In this respect, he felt, previous historians had not been scientific enough. "Science is studied by the examination of specimens, and general truths are discovered through the investigations of typical forms," he asserted. In contrast, "history has been studied mainly by national units, and the field is too broad to allow of minute examination." But Tennessee provided a perfect "specimen" of the western state. It broke away from its parent, North Carolina, during its frontier days; it was the first area of the nation to undergo territorial status; and from its backwoods settlements came Andrew Jackson himself. Why not trace the leavening effects of the frontier within this narrower compass? Abernethy set out to do just that in his book *From Frontier to Plantation in Tennessee.*

He had learned the techniques of his mentor well. Turner encouraged students to trace the effects of geography and environment on politics. Abernethy perceived that Tennessee's geography divided it into three distinct agricultural regions, providing a "rare opportunity to study the political effects of these several types of agricultural economy." Turner emphasized the role of free land as a crucial factor in the West. Abernethy agreed that land was "the chief form of wealth in the United States in its early years" and carefully studied the political controversies over Tennessee's vast tracts of land. Always he determined to look beyond the surface of the political arena to the underlying economic and geographic considerations.

These techniques were Turner's, but the results produced anything but Turner's conclusions. *From Frontier to Plantation* is dedicated to Frederick Jackson Turner, but the book directly refutes Turner's optimistic version of western history.

As Abernethy began unraveling the tangled web of Carolina-Tennessee politics, he discovered that Americans interested in western land included more than pioneer squatters and yeoman farmers of the "interior democracy." Prosperous speculators who preferred the comforts of the civilized East saw equally well that forested, uncultivated land would skyrocket *in* value once settlers poured over the Appalachians in search of homesteads.

The scramble for land revealed itself in the strange and contradictory doings of the North Carolina legislature. During the Revolution, inflation had plagued the state, largely because the legislature had continuously issued its own paper money when short of funds. The value of this paper money plummeted to a fraction of its original face value. After the war, the legislature retrenched by proclaiming that all debtors would have to repay their debts *in specie* (that is, in gold or silver coins) or its equivalent in paper money. If, for example, the going rate set $1 in silver or gold as equal to $400 in paper notes, and a person owed $10, debtors who repaid using paper money would owe $4,000. In effect, the legislature was repudiating its paper currency and saying that only gold or silver would be an acceptable medium of exchange.

This move made sense if the legislature was trying to put the state's finances on a stable footing. But Abernethy noticed that in the same session, the legislature turned around and issued a new run of paper money—printing up $100,000. Why issue more paper money when you've just done your best to get rid of the older stuff?

Abernethy also noticed that during the same legislative session, land offices were opened up to sell western lands—but only under certain conditions. The claimant had to go out into the woods and mark some preliminary boundaries, then come back and enter the claim at a designated land office. Finally, a government surveyor would survey the lot, submit a report to the secretary of state for the governor's authentication, and enter it in the county register.

The situation hardly confirmed Turner's democratic conception of the frontier, Abernethy concluded. First, who ended up being able to buy the new land? Not the squatter or yeoman farmer, certainly—few of them could fulfill the requirements of marking out land, returning East to register it, having it officially surveyed, and entering it. Instead, land speculators in the East, including state legislators, stepped in to make a killing. The career of William Blount, one of the most successful speculators, illustrated the process at work. As a state legislator, Blount helped write the new land laws. At the same time, he hired a woodsman to go west and mark out vast tracts. Blount, for his part, registered the claim and paid for the land.

Sometimes the money that paid for the land was the old paper currency, bought up for a fraction of its original price from poorer folk who had no means of claiming their own land. But the legislature also allowed purchasers to pay for the lands using the new paper money at face value. Was it coincidence only that Blount had been the legislator proposing the new issue of paper money? Abernethy thought not.

Instead of confirming Turner's version of a hardy democracy, then, Abernethy painted a picture of "free" Tennessee lands providing fortunes for already powerful men. Blount used "the entire Southwest [as] his hunting ground and he stuffed his pockets with the profits of his speculations in land. In the maw of his incredible ambition—or greed—there originated land grabs involving thousands of choice acres." And Blount was only one of many across the country. "In those days," Abernethy concluded, "America was run largely by speculators in real estate."

It was into this free-for-all country that Andrew Jackson marched in 1788, but Abernethy's new frame of reference placed his career in a different light. Compare Turner's description of Jackson's "pioneer" ride to Philadelphia with Abernethy's version of Jackson's horseback arrival in Tennessee. "Tradition has it," reported Abernethy, that Jackson

> arrived at Jonesboro . . . riding a fine horse and leading another mount, with saddlebags, gun, pistols, and fox-hounds. This was elaborate equipment for a struggling young lawyer, and within the year he increased it by the purchase of a slave girl. . . . Jackson still found time to engage in his favorite sport of horse-racing, and he fought a bloodless duel with Waightstill Avery, then the most famous lawyer in western North Carolina. All this makes it clear that the young man had set himself up in the world as a "gentleman." Frontiersmen normally fought with their fists rather than with pistols, and prided themselves more upon physical prowess, than upon manners. Though commonly looked upon as a typical Westerner, Jackson was ever an aristocrat at heart.

Jackson cemented his ties with the upper layers of society in more substantial ways. Turner had noted Jackson's practice as a "public prosecutor—an office

Jackson the gentleman: Thomas Abernethy argued that the history of Jackson's Tennessee demonstrated how "the wealthy rose to the top of affairs even on the frontier, and combined through their influence and common interests to control economic legislation. From time to time they found it necessary to make some obvious concession to democracy, such as broadening the suffrage or lowering the qualifications for office. But, while throwing out such sops with one hand, they managed to keep well in the other the more obscure field of economic legislation." The aristocratic portrait of Jackson is by Thomas Sully.

that called for nerve and decision, rather than legal acumen." What frontier lawyering also called for, which Turner neglected to mention, was a knack for collecting debts, since Jackson most often represented creditors intent on recovering loans. During his first month of legal practice, he issued some seventy writs to delinquent debtors. This energetic career soon came to the notice of William Blount, who had by this time gotten himself appointed governor of the newly created Tennessee territory. He and Jackson became close political allies.

Jackson too had an eye for speculating, and it almost ruined him. Like Blount, he had cashed in on Tennessee's lands, buying 50,000 acres on the site of the future city of Memphis. In 1795 Jackson took his first ride to Philadelphia, a year before the one Turner eloquently described, in order to sell the Memphis land at a profit. Few Philadelphians wanted to buy, but Jackson finally closed a deal with David Allison, another of Blount's cronies. Allison couldn't pay in cash, so he gave Jackson promissory notes. Jackson, in turn, used the notes to pay for goods to stock a trading post he wanted to open in Tennessee.

Scant months after Jackson returned home, he learned that David Allison had gone bankrupt. Even worse, since Jackson had signed Allison's promissory notes, Allison's creditors were now after Jackson. "We take this early opportunity to make known to you that we have little or no expectations of getting paid from him," they wrote, "and that we shall have to get our money from you." This financial nightmare left Jackson "placed in the Dam'st situation ever a man was placed in," he admitted. To get himself out, he was forced to speculate even more. Buy a parcel of land here, sell it there. Cash in the trading post, make a small profit, invest it in more land, exchange the new land for another buyer's promissory note. And so on. Not until 1824 did he settle the final claims in the tangle. Clearly, Abernethy believed that Jackson's horseback rides on behalf of real estate deserved more emphasis than any romantic notions of a galloping frontier democrat.

Despite such a devastating attack on the frontier thesis, Abernethy's admiration for Turner was genuine, no doubt because he recognized how much the thesis had guided his research. It is easy to conclude that the value of a theory rests solely on its truth. Yet even if Turner's hypothesis erred on many points, it provided a focus that prodded Abernethy to investigate important historical questions—the implications of western land policy, the effect of environment on character, the social and geographic foundations of democracy. All these topics had been slighted by historians.

Theory, in other words, is often as important for the questions it raises as for the answers it provides. In this sense it performs the same function in the natural sciences. Thomas Kuhn, a historian of science, has demonstrated how indispensable an older scientific theory is in pointing the way to the theory that replaces it. As the old theory is tested, attention naturally turns to problem areas—places where the results are not what the old theory predicts. The new theory emerges, Kuhn pointed out, "only for the man who, knowing with precision what he should expect, is able to recognize that something has gone wrong." Abernethy was able to discern that something had "gone wrong" in Tennessee politics, but only because Turner's hypothesis showed him what questions needed to be asked and where to look for answers.

JACKSON: LABORER'S FRIEND

Theory, then, can actually sharpen a historian's vision by limiting it—aiding the process of selection by zeroing in on important issues and data. It stands to reason, however, that trade-offs are made in this game. If a theory focuses attention on certain questions, it necessarily also causes a historian to ignore other facts, trends, or themes. Theory can limit in a negative as well as a positive sense.

Abernethy's disagreement with Turner illustrates this problem. Although the two historians reached diametrically opposed conclusions about Jackson, they carried on the debate within the framework of Turner's thesis. Did Jackson embody the democratic, individualistic West? Yes, argued Turner. No, countered Abernethy. Yet both accepted the premise suggested by the thesis, that the influence of the West was crucial.

That conclusion might serve well enough for a study limited to Tennessee politics, but Jackson went on to achieve national fame by winning the Battle of New Orleans and was elected to the presidency in 1828. He triumphed in all the southern coastal states and in Pennsylvania, and he also received a majority of New York's electoral votes. In New York too he cemented an alliance with Martin Van Buren, the sophisticated eastern leader of the Albany Regency political faction.

Such facts call attention to something that Turner's frame of reference overlooked. As a national leader, Jackson made friends in the East as well as the West, in cities as well as in the country. Historian Arthur Schlesinger Jr., believing that Abernethy as well as Turner overemphasized the importance of Jackson's western roots, determined to examine the eastern sources of Jackson's democratic coalition. The result was *The Age of Jackson* (1945), a sweeping study that highlighted the influence of eastern urban laboring classes on Jacksonian democracy.

In part, Schlesinger's theoretical approach was influenced by his upbringing. He spent his childhood within the civilized environs of Cambridge, Massachusetts, where his father, Arthur Meier Schlesinger Sr., held a chair in history at Harvard. Unlike Frederick Jackson Turner, the senior Schlesinger emphasized the role of urban society and culture in American life. His article "The City in American History" sparked a generation of scholarship on peculiarly urban problems such as industrial labor and immigration. The article, Schlesinger later suggested generously, "did not seek to destroy the frontier theory but to substitute a balanced view: an appreciation of both country and city in the rise of American civilization." Nevertheless, Schlesinger Sr.'s interest clearly lay with the cities.

The younger Schlesinger admired his father and his work—so much so that at the age of fifteen he changed his name from Arthur Bancroft Schlesinger to Arthur Meier Schlesinger Jr. After schooling at the prestigious Phillips Exeter Academy, Arthur completed a brilliant undergraduate and graduate career at Harvard.[2] It was out of this intellectual training that Schlesinger wrote his book.

The Age of Jackson also reflected a set of attitudes and emphases popular in the 1930s that distanced Schlesinger from the Progressive outlook Turner

2. In fact, Schlesinger Sr. firmly believed in the virtues of public education. But he felt compelled to send Arthur Jr. to Exeter after discovering that his tenth-grade public school teacher taught that "the inhabitants of Albania were called Albinos because of their white hair and pink eyes."

had shared at the turn of the century. The thirties saw the country plunged into a depression so severe that it shook many Americans' faith in the traditional economic system. Theories of class struggle, of conflict between capital and labor, became popular in scholarly circles. As an avid supporter of Franklin Roosevelt, Schlesinger by no means accepted the doctrines of the communist left, but he did believe that class conflict played a greater role in American history than the sectional disputes that Turner had emphasized.

Given Schlesinger's background, his research focused on substantially different aspects of Jackson's career. It portrayed Old Hickory as a natural leader who, though he came from the West, championed the cause of laborers in all walks of life—city "mechanicks" as well as yeoman farmers. Jackson's chief political task, argued Schlesinger, was "to control the power of the capitalist groups, mainly Eastern, for the benefit of the noncapitalist groups, farmers and laboring men, East, West, and South." Schlesinger made his opposition to Turner abundantly clear:

> The basic Jacksonian ideas came naturally enough from the East, which best understood the nature of business power and reacted most sharply against it. The legend that Jacksonian democracy was the explosion of the frontier, lifting into the government some violent men filled with rustic prejudices against big business does not explain the facts, which were somewhat more complex. Jacksonian democracy was rather a second American phase of that enduring struggle between the business community and the rest of society which is the guarantee of freedom in a liberal capitalist state.

Consequently, much of *The Age of Jackson* is devoted to people the Turner school neglected entirely: the leaders of workingmen's parties, the broader labor movement, and the efforts of Democratic politicians to bring laborers within the orbit of Jackson's party. Abernethy's treatment of Jackson as land speculator is replaced by attention to Jackson's vigorous war on the Second Bank of the United States, where Democratic leaders are shown forging an alliance with labor. "During the Bank War," Schlesinger concluded, "laboring men began slowly to turn to Jackson as their leader, and his party as their party."

Like Turner, Schlesinger came under critical fire. Other historians have argued that much of Jackson's so-called labor support was actually middle- or even upper-class leaders who hoped to channel worker sentiments for their own purposes. At the same time, many in the real laboring classes refused to support Jackson. But again—what is important for our present purposes is to notice how Schlesinger's general concerns shaped his research. It is not coincidental that Jackson's celebrated kitchen cabinet, in Schlesinger's retelling, bears a marked resemblance to the "brain trusters" of Franklin Roosevelt's cabinet. It is not coincidental that Jackson attacks the "monster Bank" for wreaking economic havoc much the way that FDR inveighed against the "economic royalists" of the Depression era. Nor is it coincidental that *The Age of Jackson* was followed, in 1957, by *The Age of Roosevelt*. Schlesinger may have displayed his political and economic philosophy more conspicuously than most historians, but no scholar can escape bringing some

Jackson, champion of the working people: "The legend that Jacksonian democracy was the explosion of the frontier, lifting into the government some violent men filled with rustic prejudices against big business does not explain the facts," wrote Arthur Schlesinger Jr. Here, the general public (dubbed "King Mob" by Jackson's genteel opponents) goes to work on a giant cheese at a White House celebration in 1837. The odor of the cheese lingered for months.

theoretical framework to his or her research. One way or another, theory inevitably limits and focuses the historian's perspective.

JACKSON AND THE NEW WESTERN HISTORY

Perhaps precisely because Schlesinger does wear his political heart on his sleeve, we are forced to consider a notion that is potentially more troubling. The term *theory* implies that a historian, like some scientist in a lab, arrives at his or her propositions in a rigorous, logical way, setting aside the controversies of the present in order to study the past on its own terms. But in Schlesinger's case—like it or not—the events of his day clearly influenced his approach to Andrew Jackson. For that matter, Turner's original frontier thesis was a product of his times. It was the census of 1890, after all, that caught Turner's attention, with its declaration that the frontier was essentially closed. It was Turner's rural, midwestern upbringing that encouraged him to dissent from eastern-trained historians in his search for an explanation of democracy in America. Indeed, Turner would have been the first to recognize the pull of contemporary affairs. "Each age writes the history of the past anew with reference to the conditions uppermost in its own time," he commented in 1891.

The notion that historians' theories are tainted by a kind of presentism troubles many, including some historians. "The present-minded contend that in writing history no historian can free himself of his total experience," complained one scholar, who was clearly unhappy with the notion that others might think he could not help being swayed by contemporary "passions, prejudices, assumptions, prepossessions, events, crises and tensions." Surely he was right in believing that those who reconstruct the past should not do violence to it by making it over in the image of the present. Yet for better or for worse—perhaps we should say, for better *and* for worse—historical theories are shaped by the present in which they arise. There is no escaping current events—only, through careful self-discipline, the opportunity of using the perspectives of the present to broaden our understanding rather than lessen it. A case study of present-mindedness at work can be found among those historians who more recently have reexamined the field Turner championed. Their movement has come to be known as the "new western history."

The generation of historians spearheading the new western history came of age, by and large, during the social upheavals of the 1960s and 1970s, an era during which African Americans led a revolution for civil rights and equal treatment under the law. Other minorities too sought a greater voice in American society, whether they were Indians seeking tribal lands and tribal rights or Chicano migrant laborers organizing for fair working conditions. During these same years feminists rallied to obtain equal treatment, and an environmental movement questioned the prevailing boom mentality in American life that equated all economic growth with progress. All these forces for change challenged traditional ways of thinking, and regardless of whether historians themselves became social activists, many were moved to reevaluate their perspectives on history. For historians of the West, the experiences of these decades were eye-opening in a host of different ways.

Return for a moment to Turner's central proposition: "The existence of an area of free land, its continuous recession, and the advance of American settlement westward, explain American development." For historian Patricia Limerick, that seemingly innocuous phrase "free land" served as a big, flapping red flag. The ferment of the sixties and seventies made it much more evident that calling such land "free" loaded the dice. In framing a working hypothesis, historians glided over the inconvenient fact that the lands "were not vacant, but occupied," as Limerick pointed out, by Indians who used them either for hunting or for the cultivation of their own crops. "Redistributing those lands to the benefit of white farmers required the removal of Indian territorial claims and of the Indians themselves—a process that was never simple." The title of Limerick's book, *The Legacy of Conquest* (1987), framed the issue in blunt terms. Conquest was what made land "free," for the land had been taken either without permission or with only the most token of payments dispensed under dubious circumstances.

Consider another phrase plucked out of Turner's sentence: "the advance of American settlement westward." Turner tended to view the frontier as essentially one-dimensional. Americans—by which he meant Americans primarily of English heritage—moved westward across the "wilderness," evolving a new democratic society as they went. But the notion of wilderness was a theoretical construct that implicitly denied the existence of any significant borderland cultures other than Anglo-American. The new voices of the sixties and seventies—Indian, Latino, and African American—pushed historians to recognize that the frontiers of North America were both multicultural and multidirectional. Spanish settlers spread northward from Central America and the Caribbean into Florida, Texas, New Mexico, and California. Chinese and Japanese immigrants of the mid-nineteenth century moved from west to east as they crossed the Pacific to California. And for the various Indian tribes themselves, frontier lines were shifting in all directions during the unsettled centuries following European contact.

Turner showed little interest in the cultural mixing that went on in these regions, a defect the new western history sought to correct. "The invaded and subject peoples of the West must be given a voice in the region's history," argued Donald Worster in 1989. "Until very recently many western historians acted as though the West had either been empty of people prior to the coming of the white race or was quickly, if bloodily, cleared of them, once and for all, so that historians had only to deal with the white point of view." But Worster suggested that the "younger generation appearing in the 1970s and '80s" made the "new multicultural perspective their own." They replaced Turner's unidirectional frontier with a portrait of a West that "has been on the forward edge of one of modern history's most exciting endeavors, the creation, in the wake of European expansion and imperialism, of the world's first multi-racial, cosmopolitan societies." Newcomers to western cities often found as many or more foreign languages spoken there than in New York, Paris, or Moscow.

Historians' attitudes toward Andrew Jackson could hardly be expected to remain untouched by these currents of change. Even before the new western history came into vogue, historians had begun reevaluating Jackson's career. For historian Michael Rogin, who wrote about Jackson during the tumultuous seventies, Old Hickory was the "embodiment" of the West for reasons entirely different from Turner's. Jackson embodied the West simply because he was instrumental in driving the Indians from their lands. "Historians have failed to place Indians at the center of Jackson's life," Rogin argued. "They have interpreted the Age of Jackson from every perspective but Indian destruction, the one from which it actually developed historically."

Robert Remini made a similar case in his biography of Jackson, the first volume of which appeared in 1977. Time after time, Jackson led efforts to force Indians to sign treaties ceding millions of acres. While he served as major general of the Tennessee militia and later as major general in the U.S. army, Jackson consistently exceeded his instructions on such matters. At the conclusion of his war against the Creek Indians, the remnants of the Creek Red Stick faction (whom Jackson had been fighting) retreated to Florida in hopes of continuing their war. Since the general could not compel his enemies to cede land, he turned around and demanded 23 million acres from his Indian *allies*, signing the treaty instead with them! Fearing that the government might revoke such a brazen action, he called for the new boundary lines to be run and land sold to settlers as quickly as possible. "The sooner this country is brought in the market the better," he advised President-Elect James Monroe, on yet another occasion. Over the years, Jackson's negotiations led to the acquisition by the United States of Indian lands amounting to one-third of Tennessee, three-quarters of Alabama and Florida, one-fifth of Georgia and Mississippi, and one-tenth of Kentucky and North Carolina.

Of course, Jackson's involvement in land acquisition did not end with his military career. As president, he championed the movement to force the remaining 125,000 Indians east of the Mississippi onto much less valuable lands west of the river, freeing up additional millions of prime acres in the midst of the booming cotton kingdom. At the president's urging, Congress set the policy of Indian removal into motion in 1830. "In terms of acquisition," commented Remini, "it is not too farfetched to say that the physical shape of the United States today looks pretty much like it does largely because of the intentions and efforts of Andrew Jackson."

Perhaps ironically, none of the new western historians has yet stepped forward to recast Jackson in light of recent scholarship. In part, the lack of attention arises because many younger scholars have preferred to focus on the trans-Mississippi West, well beyond the territory Andrew Jackson roamed. Yet there is more at work here than a different geographic focus. In many ways, the questions posed by the new western historians cannot be answered by making Jackson the center of attention. Focusing on the actions of the Anglo conquerors like Jackson tells us little about the intermixture of cultures that arose *before* removal began, during an era when both whites and Indians held significant power along the frontier.

One of the new western historians, Richard White, has examined the frontier of the seventeenth and eighteenth century along the Great Lakes in a book suggestively titled *The Middle Ground.* White argued that older discussions of the frontier portrayed the contrasting cultures as essentially and always in opposition. In contrast, White preferred to highlight a process of accommodation at work. By adopting the metaphor of a "middle ground," he highlighted a situation in which "whites could neither dictate to Indians nor ignore them. Whites needed Indians as allies, as partners in exchange, as sexual partners, as friendly neighbors." Only with the passing of this frontier did the middle ground break down, accompanied by a hardening of attitudes among whites, a "re-creation of the Indians as alien, as exotic, as other."

From this perspective, Jackson and his policies of Indian removal seem only the depressing endgame of what is the more interesting and neglected

This Chickasaw Indian girl's elegant hair and fashionable dress suggest the complexity of cultural relations in the middle ground of the Old Southwestern frontier in Andrew Jackson's time. The girl was among the thousands of Indians removed to territory west of the Mississippi.

territory of the middle ground. Indeed, the Old Southwest from about 1780 to 1820—the middle ground Jackson traveled—was a region rich in cultural accommodation. For two hundred years the land had witnessed a remarkable intermingling of Indian, French, Spanish, and English cultures. From its base in Florida, Spain actively courted trade with Indians, many of whom had intermarried with whites. The trader Alexander McGillivray, for example, was not the white European his name conjures up, but an influential Indian leader of the Creeks who concluded a treaty of alliance between his people and the Spanish in 1784. His parentage reflected the mixed heritage of the middle ground: a mother of French-Creek descent and a father who was a Scots trader.

Adding to the regional mixture of the Old Southwest were African Americans. White traders who intermarried with Indians were the first among the

Cherokees, Creeks, and other tribes to clear cotton plantations and use slaves to work them. Often these slaves were runaways whose skills the Indians drew upon in their attempt to emulate white plantation owners. African Americans knew how to spin and weave, shoe horses, and repair guns. Often they served as translators. Ironically, as a minority of Cherokees adopted a frame of government similar to the U.S. Constitution, they also set up slave codes similar to those in the white antebellum South.

Seminole Indians also held slaves, although they gave more autonomy to these "black Seminoles," as the slaves were known. When runaways fled Spanish or American plantations for Seminole lands, the Seminoles allowed the newcomers to live in separate villages, often far from their Indian owners. In return for being allowed to raise crops, black Seminoles paid a portion of the harvest to their masters—in effect, sharecropping. If, as Donald Worster suggested, the lure of the new western history involved tracing a process of multiracial, multicultural mixing along the frontier, topics such as the middle ground held a greater attraction than did rehashing the traditional stories of Andrew Jackson as Indian fighter.

After such a procession of grand historical theories, what may be said of the "real" Andrew Jackson? Skeptics may be tempted to conclude that there was not one but four Old Hickories roaming the landscape of Jacksonian America: Jackson the frontier democrat; Jackson the aristocratic planter and speculator; Jackson, friend of labor; and Jackson, taker of Indian lands. The use of historical theory seems to have led the reader into a kind of boggy historical relativism where there is no real Jackson, only men conjured up to fit the formulas of particular historical theories or the fashionable currents of the day.

But that viewpoint is overly pessimistic. It arises from the necessary emphasis of this chapter, where our concern has been to point out the general effects of grand theory rather than to evaluate the merits of each case. Theory, we have stressed, provides a vantage point that directs a researcher's attention to significant areas of inquiry. But the initial theorizing is only the beginning. Theories can be and are continually tested. Sometimes old theories are thrown out, replaced by new ones. In such fashion did Copernicus replace Ptolemy. On the other hand, some theories stand up to testing or are merely refined to fit the facts more closely. In yet other instances, old theories are incorporated into more encompassing frameworks. Newtonian mechanics are still as valid as ever for the everyday world, but they have been found to be only a special case of the broader theories of relativity proposed by Einstein.

Historical theory will probably never attain the precision of its counterparts among the natural sciences. In part, such precision remains beyond our reach because historical narrative seeks to account for specific, unique chains of events—events that can never be replicated in the way scientists replicate experiments in the lab. The complexity of the task will no doubt ensure that our explanations will remain subject, for better *and* for worse, to contemporary concerns. Of all people, historians should be the first to acknowledge that they are shaped by the currents of their own times.

But that does not mean historians must give up on the possibility of describing and explaining an objective reality. In the present example, we may argue that far from having four different Jacksons roaming the historical landscape, we are seeing various aspects of Jackson's personality and career that need to be incorporated into a more comprehensive framework. It is the old tale of the blind men describing the different parts of an elephant: the elephant is real enough, but the descriptions are partial and fragmentary. Frederick Jackson Turner was writing about a nebulous Jacksonian style. Indeed, one may as well come out with it—"democracy" and "individualism" were, for Turner, little more than styles. Abernethy, on the other hand, was looking at the concrete material interests and class alliances that Jackson developed during his Tennessee career and paid almost no attention to the presidential years. Schlesinger did precisely the opposite: he picked up Jackson's story only after 1824 and in the end was more concerned with the Jacksonian movement than with its nominal leader. The historians who came of age in the 1960s and 1970s have replaced Turner's imaginary frontier line with a contested cultural space whose middle grounds are populated with a Jacksonian "common people" more multiracial and diverse than Turner was ever able to conceive.

A unified field theory for Jacksonian America? Perhaps the outlines are there, but the task of deciding must be left to some future Turner of the discipline. What remains clear is that though particular theories continue to be revised or rejected, theory itself will accompany historians always. Without it, researchers cannot begin to select from among an infinite number of facts; they cannot separate the important from the incidental; they cannot focus on a manageable problem. Albert Einstein put the proposition succinctly. "It is the theory," he concluded, "which decides what we can observe."

Additional Reading

Grand theory begets grand bibliography. Edward Pessen's *Jacksonian America*, rev. ed. (Homewood, IL, 1978), which lists only the "more important" books and articles on Jacksonian America, contains more than 700 entries. Robert V. Remini and Robert O. Rupp devote an entire book to the writings about Jackson in *Andrew Jackson: A Bibliography* (Westport, CT, 1991).

Old Hickory himself may be approached through a number of traditional biographies. Earliest is John Reid and John Henry Eaton, *The Life of Andrew Jackson* (Philadelphia, 1817; reissued 1974). The volume has much authentic material for Jackson's early years, but beware later "campaign" editions of 1824 and 1828, to which chunks of political puffery were added. James Parton, *The Life of Andrew Jackson*, 3 vols. (Boston, 1866) includes the recollections of Jackson's boyhood neighbors, whom Parton interviewed years later. Robert Remini's eminently readable *The Life of Andrew Jackson* (New York, 1988) is a condensation of his three-volume study *Andrew Jackson and the Course of American Empire, 1767–1821; Andrew Jackson and the Course of American Democracy, 1822–1832;* and *Andrew Jackson and the Course of American Freedom, 1833–1845* (New York, 1977–1984). Although Remini provides valuable and unsparing detail on Jackson's aggressive treaty signing, the author's approach nonetheless reflects the perspectives of an older generation whose admiration for Jackson remains uppermost. For a balanced recent portrait of Jackson's place in in the political landscape, see Harry L. Watson, *Liberty and Power* (New York, 1990).

To understand the role of theory in both science and history, readers will profit from Thomas Kuhn, *The Structure of Scientific Revolutions* (Chicago, 1962). The revised edition (1970) contains a few remarks by Kuhn on the applicability of his theory to social science disciplines. For a recent critique of Kuhn's work as it relates to the natural sciences, see Steven Weinberg, "The Revolution That Didn't Happen," *New York Review of Books* 45, 15 (8 October 1998): 48–52.

Frederick Jackson Turner's key essays are reprinted in *The Frontier in American History* (New York, 1920). He also wrote *The Rise of the New West* (New York, 1906). The best accounts of Turner's life and work are by Ray Billington, the last major Turnerian, who set to print more words on Turner than Turner himself ever sent to press on American history. *Frederick Jackson Turner: Historian, Scholar, Teacher* (New York, 1973) is an entertaining biography, while *The Genesis of the Frontier Thesis* (San Marino, CA, 1971) describes just that. A contrasting view may be found in Richard Hofstadter, *The Progressive Historians: Turner, Beard, Parrington* (New York, 1968).

In addition to Thomas Abernethy's *From Frontier to Plantation in Tennessee* (Chapel Hill, NC, 1932), see his views in "Andrew Jackson and the Rise of Southwestern Democracy," *American Historical Review* 33 (October, 1927): 64–77, and his biography of Jackson in the *Dictionary of American Biography*. Arthur Schlesinger Jr.'s *Age of Jackson* (Boston, 1945) has generated much discussion among historians, discussion that is summarized well in Pessen's bibliographical essay. Information on Schlesinger's career may be gained from an essay on him in Marcus Cunliffe and Robin Winks, eds., *Pastmasters: Some Essays on American Historians* (New York, 1969). Although a great many scholars would probably agree with Michael Rogin on the importance of Indian removal to Jackson's career, the Marxian and Freudian approach that Rogin employs in *Fathers and Children: Andrew Jackson and the Subjugation of the American Indian* (New York, 1975) has been hotly challenged. Remini carries on a polite but firm running war with Rogin in the footnotes of his biography. From the radical end of the spectrum, Elizabeth Fox-Genovese offers a critique in *Reviews in American History* 3 (December 1975): 407–17.

The views of the new western history are expounded in Patricia Limerick, *The Legacy of Conquest: The Unbroken Past of the American West* (New York, 1987); Donald Worster, *Under Western Skies: Nature and History in the American West* (New York, 1992); and William Cronon, George Miles, and Jay Gitlin, eds., *Under an Open Sky: Rethinking America's Western Past* (New York, 1992). All discuss Turner as a jumping-off point for newer perspectives. Richard White's *The Middle Ground: Indians, Empires, and the Republics in the Great Lakes Region, 1650–1815* (New York, 1991) provides one of the best models of the new approaches.

Although no single work has done for the Old Southwest what White did for the Great Lakes region, many studies have been perceptive. For the Spanish influence, see the relevant chapters of David J. Weber, *The Spanish Frontier in North America* (New Haven, 1992). For a recent overview of Indian removal, see Anthony F. C. Wallace, *The Long, Bigger Trail: Andrew Jackson and the Indians* (New York, 1993). On Indians and African Americans, see Theda Perdue, *Slavery and the Evolution of Cherokee Society, 1540–1866* (Knoxville, TN, 1979) and Daniel F. Littlefield Jr., *Africans and Creeks: From the Colonial Period to the Civil War* (Westport, CT, 1979). Writing in the 1930s, Kenneth W. Porter provided much useful information about black Seminoles, later reprinted in *The Negro on the American Frontier* (New York, 1971). (Readers of this chapter should now be able to hypothesize why Porter's research, published originally in the *Journal of Negro History*, was not elaborated on by mainstream historians and was only reprinted in 1971.) More recently, Quintard Taylor, *In Search of the Racial Frontier: African Americans in the American West, 1528–1990* (New York, 1998) provides an excellent portrait of the roles played by African Americans in the emerging new western history.

Interactive Learning

The *Primary Source Investigator* provides materials that explore the role of the frontier in developing and shaping American character in the mid-nineteenth century. Images of Andrew Jackson at the various stages of his career—as a general, a justice, a president, and frontiersman—reveal the many faces of this powerful American. Other documents, including speeches by Cherokee Indian leaders, illuminate the darker side of Jackson's fierce nationalism and commitment to territorial expansion. Also included are documents by Fredrick Jackson Turner, who famously decried the closing of the American frontier.

CHAPTER 6
The Invisible Pioneers

Sometime in the early 1700s, somewhere along the rolling foothills of Montana, a man named Shaved Head lay in hiding, staring into the distance at a group of very big dogs.

To the west lay the peaks of the Rockies and the Continental Divide; to the east, the short-grass plains stretching for hundreds of miles. Shaved Head's usual haunts were some distance to the north, in what is now Saskatchewan. But together with a group of Blackfeet comrades, he had run and walked south for several days, leading a war party in search of the people who came from across the mountains to hunt buffalo—probably the Snake Indians. At last he had discovered one of their camps.

And in it stood a number of these strange big dogs.

The Blackfeet had dogs, of course. They used them to haul skin lodges, cooking pots, and utensils whenever they moved camp. But these dogs were different from any Shaved Head had ever seen. They were tall as a man and more the size of elk, except they seemed to have lost their horns. Still, they couldn't be elk, for they were obviously slaves to the Snake people, just as dogs were slaves to the Blackfeet.

Shaved Head managed to steal a few of the animals. But when his warriors tried to mount them, the creatures began walking and the men quickly jumped off. Cautiously, they led the animals home, where everyone in the band gathered around and marveled. At first, people tried putting robes on the animals' backs, but that made them jump. After a time a woman said, "Let's put a travois on one of them, just like we do on our small dogs." So they made a travois and attached it to one of the gentler animals. He didn't kick or jump. Then the people led him around with the travois attached. Finally a woman mounted the animal and rode it. In years after, they called these creatures *ponokamita*, or "elk dogs."

The elk dogs, so strange to the Blackfeet, were actually horses. Such creatures had been extinct in North America for ten thousand years, until the Spanish reintroduced them in the sixteenth century. From Spanish outposts

124

"Let's put a travois on one of them, just like we do on our small dogs." This Blackfoot oral tradition related how horses were first tamed in the early 1700s. The use of horses to draw travois, as in this photograph, meant important changes in the life of a nomadic tribe, especially for women. Larger pack animals meant larger loads; hence larger, more spacious teepees could be made and carried.

horses gradually spread north and east, finally reaching the Blackfeet early in the eighteenth century. Shaved Head's account of their arrival is noteworthy because it rests on a remarkable oral tradition. Anthropologist John Ewers heard the story in the 1940s from an eighty-year-old Blackfoot named Weasel Tail, who, in turn, had heard it growing up as a boy, in the 1860s and 1870s, from an elderly member of the tribe named Two Strikes Woman. She was passing along accounts that her great-grandfather had given her father. Thus the tradition passed through at least four generations. To be sure, such oral evidence lacks the authority of written or eyewitness accounts, especially since the events in question took place more than two hundred years earlier. (In Chapter 8, we examine in more detail the problems of oral evidence.) Still, other available records suggest that however the details fell out, the Blackfeet first gained the use of horses sometime in the early 1700s, well before the region was ever visited by whites.

Weasel Tail's story is useful for another reason. It suggests some of the complexity involved in portraying "the middle ground"—historian Richard White's metaphor for the borderlands in which various cultures met, mixed, and accommodated one with another. As we saw in Chapter 5, the new western historians have insisted that the interactions between peoples and cultures in North America amounted to more than just a process of "westward advance" into "wild forests, trackless plains, [and] untrodden valleys," to quote one Overland Trail guidebook of the 1840s. Weasel Tail's story reminds us that just as Europeans were discovering and adapting to conditions in their "New World," Native Americans were discovering and adapting to the cultures that came to them from across the oceans. And the crucial adaptations cannot be described in terms of human contact alone. Horses from European culture interacted with Blackfoot society years before whites themselves appeared. There was not only a human frontier line but also a "horse frontier," as well as myriad other plant and animal frontiers—not the least of them a critical frontier of microorganisms.

We may rephrase this insight in more basic terms: human history is not merely the history of humans. Although historians have traditionally focused on the creations of humankind—social and political institutions, wars, economic and cultural systems—all human societies are inevitably constructed within a larger natural setting: physical, geographical, biological. Historians need to be aware of the interactions of human actors and their larger environment.

The boundaries that must be drawn, then, are not simply between differing cultures but between differing ecological systems. And although such lines may at first seem unimportant, they exerted a profound impact on the settlement of North America. Europeans and Indians had developed different ways of exploiting the plants and animals of their environments. When these competing methods intermingled along the middle grounds of frontier borderlands, they were all too often disastrously incompatible. A full understanding of the expansion of the United States to the Pacific must take account of these ecological conflicts. In many ways, European flora and fauna were invisible pioneers along shifting frontiers.

To watch these larger movements in action, our approach in this chapter must be nearly the opposite of the microcosmic focus used to examine the witchcraft outbreak at Salem. Instead of looking at a small patch of ground in detail, we must pull on the proverbial seven-league boots and seek out trends at work over centuries and across an entire continent. The center of the story will remain the expansion of the United States during the nineteenth century. But it is important to look first at North America when the Atlantic Ocean remained the boundary between European and American cultures. What were some of the features of this precontact era? How did the new frontier affect not only European cultures and ecologies but also those of Native Americans?

SHAPERS OF THE ENVIRONMENT

If modern Americans were somehow able to return to the North America of 1450 and trek across it, they would most likely be struck by the sheer abundance of wildlife. Certainly, the first European colonists remarked on the profusion of birds, beasts, and fish.

Francis Higginson, an early settler of Massachusetts Bay, knew that his friends in England would be skeptical of the reports he was sending. "The aboundance of Sea-Fish are almost beyond beleeving," he noted, "and sure I should scarce have beleeved it except I had seene it with mine owne eyes." In Virginia, settlers fording streams on horseback sometimes found that the hooves of their mounts killed fish, the rivers were so thick with them. Governor Thomas Dale, in one setting of his seine, hauled in 5,000 sturgeon.

And size! Some of the sturgeon in Governor Dale's nets were 12 feet long, while Virginia crabs ran to a foot in length. A Dutch visitor to Brooklyn reported being treated to a pail of "Gowanes oysters which are the best in the country . . . large and full, some of them not less than a foot long." As for the lobsters coming out of New York Bay, another traveler reported that "those a foot long are better for serving at table." He meant in comparison to the 5- and 6-footers that were being taken. Such granddaddy lobsters continued to be trapped from time to time through much of the eighteenth century.

As with fish, so with wildfowl. Governor Berkeley of Virginia spoke of massive flocks of ducks, geese, brant, and teal, whose beating wings sounded "like a great storm coming over the water." And the number of passenger pigeons—a bird that had been hunted into extinction by 1914—astounded everyone, including naturalist John James Audubon. In 1813, along the banks of the Ohio River, Audubon watched flocks pass that darkened the sun with their numbers. In "almost solid masses, they darted forward in undulating and angular lines, descended and swept close over the earth with inconceivable velocity, mounted perpendicularly so as to resemble a vast column, and, when high, were seen wheeling and twisting within their continued lines, which then resembled the coils of a gigantic serpent." At night when they arrived at their roosting place, Audubon was waiting, along with hunters who had come with poles to knock them down.

> As the birds . . . passed over me, I felt a current of air that surprised me. . . . The fires were lighted [by the hunters], and a magnificent as well as wonderful and almost terrifying sight presented itself. The pigeons, arriving by thousands, alighted everywhere, one above another, until solid masses, as large as hogsheads, were formed on the branches all round . . . it was a scene of uproar and confusion. I found it quite useless to speak or even to shout to those persons who were nearest to me.

Similar tales were told of mammals. Red and fallow deer congregated along the Virginia coasts in the hundreds. Gray and black squirrels ate so much of the colonists' grain that colonials in Pennsylvania killed more than 600,000 squirrels in one year alone. When settlers crossed the Great Plains in the 1840s and 1850s, they sometimes encountered entire "cities" of prairie dogs. In 1905 a scientist from the U.S. Biological Survey reported finding the remnants of a Texas prairie dog colony whose underground passages stretched for nearly 25,000 square miles, an area the size of West Virginia. The colony's estimated population had been 400 million.

Above ground, bison roamed the prairies in herds estimated to number 50 million, and not only on the prairies and plains. Herds had moved east as far as Pennsylvania, Kentucky, and a few even into Virginia along the Potomac River. Pronghorn antelope may have even outnumbered buffalo. Beaver swelled the streams of eastern forests as well as those of the Rockies, and grizzly bears "were everywhere," reported one mountain man, ". . . and it is not unusual to see fifty or sixty within the twenty-four hours." Another trapper, James Ohio Pattie, claimed to have sighted 220 in one day.

It is possible, then, to assemble a picture of the North American continent as a sort of natural Eden teeming with life. Yet although this picture is accurate in many details, it presents problems. The accounts from which it is drawn were written by a wide variety of people. Some, like Audubon, possessed well-deserved reputations for accuracy; a few, like the scientists from the U.S. Biological Survey, were even conducting systematic research. On the other hand, how seriously are we to take James Ohio Pattie's report of seeing 220 grizzlies in one day? (In ten hours of wandering, 220 grizzlies would mean sighting an average of twenty-two bears every hour, or about one every three minutes.) Was 220 based on an actual count, or was it merely his rough translation for "a hell of a lot more bears than I saw most days"? Even if we believe Pattie, we cannot assume that such densities applied equally throughout the Rockies or even in that particular region at all times. (Grizzlies, for example, are more likely to congregate during mating season than other times of the year.) Individual observations, in other words, must be evaluated as critically in ecology as in history.

There is a second reason for proceeding cautiously. We must be critical not only of data provided by observers but also of ecological theory itself. Ecologists, like historians, need coherent hypotheses to organize their information; and as with historians, theory shapes the way facts are analyzed. In describing the ecological systems of precontact America, it is easy to assume not only that existing plants and animals were abundant but that they lived together in a kind of mutually adjusting, harmonious balance. Indeed, ecologists of the early twentieth century encouraged this notion. The influential Frederic Clements argued that although natural systems went through certain stages of growth, eventually they reached a "climax," or mature phase. At that point, the animals and plants within the system remained in dynamic balance. Under such conditions, stability was the norm.

More recently, ecologists have suggested that this model idealizes too much the notion of stability. Few ecosystems settle into a long-term equilibrium without experiencing disruptions. Such changes ought not to be seen as aberrations but as something to be expected. Even without human intervention, instability is normal. As a case in point, the abundant beaver of the Rockies were subject to cycles of disruption. When populations built up along streams, closer contact allowed disease to spread from one colony to another. At such times, epizootics (epidemics in animal populations) wiped out large numbers of beaver. A dry year, too, lowered stream levels, making the spread of disease easier.

Epizootics are only one example of dramatic change. The overabundance of a particular species often altered other parts of the ecosystem. As large herds of buffalo cropped the grasses of the plains too closely, the older vegetation was driven out by faster-growing, hardier weeds. When Lewis and Clark complained that their moccasins were constantly pierced by spikes of the prickly pear cactus along the upper Missouri, they were describing not vegetation that had grown there since time immemorial but relatively new growth that was taking advantage of the conditions of overgrazing.

It would be equally misleading to assume that Native Americans before 1492 harmonized so well with their world that they were a "natural" part of the system's ecology, unlike the white invaders of 1492. That idea is only a more sophisticated version of the pioneers' belief that the Indians were "children of nature" and the land still virgin wilderness. In truth, Native Americans were active in altering and controlling their environment.

To begin with, horticulture played a crucial role in many Native American cultures. In the Southwest, the Anasazi devised a sophisticated system of dikes and dams to flood their fields, while the Hohokam dug canals, some of them thirty miles long. The peoples east of the Mississippi, whom popular literature tends to portray primarily as hunters, in fact regularly raised "vast quantities of pease, beans, potatoes, cabbages, Indian corn, pumpions [pumpkins], melons" to supply the greater part of their food needs. Both men and women worked to clear fields, plow, sow, and weed. In the early years of the Virginia colony, it was Indian surplus corn that kept the English alive. Even in the plains region, horticulture was important to many tribes.

The most widespread way in which Native Americans altered their environment was through fire. All across the continent, Indians regularly burned large tracts of land. Cabeza de Vaca, the Spanish explorer who crossed much of the Southeast during the 1530s, noted that the Ignaces Indians of Texas went about

> with a firebrand, setting fire to the plains and timber so as to drive off the mosquitoes, and also to get lizards and similar things which they eat, to come out of the soil. In the same manner they kill deer, encircling them with fires, and they do it also to deprive the animals of pasture, compelling them to go for food where the Indians want.

Plains Indians used fires for communication—to report a herd of buffalo or warn of danger—as well as to drive off enemies in war. In California, where grass seeds were an important food, Indians burned fields annually to remove old stocks and increase the yield.

Along the Atlantic Coast, Indians regularly set fires to keep down the scrub brush. As William Wood observed in New England, fire consumed "all the underwood and rubbish which otherwise would overgrow the country, making it unpassable, and spoil their much affected hunting." The resulting forest was almost parklike, with large, widely spaced trees, few shrubs, and plenty of succulent grasses. Historian William Cronon has pointed out that such tended forests not merely attracted game but helped create much larger populations of it. Indian burning promoted the increase of exactly those species whose abundance so impressed English colonists: elk, deer, beaver, hare, porcupine, turkey, quail, ruffed grouse, and so on. When these populations increased, so did the carnivorous eagles, hawks, lynxes, foxes, and wolves. In short, Indians who hunted game animals were not just taking the

Fires could spread quickly through parched prairie grass, and in such cases
Indians of the plains used fire defensively, as artist Alfred Jacob Miller recorded in
this 1837 watercolor. "All hands in the camp are immediately busy in setting fire to
the long grass about them;" Miller noted, "—not suffering it to make much
headway, but beating it down with cloths & blankets. In this manner large spaces
are cleared, horses, mules, and tents are secured in the burnt areas, which are
enlarged as time permits, and escape from certain death is thus averted. . . . The
fire sweeps round with the speed of a race horse, licking up every thing that it
touches with its fiery tongue,—leaving nothing in its train but a blackened heath."

"unplanted bounties of nature"; in an important sense, they were harvesting
a foodstuff that they had worked to create.

Such carefully nurtured abundance did not mean that Native Americans
lived free from want in a land of milk and honey. Scarcity was an equally crucial element of their ecology. For abundance was above all seasonal, a fact
many enthusiastic European explorers failed to take into account. "When I
remember the high commendations some have given of the place," wrote
one New Englander, "I have thought the reason thereof to be this, that they
wrote surely in strawberry time." Governor Thomas Dale's five thousand
sturgeon were caught in spring or summer, when the fish were running, not
during the sluggish days of February. Furthermore, animal populations fluctuated from year to year, and herds of antelope, bison, and caribou migrated
along unpredictable routes. To survive, Indians had to take advantage of different seasons of abundance at different locations as well as get through the
lean winter. Ecologists summarize these constraints in what is known as
Liebig's law: that biological populations are limited not by the total re-

sources available but by the minimum amount of food that can be found during the scarcest times of the year.

Often, scarcity led Indians to extract every conceivable benefit from available resources. The buffalo, for example, provided not only meat but also hides for teepees and clothing, sinew for thread and bowstrings, bones for tools, and horns for eating utensils. Even the dung was burned as fuel. On the other hand, a "feast or famine" attitude also developed, encouraging practices of questionable ecological value. Before the coming of horses, Plains Indians most often caught buffalo by stampeding them over cliffs or into rude corrals. Such stampedes could kill many more buffalo than were needed. "Today we passed . . . the remains of a vast many mangled carcases of Buffalow," wrote Lewis in 1804, "which had been driven over a precipice of 120 feet by the Indians & perished; the water appeared to have washed away a part of this immence pile of slaughter and still there remained the fragments of at least a hundred carcases, they created a most horrid stench."

From the Indian point of view, such practices were defensible. While a successful hunt might lead to waste, success itself was never certain. A herd might easily flee if it scented its pursuers; or only a few animals might be killed while the rest broke through the ranks of Indian herders. Yet for all that, Indians ought not to be portrayed merely as the spiritual forerunners of today's environmentalists. They had developed many ways of controlling and altering their surroundings—some remarkably ingenious in terms of husbanding resources, others relatively wasteful.

THE QUESTION OF NUMBERS

The frontier, then, was not merely a buffer zone between settled white regions and untouched wilderness. Indians actively shaped the land in which they lived. But a more vexing question remains: how many Native Americans were living in the land when Europeans first came into it? The image of an untamed wilderness encourages the notion that the Indians of North America were relatively few, scattered in small villages and separated by miles of dense forest or empty, rolling plains.

Unfortunately, the question of population in the precontact era is immensely difficult. Hundreds of separate cultures spread across North America with no census to enumerate them. How can historians even begin to calculate a precontact population?

One common method has been to collect, adjust, and average available estimates from early white explorers and settlers. By proceeding across the continent, region by region and tribe by tribe, numbers can be assembled to provide an approximate total. During the early years of the twentieth century, anthropologist James Mooney did precisely that. His estimates, published in 1928, proposed a precontact North American population of approximately 1.1 million. Because Mooney was a respected researcher (and no one before had attempted so systematic an enumeration), his estimate was frequently cited in textbooks and other surveys. A decade later anthropologist Alfred

Kroeber reduced the estimate to 1 million or less. (Mooney's figures were "probably mostly too high rather than too low," Kroeber asserted.)

But if we examine Mooney's original computations (his notes have been preserved at the Smithsonian Institution), a disquieting pattern emerges. Mooney died before he could actually publish his work. For unstated reasons, the editor who published his final figures often reduced these numbers by 5 or 10 percent. In addition, Mooney's notes show that his numbers were not necessarily what he believed to be the true precontact population, but merely a bedrock minimum on which even the most conservative scholars could agree. In many cases, his preliminary notes show even larger totals, which he cautiously reduced for the final tally.

For example, in 1674 Daniel Gookin, a missionary, tried to calculate the precontact population of New England. To do so, he asked Indian elders to estimate the number of adult males each tribe could have marshaled for a war in the years before whites arrived. When combined, the elders' estimates came to a total of 18,000. Assuming that for every able-bodied male there might be three or four additional women, children, and old men, Gookin estimated a total population anywhere from 72,000 to 90,000. His number was noted by a nineteenth-century historian, John Palfrey, but Palfrey lowered it to about 50,000, for reasons he never stated. Mooney took that figure and conservatively cut it to "about 25,000 or about one-half what the historian Palfrey makes it." Similar reductions were repeated elsewhere in Mooney's notes.

Of course, even a quick look at such calculations shows how difficult it is to arrive at reliable figures. For the Narraganset tribe, the minister Edward Johnson's estimate of 30,000 warriors was six times higher than Gookin's claim of 5,000. Mooney laughed off Johnson's number as ridiculously high and also rejected Gookin's ("his usual exaggeration"), choosing rather to accept a figure of 1,000 warriors, which was Gookin's estimate of the adult male population in his own day, half a century after whites had arrived in New England. Mooney did not explain his reasoning, but we might guess that he decided Gookin's information about his own times was more accurate than numbers supplied by elderly chiefs about bygone days when their tribes were supposed to have been much more powerful.

Perhaps these suppositions are valid. But when such imprecise calculations become a part of the "judgment" involved in adjusting estimates, there is room for unstated assumptions to influence the results. Why was it that Mooney, Kroeber, and older historians like Palfrey always tended to reduce estimates rather than increase them? Could it have been partly because they viewed Indian societies as primitive and therefore unable to support such relatively large populations? Palfrey certainly made no attempt to hide his disdain for Indian culture. "These people held a low place on the scale of humanity," he wrote:

> Even their physical capacities contradicted the promise of their external conformation. Supple and agile, so that it was said they would run eighty or a hun-

dred miles in a day, and back again in the next two, they sank under continuous labor. The lymphatic temperament indicated the same preponderance in them of "vegetative nature" which marked other animals of the same continent.

Alfred Kroeber, who reduced Mooney's calculations even further, shunned the racism evident in Palfrey's remarks. Nevertheless, Kroeber hesitated to accept the high population estimates of many sixteenth- and seventeenth-century observers. Indian societies in general, he explained, were characterized by "insane, unending, continuously attritional" warfare, which would prevent tribes from becoming too large. Kroeber admitted that Indians along the eastern lands of North America grew crops and that the practice of agriculture in Europe and Asia had led to larger populations. But the Indians along the Atlantic "were agricultural hunters," not really "farmers," he argued.

> Every man, or his wife, grew food for his household. The population remaining stationary, excess planting was not practiced, nor would it have led to anything in the way of economic or social benefit nor of increase of numbers. Ninety-nine per cent or more of what might have been developed remained virgin.

"The population remaining stationary": here Kroeber's argument was circular—for of course he possessed no hard information about whether the population was expanding or decreasing. It *must* have remained stationary, he assumed, because Indians lacked the skills to expand. Therefore no one planted extra food, because it wouldn't be of any use. But we have already seen that in early Virginia, the Indians did plant enough corn to amass surpluses. More than once they gave or sold it to the fledgling Virginia colony, which sorely needed it to stave off starvation. Kroeber seems to have ignored evidence that did not fit his assumptions.

Indeed, more recent historians have criticized the readiness of many to explain away the large estimates of contemporary observers. Early-twentieth-century scholars discounted Spanish estimates of 40 to 60 million Indians in Central and South America, suggesting that "all parties were equally interested in exaggerating the flourishing state of the recently discovered nations." Another scholar approvingly quoted an old truism: "To count is a modern practice; the ancient method was to guess; and when numbers are guessed they are always magnified." But those who proposed such hypotheses offered no concrete evidence of exaggeration.

By the mid-1970s, many anthropologists had come to believe that conservative population estimates were seriously flawed. In arriving at new ones, especially in Mexico and Spanish California, they developed a number of useful techniques. One, known as "projection," focused on the detailed study of a smaller region, where population could be determined more accurately. Having established a density for that limited area, anthropologists could project the result over larger regions, making allowances for varying conditions, climates, and patterns of settlement. Anthropologists also used the technique of "cross-checking" to compare the results of different methods of calculation. For example, some Spanish churches recorded the number of Indian children brought to be baptized during their "age of innocence"—that is, age four or younger. By drawing on population studies to determine what percentage of Indians would have been four or under (perhaps 10 percent), it became possible to calculate a rough total population. At the same time, the records sometimes supplied a conquistador's estimate of warriors from the same village. Using the kind of technique applied to Daniel Gookin's figures, a second population estimate could be derived. In addition, if archaeological studies revealed the number of houses in a particular village, a third calculation might be made. By a cross-check of these different estimates, it was possible to see whether the results reinforced each other, which improved reliability.

By the 1960s and 1970s, enough studies had been done to suggest that older estimates of precontact population were markedly low. Earlier figures had set the total population in North and South America at no more than 8 to 14 million; more recent studies suggest anywhere from 57 to 112 million, 5 to 10 million of whom lived north of Mexico. Such figures undermine the stereotype of precontact America as virgin, untamed wilderness. If these figures are correct, when Columbus landed in 1492 on Hispaniola, that island alone was inhabited by as many as 7 or 8 million people, compared with about 6 to 10 million for all of Spain, an area seven times as large. (England's population at the time was only about 5 million.) The Aztec capital of Tenochtitlán, estimated to have held anywhere from 165,000 to 250,000 inhabitants, was larger than the greatest European cities of the day: Constantinople, Naples, Venice, Milan, and Paris. In fact, more people may have been living in the Americas in 1492 than in western Europe.

THE MIGRATION OF MICROBES

It would be natural to expect that figures compiled from existing records might be somewhat inaccurate. But why were such estimates as much as ten times too low? Some hint of the answer can be found in the classic story of the Pilgrims, who arrived in December 1620 on the shores of Cape Cod unsure of how they would survive in a "hideous and desolate wilderness." As they began to explore what they feared would be wild forest, they discovered instead many acres of open fields, ready for crops to be planted. Obviously, the lands had been cleared by Indians, but none were now living there.

What had happened? The Pilgrims learned that not many years earlier, an epidemic had devastated the population, causing the villages in the area to be abandoned. The epidemic, most likely chicken pox, had been brought by fishermen to American shores around 1616 and then raged for three years from Maine to Cape Cod. Devoutly, the Pilgrims thanked God for "sweeping away great multitudes of natives . . . that he might make room for us there."

Even before the Pilgrims arrived, in other words, Native Americans had been decimated by diseases brought from Europe. Before 1492 Native Americans had never been exposed to smallpox, measles, malaria, or yellow fever. When their ancestors came to America, tens of thousands of years earlier, the process of migration cut them off from the major disease pools of the world. In order to survive, disease-carrying microorganisms need a host population large and dense enough to prevent the disease from gradually running out of new victims. Thus, large cities or any large groups of people (armies, schools) are prime disease pools. The pools need not be human: domestic animals such as cattle and horses are often hosts for infections that periodically spread to their caretakers.

But the first hunters who made their way over the Asian land bridge to America migrated in sparsely populated bands. They did not bring herds of domestic animals, and the cold climates through which they passed served as a barrier to many disease-carrying microorganisms. As a result, Indians were not subjected to cycles of epidemics like those that drastically reduced populations in Europe and Asia.

Because European and Asian populations were periodically reexposed to diseases like smallpox, a significant portion developed immunities. For some diseases, such as measles, protection was acquired during childhood (when the body is constitutionally better able to build immunity). By the sixteenth century, much of Europe's adult population was protected when outbreaks periodically reappeared. For virgin populations, however, such diseases were deadly. The Indian villages near the Pilgrim settlements had experienced mortality rates as high as 95 percent, and the first European colonists were often astonished to find pile after pile of unburied bones, picked clean by the wolves and bleached by the sun. Similar epidemics struck down Native Americans along the Great Lakes. Farther south, Cortés was able to conquer the mighty Aztec empire in large part because smallpox ravaged the capital of Tenochtitlán. When the Spanish finally entered the conquered city, "the streets, squares, houses, and courts were filled with bodies, so that it was almost impossible to pass. Even Cortés was sick from the stench in his nostrils."

Anthropologists such as Mooney had been aware of the diseases that afflicted Indians. But they had not calculated how severely such epidemics might have affected total populations. More recently, researchers have attempted to establish depopulation ratios in order to project population trends backward over time. If the records from a region provide two population estimates a number of years apart, a ratio of depopulation can be established. For example, Spanish tax records might indicate that in some villages the Indian population dropped by 50 percent over forty years. Using that ratio, it is possible to project earlier populations for regions that have figures only for the later period. Cross-checking this technique with others, historians have concluded that the population of Mexico dropped from perhaps 25 million in 1500 to only 3 million in 1568—a mortality rate of 88 percent in only two-thirds of a century.

Textbooks have finally begun to take note of these large-scale epidemics, but the focus has centered largely on the depopulation of the sixteenth and seventeenth centuries. Yet as the frontiers of white settlement continued to move across the continent, so did the invisible pioneers. During the eighteenth century, smallpox epidemics broke out in the Northeast, the Southwest, and along the California coast, and up and down the Mississippi Valley. During the nineteenth century, as fur traders and pioneers began pushing across the Great Plains and through the Rockies, no fewer than twenty-seven epidemics decimated the continent: thirteen of smallpox, five of measles, three of cholera, two of influenza, and one each of diphtheria, scarlet fever, tularemia, and malaria. These numbers were greater than those recorded for any previous century of contact.

We can perhaps sense the magnitude of the disaster by following the course of one epidemic. In 1837 the American Fur Company steamer the *St. Peter* left St. Louis carrying supplies and passengers for the trading posts along the upper Missouri. When the boat stopped near Fort Clark on June 18, all seemed well. But by a week later, when it pulled into Fort Union, at least one person on board had broken out with smallpox. The traders, well aware of the disease's effect, tried to protect the Indians at the fort by inoculating them with smallpox pus.[1] Unfortunately, the attempt miscarried and most of the Indians died. At the same time, a band of forty Indians arrived at the fort, eager to barter. The trader in charge refused to admit them, but they kept pounding at the gate until finally he opened it briefly to exhibit a boy whose face was covered with a mass of smallpox scabs. The Indians retreated, but they took the disease with them. More than half the party died.

Traders tried to keep smallpox from Fort McKenzie, the next stop upstream, by unloading their cargo halfway and sending word to the fort not to come for it until the risk of catching the disease had passed. But the Indians, eager for goods and suspicious of white motives, pressed the chief trader to bring the boat up, and again the epidemic spread.

The map on page 137 shows the depressing progress of the disease. Near Fort Clark, smallpox appeared among the Mandan a month after the *St. Peter* passed through. From there it spread to the Arikara during the summer and to the Sioux by October. The Assiniboin picked up the disease, probably from Fort Union, and soon after, the Crow got it. The Gros Ventres were infected by December. Because the disease often spread far from white posts, its route was not always easy to trace; but by 1838 it had apparently crossed the Rockies to the Cayuse, who blamed missionary Marcus Whitman and attacked his settlement. In 1838 it also moved south, reaching the Pawnee by way of several Sioux prisoners taken that spring. From the Pawnee it spread to the Osage and thence to the Kiowa and other Texas tribes, killing many Apache and Comanche. Moving west into New Mexico, it reached Santa Fe, and from there white traders carried it full circle, back to the frontiers of the United States.

Loss of life ran anywhere from 50 to 95 percent of the populations affected. But horrifying as these numbers are, they fail to tell the whole tale.

1. The technique of variolation, or transferring pus from a smallpox victim to a healthy subject, was often used before vaccination with cowpox became common. Although riskier, variolation often reduced mortality rates significantly.

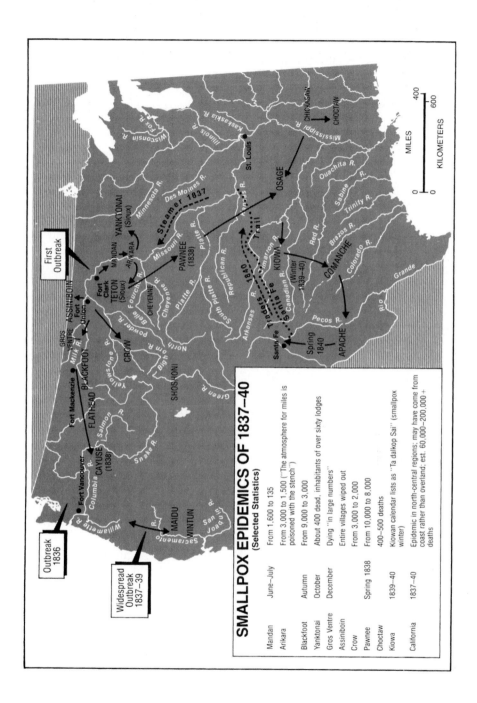

At stake were not only lives but the viability of entire cultures. The dislocations caused by disease were economic, social, and spiritual.

Economically, many Indian peoples could not carry out even their basic day-to-day work. In part, this was because the epidemics proved most deadly to those between the ages of fifteen and forty. (Scientists are still not sure why, in unexposed populations, this age group seems to be the hardest hit.) Healthy, in the prime of life, these victims were precisely those members of the community who contributed the most economically, as hunters, farmers, or food gatherers. Furthermore, the survivors of an epidemic often fled in terror from their traditional homelands. Resettling, they were obligated to discover anew the best hunting spots, places to gather nuts or berries, and sites with rich soils.

Socially, the disruptions were equally severe. Because male warriors were among those hit hardest, hostile neighbors, either white or Indian, were more difficult to resist. The plague-stricken Indians of New England had "their courage much abated," reported one colonist; "their countenance is dejected, and they seem as a people affrighted." Near Charleston, South Carolina, an Indian told a settler they had "forgotten most of their traditions since the Establishment of this Colony, they keep their Festivals and can tell but little of the reasons: their Old Men are dead." Farther west, Lewis and Clark traveled up the Missouri only a few years after the smallpox epidemic of 1801–1802. Clark reported that the remnant of the Omaha nation, "haveing no houses no Corn or anything more than the graves of their ansesters to attach them to the old Village," led a much more nomadic existence. "I am told when this fatal malady [smallpox] was among them they Carried their franzey to verry extraordinary length, not only of burning their Village, but they put their wives and children to *Death* with a view of their all going together to some better Countrey."

Even when despair did not lead to suicide, Native Americans were severely challenged by what seemed to be the Europeans' superior gods. Both Indians and whites read supernatural meaning into the epidemics, attributing such outbreaks to divine anger. Yet because the new diseases singled out nonimmune Native Americans and spared Europeans, both peoples tended to credit the superiority of the European deity. When Francis Drake's sailors brought illness to Florida in 1585, "the wilde people . . . died verie fast and said amongst themselves, it was the Inglisshe God that made them die so fast." More cynical whites were not above capitalizing on this dread. In 1812 James McDougall warned the Chinook Indians of the Columbia River not to carry out an attack against the whites:

> You imagine that because we are few you can easily kill us, but it is not so; or if you do you will only bring the greater evils upon yourselves. The medicine of the white man dead is mightier than that of the red man living. . . . You know the smallpox. Listen: I am the smallpox chief. In this bottle I have it confined. All I have to do is to pull the cork, send it forth among you, and you are dead men. But this is for my enemies and not for my friends.

The pustules from smallpox were horrifying and painful. In their own drawings, the Lakota Sioux Indians used a spiral symbol to indicate the intense pain associated with the disease.

Given that disease did strike Indians more severely than whites, it is no wonder many believed such claims. In any case, the result was to severely strain Native Americans' traditional beliefs.

COMPETING ECOLOGICAL SYSTEMS

Undoubtedly, the spread of European microorganisms had an immense effect on the cultural balances of North America. But other ecological pioneers played important roles. Colonists imported plants and animals that were new to America, and the ways settlers made use of them differed markedly from the ways Native Americans used their own natural resources. In large part, the Old World meeting the New World became a clash between competing ecological systems. In the ensuing struggle, the European ecologies often prevailed.

Many European plants that came to America spread for the same reasons European diseases did. Because American plants had been relatively isolated from competition for thousands of years, many yielded to hardier European stocks. Some plants spread so widely that today they are commonly taken to be native. "Kentucky" bluegrass originated in Europe. So did the dandelion, the daisy, white clover, ragweed, and plantain. (The last was called "the Englishman's foot" by New England Indians, for it seemed to sprout wherever the new settlers wandered.)

Many of these plants were introduced purely by accident. Seeds might arrive in chests of folded clothes or in clods of mud or dung. But settlers also deliberately imported many plants. On the Oregon trail, several overlanders made a business of carrying trees and fruits across the country. The most successful was an Iowa Quaker, Henderson Welling, who in 1847 hauled seven hundred trees, vines, and shrubs in his wagons, including such varieties as apple, cherry, pear, plum, black walnut, and quince. His imports helped launch a multimillion-dollar orchard business in California and Oregon.[2]

As for the animal frontier, we have already seen that the horse outran Europeans in crossing the continent. Most Indian peoples took to the horse rapidly; in performance they soon outstripped the Spaniards, who were a horse-loving people to begin with. Male Plains Indians learned to ride bareback, controlling their mounts with a gentle pressure of the knees instead of using reins. This ability left a rider's hands free to use a bow and arrow. A good hunter-warrior could travel at full gallop, drop to one side of his pony for cover, and launch a continuous stream of arrows with such force that a shaft might bury itself entirely in a buffalo. The Comanche men were such accomplished riders that a unit of the U.S. Cavalry was in one contest disgusted to find its finest Kentucky mare beaten by a "miserable sheep of a pony" upon which a Comanche rider was mounted backward so he could mockingly wave (with "hideous grimaces") for his American rival to "come on a little faster!"

Above all, horses gave those Indians who possessed them immensely greater mobility. Previously, hunting was done on foot by male tribe members; mounted, they searched out the buffalo with comparative ease. In addition, mounted nations were able to drive rivals from long-held territories. By 1826, according to an early fur trader, the Klamath Indians along the California-Oregon border had been raided so often by their well-mounted enemies that one village was forced in desperation to relocate on land surrounded by marsh and water, "approachable only by canoes."

While the supply of horses diffused toward the north and east, another frontier—that of guns—moved in the opposite direction, west and south. The Spanish possessed firearms, but their laws forbade selling any to Indians. English and French fur traders of the Northeast, however, operated under no such restraints. The gun and horse frontiers met along the upper Missouri

---

2. Limitations of space make it impossible to discuss an equally important topic, the migration of American flora and fauna to Europe. Perhaps the most influential Native American contributions to world civilization were agricultural products. Maize corn, unknown in Europe, had been developed by Indians over thousands of years from ears that were originally the size of a finger. The tomato, now so closely linked with Italian cuisine, was an American product; so too was the potato, before it ever reached Ireland. These imports may have contributed significantly to the rise of population in Europe, which began an upward trend in the sixteenth century.

While Indian men often road bareback, women such as this Sioux used a saddle with high ends fore and aft to keep from being pitched off. Decorations included brightly colored cloth bordered by porcupine quills and beads. Even the horses had pendants dangling from their ears!

during the first half of the eighteenth century and, in crossing, touched off an extremely unsettled period for western Indians. In the late 1700s the Cree, Assiniboin, and Ojibwa, with their guns, forced the Teton Sioux, Cheyenne, Arapaho, and Crow south across the Missouri River. Agricultural peoples, such as the Mandan and Arikara, found themselves more frequently attacked, while tribes that were originally nomadic became even more so.

Women of nomadic tribes were also affected by the coming of the horse. With mounts available as beasts of burden, women were required to do much less hauling when camps were moved. In some tribes, women were even allowed to own their own horses. Homes, too, became more spacious: in "dog days," teepees had been constructed of five or six skins, small enough to be carried on the dog travois. With horses to carry them, the teepees grew to fifteen or twenty skins. A fur trader in 1805 summed the situation up by noting that while Crow women did "most of the work," they were "not so wretchedly situated as those nations who live in the forests. . . . [and] are indebted solely to their having horses for the ease they enjoy more than their neighbors." Older people may well have benefited too, for nomadic tribes sometimes abandoned or killed those who were too feeble to travel. With horses to carry the infirm, such practices seem to have lessened.

While the horse changed the lives of Plains Indians, it did not radically alter their cultures. It was as "an intensifier of original Plains traits" that the horse presented its strongest claim, noted anthropologist Clark Wissler. The situation was far different once whites themselves reached Native American lands. Their coming fundamentally changed the relationships between the land and the Indians who used it.

Underlying this change was the apparently simple fact that from the very first, European explorers came to America in search of resources that were scarce in Europe. Invariably, they returned home praising the many precious "commodities" that were available. Spain reaped vast profits from the gold and silver of Central and South America, and the French and English hoped to follow suit. In the end, though, they discovered that the most easily extractable commodities of North America were the animals of the forest: beaver, fox, marten, muskrat, otter.

Native Americans had hunted such animals since time immemorial; Europeans merely encouraged them to trap a larger surplus. But the act of creating this surplus, and then linking it to a worldwide economy, meant that trading took on a different aspect for Indians. As William Cronon has pointed out, the fur trade was

> far more complicated than a simple exchange of European metal goods for Indian beaver skins. . . . Trade linked these groups with an abstract set of equivalent values measured in pelts, bushels of corn, fathoms of wampum, and price movements in sterling on London markets. The essential lesson for the Indians was that certain things began to have prices that had not had them before. In particular, one could buy personal prestige by killing animals and exchanging their skins for wampum or high-status European goods.

Even by the 1640s, the demand for furs had depleted beaver near the New England coast. By the end of the century, most of the region's streams and forests were trapped out. And the pattern repeated itself as the frontier moved westward. Lewis and Clark's Rocky Mountains, which in 1804 were "richer in beaver and otter than any country on earth," by 1840 were so poor, according to one trapper, "that one would stand a right good chance of starving, if he were obliged to hang up here for seven days. The game is all driven out."

The pressure on resources increased once pioneers began to cross the plains. The case of timber provides a good example. Wood is a resource not usually associated with the vast plains and open prairies. Yet precisely because trees were scarce, they played an important part in Indian ecology. Cottonwood, clustered along the richer bottomlands of plains rivers, offered crucial protection during winter blizzards as well as concealment of a village's smoke from its enemies. In lean seasons, horses fed on its bark, which was surprisingly nourishing. And along rivers during spring breakup, men, women, and children could be seen leaping onto the ice floes as they swirled downstream, tying cords to floating deadwood and hauling it ashore. Timber was worth taking big risks to obtain.

The overland migrations of the 1840s and 1850s created severe wood shortages in many areas along the trails. Although most settlers were only passing through, fully a quarter of a million whites made the trip before the

The flood of wagon trains onto the plains was often wider than the procession depicted here. Aerial photographs of old wagon routes show them spreading as much as thirty times wider than modern paved roads nearby. It was not so much the people as the animals that came with them—oxen, mules, horses, cattle, sheep—that damaged the plains environment. In 1853 there were about eleven animals for every human along the Platte River route.

Civil War, and the pressure of such numbers soon showed itself. "The road, from morning till night, is crowded like Pearl Street or Broadway," wrote a traveler in 1850. It was not uncommon for several thousand people to pass Fort Laramie in a single day. Such hordes inevitably destroyed many of the best timber stands. "By the Mormon guide we here expected to find the last timber," wrote A. W. Harlan, along the Platte, "but all had been used up by others ahead of us so we must go about 200 miles without any provisions cooked up."

Faced by this procession of wagon trains, many Indian nations responded by demanding payment, usually in provisions, for the privilege of passing through their homelands. Some bands even erected bridges and attempted to collect tolls at strategic stream crossings. In either case, they made it clear that they regarded such fees as compensation for the use of their lands—for the rights to timber, grazing, and the animals shot in their hunting territories. Some emigrants grudgingly paid the fees, but others forced their way through.

The loss of timber or grazing areas was bad enough, but Native Americans had an even more serious complaint—that "the buffalo are wantonly killed and scared off," as one white observer noted, "which renders their only means of subsistence every year more precarious." This complaint was especially grave not only because the bison became an important commodity in the trading economy but also because white settlers were replacing such wildlife with their own livestock. A large part of Indian life revolved around the hunting of wild creatures: deer, moose, buffalo, antelope. Over time, the land occupied by these animals came to be seen by whites as desirable for cattle, sheep, or pigs. The resulting competition for grazing lands spelled the death knell for Native American ways. Next to the invisible pioneers of disease, the "emigrants" that most threatened Indian cultures were European domestic animals.

In the precontact era, Native Americans had only a few domesticated animals—in North America, primarily the dog. Wild animals, on the other hand, were viewed as property only after they had been killed. This attitude differed from the European notion that a person might raise and own animals as a source of food. Even if such stock was allowed to roam free, it was still owned by individuals, as the brand on a cow's flank or the cut on a sheep's ear signified. Domestic animals such as oxen also allowed Europeans to use plows on a widespread scale, which meant more fields could be cultivated and their surpluses sold in an expanding capitalist economy. All these customs—central to the way Europeans managed their resources—were foreign to Native Americans.

On the Great Plains, domestic cattle and sheep replaced bison and antelope, just as cattle, swine, and sheep had replaced deer in the East. Although the cowboy came into his own only after the Civil War, livestock drives were common along the overland trails in the 1850s. Perhaps a half million cattle and another half million sheep made the trek. At first, such drives did not destroy the traditional plains ecology. In California, early ranching even seemed to help some wildlife temporarily, like the grizzly, who gorged on the corpses of stock skinned for their hides. But hunting pressure on the bison steadily increased. In the 1850s a traveler was already writing that "the valley of the Platte for 200 miles presents the aspect of the vicinity of a slaughter yard; dotted all over with skeletons of buffalos." By the 1860s wagon trains could no longer count on hunting food on the way across; grocery stores had sprung up instead.

Pressure on the bison herds came not only from white emigrants. As European settlement pressed westward toward the open prairies and plains, Indians were either driven or moved out onto the plains ahead of white settlement. Historians estimate that the Indian population of the central plains grew from perhaps 8,000 Indians in 1820 to as many as 20,000 in the

1850s, despite the periodic toll of epidemic disease. For a time, increased competition for hunting grounds actually helped protect the bison. The contested borderlands between rival tribes served in effect as refuges, since hunting could be conducted only sporadically in these buffer zones. But after 1840 Indian diplomacy brought relative peace to the plains. Under such conditions hunting pressures mounted, with Indian hunters especially setting their sights on two- to five-year-old bison cows for their tender meat and their thinner, more easily processed hides. Because these cows were the most fertile members of the herd, their deaths sharply reduced the number of new births.

Once the transcontinental railroad was completed, the slaughter of the herds accelerated. "Buffalo Bill" Cody gained prominence as a hunter for the train crews of the Kansas Pacific. Sportsmen riding the rails took potshots from the passing cars or, seeking better yields, tracked down the big herds and opened fire with such abandon that their gun barrels overheated after a time. A single hunter could kill more than a hundred animals in an hour. By the early 1870s the demand for buffalo robes had risen sharply in the East, so commercial companies hauled out perhaps as many as 10 million hides. A decade later the herds were nearly gone, their lands being swiftly occupied by cattle, sheep, cowpunchers, and sodbusters.

America had been transformed. The land of 1890 was vastly different from the precontact world of 1490, in large part because of the series of ecological frontiers that had crossed the continent. Beyond doubt, the most important was the frontier of disease, which provided Europeans with nothing less than the opportunity to remake the Americas in their own image. Today, having lived so long with the outcome, we tend to take the results as a foregone conclusion. We assume that European success in America was due to superior technology and efficient social and economic organization. No doubt these elements played a role. But during the same era Spain, England, France, and Portugal were also expanding eastward with markedly different results. In China and India, where diseases did not decimate the local populations, Asian cultural and political traditions remained strong, regardless of "superior" European technology. European merchants and settlers were confined to trading stations and coastal enclaves. Even where western elites came to rule a country, as the British did in India, they remained only the upper stratum of a colonial system. In the twentieth century, when nationalist movements ejected the colonial powers, Asian cultures played a renewed and revitalized role.

But in the Americas? The Aztecs and Incas had complex civilizations and, if they had not been decimated by disease, they too might have kept the Spanish pinned down along the coast. Farther north, the English found it difficult enough as it was to establish colonies. They might have been even less successful if the full complement of Native Americans had survived to resist them. But with 50 to 90 percent of the population wiped out within a century, not only peoples but cultures suffered. And hard upon the heels of disease came a host of other European "pioneers"—horses, pigs, and cattle—led by masters who employed these new beasts to organize society in foreign ways.

Even after the frontier passed into history, ecological constraints continued to influence American development. Newcomers to the plains soon found that natural limits forced them to change their ways. Barbed wire and sod huts replaced the wood traditionally used for fences and homes. Dry farming techniques were needed to make the land yield adequate harvests. Windmills used the ample resource of the wind to secure the much scarcer resource of water. But these stories belong to a later era; even in this chapter, seven-league boots have their limits. What remains clear is that on both sides of the frontier, American history has been shaped and altered by ecological factors that historians have too often lightly passed over.

Additional Reading

The subject of this chapter (not to mention its chronological span) is so vast that we can only make the briefest attempt at a bibliography. Almost every topic discussed—the effect of the horse on Native American cultures, of human-caused fires on the environment, of epidemic disease on native populations—has produced a sizable literature.

For an introduction to ecology, especially as it relates to history, see John W. Bennett, *The Ecological Transition: Cultural Anthropology and Human Adaptation* (New York, 1976). William L. Thomas, ed., *Man's Role in Changing the Face of the Earth* (Chicago, 1956) is a wide-ranging collection of papers, including some on the Indians' use of fire and the effect of domestic livestock on the grasslands of the plains. For information on the history of ecology, see Donald Worster, *Nature's Economy*, 2d ed. (New York, 1994), and Ronald C. Tobey, *Saving the Prairies: The Life Cycle of the Founding School of American Plant Ecology, 1895–1955* (Berkeley, CA, 1981). Alfred W. Crosby Jr. provides excellent overviews of ecological frontiers in *The Columbian Exchange: Biological and Cultural Consequences of 1492* (Westport, CT, 1972) and *Ecological Imperialism: The Biological Expansion of Europe, 900–1900* (Cambridge, 1986). For a model of how ecology and history may be united in the study of one region, it would be hard to surpass William Cronon's *Changes in the Land: Indians, Colonists, and the Ecology of New England* (New York, 1983), a work that has been most helpful to us.

The abundance of flora and fauna of precontact North America may be inferred from the descriptions left by early white visitors. Among many travelers' accounts worth consulting, Peter Kalm's *Travels in North America* (New York, 1964) provides material for the mid-eighteenth century. For the early nineteenth century, Lewis and Clark's journals, available in a number of editions, are informative, as is Paul Cutright's *Lewis and Clark: Pioneering Naturalists* (Urbana, IL, 1969).

For an introduction to the difficulties of estimating precontact populations, see Russell Thornton, *American Indian Holocaust and Survival: A Population History since 1492* (Norman, OK, 1987). The move toward sharply higher estimates received impetus from Henry F. Dobyns, "Estimating Aboriginal Population: An Appraisal of Techniques with a New Hemispheric Estimate," *Current Anthropology* 7 (1966): 395–416. Dobyns raised his earlier estimate of 10 million Indians in precontact North America to 18 million in *Their Number Become Thinned: Native American Population Dynamics in Eastern North America* (Knoxville, TN, 1983), but scholars have been much more wary of these calculations. The most sophisticated treatment of the effect of epidemics on precontact populations is John W. Verano and Douglas H. Ubelaker, eds., *Disease and Demography in the Americas* (Washington, DC, 1992). Francis Jennings explores some of the racist assumptions underlying earlier population estimates in *The Invasion of America* (Chapel Hill, NC, 1975). For a survey of other hemispheric studies, see William M. Denevan, ed., *The Native Population of the Americas in 1492* (Madison, WI, 1976), which includes a discussion of James Mooney's estimates.

William McNeill's superb *Plagues and Peoples* (Garden City, NY, 1976) is the starting point for understanding the effects of disease in history. For a sense of how archaeological evidence may be used to substantiate depopulation estimates, see the papers in Verano and Ubelaker. One essay by Michael K. Trimble reviews the 1837 smallpox epidemic on the upper Missouri (pp. 257–264). Elizabeth Anne Fenn chronicles an earlier outbreak in *Pox Americana: The Great Smallpox Epidemic of 1775–82* (New York, 2001).

Of the innumerable works on Indian-white relations, we list here only a handful whose ecological perspective we have found helpful. Cronon covers early New England, while the southeastern frontier is surveyed by James H. Merrell, *The Indians' New World: Catawbas and Their World from European Contact through the Era of Removal* (Chapel Hill, NC, 1989). The work of John Ewers, always lively and astute, can be sampled in *Indian Life of the Upper Missouri* (Norman, OK, 1968); he is the source of Weasel Tail's account of how the Blackfeet discovered horses. Shepard Krech III, *The Ecological Indian* (New York, 1999) corrects the myth of Indians as protoecologists.

For animal frontiers, see the exhaustive (and sometimes exhausting) Frank Gilbert Roe, *The North American Buffalo: A Critical Study of the Species in Its Wild State* (Toronto, 1970). With equal pertinacity, Roe has surveyed *The Indian and the Horse* (Norman, OK, 1955). Frank R. Secoy traces how the horse and gun frontiers affected Indian life in *Changing Military Patterns on the Great Plains: 17th Century through Early 19th Century* (Locust Valley, NY, 1953). Our own chapter has given only scant attention to the important effects of the fur trade on Native American life. For one ecologically sensitive introduction, see David J. Wishart, *The Fur Trade of the American West, 1807–1840: A Geographical Synthesis* (Lincoln, NE, 1979). Calvin Martin's *Keepers of the Game* (Berkeley, CA, 1978) is a controversial attempt to see Indian overtrapping as a consequence of the newly introduced epidemics; for a response, see Shepard Krech III, ed., *Indians, Animals, and the Fur Trade* (Athens, GA, 1981). Eric Wolf adopts a global perspective in *Europe and the People without History* (Berkeley, CA, 1982).

For the traditional frontier of the overland trail, John D. Unruh, *The Plains Across: Overland Emigrants and the Trans-Mississippi West, 1840–60* (Urbana, IL, 1982) dispels the myth of the lonely trail. The demise of the bison is covered in a pathbreaking article by Dan Flores, "Bison Ecology and Bison Diplomacy: The Southern Plains from 1800 to 1840," *Journal of American History* (September 1991): 465–485. Flores shows that the traditional explanation, that white hunters decimated the herd in the 1870s, is only a partial explanation. Elliott West has come to similar conclusions about the central plains in his eminently readable *The Way to the West: Essays on the Central Plains* (Albuquerque, NM, 1995). See also his *The Contested Plains: Indians, Goldseekers, and the Rush to Colorado* (Lincoln, NE, 1998).

Interactive Learning

The *Primary Source Investigator* provides materials exploring the role of the "invisible pioneers" in American history. Journal entries by travelers depict the sheer volume of passenger pigeons and bison on the plains. Other entries discuss time spent with Native American tribes and the various methods Native Americans used to shape their environment and the world around them. Charts illuminate the devastating effects of disease, and images of dwindling Native American encampments reinforce this loss.

CHAPTER 7
The Madness of John Brown

For more than two months the twenty-one men hid in the cramped attic. They were mostly idealistic young men in their twenties, bound together during the tedious waiting by a common hatred of slavery. Now, on October 16, 1859, their leader, Old John Brown, revealed to them his final plan. The group comprised five blacks and sixteen whites, including three of the old man's sons, Owen, Oliver, and Watson. For years Brown had nurtured the idea of striking a blow against the southern citadel of slavery. Tomorrow, he explained, they would move into Harpers Ferry, Virginia, and capture the town and its federal arsenal. As they gathered arms, slaves would pour in from the surrounding countryside to join their army. Before the local militia had time to organize, Brown's forces would escape to the nearby hills. From there, they would fight a guerilla war until the curse of slavery had been exorcised and all slaves freed from bondage. No one among them questioned Brown or his plan.

An autumn chill filled the air, and a light rain fell as the war party made its way down the dark road toward Harpers Ferry. Three men had remained behind to handle supplies and arm slaves who took up the fight. A sleepy stillness covered the small town nestled in the hills where the Shenandoah joined the Potomac sixty miles from Washington, DC. It was a region of small farms and relatively few slaves. Most likely, the presence of the arsenal and an armory explains why Brown chose to begin his campaign there.

The attack began without a hitch. Two raiders cut telegraph lines running east and west from the town. The others seized a rifle works, the armory, and three hostages, including a local planter descended from the Washington family. Soon the sounds of gunfire drew the townspeople from their beds. Amid the confusion, the church bell pealed the alarm dreaded by so many whites throughout the South—slave insurrection! By late morning the hastily joined militia and armed farmers had trapped Brown and his men in the engine house of the Baltimore and Ohio Railroad. One son had been killed and another lay dying at his father's side. Drunken crowds thronged

John Brown, man of action:
After leading the
Pottawatomie Massacre in
Kansas in 1856, Brown grew
a beard to disguise his
appearance. His eastern
abolitionist backers were
impressed with the aura he
radiated as a western man of
action. The image was not
hurt by the fact that Brown
carried a bowie knife in his
boot and regularly barricaded
himself nights in his hotel
rooms as a precaution against
proslavery agents.

the streets crying for blood and revenge. When news of the raid reached Washington, President Buchanan dispatched federal troops under Colonel Robert E. Lee to put down the insurrection.

Thirty-six hours after the first shot, John Brown's war on slavery ended. By any calculation the raid had been a total failure. Not a single slave had risen to join Brown's army. Ten of the raiders lay dead or dying; the rest had been scattered or captured. Although wounded himself, Brown had miraculously escaped death. The commander of the assault force had tried to kill him with his dress sword, but it merely bent double from the force of the blow. Seven other people had been killed and nine more wounded during the raid.

Most historians would agree that the Harpers Ferry raid was to the Civil War what the Boston Massacre had been to the American Revolution: an incendiary event. In an atmosphere of aroused passions, profound suspicions, and irreconcilable differences, Brown and his men put a match to the fuse. Once their deed had been done and blood had been shed, there seemed to be no drawing back for either North or South. The shouts of angry men overwhelmed the voices of compromise.

From pulpits and public platforms across the North, leading abolitionists leapt to Brown's defense. No less a spokesman than Ralph Waldo Emerson pronounced the raider a "saint . . . whose martyrdom, if it shall be perfected, will make the gallows as glorious as the cross." Newspaper editor Horace Greeley called the raid "the work of a madman," for which he had nothing but the highest admiration. At the same time the defenders of national union and of law and order generally condemned Brown and his violent tactics. Such northern political leaders as Abraham Lincoln, Stephen Douglas, and William Seward spoke out against Brown. The Republican Party in 1860 went so far as to adopt a platform censuring the Harpers Ferry raid.

Moderate northern voices were lost, however, on southern fire-eaters, to whom all abolitionists and Republicans were potential John Browns. Across the South angry mobs attacked northerners regardless of their views on the slave question. Everywhere the specter of slave insurrection fed fears, and the uproar strengthened the hand of secessionists, who argued that the South's salvation lay in expunging all traces of northern influence.

THE MOTIVES OF A FANATIC

And what of the man who triggered all those passions? Had John Brown foreseen that his quixotic crusade would reap such a whirlwind of violence? On that issue both his contemporaries and historians have been sharply divided. Brown himself left a confusing and often contradictory record of his objectives. To his men, and to Frederick Douglass, the former slave and black abolitionist, Brown made clear he intended nothing less than to provoke a general slave insurrection. His preparations all pointed to that goal. He went to Harpers Ferry armed for such a task, and the choice of the armory as the raid's target left little doubt he intended to equip a slave army. But throughout the months of preparation, Brown had consistently warned the coconspirators financing his scheme that the raid might fail. In that event, he told them, he still hoped the gesture would so divide the nation that a sectional crisis would ensue, leading to the destruction of slavery.

From his jail cell and at his trial Brown offered a decidedly contradictory explanation. Ignoring the weapons he had accumulated, he suggested that the raid was intended as an extension of the Underground Railroad work he had previously done. He repeatedly denied any intention to commit violence or instigate a slave rebellion. "I claim to be here in carrying out a measure I believe perfectly justifiable," he told a skeptical newspaper reporter, "and not to act the part of an incendiary or ruffian, but to aid those [slaves] suffering great wrong." To Congressman Clement Vallandigham of Ohio, who asked Brown if he expected a slave uprising, the old man replied, "No sir; nor did I wish it. I expected to gather them up from time to time and set them free." In court, with his life hanging in the balance, Brown once again denied any violent intent. He sought only to expand his campaign for the liberation of slaves.

Brown's contradictory testimony has provoked much speculation over the man and his motives. Was he being quite rational and calculating in abruptly

John Brown, the impractical idealist: "The old idiot—the quicker they hang him and get him out of the way, the better." So wrote the editor of a Chicago paper to Abraham Lincoln. Many contemporaries shared the view of the cartoon reprinted here, that Brown was a foolish dreamer. Yet Brown had other ideas. "I think you are fanatical!" exclaimed one southern bystander after Brown had been captured. "And I think you are fanatical," Brown retorted. "'Whom the Gods would destroy they first made mad,' and you are mad."

changing his story after capture? Certainly, Brown knew how much his martyrdom would enhance the abolitionist movement. His execution, he wrote his wife, would "do vastly more toward advancing the cause I have earnestly endeavored to promote, than all I have done in my life before." On the other hand, perhaps Brown was so imbued with his own righteousness that he deceived himself into believing he had not acted the part of "incendiary or ruffian," but only meant to aid those slaves "suffering great wrong." "Poor old man!" commented Republican presidential hopeful Salmon Chase. "How sadly misled by his own imaginations!"

Yet for every American who saw Brown as either a calculating insurrectionist or a genuine, if self-deluded, martyr, there were those who thought him insane. How else could they explain the hopeless assault of eighteen men against a federal arsenal and the state of Virginia—where slaves were "not abundant" and where "no Abolitionists were ever known to peep"? Who but a "madman" (to quote Greeley) could have concocted, much less attempted, such a wild scheme?

Nor was the issue of John Brown's sanity laid to rest by his execution on December 2, 1859. Brown had become a symbol, for both North and South, of the dimensions of the sectional struggle, embodying the issues of the larger conflict in his own actions. Inevitably, the question of personal motivation becomes bound up in historians' interpretations of the root causes of sectional and social conflict. Was Brown a heroic martyr—a white man in a racist society with the courage to lay down his life on behalf of his black brothers and the principles of the Declaration? Or was he an emotionally unbalanced fanatic whose propensity for wanton violence propelled the nation toward avoidable tragedy?

During the middle years of the twentieth century the view of Brown as an emotional fanatic gained ground. John Garraty, in a popular college survey text, described Brown as so "deranged" that rather than hang him for his "dreadful act. . . . It would have been far wiser and more just to have committed him to an asylum." Allen Nevins defined a middle ground when he argued that on all questions except slavery, Brown could act coherently and rationally. "But on this special question of the readiness of slavery to crumble at a blow," Nevins thought, "his monomania . . . or his paranoia as a modern alienist [psychoanalyst] would define it, rendered him irresponsible."

In 1970 Brown's academic biographer, Stephen Oates, agreed that in many ways Brown was not "normal." Yet Oates rejected the idea that insanity could either be adequately demonstrated or used in any substantive way to explain Brown's actions. That Brown had an "excitable temperament" and a single-minded obsession with slavery Oates conceded. He concluded, too, that Brown was egotistical, an overbearing father, an often inept man worn down by disease and suffering, and a revolutionary who believed himself called to his mission by God.

But having said all that, Oates demanded that before they dismissed Brown as insane, historians must consider the context of Brown's actions. To call him insane, Oates argued, "is to ignore the tremendous sympathy he felt for the black man in America." And, he added, "to label him a 'maniac' out of touch with 'reality' is to ignore the piercing insight he had into what his raid— whether it succeeded or whether it failed—would do to sectional tensions."

Given such conflicting views on the question of John Brown's sanity, it makes sense to examine more closely the evidence of his mental state. The most readily available material, and the most promising at first glance, was presented after the original trial by Brown's attorney, George Hoyt. As a last-minute stratagem, Hoyt submitted nineteen affidavits from Brown's friends and acquaintances, purporting to demonstrate Brown's instability.

Two major themes appear in those affidavits. First, a number of people testified to a pronounced pattern of insanity in the Brown family, particularly on his mother's side. In addition to his maternal grandmother and numerous uncles, aunts, and cousins, Brown's sister, his brother Salmon, his

John Brown, martyr of freedom:

> John Brown of Ossawatomie, they led him out to die;
> And lo! a poor slave-mother with her little child pressed nigh,
> Then the bold, blue eye grew tender, and the harsh face grew mild,
> And he stooped between the jeering ranks and kissed the Negro's child!

John Greenleaf Whittier based this incident in his poem, "Brown of Ossawatomie" (December 1859), on an erroneous newspaper report. Apparently Brown did kiss the child of a white jailor he had befriended. Brown also remarked to the same jailer that "he would prefer to be surrounded in his last moments by a poor weeping slave mother with her children," noting that this "would make the picture at the gallows complete."

first wife, Dianthe, and his sons Frederick and John Jr. were all said to have shown evidence of mental disorders. Second, some respondents described certain patterns of instability they saw in Brown himself. Almost everyone

John Brown, the terrorist:
Mahala Doyle, the wife of James P. Doyle, one of the men Brown killed at Pottawatomie, testified of Brown, "He said if a man stood between him and what he considered right, he would take his life as cooly as he would eat his breakfast. His actions show what he is. Always restless, he seems never to sleep. With an eye like a snake, he looks like a demon."

agreed he was profoundly religious and that he became agitated over the slavery question. A few traced Brown's insanity back through his years of repeated business failures. The "wild and desperate" nature of those business schemes and the rigidity with which he pursued them persuaded several friends of his "unsound" mind and "monomania."

Many old acquaintances thought that Brown's controversial experiences in Kansas had unhinged the man. There, in May 1856, proslavery forces had attacked the antislavery town of Lawrence. In retaliation, Brown led a band of seven men (including four of his sons) in a midnight raid on some proslavery settlers at Pottawatomie Creek. Although the Pottawatomie residents had taken no part in the attack on faraway Lawrence, Brown's men, under his orders, took their broadswords and hacked to death five of them. That grisly act horrified free-state and proslavery advocates alike. John Jr., one of Brown's sons who had not participated in the raid, suffered a nervous breakdown from his own personal torment and from the abuse he received after being thrown into prison. Another of Brown's sons, Frederick, was murdered a few months later in the civil war that swiftly erupted in Kansas.

Thus a number of acquaintances testified in 1859 that from the time of the Pottawatomie killings onward, Brown had been mentally deranged. E. N. Sill, an acquaintance of both Brown and his father, admitted that he had once had considerable sympathy for Brown's plan to defend antislavery families in Kansas. "But from his peculiarities," Sill recalled, "I thought Brown an unsafe man to be commissioned with such a matter." It was Sill who suggested the idea, which Allen Nevins later adopted, that on the slavery question alone Brown was insane. "I have no confidence in his judgment in matters appertaining to slavery," he asserted. "I have no doubt that, upon this subject . . . he is surely as monomaniac as any inmate in any lunatic asylum in the country." David King, who talked to Brown after his Kansas experience, observed that "on the subject of slavery he was crazy" and that Brown saw himself as "an instrument in the hands of God to free slaves."

Such testimony seems to support the view that Harpers Ferry was the outcome of insanity. Yet even then and ever since, many people have rejected that conclusion. Confronted with the affidavits, Governor Henry Wise of Virginia thought to have Brown examined by the head of the state's insane asylums. Upon reflection he changed his mind. Wise believed Brown perfectly sane and had even come to admire begrudgingly the old man's "indomitable" spirit. Wise once described Brown as "the gamest man I ever saw."

For what it is worth, Brown himself rejected any intimation that he was anything but sane. He refused to plead insanity at his trial and instead adopted the posture of the self-sacrificing revolutionary idealist. For him, slavery constituted an unethical and unconstitutional assault of one class of citizens against another. Under that assault, acts that society deemed unlawful—dishonesty, murder, theft, or treason—could be justified in the name of a higher morality.

Furthermore, Oates and other historians have attacked the affidavits presented by Hoyt as patently unreliable. Many people had good reason to have Brown declared insane. Among those signing the affidavits were friends and relatives who hoped Governor Wise would spare Brown's life. Might they not have exaggerated the instances of mental disorders in his family to make their case more convincing? Most had not taken Brown's fanaticism seriously until his raid on Harpers Ferry. That event, as much as earlier observation, had shaped their opinions. Just as important, none of them had any medical training or experience that would qualify them to determine with any expertise whether Brown or any member of his family could be judged insane. Only one affidavit came from a doctor, and like most physicians of the day, he had no particular competence in psychological observation.

Although it would be foolish to suggest that we in the twentieth century are better judges of character than our forebears, it is fair to say that at least we have a better clinical understanding of mental disorders. Many symptoms that in the nineteenth century were lumped together under the term *insanity* have since been identified as a variety of very different diseases, each with its own distinct causes. Among those "crazy" Brown relatives were those who, based on the descriptions in the affidavits, may have suffered from senility, epilepsy, Addison's disease, or brain tumors. Thus the "preponderance" of insanity in Brown's family could well have been a series of unrelated disorders. Even if the disorders were related, psychologists today still hotly debate the extent to which psychological disorders are inheritable.

The insanity defense also had considerable appeal to political leaders. Moderates from both North and South, seeking to preserve the Union, needed an argument to soften the divisive impact of Harpers Ferry. If Brown were declared insane, northern abolitionists could not so easily portray him as a martyr. Southern secessionists could not treat Brown as typical of all northern abolitionists. As a result, their argument that the South would be safe only outside the Union would have far less force. Even antislavery Republicans tried to dissociate themselves from Brown's more radical tactics. During the 1859 congressional elections, the Democrats tried to persuade voters that Harpers Ferry resulted inevitably from the Republicans' appeal to the doctrine of "irresistible conflict" and "higher law" abolitionism. To blunt such attacks, leading Republicans regularly attributed the raid to Brown's insanity.

Clearly, the affidavits provide only the flimsiest basis for judging the condition of Brown's mental health. But some historians have argued that the larger pattern of Brown's life demonstrated his imbalance. Indeed, even the most generous biographers must admit that Brown botched miserably much that he attempted to do. In the years before moving to Kansas, Brown had tried his hand at tanning, sheepherding, surveying, cattle driving, and wool merchandising—all with disastrous results. By 1852 he had suffered fifteen business failures in four different states. Creditors were continually hounding him. "Over the years before his Kansas escapade," John Garraty concluded, "Brown had been a drifter, horse thief and swindler, several times a bankrupt, a failure in everything he attempted."

But this evidence, too, must be considered with circumspection. During the period Brown applied himself in business, the American economy went through repeated cycles of boom and bust. Many hardworking entrepreneurs lost their shirts in business despite their best efforts. Brown's failures over the years may only suggest that he did not have an aptitude for business. His schemes were usually ill-conceived, and he was too inflexible to adapt to the rapidly changing business climate. But to show that Brown was a poor businessman and that much of his life he pursued the wrong career hardly proves him insane. Under those terms, much of the adult population in the United States would belong in asylums.

To call Brown a drifter is once again to condemn most Americans. Physical mobility has been such a salient trait of this nation that one respected historian has used it to distinguish the national character. During some periods of American history as much as 20 percent of the population has moved *each year*. In the 1840s and 1850s, a whole generation of Americans shared Brown's dream of remaking their fortunes in a new place. Many like him found the lure of new frontiers irresistible. And just as many failed along the way, only to pack up and try again.

The accusation that Brown was a swindler, while containing a measure of truth, convicts him on arbitrary evidence. After several of his many business disasters, creditors hounded him in the courts. A few accused him of fraud. Yet Simon Perkins, an Ohio businessman who lost more money to Brown and who was more familiar with his business practices than anyone else, never accused Brown of swindling, even when the two dissolved their partnership in 1854. Again, it was poor business sense rather than a desire to swindle that led Brown into his difficulties.

The horse-thievery charge hinges on the observer's point of view. During the years of fighting in Kansas, Brown occasionally "confiscated" horses from proslavery forces. Those who supported his cause treated the thefts as legitimate acts of war. Brown's enemies never believed he was sincere in his convictions. They accused him of exploiting the tensions in Kansas to act like a brigand. But it is far from clear that Brown ever stole for personal gain. Whatever money he raised, save for small sums he sent his wife, went toward organizing his crusade against slavery. Besides, it is one thing to establish Brown's behavior as antisocial and quite another to find him insane.

From the point of view of the "facts of the case," the question of insanity cannot be easily resolved. The issue becomes further muddled when we consider its theoretical aspects. Theory, as we saw when examining Andrew Jackson, will inevitably affect any judgment in the case. The question, was John Brown insane? frames our inquiry and determines the kind of evidence being sought. And in this case, the question is particularly controversial because it remains unclear just exactly what we are asking. What does it mean, after all, to be "insane"?

Modern psychologists and psychiatrists have given up using the concept of insanity diagnostically because it is a catchall term and too unspecific to have definite meaning. The only major attempt to define the concept more precisely has been in the legal world. In civil law, insanity refers to the inability of individuals to maintain contractual or other legal obligations. Thus, to void a will, an injured party might try to demonstrate that at the time of composition its author was not "of sound mind"—that is, not responsible for his or her actions. Insanity is considered sufficient grounds to commit an individual to a mental hospital. But since it involves such a curtailment of rights and freedom, it is extremely difficult to prove and generally requires the corroboration of several disinterested professionals.

Insanity has been widely used as a defense in criminal cases. By demonstrating that at the time of the crime a client could not distinguish right from wrong or was incapable of determining the nature of the act committed, a lawyer can protect the accused from some of the legal consequences of the act. To find Brown insane, as attorney Hoyt attempted to have the court do, would have been to assert Brown's inability to understand the consequences of his actions at Harpers Ferry. The raid would represent the irrational anger of a deranged man, deserving pity rather than hatred or admiration.

In the legal sense, then, Brown would have to be considered fit to stand trial. He may have been unrealistic in estimating his chance of success at Harpers Ferry, but he repeatedly demonstrated that he knew the consequences of his actions: that he would be arrested and punished if caught; that large portions of American society would condemn him; that, nevertheless, he believed himself in the right. In the legal sense, Brown was quite sane and clearheaded about his actions.

THE TURBULENT CURRENTS OF PSYCHOHISTORY

Yet the court's judgment, accurate as it may have been, is likely to leave us uneasy. To have Brown pronounced sane or insane, in addition to guilty or not guilty, does little to explain, deep down, why the man acted as he did. The verdict leaves us with the same emptiness that impelled psychologists to reject the whole concept of insanity. What drove John Brown to crusade against slavery? To execute in cold blood five men along a Kansas creek? To lead twenty-one men to Harpers Ferry? Other northerners abhorred the institution of slavery, yet only John Brown acted with such vehemence. In that sense he was far from being a normal American; far, even, from being a normal abolitionist. How can we begin to understand the intensity of his deeds?

Here we approach the limits of explanations based on rational motives. To describe John Brown simply by referring to his professed and undoubtedly sincere antislavery ideology is to leave unexplored the fire in the man. Such an approach assumes too easily that consciously expressed motives can be taken at face value. Yet we have already seen, in the case of the bewitched at Salem, that unconscious motivations often play important roles in human behavior. If we are willing to grant that apparently "normal" people sometimes act for reasons beyond those they consciously express, how much more likely is it that we must go beyond rational motives in understanding Brown? It seems only logical that historians should bring to bear the tools of modern psychology to assess the man's personality.

Indeed, a subbranch of history has applied such methods to a wide variety of historical problems. Known as psychohistory, this approach has most often drawn on the discipline of psychoanalysis pioneered by Sigmund Freud, an Austrian physician who propounded his theories during the early twentieth century. Freud assumed that every individual experiences intensely personal conflicts in life that are extremely difficult to resolve. When a person resists coming to terms with such situations in an open and direct manner, that person represses the conflict; that is, he or she is *unable* to think about it consciously. Under such conditions the conflict does not go away; it is merely forced to express itself indirectly. The surface manifestations are disguised in neurotic symptoms such as obsessions, nervous tics, or hysterical behaviors.

By exploring a patient's life history through a process of free association about memories, dreams, and fantasies, the psychoanalyst takes the fragments of evidence presented by the patient and guides him or her toward a recognition of the unconscious forces that have shaped the personality. Thus the analyst seeks to explore the territory of the unconscious much as the historian seeks to make sense out of the jumble of documentary evidence.

What sort of map to the unconscious does Freudian analysis supply? Freud called special attention to two areas he believed were the source of much tension and conflict: instinctual sexual drives and the formative experiences of infancy and childhood. Consider two examples. Every infant receives its first nourishment of mother's milk from the nipple. (More recently, of course, the baby bottle has sometimes served as a substitute.) Freud suggested that every baby experiences a crisis when the mother weans the child from her breast. The infant, Freud argued, has become accustomed to this constant gratification from the mother and experiences rage when the breast is withheld.

Even more famous among Freudian concepts is the notion of an oedipal conflict in young boys. The concept draws its name from Sophocles' *Oedipus Rex*, a Greek tragedy in which Oedipus unknowingly commits incest with his mother. For this "crime" he suffers blindness and exile. Freud contended that somewhere between the ages of three and six, every boy normally passes through an "oedipal phase," during which his consciousness of erotic gratification intensifies. The natural object of attraction is the woman closest to the boy—his mother. Yet the child is aware that this love object is forbidden; it belongs to his father, and therefore the child fears his father's imagined jealous rage.

Many of Freud's concepts—and these examples are only two, sketched in briefest outline—strike laypeople as not only counterintuitive but far-fetched. Yet Freud's psychological principles received increasing respect and attention in the first three decades of the twentieth century, both in the medical community and among the broader public. Psychoanalysts were (and still are) trained in his methods, and patients undergo therapy that often lasts for years.

Although controversial among historians, psychoanalytic theory came to be used by an increasing minority of them. In Chapter 5 for example, we noted that Michael Rogin, writing in the 1970s, analyzed Andrew Jackson from the point of view of his role in removing Indians from the Old Southwest. But Rogin also argued that to explain Indian removal, historians could not rely merely on the motives of simple land hunger and material greed. Using Freudian theory, he pointed out that white-Indian relations during the Jacksonian era were fraught with parent-child symbolism. White treaty negotiators constantly urged Indians to make peace with their "white father," the president of the United States. If friendly tribes did not conclude treaties, Jackson once warned, "We may then be under the necessity of raising the hatchet against our own friends and brothers. Your father the President wishes to avoid this unnatural state of things."

Pursuing the Freudian focus on childhood, Rogin suggested that Jackson's well-known temper as an adult might be connected to the kinds of infant rages posited by Freud. Did the death of Jackson's father before he was born affect Jackson's mother during his infancy? Rogin wondered. "Problems in infancy, involving feeding, weaning, or holding the child, often intensify infantile rage and accentuate later difficulties in the struggle of the child to break securely free of the mother." Rogin quoted Jefferson's description of Jackson "choking with rage" on the Senate floor; he also noted that according to eyewitnesses, Jackson often slobbered and spoke incoherently when excited or angry. "Jackson's slobbering," argued Rogin, "suggests early problems with speech, mouth, and aggression. Speech difficulties often indicate a problematic oral relationship."

In the 1980s and 1990s, however, Freudian theory came under broad attack. Medicine, which for many years had been an art as much as a science, increasingly demanded that hypotheses be rigorously tested and confirmed by replicable experiments. By their very nature, Freudian theories about the unconscious dealt with propositions that were either unverifiable or extremely difficult to confirm. In addition, as more of Freud's letters and papers became public, they shed doubts on the methods of the master. (For years many papers had been available only to scholars sympathetic to psychoanalysis.) Freud established his psychoanalytic method, for example, when treating thirteen young women who he said recounted tales of being seduced when they were children. In fact, Freud's papers reveal that the girls had no such recollections until *after* his analysis was in full swing. Even after Freud used, in his own words, the "strongest compulsion" to "induce" his patients to free-associate or fantasize such stories, he admitted that "they have no feeling of remembering the scenes." This revelation goes to the heart of the evidentiary problem. If such memories are not part of the patient's recollection until an analyst strongly induces them, how can we decide whether the memories truly spring from the unconscious rather than merely from the suggestive comments of the analyst?

Given the strong challenges to Freudian theory, its value for analyzing *any* person seems at the very least in serious doubt—let alone for analyzing a historical figure like John Brown, who cannot be subjected to a process of lengthy psychoanalysis on the couch. Must we throw up our hands at the possibility of understanding the inner workings of Brown's deepest motivations? It seems to us that the historian still has options.

Even Frederick Crews, one of Freud's most vocal literary critics, has suggested that it is possible to "dissent" from the rigid orthodoxy of psychoanalytic theory "without forsaking the most promising aspects of psychoanalysis—its attentiveness to signs of conflict, its hospitality to multiple significance, its ideas of ambivalence, identification, repression, and projection." Freud wished his patients to free-associate about childhood experiences in part because he recognized that unexpected patterns often emerged from these memories: recurring images, fears, preoccupations. Psychologists—whether they are strict Freudians or not—have learned to pay close attention to such patterns.

THE MOTIVES OF A SON— AND A FATHER

Although John Brown never underwent a psychological examination about his childhood, he has provided us, as it happens, with the means of conducting one ourselves. At the age of fifty-seven, Brown wrote a long letter addressed to a thirteen-year-old boy named Harry Stearns. Harry was the son of one of Brown's wealthiest financial patrons. In the letter, Brown told the story of "a certain boy of my acquaintance" who, "for convenience," he called John. This name was especially convenient because the boy was none other than Brown himself. The letter is one of the few suriving sources of information about Brown's childhood. It is reprinted here with only a few omissions of routine biographical data.

I can not tell you of anything in the first Four years of John's life worth mentioning save that at that *early age* he was tempted by Three large Brass Pins belonging to a girl who lived in the family & *stole them*. In this he was detected by his Mother; & after having a full day to think of the wrong; received from her a thorough whipping. When he was Five years old his Father moved to Ohio; then a wilderness filled with wild beasts, & Indians. During the long journey, which was performed in part or mostly with an *ox-team*; he was called on by turns to assist a boy Five years older (who had been adopted by his Father & Mother) & learned to think he could accomplish *smart things* by driving the Cows; & riding the horses. Sometimes he met with Rattle Snakes which were very large; & which some of the company generally managed to kill. After getting to Ohio in 1805 he was for some time rather afraid of the Indians, & of their Rifles; but this soon wore off: & he used to hang about them quite as much as was consistent with good manners; & learned a trifle of their talk. His father learned to dress Deer Skins, & at 6 years old John was installed a young Buck Skin. He was perhaps rather observing as he ever after remembered the entire process of Deer Skin *dressing;* so that he could at any time dress his own leather such as Squirel, Raccoon, Cat, Wolf and Dog Skins, and also learned to make Whip Lashes, which brought him some change at times, & was of considerable service in many ways. At Six years old he began to be a rambler in the wild new country finding birds and squirrels and sometimes a wild Turkey's nest. But about this period he was placed in the school of *adversity;* which my young friend was a most necessary part of his early training. You may *laugh* when you come to read about it; but these were *sore trials* to John: whose earthly treasures were very *few & small*. These were the beginning of a severe but *much needed course* of discipline which he afterwards was to pass through; & which it is to be hoped has learned him before this time that the Heavenly Father sees it best to take all the little things out of his hands which he has ever placed in them. When John was in his Sixth year a poor *Indian boy* gave him a Yellow Marble the first he had ever seen. This he thought a great deal of; & kept it a good while; but at last *he lost* it beyond recovery. *It took years to heal the wound* & I *think* he cried at times about it. About Five months after this he caught a young Squirrel tearing off his tail in doing it; & getting severely bitten at the same time himself. He however held on *to the little bob tail Squirrel;* & finally got him perfectly tamed, so that he almost idolized his pet. *This too he lost;* by its wandering away; or by getting killed; & for a year or two John was *in mourning;* and looking at all the Squirrels he could see to try & discover Bobtail, *if possible.* I must not neglect to tell you of a verry *bad and foolish* habbit to which John was somewhat addicted. I mean *telling lies;* generally to screen himself from blame; or from punishment. He could not well endure to be reproached; & I now think had he been oftener encouraged to be entirely frank; *by making frankness a kind of atonement* for some of his faults; he would not have been so often guilty of this fault; nor have been (in after life) obliged to struggle *so long* with *so mean* a habit.

John was never *quarelsome;* but was *excessively* fond of the *hardest & roughest* kind of plays; & could *never get enough* [of] them. Indeed when for a short time he was sometimes sent to School the opportunity it afforded to wrestle & Snow ball & run & jump & knock off old seedy Wool hats; offered to him almost the only compensation for the confinement, & restraints of school. I need not tell you that with such a feeling & but little chance of going to school *at all:* he did not become much of a schollar. He would always choose to stay at home & work hard rather than be sent to school; & during the warm season might generally be seen *barefooted & bareheaded:* with Buck skin Breeches suspended often with one leather strap over his shoulder but sometimes with Two. To be sent off through the wilderness alone to very considerable distances was particularly his delight; & in this he was often indulged so that by the time he was Twelve years old he was sent off more than a Hundred Miles with companies of cattle; & he would have thought his character much injured had he been obliged to be helped in any such job. This was a boyish kind of feeling but characteristic however.

At Eight years old, John was left a Motherless boy which loss was complete and pearmanent for notwithstanding his Father again married to a sensible, intelligent, and on many accounts a very estimable woman; yet he never *adopted her in feeling;* but continued to pine after his own Mother for years. This opperated very unfavorably upon him; as he was both naturally fond of females; &, withall, extremely diffident; & deprived him of a suitable connecting link between the different sexes; the want of which might under some circumstances, have proved his ruin. . . .

During the war with England [in 1812] a circumstance occured that in the end made him a most *determined Abolitionist:* & led him to declare, or *Swear: Eternal war* with Slavery. He was staying for a short time with a very gentlemanly landlord since a United States Marshall who held a slave boy near his own age very active, inteligent and good feeling; & to whom John was under considerable obligation for numerous little acts of kindness. *The master* made a great pet of John: brought him to table with his first company; & friends; called their attention to every little smart thing he *said or did:* & to the fact of his being more than a hundred miles from home with a company of cattle alone; while the *negro boy* (who was fully if not more than his equal) was badly clothed, poorly fed; *& lodged in cold weather;* & beaten before his eyes with Iron Shovels or any other thing that came first to hand. This brought John to reflect on the wretched, hopeless condition, of *Fatherless & Motherless* slave *children:* for such children have neither Fathers or Mothers to protect, & provide for them. He sometimes would raise the question *is God their Father? . . .*

I had like to have forgotten to tell you of one of John's misfortunes which set rather hard on him while a young boy. He had by some means *perhaps* by gift of his father become the owner of a little Ewe Lamb which did finely till it was about Two Thirds grown; & then sickened & died. This brought another protracted *mourning season:* not that he felt the pecuniary loss so much: for that was never his disposition; but so strong & earnest were his attachments.

John had been taught from earliest childhood to "fear God and keep his commandments;" & though quite skeptical he had always by turns felt much serious doubt as to his future well being; & about this time became to some extent a convert to Christianity & ever after a firm believer in the divine authenticity of the Bible. With this book he became very familiar, & possessed a most unusual memory of its entire contents.

Now some of the things I have been *telling of;* were just such as I would recommend to you: & I would like to know that you had selected these out; & adopted them as part of your own plan of life; & I wish you to have some *deffinite plan.* Many seem to have none; & others never stick to any that they do form. This was not the case with John. He followed up with *tenacity* whatever he set about so long as it answered his general purpose; & hence he rarely failed in some good degree to effect the things he undertook. This was so much the case that he *habitually expected to succeed* in his undertakings. With this feeling *should be coupled;* the consciousness that our plans are right in themselves.

During the period I have named, John had acquired a kind of ownership to certain animals of some little value but as he had come to understand that the *title of minors* might be a little imperfect: he had recourse to various means in order to secure a more *independent;* & perfect right of property. One of those means was to exchange with his Father for something of far less value. Another was by trading with others persons for something his Father had never owned. Older persons have some times found difficulty with *titles.*

From Fifteen to Twenty years old, he spent most of his time working at the Tanner & Currier's trade keeping Bachelors hall; & he officiating as Cook; & for most of the time as foreman of the establishment under his Father. During this period he found much trouble with some of the bad habits I have mentioned & with some that I have not told you off: his conscience urging him forward with great power in this matter: but his close attention to *business;* & success in its management, together with the way he got along with a company of men, & boys; made him quite a favorite with the serious & more inteligent portion of older persons. This was so much the case; & secured for him so many little notices from those he esteemed; that his vanity was very much fed by it: & he came forward to manhood quite full of self-conceit; & self-confident; notwithstanding his *extreme* bashfulness. A younger brother used sometimes to remind him of this: & to repeat to him *this expression* which you may somewhere find, "A King against whom there is no rising up." The habit so early formed of being obeyed rendered him in after life too much disposed to speak in an imperious or dictating way. From Fifteen years & upward he felt a good deal of anxiety to learn; but could only read & studdy a little; both for want of time; & on account of inflammation of the eyes. He however managed by the help of books to make himself tolerably well acquainted with common arithmetic; & Surveying; which he practiced more or less after he was Twenty years old.

Before exploring the letter's deeper psychological significance, it may be worth reminding ourselves what a straightforward reading of the document provides. Attention would naturally center on Brown's striking tale of how, as a twelve-year-old, he was first roused to oppose slavery. Shocked by the cruel treatment of his young black friend, John was further incensed by the unfair and contrasting treatment he benefited from simply because he was white. This vivid, emotional experience seems to go a good way toward explaining why the evil of slavery weighed so heavily on Brown's mind. In an article on the motivations behind the raid at Harpers Ferry, this anecdote is quite clearly the one piece of evidence worth extracting from the long letter. The additional material on Brown's childhood, which often seems to ramble incoherently, might be included in a book-length biography of Brown but hardly seems relevant to an article that must quickly get to the heart of the man's involvement with abolition.

Yet when we look more closely, Brown's story of the mistreated young slave does not go very far toward explaining Brown's motives. In a land where slavery was central to the culture, hundreds, even thousands, of young white boys must have had experiences in which black playmates were unfairly whipped, degraded, and treated as inferiors. Nonetheless, many of those boys went on to become slaveholders. Furthermore, although some undoubtedly developed a strong dislike of slavery (Abraham Lincoln among them[1]), none felt compelled to mount the kind of campaigns Brown did in Kansas and at Harpers Ferry. Why did Brown's rather commonplace experience make such a strong impression on him?

The answer to that question may be learned if we do not dismiss the other portions of Brown's childhood experiences as irrelevant but instead examine them for clues to his psychological development. So let us turn, for a moment, from a direct examination of Brown's abolitionism to the other elements of the letter to Harry Stearns. In doing so we must consider each of Brown's stories, illustrations, and comments with care, keeping in mind Freud's stress on unconscious motivations. In previous chapters we have seen that historians must always treat primary sources skeptically, identifying the personal perspectives and biases that may influence the writer. Psychoanalytic theory requires us to take that skepticism one step further, assuming not only that the evidence may be influenced by unstated motivations (such as Brown's wishing to impress Harry Stearns's father with his virtue) but also that some, even the most powerful of Brown's motivations, may be unconscious—hidden even from Brown himself.

At first glance the narrative appears to recount fairly ordinary events in a child's life. Who, after all, has not cried one time or another at the loss of a pet, or has not been proud of accomplishments like driving cows and riding horses? Yet we must remember that these events are only a few selected from among thousands in Brown's childhood, events meaningful enough to him

---

1. As a young man, Lincoln was reputed to have been strongly moved by the sight of slaves being auctioned in New Orleans.

that he has remembered and related them more than fifty years later. Why did Brown retain these memories rather than others? What suggestive images and themes recur? Because psychoanalytic theory emphasizes the importance of parental relationships, we may begin by examining Brown's relationship with his mother and father.

Of the two parents, John's mother is the most visible in this letter, and it is clear that Brown loved her dearly. Notice the language describing his mother's death. "John was left a Motherless boy," he writes—not the simpler and less revealing, "John's mother died," which places the emphasis on the mother rather than on the loss incurred by the "Motherless boy." Furthermore, the loss was "complete and pearmanent." Brown never grew to love his new mother and "continued to pine after his own Mother for years."

John's father, at first glance, appears to have taken a less prominent role in the letter, either positively or negatively. True, Owen Brown does teach John the art of dressing skins (and also, John takes care to note, of making "Whip Lashes"); but the attention centers not on the father's devoted teaching so much as John's remarkable ability to learn by watching his father only once. Perhaps most revealing, however, is an ambiguous passage in which Brown's father does *not* appear yet plays a substantial, hidden role. The relevant paragraph begins by noting that John "had acquired a kind of ownership to certain animals of some little value." From earlier parts of the letter, we are aware how much these pets meant to him—the loss of the squirrel "Bobtail" (which he "almost idolized") and later the ewe lamb (which he had *"perhaps"* by gift of his father become the owner). Now, Brown indicates that he had owned other animals, but apparently not completely. He is curiously circumspect about explaining why: the ownership, he says, was incomplete because "the *title of minors*" was "a little imperfect." Apparently, animals that he thought he owned were taken away from him, on the grounds that he did not have "title" to them as a minor. So John, being extremely strong-willed despite his bashfulness, determinedly set out "to secure a more *independent;* & perfect right of property." Significantly, this question of ownership appears to have occurred more than once, for Brown noted that he devised "various means" to deal with it.

What is happening here? Brown's evasive language makes the situation difficult to reconstruct, but certain outlines emerge. The only logical person who might repeatedly prevent John from obtaining full "title" to his pets was his father, Owen. Why Owen objected is never stated, but several ideas suggest themselves. Conceivably the elder Brown needed one of John's "pet" sheep or cows to feed the family or to sell for income. Furthermore, in a frontier settlement where unfenced woodlands merged with small farms, wild or stray domestic animals might have roamed onto the Brown farm from time to time. If young John Brown found them, he would likely have claimed them as pets, only to discover that the animal was on father Owen's land—and duly appropriated for food or income.

Whatever the specific situations, young Brown repeatedly attempted to secure his property through one of two means. "One of those means was to exchange with his Father for something of far less value." The implication is that in some cases Owen Brown allowed John to treat animals as pets if they were formally "purchased" from his father for a token fee ("something of far less value"). In such cases, Owen Brown acted kindly toward his son, though rigorously insisting that the formalities of "property" and "title" be observed. But on other occasions John apparently could not convince his father to spare such pets, for the letter indicates that another means of obtaining them "was by trading with others persons for something his Father had never owned." If Owen would not give him pets, John would be able to get them from more willing neighbors.

The conflict of ownership between father and son obviously left a strong imprint. More than forty years later, Brown still vividly remembered how Owen confiscated his pets, as well as the means he worked out to satisfy, or in some cases actually to evade, his father's authority. Even more important, the evasive language in the passage demonstrates that Brown remained unable to acknowledge his anger openly. In effect, the paragraph reveals a concealed hostility that Brown was still carrying toward his father. The last sentence amounts to a condemnation, but the son could only express his anger indirectly, through use of a generality: "Older persons have some times found difficulty with *titles.*"

Unconsciously, Brown may have been applying the last phrase to himself as well. For the crucial message of the passage is not Brown's hostility toward his father, but the issues through which the hostility is expressed, that is to say, title and ownership. Indeed, a psychoanalytic interpretation of Brown's childhood suggests that throughout his life, Brown never fully resolved the question of "titles" of his own identity. The more the letter is probed, the more it reveals an obsession with property and title. Brown continually describes himself as finding some piece of "property," forming strong attachments to it, and then losing it and severely mourning the loss.

What, after all, is the very first experience in Brown's life that he can recall? Before the age of four, John steals three brass pins, discovers that his title to them is imperfect, has them taken away, and is severely whipped. At six, John receives a treasured yellow marble, loses it, and mourns for "years." Soon afterward, John catches a squirrel, pulling its tail off in the process; then tames and idolizes it; then loses it and mourns another year or two. At eight, John loses another precious possession—his mother—and pines after her for years. Then comes the story of the lamb and, later, his conflicts with his father over the ownership of other pets. The religious moral drawn from these lessons ("a severe but *much needed course* of discipline") was that "the Heavenly Father sees it best to take all the little things out of his hands which he has ever placed in them." Clearly, the process of becoming an independent adult was for John Brown a continuing effort to reconcile his guilt and anger over losing property with his fierce desire to become truly independent, to possess clear title to his own pets, to become a "propertied" father like Owen and—dare we say it?—even like God the father himself. Paradoxically, only when Brown internalized and accepted the authority of

John Brown, the kindly father: Brown's daughter Ruth remembered the following incident from her childhood: "When I first began to go to school, I found a piece of calico one day behind one of the benches,—it was not large, but seemed quite a treasure to me, and I did not show it to any one until I got home. Father heard me then telling about it, and said, 'Don't you know what girl lost it?' I told him I did not. 'Well, when you go to school tomorrow take it with you, and find out if you can who lost it. It is a trifling thing, but always remember that if you should lose anything you valued, no matter how small, *you* would want the person that found it to give it back to you.'"

his fathers could he then act the part of a stern, loving parent himself. Submission to his father's authority made it possible for him to accept as legitimate his authority over his own "pets."

The pattern of Brown's struggle for autonomy is reflected in the role he played as father to his own children. Owen Brown had been a stern disciplinarian, in part because he had felt the lack of a strong hand in his own childhood. John internalized and emulated this severe approach early on. When his younger brother, Salmon, had been pardoned for some misdeed by a boarding-school teacher, John went to the teacher and told him that "if Salmon had done this thing at home, father would have punished him. I know he would expect you to punish him now for doing this—and if you don't, I shall." When the schoolmaster persisted in his lenience, John was reported to have given Salmon a "severe flogging." As a parent, Brown's discipline was equally harsh. When his three-year-old son Jason claimed that a certain dream actually had occurred, Brown felt obliged to whip the boy for lying. The father's immense ambivalence in such a situation was evidenced by the tears that welled up in his eyes as he performed the whipping.

For Brown, even sins took on an aspect of property. The father kept a detailed account book of his son John Jr.'s transgressions, along with the number of whiplashes each sin deserved. Recalled the son:

> On a certain Sunday morning he invited me to accompany him from the house to the tannery, saying that he had concluded it was time for a settlement. We

went into the upper or finishing room, and after a long and tearful talk over my faults, he again showed me my account, which exhibited a fearful footing up of *debits*. . . . I then paid about one-third of the debt, reckoned in strokes from a nicely-prepared blue-beech switch, laid on "masterly." Then, to my utter astonishment, father stripped off his shirt, and, seating himself on a block, gave me the whip and bade me "lay it on" to his bare back. I dared not refuse to obey, but at first I did not strike hard. "Harder!" he said; "harder, harder!" until he received the *balance of the account*. Small drops of blood showed on his back where the tip end of the tingling beech cut through. Thus ended the account and settlement, which was also my first practical illustration of the Doctrine of Atonement.

In this astonishing tableau, Brown's personal conflicts are vividly reflected. The father punishes the son as justice demands, yet Brown also plays the wayward son himself. And as John Brown Jr. recognized only later, his father was consciously assuming the mantle of Christ, whom the heavenly Father had permitted humankind to crucify and punish, in order that other children's sins would be forgiven.

The upshot of such discipline was that Brown's sons harbored a similar ambivalence toward their father—an intense feeling of loyalty and submission countered by a strong desire for independence. The contradiction of such training became apparent to one of Brown's sons, Watson, during the raid on Harpers Ferry. "The trouble is," Watson remarked to his father, "you want your boys to be brave as tigers, and still afraid of you." "And that was perfectly true," agreed Salmon Brown, another son.

Psychoanalytic insight has thus helped to reveal some of John Brown's most intense personal conflicts: his ambivalence toward his father's strict discipline, the paradox of his struggle to internalize and accept his father's authority in order to become independent himself, and his excessive concern with property and "pets" as a means of defining his independence. Having exposed these themes, let us now return to the starting point of our original analysis of the letter—the anecdote about Brown and the young slave. Suddenly, what had seemed a straightforward tale is filled with immensely suggestive vocabulary, whose overtones reveal a great deal. The passage is worth reading once again:

During the war with England a circumstance occurred that in the end made him a most *determined Abolitionist*: & led him to declare, or *Swear: Eternal war* with Slavery. He was staying for a short time with a very gentlemanly landlord since a United States Marshall who held a slave boy near his own age very active, inteligent and good feeling; & to whom John was under considerable obligation for numerous little acts of kindness. *The master* made a great pet of John: brought him to table with his first company; & friends; called their attention to every little smart thing he *said or did*; & to the fact of his being more than a hundred miles from home with a company of cattle alone; while the *negro boy* (who was fully if not more than his equal) was badly clothed, poorly fed; *& lodged in cold weather*; & beaten before his eyes with Iron Shovels or any other

John Brown, the stern father: Brown was influenced in his harsh discipline by his father, Owen (*left*), and in turn influenced his own son, John Jr. (*right*). Father John kept a detailed account book of young John's sinful acts, along with the number of whiplashes each sin deserved. Even sins, it seemed, were carefully enumerated as property.

thing that came first to hand. This brought John to reflect on the wretched, hopeless condition, of *Fatherless & Motherless* slave *children:* for such children have neither Fathers or Mothers to protect, & provide for them. He sometimes would raise the question *is God their Father?*

Upon this second reading, it becomes evident that Brown's language and metaphors here are full of references to parental relationships, dependence, and authority. John stayed with a "very gentlemanly landlord" who "made a great pet of John," treating the boy just as John treated his own pets. At the same time, however, this gentlemanly father acted like no father at all to the negro boy, beating him unmercifully. This led John "to reflect on the wretched, hopeless condition, of *Fatherless & Motherless* slave *children*." "Is God their Father?" he asked himself.

The situation confronted young Brown with two starkly contrasting models of a father, corresponding with the boy's own ambivalent feelings toward Owen. Naturally, John wanted his own father to discipline him less harshly. He wanted to be treated as a "pet," as his own animals were treated, as this gentleman treated him. Similarly, he identified with the negro boy, an innocent lad who was being punished just as Owen Brown sometimes punished John. Yet like all boys, he also identified with his own father. He desired as well as hated the power that Owen wielded over him and that this gentleman wielded over the negro boy. He thus felt the tug of two conflicting loyalties. To use the religious imagery so familiar to that age, John Brown wanted to grow up and act both as God the merciful Father and as God the righteous Judge.

This ambivalent father-son relationship suggests that Brown's intense life-long identification with black slaves might well have sprung from the struggle he experienced with paternal discipline. Helping slaves was ultimately a means of helping himself without consciously recognizing the source of his emotions and convictions. He could channel the repressed hostility toward his father into a more acceptable form—hatred of the slaveholders, another class of paternalistic oppressors who cruelly whipped their charges. In attacking the planters, Brown relieved the sense of guilt he harbored for secretly wishing to destroy his father. After all, God the implacable Father and Judge was using Brown as his instrument for bringing justice to the world. At the same time, by protecting and defending the helpless slaves, Brown carried out God's will as a merciful father. In liberating the black nation, he could free himself. In some indirect yet significant way, the raid at Harpers Ferry involved the working out of psychological turmoil that had troubled Brown since childhood.

Does all this speculation lead us then to assume that childhood neuroses rather than moral conviction dictated Brown's actions? Few historians would go that far. A full explanation of any person's actions and beliefs must, in the end, be multicausal if it is to reflect the complexity of real life. We cannot minimize the sincerity—nor the nobility—of Brown's belief in the brotherhood of black people and white people. Yet the stirrings of deeply rooted unconscious forces can be neglected no more than the more rational components of behavior can.

This psychological interpretation, then, is not offered as definitive or exclusive. And our brief exposition of one letter constitutes only one small part of what should properly be a much larger analysis of Brown's personality and career. But the exposition is ample enough to suggest how fruitful a broadly psychoanalytical approach can be. As Michael Rogin suggested in the case of Andrew Jackson, psychohistory provides historians with a theory that sensitizes them to profitable themes, motifs, and vocabularies. An awareness of recurring tensions stemming from Brown's childhood makes it possible to appreciate how his personal sufferings incorporated the larger events of the period.

At the moment Brown transcended his life of failure, he forced his generation to identify either positively or negatively with the action he took to liberate black Americans. His act of violence was appropriate to what Oates described as "the violent, irrational, and paradoxical times in which he lived." Given Brown's profoundly religious nature and commitment to human liberty and equality, he could not be at peace until his society recognized the contradiction between its religious and political ideals and the existence of slavery.

In the end, John Brown turned the tables on society. His raid on Harpers Ferry pressed his fellow Americans to consider whether it was not actually their values, and society's, that were immoral and "abnormal." The outbreak of civil war, after all, demonstrated that American society was so maladjusted and so divided that it could not remain a "normal," integrated whole without violently purging itself. If Brown's raid was an isolated act of a disturbed man, why did it drive an entire generation to the brink of war? Why did Brown's generation find it impossible to agree about the meaning of Harpers Ferry? As C. Vann Woodward concluded, the importance lay not so much in the man or event, but in the use made of them by northern and southern partisans. For every Emerson or Thoreau who pronounced the raid the work of a saint, a southern fire-eater condemned the venture as the villainy of all northerners.

None of these actors in the historical drama paid much attention to evidence. A crisis mentality thwarted any attempts at understanding or reconciliation. In the fury of mutual recrimination, both sides lost sight of the man who had provoked the public outcry and propelled the nation toward war. In such times it will always be, as abolitionist Wendell Phillips remarked, "hard to tell who's mad."

Additional Reading

The best of modern biographies on John Brown is Stephen Oates, *To Purge This Land with Blood* (New York, 1970). Oates's treatment is evenhanded, scholarly, and stirring in its narrative. (Other modern biographies include studies by Jules C. Abels and Richard O. Boyer, both published during the 1970s.) Oswald Garrison Villard, *John Brown, 1800–1859: A Biography Fifty Years After* (Boston, 1910) is an older work worth reading. It draws on and excerpts many primary sources. C. Vann Woodward, "John Brown's Private War" is one of the best short interpretive essays available on the raid and can be found in his *Burden of Southern History* (Baton Rouge, LA, 1968). For a detailed account of Brown's earlier doings in Kansas, see James C. Malin, *John Brown and the Legacy of Fifty-Six* (Philadelphia, 1942). Brown's relationship with his conspirators is grippingly told in Edward J. Renehan Jr., *The Secret Six: The True Tale of the Men Who Conspired with John Brown* (New York, 1995). Franklin B. Sanborn, *The Life and Letters of John Brown* (Boston, 1891), an older biography unabashedly sympathetic to Brown, contains many valuable personal letters. The fullest collection of materials on the raid and trial is *The Life, Trial, and Execution of John Brown* (New York, 1859).

The debate over John Brown's mental state continues. For additional perspectives see Paul Finkelman, ed., *His Soul Goes Marching On: Responses to John Brown and the Harpers Ferry Raid* (Charlottesville, VA, 1995), in particular the essays by Bertram Wyatt-Brown (pp. 10–40) and Robert E. McGlone, who discusses the political considerations of contemporaries' debates about Brown's sanity (pp. 213–252). McGlone's forthcoming *Apocalyptic Visions: John Brown's Witness against Slavery* will argue that Brown suffered from a bipolar depressive condition.

With so little space available in this chapter, we chose to avoid the intricacies of the debates over the present state of Freudian psychology. Readers who would like a biography of Sigmund Freud should turn to Peter Gay's sympathetic *Freud: A Life for Our Time* (New York, 1988). For a good introduction to Freudian theory, see Charles Brenner, *An Elementary Textbook of Psychoanalysis* (New York, 1974). In 1998 the Library of Congress (which holds many of Freud's papers, some of them still restricted in access) mounted an exhibition on Freud. The accompanying book provides a number of useful perspectives: Michael S. Roth, ed., *Freud: Conflict and Culture—Essays on His Life, Work, and Legacy* (New York, 1998). The assault on Freud and his methods receives the best brief treatment in Frederick Crews, ed., *Unauthorized Freud: Doubters Confront a Legend* (New York, 1998). One of the weightiest challenges to the scientific validity of Freudian theory came from Adolf Grünbaum, *The Foundations of Psychoanalysis* (Berkeley, CA, 1984). Other critical works include another voluminous study, Malcolm Macmillan's *Freud Evaluated: The Completed Arc* (Cambridge, MA, 1997), and the more succinct analysis by Allen Esterson, *Seductive Mirage: An Exploration of the Work of Sigmund Freud* (Chicago, 1993).

Like psychoanalysis itself, psychohistory has always been a tempestuous field. It was formally acknowledged when historian William L. Langer used his presidential address to the American Historical Association to call for increased use of psychoanalytic techniques. "The Next Assignment," Langer's address, appears in the *American Historical Review* 63 (January 1958): 283–304. But Freud himself had dabbled in historical waters, with disastrous results, in (among other studies) a psychobiography coauthored with William Bullitt entitled *Thomas Woodrow Wilson* (Boston, reprinted 1968). More responsible efforts include Erik Erikson's biographies *Young Man Luther* (New York, 1958) and *Gandhi's Truth* (New York, 1969). The methods of psychohistory are discussed in Robert J. Lifton, ed., *Explorations in Psychohistory* (New York, 1974). George M. Kren and Leon H. Rappoport, eds., *Varieties of Psychohistory* (New York, 1976), and Robert J. Brugger, ed., *Our Selves/Our Past: Psychological Approaches to American History* (Baltimore, 1981) are also useful. For recent examples of the discipline, see current issues of the *Journal of Psychohistory*. David E. Stannard applies the Freudian critique to the problems of psychohistory in *Shrinking History* (New York, 1980). Peter Gay's brief for the defense, *Freud for Historians* (New York, 1985), strikes us as disappointing, and Stannard provides a scathing commentary in "Grand Illusions," *Reviews in American History* 14, 2 (June 1986): 289–308.

As professed amateurs in the psychoanalytic field, we would like to thank Dr. David Musto, able psychiatrist and historian, for a fine introduction to the territory in his graduate seminars at Yale University. In evaluating John Brown, we also consulted with two practicing psychiatrists, both aware of the possibilities and limitations of their discipline: Dr. Geoff Linburn of the MIT mental health staff and Dr. Eric Berger of Yale psychiatric faculty. Finally, our friend Dr. John Rugge brought into focus Brown's striking concern for property and ownership.

Interactive Learning

The *Primary Source Investigator* provides materials that explore the question of the "madness of John Brown." Images depicting Brown as the kindly father, the terrorist, and the martyr illustrate the many sides of Brown. Newspaper articles, military demands for surrender, and depictions of Brown just before his death probe the questions of Brown's responsibility and his sanity.

CHAPTER 8
The View from the Bottom Rail

Thunder. From across the swamps and salt marshes of the Carolina coast came the distant, repetitive pounding. Thunder out of a clear blue sky. Down at the slave quarters, young Sam Mitchell heard the noise and wondered. In Beaufort, the nearby village, planter John Chaplin heard too, and dashed for his carriage. The drive back to his plantation was as quick as Chaplin could make it. Once home, he ordered his wife and children to pack; then he looked for his slaves. The flatboat must be made ready, he told them; the family was going to Charleston. He needed eight men at the oars. One of the slaves, Sam Mitchell's father, brought the news to his wife and son at the slave quarters. "You ain't gonna row no boat to Charleston," the wife snapped, "you go out dat back door and keep agoing." Young Sam was mystified by all the commotion. How could it thunder without a cloud in the sky? "Son, dat ain't no t'under," explained the mother, "dat Yankee come to gib you freedom."

The pounding of the guns came relatively quickly to Beaufort—November of 1861, only seven months after the first hostilities at Fort Sumter. Yet it was only a matter of time before the thunder of freedom rolled across the rest of the South, from the bayous and deltas of Louisiana in 1862 to the farms around Richmond in 1865. And as the guns of the Union spoke, thousands of Sam Mitchells experienced their own unforgettable moments. Freedom was coming to a nation of four million slaves.

To most slaves, the men in the blue coats were foreigners. As foreigners, they were sometimes suspect. Many southern masters painted the prospect of northern invasion in deliberately lurid colors. Union soldiers, one Tennessee slave was told, "got long horns on their heads, and tushes [pointed teeth] in their mouths, and eyes sticking out like a cow! They're mean old things." A fearful Mississippi slave refused to come down out of a tree until the Union soldier below her took off his cap and demonstrated he had no horns. Many slaves, however, took such tales with more than a grain of salt. "We all hear 'bout dem Yankees," a Carolina slave told his overseer. "Folks tell we they has horns and a tail . . . Wen I see dem coming I shall run like

177

This slave family lived on a plantation at Beaufort, South Carolina, not far from the plantation where Sam Mitchell heard the thunder of northern guns in 1861. The photograph was taken after northern forces had occupied the Sea Islands area.

all possess." But as soon as the overseer fled, leaving the plantation in the slaves' care, the tune changed: "Good-by, ole man, good-by. That's right. Skedaddle as fast as you kin. . . . We's gwine to run sure enough; but we knows the Yankees, an' we runs that way."

For some slaves, the ingrained habits, the bond of loyalty, or the fear of alternatives led them to side with their masters. Faithful slaves hid valuable silver, persuaded Yankees that their departed masters were actually Union sympathizers, or feigned contagious illness in order to scare off marauding soldiers. One slave even led Yankees right to the plantation beehives. "De Yankees forgot all about de meat an' things dey done stole," she noted with satisfaction; "they took off down de road at a run." But in many cases, the conflict between loyalty and freedom caused confusion and anguish. A Georgia couple, both more than sixty years old, greeted the advance of Sherman's soldiers calmly and with apparent lack of interest. They seemed entirely content to remain under the care of their master instead of joining the mass of slaves flocking along behind Sherman's troops. As the soldiers prepared to leave, however, the old woman suddenly stood up, a "fierce, almost devilish" look in her eyes, and turned to her husband. "What you sit dar for?" she asked vehemently. "You s'pose I wait sixty years for nutten? Don't yer see de door open? I'se follow my child; I not stay. Yes, anudder day I goes 'long wid dese people; yes, sar, I walks till I drop in my tracks."

Other slaves felt no hesitation about choosing freedom; indeed, they found it difficult to contain their joy. One woman, who overheard the news of emancipation just before she was to serve her master's dinner, asked to be excused because she had to get water from a nearby spring. Once she had reached the seclusion of the spring, she allowed her feelings free rein.

> I jump up and scream, "Glory, glory hallelujah to Jesus! I'se free! I'se free! Glory to God, you come down an' free us; no big man could do it." An' I got sort o' scared, afeared somebody hear me, an' I takes another good look, an' fall on de goun' an' roll over, an' kiss de gound' fo' de Lord's sake, I's so full o' praise to Masser Jesus.

To the newly freed slaves, it seemed as if the world had been turned upside down. Rich and powerful masters were fleeing before Yankees, while freed slaves were left with the run of the plantation. The situation was summed up succinctly by one black soldier who was surprised—and delighted—to find his former master among the prisoners he was guarding. "Hello, massa!" he said cheerfully, "bottom rail top dis time!"

RECOVERING THE FREEDPEOPLE'S POINT OF VIEW

The freeing of four million black slaves surely ranks as one of the major events in American history. Yet the story has not been an easy one to tell. To understand the personal trials and triumphs of the newly liberated slaves, or "freedpeople" as they have come to be called,[1] historians must draw on the personal experiences of those at the center of the drama. They must recreate the freedpeople's point of view. But slaves had occupied the lowest level of America's social and economic scale. They sat, as the black soldier correctly noted, on the bottom rail of the fence. For several reasons, that social reality has made it more difficult for historians to recover the freedpeople's point of view.

In the first place, most traditional histories have suffered from a natural "top-rail" bias. They have most often taken as their subjects members of the higher social classes. Histories cannot be written without the aid of documentary raw material, and by and large, those on the top rails of society have produced the most voluminous records. Having been privileged to receive

---

1. White contemporaries of the newly freed slaves referred to them as freedmen. More recently historians have preferred the gender-neutral term *freedpeople*, which we will use here except when quoting primary sources.

"**Git away from dat dar fence white man** or I'll make Old Abe's Gun smoke at you. I can hardly hold de ball back now.—De bottom rails on top now." More than one former slave used the image of the "bottom rail on top" to define the transformation wrought by the Civil War. This watercolor sketch was made by a Confederate soldier being held prisoner by Union forces at Point Lookout, Maryland.

an education, members of the middle and upper classes are more apt to publish memoirs, keep diaries, or write letters. As leaders of society who make decisions, they are the subjects of official minutes and records. They are more often written about and commented on by their contemporaries.

At the other end of the social spectrum, ordinary folk lead lives that are often less documented. While political leaders involve themselves in what appears to be one momentous issue after another, the work of farmers and laborers is often repetitive and appears to have little effect on the course of history. The decade of the 1970s, however, saw an increasing interest by historians in the writing of social histories that would shed greater light on the lives of ordinary people. In Chapter 1, for example, we saw that a knowledge of the social and economic position of the serving class was essential to understanding the volatile society of early Virginia. Similarly, in Chapter 2 we turned to the social tensions of ordinary farmers in order to explore the alliances behind the witchcraft controversy at Salem.

Although social historians have found it challenging to piece together the lives of any anonymous class of Americans, reconstructing the perspective of enslaved African Americans has proved particularly challenging. In the years before the Civil War, not only were slaves discouraged from learning to read and write, southern legislatures passed slave codes that flatly forbade whites to teach them. The laws were not entirely effective. A few blacks employed as drivers on large plantations learned to read and correspond so that their absent masters might send them instructions. Some black preachers were also literate. Still, most reading remained a clandestine affair, done out of sight of the master or other whites. During the war, a literate slave named Squires Jackson was eagerly scanning a newspaper for word of northern victories when his master unexpectedly entered the room and demanded to know what the slave was doing. The surprised reader deftly turned the newspaper upside down, put on a foolish grin, and said, "Confederates done won the war!" The master laughed and went about his business.

Even though most slaves never wrote letters, kept diaries, or left other written records, it might at first seem easy enough to learn about slave life from accounts written by white contemporaries. Any number of letters, books, travelers' accounts, and diaries survive, after all—full of descriptions of life under slavery and of the experiences of freedpeople after the war. Yet the question of perspective raises serious problems. The vantage point of white Americans observing slavery was emphatically not that of slaves who lived under the "peculiar institution" nor of those freedpeople forced to cope with their dramatically changed circumstances. The marked differences between the social and psychological positions of blacks and whites make it extremely difficult to reconstruct the black point of view solely from white accounts.

Consider, first, the observations of those white people who associated most often and most closely with black slaves: their masters. The relationship between master and slave was inherently unequal. Slaves could be whipped for trifling offenses; they could be sold or separated from their families and closest friends; even under "kind" masters, they were bound to labor as ordered if they wanted their ration of food and clothing. With slaves so dependent on the master's authority, they were hardly likely to reveal their true feelings; the dangerous consequences of such indiscretion were too great.

In fact, we have already encountered an example in which a slave deceived his master: the case of Squires Jackson and his newspaper. Think for a moment about the source of that story. Even without a footnote to indicate where the information came from, readers of this chapter can deduce that it was left in the historical record by Jackson, not the planter. (The planter, after all, went away convinced Jackson could not read.) And indeed, Jackson is the source of the story. But imagine how much different our impression would be if the only surviving record of Jackson's conduct were the planter's diary. No such diary has survived, but if it had, we might have read an entry something like the following:

"They are having a merry time, thoughtless creatures, they think not of the morrow." This scene of a Christmas party, similar to the one described by the Louisiana planter, appeared with an article written by a northern correspondent for *Frank Leslie's Illustrated Newspaper* in 1857. The picture, reflecting the popular stereotype of slaves as cheerful and ignorantly content with their lot, suggests that the social constraints of the times made it as difficult for southern African Americans to be completely candid with their northern liberators as it had been to be candid with their southern masters.

> A humorous incident occurred today. While entering the woodshed to attend some business, I came upon my slave Squires. His large eyes were fixed with intense interest upon an old copy of a newspaper he had come upon, which alarmed me some until I discovered the rascal was reading its contents upside down. "Why Squires," I said innocently. "What is the latest news?" He looked up at me with a big grin and said, "Massa, de 'Federates jes' won de war!" It made me laugh to see the darkey's simple confidence. I wish I could share his optimism.

This entry is fictional, but having Jackson's version of the story serves to cast suspicion on similar entries in real planter diaries. One Louisiana slave owner, for instance, marveled that his field hands went on with their Christmas party apparently unaware that Yankee raiding parties had pillaged a nearby town. "We have been watching the negroes dancing for the last two hours. . . . They are having a merry time, thoughtless creatures, they think not of the morrow." It apparently never occurred to the planter that the "thoughtless" merriment may have been especially great because of the northern troops nearby.[2]

The harsh realities of the war caused many southerners to realize for the first time just how little they really knew about their slaves. In areas where Union troops were near, slaves ran for freedom—often the very servants that masters had deemed most loyal. Mary Chesnut, whose house was not far from Fort Sumter, sought in vain to penetrate the blank expressions of her slaves. "Not by one word or look can we detect any change in the demeanor of these Negro servants. . . . You could not tell that they even hear the aw-ful noise that is going on in the bay [at Fort Sumter], though it is dinning in their ears night and day. . . . Are they stolidly stupid, or wiser than we are, silent and strong, biding their time?"

It is tempting to suppose that white northerners who helped liberate slaves might have provided more sympathetic or accurate accounts of freed-people's attitudes. But that assumption is dangerous. Although virtually all northern slaves had been freed by 1820, race prejudice remained over-whelmingly evident. Antislavery forces often combined a vehement dislike of slavery with an equally vehement desire to keep the freedpeople out of the North. For African Americans who did live there, most housing and trans-portation facilities were segregated. Whites and blacks had much less con-tact than that afforded by the easy, if unequal, familiarity common in the South.

Consequently, while some Union soldiers went out of their way to be kind to the slaves they encountered, many more looked upon African Americans with distaste and open hostility. Many Yankees strongly believed that they were fighting a war to save the Union, not to free the "cursed Nigger," as one recruit put it. Even white officers who commanded black regiments could be remarkably unsympathetic. "Any one listening to your shouting and singing can see how grotesquely ignorant you are," one officer lectured his troops when they refused to accept less than the pay promised them on enlistment. Even missionaries and other sympathetic northerners who came to occupied territory had preconceptions to overcome. "I saw some very low-looking women who answered very intelligently, contrary to my expec-tations," noted Philadelphia missionary Laura Towne. Another female mis-sionary, much less sympathetic than Towne, bridled when a black child greeted her with too much familiarity. "I say good-mornin' to my young missus," recounted the child to a friend, "and she say, 'I slap your mouth for your impudence, you nigger.'" Such callousness underlines the need for cau-tion when reviewing northern accounts.

2. Readers who review the opening narrative of this chapter will discover that they have already en-countered quite a few other examples of deception arising out of the social situations in which the actors found themselves. In fact, except for the black soldier's comment about the bottom rail being top, every example of white-black relationships cited in the opening section has some element of concealment or deception. It may be worth noting that we did not select the opening incidents with that fact in mind. The preponderance of deception was noted only when we reviewed the draft sev-eral days after it had been written.

Indeed, perceptive northern whites recognized that black people would continue to be circumspect around white people. Just as the slave had been dependent on his southern masters, so freedpeople found themselves similarly vulnerable to the new class of conquerors. "One of these blacks, fresh from slavery, will most adroitly tell you precisely what you want to hear," noted northerner Charles Nordhoff.

> To cross-examine such a creature is a task of the most delicate nature; if you chance to put a leading question he will answer to its spirit as closely as the compass needle answers to the magnetic pole. Ask if the enemy had fifty thousand men, and he will be sure that they had at least that many; express your belief that they had not five thousand, and he will laugh at the idea of their having more than forty-five hundred.

Samuel Gridley Howe, a wartime commissioner investigating the freedpeople's condition, saw the situation clearly. "The negro, like other men, naturally desires to live in the light of truth," he argued, "but he hides in the shadow of falsehood, more or less deeply, according as his safety or welfare seems to require it. Other things equal, the freer a people, the more truthful; and only the perfectly free and fearless are perfectly truthful."

Even sympathetic northerners were at a disadvantage in recounting the freedpeople's point of view, simply because the culture of southern African Americans was so unfamiliar to them. The first hurdle was simple communication, given the wide variety of accents and dialects spoken by northerners and southerners. Charles Nordhoff noted that often he had the feeling that he was "speaking with foreigners." The slaves' phrase "I go shum" puzzled him until he discovered it to be a contraction of "I'll go see about it." Another missionary was "teaching the little darkies gymnastics and what various things were for, eyes, etc. He asked what ears were made for, and when they said, 'To yer with,' he could not understand them at all."

If black dialect was difficult to understand, black culture and religion could appear even more unfathomable. Although most slaves nominally shared with northerners a belief in Christianity, black methods of worship shocked more than one staid Unitarian. After church meetings, slaves often participated in a singing and dancing session known as a "shout," in which the leader would sing out a line of song and the chorus would respond, dancing in rhythm to the music. As the night proceeded, the music became more vocal and the dancing more vigorous. "Tonight I have been to a 'shout'," reported Laura Towne, "which seems to me certainly the remains of some old idol worship . . . I never saw anything so savage." Another missionary noted, "It was the most hideous and at the same time the most pitiful sight I ever witnessed."

Thus, as sympathetic as many northerners wished to be, significant obstacles prevented them from fully appreciating the freedpeople's point of view. The nature of slave society and the persistence of race prejudice made it virtually impossible for blacks and whites to deal with one another in open, candid ways.

THE FREEDPEOPLE SPEAK

Given the scarcity of first-person African American accounts, how can we fully recover the freedpeople's point of view? From the very beginning, some observers recognized the value of the former slaves' perspective. If few black people could write, their stories could be written down by others and made public. Oral testimony, transcribed by literate editors, would allow black Americans to speak out on issues that affected them most.

The tradition of oral evidence began even before the slaves were freed. Abolitionists recognized the value of firsthand testimony against the slave system. They took down the stories of fugitive slaves who had made their way north, and they published the accounts. During the war Congress also established the Freedman's Inquiry Commission, which collected information that might aid the government in formulating policies toward the newly freed slaves.

In the half century following Reconstruction, however, interest in preserving black history generally languished. An occasional journalist or historian traveled through the South to interview former slaves. Educators at black schools, such as the Hampton Institute, published recollections. But a relatively small number of subjects were interviewed. Often the interviews were published in daily newspapers whose standards of accuracy were not high and in which the interviews were severely edited to fit limited space.

Furthermore, the vast majority of professional historians writing about Reconstruction ignored these interviews, as well as the freedpeople's perspective in general. Historians most often relied on white accounts, which, not unexpectedly, painted a rather partial picture. William A. Dunning, a historian at Columbia University, was perhaps the most influential advocate of the prevailing viewpoint. He painted the freedpeople as childish, happy-go-lucky creatures who failed to appreciate the responsibilities of their new status. "As the full meaning of [emancipation] was grasped by the freedmen," Dunning wrote, "great numbers of them abandoned their old homes, and, regardless of crops to be cultivated, stock to be cared for, or food to be provided, gave themselves up to testing their freedom. They wandered aimless but happy through the country." At the same time Dunning asserted that Confederate soldiers and other southern whites had "devoted themselves with desperate energy to the procurement of what must sustain the life of both themselves and their former slaves." Such were the conclusions deduced without the aid of the freedpeople's perspectives.

Only in the twentieth century were systematic efforts made to question blacks about their experiences as slaves and freedpeople. Interest in the African American heritage rose markedly during the 1920s, in great part spurred by the efforts of black scholars such as W. E. B. DuBois, Charles Johnson, and Carter Woodson, the editor and founder of the *Journal of Negro History*. Those scholars labored diligently to overturn the Reconstruction stereotypes promoted by the Dunning school. Moreover, the growth of both sociology and anthropology departments at American universities encouraged scholars to analyze southern culture using the tools of the new social sciences. By the beginning of the 1930s, historians at Fisk University, in Nashville, and Southern University, in Baton Rouge, had instituted projects to collect oral evidence.

Ironically, the economic adversity of the Depression sparked the greatest single effort to gather oral testimony from the freedpeople. One of the many alphabet-soup agencies chartered by the Roosevelt administration was the Federal Writers' Project (FWP). The project's primary goal was to compile cultural guides to each of the forty-eight states, using unemployed writers and journalists to collect and edit the information. But under the direction of folklorist John Lomax, the FWP also organized staffs in many states to interview former slaves.

Although Lomax's project placed greatest emphasis on collecting black folklore and songs, the FWP's directive to interviewers included a long list of historical questions that interviewers were encouraged to ask. The following sampling gives an indication of the project's interests:

> What work did you do in slavery days? Did you ever earn any money?
> What did you eat and how was it cooked? Any possums? Rabbits? Fish?
> Was there a jail for slaves? Did you ever see any slaves sold or auctioned off?
>   How and for what causes were the slaves punished? Tell what you saw.
> What do you remember about the war that brought you your freedom? When the Yankees came what did they do or say?
> What did the slaves do after the war? What did they receive generally? What do they think about the reconstruction period?

The results of these interviews are remarkable, even in terms of sheer bulk. More than 2,300 were recorded and edited in state FWP offices and then sent to Washington, assembled in 1941, and published in typescript. A facsimile edition, issued during the 1970s, takes up nineteen volumes. Supplementary materials, including hundreds of interviews never forwarded to Washington during the project's life, comprise another twenty-two volumes. Benjamin Botkin, the series' original editor, recognized the collection's importance:

> These life histories, taken down as far as possible in the narrator's words, constitute an invaluable body of unconscious evidence or indirect source material, which scholars and writers dealing with the South, especially, social psychologists and cultural anthropologists, cannot afford to reckon without. For the first and last time, a large number of surviving slaves (many of whom have since died) have been permitted to tell their own story, in their own way.

At first glance, the slave narrative collection would appear to fulfill admirably the need for a guide to the freedpeople's point of view. But even Botkin, for all his enthusiasm, recognized that the narratives could not simply be taken at face value. Like other primary source materials, they need to be viewed in terms of the context in which they originated.

To begin with, no matter how massive the nineteen volumes of interviews may appear on the library shelf, they still constitute a small sampling of the original four million freedpeople. What sort of selection bias might exist? Geographic imbalance comes quickly to mind. Are the slave interviews drawn from a broad cross section of southern states? Counting the number of slaves interviewed from each state, we discover only 155 interviews from African Americans living in Virginia, Missouri, Maryland, Delaware, and Kentucky—about 6 percent of the total number of interviews published. Yet in 1860, 23 percent of the southern slave population lived in those states. Thus the upper South is underrepresented in the collection.

What about age? Because the interviews took place primarily between 1936 and 1938, former slaves were fairly old: fully two-thirds of them were more than eighty years of age. The predominance of elderly interviewees raises several questions, most obviously, how sharp were the informants' memories? The Civil War was already seventy years in the past. The ability to recall accurately varies from person to person, but common sense suggests that the further away from an event, the less detailed a person's memory is likely to be. In addition, age may have biased the type of recollections as well as their accuracy. Historian John Blassingame has noted that the average life expectancy of a slave in 1850 was less than fifty years. Those who lived to a ripe old age might well have survived because they were treated better than the average slave. If so, their accounts would reflect some of the milder experiences of slaves.

Also, if those interviewed were predominantly old in 1936, they were predominantly young during the Civil War. Almost half (43 percent) were less than ten years old in 1865. Sixty-seven percent were under age fifteen, and 83 percent were under age twenty. Thus, many interviewers remembered slavery as it would have been experienced by a child. Since the conditions of bondage were relatively less harsh for a child than for an adult slave, once again the FWP narratives may be somewhat skewed toward an optimistic view of slavery. (On the other hand, it might be argued that because children are so impressionable, memories both good and bad might have been vividly magnified.)

Other possible sampling biases come to mind—the sex of the subjects or the kinds of labor they performed as slaves. But distortions may be introduced into the slave narratives in ways more serious than sample bias. Interviewers, simply by choosing their questions, define the kinds of information a subject will volunteer. We have already seen that sensitive observers, such as Charles Nordhoff, recognized how important it was not to ask leading questions. But even Nordhoff may not have realized how many unconscious cues the most innocent questions carry.

Social scientists specializing in interviewing have pointed out that even the grammatical form of a question will influence a subject's response. Take, for example, the following questions:

Where did you hear about this job opening?
How did you hear about this job opening?
So you saw our want ad for this job?

Each question is directed at the same information, yet each suggests to the subject a different response. The first version ("Where did you hear . . .")

implies that the interviewer wants a specific, limited answer ("Down at the employment center."). The second question, by substituting "how" for "where," invites the subject to offer a longer response ("Well, I'd been look- ing around for a job for several weeks, and I was over at the employment of- fice when . . ."). The final question signals that the interviewer wants only a yes or no confirmation to a question whose answer is believed to be already known.

Interviewers, in other words, constantly communicate to their subjects the kinds of evidence they want, the length of the answers, and even the manner in which answers ought to be offered. If such interviewing cues influence rou- tine conversations, they prove even more crucial when a subject as controver- sial as slavery is involved, and when relations between blacks and whites continue to be strained. In fact, the most important cue an interviewer was likely to have given was one presented before any conversation took place. Was the interviewer white or black? William Ferris, a sociologist obtaining oral folklore in the Mississippi Delta region in 1968, discussed the problem. "It was not possible to maintain rapport with both Whites and Blacks in the same community," he noted,

> for the confidence and cooperation of each was based on their belief that I was "with them" in my convictions about racial taboos of Delta society. Thus when I was "presented" to Blacks by a white member of the community, the infor- mants regarded me as a member of the white caste and therefore limited their lore to noncontroversial topics.

Such tensions were even more prevalent throughout the South during the 1930s. In hundreds of ways, black people were made aware that they were still considered inferior to white people, and that they were to remain within strictly segregated and subordinate bounds. From 1931 to 1935, more than seventy African Americans were lynched in the South, often for minor or nonexistent crimes. Black prisoners found themselves forced to negotiate grossly unfavorable labor contracts if they wished to be released. Many share- croppers and other poor farmers were constantly in debt to white property owners.

Smaller matters of etiquette reflected the larger state of affairs. A white southerner would commonly address black adults by their first names, or as "boy," "auntie," "uncle," regardless of the black person's status and even if the white person knew the black person's full name. Black people were re- quired to address white people as "ma'am" or "mister." Such distinctions were maintained even on the telephone. If an African American placed a long-distance call for "Mr. Smith" in a neighboring town, the white opera- tor would ask, "Is he colored?" The answer being yes, her reply would be, "Don't you say 'Mister' to me. He ain't 'Mister' to me." Conversely, an op- erator would refuse to place a call by a black caller who did not address her as "Ma'am."

In such circumstances, most African Americans were naturally reticent about volunteering information to white FWP interviewers. "Lots of old

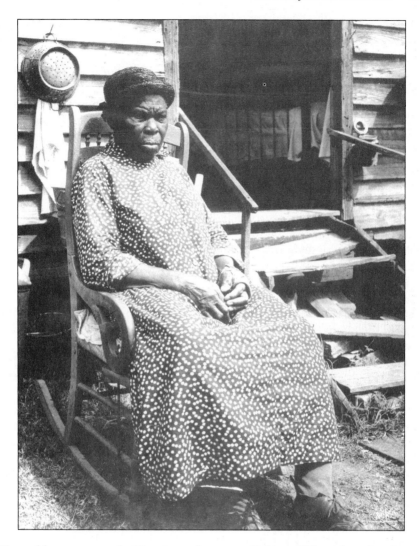

"I've told you too much. How come they want all this stuff from the colored people anyway? Do you take any stories from the white people? . . . They don't need me to tell it to them." This Georgia woman, like many of the subjects interviewed for the Federal Writers' Project, was still living in the 1930s on the plantation where she had grown up as a slave child. The plantation was still owned by descendants of her former master. Under such conditions, suspicion toward FWP interviewers was a predictable reaction, even if the interviewer was black; doubly so if he or she was white and a resident of the community.

slaves closes the door before they tell the truth about their days of slavery," noted one black Texan to an interviewer. "When the door is open, they tell how kind their masters was how rosy it all was." Samuel S. Taylor, a skilled black interviewer in Arkansas, found that he had to reassure informants that the information they were giving would not be used against them. "I've told you too much,"one subject concluded. "How come they want all this stuff from the colored people anyway? Do you take any stories from the white people? They know all about it. They know more about it than I do. They don't need me to tell it to them."

Often the whites who interviewed blacks lived in the same town and were long acquaintances. "I 'members when you was barefoot at de bottom," one black interviewee told his white (and balding) interviewer; "now I see you a settin' dere, gittin' bare at de top, as bare as de palm of my hand." Another black man revealed an even closer relationship when he noted that his wife, Ellen, "'joy herself, have a good time nussin' [nursing] white folks chillun. Nussed you; she tell me 'bout it many time." In such circumstances African Americans could hardly be expected to speak frankly. One older woman summed up the situation quite cheerfully. "Oh, I know your father en your granfather en all of dem. Bless Mercy, child, I don't want to tell you nothin' but what to please you."

The methods used to set down FWP interviews raise additional problems. With only a few exceptions (see our bibliography at the end of the chapter), tape recorders were not used. Instead, interviewers took written notes of their conversations, from which they later reconstructed their interview. In the process, interviewers often edited their material. Sometimes changes were made simply to improve the flow, so that the interview did not jump jarringly from topic to topic. Other interviewers edited out material they believed to be irrelevant or objectionable.

Furthermore, no protocol existed for transcribing African American dialect onto the written page. A few interviewers took great pains to render their accounts in correct English, so that regional accents and dialect disappeared. ("Fo'" became "for," "dem" became "them," and so forth.) But most interviewers tried to provide a flavor of black dialect, with wildly varying success. In some cases the end result sounded more like the stereotypical "darky dialect" popular with whites of the period. "I wuz comin' frum de back uv de stable," an interviewer might quote his subject as saying—a colloquial approach that, to some readers, might at first seem unobjectionable. Yet few of the same interviewers would have thought it necessary to render, with similar offbeat spelling, the accents of a white "southun plantuh," whose speech might seem equally exotic to an American from another region of the United States. For that matter, consider the spellings used in "I wuz comin' frum de back uv de stable." In fact, there is no difference in pronunciation between "was" and "wuz"; or "frum" and "from"; or "uv" and "of." In effect, those transcriptions are simply cultural markers conveying the unspoken message that, in the eyes of the interviewer, the speaker comes from a different (read: less cultured and less educated) social class. Eventually, the FWP sent its interviewers a list of "Approved Dialect Expressions": "dem," "dose," and "gwine" were among the permitted transcriptions; "wuz," "ovah," and "uv" were not allowed.

By understanding the difficulties of gathering oral evidence, researchers are able to proceed more carefully in evaluating the slave narrative collection.

Even so, readers new to this field may find it difficult to appreciate the varying responses that different interviewers might elicit. In order to bring the point home, it may be helpful to analyze material that we came across during our own research in the slave narrative collection. The first interview is with Susan Hamlin, a black woman who lived in Charleston, and we reprint it below exactly as it appears in typescript.

Interview with Ex-Slave

On July 6th, I interviewed Susan Hamlin, ex-slave, at 17 Henrietta street, Charleston, S. C. She was sitting just inside of the front door, on a step leading up to the porch, and upon hearing me inquire for her she assumed that I was from the Welfare office, from which she had received aid prior to its closing. I did not correct this impression, and at no time did she suspect that the object of my visit was to get the story of her experience as a slave. During our conversation she mentioned her age. "Why that's very interesting, Susan," I told her, "If you are that old you probably remember the Civil War and slavery days." "Yes, Ma'am, I been a slave myself," she said, and told me the following story:

"I kin remember some things like it was yesterday, but I is 104 years old now, and age is starting to get me, I can't remember everything like I use to. I getting old, old. You know I is old when I been a grown woman when the Civil War broke out. I was hired out then, to a Mr. McDonald, who lived on Atlantic Street, and I remembers when de first shot was fired, and the shells went right over de city. I got seven dollars a month for looking after children, not taking them out, you understand, just minding them. I did not got the money, Mausa got it." "Don't you think that was fair?" I asked. "If you were fed and clothed by him, shouldn't he be paid for your work?" "Course it been fair," she answered, "I belong to him and he got to get something to take care of me."

"My name before I was married was Susan Calder, but I married a man named Hamlin. I belonged to Mr. Edward Fuller, he was president of the First National Bank. He was a good man to his people till de Lord took him. Mr. Fuller got his slaves by marriage. He married Miss Mikell, a lady what lived on Edisto Island, who was a slave owner, and we lived on Edisto on a plantation. I don't remember de name cause when Mr. Fuller got to be president of de bank we come to Charleston to live. He sell out the plantation and say them (the slaves) that want to come to Charleston with him could come and them what wants to stay can stay on the island with his wife's people. We had our choice. Some is come and some is stay, but my ma and us children come with Mr. Fuller.

"We lived on St. Philip street. The house still there, good as ever. I go 'round there to see it all de time; the cistern still there too, where we used to sit 'round and drink the cold water, and eat, and talk and laugh. Mr. Fuller have lots of servants and the ones he didn't need hisself he hired out. The slaves had rooms in the back, the ones with children had two rooms and them that didn't have any children had one room, not to cook in but to sleep in.

They all cooked and ate downstairs in the hall that they had for the colored people. I don't know about slavery but I know all the slavery I know about, the people was good to me. Mr. Fuller was a good man and his wife's people been grand people, all good to their slaves. Seem like Mr. Fuller just git his slaves so he could be good to dem. He made all the little colored chillen love him. If you don't believe they loved him what they all cry, and scream, and holler for when dey hear he dead? 'Oh, Mausa dead my Mausa dead, what I going to do, my Mausa dead.' Dey tell dem t'aint no use to cry, dat can't bring him back, but de chillen keep on crying. We used to call him Mausa Eddie but he named Mr. Edward Fuller, and he sure was a good man.

"A man come here about a month ago, say he from de Government, and dey send him to find out 'bout slavery. I give him most a book, and what he give me? A dime. He ask me all kind of questions. He ask me dis and he ask me dat, didn't de white people do dis and did dey do dat but Mr. Fuller was a good man, he was sure good to me and all his people, dey all like him, God bless him, he in de ground now but I ain't going to let nobody lie on him. You know he good when even the little chillen cry and holler when he dead. I tell you dey couldn't just fix us up any kind of way when we going to Sunday School. We had to be dressed nice, if you pass him and you ain't dress to suit him he send you right back and say tell your ma to see dat you dress right. Dey couldn't send you out in de cold barefoot neither. I 'member one day my ma want to send me wid some milk for her sister-in-law what lived 'round de corner. I fuss cause it cold and say 'how you going to send me out wid no shoe, and it cold?' Mausa hear how I talkin and turn he back and laugh, den he call to my ma to gone in de house and find shoe to put on my feet and don't let him see me barefoot again in cold weather.

"When de war start going good and de shell fly over Charleston he take all us up to Aiken for protection. Talk 'bout marching through Georgia, dey sure march through Aiken, soldiers was everywhere.

"My ma had six children, three boys and three girls, but I de only one left, all my white people and all de colored people gone, not a soul left but me. I ain't been sick in 25 years. I is near my church and I don't miss service any Sunday, night or morning. I kin walk wherever I please, I kin walk to de Battery if I want to. The Welfare use to help me but dey shut down now, I can't find out if dey going to open again or not. Miss (Mrs.) Buist and Miss Pringle, dey help me when I can go there but all my own dead."

"Were most of the masters kind?" I asked. "Well you know," she answered, "times den was just like dey is now, some was kind and some was mean; heaps of wickedness went on just de same as now. All my people was good people. I see some wickedness and I hear 'bout all kinds of t'ings but you don't know whether it was lie or not. Mr Fuller been a Christian man."

"Do you think it would have been better if the Negroes had never left Africa?" was the next question I asked. "No Ma'am, (emphatically) dem heathen didn't have no religion. I tell you how I t'ink it is. The Lord made t'ree nations, the white, the red and the black, and put dem in different places on de earth where dey was to stay. Dose black ignoramuses in Africa forgot God, and didn't have no religion and God blessed and prospered the white people dat did remember Him and sent dem to teach de black people even if dey have to grab dem and bring dem into bondage till dey learned some sense. The Indians forgot God and dey had to be taught better so dey land was taken away from dem. God sure bless and prosper de white people and He put de red and de black people under dem so dey could teach dem and bring dem into sense wid God. Dey had to get dere brains right, and honor God, and learn uprightness wid God cause ain't He make you, and ain't His Son redeem you and save you wid His Precious blood. You kin plan all de wickedness you want and pull hard as you choose but when the Lord mek up His mind you is to change, He can change you dat quick (snapping her fingers) and easy. You got to believe on Him if it tek bondage to bring you to your knees.

"You know I is got converted. I been in Big Bethel (church) on my knees praying under one of de preachers. I see a great, big, dark pack on my back, and it had me all bent over and my shoulders drawn down, all hunch up. I look up and I see de glory, I see a big beautiful light, a great light, and in de middle is de Sabior, hanging so (extending her arms) just like He died. Den I gone to praying good, and I can feel de sheckles (shackles) loose up and moving and de pack fall off. I don't know where it went to, I see de angels in de Heaven, and hear dem say 'Your sins are forgiven.' I scream and fell off so. (Swoon.) When I come to dey has laid me out straight and I know I is converted cause you can't see no such sight and go on like you is before. I know I is still a sinner but I believe in de power of God and I trust his Holy name. Den dey put me wid de seekers but I know I is already saved."

"Did they take good care of the slaves when their babies were born?" she was asked. "If you want chickens for fat (to fatten) you got to feed dem," she said with a smile, "and if you want people to work dey got to be strong, you got to feed dem and take care of dem too. If dey can't work it come out of your pocket. Lots of wickedness gone on in dem days, just as it do now, some good, some mean, black and white, it just dere nature, if dey good dey going to be kind to everybody, if dey mean dey going to be mean to everybody. Sometimes chillen was sold away from dey parents. De Mausa would come and say 'Where Jennie,' tell um to put clothes on dat baby, I want um. He sell de baby and de ma scream and holler, you know how dey carry on. Geneally (generally) dey sold it when de ma wasn't dere. Mr. Fuller didn't sell none of us, we stay wid our ma's till we grown, I stay wid my ma till she dead.

"You know I is mix blood, my grandfather bin a white man and my grandmother a mulatto. She been marry to a black so dat how I get fix like I is. I got both blood, so how I going to quarrel wid either side?"

SOURCE: Interview with Susan Hamlin, 17 Henrietta Street

NOTE   Susan lives with a mulatto family of the better type. The name is Hamlin not Hamilton, and her name prior to her marriage was Calder not Collins. I paid particular attention to this and had them spell the names for me. I would judge Susan to be in the late nineties but she is wonderfully well preserved. She now claims to be 104 years old.

From the beginning, the circumstances of this conversation arouse suspicion. The white interviewer, Jessie Butler, mentions that she allowed Hamlin to think she was from the welfare office. Evidently, Butler thought Hamlin would speak more freely if the real purpose of the visit was hidden. But surely the deception had the opposite effect. Hamlin, like most of the black people interviewed, was elderly, unable to work, and dependent on charity. If Butler appeared to be from the welfare office, Hamlin would likely have done whatever she could to ingratiate herself. Many black interviewees consistently assumed that their white interviewers had influence with the welfare office. "You through wid me now, boss? I sho' is glad of dat," concluded one subject. "Help all you kin to get me dat pension befo' I die and de Lord will bless you, honey. . . . Has you got a dime to give dis old nigger, boss?"

Furthermore, Butler's questioning was hardly subtle. When Hamlin noted that she had to give her master the money she made from looking after children, Butler asked, "Don't you think that was fair?" "Course it been fair," came the quick response. Hamlin knew very well what was expected, especially since Butler had already answered the question herself: "If you were fed and clothed by him, shouldn't he be paid for your work?"

Not surprisingly, then, the interview paints slavery in relatively mild colors. Hamlin describes in great detail how good her master was and how she had shoes in the winter. When asked whether most masters were kind, Hamlin appears eminently "fair"—"some was kind and some was mean." She admits hearing "all kinds of t'ings but you don't know whether it was lie or not." She does note that slave children could be sold away from parents and that black mothers protested; but she talks as if that were only to be expected ("de ma scream and holler, you know how dey carry on").

Equally flattering is the picture Hamlin paints of relations between the races. "Black ignoramuses" in Africa had forgotten about God, she explains, just as the Indians had; but "God sure bless and prosper de white people." So Africans and the Indians are placed under white supervision, "to get dere brains right, and honor God, and learn uprightness." Those were not exactly the words proslavery apologists would have used to describe the situation, but they were the same sentiments. Defenders of slavery constantly stressed that Europeans served as benevolent models ("parents," Andrew Jackson might have said) leading Africans and Indians on the slow upward road to civilization.

All these aspects of the interview led us to be suspicious about its content. Moreover, several additional clues in the document puzzled us. Hamlin had mentioned a man who visited her "about a month ago, say he from de Government, and dey send him to find out 'bout slavery." Apparently her interview with Jessie Butler was the second she had given. Butler, for her part, made a fuss at the end of the transcript over the spelling of Hamlin's name ("I paid particular attention to this."). It was "Hamlin not Hamilton" and her maiden name was "Calder not Collins." The phrasing indicates that somewhere else Butler had seen Hamlin referred to as "Susan Hamilton." If someone had interviewed Hamlin earlier, we wondered, could Hamilton have been the name on that original report?

We found the answer when we continued on through the narrative collection. The interview following Butler's was conducted by a man named Augustus Ladson, with a slave named "Susan Hamilton." When compared with Jessie Butler's interview, Augustus Ladson's makes absorbing reading. Here it is, printed exactly as it appears in the collection:

Ex-Slave 101 Years of Age

Has Never Shaken Hands Since 1863

Was on Knees Scrubbing when Freedom Gun Fired

I'm a hund'ed an' one years old now, son. De only one livin' in my crowd frum de days I wuz a slave. Mr. Fuller, my master, who was president of the Firs' National Bank, owned the fambly of us except my father. There were eight men an' women with five girls an' six boys workin' for him. Most o' them wus hired out. De house in which we stayed is still dere with de sisterns an' slave quarters. I always go to see de old home which is on St. Phillip Street.

My ma had t'ree boys an' t'ree girls who did well at their work. Hope Mikell, my eldest brodder, an' James wus de shoemaker. William Fuller, son of our Master, wus de bricklayer. Margurite an' Catharine wus de maids an' look as de children.

My pa b'long to a man on Edisto Island. Frum what he said, his master was very mean. Pa real name wus Adam Collins but he took his master' name; he wus de coachman. Pa did supin one day en his master whipped him. De next day which wus Monday, pa carry him 'bout four miles frum home in de woods an' give him de same 'mount of lickin' he wus given on Sunday. He tied him to a tree an' unhitched de horse so it couldn't git tie-up an' kill e self. Pa den gone to de landin' an' cetch a boat dat wus comin' to Charleston wood fa'm products. He (was) permitted by his master to go to town on errands, which helped him to go on de boat without bein' question'. W'en he got here he gone on de water-front an' ax for a job on a ship so he could git to de North. He got de job an' sail' wood de ship. Dey search de island up an' down for him wood houndogs en w'en it wus t'ought he wus drowned, 'cause dey track him to de river, did dey give up. One of his master' friend gone to New York en went in a store w'ere pas wus employed as a clerk. He reconize' pa is easy is pa reconize' him. He gone back home an' tell pa master who know den dat pa wusn't comin' back an' before he died he sign' papers dat pa wus free. Pa' ma wus dead an' he come down to bury her by de permission of his master' son who had promised no ha'm would come to him, but dey wus' fixin' plans to keep him, so he went to de Work House an' ax to be sold 'cause any slave could sell e self if e could git to de Work House. But it wus on record down dere so dey couldn't sell 'im an' told him his master' people couldn't hold him a slave.

People den use to do de same t'ings dey do now. Some marry an' some live together jus' like now. One t'ing, no minister nebber say in readin' de matrimony "let no man put asounder" 'cause a couple would be married tonight an' tomorrow one would be taken away en be sold. All slaves wus married in dere master house, in de livin' room where slaves an' dere missus an' mossa wus to witness de ceremony. Brides use to wear some of de finest dress an' if dey could afford it, have de best kind of furniture. Your master nor your missus objected to good t'ings.

I'll always 'member Clory, de washer. She wus very high-tempered. She was a mulatto with beautiful hair she could sit on; Clory didn't take foolishness frum anybody. One day our missus gone in de laundry an' find fault with de clothes. Clory didn't do a t'ing but pick her up bodily an' throw 'er out de door. Dey had to sen' fur a doctor 'cause she pregnant an' less than two hours de baby wus bo'n. Afta dat she begged to be sold fur she didn't [want] to kill missus, but our master ain't nebber want to sell his slaves. But dat didn't keep Clory frum gittin' a brutal whippin'. Dey whip' 'er until dere wusn't a white spot on her body. Dat wus de worst I ebber see a human bein' got such a beatin'. I t'ought she wus goin' to die, but she got well an' didn't get any better but meaner until our master decide it wus bes' to rent her out. She willingly agree' since she wusn't 'round missus. She hated an' detest' both of them an' all de fambly.

W'en any slave wus whipped all de other slaves wus made to watch. I see women hung frum de ceilin' of buildin's an' whipped with only supin tied 'round her lower part of de body, until w'en dey wus taken down, dere wusn't breath in de body. I had some terribly bad experiences.

Yankees use to come t'rough de streets, especially de Big Market, huntin' those who want to go to de "free country" as dey call' it. Men an' women wus always missin' an' nobody could give 'count of dere disappearance. De men wus train' up North fur sojus.

De white race is so brazen. Dey come here an' run de Indians frum dere own lan', but dey couldn't make dem slaves 'cause dey wouldn't stan' for it. Indians use to git up in trees an' shoot dem with poison arrow. W'en dey couldn't make dem slaves den dey gone to Africa an' bring dere black brother an' sister. Dey say 'mong themselves, "we gwine mix dem up en make ourselves king. Dats d only way we'd git even with de Indians."

All time, night an' day, you could hear men an' women screamin' to de tip of dere voices as either ma, pa, sister, or brother wus take without any warnin' an' sell. Some time mother who had only one chile wus separated fur life. People wus always dyin' frum a broken heart.

One night a couple married an' de next mornin' de boss sell de wife. De gal ma got in in de street an' cursed de white woman fur all she could find. She said: "dat damn white, pale-face bastard sell my daughter who jus' married las' night," an' other t'ings. The white man tresten' her to call de police if she didn't stop, but de collud woman said: "hit me or call de police. I redder die dan to stan' dis any longer." De police took her to de Work House by de white woman orders an' what became of 'er, I never hear.

W'en de war began we wus taken to Aiken, South Ca'lina were we stay' until de Yankees come t'rough. We could see balls sailin' t'rough de air w'en Sherman wus comin'. Bumbs hit trees in our yard. W'en de freedom gun wus fired, I wus on my 'nees scrubbin'. Dey tell me I wus free but I didn't b'lieve it.

In de days of slavory woman wus jus' given time 'nough to deliver dere babies. Dey deliver de baby 'bout eight in de mornin' an' twelve had to be back to work.

I wus a member of Emmanuel African Methodist Episcopal Church for 67 years. Big Zion, across de street wus my church before den an' before Old Bethel w'en I lived on de other end of town.

Sence Lincoln shook hands with his assasin who at de same time shoot him, frum dat day I stop shakin' hands, even in de church, an' you know how long dat wus. I don't b'lieve in kissin' neider fur all carry dere meannesses. De Master wus betrayed by one of his bosom frien' with a kiss.

SOURCE: Interview with (Mrs.) Susan Hamilton, 17 Henrietta Street, who claims to be 101 years of age. She has never been sick for twenty years and walks as though just 40. She was hired out by her master for seven dollars a month which had to be given her master.

Susan Hamlin and Susan Hamilton are obviously one and the same, yet by the end of Ladson's interview, we are wondering if we have been listening to the same person! Kindness of the masters? We hear no tales about old Mr. Fuller; only vivid recollections of whippings so harsh "dere wusn't a white spot on her body." To Butler, Hamlin had mentioned only cruelties that she had heard about secondhand ("you don't know whether it was lie or not"); to Ladson, she recounts firsthand experiences ("I see women hung from de ceilin' of buildin's an' whipped with only supin tied 'round her lower part of de body").

Discussions of happy family relations? Instead of tales about shoes in the winter, we hear of Hamlin's father, whipped so severely, he rebels and flees. We hear of family separations, not downplayed with a "you know how dey carry on," but with all the bitterness of mothers whose children had been taken "without any warnin'." We hear of a couple married one night, then callously separated and sold the next day. In the Butler account, slave babies are fed well, treated nicely; in the Ladson account, the recollection is of mothers who were given only a few hours away from the fields in order to deliver their children.

Benevolent white paternalism? This time Hamlin's tale of three races draws a different moral. The white race is "brazen," running the Indians off their land. With a touch of admiration, she notes that the Indians "wouldn't stan' for" being made slaves. White motives are seen not as religious but as exploitative and vengeful: "Dey say 'mong themselves, 'we gwine mix dem up en make ourselves king. Dats d only way we'd git even with de Indians.'" The difference between the two interviews, both in tone and substance, is astonishing.

How do we account for this difference? Nowhere in the South Carolina narratives is the race of Augustus Ladson mentioned, but internal evidence would indicate he is black. In a culture in which blacks usually addressed whites respectfully with a "sir," "ma'am," or "boss," it seems doubtful that Susan Hamlin would address a white man as "son" ("I'm a hund'ed an' one years old now, son"). Furthermore, the content of the interview is just too

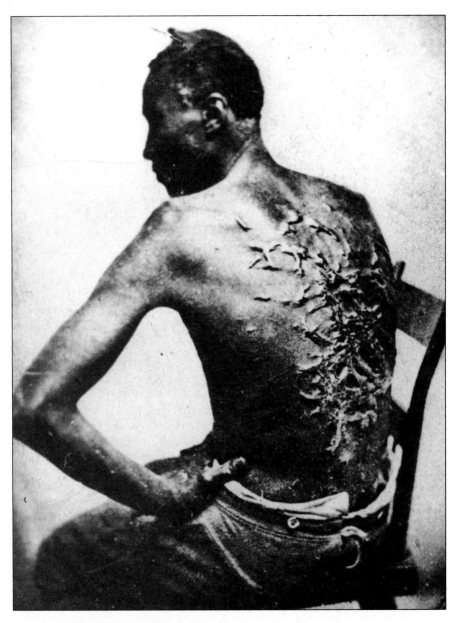

"W'en any slave wus whipped all de other slaves was made to watch. . . . I had some terribly bad experiences." The scars from whippings on this slave's back were recorded in 1863 by an unknown photographer traveling with the Union army.

consistently critical of whites. Hamlin would never have remarked, "De white race is so brazen," if Ladson had been white, especially given the reticence demonstrated in her interview with Butler. Nor would she have been so specific about the angry mother's curses ("damn white, pale-face bastard"). It would be difficult to conceive of a more strikingly dramatic demonstration of how an interviewer can affect the responses of a subject.

FREEDOM AND DECEPTION

The slave narrative collection, then, is not the direct, unfiltered perspective that it first appears to be. In fact, interviews like the ones with Susan Hamlin seem to suggest that the search for the "true" perspectives of the freedpeople is bound to end in failure and frustration. We have seen, first, that information from planters and other white sources must be treated with extreme skepticism and, second, that northern white sources deserve similar caution. Finally, it appears that even the oral testimony of African Americans themselves must be questioned, given the circumstances under which much of it was gathered. It is as if a detective discovered that all the clues so carefully pieced together were hopelessly biased, leading the investigation down the wrong path.

The seriousness of the problem should not be underestimated. It is fundamental. We can try to ease out of the dilemma by noting that differing degrees of bias undoubtedly exist—that some accounts, relatively speaking, are likely to be less deceptive than others. It can be argued, for instance, that Susan Hamlin's interview with Ladson is a more accurate portrayal of her feelings than the interview with Butler. In large measure that assumption is probably true. But does that mean we must reject all of the Butler interview? Presumably, Susan Hamlin's master did give her a pair of shoes one cold winter day. Are we to assume, because of Ladson's interview, that the young child felt no gratitude or obligation to "kind old" Mr. Fuller? Or that the old woman did not look back on those years with some ambivalence? For all her life, both slave and free, Susan Hamlin lived in a world where she was required to "feel" one set of emotions when dealing with some people and a different set when dealing with other people. Can we rest completely confident in concluding that the emotions she expressed to Ladson were her "real" feelings, while the ones to Jessie Butler were her "false" feelings? How can we possibly arrive at an objective conclusion about "real" feelings in any social situation in which such severe strains existed?

Yet putting the question in this light offers at least a partial way out of the dilemma. If so many clues in the investigation are hopelessly "biased"—that is, distorted by the social situation in which they are set—then the very pervasiveness of the distortion may serve as a key to understanding the situation. The evidence in the case is warped precisely because it accurately reflects a distortion in the society itself. The elements of racism and slavery determined a culture in which personal relations were necessarily grounded in mistrust and deception, in which slaves could survive only if they remained acutely conscious of the need to adapt their feelings to the situation. The distortion in the evidence, in other words, speaks eloquently of the hurt inflicted in a society in which personal behavior routinely operated under an economy of deception.

The deception was mutual—practiced by both sides on each other. Susan Hamlin was adapting the story of her past to the needs of the moment at the same time that Jessie Butler was letting Hamlin believe her to be a welfare agent. White masters painted lurid stories of Yankee devils with horns, while slaves, playing roles they were expected to play, rolled their eyes in fear until they had the chance to run straight for Union lines. The deceptions fed on each other and were compounded, becoming an inextricable part of daily life.

It would be tempting, given our awareness of this situation, simply to turn previous historical interpretations on their heads. Whereas William Dunning and his disciples took most of their primary sources at face value and thus saw only cheerful, childlike Sambos, an enlightened history would read the documents upside down, so to speak, stripping away the camouflage to reveal slaves who, quite rationally, went about the daily business of "puttin' on ole massa." And of course we have already seen abundant evidence that slaves did use calculated deception in order to protect themselves.

But simply to replace one set of feelings with another is to ignore the intricate and tense relationships between them. It drastically underestimates the strains that arose out of an economy of deception. The longer and more consistently that masters and slaves were compelled to live false or inauthentic lives, the easier it must have been for them to mislead themselves as well as others. Where white and black people alike engaged in daily dissimulation, some of the deception was inevitably directed inward, simply to preserve the fiction of living in a tolerable, normally functioning society.

When the war came, shattering that fiction, whites and blacks were exposed in concrete and vivid ways to the deception that had been so much a part of their lives. For white slaveholders, the revelation usually came when Union troops entered a region and slaves deserted the plantations in droves. Especially demoralizing was the flight of slaves whom planters had believed most loyal. "He was about my age and I had always treated him more as a companion than a slave," noted one planter of the first defector from his ranks. Mary Chesnut, the woman near Fort Sumter who had tried to penetrate the blank expressions of her slaves, discovered how impossible the task had been. "Jonathan, whom we trusted, betrayed us," she lamented, while "Claiborne, that black rascal who was suspected by all the world," faithfully protected the plantation.

Many slaveholders, when faced with the truth, refused to recognize the role that deception had played in their lives, thereby deceiving themselves further. "The poor negroes don't do us any harm except when they are put up to it," concluded one Georgia woman. A Richmond newspaper editor demanded that a slave who had denounced Jefferson Davis "be whipped every day until he confesses what white man put these notions in his head." Yet the war brought painful insight to others. "We were all laboring under a delusion," confessed one South Carolina planter. "I believed that these people were content, happy, and attached to their masters. But events and reflection have caused me to change these opinions. . . . If they were content, happy and attached to their masters, why did they desert him in the moment of his need and flock to an enemy, whom they did not know?"

For slaves, the news of emancipation brought an entirely different reaction, but still one conditioned by the old habits. We have already seen how one old Georgia slave couple remained impassive as Sherman's troops passed through, until finally the wife could restrain herself no longer. Even the servant who eloquently shouted the praises of freedom at a secluded brook instinctively remembered the need for caution: "I got sort o' scared, afeared somebody hear me, an' I takes another good look." Although emancipation promised a society founded on equal treatment and open relations, slaves could not help wondering whether the new order would fully replace the old. That transformation would occur only if freedpeople could forge relationships that were no longer based on the customs of deception nor rooted in the central fiction of slavery: that blacks were morally and intellectually incapable of assuming a place in free society.

As historians increasingly came to recognize the value of the slave narrative collection, they drew upon its evidence, along with the standard range of primary sources, to re-create the perspectives of freedpeople as they sought the real meaning of their new freedom. Certainly that meaning was by no means evident once the first excitement of liberation had passed. James Lucas, a slave of Jefferson Davis, recalled the inevitable confusion: "Dey all had diffe'nt ways o' thinkin' 'bout it. Mos'ly though dey was jus' lak me, dey didn' know jus' zackly what it meant. It was jus' somp'n dat de white folks an' slaves all de time talk 'bout. Dat's all. Folks dat ain' never been free don' rightly know de feel of bein' free. Dey don' know de meanin' of it." But former slaves were not long in taking their first steps toward defining freedom. On the surface, many of these steps seemed small. But however limited, they served to distance the freedpeople in significant ways from the old habits of bondage.

The taking of new names was one such step. As slaves, African Americans often had no surname or took the name of their master. Equally demeaning, given names were often casually assigned by their owners. Cicero, Pompey, and other Latin or biblical names were commonly bestowed in jest. And whether or not slaves had a surname, they were always addressed familiarly, by their given names. Such customs were part of the symbolic language of deception, promoting the illusion that black people were helpless and even laughable dependents of the planter's family.

Thus many freedpeople took for themselves new names, severing the symbolic tie with their old masters. "A heap of people say they was going to name their selves over," recalled one freedman. "They named their selves big names. . . . Some of the names was Abraham an' some called their selves Lincum. Any big name 'ceptin' their master's name. It was the fashion." Even former slaves who remained loyal to their masters recognized the significance of the change. "When you'all had de power you was good to me," an older freedman told his master, "an I'll protect you now. No niggers nor Yankees shall touch you. If you want anything, call for Sambo. I mean, call for Mr. Samuel—that's my name now."

Just as freedpeople took new names to symbolize their new status, so also many husbands and wives reaffirmed their marriages in formal ceremonies. Under slavery, many marriages and family ties had been ignored through the convenient fiction that Africans were morally inferior. Black affections, the planters argued, were dominated by impulse and the physical desires of the moment. Such self-deception eased many a master's conscience when slave families were separated and sold. Similarly, many planters married slaves only informally, with a few words sufficing to join the couple. "Don't mean nuthin' less you say, 'What God done jined, cain't no man pull asunder,'" noted one Virginia freedman. "But dey never would say dat. Jus' say, 'Now you married.'" For obvious reasons of human dignity, black couples moved to solemnize their marriage vows. There were practical reasons for an official ceremony too: it might qualify families for military pensions or the division of lands that was widely rumored to be coming.

Equally symbolic for most former slaves was the freedom to travel where they wished. As we have seen, historian William Dunning recognized this fact but interpreted it from the viewpoint of his southern white sources as "aimless but happy" wandering. Black accounts make abundantly clear how travel helped freedpeople to rid themselves of the role they had been forced to play during their bondage. Richard Edwards, a preacher in Florida, explicitly described the symbolic nature of such a move:

> You ain't, none o' you, gwinter feel rale free till you shakes de dus' ob de Old Plantashun offen yore feet an' goes ter a new place whey you kin live out o' sight o' de gret house. So long ez de shadder ob de gret house falls acrost you, you ain't gwine ter feel lak no free man, an' you ain't gwine ter feel lak no free 'oman. You mus' all move—you mus' move clar away from de ole places what you knows, ter de new places what you don't know, whey you kin raise up yore head douten no fear o' Marse Dis ur Marse Tudder.

And so, in the spring and summer of 1865, southern roads were filled with black people, hiving off "like bees trying to find a setting place," as one former slave recalled. Most freedpeople preferred to remain within the general locale of family and friends, merely leaving one plantation in search of work at another. But a sizable minority traveled farther, to settle in cities, move west, or try their fortunes at new occupations.

Many former slaves traveled in order to reunite families separated through previous sales. Freedpeople "had a passion, not so much for wandering, as for getting together," a Freedman's Bureau agent observed, "and every mother's son among them seemed to be in search of his mother; every mother in search of her children." Often, relatives had only scanty information; in other cases, so much time had passed that kin could hardly recognize each other, especially when young children had grown up separated from their parents.

A change of name or location, the formalization of marriages, reunion with relatives—all these acts demonstrated that freedpeople wanted no part of the old constraints and deceptions of slavery. But as much as these acts defined black freedom, larger issues remained. How much would emancipation broaden economic avenues open to African Americans? Would freedom provide an opportunity to rise on the social ladder? The freedpeople looked anxiously for signs of significant changes.

Perhaps the most commonly perceived avenue to success was through education. Slavery had been rationalized, in part, through the fiction that blacks were incapable of profiting from an education. The myth of intellectual inferiority stood side by side with that of moral inferiority. Especially in areas where masters had energetically prevented slaves from acquiring skills in reading, writing, and arithmetic, the freedpeople's hunger for learning was intense. When northerners occupied the Carolina Sea Islands during the war, Yankee plantation superintendents found that the most effective way to force unwilling laborers to work was to threaten to take away their schoolbooks. "The Negroes . . . will do anything for us, if we will only teach them," noted one missionary stationed on the islands.

After the war, when the Freedman's Bureau sent hundreds of northern schoolteachers into the South, black students flocked enthusiastically to the makeshift schoolhouses. Often, classes could be held only at night, but the freedpeople were willing. "We work all day, but we'll come to you in the evening for learning," Georgia freedpeople told their teacher. Some white plantation owners discovered that if they wished to keep their field hands, they would have to provide a schoolhouse and teacher.

Important as education was, the freedpeople were preoccupied even more with their relation to the lands they had worked for so many years. The vast majority of slaves were field hands. The agricultural life was the one they had grown up with, and as freedpeople they wanted the chance to own and cultivate their own property. Independent ownership would lay to rest the lie that black people were incapable of managing their own affairs, but without land, the idea of freedom would be just another deception. "Gib us our own land and we take care of ourselves; but widout land, de ole massas can hire us or starve us, as dey please," noted one freedman. In the heady enthusiasm at the close of the war, many former slaves were convinced that the Union would divide up confiscated Confederate plantations. Each family, so the persistent rumor went, would receive forty acres and a mule. "This was no slight error, no trifling idea," reported one white observer, "but a fixed and earnest conviction as strong as any belief a man can ever have." Slaves had worked their masters' lands for so long without significant compensation, it seemed only fair that recompense should finally be made. Further,

"My Lord, ma'am, what a great thing larning is!" a freedman exclaimed to a white teacher. Many white people were surprised by the intensity of the ex-slaves' desire for an education. To say that the freedpeople were "anxious to learn" was not strong enough, one Virginia school official noted; "they are *crazy* to learn." These schoolboys were from South Carolina.

the liberated had more than hopes to rely on. Ever since southern planters had fled from invading Union troops, some black workers had been allowed to cultivate the abandoned fields.

The largest occupied region was the Sea Islands along the Carolina coast, where young Sam Mitchell had first heard the northern guns. As early as March 1863, freedpeople were purchasing confiscated lands from the government. Then in January 1865, after General William Sherman completed his devastating march to the sea, he extended the area that was open to confiscation. In his Special Field Order No. 15, Sherman decreed that a long strip of abandoned lands, stretching from Charleston on the north to

Jacksonville on the south, would be reserved for the freedpeople. The lands would be subdivided into forty-acre tracts, which could be rented for a nominal fee. After three years, the freedpeople had the option to purchase the land outright.

Sherman's order was essentially a tactical maneuver, designed to deal with the overwhelming problem of refugees in his path. But black workers widely perceived this order and other promises by enthusiastic northerners as a foretaste of Reconstruction policy. Consequently, when white planters returned to their plantations, they often found blacks who no longer bowed obsequiously and tipped their hats. Thomas Pinckney of South Carolina, having called his former slaves together, asked them if they would continue to work for him. "O yes, we gwi wuk! we gwi wuk all right," came the angry response. "We gwi wuk fuh ourse'ves. We ain' gwi wuk fuh no white man." Where would they go to work, Pinckney asked—seeing as they had no land? "We ain't gwine nowhar," they replied defiantly. "We gwi wuk right here on de lan' whar we wuz bo'n an' whar belongs tuh us."

Despite the defiance, Pinckney prevailed, as did the vast majority of southern planters. Redistribution of southern lands was an idea strongly supported only by more radical northerners. Thaddeus Stevens introduced a confiscation bill in Congress, but it was swamped by debate and never passed. President Johnson, whose conciliatory policies pleased southern planters, determined to settle the issue as quickly as possible. He summoned General O. O. Howard, head of the Freedman's Bureau, and instructed him to reach a solution "mutually satisfactory" to both blacks and planters. Howard, though sympathetic to the freedpeople, could not mistake the true meaning of the president's order.

Regretfully, the general returned to the Sea Islands in October and assembled a group of freedpeople on Edisto Island. The audience, suspecting the bad news, was restless and unruly. Howard tried vainly to speak and made "no progress" until a woman in the crowd began singing, "Nobody knows the trouble I've seen." The crowd joined, then was silent while Howard told them they must give up their lands. Bitter cries of "No! No!" came from the audience. "Why, General Howard, why do you take away our lands?" called one burly man. "You take them from us who have always been true, always true to the Government! You give them to our all-time enemies! That is not right!"

Reluctantly, and sometimes only after forcible resistance, African Americans lost the lands to returning planters. Whatever else freedom might mean, it was not to signify compensation for previous labor. In the years to come Reconstruction would offer freedom of another sort, through the political process. By the beginning of 1866 the radicals in Congress had charted a plan that gave African Americans basic civil rights and political power. Yet even that avenue of opportunity was quickly sealed off. In the decades that followed the first thunder of emancipation, black people would look back on their early experiences almost as if they were part of another, vanished world. The traditions of racial oppression and the daily deceptions that went with them were too strong to be thoroughly overturned by the war.

"I was right smart bit by de freedom bug for awhile," Charlie Davenport of Mississippi recalled.

> It sounded pow'ful nice to be tol: "You don't have to chop cotton no more. You can th'ow dat hoe down an' go fishin' whensoever de notion strikes you. An' you can roam 'roun' at night an' court gals jus' as you please. Aint no marster gwine a-say to you, 'Charlie, you's got to be back when de clock strikes nine.'"
> I was fool 'nough to b'lieve all dat kin' o' stuff.

Both perceptions—the first flush of the "freedom bug" as well as Davenport's later disillusionment—accurately reflect the black experience. Freedom had come to a nation of four million slaves, and it changed their lives in deep and important ways. But for many years after the war put an end to human bondage, too many freedpeople still had to settle for a view from the bottom rail.

Additional Reading

Leon Litwack's superb *Been in the Storm So Long: The Aftermath of Slavery* (New York, 1979) was a seminal work incorporating the evidence from the slave narrative collections into a reevaluation of the Reconstruction era. It serves as an excellent starting point for background on the freedpeople's experience after the war. For an overview of Reconstruction, the definitive account is Eric Foner, *Reconstruction: America's Unfinished Revolution* (New York, 1988). Foner places the contributions of African Americans at the center of his account. Herbert Gutman, *The Black Family in Slavery and Freedom, 1750–1925* (New York, 1976) is another influential work.

African American experiences can be traced in a host of state histories that give more attention to grassroots effects of the new freedom: for Maryland, see Barbara Jeanne Fields, *Slavery and Freedom on the Middle Ground* (New Haven, 1985); for Virginia, Lynda J. Morgan, *Emancipation in Virginia's Tobacco Belt, 1850–1870* (Athens, GA, 1992); for Georgia, Joseph P. Reidy, *From Slavery to Agrarian Capitalism in the Cotton Plantation South* (Chapel Hill, NC, 1992), and Jonathan M. Bryant, *How Curious a Land* (Chapel Hill, NC, 1996); for South Carolina, Julie Saville, *The Work of Reconstruction* (New York, 1996) and Joel Williamson, *After Slavery* (Chapel Hill, NC, 1965); for Alabama, Peter Kolchin, *First Freedom* (Westport, CT, 1972); and for Mississippi, William C. Harris, *Day of the Carpetbagger* (Baton Rouge, LA, 1979).

A pioneering work on the experiences of black women is Jacqueline Jones, *Labor of Love, Labor of Sorrow: Black Women, Work, and the Family, from Slavery to the Present* (New York, 1985). More recent treatments include Tera W. Hunter, *To 'Joy My Freedom: Southern Black Women's Lives and Labors after the Civil War* (Cambridge, MA, 1997), and Leslie A. Schwalm, *A Hard Fight for We: Women's Transition from Slavery to Freedom in South Carolina* (Urbana, IL, 1997). Willie Lee Rose, *Rehearsal for Reconstruction: The Port Royal Experiment* (Indianapolis, 1964) tells the story of the Union occupation of the Carolina Sea Islands, where the North first attempted to forge a coherent Reconstruction policy. For the Freedmen's Bureau, see William O. McFeely's biography of its leader, General O. O. Howard, *Yankee Stepfather* (New Haven, 1968), and Donald Nieman, *To Set the Law in Motion: The Freedmen's Bureau and the Legal Rights of Blacks* (Millwood, NY, 1979).

Although oral history has provided one crucial means of recapturing the experiences of the freedpeople, the past two decades have witnessed a complementary revolution in unearthing manuscript primary sources for the period. The leaders of this movement are the scholars working on the Freedmen and Southern Society Project, based at the University of Maryland and overseen by Ira Berlin and Leslie Rowland. To date, the project has issued four volumes of documentary evidence—letters, surveys, court depositions, military reports—gathered from twenty-five collections in the bureaucratic recesses of the National Archives: *Freedom: A Documentary History of Emancipation,*

1861–1867 (New York, 1982–). More volumes are promised. The editors have also issued two briefer, easier-to-manage selections from the collection: Ira Berlin et al., eds., *Free at Last: A Documentary History of Slavery, Freedom, and the Civil War* (New York, 1992), and *Families and Freedom: A Documentary History of African-American Kinship in the Civil War Era* (New York, 1997). The editors discuss these documents in Ira Berlin, Barbara J. Fields, Steven F. Miller, and Leslie S. Rowland, *Slaves No More: Three Essays on Emancipation and the Civil War* (New York, 1992). Other sources for the freedpeople's perspective include Octavia V. Rogers Albert, *The House of Bondage* (New York, 1891); Orland K. Armstrong, *Old Massa's People* (Indianapolis, IN, 1931); M. F. Armstrong and Helen W. Ludlow, *Hampton and Its Students* (New York, 1875); and Laura Haviland, *A Woman's Life Work* (Cincinnati, OH, 1881).

A selection of oral interviews from the Federal Writers' Project (again, edited by Ira Berlin and his associates) appears in *Remembering Slavery: African Americans Talk about Their Personal Experiences of Slavery and Freedom* (New York, 1998). But the highlight of this collection is an audiocassette containing more than a dozen of the only known original recordings of former slaves. For the full collection of interviews, see George P. Rawick, *The American Slave: A Composite Autobiography*, 19 vols. and suppl. (Westport, CT, 1972–). The collection invites use in many ways. Intriguing material is available on the relations between African Americans and Indians, for example, especially in the Oklahoma narratives. Because one interviewer often submitted many interviews, readers may wish to analyze strengths and weaknesses of particular interviewers. The Library of Congress, under Benjamin Botkin's direction, began such an analysis; its records can be examined at the National Archives, cataloged under Correspondence Pertaining to Ex-Slave Studies, Records of the Federal Writers' Project, Records Group 69, Works Progress Administration.

Further information on the slave narratives may be found in Norman Yetman, "The Background of the Slave Narrative Collection," *American Quarterly* 19 (fall 1967): 534–553, and John Blassingame, "Using the Testimony of Ex-slaves: Approaches and Problems," *Journal of Southern History* 41 (November 1975): 473–492, available in expanded form in the introduction to his *Slave Testimony* (Baton Rouge, LA, 1977). Paul D. Escott, *Slavery Remembered: A Record of Twentieth-Century Slave Narratives* (Chapel Hill, NC, 1979) provides a quantitative analysis, including the percentage of interviews with field hands, house servants, and artisans; the occupations they took up as freedpeople; and the destinations of those who migrated.

Finally, those wishing to try their hand at oral history should consult David K. Dunaway and Willa K. Baum, eds., *Oral History: An Interdisciplinary Anthology*, 2d ed. (Walnut Creek, CA, 1996). The volume balances good discussions of methodology and technique with more wide-ranging explorations of the ethical questions involved in interviewing as well as international perspectives. Additional nuts-and-bolts information can be found in James Hoopes's excellent *Oral History: An Introduction for Students* (Chapel Hill, NC, 1979). See also Cullom Davis et al., *Oral History: From Tape to Type* (Chicago, IL,

1977), and Ramon I. Harris et al., *The Practice of Oral History* (Glen Rock, NJ, 1975).

Interactive Learning

The *Primary Source Investigator* provides materials that explore the "view from the bottom rail." Included are photographs of former slaves, slave accounts from the end of the Civil War, early Black Codes instituted to firmly establish racial segregation, and personal accounts from both whites and blacks commenting on the uncertainties of the future.

CHAPTER 9
The Mirror with a Memory

At the same time that freedpeople all across the South were struggling to become an integral part of a free and equal society, millions of other Americans in the urbanized North and Midwest were searching for a place in the new industrial society of the late nineteenth century. In the forty years following the Civil War more than 24 million people flooded into American cities. While the population of the agricultural hinterlands doubled during these years, urban population increased by more than 700 percent. Sixteen cities could boast populations over 50,000 in 1860; by 1910 more than a hundred could make that claim. New York City alone grew by 2 million.

Urban areas changed not only in size but also in ethnic composition. While many of the new city-dwellers had migrated from rural America, large numbers came from abroad. Most antebellum cities had been relatively homogeneous, with perhaps an enclave of Irish or German immigrants; the metropolises at the turn of the century were home to large groups of southern as well as northern European immigrants. Again, New York City provides a striking example. By 1900 it included the largest Jewish population of any city in the world, as many Irish as Dublin, and more Italians and Poles than any city outside Rome or Warsaw. Enclaves of Bohemians, Slavs, Lithuanians, Chinese, Scandinavians, and other nationalities added to the ethnic mix.

The quality of living in cities changed too. As manufacturing and commerce crowded into city centers, the wealthy and middle classes fled along newly constructed trolley and rail lines to the quiet of developing suburbs. Enterprising realtors either subdivided or replaced the mansions of the rich with tenements in which a maximum number of people could be packed into a minimum of space. Crude sanitation transformed streets into breeding grounds for typhus, scarlet fever, cholera, and other epidemic diseases. Few tenement rooms had outside windows; less than ten percent of all buildings had either indoor plumbing or running water.

The story of the urban poor and their struggle against the slum's cruel waste of human beings is well known today—as it was even at the turn of the

210

century—because of a generation of social workers and muckrakers who studied the slums firsthand and wrote indignantly about what they found. Not only did they collect statistics to document their general observations, they compiled numerous case studies that described the collective experience in compelling stories about individuals. The pioneer in this endeavor was Jacob Riis. Few books have had as much impact on social policy as his landmark study of New York's Lower East Side, *How the Other Half Lives*. It was at once a shocking revelation of the conditions of slum life and a call for reform. As urban historian Sam Bass Warner concluded, "Before Riis there was no broad understanding of urban poverty that could lead to political action."

Riis had come to know firsthand the degrading conditions of urban life. In 1870 at the age of twenty-one he joined the growing tide of emigrants who fled the poverty of the Scandinavian countryside for the opportunities offered in America. Riis was no starving peasant; in fact his father was a respected schoolmaster and his family comfortably middle class. But Jacob had rejected professional training in order to work with his hands as a carpenter. Unable to find a job in his hometown and rejected by his local sweetheart, he set out for the United States.

Once there, Riis retraced the pattern that millions of immigrants before him had followed. For three years he wandered in search of the promise of the new land. He built workers' shacks near Pittsburgh, trapped muskrats in upstate New York, sold furniture, did odd jobs, and occasionally returned to carpentry. In none of those lines of work did he find either satisfaction or success. At one point poverty reduced him to begging for crumbs outside New York City restaurants and spending nights in a police lodging house. His health failed. He lingered near death until the Danish consul in Philadelphia took him in. At times his situation grew so desperate and his frustration so intense that he contemplated suicide.

Riis, however, had a talent for talking and the hard sell. Eventually he landed a job with a news association in New York and turned his talent to reporting. The direction of his career was determined in 1877, when he became the police reporter for the *New York Tribune*. He was well suited for the job; his earlier wanderings having made him all too familiar with the seamy side of urban life. The police beat took him to headquarters near "The Bend," what Riis referred to as the "foul core of New York's slums." Every day he observed the symptoms of urban poverty. Over the course of a year police dragnets collected some forty thousand indigents who were carted off to the workhouses and asylums. And at night Riis shadowed the police to catch a view of the neighborhood "off its guard." He began to visit immigrants in their homes, where he observed their continual struggle to preserve a measure of decency in an environment of chronic unemployment, disease, crime, and cultural dislocation.

As a *Tribune* reporter, Riis published exposé after exposé on wretched slum conditions. In so doing he followed the journalistic style of the day. Most reporters had adopted the strategies found in Charles Dickens's novels, personifying social issues through the use of graphic detail and telling vignettes. Such concrete examples involved readers most directly with the squalor of city slums. The issue of female exploitation in sweatshops became the story of an old woman Riis discovered paralyzed by a stroke on her own doorstep. The plight of working children, who had neither education nor more than passing familiarity with the English language, was dramatized by the story of Pietro, the young Italian boy who struggled to keep awake at night school. Touching stories brought home the struggles of the poor better than general statistics. They also sold newspapers.

But Riis found the newspaper life frustrating. His stories may have been vivid, but apparently not vivid enough to shock anyone to action. New York authorities had made token efforts at slum clearance, but by 1890 the conditions about which Riis protested had grown steadily worse. The Lower East Side had a greater population density than any neighborhood in the world—335,000 people to one square mile of the tenth ward and as many as one person per square foot in the worst places.[1]

In frustration, Riis left the *Tribune* to write *How the Other Half Lives*. He wanted to make a case for reform that even the most callous officials could not dismiss, and a full-length book was more likely to accomplish what a series of daily articles could not. The new format enabled Riis to weave his individual stories into a broader indictment of urban blight. It allowed him to buttress concrete stories with collections of statistics. And perhaps most important, it inspired him to provide documentary proof of a new sort—proof so vivid and dramatic that even the most compelling literary vignettes seemed weak by comparison. Riis sought to document urban conditions with the swiftly developing techniques of photography.

From the experience of other urban reformers, Riis had learned that photographs could be powerful weapons to arouse popular indignation. In a book on London slums, *Street Life in London* (1877), authors John Thompson and Adolph Smith had decided to include photographs because, as they explained, "The unquestionable accuracy of this testimony will enable us to present true types of the London poor and shield us from accusations of either underrating or exaggerating individual peculiarities of appearance." For Riis their argument was a compelling one. If photographs accompanied *How the Other Half Lives*, no corrupt politician could dismiss its arguments as opinionated word-paintings spawned by the imagination of an overheated reformer. Photography indisputably showed life as it really was.

"REALITY" AND PHOTOGRAPHIC EVIDENCE

From the moment in 1839 when the French pioneer of photography Louis-Jacques Daguerre announced his discovery of a process to fix images perma-

---

1. Those readers conjuring up a picture of slum-dwellers standing like sardines row on row, each with his or her own square foot, must remember that tenement space reached upward through several stories. The statistic refers to square footage of ground area, not square footage of actual floor space.

nently on a copper plate, observers repeatedly remarked on the camera's capacity to record reality. More than anything else, the seeming objectivity of the new medium caught the popular imagination. The camera captured only those objects that appeared before the lens—nothing more, nothing less. So faithful was the camera that people often commented that the photographic image recorded the original with an exactness "equal to nature itself." Indeed, one of the attractions of the new medium was that it could accurately reveal the look of other parts of the United States and the world. Nineteenth-century Americans were hungry for visual images of unseen places. Few had ever seen the trans-Mississippi West, much less Europe or the South Pacific. Almost no one had access to pictures that satisfied curiosity about exotic lands or people. As a result, crowds flocked to the galleries of a painter such as Albert Bierstadt when he displayed his grand landscapes of the Rocky Mountains. Even Bierstadt's paintings, though, were colored by his romantic vision of the West, just as all artists' work reflects their own personal styles and quirks.

The new photography seemed to have no style—that was its promise. It recorded only what was before the camera. Reproductions were so faithful to the original that close observation with a magnifying glass often revealed details that had been invisible to the naked eye. The American writer and physician Oliver Wendell Holmes summed up the popular conception when he noted that the camera was even more than "the mirror of reality"; it was "the mirror with a memory."

Certainly, there was no denying the camera's unprecedented ability to record detail in a way that paintings could not. Yet from today's vantage point, it is easier to see the limits of the camera's seeming objectivity. Any modern amateur photographer who is familiar with the features of a single-lens reflex camera will appreciate immediately how deceptive the camera's claim to mirroring reality can be. Merely to sight through the viewfinder reminds us that every photograph creates its own frame, including some objects and excluding others. The problem of selection of evidence, which is at the heart of the historian's task, remains of paramount importance in photography.

The situation becomes even more complex when we begin to make simple photographic adjustments once the frame has been selected. Far from recording every detail within the lens's reach, we immediately begin excluding details by turning the focusing ring: in choosing a closeup, background details blur; if aiming for a distant subject, it is the foreground that becomes hazy. The technical constraints of the camera thus limit what can be recorded on the negative's frame. If we close down the aperture of the camera's lens (the circular hole that allows light to pass through the lens), the camera's depth of field is increased, bringing into focus a larger area within the path of the lens. On the other hand, photographers who wish to concentrate the viewer's attention on a central subject will eliminate cluttering detail by decreasing their depth of field.

Of course, it may be argued with a good deal of justice that many, if not all, of these distorting capabilities of the camera are irrelevant when

The cumbersome technology of early photography restricted the use of photography largely to professionals. Field photographers had to take along darkrooms in which they prepared the photographic plates that went into a heavy box camera. The van pictured here was used by a photographer during the Crimean War. Matthew Brady and his assistants employed similar large wagons during the Civil War. They soon discovered, much to their chagrin, that such rolling darkrooms made uncomfortably obvious targets for enemy artillery and sharpshooters.

discussing the work of Jacob Riis. Riis worked with neither a sophisticated single-lens reflex camera nor a particularly extensive knowledge of photographic principles. His primary goals were not to record scenes aesthetically and artistically but to capture the subject matter before his camera. The niceties of art would have to wait.

Indeed, when Riis began his photographic efforts he quickly discovered that the primitive nature of photography precluded too much attention to aesthetic details, especially in his line of work. In the 1880s taking pictures was no simple matter. Each step in the photographic process presented formidable obstacles. First, would-be photographers had to learn to prepare a light-sensitive chemical mixture and spread it evenly on the glass plates that served as photographic negatives. For work in the field, they had to take along a portable darkroom, usually a clumsy tent perched on a tripod. Here the negatives were taken from the cumbersome box camera and developed in chemical baths. Additional solutions were necessary to transfer the image from the plate to the final paper print. Such a process taxed the ingenuity and dedication of even the most avid practitioners.

Fortunately, advances in chemistry, optics, and photographic technology had given birth to a new generation of equipment, the "detective camera." Wily photographers took to disguising cameras as doctors' satchels, briefcases, books, revolvers, and vest buttons—hence the nickname detective camera. To ease the burden of field photographers and make possible the candid shot, a number of companies had introduced small cameras about the size of a cigar box. Some carried as many as twelve photographic plates that could be used before the camera required reloading.

George Eastman simplified the process even further with his Kodak camera. Introduced to the public in 1888, the Kodak was more than an improved detective camera; it was the first model that replaced glass negatives with a photographic emulsion coated on paper rolls. For twenty-five dollars, an aspiring photographer could acquire the camera loaded with a hundred shots. Once the film had been exposed, the owner simply returned the camera to the dealer, who removed the spool in a darkroom and shipped it to Eastman's factory for processing. For an additional ten dollars, the dealer would reload the camera with new film. So successfully had Eastman reduced the burden on amateur photographers that his ads could boast, "You press the button, we do the rest."

But even the advances in photographic technology did not eliminate Riis's difficulties. When he began his photographic work, he knew nothing of photography. To help him, he enlisted the assistance of several friends in the Health Department who also happened to be amateur photographers. Together they set out to catch their subjects unawares. That meant skulking around the Bend in the dead of night, with the normal photographic paraphernalia increased by bulky and primitive flash equipment. For a flash to work, a highly combustible powder was spread along a pan. The pan was then held up, and Riis exploded a blank cartridge from a revolver to ignite the powder. This photographic entourage sneaking about town after hours made a remarkable sight, as the *New York Sun* reported:

> Somnolent policemen on the street, denizens of the dives in their dens, tramps and bummers in their so-called lodgings, and all the people of the wild and wonderful variety of New York night life have in turn marvelled at and been frightened by the phenomenon. What they saw was three or four figures in the gloom, a ghostly tripod, some weird and uncanny movements, the blinding flash, and then they heard the patter of retreating footsteps and their mysterious visitors were gone before they could collect their scattered thoughts.

The results from using such finicky equipment were not always predictable. Sometimes the noise would awaken unsuspecting subjects and create a disturbance. On one particularly unfortunate occasion Riis had gone to "Blind Man's Alley" to photograph five sightless men and women living in a cramped attic room. Soon after his eyes cleared from the blinding flash, he

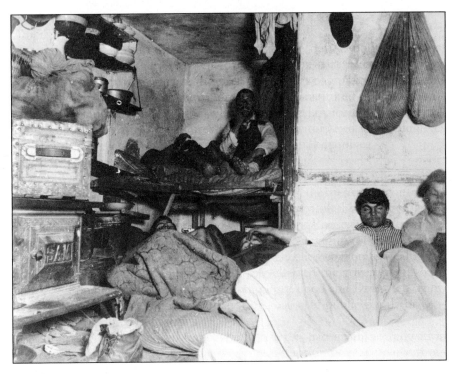

Lodgers in a crowded Bayard Street tenement—"Five Cents a Spot"

saw flames climbing up the rags covering the walls. Fear gripped him as he envisioned the blaze sweeping through twelve rickety flights of stairs between the attic and safety. Fighting the impulse to flee, he beat out the flames with his coat and then rushed to the street seeking help. The first policeman who heard his story burst out laughing. "Why, don't you know that's the Dirty Spoon?" he responded. "It caught fire six times last winter, but it wouldn't burn. The dirt was so thick on the walls it smothered the fire."

Under such precarious circumstances, it might be argued that Riis's photography more closely mirrored reality precisely because it was artless, and that what it lacked in aesthetics it gained in documentary detail. Above, for example, we see a picture taken on one of Riis's night expeditions, of lodgers at one of the crowded "five cents a spot" tenements. The room itself, Riis informs us in *How the Other Half Lives*, is "not thirteen feet either way," in which "slept twelve men and women, two or three in bunks in a sort of alcove, the rest on the floor." The sleepy faces and supine bodies reflect the candid nature of the picture; indeed, Riis had followed a policeman who was raiding the room in order to drive the lodgers into the street. The glare of the flash, casting distinct shadows, reveals all of the crowding, dirt, and disorder. This photograph is no aesthetic triumph, perhaps, but it does reveal a wealth of details that prove most useful to the curious historian.

In the original edition of *How the Other Half Lives*, seventeen of the
photographs appeared as blurry halftones and nineteen as artists' engravings, such
as this rendering of the "Five Cents a Spot" photograph. A comparison of the two
illustrations quickly demonstrates how much more graphically the photograph
presented Riis's concerns. Riis continued to take photographs for other books he
published, although it was not until well into the twentieth century that mass
reproduction techniques could begin to do justice to them.

We notice, for instance, that the stove in the foreground is a traditional
wood-burning model, with its fuel supply stacked underneath. Space in the
apartment is so crowded that footlockers and bundles have been piled directly
on top of the stove. (Have they been moved from their daytime resting places
on the bunks? Or do these people carry their possessions onto the street during the day?) The dishes and kitchen utensils are piled high on shelves next
to the stove. The bedding is well used, dirty, and makeshift. Such details are
nowhere near as faithfully recorded in the line drawing originally published
in *How the Other Half Lives*.

Yet no matter how "artless" the photographs of Jacob Riis may be in terms
of their aesthetic control of the medium, to assume they are bias-free seriously underestimates their interpretive content. However primitive a photographer Riis may have been, he still influenced the messages he presented
through an appropriate selection of details. Even the most artless photographers make such interpretive choices in every snapshot they take.

Let us look, for example, at the most artless photographic observations of all: the ordinary family scrapbook found in most American homes. When George Eastman marketed his convenient pocket camera, he clearly recognized the wide appeal of his product. At long last the ordinary class of people, not just the rich and wellborn, could create for themselves a permanent documentary record of their doings. "A collection of these pictures may be made to furnish a pictorial history of life as it is lived by the owner," proclaimed one Kodak advertisement.

But while family albums provide a wide-ranging "pictorial history," they are still shaped by conventions every bit as stylized as the romantic conventions of Bierstadt or other artists with equally distinct styles. The albums are very much ceremonial history—birthdays, anniversaries, vacations. Life within their covers is a succession of proud achievements, celebrations, and uncommon moments. A father's retirement party may be covered, but probably not his routine day at the office. We see the sights at Disney World, not the long waits at the airport. Arguments, rivalries, and the tedium of the commonplace are missing.

If the artless photographers of family life unconsciously shape the records they leave behind, then we must expect those who self-consciously use photography to be even more interpretive with their materials. This manipulation is not a matter of knowing the tricks of the trade about depth of field or shutter speed, but simply intelligent people wishing to convey a coherent message with their photographs. Civil War photographer Matthew Brady wanted to capture the horrific carnage of the war. To achieve it, he did not hesitate to drag dead bodies to a scene in order to further the composition or the effect he desired.

But to point out such literal examples of the photographer's influence almost destroys the point by caricaturing it. The photographer need not rearrange compositions in order to be photographing for interpretive, even propagandistic purposes. The western land surveys of the 1860s and 1870s, for instance, discovered that their photographs had social uses that extended beyond the narrowly geologic. Although the surveys' missions were ostensibly scientific, they required the financial patronage of Congress. As rival surveys vied for an adequate share of the limited funds, they discovered that photographs of scenic wonders produced the desired results back East. The survey headed by F. V. Hayden in 1871 verified the tall tales that had long circulated about natural wonders in northwest Wyoming. The photographs of spectacular vistas, towering waterfalls, Mammoth Hot Springs, Old Faithful, and the geyser basins justified survey appropriations as well as helped persuade Congress to establish Yellowstone as the first national park safe from commercial development.

A later generation of government photographers, those who worked during the Great Depression of the 1930s, also viewed photographs as vehicles to convey their social messages. Few photographers were more dedicated to the ideal of documentary realism than Walker Evans, Dorothea Lange, Ben Shahn, and others who photographed tenant farmers and sharecroppers for

"A collection of these pictures may be made to furnish a pictorial history of life as it is lived by the owner." Following the dictum in the Kodak advertisement, these two men pose happily, one holding one of the new Kodak cameras while a friend uses another to record the scene. Like so many family album "candids," this shot follows the tradition of ceremonial history—proud achievements, celebrations, and uncommon moments. These men, dressed in their best, are tourists from Pennsylvania enjoying spring on the White House lawn in April 1889.

the Farm Security Administration. Yet these photographers also brought to their work preconceived notions about how poverty should look. As critic Susan Sontag has noted, they "would take dozens of frontal pictures of one of their sharecropper subjects until satisfied that they had gotten just the right look on film—the precise expression on the subject's face that supported their own notions about poverty, light, dignity, texture, exploitation,

"Photographing in High Places," Teton range 1872, by William Henry Jackson. A member of John Wesley Powell's earlier expedition down the Colorado River recalled the effort involved in handling the unwieldy photographic equipment: "The camera in its strong box was a heavy load to carry up the rocks, but it was nothing to the chemical and plate-holder box, which in turn was feather weight compared to the imitation hand organ which served as a darkroom." Mishaps along the way were not uncommon. "The silver bath had gotten out of order," reported one of Powell's party, "and the horse bearing the camera fell off a cliff and landed on top of the camera . . . with a result that need not be described."

and geometry. In deciding how a picture should look . . . photographers are always imposing standards on their subjects."

Thus any series of photographs—including those Jacob Riis took for his books—must be analyzed in the same way a written narrative is. We can appreciate the full import of the photographs only by establishing their historical context. What messages are they meant to convey? What are the premises—stated or unstated—that underlie the presentation of photographs? Ironically, in order to evaluate the messages in the Riis photographs, we must supplement our knowledge of his perspectives on the city by turning to his writings.

IMAGES OF THE OTHER HALF

Jacob Riis was an immigrant to America, like so many of those he wrote about. He had tasted poverty and hardship. Yet in a curious way, Riis the social reformer might best be understood as a tourist of the slums, wandering from tenement to tenement, camera in hand. To classify him as such is to suggest that despite his immigrant background, he maintained a distance between himself and his urban subjects.

In part, that distance can be explained by Riis's own background as an immigrant. Despite his tribulations, he came from a middle-class family, which made it easy to choose journalism as a career. As a boy, in fact, Riis had helped his family prepare copy for a weekly newspaper. Once established in a job commensurate with his training, Riis found it easy to accomplish the goal of so many immigrants—to rise to middle-class dignity and prosperity and to become, in the most respectable sense, not a newcomer but an American.

Furthermore, because Riis emigrated from Denmark, his northern European background made it more difficult for him to empathize with the immigrant cultures of southern and eastern Europe, increasingly the source of new immigrants in the 1880s and 1890s. Like many native-born Americans, Riis found most of these immigrants' customs distasteful and doubted whether they could successfully learn the traditional American virtues. As Sam Warner remarked, Riis ascribed a "degree of opprobrium to each group directly proportional to the distance from Denmark."

Yet for all that, Riis retained a measure of sympathy and understanding for the poor. He did not work his way out of poverty only to find a quiet house far from the turmoil of the urban scene. He was unable to ignore the squalor that so evidently needed the attention of concerned Americans. Thus an ambivalence permeated Riis's writings. On the one hand he sympathized with the plight of the poor and recognized how much they were the victims of their slum environment. "In the tenements all the elements make for evil," he wrote. He struggled to maintain a distinction between the "vicious" classes of beggars, tramps, and thieves and the working poor who made the slum their home because they had no other choice. On the other hand, Riis could not avoid using language that continuously dismissed whole classes of immigrants as inherently unable to adapt themselves to what he considered acceptable American behavior.

When he visited "Jewtown," for example, Riis scarcely commented on the strong bonds of faith and loyalty that held families and groups together in the face of all the debilitating aspects of slum life. Instead, he dwelt on the popular "Shylock" stereotype. "Money is their God," he wrote. "Life itself is of little value compared to even the leanest bank account." Upon the Irish, of course, he bestowed a talent for politics and drink. "His genius runs to public affairs rather than domestic life," said Riis of the Irish politician; "wherever he is mustered in force the saloon is the gorgeous center of political activity."

To southern and eastern Mediterranean people, Riis was least understanding. The "happy-go-lucky" Italians, he observed, were "content to live in a pig sty." Not only did they "come in at the bottom," but also they managed to stay there. They sought to reproduce the worst of life in Italy by flocking to slum tenements. When an Italian found better housing, "he soon reduced what he did find to his own level, if allowed to follow his natural bent." These affable and malleable souls "learned slowly, if at all." And then there was the passion for gambling and murder: "[The Italian's] soul is in the game from the moment the cards are on the table, and very frequently his knife is in it too before the game is ended." Such observations confirm our sense of Riis as a tourist in the slums, for he seemed only to have educated his prejudices without collecting objective information.

A second quality that strikes the reader of *How the Other Half Lives* is its tone of Christian moralism. Riis blamed the condition of the urban poor on the sins of individuals—greedy landlords, petty grafters, corrupt officials, the weak character of the poor, and popular indifference. Insensitive to the economic forces that had transformed cities, he never attempted a systematic analysis of urban classes and institutional structures. Instead, he appealed to moral regeneration as the means of overcoming evil, and approvingly cited the plea of a philanthropic tenement builder: "How are these men and women to understand the love of God you speak of, when they see only the greed of men?" In his own ominous warning to his fellow New Yorkers, Riis struck an almost apocalyptic note: "When another generation shall have doubled the census of our city," he warned, "and to the vast army of workers, held captive by poverty, the very name of home shall be a bitter mockery, what will the harvest be?" If conditions worsened, the violence of labor strikes during the 1870s and 1880s might seem quite tame in comparison.

Given those predispositions, how do we interpret Riis's photographs? Like the arrangers of family albums, his personal interests dictated the kind of photographs he included in his books. And as with the family albums, by being aware of these predispositions we can both understand Riis better by consciously examining his photographic messages and at the same time transcend the original intent of the pictures.

For example, Riis's Christian moralism led him to emphasize the need for stable families as a key to ameliorating slum conditions. Many American Protestants in his audience thought of the home and family as a haven from the bustle of the working world as well as a nursery of piety and good morals. Fathers could return at the end of the day to the warm, feminine environment in which their children were carefully nurtured. Thus the picture we have already examined of the "five cents a spot" lodgings takes on added

Bohemian cigar makers at work in their tenement

significance in light of these concerns. It is not simply the lack of cleanliness or space that would make such an apartment appalling to many viewers, but the corrosive effect of such conditions on family life. Yet this building was a family dwelling, for Riis heard a baby crying in the adjoining hall-room. How could a family preserve any semblance of decency, Riis asked his readers, in a room occupied by twelve single men and women?

Let us turn from that photograph to another, shown on this page, which is more obviously a family portrait. The middle-class Protestant viewer of Riis's day would have found this picture shocking as well. The home was supposed to be a haven away from the harsh workaday world, yet here the factory has invaded the home. This small room of an immigrant Bohemian family is crowded with the tools and supplies needed to make a living. The business is apparently a family enterprise, since the husband, wife, and at least one child assist in the work. Although the young boy cannot keep his eyes off the camera, he continues to stretch tobacco leaves from the pile on his lap.

The room speaks of a rather single-minded focus on making a living. All the furnishings are used for cigar making, not for creature comforts or living after work. The only light comes from a small kerosene lamp and the indirect sunlight from two windows facing out on the wall of another building. Yet Riis had a stronger message for the picture to deliver. The text stresses the exploitation of Bohemians in New York, most of whom worked at cigar making in apartments owned by their employers, generally Polish Jewish immigrants.

The cigar trade dominated all aspects of life: "The rank smell that awaited us on the corner of the block follows us into the hallways, penetrates every nook and cranny of the house." This particular family, he noted, turned out 4,000 cigars a week, for which it was paid $15. Out of that amount the landlord-employer deducted $11.75 in rent for three small rooms, two of which had no windows for light or air. The father was so tied to his workbench that in six years he had learned no English and, therefore, made no attempt to assimilate into American life.

It is interesting to contrast the portrait of the Bohemian family with a different family portrait, this one taken by another reforming photographer, but still often published in reprints of *How the Other Half Lives*.[2] Unlike the photograph of the cigar makers' lodgings, the photograph on page 225 is a more formal family portrait. Very much aware of the camera's presence, everyone is looking directly at the lens. Perhaps the photographer could gain consent to intrude on their privacy only by agreeing to do a formal photograph. The children have been scrubbed and dressed in what appear to be their good clothes—the oldest son in his shirt and tie, his sister in a taffeta dress, and a younger girl in a frock. Unlike the "five cents a spot" lodging, where dishes were stacked one upon the other, here the family china is proudly displayed in the cabinet. Perhaps it was a valued possession carefully guarded on the journey from Europe.

Other details in the picture suggest that this family enjoyed a more pleasant environment than was seen in the previous photos. We notice on the left a gas stove, a relatively modern improvement in an age when coal and wood were still widely used for heating and cooking. Perhaps these people had found a room in a once-elegant home divided by the realtor into a multiple dwelling. Certain details suggest that may be the case. Few tenements would have had gas, much less built-in cupboards or the finished moldings around doors and windows. The window between the kitchen-bedroom and closet-bedroom indicates that the room may have once looked out on open space.

By contrast, the picture communicates a sense of crowding. This image hardly seems an accident. Had the photographer wished to take only a family portrait, she could have clustered her subjects in the center of her lens. Instead, she placed them around the room, so that the camera would catch all the details of their domestic circumstance. We see not just a family, but the conditions of their lives in an area far too small for their needs. Each space and almost all the furnishings are used for more than one purpose. The washtub just before the window and washboard behind it indicate that the kitchen doubles as a laundry room—and the tub was probably used for

---

2. The photographer is Jessie Tarbox Beals, and the picture was taken in 1910. Although not included in the original edition of *How the Other Half Lives*, it is among the photographs in the Riis collection held by the Museum of the City of New York.

Room in a tenement flat, 1910

baths as well. The bed serves during the day as a sofa. To gain a measure of privacy the parents have crowded their bed into a closet stuffed with family possessions. Seven people seem to share a room perhaps no more than 250 square feet in total. The children appear to range in age from one to twelve. If the mother is again pregnant, as the picture hints, that means every two years another person enters that cramped space.

This portrait, then, does not conform to the stereotype we would expect to find of urban immigrant slum dwellers. In the first place, many immigrants came to America without families. Of those, a majority were young men who hoped to stay just long enough to accumulate a small savings with which to improve their family fortunes upon returning to Europe. On the other hand, immigrant families tended to be much larger than those of middle-class native-born Americans. Rather than evoking a sympathetic response among an American audience, the picture might, instead, reinforce the widespread fear that prolific breeding among foreign elements threatened white Protestant domination of American society.

What then does the modern viewer derive from this family portrait? Over all, it seems to say that immigrants, like other Americans, prized family life. The father perches at the center almost literally holding his family together,

"Street arabs" in sleeping quarters

though with a rather tenuous grip. The son with his tie appears to embody the family's hopes for a better future. His mother securely holds the baby in her arms. Each element, in fact, emphasizes the virtues of the domestic family as it was traditionally conceived in America. The picture, while sending a mixed message, conveys less a sense of terrible slum conditions than a sense of the middle-class aspirations among those forced to live in inadequate housing.

Does the fact that the picture is posed make it less useful as historical evidence? Not at all. Even when people perform for the camera, they communicate information about themselves. There is no hiding the difficulty of making a decent life for seven people in a small space. Nor can the viewer ignore the sense of pride of person and place, no matter how limited the resources. What remains uncertain, however, is what message the photographer meant to convey. The scene could serve equally well to arouse nativist prejudice or to extol the strength of family ties in the immigrant community. Both were concerns that Riis addressed in his writing and photographs.

Concern over the breakdown of family life drew Riis to children. They are among his most frequently photographed subjects. He shared the Victorian notion of childhood innocence and, therefore, understood that nothing could be more disturbing to his middle-class audience than scenes of homeless children, youth gangs, and "street arabs" sleeping in alleys, gutters, and empty stairways. At first glance, the three "street arabs" pictured above ap-

Hell's Kitchen boys—"Showing Their Tricks"

pear as if they might even be dead. A closer look suggests helpless innocence—children alone and unprotected as they sleep. Their ragged clothes and bare feet advertise poverty and the absence of parents to care for them. In each other, though, they seem to have extracted a small measure of warmth, belonging, and comfort. It would be almost impossible for any caring person to view the picture without empathy for its subjects and anger at a society that cares so little for its innocent creatures.

Riis hints at his sympathies through the location of the camera. He did not stand over the boys to shoot the picture from above. That angle would suggest visually the superiority of the photographer to his subjects. From ground level, however, observer and subject are on the same plane. We look at the boys, not down on them. And should we dismiss as accidental his inclusion of the prisonlike bars over the small window? From another angle Riis could have eliminated that poignant symbol from his frame.

Certainly, we know that Riis feared that all too soon those "innocents" would become the members of slum gangs, operating outside the law with brazen disregard for society or its values. In a second picture of lost innocence

Tenement-house yard

on page 227, Riis persuaded some gang members to demonstrate how they "did the trick"—that is, robbed the pockets of a drunk lying in an alley. The mere fact that Riis had obviously arranged the content of the picture, indicating that some relationship existed between the photographer and his subjects,

"Bottle Alley"

would have made the image even more shocking. These young men were clearly proud of their acts and so confident that they were beyond the reach of the law that they could show off for the camera. We see smiles and smug satisfaction on their faces. Other members (not shown) gather around to enjoy the novelty of the situation. Riis's audience would have understood quite clearly that the slums as breeding grounds for crime drove the innocence out of childhood.

Space was scarce not only in the homes of the poor. Crowding extended into public places as well. Without parks or wide streets, children were forced to play in filthy alleys and garbage heaps. Adults had no decent communal space in which to make contact with the community. The picture of a tenement yard on page 228 immediately reveals a scene of chaos and crowding. As in slum apartments, every open area had to serve more than one purpose. Women doing the wash and children playing appear to fall all over one another. The fire escape doubles as a balcony. Any of Riis's readers with a small yard, separate laundry room or laundress, and nearby park surely thanked their good fortune not to be part of this confusion.

Once again, however, closer scrutiny may lead us to reconsider our initial impressions. This place seems alive with energy. We see that the women and children are all part of a community. They have given their common space, restricted as it may be, to shared activities. Everyone seems to have a place in the scheme of things. All that laundry symbolizes a community concern with cleanliness and decency. On the balcony some people have flower boxes to add a touch of color and freshness to the drab landscape. Our initial shock gives way to a more complex set of feelings. We come to respect the durability of spirit that allowed people to struggle for a small measure of comfort amid such harsh surroundings. The message that at first seemed obvious is not so clear after all.

In the photograph titled "Bottle Alley," on page 229, Riis has editorialized on the same theme with more telling effect. In this dingy slum, along the infamous Bend, we are still among tenements. Laundry again hangs from the balcony. A few isolated men look upon the camera as it takes in the scene. Their presence during the day suggests they are among the army of unemployed who sit aimlessly waiting for time to pass. They seem oblivious to the filth that surrounds them. We cannot help but feel that they are as degraded as the conditions in which they live. The dilapidated buildings and rickety stairs create an overall sense of decay; nothing in the picture relieves the image of poverty and disorder Riis wanted to capture. The message is all too clear.

As Jacob Riis and his camera demonstrate, photography is hardly a simple "mirror of reality." The meanings behind each image must be uncovered through careful exploration and analysis. On the surface, certainly, photographs often provide the historian with a wealth of concrete detail. In that sense they do convey the reality of a situation with some objectivity. Yet Riis's relative inexperience with a camera did not long prevent him from learning how to frame the content to create a powerful image. The photographic details communicate a stirring case for social reform, full of subjective as well as objective intent. Riis did not simply want us to see the poor or the slums; he wanted us to see them as he saw them. His view was that of a partisan, not an unbiased observer.

In that sense the photographic "mirror" is silvered on both sides, catching the reflections of its user as well as its subjects. The prints that emerge from the twilight of the darkroom must be read by historians as they do all evidence—appreciating messages that may be simple and obvious or complex and elusive. Once these evidentiary limits are appreciated and accepted, the historian can recognize the rueful justice in Oliver Wendell Holmes's definition of a photograph: an illusion with the "appearance of reality that cheats the senses with its seeming truth."

Additional Reading

Readers wishing to examine more visual evidence from Jacob Riis's *How the Other Half Lives* should consult the Dover Publications edition (New York, 1971) of his book. It has a good introduction by Charles Madison, but most important, it includes 100 photographs and several reproductions of line illustrations from the original version. Another edition of *How the Other Half Lives* (Cambridge, MA, 1970) has an excellent introduction by urban historian Sam Bass Warner but suffers because of a limited number of photos. A more comprehensive collection is Robert J. Doherty, ed., *The Complete Photographic Work of Jacob Riis* (New York, 1987). The Riis photographs are also available on microfiche from the International Archives of Photography (New York, 1981). Peter B. Hales, *Silver Cities: Photography of Urban America, 1839–1915* (Philadelphia, 1984) has offered a persuasive interpretation of Riis's place in the tradition of urban photography and social reform. Hales makes clear the extent to which Riis redirected both urban photography away from the celebration of an idealized urban order and social reform away from its ignorance of slum conditions and its sentimentalized view of the poor.

Riis's account of his life is found in Roy Lubove, ed., *The Making of an American* (New York, 1966). An interesting but dated biography exists in Louise Ware, *Jacob A. Riis, Police Reporter* (New York, 1938); see also the more recent study by Edith P. Mayer, *"Not Charity But Justice": The Story of Jacob A. Riis* (New York, 1974). One of America's finest photographers and critics, Ansel Adams, has also done the preface to an important book on Riis: Alexander Alland, *Jacob Riis: Photographer and Citizen* (Millerton, NY; reissued 1993).

Even for those readers whose photographic expertise is limited to a mastery of George Eastman's injunction ("You press the button . . . "), a number of books provide clear discussions of the photographic medium, its potentialities, and its limitations. Susan Sontag, in her *On Photography* (New York, 1977), provides many stimulating ideas, particularly in her first essay, "In Plato's Cave," and, most recently, in *Regarding the Pain of Others* (New York, 2003). All followers of photographic art owe a debt to Beaumont Newhall, *The History of Photography from 1839 to the Present Day* (New York, 1964). Besides his work as photo-historian and critic, Newhall helped establish the photographic wing of the Museum of Modern Art. Also useful for background on the technical and aesthetic developments in photography is Robert Taft, *Photography and the American Scene* (New York, 1938; reissued 1964). For views that contrast with Riis's scenes of New York, see the Museum of the City of New York's *Once Upon a City: New York from 1890 to 1910* (New York, 1958).

Discussions of immigration, urbanization, and industrialization abound; here we mention only a representative and useful sampling. Among the histories and novels of the immigration experience, few have the impact of Anzia Yezierska, *Breadgivers* (New York, 1925), reissued in 1975 with a fine introduction by Alice Kessler Harris. Umberto Nelli, *Italians of Chicago* (New York, 1972) is worth reading as a corrective to Riis's stereotypes of Italians. For more general discussions about immigration we recommend Roger Daniels, *Coming to America: A History of Immigration and Ethnicity in American Life* (New York, 1990), and Ronald Takaki, *A Different Mirror: A History of Multicultural America* (Boston, 1993). On the story of Jews, Ronald Sanders, *Shores of Refuge: A Hundred Years of Jewish Emigration* (New York, 1988) is a readable account. To appreciate Riis's impact on other urban reformers, we suggest Robert Hunter, *Poverty* (New York, 1904; reissued 1965), supplemented by Keith Gandal, *The Virtues of the Vicious: Jacob Riis, Stephen Crane, and the Spectacle of the Slum* (New York, 1997).

Two brief yet informed analyses of late-nineteenth-century economic development are Stuart Bruchey, *The Growth of the American Economy* (New York, 1975), and Robert Heilbroner, *The Economic Transformation of America* (New York, 1977). For the concurrent transformation of cities, see Zane Miller, *The Urbanization of Modern America* (New York, 1973), and even more stimulating, Sam Bass Warner, *The Urban Wilderness* (New York, 1972). Nor should readers miss Ray Ginger's lively discussion of urban Chicago in *Altgeld's Illinois* (Chicago, 1958). The problems and challenges of technology are treated in Ruth Cowan Schwartz, *A Social History of American Technology* (New York, 1996), and Nathan Rosenberg, *Technology and American Growth* (White Plains, NY, 1972).

One significant pleasure in a field as untapped as photographic evidence comes from doing original research yourself. Many photographs of historic value are on file and readily available to the public in the Library of Congress Prints and Photographs Division and the National Archives Still Picture Branch. At quite reasonable prices, interested researchers may obtain their own 8 × 10 inch glossy reproductions printed from copy negatives made of the original photographs, or they may download them from the Library's *American Memory* Web site (http://memory.loc.gov). The Library of Congress is easier for novices to use than is the National Archives, although the staffs at both institutions are extremely helpful. Two books provide a sampling of each institution's collections: from the Library of Congress, *Viewpoints* (Washington, DC, 1975); from the National Archives, *The American Image* (New York, 1979). The latter volume contains an excellent introduction by Alan Trachtenberg, whose discussions of photographic images planted the seed for this essay. Both books provide ordering numbers for the photographs that were reproduced so that interested readers may order their own prints. Michael Lesy, *Wisconsin Death Trip* (New York, 1973) opened up the possibilities of doing photographic research, though not without disturbing other historians. Almost all readers will have access to family albums, yearbooks, newspaper files, Web sites, and other sources from which to do their own investigating.

Interactive Learning

The *Primary Source Investigator* includes materials that explore early photographic images of immigrants in tenements during the late-nineteenth and early-twentieth centuries. These photographs provide a telling story of what city life was like for immigrants at this time. Also included are images of early photography equipment and personal accounts of "how the other half lives."

CHAPTER 10
USDA Government Inspected

All our essays tell a story, and this one is no exception. But our present tale, by its very nature, partakes in large measure of the epic and the symbolic. It is a political tale, compiled largely from the accounts of politicians and the journalists who write about politicians; which is to say, it possesses much of the charm and innocence of a good, robust fairy tale. As we shall shortly discover, there are logical reasons for such larger-than-life overtones, and they deserve serious scrutiny. But the story must come first: an exciting tale of a bold president, an earnest reformer, some evil political bosses, and a lot of pork and beef.

It begins ("once upon a time") with the president, Teddy Roosevelt, who turns out to be the hero of the tale. There was nothing ordinary about Teddy, including the fact that he was ever president at all. People from the Roosevelts' social class disdained politics and would never encourage their sons to take it up as a profession. But then again Teddy was not like other members of his social class nor like his fellow students at Harvard. Anything he did, he did with gusto, and if being the best meant being president, then Teddy would not stop short of the White House.

His path to success was not an easy one. As a child Teddy was sickly, asthmatic, and nearsighted. He spent long hours pummeling punching bags, swinging on parallel bars, doing push-ups, and boxing in the ring to build a body as robust as his mind. When he went west in the 1880s to take up ranching, he had to overcome his image as an effete eastern "dude." He soon amazed many a grizzled cowboy by riding the Dakota badlands in spring mud, blasts of summer heat, and driving winter storms. He fought with his fists and once rounded up a band of desperados at gunpoint. Back East, when Teddy played tennis, he showed the same determination, his record being ninety-one games in a single day. When he led the Rough Riders through Cuba in 1898, he raised troop morale by walking the sentry line, whistling cheerfully while his men crouched low to avoid the bullets flying overhead. As president he advised others to speak softly and carry a big stick, though he himself more often observed only the latter half of his maxim. Teddy's

TR, displaying characteristic gritted teeth and holding a moderately big stick. When he spoke, Roosevelt chopped every word into neat, staccato syllables, with a rhythm that bore no resemblance to the ordinary cadences of the English language. "I always think of a man biting tenpenny nails when I think of Roosevelt making a speech," remarked one acquaintance.

favorite expressions, seldom spoken softly, were "Bully!" and "Dee lighted!" —uttered because he usually got his way.

By 1906 Teddy had the White House firmly in his grasp. Just two years earlier he had engineered an impressive victory to become president in his own right. He had collected a record of achievements to which he would soon add the Nobel Peace Prize for his role in bringing an end to the Russo-Japanese War. But Teddy could never rest on his laurels. In February a storm broke that challenged his skill as leader of both the nation and the Republican Party.

The thunderclap that shattered the calm was the publication of *The Jungle*. The book told a lurid tale about Chicago's meatpacking industry. Its author, Upton Sinclair, was not only a reformer but a socialist as well. Most Americans of the day believed that socialists were dangerous people who held extreme and impractical opinions. Despite that skepticism, readers could not ignore the grisly realities recounted in *The Jungle*. It related, in often revolting detail, the conditions under which the packers processed pork and beef, adulterated it, and shipped it to millions of American consumers. Breakfast sausage, Sinclair revealed, was more than a tasty blend of ground meats and spices. "It was too dark in these storage spaces to see clearly," he reported,

Hogs being scalded preparatory to scraping at a Swift and Company plant, 1905. The packers boasted that they used every bit of the pig "except the squeal," and they were probably more than right, given some of the extraneous ingredients that went into the canned goods of the period. Although modern viewers may be taken aback at the unsanitary appearance of the plant, this photograph was a promotional shot illustrating some of the better conditions in packing facilities.

but a man could run his hands over the piles of meat and swap off handfulls of dry dung of rats. These rats were nuisances, and the packers would put out poisoned bread for them; they would die; and then rats, bread, and meat would go in the hoppers together. This is no fairy story and no joke; the meat would be shoveled into carts, and the man who did the shoveling did not trouble to lift out a rat even when he saw one.

Rats were but one tasty additive in the meat sent to dinner tables. Potted chicken contained no chicken at all, only beef suet, waste ends of veal, and tripe. Most shocking of all, Sinclair told of men in cooking rooms who fell into vats and, after being cooked for days, "all but the bones had gone out into the world as Durham's Pure Leaf Lard!"

In just one week a scandalized public had snapped up some 25,000 copies of *The Jungle*. Most readers missed the socialist message. Sinclair had hoped to draw their attention to "the conditions under which toilers get their bread." The public had responded instead to the disclosures about corrupt federal meat inspectors, unsanitary slaughterhouses, tubercular cattle, and the packers' unscrupulous business practices.

One of the most outraged readers was President Theodore Roosevelt. Few politicians have ever been as well informed as TR, who devoured books at more than 1,500 words per minute, published works of history, and corresponded regularly with leading business, academic, and public figures. Roosevelt recognized immediately that the public would expect government at some level—local, state, or federal—to clean up the meat industry. He invited Sinclair for a talk at the White House, and though he dismissed the writer's "pathetic belief" in socialism, he promised that "the specific evils you point out shall, if their existence be proved, and if I have the power, be eradicated."

Roosevelt kept his promise. With the help of allies in Congress, he quickly brought out a new bill, along with the proverbial big stick. Only four months later, on June 30, he signed into law the Meat Inspection Act that banned the packers from using any unhealthy dyes, chemical preservatives, or adulterants. The bill provided $3 million toward a new, tougher inspection system, one in which government inspectors could be on hand day or night to condemn animals unfit for human consumption. Senator Albert Beveridge of Indiana, Roosevelt's progressive ally in Congress, gave the president credit for the new bill. "It is chiefly to him that we owe the fact that we will get as excellent a bill as we will have," he told reporters. Once again, Americans could put canned meats and sausages on the dinner table and eat happily ever after. Or so it would seem.

THE SYMBOLS OF POLITICS

The story you have just read is true—as far as it goes. It has taken on a legendary, even mythic quality in the telling. Politics is, after all, public business. And the public, especially in that era, treated their politicians a bit like celebrities. Politicians provide entertainment along with public service. The tales of national politics almost inescapably take on epic proportions. In such situations, symbolic language serves to simplify highly complex realities. It makes those realities more comprehensible by substituting concrete and recognizable actors and objects in the place of complicated, though often ordinary, situations. In doing so, symbols and symbolic language serve as a means of communication between political leaders and their constituencies. Skillful politicians generally have the ability to dramatize their actions so as to appear to address deeply felt public concerns.

Boss William Tweed of New York, in life and in art. During the latter half of the nineteenth century, cartoons played an important part in defining the symbols of political discourse. Occasionally the representations were readily recognizable in more than a symbolic sense. When Tweed fled the United States to escape a jail term, he was arrested in an out-of-the-way Spanish village. The Spanish constables, it turned out, had recognized him from this Thomas Nast cartoon. The symbolic aspect of the drawing escaped them, however; they thought they had apprehended a notorious child kidnapper.

Jacksonian Democrats pioneered many of the modern uses of campaign imagery. They touted their candidate, Old Hickory, as the symbolic embodiment of the American frontier tradition. In their hands Jackson became the uncommon "Common Man." As president, he waged war against the Second Bank of the United States, fittingly symbolized by its enemies as the Monster Bank. His Whig opposition had quickly grasped the use of such symbols; they nominated a popular general of their own, William Henry "Tippecanoe" Harrison. Their campaign rhetoric invoked a log cabin motif and other appropriate frontier images, although in reality Harrison came from a distinguished Virginia family and lived in an elegant house. Thus, along with a two-party system of politics, Americans had developed a body of symbols to make complex political issues familiar and comprehensible to the voters.

Symbols as a mode of political discourse took on a new power in a form that matured in the late nineteenth century: the political cartoon. Earlier cartoonists had portrayed Old Hickory's epic struggle with the Monster Bank, but they lacked the sophistication and draftsmanship achieved by Gilded Age caricaturists such as Thomas Nast. Week after week, newspapers carried cartoons that established readily identifiable symbols. Nast conceived the elephant as a representation of the GOP (the Republicans, or Grand Old Party) and the donkey for the Democrats. To Nast and his fellow cartoonists we owe our image of the Political Boss, decked out in his gaudy suit that assumes a striking resemblance to a convict's striped outfit. So too, we have the Monopolist, or greedy capitalist, his huge, bloated waistline taking on the aspect of a bag of silver dollars. A scraggly beard, overalls, and wild, crazed eyes denoted the Populist. In place of the Monster Bank stood the Trust, vividly pictured as a grasping octopus. Such cartoons by their very nature communicated political messages of their day.

The cartoonists seldom had a better subject than Teddy Roosevelt. His gleaming, oversized front teeth, bull neck, pince-nez glasses, and, of course, big stick begged to be caricatured. Cartoonists did not have to stretch the imagination to cast Teddy larger than life; he specialized in that department long before he reached the White House. He offered himself up as the gun-toting cowboy, the New York police commissioner in his long, black cape, and the Rough Rider charging up Tea Kettle Hill. Thus it was easy during the political battles of the Progressive Era to conceive of the actors in symbolic terms. In one corner stood the reformers: Roosevelt, a policeman, clubbing the opposition with his big stick; or Sinclair, wild-eyed like all political radicals. In the other corner, during the meat-inspection fight, stood the Beef Trust—Armour, Swift, and the other packers with their "public-be-damned" attitudes.

Yet as we have already noted, such symbolic representations inevitably oversimplify the political process to the point of distortion. As rendered by the cartoonist, shades of gray become black and white, and political conflict becomes a Manichaean struggle between good and evil. Even more subtly, distortion arises because symbols come to personalize complex situations and processes. Inanimate institutions (trusts, political machines, Congress) appear as animate objects (a grasping octopus, predatory tigers, braying donkeys) with human motives and designs.

Consequently, we tend to visualize political events as being primarily the result of individuals' actions. The story of the meat-inspection law is reduced to the tale of Roosevelt, Sinclair, and their enemies. The tale, as we saw, is quite simple: (1) Sinclair's revelations scandalize the president; (2) Roosevelt determines to reform the meatpacking industry; (3) with his usual energy, Roosevelt overwhelms the opposition and saves the consumer. Such an explanation masks the crucial truth that the actors—whether individuals, groups, or institutions—often have complicated motives and confused objectives. The outcome of a situation may bear slight resemblance to the original design of any of the participants. As a result, symbolic explanations do not adequately portray the process through which political actors turn their intentions, both good and bad, into law.

Caricaturists had a field day with Roosevelt's energetic and good-natured self-aggrandizement. In this cartoon by Frederick Opper, Vice-President-Elect Roosevelt has rearranged the inaugural parade of 1901 so that President William McKinley is forced to bring up the rear. Teddy, of course, displays his teeth as well as a load of hunting trophies from western exploits, while the characteristic Trust figure looms in the background as "Willie's Papa."

Political historians, then, must handle symbolic language and explanations with caution. They cannot simply dismiss or debunk the symbolism, for it can, by influencing opinion, affect the political process. At the same time, historians cannot allow symbols to obscure the information necessary to narrate and explain political events. Granted, Roosevelt played the reformer in seeking to curb the packers' worst abuses, but how successfully did he translate his intentions into an effective political instrument? Senator Beveridge, it is true, praised both the new law and the president's role in securing its passage, yet other supporters of inspection reform did not share Beveridge's enthusiasm. "The American consumer and the ordinary American farmer have been left out of the question," Senator Knute Nelson complained shortly after the act passed. "I must say I feel disappointed. . . . When I go home I will go home like a licked dog."

In fact, prominent Republicans in the Senate led by Beveridge himself and Roosevelt's good friend, Henry Cabot Lodge of Massachusetts, had fought to defeat the law only a few days before Roosevelt signed it. They believed, as Nelson had argued, that the bill was intended "to placate the packers; next to placate the men who raise cattle; and, third to get a good market for the packers abroad." In short, many senators viewed the Meat Inspection Act as a victory for the packers and a defeat for reform. In that light, Beveridge's praise has a symbolic meaning that our story thus far cannot explain.

So the historian must seek to set aside the mythic story and its symbols in order to reconstruct the way in which the real story unfolded. Individual actions must be made to square with motives. The outcome must be treated not as the inevitable triumph of good over evil but as just one of the many possible outcomes and not necessarily the best at that. The political historian's task is also to determine how the complex procedural tangle by which a bill becomes law limits the impact of individual actors no matter how lofty or base their motives.

THE TANGLE BEHIND *THE JUNGLE*

The mythic tale of the Meat Inspection Act begins with the publication of *The Jungle* in February 1906. That, so the story goes, sparked the outrage against the packers and their unscrupulous methods. Yet although as many as one million people read *The Jungle*, we may legitimately wonder whether a single book could by itself generate such widespread controversy. For better or worse, we have no opinion polls from 1906 to measure public response to Sinclair's lurid exposé. But if we poke around in earlier stories about the meat industry, we find that *The Jungle* was merely a final chapter, albeit a telling one, in a long train of unfavorable stories about the packers.

As early as the 1870s some European governments had begun to ban what they had found to be unhealthy American meat products. Over the years American exports declined as the Europeans tightened their restrictions. In 1891 the worried packers persuaded Congress to pass a federal meat-inspection act in order to win back their foreign customers. The federal stamp would show that all meats in interstate and foreign sales had been subjected to antemortem (preslaughter) inspection. That measure succeeded until 1897, when "embalmed meat" scandals renewed outrage at the industry's unsavory practices. A few unscrupulous packers had supplied the army fighting in Cuba with rotten and chemically adulterated meats. As the commander of the Rough Riders, Colonel Teddy Roosevelt had seen troops die from poisonous meats, as well as from Spanish bullets.

Roosevelt with his Rough Riders. TR's distrust of the packers reached as far back as the Spanish-American War, when packers had sold the American army quantities of rotten and chemically adulterated meats. Humorist Finley Peter Dunne took note of the situation—as well as the disorganized state of the regular army—when he had his fictional Irish bartender, Mr. Dooley, remark on the invincible American army of "injineers, miners, plumbers, an' lawn tinnis experts, numberin' in all four hundhred an' eighty thousand men," sent to do battle against the Spanish "ar-rmed with death-dealin' canned goods."

Roosevelt had not forgotten what he interpreted as treachery. In 1905 he found an opportunity to punish the packers. He ordered his attorney general to bring suit against the packinghouse trust under the Sherman Antitrust Act. The president was particularly offended by what he viewed as the packers' brazen disregard for public safety. In building their industry into one of the nation's ten largest, Armour, Swift, and others boasted openly that they used every bit of the pig "except the squeal." Roosevelt was therefore beside himself when he heard that the judge had dismissed the government's suit on narrow procedural grounds. Suspicious that the packers had bribed the judge, he instructed his attorney general to release a confidential report revealing perjury in the Beef Trust case. Roosevelt scarcely needed to read *The Jungle* to believe that with their public-be-damned attitude the meat barons might be guilty of any manner of irresponsible behavior. *The Jungle* merely provided a new weapon for Roosevelt's ongoing fight.

Furthermore, the president recognized that the existing meat-inspection law left much to be desired. Under it, Congress allocated money for an inspection force, but those appropriations were usually inadequate. Given the limited funds, most inspectors worked only during the day, leaving the packers free to commit their worst abuses at night. Even if inspectors did find diseased cattle at antemortem inspection, they had no power to have the animals destroyed. In fact, the packers often sold those tainted animals to other plants not under federal supervision.

The federal government actually had almost no authority over the packers. Nothing under the system forced compliance with government standards. The inspectors could only threaten to leave the premises (and take their stamps with them) if the packers ignored their rulings. And though the law did prevent the industry from exporting meat without the federal stamp of approval, no similar provision protected American consumers. Once a carcass passed the inspector, the government had no further power to impose sanitary standards anywhere in the plants. Roosevelt was aware of these deficiencies and eager to see them corrected.

The public, too, had grounds for suspicion even before *The Jungle* hit the bookstores. Sinclair's accusations had already been published in a popular socialist journal. In doing his research, Sinclair had received information from the *Lancet*, a distinguished British medical journal that had investigated earlier meat-industry scandals. In 1905 *The Lancet* renewed its investigation of the packinghouses. Investigators discovered filth that jeopardized both workers and consumers. At the same time, Samuel Merwyn, a well-known muckraking journalist, had written articles charging the packers with deliberately selling diseased meats.

Muckrakers like Merwyn had much in common with the political cartoonists. Toward the turn of the century, journalists had discovered that the public possessed an almost insatiable appetite for sensational stories. Muckrakers' investigations uncovered villains who made convenient, easily recognizable symbols. Evil could be personified as the Monster Trust, the Self-Serving Politician, or the Avaricious Capitalist. These villains were much like the greedy landlords Jacob Riis had condemned. Like Riis, muckrakers told Americans what was wrong with their society, but not how the problems arose nor what could be done about them. Somehow the exposure of the symptoms of evil was supposed to motivate reformers and an aroused public to cure the disease. In keeping with the popular style of muckraking, Sinclair had pointed an accusing finger at the packers without offering any specific suggestions for cleaning up the meat industry.

But just as *The Jungle* can be understood only within the context of the muckraking era, so too the Meat Inspection Act stood within the context of Progressive reform. Despite Sinclair's lack of analysis, many Americans had identified the sources of such corporate arrogance and had prepared an agenda for politics. Theodore Roosevelt embodied much of the temperament

"An Alphabet of Joyous Trusts" was Frederick Opper's subject in a 1902 series of cartoons. Predictably, "B" stood for the Beef Trusts. The same Trust figure is back (compare it with the one in Opper's Roosevelt cartoon on page 240), although here Opper plays on the monopolist's traditional control over market prices rather than on the unsanitary practices of the packing industry.

of those Progressive reformers. He shared their hostility to excessive concentrations of power in private hands, their approval of executive regulatory agencies, their faith in democratic forms of government, their humanitarian sensibilities, and their confidence in the people's capacity to shape their future intelligently.

The Progressives were actually a diverse group seeking to turn government at all levels into a weapon for social justice. They included rural reformers, good government and moral uplift advocates, economic regulators, antitrusters, and political liberals and conservatives. Roosevelt's faith in traditional institutions might easily have led him to oppose the reformers, but he was never a diehard conservative who railed against change in any form. "The only true conservative is the man who resolutely set his face to the future," he once told a Progressive supporter.

It was preoccupation with morality that brought the reform movement together and that attracted Roosevelt to Progressivism. "His life, he felt, was a quest for the moral," wrote one biographer. The reformers of the early twentieth century saw themselves rooting out evil, which more often than not they defined as "corporate arrogance." Thus when Roosevelt set out to bust a trust, he did not always pick the biggest corporations. Rather, he picked the more notorious companies, like the Northern Securities railroad combination, whose reputation for stock manipulation and rate gouging against farmers and small shippers had outraged popular opinion. Corporate misconduct would not have spurred moral outrage had the misconduct not frequently resulted in tragedy. Seeking to maximize profits, a railroad might leave a road crossing unguarded; a water company might eliminate safeguards against typhoid fever. "Such incidents made the corporation look like a killer," wrote historian David Thelen. "These specific threats united all classes; anyone's child might be careless at a railroad crossing; and typhoid fever was no respecter of social origins."

Such problems were particularly acute because the explosive growth of cities had created a huge demand for processed foods. Other food industries had no better sanitary standards than the meatpackers. Milk dealers, for example, regularly increased their profits by diluting their product, using chalk, plaster, and molasses to fortify the color and taste. A popular ditty of the day expressed the widespread skepticism with processed foods:

> Things are seldom what they seem;
> Skim milk masquerades as cream;
> Lard and soap we eat for cheese;
> Butter is but axle grease.

As a result, the public was prepared to think the worst of the meat industry. The campaign for improved meat inspection had all the ingredients that aroused Progressive ire. The packing industry fit Roosevelt's definition of a "bad" trust, since its apparent disregard for even minimum health standards threatened all classes of Americans.

Yet we must remember how politicians like to cast issues in black and white terms. Were the packers the villains that reformers painted them to be? To be fair, we should hear the packers' side of the case before we rush to judgment. Some packers stated publicly that improved federal inspection was the best way to restore public confidence in their products. J. Ogden Armour, head of the packinghouse that bore his name, confidently invited the

Chicago packers pioneered the moving (dis)assembly line. Live pigs were lifted by their hind feet onto the overhead rail. Their throats were cut, and after they bled to death, the carcasses moved along as each worker cut off a particular part until nothing was left "but the squeal." This process revolutionized work by reducing complex operations to simple steps.

public to visit local packing plants "to see for yourself how the hated packer takes care of your meat supply." But he frankly admitted that "no packer can do an interstate or export business without government inspection."

In their way, the packers were as revolutionary as the crazed socialists that Roosevelt condemned. Over a twenty-year period the industry had fundamentally altered the way Americans bought and ate meat. Whereas at one time customers would buy meat only from a local butcher, they now felt confident eating meats prepared in distant packinghouses. To get meat safely to consumers, the packers had invented the moving assembly line (*disassembly* might be a better term as the engraving above indicates), refrigerated railroad cars, and a national marketing system. Urban consumers benefited because they had a greater variety of meat products at lower costs.

Packers had succeeded in large part because they used "everything but the squeal." Put another way, packers made a profit from what local butchers threw away. As one historian wrote, "[Armour] had built his empire on waste." To reformers, "this seemed akin to making something out of noth-

Armour's Estimates of Dressed Beef By-Product Costs and Profits

Steer, 1,260 lbs @ $3.25 per cwt* (becomes 710 lbs dressed beef)	$ 40.95
Cost of killing, processing, salt, icing, etc.	1.75
Freight on 710 lbs @ $0.45 per cwt	3.20
New York selling charges @ $0.35 per cwt	2.48
Costs of purchase, processing, and transport	$ –48.38
Sale in NW of 710 lbs dressed beef @ 5⅜¢ per lb	$ 38.17
(Net loss on dressed beef in NW)	–$10.21
Sale of hide, 70 lbs @ $.09 per lb	6.30
Sale of by-products	4.50
Yield from all by-product sales	10.80
Net profit from all transactions	0.59

From *Nature's Metropolis: Chicago and the Great West* by William Cronon. Copyright © 1991 by William Cronon. Reprinted by permission of W. W. Norton & Company, Inc.

*hundred-weight

ing." Look at the table above and you can see what these comments mean. Had Armour sold only the dressed beef, how much money would he have lost per head? Instead, the packers established chemical research labs that developed products out of the wastes once flushed down the sewers. Margarine, bouillon, brushes, combs, gut stringing, stearin (used in soap and candles), and pepsin (to aid digestion) were among their innovations. They even found uses for ground bones, dried blood, and hooves and feet (for glues). Today we might praise the packers for their aggressive approach to recycling. Reformers, however, mistook the careful attention to profit margins as corporate greed and a disregard for public health. Much of what the packers sold to make a profit, the reformers thought they should throw away.

The innovative side of the packers' success was lost in the outcry over *The Jungle*. Under the shadow Sinclair had cast, millions of Americans altered their eating habits. Many foreign countries banned American meats. An industry representative confessed that the loss of public confidence was "hurting us very, very materially." The decline in both domestic and foreign meat sales persuaded Armour that only improved inspection would save the industry.

Thus the historical context surrounding meat-inspection reform reveals that the dramatic appearance of *The Jungle* was only the most conspicuous—and therefore the most obviously symbolic—event among a whole series of developments. All the necessary ingredients were on hand to produce legislation for a more stringent federal law. And on hand was Theodore Roosevelt, the master political chef who would whip all the ingredients into a dish that consumers could taste with confidence.

THE LEGISLATIVE JUNGLE

In order for public outrage to find a constructive outlet, politicians must translate that anger into law. And historians, for their part, must trace a path through the congressional maze in order to see what compromises and deals shaped the final bill. The legislative process is so constituted that willful minorities can sometimes thwart the will of determined majorities. Skillful manipulation of legislative procedures may allow senators and representatives to delay the legislative process until support for a bill dissolves.

It is during the legislative phase that the historian discovers that support for improved inspection was not so universal as it first seemed. Meat inspection, like many reforms of the Progressive Era, raised issues more controversial than the question of sanitary standards. Many of those larger issues affected the roles of the individual actors. President Roosevelt, for example, had expressed his determination "to assert the sovereignty of the National Government by affirmative action" against unchecked corporate wealth and power. When added to the Hepburn bill that allowed the government to set railroad shipping rates and that included the Pure Food and Drug Act, a new meat-inspection bill would mark a major extension of public regulatory authority over private corporations.

Many people who favored improved inspection had given no indication that they would accept Roosevelt's sweeping definition of executive authority. The popular doctrine of *caveat emptor* (let the buyer beware) placed the burden for policing the marketplace on the consumer, not the government. As recently as 1895 in the case of *E. C. Knight* the Supreme Court had severely restricted government regulation of commerce. The packers, for their part, had given no indication that in agreeing to inspection reform they would accept a bill that in any way impinged on their control of the meat industry. Misguided rules might ruin their business. So behind a mask of general agreement, many actors entered the legislative process with conflicting motives and objectives. Much of that conflict would be expressed not as disagreement on major legal or philosophical issues, but as seemingly petty bickering over the details of the proposed law.

From the outset Roosevelt knew he faced a struggle in Congress. What he sometimes thought of as Sinclair's socialist rantings would not persuade congressional conservatives to support the tough bill he wanted. Nor had the government yet taken adequate steps to investigate the misconduct of its own officials. Immediately after the furor over *The Jungle*, Agriculture Secretary James Wilson had ordered an internal investigation of the Bureau of Animal Industry (BAI), which ran the inspection system. But Wilson and Roosevelt both suspected that the investigation would not "get to the bottom of this matter." Therefore, they asked Commissioner of Labor Charles P. Neill and New York attorney James Reynolds to undertake an independent investigation. Both men had been active in "good government" causes, though neither had any familiarity with the meat industry. Once they reported back, Roosevelt would have the evidence he needed to determine whether Sinclair or the meatpackers were the "malefactors" in this case.

Agriculture Department investigators whitewashed the BAI, just as Roosevelt suspected they would. Sinclair had grossly exaggerated conditions in the plants and treated "the worst . . . which could be found in any establishment as typical of the general conditions," the investigators charged. Although the system could stand reforming, they argued that Sinclair's accusations were "willful and deliberate misrepresentations of fact."

Neill and Reynolds suggested quite the contrary. If anything, they found conditions in the packinghouses were even worse than Sinclair had claimed. Their official report contained even more lurid details. Slime and manure covered the walks leading into the plants. The buildings lacked adequate ventilation and lighting. All the equipment—the conveyors, meat racks, cutting tables, and tubs—rotted under a blanket of filth and blood. Meat scraps for canning or sausages sat in piles on the grimy floors. Large portions of ground rope and pigskin went into the potted ham. Just as Sinclair had charged, foul conditions in the plant proved harmful to the health of both the workers and the consumers of the products they prepared.

The Neill-Reynolds report gave Roosevelt the big stick he liked to carry into any political fight. Should the packers prove resistant, he could threaten to make the secret report public. "It is absolutely necessary that we shall have legislation which will prevent the recurrence of these wrongs," he warned. In Senator Albert Beveridge of Indiana he found a willing ally, already at work on a new inspection bill. Beveridge, like Roosevelt, had caught the rising tide of Progressive discontent over corporate misconduct. He sensed, too, that leadership on this issue would win him the popular acclaim he craved. Assisted by Agriculture Department experts, Beveridge had a bill drafted by the middle of May 1906. He urged Roosevelt to pave the way for Senate approval by releasing the damning Neill-Reynolds report.

For the moment, the politically adept Roosevelt heeded his own admonition to speak softly. For all his bluster, the president was generally a cautious man. An unnecessary confrontation with the powerful Beef Trust offended his sense of political practicality. Why waste his political ammunition if he could have his way without a fight? "The matter is of such far-reaching importance," he confided to Neill, "that it is out of the question to act hastily." Besides, having once been a rancher himself, he was reluctant to injure the livestock raisers, who bore no responsibility for the packers' scandalous behavior.

The packers had indicated that they would resist efforts to regulate their business, but had privately admitted that all was not well in their plants. One had begged Neill to withhold his report, promising in return that the packers would carry out any "reasonable, rational, and just recommendations" within thirty days. After that Neill and Reynolds would be free to reexamine the plants. When Neill refused, packer Louis Swift rushed off to confront the president. He found Roosevelt equally unsympathetic to any scheme

Following the public outcry, meatpackers tried to create a better image of conditions in their plants and of the thoroughness of government inspection. In fact, when this picture was taken in 1906, postmortem inspection as shown here had not been at all common.

involving voluntary compliance. The president assured Swift that he would settle for no less than legislation to "prevent the recurrence of these wrongs."

Beveridge by now had his bill ready. On May 2, 1906, he introduced it as a Senate amendment to the House Agricultural Appropriations bill. Why, we might well ask, did such a major reform make its debut as an amendment tacked on to a House bill? Here, we begin to see how the legislative process affects political outcomes. Beveridge recognized that effective inspection required adequate funds. Previous congresses had undermined the system by refusing to vote the money needed. Many smaller plants had no inspection at all, and the largest ones had no inspectors at night. Beveridge, therefore, had proposed to shift the funding from the small amount allotted in the House Appropriations bill to a head fee charged for each animal inspected.

As the industry grew, so would the funds for the Bureau of Animal Industry. But since the Constitution requires the House to initiate all money bills, Beveridge had to amend a House bill pending before the Senate rather than introduce a separate measure.

Beveridge included two other important changes. The old law did nothing to force the packers to indicate on the label of canned meats either the date on which they were processed or the actual contents. (Neill and Reynolds, for example, discovered that the product called potted chicken contained no chicken at all.) The new law required dating and accurate labeling. It also invested the secretary of agriculture with broad authority to establish regulations for sanitary standards in the plants. Inspectors could then enforce those conditions as well as ensure the health of animals prior to and after slaughtering. If the owners challenged an inspector, the secretary had authority to make a "final and conclusive" ruling.

Yet this bill, which Beveridge confidently introduced in May, was hardly the same bill Roosevelt signed on June 30, 1906. By then an annual $3-million appropriation replaced the small head fee. No longer did the secretary of agriculture have "final and conclusive" authority. That authority was shifted to the federal courts, which could review his rulings. And the final measure said nothing about dating canned meats. In those discrepancies undoubtedly lies the source of Senator Nelson's dismay with the outcome of the meat-inspection battle. What the historian must now explain is why, if the reformers entered the fray holding the high cards, they had given so much away.

In fact the battle had begun well for Roosevelt and Senate reformers. When the packers first tried to stall Beveridge with promises to make voluntary improvements, the senator threatened them with more damaging disclosures. To show he meant business, he had Neill brief representatives for livestock raisers and western cattle state senators on the contents of his report. The packers had counted on those men as allies in their fight against overly stringent federal regulation. But faced with the prospect of more adverse publicity, the meat and cattle interests beat a hot retreat. The Beveridge Amendment passed in the Senate without a single negative vote. Never known for his modesty, Beveridge touted his measure as "the most perfect inspection bill in the world."

Roosevelt hoped that the smashing Senate victory would lead to equally swift action by the House. The packers, however, had no intention of giving up without a fight. In the House, they had far more substantial support, particularly on the critical Agriculture Committee. Its chairman, James Wadsworth, a Republican from New York, was himself a cattle breeder. He regarded *The Jungle* as a "horrid, untruthful book" that, he claimed, had temporarily unhinged the president. To orchestrate the opposition, Wadsworth could count on the unflagging support of "Blond Billy" Lorimer, a senior committee member, a notorious grafter, and the Republican representative from Chicago's packinghouse district. The Beveridge bill roused Lorimer like a red flag waved before a bull: "This bill will never be reported by my committee—not if little Willie can help it."

The packers had another, even more powerful, ally—time. Summer adjournment for Congress was only six weeks away. In the days before air conditioning, most public officials left Washington to escape the oppressive summer heat. While Congress vacationed, the public would most likely forget all about *The Jungle*, and as popular outrage waned, so would much of the pressure for reform. Only new and more damaging disclosures could rekindle the fervor that had swept Beveridge's amendment through the Senate. So long as the Neill-Reynolds report remained secret, Roosevelt could save it as a way to rekindle the public outcry. Upton Sinclair had promised Roosevelt that he would say nothing more until his accusations had been proven. But by the time the Beveridge bill reached the House, Sinclair had grown impatient. To goad the president, he published new charges embellished with even more lurid details. Finally, unable to contain his frustration, he leaked the details of the Neill-Reynolds report to the *New York Times*, and newspapers across the country picked up the story. Having lost its shock value, Roosevelt's big stick had become a twig.

With the worst behind them, the packinghouse forces could now afford to delay a vote on the Beveridge bill. Reformers would then be more inclined to make vital concessions. The requirement for stringent labeling, packers argued, would force the industry to abandon many well-known brand names. Dating would prejudice consumers against perfectly healthy canned meats. Nor could the packers abide investing such broad discretionary powers in the secretary of agriculture. Such a step, one spokesman claimed, would in effect "put our business in the hands of theorists, chemists, and sociologists, etc., and the management and control taken away from men who devoted their lives to the upbuilding and perfecting of this great American industry." In short, the packers argued that the secretary's arbitrary authority could deprive them of their property without the constitutional safeguard of due process in the courts.

Although they were likely to gain materially from more effective inspection, the packers called the head fees the most unfair aspect of the bill. Condemned animals, they claimed, already cost them millions each year. Now, the government proposed to saddle them with the additional burden of paying inspectors' salaries. Given the thin margins on which they operated, even a few pennies could make a difference. But that argument artfully concealed another reason the packers opposed a self-financing system. As many reformers pointed out, the small head fee (no more than 3 to 5 cents per animal) could easily be passed on to consumers. But a more effective inspection service might force the packers to abandon some of their most profitable, if unhealthy, practices. They could, for example, reroute cattle rejected at antemortem inspection to other parts of their plants. Furthermore, the old law allowed the packers to undermine the inspection system whenever it hurt profits, simply by arranging for their congressional allies, Lorimer and Wadsworth, to cut the BAI budget in the name of government economy. Forced to lay off inspectors, the BAI could not effectively supervise the plants. The Beveridge head-fee system eliminated that possibility. So what seemed like a minor issue had the potential to make or break the new inspection system.

When the packers lobbyed in Congress, they shrewdly pitched their arguments to other interests as well as their own. Control over annual appropriations gives the House and its members much of their political clout. By making his system self-financing, Beveridge would have weakened the House's jealously guarded grip on federal purse strings, depriving some congressional representatives of potential influence. Other representatives who were traditional champions of private enterprise agreed that restrictions on labels and dates, combined with the secretary of agriculture's discretionary authority, constituted unwarranted government interference in private enterprise. Beveridge had unwittingly reinforced his opponents' claims when he boasted that his bill was "THE MOST PRONOUNCED EXTENSION OF FEDERAL POWER IN EVERY DIRECTION EVER ENACTED." Representative E. D. Crumpacker of Indiana warned House members that "the passage of the meat inspection bill as it came from the Senate would mean the ultimate federalization of every industry in the United States."

With support growing in the House and the damning Neill-Reynolds report defanged, the packers went on the offensive. Wadsworth and Lorimer introduced a substitute bill in late May. Their draft eliminated each feature the packers opposed. They authorized the continued use of misleading brand names and preservatives. Dates on the cans were not required. In place of the head fee they had restored the annual appropriation. And in two other sweeping revisions, they removed the proposed ban on interstate transportation of uninspected meats and gave packing firms the right to appeal any Agriculture Department ruling to the federal courts. That last provision promised to be the most destructive of all, for private business had no more sympathetic audience than the champions of laissez-faire who sat on the federal judiciary. By appealing each unfavorable decision to the courts, the packers could paralyze the inspection system.

The Wadsworth-Lorimer substitute outraged President Roosevelt. "It seems to me," he wrote Wadsworth, "that each change is for the worse and in the aggregate they are ruinous, taking every particle of good from the suggested Beveridge amendment." He then made good on his threat to expose the packers. On June 4 he sent the Neill-Reynolds report to Congress along with a sharply worded message calling for a stringent inspection bill.

As might have been expected, Roosevelt's message in no way routed the packinghouse forces. Lorimer returned from a hasty trip to Chicago in time to denounce the Neill-Reynolds report as a "gross exaggeration of conditions." Armour accused the president of doing "everything in his power to discredit them and their business." The packers even produced two University of Illinois professors to rebut Neill and Reynolds.

All that rhetoric, of course, is a part of the symbolic language that so often monopolizes the public stage of politics. Each side adopts an uncompromising posture and accuses the opposition of all manner of villainy. The combatants strike heroic postures as champions of a larger public or national interest. They use such "disinterested" allies as Neill and Reynolds or university professors to legitimize their position. But at this point, when no accommodation seems possible, the negotiation and compromise begin. After all, both sides preferred some bill to no bill at all.

Faced with Roosevelt's demand for quick action, the House sent both the Beveridge bill and the Wadsworth-Lorimer substitute measures to the Agriculture Committee. In doing so, it followed a well-established procedure for reviewing legislation through its committee system. No handbook exists that explains how the committee system works; nor does the Constitution make any mention of it. Congress first established committees to streamline its functioning. Rather than have the entire body deliberate every bill, these smaller groups consider measures relevant to their areas of special interest before making recommendations to the entire House or Senate. A trade bill may go to the Commerce or Foreign Relations Committees, a pork barrel water project to the Rivers and Harbors Committee, and a farm bill to the Agriculture Committee. Those bills, encompassing a variety of features, have to go through several committees. All bills must eventually pass through the Rules Committee, which establishes parliamentary rules, such as the time allotted for floor debate or the conditions for amendment.

Yet if the committee system promotes efficiency, it also can provide an undemocratic means to defeat a popular bill. Committees can eliminate or amend central provisions or even refuse to return a bill to the floor for a vote. In sending the Beveridge bill to the Agriculture Committee, the House had routed it through an enemy stronghold. Wadsworth and Lorimer were both members of the committee; they had only to gain ten of eighteen votes from their colleagues in order to replace the Beveridge bill with their substitute. Other members of the House might never have a chance to vote on the original bill, even if a majority favored it.

Diligently, Wadsworth and Lorimer set out to undermine the Beveridge bill. They opened their attack by holding committee hearings to which they invited only witnesses sympathetic to the packers. Hearings are ostensibly a means to collect information that guides Congress as it formulates legislation. But they can be used to delay, to discredit opponents, or to gain publicity for committee members. So for four days the Agriculture Committee heard a parade of witnesses defend the packers. The testimony of Thomas Wilson, a leading packer lobbyist, set the tone. He attacked the Neill-Reynolds report as a "compendium of inaccuracies of fact," impugned the two men's competence, and stressed the "non-practical nature" of their background. And though under oath, Wilson swore that no condemned meat ever entered the market! The packers, he explained, were reasonable, public-spirited men. They would support a fair measure, such as Wadsworth and Lorimer had proposed, but not the government interference Beveridge called for.

More moderate committee members finally insisted that the committee hear opposing witnesses as well. That suited Wadsworth and Lorimer, for the longer the hearings lasted, the closer Congress came to adjourning. They also gained an opportunity to confront Neill and Reynolds directly. Neill attempted to refute his critics by stating that "we only reported what we could see, hear, and smell." He soon withered, however, under an unending barrage of hostile questions from the chairman and his crony. Reynolds, the Washington lawyer, was more accustomed to such abusive tactics. He coolly pointed out that while he had based his conclusions on direct observation, Wilson had relied solely on hearsay gathered from packinghouse employees.

As the hearings closed on June 9, Wadsworth eked out a narrow margin of victory, his substitute bill passing by only eleven to seven. Four Republicans had been so disgusted by the "bullyragging" aimed at Neill and Reynolds that they voted against the substitute. The president exploded when he saw Wadsworth's handiwork. The provisions in the new bill struck him as "so bad that . . . if they had been deliberately designed to prevent remedying of the evils complained of, they could not have been worse."

Historians recognize that parties to a negotiation often inflate their initial demands to allow room for compromise. Still, Wadsworth and Lorimer had been unusually brazen in attacking the heart of Beveridge's inspection system. In their substitute, they made no provision for night inspection. Lorimer had also included a clause that waived for one year the civil service requirements for new inspectors. In that year, he could personally control the list of new appointments. The BAI would be saddled with political hacks loyal only to Lorimer and the packers.

Two provisions particularly infuriated Roosevelt. The agriculture department had suggested as a compromise that Congress authorize an annual appropriation, but also grant the secretary standby power to levy a head fee if the appropriation proved inadequate. Lorimer and Wadsworth insisted on an annual sum of $1 million, scarcely enough to meet current costs. And once again, they had shifted final authority under the act from the secretary of agriculture to the federal courts.

The president did not deny that the packers, like anyone else, were entitled to "due process." But he also believed that court review should be restricted to a narrow procedural question: had the secretary been fair in reaching his decision? The committee granted the courts power to rule on substantive questions of fact. "You would have the functions of the Secretary of Agriculture narrowly limited so as to be purely ministerial," Roosevelt told Wadsworth, "and when he declared a given slaughter house unsanitary, or a given product unwholesome, acting upon the judgment of government experts, you would put on a judge, who had no knowledge of conditions, the burden of stating whether the Secretary was right."

Wadsworth refused to be cowed by the president's angry outburst. "You are wrong, very, very wrong in your estimate of the committee's bill," he responded. He even criticized the president for "impugning the sincerity and competency of a Committee of the House of Representatives" and called his substitute measure "as perfect a piece of legislation to carry into effect your own views on this question as was ever prepared by a committee of Congress." Lorimer, too, vowed to continue his defiance of the president.

All that sniping would not deserve a historian's attention except for one important detail—all the antagonists belonged to the same party. The meat-inspection battle had pitted a popular and powerful Republican president and his

Senate friends against the Republican majority in the House. Senator Henry Cabot Lodge of Massachusetts, perhaps the president's closest political ally, had made the intraparty schism that much more public when he denounced the "greedy" packers for their attempt to derail the reform bill. Sensing the growing embarrassment among Republicans, House Democrats sought to deepen the rift. They insisted that the Beveridge bill be given a full vote on the House floor, even though it had not been voted out of the Agriculture Committee. "Czar" Joseph Cannon, the dictatorial Republican speaker, temporarily retrieved the situation for his party by ruling the motion out of order.

Cannon was now the man on the hot seat. The catfight among Republicans threatened to destroy party unity and with it the political empire he ruled so ruthlessly. His personal and political sympathies lay with the packers and conservatives who opposed government regulation of the free enterprise system. His power came, however, not from leading any particular faction, but from bringing together all the elements of his party. As speaker and chairman of the powerful Rules Committee, he had the means to keep unruly representatives in line because he handed out all committee assignments. Members of Congress prefer to sit on those committees that deal with issues important to their constituents. Industrial state representatives may want positions on the Labor or Commerce Committees, whereas a representative from a mining state such as Nevada might prefer to serve on the Interior Committee. To earn Cannon's favor, many representatives found themselves forced to vote with the speaker and against their consciences.

With his power base wobbling, Cannon sought some way to break the impasse between Republican reformers and conservatives. Since Roosevelt, too, had an interest in party unity, the speaker went to see him at the White House. The president proved amenable to a suitable compromise. They agreed that Wisconsin Representative Henry Adams, a moderate and a member of the Agriculture Committee, was the best person to work out the details. Adams had endorsed earlier compromises and, as a former food commissioner and champion of pure foods legislation, he was free of the taint that clung to Wadsworth and Lorimer. Adams, Reynolds, and Agriculture Department lawyers had soon produced a new bill. From the Wadsworth-Lorimer measure, they dropped the civil service waiver, added a provision for dating canned meats, gave the secretary standby fee authority, and eliminated the section on broad court review. Roosevelt declared their measure "as good as the Beveridge amendment."

While Cannon and Roosevelt negotiated, Wadsworth and Lorimer were away from Washington. When they returned, they vowed to reverse the president's apparent victory. Cannon, however, had no appetite for further infighting. He urged the Agriculture Committee to work out yet another compromise. Wadsworth and Lorimer immediately deleted the secretary's standby fee authority from the Adams bill, though they did raise the appropriation to $3 million, more than enough to meet current costs. Their axe next fell on the dating requirement and, in return, they kept out the civil service waiver, while explicitly authorizing inspectors to visit plants "day or night."

One crucial issue remained. What would be the scope of court review? Wadsworth was willing to drop his demand for broad review if the president took out the Senate's phrase giving the secretary "final and conclusive" authority. Roosevelt agreed to that horse trade, which one historian aptly described as "purposeful obscurity." In other words the bill obscured whether final authority would rest with the secretary or with the courts. To achieve improved inspection, Roosevelt was willing to have the courts decide the actual scope of judicial review. He regretted the absence of mandatory dating but did not consider the issue sufficiently important to upset the hard-won compromise. Roosevelt often criticized those diehards who would go down fighting for a "whole loaf" when "half a loaf" was the best they could expect. With the president behind the final committee bill, the entire House passed it on June 19.

The battle was not yet won, however, for Beveridge and the reformers in the Senate continued their fight, threatening to keep the two Houses deadlocked until recess. The Indiana senator had strong support from Redfield Proctor, chairman of the Senate Agriculture Committee. Although nearly crippled by rheumatism, Proctor had stayed on in Washington to ensure passage of an effective meat bill. Like Beveridge, he believed a consumer had the right to know whether canned meats were five days or five years old. And if the government stamp would be worth millions in free advertising for the packers, Proctor thought the industry, not the taxpayer, should bear the cost. The Senate, therefore, voted to reject the House bill in favor of its own.

Once again, process more than substance determined the outcome. When the two Houses pass different versions of the same bill, they create a conference committee to iron out the discrepancies. With time too short for long wrangling over each point, Roosevelt intervened. He first urged the House members to reconsider their position on dating and fees. They refused so vehemently that Roosevelt turned to the Senate conferees instead. Proctor and Beveridge recognized that further resistance meant total defeat. On June 29, the day before adjournment, they raised the white flag "to make sure of the greater good," and the Senate passed the House bill. The next day, after Roosevelt signed, the Meat Inspection Act of 1906 became the law of the land.

OUT OF *THE JUNGLE*

Was it time to uncork the champagne for a celebration? Despite their opposition to certain compromises, Roosevelt and Beveridge had endorsed the final measure as a triumph for reform. If historians let the case rest here, however, they would not know whether to accept Roosevelt and Beveridge's enthusiasm or Knute Nelson's despair. Who, after all, had won this legislative battle? Certainly, reformers were heartened to see that the old toothless law had been replaced by a system that required "day and night" inspection, banned uninspected meats from interstate commerce, gave the secretary authority to establish sanitary standards, and provided ample funding for the immediate future at least. Yet the final bill contained no provisions for head fees or dating and still left the courts as the final judge of the secretary of agriculture's rulings.

Roosevelt, Beveridge, and Nelson had reacted to the provisions in the bill as Congress passed it. The real impact of a new law, however, remains uncertain until it is applied by the executive branch and tested in the courts. In the case of the Meat Inspection Act, future presidents might appoint agriculture secretaries sympathetic to the packers. The standards established might be either too vague or too lax to enforce proper sanitation. More important, the courts might yet call Roosevelt's bluff and assume their prerogative for broad review. Only after historians learn how the new system worked over time can they decide whether the compromises vindicated Roosevelt or proved "half a loaf" worse than none at all.

As it happens, the subsequent history of meat inspection confirms the wisdom of the president's compromise strategy. The $3-million appropriation more than adequately funded the "beefed-up" inspection system. By the end of 1907 Secretary Wilson reported that new and more efficient procedures had substantially reduced operating costs. The BAI spent only $2 million the first year, and costs dropped even though the industry grew.

Roosevelt had been shrewdest in his resort to "purposeful obscurity." The packers made no attempt to dismantle the inspection system in the courts—the first important case did not arise for more than ten years. Then in 1917, in *United States v. Cudahy Packing Co., et al.*, a federal judge affirmed the secretary's authority. Congress, he ruled, could "delegate authority to the proper administrative officer to make effective rules." Two years later the Supreme Court adopted narrow rather than broad review. In an opinion for a unanimous Court in the case of *Houston v. St. Louis Independent Packing Company*, Justice John Clarke wrote that a decision over proper labeling of meat "is a question of fact, the determination of which is committed to the Secretary of Agriculture . . ., and the law is that the conclusion of the head of an executive department . . . will not be reviewed by the Courts, where it is fairly arrived at with substantial support." After thirteen years, the reformers could finally claim victory, though the outcome by then was scarcely in doubt. Not until 1968 did another generation of reformers, spurred by Ralph Nader, find it necessary to launch a new campaign to strengthen the inspection system.

The controversy over meat inspection reminds the historian that when a legislative issue involves the disposition of economic and political power, all three branches of government influence the outcome. This input does not mean, however, that their roles are equal. In this case a politically shrewd and popular executive had shown greater capacity to affect the political process at critical moments. Roosevelt used the power of his office, his control over the Republican Party, and his ability to generate publicity to overcome opposition on both sides. Beveridge admitted that even in the face of widespread public outrage, Congress would not have acted "if the President had not picked up his big stick and smashed the packers and their agents in the House

and Senate over the head with it." Yet Roosevelt prevailed in the end only because he recognized compromise as an essential feature of the political
process. He had yielded on points he considered less consequential in order
to achieve his larger objective.

Just as historians must expand their field of vision to weigh the effects on
a law of all three branches of government, so too they must establish the historical context of a bill over time. As we discovered, the meat scandal had a
long history before the publication of *The Jungle*. We discovered, too, the
existence of near-unanimous support for stricter inspection, though there
was little understanding of what form a new law might take. Only when the
bill made its way through the legislative process did we find that the widespread cry for reform masked a deep conflict over the roles of private and
public agencies in determining satisfactory standards. The packers wanted
the benefits of a new bill without having to relinquish control over their
business. Reformers had both a moral goal and a political one. First, they
wanted to punish the packers for their disregard for the public good. Second, and more consequentially, reformers sought to assert the authority of
the federal government to police "corporate arrogance." The success of that
effort remained in doubt until well after the bill's enactment, when the
Supreme Court adopted narrow review.

It becomes clear, then, why the Meat Inspection Act could generate both
Beveridge's enthusiasm and Nelson's dismay. The outcome had been a total
victory for neither reformers nor packers. As is so often the case, the political system achieved results only after the visible symbols and myths of public discourse had been negotiated, debated, and compromised in the
procedural tangle at the heart of the legislative process. Gone from our
analysis are those wonderful symbols of corporate villainy and presidential
heroism. But in their place we have a more complex story revealing the political processes that shape our history.

Additional Reading

This chapter grew out of an Early Concentration History Seminar at Yale University. To give students their own experience at reconstructing history from primary sources, Mark Lytle put together a package of documents on the Meat Inspection Act of 1906. Many of the students in that seminar showed remarkable initiative in locating additional materials. In particular, they discovered the section in John Braeman, "The Square Deal in Action: A Case Study in the Growth of 'National Police Power'" that discusses the constitutional questions the new meat-inspection law raised. That essay appears in Braeman et al., *Change and Continuity in Twentieth Century America*, vol. 1 (Columbus, OH, 1964), pp. 34–80. Historians took much longer to discover certain urban and ecological factors involved in this episode. William Cronon, *Nature's Metropolis: Chicago and the Great West* (New York, 1991) places the industry in its urban context and establishes its links to a rural hinterland. Cronon, while no fan of big-business practices, recognizes the revolutionary nature of what the Chicago packers accomplished with such innovations as the moving (dis)assembly line and the refrigerated railcar.

Cronon's view of the packers is somewhat at odds with long-standing interpretations that have generally focused on the ruthless sides of business. Like Cronon, Michael McGerr, *A Fierce Discontent: The Rise and Fall of the Progressive Movement in America, 1870–1920* (New York, 2003), and Elizabeth Sanders, *Roots of Reform: Farmers, Workers, and the American State, 1877–1917* (Chicago, 1999) offer a more modulated view of business and reform. The older muckrakers' bias is reflected in two books by Upton Sinclair, *The Jungle* (New York, 1906) and his often autobiographical *The Brass Check* (Pasadena, CA, 1919). On Theodore Roosevelt and traditional debate over Progressivism, see George Mowry, *The Era of Theodore Roosevelt* (New York, 1958); Gabriel Kolko, *The Triumph of Conservatism* (New York, 1964); and Lewis Gould, ed., *The Progressive Era* (1973). After going through the documents for themselves, our students concluded that Mowry's cursory treatment missed much of the significant political maneuvering and that Kolko misused documents and misinterpreted the meaning of the act. Another helpful secondary work is Joel Tarr, *Boss Politics* (Chicago, 1964), which examines the career of "Blond Billy" Lorimer. David Thelen, "Not Classes, But Issues," which first appeared in the *Journal of American History* 1 (September 1969): 323–334, offers a stimulating review of the many explanations of Progressivism as well as a substantial interpretation of his own. That historiography was updated by Dan Rogers, "In Search of Progressivism," *Reviews in American History* 10 (1982). Robert Crunden, *Ministers of Reform: The Progressives' Achievements in Modern America, 1889–1920* (Urbana, IL, 1982), and Arthur Link and Richard McCormick, *Progressivism* (Arlington Heights, IL, 1983) give additional insights into the reform impulse that swept the nation. A reconsideration of Sinclair and other reformers comes in Walter Brasch, *Forerunners of Revolution: Muckrakers and the Social Conscience* (New York, 1990).

Biographies help us understand Theodore Roosevelt. Among those available are John Blum, *The Republican Roosevelt* (Cambridge, MA, 1958); John Milton Cooper Jr., *The Warrior and the Priest* (Cambridge, MA, 1983); David McCullough, *Mornings on Horseback* (New York, 1981); and Edmund Morris, *The Rise of Theodore Roosevelt* (New York, 1981) and *Theodore Rex* (New York, 2002). Professor Lewis Gould of the University of Texas at Austin generously offered some important revisions to an early draft of this chapter. Students could profitably read his *The Presidency of Theodore Roosevelt* (Lawrence, KS, 1991).

The documents in this case study are available in good research libraries and can be assembled. Such newspapers as the *New York Times, Chicago Tribune, Chicago Record-Herald,* and the *Chicago Inter-Ocean* covered the entire controversy, though the Chicago papers did so in greater depth. Much of Roosevelt's thinking can be found in Elting Morison et al., *The Letters of Theodore Roosevelt,* vol. 5 (Cambridge, MA, 1953). Access to some contemporary magazines, including *Everybody's Magazine,* the *Lancet, Cosmopolitan,* and specifically J. Ogden Armour, "The Packers and the People," *Saturday Evening Post* 177, 37 (March 10, 1900)—a key document in Kolko's interpretation—will provide a picture of the debate over meatpacking and other muckraking issues.

This chapter drew most heavily on government documents. Readers should see *Congressional Record,* 59th Congress, 1st Session; House Committee on Agriculture, 59th Congress, 1st Session, *Hearings . . . on the So-called "Beveridge Amendment" to the Agriculture Appropriation Bill—H.R. 18537* (Washington, DC, 1906); Bureau of Animal Industry, *Twenty-Third Annual Report* (Washington, DC, 1906); *House Document 873,* 59th Congress, 1st Session (June 1906)—the Neill-Reynolds Report and Theodore Roosevelt's cover letter; and the Agriculture Committee's minority and majority reports in *House Report 4935,* pts. 1 and 2, 59th Congress, 1st Session (June 14 and 15, 1906) and *House Report 3468,* pt. 2, 59th Congress, 1st Session (June 15, 1906). Additional materials can be found in the Roosevelt Papers (Harvard University, Widner Library) and Beveridge Papers (University of Indiana).

Interactive Learning

The *Primary Source Investigator* provides a variety of materials on the controversy surrounding the government inspection of the meatpacking industry. Political cartoons, letters, photographic images, and newspaper articles illuminate various aspects of this debate. Investigate the photographs of the stockyards, the Neill-Reynolds report, and the Meat Inspection Act of 1906, and consider the ways in which these documents might have played off each other, motivating politicians (most notably President Theodore Roosevelt), the public, and the meatpackers themselves into action.

CHAPTER 11
Sacco and Vanzetti

In the years after World War I, crime statistics curved sharply upward. Armed robberies rose at an alarming rate, and anyone handling large sums of money had reason to exercise caution. On most paydays Frederick Parmenter, paymaster for the Slater and Morrill Shoe Company of South Braintree, Massachusetts, would have used a truck to deliver his money boxes to the lower factory building. Only a few months earlier, in December 1919, a brazen gang of bandits had attempted a daylight payroll heist in nearby Bridgewater. The bandits had fled empty-handed, and no one was hurt in the gunfight. Still, area businesses were uneasy. On the morning of April 15, 1920, however, the robbery attempt must have been far from Parmenter's mind. It was a mild spring day, and he set out on foot for the lower factory building with his assistant, Alessandro Berardelli, walking ahead.

Halfway to their destination, a man approached Berardelli from the side of the road, spoke to him briefly, and then suddenly shot him dead. As Parmenter turned to flee, the bandits fired again, mortally wounding him. A blue Buick pulled from its parking place. The two assailants and their lookout jumped into the car and fled toward Bridgewater. To discourage pursuers, the bandits threw tacks onto the streets. Two miles from Braintree they abandoned the Buick and escaped in another car.

Bridgewater Police Chief Michael Stewart thought he recognized a pattern in the Braintree crime. The same foreigners who bungled the December heist, he guessed, had probably pulled off the Braintree job. Stewart's investigation put him on the trail of Mike Boda, an Italian anarchist. Unable to locate Boda, Stewart kept watch on a car Boda had left at Simon Johnson's garage for repairs. Whoever came to get the car would, according to Stewart's theory, become a prime suspect in both crimes.

His expectations were soon rewarded. On May 5, 1920, Boda and three other Italians called for the car. Mrs. Johnson immediately slipped next door to alert the police, but the four men did not wait for her return. Boda and one friend, Riccardo Orciani, left on a motorcycle while their companions

Nicola Sacco and Bartolomeo Vanzetti, accused of committing a payroll robbery of the Slater and Morrill Shoe Company in South Braintree, Massachusetts. When police asked witnesses to identify the two men, instead of using a lineup, officers made Sacco and Vanzetti stand alone in the middle of a room and pose as bandits.

walked to a nearby streetcar stop. Apparently nervous, they moved on to another stop a half mile away. There they boarded the trolley for Brockton. As the trolley car moved down Main Street, Police Officer Michael Connolly climbed on. Having spotted the two foreigners, he arrested them. When they asked why, he replied curtly, "suspicious characters."

Thus began the epic story of Nicola Sacco and Bartolomeo Vanzetti, two obscure Italian aliens who became the focal point of one of the most controversial episodes in American history. Within little more than a year after their arrest a jury deliberated for just five hours before convicting both men of robbery and murder. Such a quick decision came as a surprise, particularly in a trial that had lasted seven weeks, heard more than 160 witnesses, and gained national attention.

Nor did the controversy end with the jury's decision. Six years of appeals turned a small-town incident of robbery and murder into a major international uproar. The Italian government indicated that it was following the case with interest. Thousands of liberals, criminal lawyers, legal scholars, civil libertarians, radicals, labor leaders, prominent socialites, and spokespersons for immigrant groups rallied to Sacco and Vanzetti's cause. Arrayed against them was an equally imposing collection of the nation's legal, social, academic, and political elite.

The case climaxed on April 9, 1927. Having denied some eight appeals, trial judge Webster Thayer sentenced Sacco and Vanzetti to die in the electric chair. His action triggered months of protests and political activities. Around Charleston Prison (where the two men were held) and the State House in Boston, Sacco and Vanzetti's supporters marched, collected petitions, and walked picket lines. Occasionally violence erupted between protesters and authorities, as mounted police attacked crowds in Boston and clubbed them off the streets in New York. On August 22, the morning before Sacco and Vanzetti were scheduled to die, Charleston Prison appeared like an embattled fortress. Ropes circled the prison grounds to keep protesters at bay as eight hundred armed guards walked the walls. In New York's Union Square, 15,000 people gathered to stand in silent vigil. Similar crowds congregated in major European cities. All awaited the news of the fate of "a good shoemaker and a poor fish peddler."

The historian confronting that extraordinary event faces some perplexing questions. How did a case of robbery and murder become an international cause célèbre? How was it that two Italian immigrants living on the fringe of American society had become the focus of a debate that brought the nation's cherished legal institutions under attack? Or as one eminent law professor rhetorically posed the question:

> Why all this fuss over a couple of "wops," who after years in this country had not even made application to become citizens; who had not learned to use our language even modestly well; who did not believe in our form of government; . . . who were confessed slackers and claimed to be pacifists but went armed with deadly weapons for the professed purpose of defending their individual personal property in violation of all the principles they preached?

THE QUESTION OF LEGAL EVIDENCE

Lawyers reviewing events might answer those questions by arguing that the Sacco and Vanzetti case raised serious doubts about the tradition of Anglo-Saxon justice so venerated in the United States. More specifically, many legal scholars then and since have asserted that the trial and appeals process failed to meet minimum standards of fairness, particularly for a criminal case in which the defendants' lives hung in the balance.

In the first flush of Sacco and Vanzetti's arrest, prosecutors seemed to have good reason to label the two men "suspicious characters." Both Sacco and Vanzetti were carrying loaded revolvers. Not only that, Sacco had twenty-three extra cartridges in his pockets, while Vanzetti carried several shotgun shells. When questioned, both men lied about their activities. They claimed not to know Mike Boda or to have been at the garage to pick up Boda's car. But suspicious behavior was one matter; proof that Sacco and Vanzetti had committed the Braintree murders was another. As the police and prosecutors went about making their case, they followed distinctly irregular procedures.

To be sure, in 1920 the police were allowed to conduct an investigation with far greater latitude than the law permits today. The Supreme Court decisions in *Miranda* (1966) and *Escobedo* (1964) established that criminal suspects have the right to remain silent, to be informed of their rights, and to stand in an impartial lineup for identification. None of those guarantees existed in 1920. Even so, District Attorney Frederick Katzmann and Chief Stewart showed unusual zeal in constructing a case against Sacco and Vanzetti. At no time during the first two days of questioning did they tell either suspect why they had been arrested. Chief Stewart repeatedly asked them not about the robbery, but about their political beliefs and associates. The district attorney did obliquely inquire about their activities on April 15, though he never mentioned the Braintree crimes. Furthermore, when the police asked witnesses to identify the suspects, they did not use a lineup. Instead, they forced Sacco and Vanzetti to stand alone in the middle of a room posing as bandits.

As the investigation continued, the case came close to collapsing for lack of evidence. Of the five suspected gang members, all but Vanzetti could prove they had not been in Bridgewater during the December holdup attempt. Despite an intensive search of the suspects' belongings, including a trunk sent to Italy, Katzmann was never able to trace the money, even among radical political groups with whom the suspects were associated. Fingerprint experts found no matches between prints lifted from the abandoned Buick and those taken from the suspects.

Faced with those gaps in the evidence, Katzmann still decided, first, to prosecute Vanzetti for the December Bridgewater holdup and, second, to charge both Sacco and Vanzetti with the Braintree murders in April. Arguing the Bridgewater case in June 1920 before Judge Webster Thayer, Katzmann presented a weak case against Vanzetti on the charge of assault with intent to rob. Still, he did manage to make the jury aware of Vanzetti's anarchist views and persuade them to convict. Judge Thayer then meted out an unusually severe sentence (twelve to fifteen years) to a defendant with no criminal record for a crime in which no one was hurt and nothing was stolen.

That conviction allowed Katzmann to proceed with the second trial, to be held in the suburban town of Dedham. Since this trial would be a special session of the superior court, a judge had to be appointed to hear the case. Judge Thayer asked his old college friend, Chief Justice John Aiken, for the assignment, even though he had presided over Vanzetti's earlier trial and could scarely consider himself impartial. Thus the second trial opened with a judge who already believed unequivocally in the defendants' guilt.

At Dedham, District Attorney Katzmann built his case around three major categories of evidence: (1) eyewitness identification of Sacco and Vanzetti at the scene, (2) expert ballistics testimony establishing Sacco's gun as the weapon that fired the fatal shot at Berardelli and Vanzetti's gun as one taken from Berardelli during the robbery, (3) the defendants' evasive behavior

both before and after arrest as evidence of what is legally termed "consciousness of guilt."

The prosecution, however, had a difficult time making its case. Of the
"eyewitnesses" claiming to place Sacco and Vanzetti at the scene, one, Mary
Splaine, claimed to have observed the shooting from a window in the Slater
and Morrill factory for no longer than three seconds at a distance of about 60
feet. In that time she watched an unknown man in a car traveling about 18
miles an hour. Immediately after the crime Splaine had difficulty describing
any of the bandits, but one year later she picked out Sacco, vividly recalling
such details as his "good-sized" left hand. She refused to recant her testimony
even after the defense demonstrated that Sacco had relatively small hands.

Louis Pelzer testified for the prosecution that upon hearing shots, he had
observed the crime from a window for at least a minute. He pointed to Sacco
as the "dead image" of the man who shot Berardelli. Two defense witnesses,
however, controverted Pelzer's story. Upon hearing the shots, they recalled,
the intrepid Pelzer had immediately hidden under his workbench—hardly a
vantage point from which to make a clear identification.

Lola Andrews, a third witness, claimed that on the morning of the crime
she had stopped near the factory to ask directions from a dark-haired man
working under a car. She later identified Sacco as that man. But a companion, Julia Campbell, denied that Andrews had ever spoken to the man under
the car. Instead, Campbell testified, Andrews had approached a pale, sickly
young man who was standing nearby. Other witnesses had recalled the same
pale person. A second friend swore that he had heard Andrews say after she
returned from police headquarters that "the government took me down and
wanted me to recognize those men and I don't know a thing about them."
Nor did Andrews's reputation as a streetwalker enhance her credibility. Yet
in his summation, prosecutor Katzmann told the jury that in eleven years as
district attorney he had not "ever before . . . laid eye or given ear to so convincing a witness as Lola Andrews."

Against Katzmann's dubious cast, the defense produced seventeen witnesses who provided the defendants with alibis for the day or who had seen
the crime, but not Sacco or Vanzetti. One, an official of the Italian Consulate
in Boston, confirmed Sacco's claim that he had been in Boston on April 15
acquiring a passport. The official remembered Sacco because he had tried to
use a picture over 10 inches square for his passport photo. "Since such a
large photograph had never been presented before," the official recalled, "I
took it in and showed it to the Secretary of the Consulate. We laughed and
talked over the incident. I remember observing the date . . . on a large pad
calendar." Others said they had met Sacco at a luncheon banquet that day.
Witnesses for Vanzetti claimed to have bought fish from him. Katzmann
could only try to persuade the jury that the witnesses had little reason to
connect such a mundane event with a specific date.

In the face of contradictory eyewitness testimony, the ballistics evidence
might have decided the case. To prove murder, Katzmann wished to show
that the fatal shot striking Berardelli had come from Sacco's gun. Ballistics

specialists can often identify the gun that fired a bullet by characteristic marks, as distinct as fingerprints, that the barrel and hammer make on the projectile and casing. Two experts, Captains William Proctor and Charles Van Amburgh, connected the fatal bullet to a Colt pistol similar to and possibly the same as Sacco's. But neither of Katzmann's witnesses made a definitive link. "It is consistent with being fired by that pistol," Proctor replied to Katzmann. Van Amburgh also indicated some ambiguity: "I am inclined to believe that it was fired . . . from this pistol."

For unknown reasons defense attorneys never pursued the equivocation of those testimonies. Instead, they called their own ballistics specialists who stated with absolute certainty that the fatal bullet could not have come from Sacco's gun. In addition, they controverted the prosecutor's claim that Vanzetti had taken Berardelli's gun during the holdup. Shortly before his murder, Berardelli had left his pistol at a repair shop to have the hammer fixed. Shop records, though imprecise, indicated that the gun was .32 caliber, not a .38 such as Vanzetti was carrying. The records also supported Mrs. Berardellis's sworn testimony that her husband had never reclaimed his pistol. The defense then argued that the hammer on Vanzetti's gun had never been repaired.

Since the defense had weakened the ballistics evidence, Katzmann based his case primarily on "consciousness of guilt." To convict on those grounds, he had to convince the jury that Sacco and Vanzetti had behaved like men guilty of the crime, both before and after arrest. Here, Katzmann made his case with telling effect. Why had the defendants been carrying guns when they were arrested? They had gone hunting that morning, they claimed. But if that were the case, why were they still carrying hunting weapons and extra ammunition at night, when they set out to pick up Mike Boda's car? They were in such a hurry, Sacco and Vanzetti replied, that they forgot to leave their revolvers at home. But Katzmann continued his onslaught. Why did the two men lie at first about knowing Mike Boda or having visited the garage? Surely this evasion indicated a clear consciousness of guilt.

To explain such evasive behavior, defense lawyers were forced to introduce the inflammatory issue of Sacco and Vanzetti's political beliefs. For indeed, both men proudly proclaimed themselves to be anarchists, rejecting the authority of any government. Capitalism, they believed, was little more than an organized system of banditry under which the rich and powerful extorted the poor. Sacco and Vanzetti had both been active in the strikes and labor unrest of the era. As a result, they had been alarmed by the government crackdown on radicals that began in 1919. When Officer Connolly arrested them, the two men assumed that they, too, had been snared in the government's dragnet. They acted evasively, defense lawyers argued, not because they were criminals but because radicals were being persecuted and deported. Once arrested, Sacco and Vanzetti's fears were only confirmed by the police's constant questions about their political beliefs.

Similar worries accounted for their peculiar actions at Johnson's garage, the defense argued. Shortly before his arrest, Vanzetti had conferred with the Italian Defense Committee of New York, then inquiring into the fate of a fellow anarchist, Andrea Salsedo. The committee knew only that Salsedo was being held by Justice Department agents; members warned Vanzetti that he and his friends might be in danger of being jailed or deported. Only a week later, newspapers across the nation reported that Salsedo had fallen to his death from a twelfth-floor window. The police insisted the case had been a suicide, but many anarchists thought Salsedo had been pushed. Before he died, had he provided the government with the names of other anarchists? If so, Vanzetti and Sacco were at risk. Anyone found with anarchist literature could be arrested and deported. It was for that reason, Sacco and Vanzetti told the court, that they had gone to retrieve Mike Boda's car: they needed it to carry away the radical pamphlets stored in their homes—something they hardly wished to admit to police questioning them about radical activities.

The revelations of the defendants' radical politics could hardly have raised the jury's opinion of the two men. And their explanations did not stop Katzmann from focusing on consciousness of guilt in his final summation. Nor did Judge Thayer take into account their explanations in his charge to jury. In theory, a judge's charge guides the jury as it interprets conflicting evidence: in separating the relevant from the irrelevant and in establishing the grounds for an objective verdict. But Thayer made his sympathies all too clear. In discussing the ballistics testimony, he wrongly assumed that Katzmann's expert witnesses had unequivocally identified Sacco's gun as having fired the fatal shot. And he spent no time weighing the defense's argument that prosecution eyewitnesses had been unreliable. Only when he discussed consciousness of guilt did the judge become expansive and specific. He lingered over the evidence offered by the police and the garage owner while ignoring Sacco and Vanzetti's explanations.

Lawyers and legal historians have raised other telling criticisms—excesses in the trial procedures, prejudice on the part of both judge and prosecutor, bungling by the defense lawyer. Inevitably, these criticisms have influenced the way historians have approached the controversy. Most of them have centered on the issue of *proof* of guilt. Contrary to popular opinion, the courts do not determine whether a person is guilty or innocent of a crime. They decide merely whether the prosecutor has assembled sufficient evidence to establish guilt. The judge may even suspect a defendant is guilty, but if the evidence does not meet minimum standards of legal proof, the court must set the accused free. As one court concluded, "the commonwealth demands no victims . . . and it is as much the duty of the district attorney to see that no innocent man suffers, as it is to see that no guilty man escapes."

Thus lawyers tend to focus on narrow, yet admittedly important, questions. They are all the more crucial when human lives are at stake, as was the case with Sacco and Vanzetti. Believing that the legal system maintains vital safeguards of individual rights, lawyers in general seek to ensure that proper legal procedures have been followed, that evidence is submitted according to established rules, and, in accordance with those procedures, that guilt has been adequately determined. A lawyer answering the question, "Why all the fuss over the Sacco and Vanzetti case?" would most likely reply, "Because the trial, by failing to prove guilt beyond reasonable doubt, perpetrated a serious miscarriage of justice."

BEYOND GUILT OR INNOCENCE

So far in these essays we have considered enough historical methods to understand that history affords far more latitude in weighing and collecting evidence than does the legal system. The law attempts to limit the flow of evidence in a trial to what can reasonably be construed as fact. A judge will generally exclude hearsay testimony, speculation about states of mind or motives, conjecture, and vague questions leading witnesses to conclusions. But those same elements are sources of information upon which historians can and do draw in their research. Historians can afford to speculate more freely, because their conclusions will not send innocent people to jail or let the guilty go free. In one instance, for example, appeals judges refused to act on defense claims that Judge Thayer had allowed his prejudices against Sacco and Vanzetti to influence his conduct of the trial. They ruled that remarks made outside the courtroom, no matter how inappropriate, had no bearing on what occurred inside. By contrast, the historian can accept the fact of Judge Thayer's prejudice regardless of where he revealed it.

Given their broader canons of evidence, historians might be tempted to go the lawyers one step further by establishing whether Sacco and Vanzetti actually did commit the robbery and murders at Braintree. To succeed in such an investigation would at least lay the controversy to its final rest. Yet that approach does not take us beyond the lawyers' questions. We are still dealing with only two men—Sacco and Vanzetti—and one central question—guilty or innocent?

We must remember, however, that when historians confront such either- or questions, their overriding obligation is to construct an interpretation that gives full play to *all* aspects of the subject being investigated, not just the question of guilt or innocence. They must look beyond Sacco and Vanzetti to the actions of the people and society around them. What political currents led the prosecutor to bring those two men to trial? How much were Judge Thayer, District Attorney Katzmann, and the men in the jury box representative of Massachusetts or of American society in general? Of just what crime did the jury actually convict the defendants? In answering those questions, historians must lift their drama out of the Dedham courtroom and into a larger theater of action. In short, we cannot answer our original question, "Why all the fuss?" merely by proving the defendants guilty or innocent. Historians want to know why this case provoked such sharp controversy for so many years.

Any historian who studies the climate of opinion in the early 1920s cannot help suspecting that those who persecuted Sacco and Vanzetti were far more concerned with who the defendants were and what they believed than with what they might have done. Throughout the nation's history, Ameri-

Going to Join the Indian and Buffalo?

The sturdy old American breed that wrested this country from the wilderness might now try a hard, quick shove toward the middle of the bench

Many "old stock" Americans from northern Europe feared that the new flood of immigrants from southeastern Europe would, by sheer force of numbers, displace them from their dominant place in society. Even a Progressive like George Creel, who had been sympathetic to immigrants during World War I, turned hostile and referred to the newcomers as "so much slag in the melting pot." Respected academics published research that purported to prove "the intellectual superiority of our Nordic groups over the Alpine, Mediterranean, and negro groups."

cans have periodically expressed hostility toward immigrants and foreign political ideas that were perceived as a threat to the "American way of life." Nativism, as such defensive nationalism has been called, has been a problem at least since the first waves of Irish immigrants came ashore in the first half of the nineteenth century. Until then, the United States had been a society dominated by white Protestants with a common English heritage. The influx of the Catholic Irish and then political refugees from the 1848 German revolution diversfied the nation's population. Native-born Americans became alarmed that immigration threatened their cherished institutions. Successive waves of newcomers from Asia, the Mediterranean, and eastern Europe deepened their fears.

In analyzing nativist ideology, historian John Higham has identified three major attitudes: anti-Catholicism, antiradicalism, and Anglo-Saxon nationalism. Anti-Catholicism reflected northern European Protestants' distrust of the Catholic Church, a rejection of its hierarchical and undemocratic structure, and a fear of the pope as a religious despot. Nativists often viewed

The rabid patriotism of the war led to widespread abuses of civil liberties. Here, angry servicemen on the Boston Commons destroy a Socialist Party flag seized during a 1918 peace march. The same spirit of intolerance was also reflected in the Red Scare, during which an Indiana jury deliberated only two minutes before acquitting a defendant who had shot and killed a radical for yelling, "To hell with the United States!"

Catholic immigrants as papal agents sent to bring the United States under the tyranny of Rome. Antiradicalism stemmed in part from an increasing rejection of America's own revolutionary tradition and in part from the American tendency to associate violence and criminal subversion with Europe's radical political creeds such as Marxism, socialism, and anarchism. Anglo-Saxon nationalism was a more amorphous blend of notions about the racial superiority of the northern European people and pride in the Anglo-Saxon heritage of legal, political, and economic institutions, one of the most cherished being the Anglo-Saxon belief in the rule of law.

The tides of nativism tend to rise and fall with the fortunes of the nation. During periods of prosperity, Americans often welcome immigrants as a vital source of new labor. In the 1860s, for example, many Californians cheered the arrival of the strange Chinese coolies, without whom the transcontinental railroad could not have been so quickly completed. In the 1870s, as the nation struggled through a severe industrial depression, nativism became a virulent social disease. The same Californians who once welcomed the Chinese now organized vigilante groups to harass them and clamored for laws to restrict the number of Asian immigrants.

The period following World War I, which Higham labeled the "Tribal Twenties," marked the high tide of nativism. No group more fully embodied the nativist impulse than the reborn Ku Klux Klan. By 1924 it claimed large chapters not only in its traditional southern strongholds but also in major cities, in Oregon and in the states of the upper Midwest—Indiana, Ohio, and Illinois in particular. The Klan's constitution unabashedly advertised the organization's commitment to all three nativist traditions:

> to unite white, male persons, native born gentile citizens of the United States of America, who owe no allegiance of any nature to any foreign government, nation, institution, sect, ruler, person or people; whose morals are good, whose reputations and vocations are exemplary . . . ; to shield the sanctity of white womanhood; to maintain forever white supremacy.

Loyalty to the church, the pope, a motherland, Old World culture, or any other tie outside the United States eliminated almost all immigrants from possible Klan membership.

Several factors accounted for the resurgence of nativism. World War I had temporarily interrupted the flow of immigrants who, since the 1880s, had increasingly included a preponderance of Catholics and Jews from countries with strong radical traditions. In 1914 alone, more than 138,000 of a total of 1.2 million immigrants to the United States were Jews. During the war, the number fell to just 3,672 newcomers in 1918 (out of a total of 110,000), but then rose to 119,000 (out of 805,000) in 1921, the last year of unrestricted immigration. A similar pattern occurred among Italians. In the entire decade of the 1870s fewer than 50,000 Italians came to the United States. In the first fifteen years of the twentieth century almost 3 million made the crossing. That torrent, which slowed to a trickle during the war years, swelled again with the return of peace. The approximately 221,000 Italians who immigrated in 1921 made up, with the Jews, more than 42 percent of the total immigrants. More than ever, nativists protested that these undesirable foreigners threatened to destroy cherished institutions, weaken the genetic pool, or in other ways undermine the American way of life.

The rocky transition to a peacetime economy only aggravated resentment toward immigrants. Returning veterans expected jobs from a grateful nation; instead, they found crowds of unemployed workers around factory gates. The army had discharged millions of soldiers almost overnight. The government dismissed hundreds of thousands of temporary wartime employees and canceled millions of dollars' worth of contracts with private businesses. As the economy plunged downward, native-born Americans once again looked on new immigrants as a threat to their livelihoods. Organized labor joined other traditional nativist groups in demanding new restriction laws.

Union leaders called for relief on another front. During the war they had cooperated with the government to control inflation by minimizing wage increases. At the same time, high wartime employment had attracted millions

Seeking to screen out those immigrants who were "undesirable," many nativists urged Congress to adopt a literacy test. Although campaigns for such a law had been mounted since the 1890s, only in 1917 did a literacy requirement pass Congress. The cartoon shown here disparages such exclusionist policies, but in the 1920s the pressure for even tighter restrictions mounted, to be embodied (as one Minnesota representative put it) in a "genuine 100 per cent American immigration law."

THE AMERICANESE WALL, AS CONGRESSMAN
BURNETT WOULD BUILD IT.
UNCLE SAM: You're welcome in—if you can climb it!

of new recruits to the union movement. The government had orchestrated labor-management harmony to ensure uninterrupted production schedules. Once the war ended, labor set out to consolidate its gains. Union leaders asked for higher wages, improved working conditions, and the recognition of collective bargaining.

Most business leaders were in no mood to compromise. They resented the assistance the government had given organized labor during the war. Now, they not only rejected even the mildest union demands but also sought to cripple the labor movement. Conservatives launched a national campaign to brand all organized labor as Bolsheviks, Reds, and anarchists. They called strikes "crimes against society," "conspiracies against the government," and "plots to establish communism." As the market for manufactures declined, employers had little reason to avoid a showdown. Strikes saved them the problem of laying off unneeded workers.

In 1919 American industry lost more labor hours to strikes than ever before in history. March brought 175 significant strikes, followed by 248 in April, 388 in May, 303 in June, 360 in July, and 373 in August. By September, strikes in the coal and steel industries alone had idled more than 700,000 workers and led to repeated violence. The average strike lasted thirty-four days, while some exceeded four months. Even employers who made minor concessions on wages or hours refused to yield on the question of collective bargaining.

Radicals played a minor role in the postwar labor unrest. Most union leaders were as archly conservative as the employers they confronted. Still, the constant barrage of anti-Red propaganda turned public opinion against the unions. And American radicals fed that hostility by adopting highly visible tactics. The success of a small band of Bolsheviks in capturing Russia's tottering government in October 1917 had rekindled waning hopes and at the same time startled most Americans. Two years later, the Bolsheviks boldly organized the Third Communist International to carry the revolution to other countries. Communist-led worker uprisings in Hungary and Germany increased conservative anxiety that a similar revolutionary fever might infect American workers, especially after a Comintern official bragged that the money spent in Germany "was as nothing compared to the funds transmitted to New York for the purpose of spreading Bolshevism in the United States."

Only a few shocks were needed to inflame the fears of Americans caught in the midst of economic distress, labor unrest, and renewed immigration from southern and eastern Europe. Those shocks were provided by a series of anarchist bombings inspired by Luigi Galleani, an Italian immigrant who had settled in New England. Although authorities at the time did not know it, members of Galleani's circle were the source of a series of thirty parcels mailed in April 1919 to eminent officials, including Attorney General A. Mitchell Palmer, Supreme Court Justice Oliver Wendell Holmes, members of Congress, mayors, as well as the industrial magnates John D. Rockefeller and J. P. Morgan. Only one of the deadly packages detonated (blowing off the hands of the unsuspecting servant who opened it), but in June a series of even more lethal explosions rocked seven cities. The most spectacular explosion demolished the entire front wall of Attorney General Palmer's home. The device exploded prematurely, blowing to bits the man who was crouching by the front steps.

The American public had already learned to associate such deeds with anarchists: the Haymarket Square explosion of 1886 as well as the assassination of President William McKinley in 1901 by radical Leon Czolgosz. ("The anarchist is the enemy of humanity, the enemy of all mankind," proclaimed McKinley's successor, Teddy Roosevelt.) Following the bombings of 1919 Attorney General Palmer reacted swiftly, launching a roundup of as many radicals as he could find, branding each "a potential murderer or a potential thief." That the majority were only philosophical anarchists who had never undertaken any violent acts toward the government did not deter Palmer. That the majority were foreign-born served only to raise his patriotic bile: "Out of the sly and crafty eyes of many of them leap cupidity, cruelty, insanity, and crime; from their lopsided faces, sloping brows, and misshapen features may be recognized the unmistakable criminal types."

For more than a year, Palmer and his young, Red-hunting assistant J. Edgar Hoover organized government raids on homes, offices, union halls, and alien organizations. Seldom did the raiders pay even passing attention to civil liberties or constitutional prohibitions against illegal search and seizure. One particularly spectacular outing netted more than 4,000 alleged subversives in some thirty-three cities. Most of those arrested, though innocent of any crime, were detained illegally by state authorities either for trial or Labor Department deportation hearings. Police jammed suspects in cramped rooms with inadequate food and sanitation. They refused to honor the suspects' rights to post bail or obtain a writ of habeas corpus.

The public quickly wearied of Palmer and the exaggerated stories of grand revolutionary conspiracies. Not one incident had produced any evidence of a serious plot. Palmer predicted that on May 1, 1920, radicals would launch a massive attempt to overthrow the government. Alerted by the Justice Department, local police and militia girded for the assault. But May Day passed without incident. The heightened surveillance did, however, have profound consequences for Nicola Sacco and Bartolomeo Vanzetti. Both men were on a list of suspects the Justice Department had sent to District Attorney Katzmann and Chief Stewart. Just four days after the May Day scare, Officer Connolly arrested the two aliens.

Sacco and Vanzetti fit the stereotypes that nativists held of foreigners. Sacco arrived in the United States in 1908 at the age of seventeen. Like so many other Italians, he had fled the oppressive poverty of his homeland with no intention of making a permanent home in America. Most of the young men planned to stay only until they had saved enough money to return home and improve their family fortunes. Although born into a modestly well-to-do family, Sacco was no stranger to hard labor. Shortly after his arrival he found steady work in the shoe factories around Milford, Massachusetts.

Sacco's resourcefulness and industry marked him as the kind of foreign worker whose competition American labor feared. Although he lacked formal schooling, Sacco understood that skilled labor commanded steadier work and higher wages, so he paid $50 out of his earnings to learn the specialized trade of edge trimming. His wages soon reached as high as $80 per week. By 1917 he had a wife and child, his own home, and $1,500 in savings. His employer at the "3 K" shoe factory described him as an excellent worker and recalled that Sacco often found time, despite his long workdays, to put in a few hours each morning and evening in his vegetable garden.

Vanzetti conformed more to the nativist stereotype of shiftless foreigners who drifted from one job to the next. Born in 1888 in the northern Italian village of Villafalletto, he had come to America in 1908 where, like many other immigrants, he found a limited range of jobs open to him. He took a job as a dishwasher in hot, stinking kitchens. "We worked twelve hours one day and fourteen the next, with five hours off every other Sunday," he recalled. "Damp food hardly fit for a dog and five or six dollars a week was the pay." Fearing an attack of consumption, Vanzetti migrated to the countryside in search of open-air work. "I worked on farms, cut trees, made bricks, dug ditches, and quarried rocks. I worked in a fruit, candy and ice cream store and for a telephone company," he wrote his sister in Italy. By 1914 he had wandered to Plymouth, where he took a job in a cordage factory.

If that sketch captured the essence of Sacco and Vanzetti's lives, they would most likely never have come to the attention of Justice Department agents. But because they were aliens and anarchists, they embodied the kind of foreign menace American nativists most feared. Although not a student of politics like Vanzetti, Sacco was a rebel. He identified closely with the workers' struggle for better wages and the right to organize. In 1912 he and Vanzetti had independently participated in a violent textile strike at Lawrence, Massachusetts. Three years later plant owners around Plymouth had blacklisted Vanzetti for his role in a local strike. Sacco had walked off his job to express sympathy for the cordage workers. Soon after a local labor leader organized a sympathy strike to support workers in Minnesota, authorities arrested Sacco and convicted him of disturbing the peace. All this time, he and his wife regularly joined street-theater productions performed to raise money for labor and radical groups.

American entry into World War I created a crisis for both men. Their anarchist beliefs led them to oppose any war that did not work to overthrow capitalism. Sacco even refused the patriotic pressures to buy war bonds. He quit his job rather than compromise his principles. Both began to dread the law requiring them to register (though in fact as aliens they were ineligible for military service). They decided to join a group of pacifists who in May 1917 fled to Mexico, where the two first became personal friends. The hard life and absence from his family finally drove Sacco to return home under an alias, though he did resume his name and former job after the war. Vanzetti returned to Plymouth and soon outfitted himself as a fish peddler.

So in the eyes of many Americans, Sacco and Vanzetti were guilty in at least one important sense. As self-proclaimed enemies of the capitalist system, they had opposed "the American way of life" that nativists cherished. Their suspicious behavior, which Katzmann successfully portrayed as consciousness of guilt, was all too real, for they knew that their radical beliefs might subject them to arrest and deportation, the fate hundreds of other friends and political associates had already faced.

Certainly, the trial record shows that nativism influenced the way judge and jury viewed the defendants. Almost all the eyewitnesses who identified Sacco and Vanzetti were native-born Americans. That they saw a resemblance between the Italian suspects and the foreign-looking criminals proved only, as Harvard law professor Felix Frankfurter remarked, that there was much truth in the popular racist song "All Coons Look Alike to Me." On the other hand, almost all the witnesses substantiating the defendants' alibis were Italians who answered through an interpreter. The jury, also all native-born Americans, would likely accept Katzmann's imputation that foreigners stuck together to protect each other from the authorities.

The choice of Fred Moore as chief defense counsel guaranteed that radicalism would become a central issue in the trial. In his earlier trial, Vanzetti had been defended by a conservative criminal lawyer, George Vahey. His conviction persuaded Vanzetti that Vahey had not done all he could have, especially when Vahey entered into a law partnership with Katzmann shortly after the trial. For the Dedham trial, friends, local labor leaders, and anarchists created a defense fund to see that no similar betrayal by counsel occurred. From Elizabeth Gurley Flynn, an Industrial Workers of the World agitator and wife of anarchist publisher Carlo Tresca, the defense-fund committee learned of Moore, who had participated in the trials of numerous radicals, including two Italian anarchists charged with murder during the Lawrence strike. Only later did the committee learn that Moore had contributed little to the acquittal of the Lawrence defendants.

Moore's participation must have reinforced the impression that Sacco and Vanzetti were dangerous radicals. He spent the bulk of defense funds to orchestrate a propaganda campaign dramatizing the plight of his clients and the persecution of radicals. He gave far less attention to planning defense strategy, left largely in the hands of two local cocounsels, Thomas and Jeremiah McAnarney.

Yet in the courtroom Moore insisted on playing the major role. The McAnarneys soon despaired of making a favorable impression on the jury. An outsider from California, Moore wore his hair long and sometimes shocked the court by parading around in his shirtsleeves and socks. Rumors abounded about his unorthodox sex life. And at critical moments he sometimes disappeared for several days. Judge Thayer once became so outraged at Moore that he told a friend, "I'll show them that no long-haired anarchist from California can run this court." Not until 1924 did Moore finally withdraw in favor of William Thompson, a respected Massachusetts criminal lawyer.

Nativism, particularly antiradicalism, obviously prejudiced Judge Thayer and District Attorney Katzmann. We have already seen how Thayer used his charge to the jury to underscore Katzmann's construction of the evidence in the trial. Outside the courtroom, Thayer consistently violated the canons of judicial discretion by discussing his views of the case. George Crocker, who sometimes lunched with Thayer, testified that on many occasions the judge "conveyed to me by his words and manner that he was bound to convict these men because they were 'reds.'" Veteran court reporter Frank Silbey had been forced to stop lunching at the Dedham Inn to avoid Thayer and his indiscreet remarks. Silbey later recalled, "In my thirty-five years I never saw anything like it. . . . His whole attitude seemed to be that the jurors were there to convict these men."

From the moment the trial opened, Thayer and Katzmann missed few opportunities to strike a patriotic pose or to remind the jury that both defendants were draft dodgers. Thayer told the prospective jurors at the outset, "I call upon you to render this service . . . with the same patriotism as was exhibited by our soldier boys across the sea." Katzmann opened his cross-examination of Vanzetti with a cutting statement dressed up as a question: "So you left Plymouth, Mr. Vanzetti, in May 1917 to dodge the draft did you?" Since Vanzetti was charged with murder, not draft evasion, the question served to arouse the jury's patriotic indignation.

Katzmann struck hardest in his questioning of Sacco, whose poor command of English often left him confused or under a misapprehension. Judge Thayer never intervened to restrain the overzealous prosecutor, even when it became clear that Sacco could neither follow a question nor express his thoughts clearly. Playing again upon the residual patriotic war fervor, Katzmann hammered away at the defendant's evident disloyalty:

> KATZMANN: And in order to show your love for this United States of America when she was about to call upon you to become a soldier you ran away to Mexico. Did you run away to Mexico to avoid being a soldier for the country that you loved?
>
> SACCO: Yes.
>
> KATZMANN: And would it be your idea of showing love for your wife that when she needed you, you ran away from her?
>
> SACCO: I did not run away from her.

When the defense objected, Thayer ruled that this line of questioning would help establish Sacco's character. But instead of showing Sacco's philosophical opposition to war, Katzmann made the defendant appear, as one critic expressed it, "an ingrate and a slacker" who invited the jury's contempt. With such skillful cross-examination Katzmann twisted Sacco's professed love of "a free country" into a preference for high wages, pleasant work, and good food.

The prosecutor summed up his strategy in his final appeal to the jury: "Men of Norfolk do your duty. Do it like men. Stand together you men of Norfolk." There was the case in a nutshell—native American solidarity against alien people and their values. Whether he had proved Sacco and Vanzetti guilty of murder mattered little, for he had revealed their disloyalty. In case the point was lost, Judge Thayer reiterated it in his charge:

> Although you knew such service would be arduous, painful, and tiresome, yet you, like the true soldier, responded to the call in the spirit of supreme American loyalty. There is no better word in the English language than "loyalty."

And just who were those "men of Norfolk" to whom the judge and prosecutor appealed? Could they put aside inflammatory rhetoric and render a just verdict? Not a single foreign name, much less an Italian one, appeared on the juror's list. Because Fred Moore had rejected any "capitalists" during jury selection, a few prospective jurors whom the McAnarneys knew to be fair-minded were kept off the jury. Those jurors selected were drawn from the tradespeople and other respectable Protestants of the town. None would share the defendants' antipathy to capitalism; few would have had any compassion for the plight of Italian immigrants or union members. Even worse, the jury foreman, Harry Ripley, was a former police chief who outdid himself in persuading his fellow jurors to convict. He violated basic rules of evidence in a capital case by bringing into the jury room cartridges similar to those placed in evidence. A short time before, he had told his friend William Daly that he would be on the jury in "the case of the two 'ginneys' charged with murder at South Braintree." When Daly suggested that they might be innocent, Ripley replied, "Damn them, they ought to hang anyway."

By using the concept of nativism to gain a broader perspective, the historian has come to understand the answer to a question lawyers need not even ask: what factors accounted for the conviction of Sacco and Vanzetti where legitimate evidence was so clearly lacking? Nativism explains many prejudices exhibited in the trial record. It also explains why those attitudes were so widespread in 1920–1921. We must accept the truth of law professor Edmund M. Morgan's assertion that it was "almost impossible to secure a verdict which runs counter to the settled convictions of the community." Sacco and Vanzetti symbolized for a majority of Americans and the "men of Norfolk" alien forces that threatened their way of life.

Yet, having answered one important question, the historian still faces another. Granted that a jury convicted two alien radicals of robbery and murder in 1921, but "why all the fuss," as we asked earlier, in the years that followed? After all, Sacco and Vanzetti were not sentenced until 1927, long after the virulent nativist mood had passed. Corruption and scandal had by then killed the Klan. Prohibition had closed that infernal den of immigrant iniquity, the saloon. The Immigration Acts of 1921 and 1924 had severely curbed the flow of newcomers from Italy and eastern Europe. The damage from unsuccessful strikes, management opposition, and government hostility had sent organized labor into a decline from which it would not recover until the New Deal years. The historian must still explain how a local case extended its impact beyond Norfolk County to the nation and even the international community.

No single answer, even one so broad as nativism, can account for the notoriety. Certainly, from the beginning the case had sent ripples across the nation. Socially prominent individuals, intellectuals, the American Federation of Labor, immigrant groups, and radicals had all contributed to the defense fund for the Dedham trial. Those people represented a small minority without great political influence. But by tracing out the appeals process, the historian discovers a series of events that enlarged the significance of the case, heightened the public's awareness of the crucial issues involved, and raised the stakes many groups risked on the judicial outcome.

A NATION STIRRED

In the American legal system, the right of appeal is designed to protect defendants against any miscarriage of justice rising out of the original trial. But in 1920 the appeals process in Massachusetts contained a provision that ultimately proved fatal to Sacco and Vanzetti. Any motion for a retrial based on new evidence had to be granted by the original trial judge. On each of eight motions made by the defense, including substantial evidence of prejudice on the part of the judge, the person who heard that appeal was none other than Webster Thayer! Thayer did not have to determine whether new information proved the men innocent, only whether another jury might reasonably reach a different verdict.

The next higher court, the Supreme Judicial Court, had only narrow grounds on which to reverse Thayer's decisions. It could review the law in each case, but not the facts. Those grounds meant that the court could determine only if the procedure conformed to the criteria of a fair trial established under state and federal constitutions. Although it found some irregularities in procedure, the Supreme Judicial Court ruled that those irregularities did not prejudice the verdict against the defendants. At no time did that court review the weight of evidence presented at the trial or on appeal. It determined, instead, that a reasonable judge might have acted as Thayer did.

And what of the American Supreme Court, the ultimate safeguard of civil liberties? On three separate occasions the defense attempted to move the case into the federal courts. Defense attorneys argued that Sacco and Vanzetti had been the victims of a sham trial, particularly given Judge Thayer's overwhelming prejudice. Justice Oliver Wendell Holmes Jr., long a champion of civil liberties, wrote that the court could rule only on the grounds of constitutional defects in Massachusetts law. Since none existed, he refused in 1927 to grant a writ of certiorari allowing the Supreme Court to review the weight of evidence. Thus the appeals procedure created a formidable barrier to reversing the verdict rendered at Dedham.

Despite such inequities, the defense spent six years in an effort to overturn the conviction. Between July 1921 and October 1924 it presented five motions for a new trial. The first involved the behavior of jury foreman Harry Ripley. In response, Thayer completely ignored the affidavit from Ripley's friend William Daly and ruled that Ripley's tampering with evidence had not materially affected the verdict. Eighteen months later the defense uncovered an important new witness, Roy Gould, who had been nearly shot at point-blank range by the fleeing bandits. Gould had told his story to police immediately afterward, but Katzmann never called him to testify. Eventually defense lawyers uncovered Gould and realized why he had been kept off the stand. Gould had been so close to the escape car that one shot passed through his overcoat; yet he swore that Sacco was not one of the men. Judge Thayer rejected that appeal on the grounds that since Gould's testimony did no more than add to the cumulative weight of evidence, it did not justify a new trial.

Later appeals attempted to show that the prosecutor had tampered with the testimony of two key witnesses. Both witnesses had recanted their courtroom statements and then later recanted their recantations. Rather than find Katzmann guilty of impropriety, Thayer condemned Moore for his "bold and cruel attempt to sandbag" witnesses. Yet another motion came after the prosecution's ballistics expert, Captain Proctor, signed an affidavit in which he swore that on many occasions he had told Katzmann that there was no evidence proving Sacco's gun had fired the fatal shot. He warned that if the prosecutor asked a direct question on that point, Proctor would answer no. Katzmann had, therefore, carefully tailored his questions during the trial. By the time Thayer heard this motion, Proctor had died. The judge ruled that the jury had understood perfectly what Proctor meant and that Katzmann had not been unfairly evasive.

After that setback, Fred Moore finally withdrew from the case in favor of William Thompson, a distinguished trial lawyer who devoted the rest of his career to Sacco and Vanzetti's cause. Thompson made the first appeal to the Supreme Judicial Court. He argued that the accumulated weight of new evidence and the repeated rejection of appeals demonstrated that Thayer had abused his authority out of hostility to the defendants. Unlike historians, who would render judgment on the basis of the totality of evidence, the appeals judges turned down the defense arguments case by case, point by point. In each separate instance, they ruled that Judge Thayer had acted within his proper authority.

Throughout this drawn-out process, public interest in the case had steadily dwindled. But after November 18, 1925, controversy exploded once again. Sacco received a note from a fellow inmate that read, "I hear by [sic] confess to being in the South Braintree shoe company crime and Sacco and Vanzetti was not in said crime. Celestino F. Medeiros." Medeiros was a young prisoner facing execution for a murder conviction.

The defense soon connected Medeiros to the Morelli gang of Providence, Rhode Island. In the spring of 1921, the Morellis badly needed money to fight a pending indictment, and so had ample reason to commit a payroll robbery. Joe Morelli carried a .32 Colt pistol and bore a striking resemblance to Sacco. Another gang member carried an automatic pistol, which could have accounted for spent cartridges found at the scene. Mike Morelli had been driving a new Buick, which disappeared after April 15. Another member fit the description of the pale, sickly driver. A number of defense and prosecution witnesses identified Joe Morelli when shown his picture. The New Bedford police had even suspected the Morellis of the Braintree crime.

Once again, the district attorney's office refused to reopen the case. The defense then appealed to Thayer to order a new trial. In reviewing the evidence, Thayer did not have to determine if it conclusively demonstrated Medeiro's guilt or Sacco and Vanzetti's innocence. He had only to decide that a new jury might now reach a different verdict. It took Thayer some 25,000 words to deny this motion.

That decision, more than any other, unleashed the torrent of outrage that surrounded the last months of the Sacco and Vanzetti case. Felix Frankfurter, an eminent Harvard Law School professor and later Supreme Court justice, published a lengthy article in the *Atlantic Monthly* in which he questioned the conduct of Thayer and Katzmann and the state appeals court's refusal to grant either clemency or a new trial. "I assert with deep regret but without the slightest fear of disproof," he wrote, "that certainly in modern times Judge Thayer's opinion [on the Medeiros motion] stands unmatched, happily, for discrepancies between what the record discloses and what the opinion conveys." Frankfurter described the document as "a farrago of misquotations, misrepresentations, suppressions, and mutilations." The *Boston Herald* rebuked Thayer for adopting "the tone of the advocate rather than the arbiter." Once a staunch supporter of the prosecution, the *Herald* now called on the Supreme Judicial Court to overturn this ruling. Once again, the court refused to weigh the evidence. It ruled in rejecting the appeal that the defense motion involved questions of fact lying totally within the purview of the trial judge.

That decision, in combination with Frankfurter's blistering attack, shifted public sympathy to Sacco and Vanzetti. A mounting body of evidence seemed to indicate that the two men were innocent. Yet, as the courts remained deaf to the defense appeals, more and more reasonable people came to suspect that, indeed, powerful men and institutions were conspiring to destroy two people perceived as a threat to the social order. Thayer's sentence of death by electrocution seemed but a final thread in a web of legal intrigue to commit an injustice.

Sacco and Vanzetti played an important part in winning broad popular support for their cause. Steadfastly, in the face of repeated disappointments, they maintained their innocence. Sacco, the more simple and direct of the two, suffered deeply as a result of separation from his family. During the first trying years, he went on a hunger strike and suffered a nervous breakdown. From that point on, he stoically awaited the end, more preoccupied with saving his wife further anguish than with saving himself. To assist the defense effort, however, he had begun in 1923 to study English, though with little success. A letter written to his teacher in 1926 conveys his energetic, simple idealism. Sacco had wanted to explain to his teacher why he had been unable to master the language:

> No, it isn't, because I have try with all my passion for the success of this beautiful language, not only for the sake of my family and the promise I have made to you—but for my own individual satisfaction, to know and to be able to read and write correct English. But woe is me! It wasn't so; no, because the sadness of these close and cold walls, the idea to be away from my dear family, for all the beauty and joy of liberty—had more than once exhaust my passion.

Vanzetti's articulate, often eloquent speeches and letters won him the respect of fellow prisoners, defenders, and literary figures drawn to the case, including Upton Sinclair, whose reformist instincts had not deserted him since writing *The Jungle* twenty years earlier. (Vanzetti was "one of the wisest and kindest persons I ever knew," Sinclair wrote, "and I thought him as incapable of murder as I was.") When at last Vanzetti stood before Judge Thayer on the day of his sentencing, he spoke passionately of the first principles that moved him:

> Now, I should say that I am not only innocent of all these things, not only have I never committed a real crime in my life—though some sins but not crimes—not only have I struggled all my life to eliminate crimes, the crimes official law and official moral condemns, but also the crime that the official moral and official law sanctions and sanctifies,—the exploitation and the oppression of man by man, and if there is reason why you in a few minutes can doom me, it is this reason and nothing else. . . . I would not wish to a dog or to a snake, to the most low and misfortunate creature of the earth—I would not wish to any of them what I have had to suffer for things that I am not guilty of. But my conviction is that I have suffered for things I am guilty of. I am suffering because I am a radical and indeed I am a radical; I have suffered because I was an Italian, and indeed I am an Italian; I have suffered more for my family and beloved than for myself; but I am so convinced to be right that if you could execute me two times, and if I could be reborn two other times, I would live again to do what I have done already.

Many artists, intellectuals, and literary figures sympathized with Sacco and Vanzetti. Maxwell Anderson wrote a play, *Gods of the Lightning;* Upton Sinclair, the novel *Boston;* and Edna St. Vincent Millay, a series of sonnets. Artist Ben Shahn, himself an immigrant from Lithuania, received recognition during the 1930s for his series of twenty-three paintings on Sacco and Vanzetti. When the painting shown here is compared with the photograph of the two men on page 263, Shahn's source becomes evident. But the artist transformed the photograph in subtle ways. Given our earlier discussion of photographic evidence, how do the changes lend more force to his painting?

The question of guilt or innocence, Vanzetti seemed to suggest, involved more than courtroom evidence. Despite the safeguards of the rule of law, society had used a broad constellation of attitudes, beliefs, and prejudices embedded in American culture to judge Vanzetti guilty. And, a historian might add, from out of Vanzetti's own constellation of beliefs, attitudes, and prejudices, he continued to condemn all governments as oppressive, all institutions as evil. This was the anarchist philosophy he lived by—the *Idea*, as he and fellow believers termed it. Vanzetti reaffirmed his right to war against American society and against "the crime that the . . . offical law sanctions and sanctifies."

    As the debate and protests continued, public support for the execution began to erode. Yet an equally vocal element of the populace hailed Thayer's conduct as a message to "Reds" that they could not subvert the Commonwealth of Massachusetts. Thus Governor Alvan Fuller faced a difficult decision when he received a plea from Vanzetti for executive clemency.[1] To ease

1. Sacco refused to sign. Although he agreed with Vanzetti's arguments, he did not want to violate his anarchist principles by appealing to government authorities—or to give his wife further vain hopes.

the political pressure on him, Fuller appointed a blue-ribbon panel to review the entire trial and appeals process. The three men he chose were symbols of the commonwealth's social and educational elite. Unfortunately, retired Judge Robert Grant was a socialite more often preoccupied with black-tie parties than public affairs. Samuel Stratton, president of Massachusetts Institute of Technology, was clearly overshadowed by the committee chair, A. Lawrence Lowell—a pillar of Boston society, a lawyer by training, and the president of Harvard. Lowell had already demonstrated his capacity for ethnocentrism, having introduced quotas to limit the number of Jewish students admitted to Harvard. As the liberal *New Republic* remarked of the committee, "the life of an Italian anarchist was as foreign to them as life on Mars."

For more than ten days the three men heard testimony on the evidence, much of it new. The defense also submitted a lengthy brief. But the committee's deliberations were short. On July 27, it filed its final report, upholding both the verdict and sentence against Sacco and Vanzetti. Sympathizers reacted with a mixture of despair and disgust. "What more can immigrants from Italy expect?" asked editorial writer Heywood Broun. "It's not every prisoner who has the President of Harvard throw the switch for him."

By the time all appeals were exhausted, the Sacco and Vanzetti case had brought to public attention not only issues of guilt and innocence, but more fundamental tensions in American society. On one side were arrayed immigrants, workers, and the poor for whom Sacco and Vanzetti stood as powerful symbols. On the other stood Thayer, the "men of Norfolk," the Protestant establishment, and those who believed that America should tolerate only certain peoples and ideas.

On the night of August 22, 1927, John Dos Passos, a young writer, stood with the crowd outside Charleston Prison waiting for news of Sacco and Vanzetti's fate. Shortly after midnight word came—the "good shoemaker and poor fish peddler" were dead. Grief and anger raked the crowd. Some wept, others cried out in the name of justice, and many tore their clothes in anguish. The scene outside the prison was repeated in New York and other cities around the world. Years later, Dos Passos expressed the outrage he felt against those who had persecuted Sacco and Vanzetti:

> they have clubbed us off the streets they are stronger they are rich they hire and fire the politicians the newspapereditors the old judges the small men with reputations the collegepresidents the ward heelers (listen collegepresidents judges America will not forget her betrayers). . . .
>
> all right you have won you will kill the brave men our friends tonight there is nothing left to do we are beaten. . . .
>
> America our nation has been beaten by strangers who have turned our language inside out who have taken the clean words our Fathers spoke and made them slimy and foul. . . .
>
> they have built the electricchair and hired the executioner to throw the switch
>
> all right we are two nations

Two nations—that was the reason for "all the fuss."

Will the real truth of the case ever be known? Perhaps not—at least not "beyond a reasonable doubt," to borrow the language of the courts. Yet historians have unearthed enough additional information to provide, if not the certainties of fact, at least a few ironies of probability. After Sacco and Vanzetti's execution, Upton Sinclair began to collect material for a novel about the case. As a socialist who had staunchly defended the two men during their years in prison, he was able to interview scores of friends and associates. While Sinclair remained convinced that Sacco and Vanzetti were innocent of the Bridgewater and Braintree robberies, he became less sure whether the two men were merely philosophical anarchists. Both had "believed in and taught violence," he discovered. "I became convinced from many different sources that Vanzetti was not the pacifist he was reported to be under the necessity of defense propaganda. He was, like many fanatics, a dual personality, and when he was roused by the social conflict he was a very dangerous man."

Historian Paul Avrich, investigating the anarchist community of which the two men were a part, noted that Vanzetti was indeed a close friend of Luigi Galleani, the firebrand whose associates had launched the letter bombs of 1919 and dynamited Attorney General Palmer's home. "We mean to speak for [the proletariat through] the voice of dynamite, through the mouth of guns," announced the anarchist leaflet found nearby. Carlo Valdinoci, the man who was blown up carrying out his mission, had been a good friend of both Sacco and Vanzetti. Indeed, after Valdinoci's death, his sister Assunta moved in with Sacco and his family. Then, too, rumors within the anarchist community suggested that Vanzetti himself had assembled the bomb that demolished a judge's home in Boston the night Valdinoci had done his work in Washington.

"But my conviction is that I have suffered for things I am guilty of," Vanzetti told Thayer at the end. Perhaps there was pride as well as indignation in this response. What, in the end, was the guilt of which Sacco and Vanzetti were so conscious during the trial? Was it merely the knowledge that their radical pamphlets, if found, would get them deported? But both men had been preparing to flee the country anyway, before being arrested. (Recall Sacco's outsized passport photo.) Could their evasive behavior have resulted from the fact that they had more to conceal at home than a few pamphlets?

Upton Sinclair came to believe so. After the execution, Fred Moore confided to him that Sacco and Vanzetti had admitted "they were hiding dynamite on the night of their arrest, and that that was the real reason why they told lies and stuck to them." If true, Sacco and Vanzetti, like Valdinoci, had been willing to commit acts of anarchism that, by the laws of American society, would have been punishable by death. Sacco made clear his own distinction between being tried for his beliefs and being arrested for mere bank robbery. "If I was arrested because of the Idea I am glad to suffer. If I must I will die for it. But they have arrested me for a gunman job."

Is the final irony that Sacco and Vanzetti were willing to die—perhaps even to kill others—for their Idea? Just as the "men of Norfolk" and the officials of Massachusetts were willing to execute Sacco and Vanzetti on behalf of *their* idea of what America should be? ("Damn them, they ought to hang anyway," remarked juror Ripley.) The historian must suspect that on that August night in 1927, citizens were not merely fighting over a matter of guilt or innocence, but (as Dos Passos put it) over the meaning of those "clean words our Fathers spoke." Sacco and Vanzetti had forced the nation to ask who in their own times best embodied the principles of freedom and equality inherited from 1776. Perhaps neither historians nor lawyers can resolve that question to the satisfaction of a divided nation.

Additional Reading

Novels often provide excellent introductions to history. Although they may play hob with facts or freely mingle real and fictitious characters, they just as often have a keen sense of the temper of the times and the issues facing a society. Thus readers interested in the Sacco and Vanzetti case in the context of the 1920s might begin with the trilogy by John Dos Passos, *U.S.A.* In volume 3, *The Big Money* (New York, 1930), Mary French, an idealistic young liberal, becomes deeply involved in the fight to save Sacco and Vanzetti. More important, Dos Passos writes about the tensions besetting American society and particularly the sense among liberals and radicals that the ruling class had betrayed the nation. Another novel, though less well written, is Upton Sinclair, *Boston: A Documentary Novel of the Sacco and Vanzetti Case* (New York, 1930).

Several general histories of the 1920s make good reading. Among the best are Lynn Dumenil, *Modern Temper: American Culture and Society in the 1920s* (New York, 1995); Geoffrey Perrett, *America in the Twenties* (New York, 1987); William Leuchtenberg, *The Perils of Prosperity* (Chicago, 1958); Frederick Lewis Allen, *Only Yesterday* (New York, 1931); and Arthur Schlesinger Jr., *The Crisis of the Old Order* (New York, 1957). All those works treat Sacco and Vanzetti briefly in the context of the time. Richard Pells, *Radical Visions and American Dreams* (New York, 1973) places the case in its intellectual context and explains how reactions among those involved set much of the radical tone of the depression era. John Higham, *Strangers in the Land* (New Brunswick, NJ, 1955) remains not only the outstanding work on nativism but also one of the best monographic treatments of modern American history. On the political repression of labor and radicals, Robert Murray, *Red Scare* (New York, 1955) is a colorful, though not deeply analytical, account. A far more sophisticated account of American urban culture of the era is Ann Douglas, *Terrible Honesty: Mongrel Manhattan in the 1920s* (New York, 1995).

Like so many controversial episodes in American history, the Sacco and Vanzetti case has become something of a cottage industry for devotees, polemicists, scholars, and writers seeking a provocative subject. Among those works that have sought to establish the guilt of Sacco, Vanzetti, or both, the most forceful presentation is made by Francis Russell, *Tragedy in Dedham* (New York, 1971). To our minds, the following works have made a far stronger case. Readers might best start with Felix Frankfurter, *The Case of Sacco and Vanzetti* (New York, 1962), an expanded version of his famous *Atlantic Monthly* critique of the case. This book reveals why the establishment reacted so violently—to the extent that the Justice Department tapped Frankfurter's phone until after the execution. The trial records, though available in some libraries in six volumes, may be found in adequate length in Robert Weeks, ed., *The Sacco-Vanzetti Case* (Englewood Cliffs, NJ, 1958). Any reader who wishes to encounter Sacco and Vanzetti through their own words can read Marion Frankfurter and Gardner Jackson, eds., *The Letters of Sacco and Vanzetti* (New York, 1960). Richard Newby, *Kill Now, Talk Forever: Debating Sacco and Vanzetti* (Bloomington, IN, 2001) provides another valuable source of documents.

One work that recognized that this case had a social as well as a legal side is Edmund M. Morgan and Louis Joughlin, *The Legacy of Sacco and Vanzetti* (New York, 1948). Morgan, like Frankfurter a Harvard law professor, used his expertise on rules of evidence to analyze the legal issues, while Joughlin, an English professor, traced the strong effects of the case on intellectuals and writers. Another compelling treatment of the evidence, trial, and appeals procedure is Herbert Ehrmann, *The Case That Will Not Die* (Boston, 1969). Erhmann entered the case as an assistant to William Thompson. His first assignment was to research the Medeiros confession. From that experience he developed a lifelong commitment to establish Sacco and Vanzetti's innocence. Reinforcement of Ehrmann's case against the Medeiros gang is offered in Frank D'Allesandro, *The Verdict of History: Sacco and Vanzetti* (Providence, 1997).

After seventy years in which many people have spent nearly a lifetime of digging, it might seem that historians would be hard-pressed to produce any new evidence about this case. But William Young and David Kaiser, *Postmortem: New Evidence in the Case of Sacco and Vanzetti* (Amherst, MA, 1985) have uncovered startling evidence of police improprieties, including extensive wiretaps of the defense and its friends and tampering with the ballistics evidence. Young and Kaiser make a powerful case that Sacco and Vanzetti were innocent of robbery and murder. Paul Avrich, *Sacco and Vanzetti: The Anarchist Background* (Princeton, 1991) focuses attention on the anarchist movement itself, including many previously untapped sources in Italian, that help clarify Sacco and Vanzetti's involvement with the Idea and with a philosophy of violence. Among the book's most startling revelations: Mike Boda, apparently outraged by the arrest of Sacco and Vanzetti, drove a wagon full of dynamite to Wall Street. The ensuing blast, notorious in American history, killed thirty-three people in September 1920. In a book about historical methods, we must mention Joseph Kadane, with David Schum, contributor, *A Probabilistic Analysis of the Sacco and Vanzetti Case* (New York, 1996). This book will be difficult for most of our readers. The authors apply Bayesian analysis using inference networks, applied probability, and statistics to determine that Sacco and Vanzetti were probably innocent of the payroll robberies and murder and that the case against them was not proven.

Interactive Learning

The *Primary Source Investigator* supplies additional materials that explore the reaction against immigrants and immigration in the early twentieth century. Photographic images of Sacco and Vanzetti posed as bandits and of American soldiers tearing apart a socialist flag offer vivid depictions of the hatred many immigrants encountered when they arrived in the United States. Also included are transcripts of Sacco and Vanzetti's trial, as well as letters written by the two men concerning their arrest. Among other things, those letters and transcripts reveal the betrayal many immigrants felt when they arrived.

CHAPTER 12
Dust Bowl Odyssey

The story begins with dust—not the thin coating on the shelf or the little balls in the corner, but huge dark clouds of it. When the winds blew, they sucked the dust into the sky to create blizzards. The dust storms began in earnest on May 9, 1934. High winds captured dirt from Montana and Wyoming—some 350 million tons of it—and carried it eastward. By noon the dust began falling in Iowa and Wisconsin. That evening a brown grit fell like snow on Chicago—four pounds for each inhabitant. Then the storm moved on. It was dark in Buffalo at noon the next day, and the midday gloom covered five states. On May 11 the dust sifted down as far south as Atlanta and as far north as Boston. The following day ships some 300 miles off the East Coast noticed a film of brown dust on their decks.

Every year more storms blew: twenty-two in 1934, to a peak of seventy-two by 1937, then a gradual decline until finally the rains returned in the 1940s. Residents of the high western plains remembered 1935 as the worst year. February brought temperatures in the seventies. With no snow cover and no vegetation to hold it, the dirt flew. Even on calm days on the southwestern plains a pervasive grit fell everywhere. "In the morning," John Steinbeck wrote, "the dust hung like fog, and the sun was as red as ripe new blood. All day the dust sifted down from the sky, and the next day it sifted down . . . It settled on the corn, piled on the tops of the fence posts, piled on the wires; it settled on roofs and blanketed weeds and trees." On May 15 Denver sent a warning that a dust storm was rolling eastward. Under a clear blue sky, folks in Kansas paid little attention until around noon, when the sky suddenly blackened. One movie patron leaving a theater expected to walk into the blinding glare of daylight. Instead, he thought a prankster had thrown a bag over his head. As he stepped outside, he bumped into a telephone pole, tripped over cans and boxes, and finally found his way by crawling along the curb. A young boy was less fortunate. He wandered out the door, became disoriented, and suffocated in a dust drift.

No matter what they tried, people could not escape the dust. Open the door and the dust beat in your face. Shut the door tight and still "those tiny

The enormity of the dust storms at first inspired amazement and awe. That sense of wonder soon gave way to despair as the constantly blowing dust turned day into night and left people asking if "this was the wrath of God."

particles seemed to seep through the very walls. It got into cupboards and clothes closets; our faces were as dirty as if we had rolled in the dirt; our hair was gray and stiff and we ground dirt between our teeth."

Was this the wrath of God, as some plains dwellers thought? "This is the ultimate darkness," one woman wrote in her diary. "So must come the end of the world." Still, though the story of the Dust Bowl remains one of the saddest chapters in American history, its coming could be explained by causes more proximate than divine wrath. Drought had been a recurring feature of the high plains that stretched northward from the Texas panhandle, New Mexico, and western Oklahoma all the way through portions of Colorado, Kansas, Nebraska, Wyoming, and the Dakotas. To survive extremes of heat and cold, wind and drought, prairie grasses had developed deep roots. Those grasses fed the buffalo and held the soil in place.

In the late nineteenth century, farmers had seen the grass as a nuisance to be plowed under so they could exploit the rich soil beneath. Land that had been suitable enough for grazing was turned into fields of cotton, wheat, and corn. Little did farmers heed the warning of those who described the area as the "Great American Desert," subscribing instead to the popular notion that "rain follows the plow." Homestead farmers sought to create an agrarian kingdom in which they "busted" and "broke" the land into farms to feed their families, the nation, and the world.

In 1934, when the dust storms arrived in the midst of the Great Depression, the ensuing disaster shattered the dreams of a people who had always seen the West as the land of opportunity. The rains failed them, their crops

Photographer Dorothea Lange liked to place displaced Oklahoma migrants against a background that suggested a central irony of the Depression era—want in the midst of plenty. This picture reminded viewers that there was more than one way to make the trip to California.

withered, and the winds hurled the loose soil across the nation. As the soil eroded year after year, so did farmers' resources and hopes.

That story was the one that John Steinbeck presented in his novel *The Grapes of Wrath* and that director John Ford turned into one of the most critically acclaimed movies of all time. Most Americans now associate the Depression era with the Okies—dispossessed farm families out of Oklahoma and other Dust Bowl states—and their rickety cars packed high with all they owned and heading along Route 66 to California. Whether in Steinbeck's words, in Ford's images, in the ballads of folk singer Woody Guthrie, or in the pictures taken by Farm Security Administration (FSA) photographers such as Dorothea Lange, the Okies and their flight from the Dust Bowl put a face on the tragedy of America during the Great Depression.

Steinbeck's novel told of the Joad family in a near-biblical parable of suffering, endurance, and dignity in the face of adversity. The name Joad echoes the name Job, and the voice of God comes through the Reverend Jim Casy, whose initials link him to Jesus Christ. The Joads' trek across the desert to the promised land reminds us of Israel's lost tribes. It is a compelling story with three major sections: the opening in Oklahoma, in which the Joads are driven from their land; their odyssey across the desert on Route 66; and their journey through California in a desperate search for work.

The Joads are a simple family who for decades struggled to wrest a living cropping cotton on a forty-acre plot near Sallisaw, Oklahoma. At first there were five years of good crops "while the wild grass was still in her." Then it became an "ever' year" kind of place. "Ever' year," Tom Joad told his friend Jim Casy, "we had a good crop comin' an' it never came." Bad crops forced the Joads to borrow from the bank. The crops kept failing, the debt kept growing, and soon the bank owned their farm. The Joads, along with hundreds of thousands of plains farmers, became sharecroppers who each year gave the better part of their crop to a landowner or the bank. When Tom Joad returns home after a stint in prison, he finds his family gone. His friend Muley Graves explains that they have been driven from their farm: "they was gonna stick her out when the bank come to tractorin' off the place." The tractor that leveled the farmhouse also severed the vital connection between the Joads and their land. They were almost literally uprooted and displaced.

Now the question became where to go. In the 1930s California beckoned more than any other destination. The agrarian dream of economic sufficiency and independence still glittered in the West. So the Joads piled all their worldly goods and a family of twelve onto a jalopy and headed down Route 66. Steinbeck described the highway as

> the path of a people in flight, refugees from dust and shrinking land, from the numbers of tractors and shrinking ownership, from the desert's slow northward invasion, from the twisting winds that howl up out of Texas, from the floods that bring no richness to the land and steal what richness is there. From all of these the people are in flight.

The road proves a cruel taskmaster. Each repair of their weather-beaten auto eats into the Joads' shrinking cash reserve. The weaker members of the family die or wander off. In the roadside camps, however, the Joads often meet other refugees who give help and comfort, share what little they have, and join the Joads in reestablishing ties to the places they have left behind.

In California the dream turns into a nightmare. The Joads do indeed discover the land of milk and honey. Rich farms and fertile fields roll across a vast landscape. Yet that abundance is off-limits to the Okies. Californians treat them like vermin, vigilante mobs attack them, labor agents cheat them, strike breakers threaten them, and worst of all, work at a living wage proves nearly impossible to find. Unable to provide, the men lose their place at the head of the family. In the end Ma Joad's faith holds the remnants of the family together, but in a final irony these Dust Bowl refugees face the peril of rising floodwaters.

THE SPECIFIC VERSUS THE COLLECTIVE

Many Americans come away from the Joads' story convinced that Steinbeck recorded the central tragedy of America in the 1930s. Yet no single story, however powerful or popular, can capture the collective experience of hundreds of thousands, even millions of people. A historian wants to know just how typical the Joads were—of Americans, of migrants to California, or even simply of Okies during the Great Depression. After all, Steinbeck was a novelist seeking to tell a story of people dispossessed from the land. Unlike a historian, he was not bound by strict rules of evidence and explanation, only by the true expression of the human condition. Yet Steinbeck gained the respect of his readers in part because he based much of his novel on direct observation. Like many writers of the 1930s he used a reporter's techniques to research his story, visiting Oklahoma, traveling Route 66, and touring California's migrant labor camps.

Social scientists and government officials of Steinbeck's day confirmed much of what he wrote. They too reported the drought conditions that drove farm families out of the plains, the hostility of Californians to refugees, and the destitution of many migrants. Yet we have already seen that the historian must rigorously question the testimony of social scientists and journalists as much as novelists. Even the apparently objective photographs taken by that "mirror with a memory" need to be scrutinized.

Take, for example, the case of photographer Dorothea Lange and her husband, Paul Taylor, an agricultural economist from the University of California at Berkeley. Like Steinbeck, Lange and Taylor followed the migrant trail from Oklahoma through Texas and across the desert to the migrant camps in California. Lange was one of many photographers hired by the FSA to document rural life in the 1930s. She and Taylor published a book, *An American Exodus: A Record of Human Erosion,* that described the destruction of the plains and the impoverishment of a proud people. Yet Taylor and Lange were hardly disinterested observers—much to their credit, one can argue. Like Steinbeck, they believed that the migrants needed help. And all three went looking for evidence to make that case.

The story of Lange's most famous photograph is instructive. One March morning in 1936 she was driving up California Highway 101 toward San Francisco. Eager to be home, she hurried past a hand-painted sign directing passersby to a pea-pickers' camp. Some impulse made her turn back. What she saw staggered her, even though she had spent months investigating the conditions of migrant farm laborers. The camp contained more than two thousand men, women, and children huddled against the cold and driving rain in ragged tents and flimsy wood shelters. They had come to pick peas, but the weather left them without work or wages. And with nowhere to go and no relief from local, state, or federal officials, they waited. First their money ran out, then their food. By the time Lange arrived they were desperate. How was she to give voice to their need?

The collection of Dorothea Lange's work in the Library of Congress shows that she was far more than a "one-picture" photographer. She traveled widely and photographed a wide variety of Depression-era scenes. "Migrant Mother," her most famous photograph, was actually taken as the final in a series of six separate shots. What is it about "Migrant Mother #6" (*left*) that makes it more affecting than "Migrant Mother #1" (*right*)?

That day Lange took a photograph that must rank as one of the most widely viewed images of the decade. She entitled it "Migrant Mother." Her subject was Florence Thompson, at age thirty-two the recently widowed mother of six children. What Lange captured was the quiet dignity of a woman at the end of hope, cradling an infant in her arms with two young children clinging to her shoulders. She had just sold the tires off her car to buy food for her family. As Lange intended, the image put a personal face to a need so compelling that few people could turn away. Along with Steinbeck's tale of the Joads, "Migrant Mother" made Americans aware of the story of the Dust Bowl refugees.

Lange and other FSA photographers did not simply arrive at a camp and begin taking pictures. To get the image she wanted, Lange often posed her subjects. She sometimes even suggested to them where to look or what to do with their hands. In the case of Florence Thompson, Lange recalled, "she seemed to know that my pictures might help her, and so she helped me. There was a sort of equality about it." Lange took six different photographs, each time looking for a more compelling shot. In the first, one child was smiling at the camera, defusing the desperation of the situation. Lange then tried a longer view of the tent; then moved in to focus on the mother and her baby. In the final, telling shot, Thompson, of her own accord, raised her hand to her chin. "LOOK IN HER EYES," ran the headline in *Midweek Pictorial*

EXTENT OF AREA SUBJECT TO SEVERE WIND EROSION
1935–1940

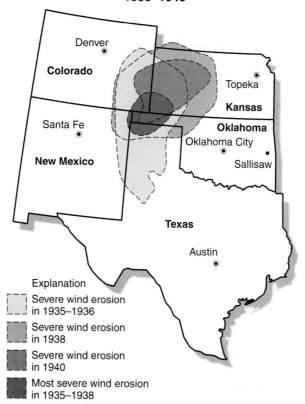

Explanation

Severe wind erosion
in 1935–1936

Severe wind erosion
in 1938

Severe wind erosion
in 1940

Most severe wind erosion
in 1935–1938

when it first ran the photo. "This woman is watching something happen to America and to herself and her children who are part of America."

Both Lange and Steinbeck adopted the time-tested literary technique of allowing a part to stand for the whole. The two created images so vivid, stories so concrete, they would be remembered long after the bland generalizations of bureaucratic reports were forgotten. Yet here, in the matter of the concrete and the specific, is precisely where historians so often begin their skeptical cross-examinations. One way of identifying biases or limiting perspectives is to examine a broader sample. To what degree are Steinbeck's vivid stories and Lange's wrenching photographs representative of the collective reality they are taken to symbolize?

Even a casual glance at the Joads' story suggests that Steinbeck painted with a broad, sometimes imprecise brush. To begin with, the Joads did not live in what was physically the Dust Bowl. While drought affected a vast region from the Dakotas to Texas, geographers place the Dust Bowl in an area in the Texas-Oklahoma panhandle that spills over into western Kansas and eastern parts of Colorado and New Mexico. Sallisaw, from which the Joads hailed, lay in the eastern part of Oklahoma, several hundred miles outside the Dust Bowl. Rolling hills and oaks, not prairie and short grasses, formed the landscape. And corn rather than cotton was the primary crop. As one historian remarked, "Steinbeck's geography, like that of most Americans, was a bit hazy; any place in Oklahoma, even on the Ozark Plateau, must be Dust Bowl country, he assumed."

Still, this point seems a small one, given the wide reach of those rolling black clouds. Even if the Joads were not technically from the Dust Bowl, surely most of the Okies who migrated to California were farm refugees from the dust storms. Or were they? Here, too, the facts get in the way of the image Steinbeck made popular. Statistics show that California gained more than a million new residents in the 1930s. In fact, however, no more than about 15,000 to 16,000 of those people came from the Dust Bowl—well under 2 percent. In imagining the Joads, Steinbeck was implicitly portraying a much broader group of southwestern emigrants from four states: "agricultural laborers" and "farm workers" not only from Oklahoma but also Arkansas, Texas, and Missouri. Because this group amounted to about one-third of the newcomers to California, we might say that, strictly speaking, the Joads are more accurately representative of displaced agricultural labor than of Dust Bowl refugees.

The minute we begin talking about collective experiences, of course, we run headlong into numbers. To understand the great migration of the Depression decade, historians must place the Joads in a statistical context. What links them to the million people who reached California between 1930 and 1940? Unfortunately the mere mention of numbers—statistics or columns of figures—is enough to make the eyes of many readers glaze over. It is only natural to prefer Steinbeck's way of personifying the Dust Bowl refugees.

Yet the numbers cannot be avoided if we are to paint an accurate picture. The challenge for the historian lies in bringing statistics to life so they tell a story with some of the human qualities that Lange and Steinbeck invested in their subjects. In looking at the 1930s in particular, historians are lucky because social scientists and government officials tried hard to quantify the human circumstances of the era. In particular, historians of the Dust Bowl era have been able to benefit from the federal population count of 1940, which was the first modern census.

The federal census had been taken every decade since 1790, because its data was needed to apportion each state's seats in the House of Representatives, in accordance with the provisions of the Constitution. For the first fifty years federal marshals did the actual counting, by locating households within their districts and recording the number of people living there. Over time the nature of the information collected became broader and more detailed; it included social statistics about taxes collected, real estate values, wages, education, and crime. In 1880 Congress shifted responsibility for the census from the marshals to specially appointed experts trained to collect not only population statistics but also data on manufacturing and other economic activities. By 1890 punch cards were being used to record data, and an electric tabulating machine was used to process those cards. Mechanization, by vastly reducing calculation time, made it possible to accumulate more complex and varied information.

The census of 1940, because of advanced statistical techniques used by the enumerators, was even more comprehensive than its predecessors. Social scientists and opinion pollsters such as George Gallup had experimented during the 1930s with probability sampling. To measure unemployment rates in 1940, for example, they constructed a group of some 20,000 households to represent a cross section of the nation as a whole. The data from this small sample gave the social scientists statistics that accurately (though not exactly) reflected the national employment pattern. Other questions in the 1940 census were asked of just 5 percent of the households. That allowed the Census Bureau to publish detailed tables on many more subjects, not the least of which was internal migration. In so doing, they provided historians with a way of determining how representative the Joads actually were of the Dust Bowl refugees.

HISTORY BY THE NUMBERS

Historian James Gregory went to the census records in his own attempt to analyze the Dust Bowl migration. In each of the censuses from 1910 to 1970, he was able to find statistics on Americans born in western regions of the South (Texas, Oklahoma, Missouri, and Arkansas) who had moved to California. By comparing these numbers decade to decade, he could also estimate how many new southwesterners arrived every ten years. Take a moment to look at the table on page 298.

The story of the Joads would lead us to hypothesize that between 1930 and 1940 a large number of migrants left the southwestern plains states for California. Drought and economic hardships drove them out. Because so many settled in California, we would further assume that conditions special to that state drew the refugees there.

At first glance, the statistics support the hypothesis. The number of southwesterners in California in 1940 was 745,934. Subtracting the residents that were already there in 1930 (430,810) we discover that some 315,124 southwesterners moved to California during the decade in which the severe dust storms took place (this number is shown for 1940 under the column heading "Net California Increase"). Of course, there is a certain false precision here. Common sense tells us that at least some southwesterners living in California who were counted in the 1930 census must have returned home, moved to an entirely new state, or died over the next ten years. In that case, the actual number of migrants arriving must have been greater, though we have no reliable way of knowing how much greater. But the bureau has estimated that the total number of southwestern emigrants might have been as many as 400,000. In other words, the number in our table—315,124—may have been off by 85,000 people, enough to populate a medium-sized city.

Western South Natives Living outside the Region, 1910–1970

	Living outside region	Living in California	Net Calif. Increase	Percentage of Calif. pop.
1910	661,094	103,241		4.3%
1920	1,419,046	187,471	84,230	5.5%
1930	2,027,139	430,810	243,339	7.6%
1940	2,580,940	745,934	315,124	10.8%
1950	3,887,370	1,367,720	621,786	12.9%
1960	4,966,781	1,734,271	366,551	11.0%
1970	5,309,287	1,747,632	13,361	8.8%

Sources: U.S. Bureau of the Census, Census of the United States, Population: 1910, Vol. 1, 732–733; 1920, Vol. 11, 628–629; 1930, Vol. H, 155–156; 1940, State of Birth, 17–18; 1950, State of Birth, 20–24; 1960, State of Birth, 22–23; 1970, State of Birth, 28–29.

A migrant total approaching half a million is surely high. But we must ask another question. Is there a *causal* connection between the drought and migration, or is the link merely coincidental? The anecdotal evidence of one journalist suggests an intriguing clue. He reported seeing Oklahoma farmers "in their second-hand flivvers [inexpensive Model-T Fords], piled high with furniture and family . . . pouring through the divides by the hundreds." It is the kind of literary detail that might have come straight out of Steinbeck. The problem is that the reporter was writing in 1926, eight years before the first dust storm. We begin to see the reason that James Gregory, in compiling his table, sought data over a sixty-year period. The broader time span provides a better yardstick of comparison. To make the point visually, we have taken the information from the "Net California Increase" column and displayed it as a bar graph (on the next page).

As the bar graph reveals, during the 1920s nearly a quarter of a million southwesterners migrated to California—nearly as many as came during the "dirty thirties" of the Dust Bowl years. Small wonder that a reporter could speak, in 1926, of hundreds of flivvers crowding the mountain passes. And the 1920s, by contrast, were years of average rainfall. Equally notable, the number of arrivals virtually doubles during the 1940s, a time when rain and better economic times had returned to the region, mostly because of massive industrial growth stimulated by World War II. Even in the postwar decade of 1950–1960, the migration of southwesterners remained heavy. Such numbers suggest that factors besides drought, dust storms, and the Depression were driving people from the southwestern plains or drawing them to California.

Steinbeck's powerful imagery provides one suggestion for explaining this broader trend: the tractor that knocked down the Joads' house. Why, we might ask, were tractors rumbling across the farmland, driving people from their homes? Steinbeck offered an explanation: "At last the owner men came

WESTERN SOUTH NATIVES ARRIVING IN CALIFORNIA, 1910–1970

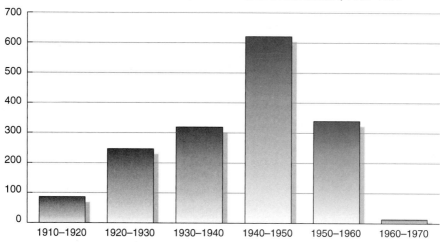

to the point. The tenant system won't work any more. One man on a tractor can take the place of twelve or fourteen families. Pay him a wage and take all the crop." The owners took no responsibility for what they and their tractors did. It was "the bank" that gave the order, and the bank was "something more than men. . . . It's the monster. Men made it, but they can't control it." When the tenants protest that their families had "killed the weeds and snakes" to make way for their farms, the owners show cold indifference. "The bank, the fifty-thousand acre owner, can't be responsible," they explain. "You're on land that isn't yours." When the tenants complain that they have no money and nowhere else to go, the owners respond, "Why don't you go to California? There's work there and it never gets cold."

The tractor is a symbol for a complex process of agricultural reorganization through absentee landownership, mechanization, and corporatization. During the late nineteenth century farmers had flooded into the southwestern plains—the nation's final agricultural frontier. Through World War I they realized generally high prices for their crops. All the same, many farmers had arrived with few resources other than the labor they and their families could perform. One bad crop, one dry year, and they were facing debt. Once in debt, they had to buy on credit and borrow on future crops. As a result, sharecropping and tenantry had become widespread even in flush times.

During the 1920s, though industry boomed, the agricultural economy went into decline. Prices for agricultural staples including cotton, wheat, and corn fell. Overfarming depleted the soil. Such factors created conditions under which too many people were trying to farm land that could no longer support them. Between 1910 and 1930, well before the great dust storms, the number of farmers and agricultural workers in the region fell by about 341,000 and some 1.3 million people left. About 430,800 settled in California. A majority of the farmers who remained in the region rented land or cropped on shares. By the 1930s landowners had come to realize that they could increase profits by driving off their tenants, by consolidating their acreage into larger, more efficient farms, and by using tractors and other machines rather than human labor.

So the explanation for the exodus from the plains would need to include a discussion of agricultural reorganization and the mechanization of farming. Steinbeck's vivid portrait of the bankers' tractors acknowledged this reality, but the novel's pervasive images of dust overwhelm it somewhat. These findings do not mean we should dismiss *The Grapes of Wrath*, merely that we should study the numbers on migration a little more closely. Were those migrants who left between 1910 and 1930 the same kinds of people who left in the 1930s? Did they leave for the same reasons?

Because the 1940 census was so much more comprehensive than those that preceded it, we actually know more about the Dust Bowl–era migrants than about those who traveled in previous decades. The 1930 census tells us, for example, that the population of rural counties in Oklahoma, Missouri, and Arkansas dropped in the 1920s, but not whether people left the region. Many may have gone into the cities or to work in the booming oil fields. All the same, it seems most likely that the migrants of the 1920s were a more prosperous group than those of the next decade. Despite the popular image of the West as a "safety valve" for the poor from the East, over the course of American history the majority of pioneer farmers were neither rich nor poor. The West attracted largely middle-class folk drawn to the promise of economic opportunity rather than driven out by harsh circumstances.

Elbert Garretson seems representative of the middling sort of people making up migrants before the Great Depression. Garretson saw that lower crop prices and declining soil fertility had weakened his chances to succeed at farming. So he packed up his family and took a job in a California steel mill. His plan was to get on his feet financially so he could continue to farm in Oklahoma. Several times the Garretsons returned to Oklahoma, but each time the lure of California proved stronger. Finally, Garretson sold the farm as a bad bet.

During the 1920s the lure for migrants was even stronger because California farmers faced a shortage of agricultural labor. To attract workers, they often paid railroad fares of southwesterners who would emigrate. "The farmers would meet you at the trains," one woman recalled. Another family went "because we could see the promise of the cotton future here, and we were cotton ranchers." Poorer people like the Joads surely felt the draw too, but they were more likely tied by debt to their "ever' year" farms.

What differed in the 1930s was not so much the numbers of those who went but their identities. Of all the regions of the United States, none suffered more economic devastation during the Great Depression than the southwest plains. The once-robust oil industry collapsed in a glut of overproduction. Unemployment in the region hit one-third of all workers. Infestations of locusts and boll weevils added to the woes of farmers long afflicted by drought and low crop prices. In the two years before Franklin Roosevelt became president, creditors foreclosed the mortgages of some 10 percent of Oklahoma's farms. As a result, the migrants of the 1930s included many more desperately poor and displaced families like the Joads.

When Franklin Roosevelt launched the New Deal in 1933, he placed the agricultural crisis at the top of his agenda. Still, it was far from clear what government could do to ease the farmers' plight. One of the New Deal's most ambitious measures during the president's Hundred Day program for relief, recovery, and reform was the Agricultural Adjustment Act. New Dealers sought to ease farm distress by providing credit, reducing overproduction, and raising prices. One strategy was to offer farmers a cash subsidy to take land out of production. Over the next eight years, desperate southwestern farmers so eagerly sought the subsidy that they reduced their cotton acreage by 12.5 million acres, or more than 50 percent.

This strategy contains one of the central ironies of the Dust Bowl crisis. Along with the drought and the "monster" bank, the good intentions of the federal government helped to account for the wave of tractors driving people like the Joads from their land. To receive a crop subsidy, landowners had to reduce the acreage they planted. The easiest way to do that was to evict tenants. Landowners could consolidate their best lands and farm them with tractors while letting tenant lands return to grass. One landlord boasted that "I bought tractors on the money the government give me and got shet o' my renters." So common was that practice that by 1940 tenancy had decreased by 24 percent. "They got their choice," the same landlord remarked curtly. "California or WPA [Works Progress Administration, a federal relief agency]."

If only the choice had been so simple. Unlike the 1920s, when California and the urban centers of the Southwest attracted rural folk with new opportunities, displaced tenants in the 1930s had few practical options. By this time California had a glut of agricultural workers, and the southwestern cities had higher unemployment than the rural counties did. The New Deal did offer help. During the early duster years of 1934 and 1935, the Federal Emergency Relief Administration provided funds to some 2.5 million southwestern families, about 20 percent of the population. But the aid proved woefully inadequate. In most areas of the country the states supplemented federal relief payments, but not in the Southwest. Throughout the 1930s some 20 percent to 35 percent of all families in the region suffered from extreme poverty and unemployment. This situation is one area in which the story of the Joads brings the plight of 1930s migrants into clear focus.

THE ROAD

As the Great Depression worsened, Roy Turner and his family migrated to a shantytown outside the Oklahoma City stockyards. These encampments (often nicknamed Hoovervilles, after President Herbert Hoover) appeared in many urban areas. In Oklahoma City, the Turners joined some 2,000 others living off a mixture of relief, part-time jobs, and declining hopes. The

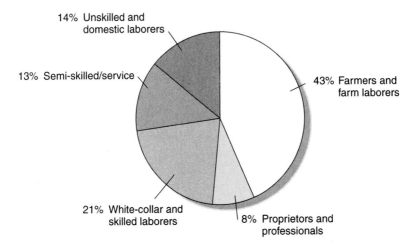

Premigration occupations of California migrants from west south-central states. (Data from *American Exodus: The Dust Bowl Migration and Okie Culture in California* by James N. Gregory. Copyright © 1991 by James N. Gregory. Used by permission of Oxford University Press, Inc.)

Turners described their home as "old automobiles, old lard cases, buckets, paste board." For food they had little more than the milk from the stockpen cows. When conditions became unbearably grim, the family pulled together what few belongings they had and headed down Route 66—"walking, me and my wife and two babies," hoping to hitch rides on the 1,200 mile trip to California.

Here indeed is a family much like the Joads, though their path to California involved a stop for several years in an urban center. But the Turners and Joads—desperately poor, without jobs, and without prospects—were only one element of the southwestern surge to California. When James Gregory examined the Census Bureau statistics as well as other surveys, he discovered some surprising percentages. For example, in 1939 the Bureau of Agricultural Economics surveyed the occupations of about 116,000 families who had come to California in the 1930s. The results of that data are displayed in the graph below.

As the chart indicates, only 43 percent of southwesterners were doing farmwork immediately before they migrated. Farmers were a definite minority. In fact, nearly one-third of all migrants were professional or white-collar workers. The 1940 census showed similar results. Southwesterners who moved to California between 1935 and 1940 were asked to list their residence as of April 1, 1935. Only 36 percent reported that they were living on a farm.

With these numbers, as with all statistics, it is important to look critically at the method of collection. The census enumerators of 1940 reported that rural residents, to simplify answering the question of residence, would sometimes merely list the nearest town or city, which gave the mistaken impression that those people lived in an urban area. Even taking these biases into account, however, it seems that Steinbeck (and many historians as well) have exaggerated the numbers of farmers in the migrant stream.

Other factors distinguish the actual migrants from the Joads. Of the twelve travelers in the Joads's old Hudson, five were well over forty years old. By contrast, most of the actual migrants were younger—60 percent of the adult travelers were under age thirty-five. Unlike the Joads, the actual migrants were slightly better educated than those who remained behind. The Joads were typical in gender balance since the majority of migrants traveled as families. (In the broader history of American migration this family movement is rather unusual, because single males more commonly predominate among migrating populations.) All the same, large extended families like the Joads were rare. The average southwestern migrant family had 4.4 members.

Finally, there is the matter of race. Like 95 percent of all southwestern migrants to California, the Joads were white. This was not because few African Americans lived in Missouri, Arkansas, Texas, or Oklahoma. In 1930 the black population in those four states was approximately 1.7 million. Many of these African Americans were farmers or agricultural laborers, and thousands left the region between 1910 and 1930. However, most migrated to urban centers in the North and upper Midwest, such as Chicago and Pittsburgh, where they already had relatives or friends. Among those black southwesterners who headed to California, the great majority settled in Los Angeles. Even so, by 1940 the black population there was only about 64,000 out of 1.5 million residents. (And a mere 5,000 African Americans resided in San Francisco.)

Steinbeck's account of the Joad's trip west leads us to another question—about the quality of the trip itself. *The Grapes of Wrath* devotes a third of its tale to the Joads' struggle to reach California. The book gives no exact dates, but the Joads were on the road long enough to have many hardships and adventures. They reached California weeks after their journey began. Reading of such tribulations, a reader might well wonder why so many people risked the trip if it was such an ordeal.

But the collective portrait that historians have assembled about migration journeys suggests that, for most people, the odyssey was not so wrenching. Here, the evidence is mostly anecdotal. The census collected no systematic information on the length of the journey or conditions along the way. But social scientists and reporters interviewed Okies and recorded oral histories of their experience. Although the individual misfortunes that Steinbeck ascribed to the Joads no doubt happened to some migrants, most found the trip less harrowing.

Take, for example, the hopes that drew people to the road. To the Joads, California was little more than a blurry set of ideas based on rumors, legends, gossip, and handbills sent to Oklahoma by labor agents. Certainly, many people headed for California with unreasonable expectations. Two young researchers who were hired by the Library of Congress to collect folklore recorded this verse:

> They said in California
> that money grew on trees,
> that everyone was going there,
> just like a swarm of bees.

State tourist agencies encouraged such illusions. California was the place to come for a grand vacation of sun and fun. The Hollywood film industry portrayed the state as a glamorous alternative to the dark urban settings it used for films about social problems and crime.

But precisely because California officials feared that their state would be overrun by destitute job seekers, they repeatedly sought to dispel such fantasies, sending word that conditions in California were desperate. A billboard along Route 66 near Tulsa announced in bold letters:

> NO JOBS in California
> If you are looking for work—KEEP OUT
> 6 men for every job
> No State Relief available for Non-residents

Neither the dire warnings nor the glamorous tourist brochures were accurate. Although California's economy suffered and unemployment remained serious, the state in the 1930s was much better off than most of the nation. Its farms grew some one hundred different crops, and such diversification made California agriculture less vulnerable to overproduction and falling prices. Other industries also weathered the depression better than most. Industrial workers in California generally received higher hourly wages than did the same workers in other regions. The state economy actually grew during the 1930s. For those unable to find work or who lost jobs, the state had the nation's best relief benefits—$40 per month as opposed to $10 to $12 in the Southwest. All these facts suggest that folks who left the southern plains had reason to pick California as their destination. As one Texan remarked, "Well, if they have lots of work out there and if relief is good, then if I don't find work I'll still be all right."

Furthermore, unlike the Joads, many of the migrants traveling along Route 66 had relatives and friends already living in California. By 1930 more than 400,000 former southwesterners resided in the state, creating a solid base for what demographers call "migration chains." Much like worldwide immigrants to America did, southwesterners wrote home to relatives. Such letters "gits the folks back home to talkin' that work is pretty good in California," explained one Oklahoman, "so they decide to pull up stakes and come." One message made a particularly powerful impression: "Everyone writes back that he's heeled. He's got him a job." Equally important, relatives offered newly arrived migrants a place to stay and help in getting started. During the 1920s and 1930s entire communities of Okies and Arkies (migrants from Arkansas) sprang up in California's agricultural valleys. Unlike the Joads, more than half of the Dust Bowl migrants left for California with a destination in mind.

Novelists and reporters dramatized the hardships of the road because it made a good story; indeed, much of *The Grapes of Wrath* fits the popular literary genre of a "road novel." Just as Huck Finn's character deepened as he and the runaway slave Jim floated down the broad Mississippi, so the Joads were transformed by their trials along Route 66. But as one historian observed, Steinbeck wrote in tones "more justly reserved for the era of covered wagons." By the 1930s good highways, bus routes, and railroads linked the southwestern plains to California. A family with a decent car could make the trip in about three or four days.

One reason that southwesterners knew so much about California was that, because the trip was not difficult, their relatives returned home to visit. People noticed the signs of prosperity that the visitors brought with them. "They left in an old wreck and come back in a good car," one migrant told a social worker. Because the trip was manageable, migrants did not necessarily see their move as permanent. Many families sent a few members to scout out the prospects. Some, such as Elbert Garretson, left their farms behind with the idea that they could always return.

CALIFORNIA

About 150 miles after crossing the state line, Route 66 entered the town of Barstow, California. There, travelers faced a significant choice. Should they follow the highway as it veered south into the sprawling city of Los Angeles? Or should they take the smaller road out of Barstow, not entirely paved, that wound through the Tehachapi Mountains and into the San Joaquin Valley? The decision was a fateful one.

The Joads chose the route to the valley. But as you may have suspected (based on the census data we have already reviewed), most southwestern migrants did not. The majority hailed from urban areas, and during the years 1935 to 1940 at least, nearly 70 percent chose to make their residence in urban California. That figure is somewhat misleading because, as we shall see, many agricultural laborers settled in cities and migrated to various farm jobs from season to season. Still, Los Angeles remained the most popular destination for southwesterners, attracting more than one-third of all migrants.

Why do we hear so little about these urban migrants? The reason, most likely, is that their stories are at once less colorful and more familiar. The movement of the American population from the country to the city had accelerated in the last half of the nineteenth century, a broad trend that continued throughout the twentieth. Furthermore, Los Angeles assimilated its new population with less strain. To be sure, many Okies were shocked by the vast, sprawling city. Arriving was "like going into an entirely different world," recalled one migrant. "It seemed like you could drive forever and never get out of a town." And the Depression's tough times made it more difficult to find work than it had been during the 1920s. But the diverse urban economy offered a wide range of jobs, which were eagerly taken by new arrivals. By 1940, 83 percent of all men in the city eligible to work had found jobs.

Only 28 percent of the Dust Bowl's refugees found their way, like the Joads, to the San Joaquin Valley. Most of those who did harbored the same dreams that had inspired so many Americans throughout the nineteenth century: to take possession of their own family farms. California, after all, boasted plenty of cotton fields, just like back home. Migrants assumed they could work in the fields at a living wage until they could save enough to purchase some land. It was the same pattern of hope that had sent many of their forebears to the Southwest. But California surprised them.

The sights greeting newcomers to the San Joaquin Valley were both tantalizing and troubling. As the Joads rolled down the highway, Pa stared at the countryside transfixed: "I never knowed they was anything like her." Before him lay the "peach trees and the walnut groves, and the dark green patches of oranges." Just the look of the place struck migrants as somehow more vast and strange than the plains they left behind. And something else seemed odd. Amidst the broad fields and orchards spreading for miles and miles, migrants saw few signs of the agrarian kingdom of small farms they were expecting. "Where are the farmers?" one newcomer asked. And even more puzzling: "Where are the farmhouses?"

Indeed, in its economic, social, and political structures, California's San Joaquin Valley—and the larger Central Valley of which it was a part—was a foreign land. By the 1920s the state had pioneered the techniques of what later would come to be called agribusiness. Again, the census data helps fill out the collective portrait. The state's farms commanded more capital and produced products worth more than twice the national average. Those crops required more water, more machinery, more chemical fertilizers and weed killers, and more paid labor than did crops grown in other areas of the United States. To exploit the valley's soils, irrigation projects initiated by large landowners and private corporations eventually fell under the control of state and federal irrigation agencies such as the Bureau of Reclamation and Army Corps of Engineers. These agencies diverted the waters of the Sacramento, San Joaquin, and other smaller rivers into the fields of valley farms and ranches.

To be sure, small farms had hardly vanished from the landscape. In 1929 some 90 percent of California's 135,000 farms produced crops valued at less than $30,000 a year. Thirty percent had crops worth less than $1,000. But those smaller farmers lacked political or economic clout. Of all American farms producing crops worth more than $30,000 a year, more than one-third lay in California. Thus the state's agriculture was dominated by large corporations and landowners. Some crops, including citrus fruits and raisins, were organized into centrally controlled marketing cooperatives. (Sunkist was one such example.) Cotton, the crop Okies knew best, was a bit less organized. Even so, just four companies ginned two-thirds of the cotton, and a web of corporate farms, banks, and the San Joaquin Valley Agricultural Bureau kept a tight rein on production levels and labor costs. In fact, California only permitted farmers to grow one kind of high-quality cotton.

Most migrants coming into the valley had little time to think of buying land; they faced the more pressing task of simply surviving. Like the Joads, most timed their arrival in California for September, the beginning of the cotton harvest. Growers estimated that a good worker might earn $3 to $4 a day, about twice the wage in the Southwest. But agricultural employment in cotton virtually ceased between December and March. That was the rainy season, when temperatures, though milder than back home, often dipped into the thirties. Some lucky families found shelter in labor camps. A few landowners allowed migrants to stay on in one-room shacks. More often, home was a squatter village of tents, old cars, and shanties made from wood scraps. Under conditions of poverty and malnutrition, disease spread quickly, especially among the old and young. This was the scene that Dorothea Lange discovered when she photographed her "Migrant Mother."

So *The Grapes of Wrath* remains closest to history when Steinbeck describes the plight of the Joads during 1937–1938, the worst and wettest California winter of the era. In 1937, when the Roosevelt administration cut back on spending in the belief that the nation was on its way to recovery, the economy collapsed. Unemployment returned to levels much like those before the New Deal. Not surprisingly, migration reached a peak that year. And then the rains came. Floods, as Steinbeck depicted, wiped out entire squatter camps, often leaving the residents homeless. The situation became so desperate that private charities and government agencies finally swung into action—just as Lange and Steinbeck had hoped. The FSA offered medical care and relief to families who could not meet California's one-year residency requirement for public assistance.

After that winter, the worst was over. Within two years the rains returned to the plains, while World War II brought back prosperity and a virtual end to unemployment. No longer did migrants face the same struggle for survival that the Joads experienced in California.

THE OTHER MIGRANTS

The collective portrait of the Okies, drawn by Gregory and other historians, demonstrates the strengths of Steinbeck's searing novel as well as its limitations. In effect, the census and other numerical data serve as a framework, within which we can set not only Steinbeck's specific tale but also the newspaper reports, photographs, contemporary sociological studies, and oral recollections that have been left behind in the historical record. The structure of the numbers allows us to give Steinbeck and the other evidence its proper due without mistaking a part for the whole.

In the same way, the discipline of the numbers is also invaluable for placing the newly arrived Okies within their larger California context. Because Steinbeck's tale focuses on the Okies alone, historians have come to appreciate that the tale is inevitably partial in the picture it gives of California's

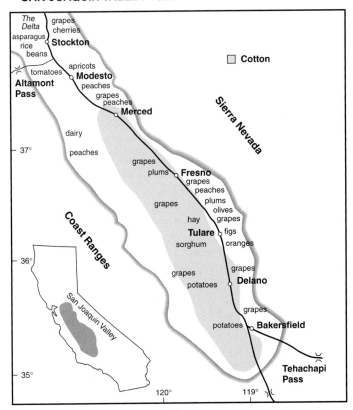

SAN JOAQUIN VALLEY 1930

A rich array of fruits and vegetables grow in California's San Joaquin Valley. Such variety reduced the impact of the Depression on the state's agricultural economy and helps explain why the valley became a destination for families like the Joads. (From *American Exodus: The Dust Bowl Migration and Okie Culture in California* by James N. Gregory. Copyright © 1991 by James N. Gregory. Used by permission of Oxford University Press, Inc.)

agricultural labor force. Another set of numbers makes the point. In 1930 that labor force was 43 percent white, 21 percent Mexican, 17 percent European, 8 percent Filipino, and 7 percent Japanese.

That multicultural influence is mirrored by another data set, this one illustrating the wide diversity of crops grown in the San Joaquin Valley. The map below shows not only cotton but also grapes, potatoes, peaches, plums, olives, figs, oranges, rice, beans, cherries, tomatoes, and so on. Small wonder Pa Joad was taken aback. And the diversity of both the agriculture and its labor force are related. Americans today take for granted the variety of California produce. But these crops are hardly "natural." Most were not raised by the original Spanish settlers, nor were they the choice of Anglo newcomers from the East during the mid-nineteenth century, whose preference was to plant familiar crops like wheat. The diversity of California agriculture arose only in the late nineteenth century—at the same time that its labor force was becoming increasingly diverse.

To begin with, the Chinese who arrived in the wake of the 1848 gold rush played a vital part in introducing fruit orchards. Many Chinese immigrants who had once farmed along the Pearl and Yellow Rivers turned their energies in America to constructing irrigation channels, dikes, and levies in the delta regions of the San Joaquin and Sacramento Rivers. Swampy land that sold for only $28 an acre in 1875 was soon being snapped up at $100 an acre. The Chinese also brought valuable horticultural experience in growing orchard and garden crops. One immigrant to the United States, Ah Bing, bred the renowned Bing cherry; in Florida, Lue Gim Gong developed a frost-resistant orange.

Anti-Asian nativism, especially strong in California, led Congress to pass the Chinese Exclusion Act, banning the entry of Chinese laborers after 1882. Nevertheless, increasing numbers of Japanese immigrants continued the transformation of California agriculture, especially after 1900. By 1910 Japanese farmers were producing 70 percent of California's strawberries. By 1940 they grew 95 percent of its snap beans as well as spring and summer celery, and they actively cultivated a host of other crops. As Colonel John Irish, president of the California Delta Association, commented in 1921, Californians

> had seen the Japanese convert the barren land like that at Florin and Livingston into productive and profitable fields, orchards and vineyards, by the persistence and intelligence of their industry. They had seen the hardpan and goose lands in the Sacramento Valley, gray and black with our two destructive alkalis, cursed with barrenness like the fig tree of Bethany, and not worth paying taxes on, until Ikuta, [a Japanese immigrant], decided that those lands would raise rice. After years of persistent toil, and enduring heartbreaking losses and disappointments, he conquered that rebellious soil and raised the first commercial crop of rice in California.

The restrictive immigration acts of the 1920s, however, once again reshaped California's labor pool, drastically limiting the inflow of workers from most nations and banning Asian immigration entirely. No longer could Californians find European or Japanese immigrants to tend their fields. Facing a labor shortage, they turned to Mexicans and, to a lesser extent, to Filipinos, who were still allowed entry because the Philippines was a U.S. territory.

A look at the numbers and background of Mexican laborers dispels a stereotype similar to the one we have already rejected about southwestern immigrants. Most Mexicans who labored in California in 1930 were hardly simple peasants straight from the Mexican countryside. More often they were laborers possessing a variety of skills, whose migration resulted from the industrialization spreading through Mexico after the 1890s. For example, Braulio

THE GOVERNOR SENDS
AID TO PIXLEY
24 BUSHELS (?)
(?) FOR (?)
(?) PEOPLE

WE WANT
FOOD!

Mexican farmworkers organized a number of major labor actions against California's growers. Such action is one reason the growers were so willing to replace them with southwestern migrants. The Dust Bowl migrants had no similar tradition of labor activism and community organization. The Mexican women on this truck were making an appeal to strikebreakers to join their strike.

López, a worker who picked cotton in the San Joaquin Valley, had worked on the Mexican railroad before coming north. In the United States López had also worked as a miner, laid tracks for the streetcar in Los Angeles, and worked on road construction between Los Angeles and San Diego.

This pattern of varied labor was common among both Mexicans and Filipinos. Although many workers called Los Angeles or some other city their home, they moved seasonally to jobs they knew they could count on. "You start out the year, January," one Filipino laborer recalled, "you'd find a place and it was usually an asparagus camp. . . . From asparagus season, we would migrate to Fairfield, to Suisin and there the men worked out in the orchards picking fruits while the women and even children, as long as they could stand on their boxes, worked cutting fruits." Historian Devra Weber has argued that these more regular patterns of migration became a source of stability in a chaotic labor regime by providing a combination of jobs that allowed families to make ends meet.

Such regular migration depended on members of the community helping one another. Mexicans had a long tradition of mutual assistance. In addition to formal community organizations—*mutualistas*—informal employment networks existed in which families and friends from the same region in Mexico would live and work together in California. Women created informal networks, sharing food when needed or cooking for several families when one mother was sick. The Japanese relied on similar social associations, called *ken-*

The faded Spanish on the older sign to the left offers mute testimony to the shift from Mexican to southwestern migrants in California agriculture. Notice that the Hotchkiss Ranch has been able to expand production of cotton despite the Depression (from 10,000 to 15,000 acres in cultivation and from 3,000 to 10,000 acres in cotton). The glowing description on the signs is a far cry from the actual conditions under which most migrants lived and worked.

jinkai. "If you hold *hashi* [chopsticks] individually," explained one farmer, "you can certainly break them all, but if you put them together, why you can't break a bunch of *hashi*. And so, like that, as a family we should stick together, but also as a community we should be sticking together."

Now that we are aware of these patterns of agricultural labor, we can place the Okies' arrival in context. In doing so, it becomes evident that not one but two large migrations were going on during the 1930s. Over the decade, as we have seen, as many as 400,000 southwesterners came to the state. During that same period, however, anywhere from half a million to a million Mexicans returned to Mexico from the United States. (Exact figures for migration in and out of Mexico are difficult to obtain.) With the coming of the Depression and scarce employment, many local governments either encouraged or coerced Mexican laborers into leaving the country. Many laborers who were forced out had been born in the United States and thus were legal citizens. "My father left his best years of his life in this country because he worked hard in the mines and in the fields," recalled one San Joaquin Valley resident, "and when hard times came around, we were expendable, to be thrown like cattle out of this country."

These odysseys were as wrenching as those of the Okies, and very similar. Life was "muy dura," recalled Lillie Gasca-Cuéllar—very hard.

> Sufrió uno mucho. Mucho trabajo. No teníamos estufa. No teníamos camas. Dormíamos no más con cartónes, no teníamos casa—y a veces en las calles durmiéndonos.
>
> [We suffered a lot. Lots of work. We didn't have a stove. We didn't have beds. We had only cartons to sleep in, we didn't have a house—and at times we slept in the streets.]

By 1940, whites constituted 76 percent of the workforce in the San Joaquin Valley, an area that formerly had been a stronghold of Mexican labor. Of those white workers, half were southwestern emigrants.

As we have seen, the Okie migration was unusual in that it consisted more often of families than of single individuals. Even so, the newcomers in the 1930s lacked the extensive network of family and community connections built up by Mexican families during the previous two decades. Those southwesterners who already had family in California adapted best. But other newcomers could not anticipate the harvest schedules of crops they had never grown, so that they sometimes arrived at picking fields early, losing precious time, or came too late, when there was no work to be had. Furthermore, the picking style for California cotton proved different from that of the plains. Jessie de la Cruz, an experienced Mexican picker, noticed that some Texans in her field "weren't used to this kind of picking. . . . It had to be clean, no leaves, you had to leave nothing but the stalk." The newcomers picked forty-five pounds to her hundred. Such difficulties compounded the problems faced by newcomers like the Joads.

In theory, southwestern migrants might have made common cause with Mexican and Filipino laborers to strike for better wages and working conditions. As migrants poured into the San Joachin Valley, established local residents treated them with increasingly open hostility. *The Grapes of Wrath* portrays the comments of a service station attendant at Needles, California: "Them Okies got no sense and no feelings. They ain't human. A human being wouldn't live like they do. A human being couldn't stand it to be so dirty and so miserable. They ain't a hell of a lot better than gorillas." Other journalists and investigators reported similar prejudices. "You take some of these

California had both ladder crops—tree fruit that workers climbed to pick—and stoop crops—those that required long hours of painful bending and squatting to pick. Growers of stoop crops generally preferred Filipino and other Asian American workers because those workers had conditioned themselves to the painful positions involved. Such conditioning did not mean they did not suffer greatly from the physical demands of the work.

guys," complained a California grower, "and give them the best land in the Garden of Eden and they'd starve to death."

But cultural prejudices made cooperation between ethnic groups difficult. Okies often found California's ethnic and racial diversity threatening. Compared to the southwest plains, California simply had too many "foreigners." As one Okie put it, "the farmers ain't got no business hirin' them fer low wages when we native white American citizens are starvin'." At an FSA labor camp in Arvin, California, migrants from Texas objected when a Mexican family moved in. "Remember the Alamo! Either us or them," they told the camp manager. "Can't have both of us here."

The competition for jobs intensified resentments. Some Okies found it degrading to pick for Italian and Japanese growers or to find work through Hispanic labor contractors—*contratistas*. There were certain kinds of farmwork the Okies could not or would not do. Vegetables like asparagus required them "to squat and walk, like a Mexican," which most could not. Mexicans and Asians did the more backbreaking work associated with ground crops like vegetables and potatoes. "White men can't do the work as well as these short men who can get down on their hands and knees, or work all day long stooping over," commented a California newspaper editor in 1930, and his sentiments were echoed by a Japanese farmer, who applied the same prejudice to the Filipino workers he hired. "The Fils do all the stoop labor. They are small and work fast." As might be expected, such judgments were not shared by the workers themselves. "Many people think that we don't suffer from stoop labor, but we do," remarked one Filipino.

In the end, the oversupply of labor drove wages down, making life worse for Okie, Mexican, Filipino, and Japanese laborers alike. The census shows that with the influx of southwestern migrants, the income for all workers fell. Even so, the Okies earned more than the minorities they displaced. Once again the census provides key evidence. In 1940 southwesterner families who arrived in the valley before 1935 had average annual incomes of $1,070. Those who arrived between 1935 and 1940 averaged $650, while other white Californians received $1,510. Those Mexican families who had not returned to their homeland earned just $555 a year and usually found even New Deal relief programs beyond their reach. California law barred alien Mexicans from public work projects, and local rules also kept many Mexicans, even those who were American citizens, from WPA jobs.

In short, the structure and dynamics of agricultural labor in California were far more complex than *The Grapes of Wrath* could suggest within the tale of a single family's tribulations. Why did Steinbeck ignore that complexity, with its often darker side? The answer is perhaps not so difficult to understand. Instinctively, he viewed the Okies as victims, not victimizers. From his perspective, the real tragedy of the farm crisis of the 1930s was the destruction of Jeffersonian agrarian ideals. Steinbeck wanted the government to give the Joads more than a handout; he advocated a second revolution that would recreate an America of small farmers rooted in the land. He failed to acknowledge that the ideals he cherished too often applied only to white Americans and, in any case, had become increasingly irrelevant to the kind of industrial agriculture that was transforming America.

In the half century since the dust storms swept across the southwestern plains, the United States has been transformed by a civil rights revolution. It has been reminded, too, of its diversity, by the renewed tide of immigration springing up in the wake of the Immigration Reform Act of 1964. Historians have worked to give voice to that diversity. In doing so, they have drawn not only on statistics but folk songs, photographs, anecdotes, and observations from ordinary people like the Turners, the Garretsons, and Lillie Gasca-Cuéllar. Among this abundance of evidence, the impersonal numbers of the census may have seemed, at first blush, the most lifeless of voices. But in the aggregate, the mass of their ones and zeros provides the structure that gives a collective portrait weight and balance. And with proper study, the tales those numbers tell can prove to be nearly as gripping as those of a novel.

Additional Reading

Because the narrative in this chapter begins with "dust," interested readers might well begin with Donald Worster, *The Dust Bowl: The Southern Plains in the 1930s* (New York, 1979). For an idiosyncratic view, Worster would direct readers to James Malin, *The Grasslands of North America* (New York, 1956). John Steinbeck actually began *The Grapes of Wrath* (New York, 1939) as a series of articles for the *San Francisco News* and published them as *Their Blood Is Strong* (New York, 1938). A similar study that historians find valuable is Carey McWilliams, *Factories in the Fields* (Boston, 1939). On "Migrant Mother" we recommend Dorothea Lange and Paul Schuster Taylor, *An American Exodus: A Record of Human Erosion* (New York, 1939). That book may be hard to find, but Lange and her work are the subject of Milton Meltzer, *Dorothea Lange: A Photographer's Life* (New York, 1978). Dorothea Lange, *Photographs of a Lifetime* (New York, 1996) is a recent reprint with much of her work. The story of "Migrant Mother," *The Grapes of Wrath* as both novel and movie, and other aspects of the Dust Bowl in American cultural memory are wonderfully told and illustrated in Charles J. Shindo, *Dust Bowl Migrants in the American Imagination* (Lawrence, KS, 1997). Many of Lange's photographs, including "Migrant Mother 6," are available on-line through the Library of Congress at its American Memory site: http://memory.loc.gov.

Two historians, through their work, have contributed heavily to this essay. James Gregory, *American Exodus: The Dust Bowl Migration and Okie Culture in California* (New York, 1989) not only conceptualizes the problem of collective history, he also models the way in which quantitative analysis and anecdotal narrative interact to produce history that is both informative and easy to read. In that same spirit, Devra Weber, *Dark Sweat, White Gold: California Farm Workers, Cotton, and the New Deal* (Berkeley, 1994) has captured the migrant farmworkers' experience with special attention to Mexicans. For a vivid account of life for middling farmers before the Dust Bowl, we commend Thad Sitton and Dan Utley, *From See to Can't See: Texas Cotton Farmers in the Southern Prairies* (Austin, 1997). The politics and labor strife in California during the 1930s are among the topics covered in Kevin Starr, *Endangered Dreams: The Great Depression in California* (New York, 1996). In an effort to obtain additional information on Mexicans in California we also consulted Ronald Takaki, *A Different Mirror: A History of Multicultural America* (New York, 1993); Leo Grabler, Joan W. Moore, and Ralph C. Guzman, *The Mexican-American People: The Nation's Second Largest Minority* (New York, 1970); Matt S. Meier and Feliciano Rivera, *The Chicanos: A History of the Mexican Americans* (New York, 1972); and Renato Resaldo et al., *Chicano: The Evolution of a People* (Minneapolis, 1973). An additional source on repatriation in the 1930s is Francisco E. Balderrama and Raymond Rodríguez, *Decade of Betrayal: Mexican Repatriation in the 1930s* (Albuquerque, 1995).

Gregory and Weber both discuss Asian American migrants, but we also found useful Ronald Takaki, *Strangers from a Different Shore: A History of Asian Americans* (New York, 1989), and Sucheng Chan, *Asian Americans: An Interpretive History* (New York, 1991). We did try to puzzle out why so few African Americans joined the Dust Bowl migration to California. In that effort we consulted Peter Gottlieb, *Making Their Own Way: Southern Blacks' Migration to Pittsburgh, 1916–1930* (Urbana, IL, 1987), and James R. Grossman, *Land of Hope: Chicago, Black Southerners, and the Great Migration* (Chicago, 1989). The footnotes from these many sources inevitably lead back to the U.S. Bureau of the Census, *Historical Statistics of the United States, Colonial Times to 1970*, 2 vols. (Washington, DC, 1975), which is supplemented annually. Internet users can access the Census Bureau at http://www.census.gov.

Interactive Learning

See the *Primary Source Investigator* for resources that illuminate the odyssey of the Dust Bowl in the 1930s. The CD-ROM contains audio clips of Woody Guthrie songs, vivid images of Americans displaced by both the Great Depression and the Dust Bowl, and the government's response to their plight. Also included are charts and maps illustrating the movement of people and the devastating effects of the Dust Bowl.

CHAPTER 13
The Decision to Drop the Bomb

Just before dawn on July 16, 1945, a few clouds hung over the still New Mexico desert. The air possessed that lucid clarity that skews all sense of distance and space. Out on the desert stood several large towers, yet from the perspective of the blockhouse, where the observers anxiously waited, they appeared as little more than a few spikes stuck in the sand.

Suddenly, one of the towers erupted into a brilliant fireball, searing the air and instantly replacing the dawn's pastels with a blazing radiance. With the radiance came heat—an incredible, scorching heat that rolled outward in waves. Where seconds before the sand had stretched cool and level in every direction, now it fused into glass pellets. The concussion from the fireball completely vaporized the tower at its center, created a crater a quarter of a mile wide, and obliterated another forty-ton steel tower one-half mile away. Above the fireball an ominous cloud formed, shooting upward, outward, then back upon itself to form the shape of a mushroom, expanding until it had reached 8 miles in the air. The effects of the fireball continued outward from its center: the light, followed by the waves of heat, and then the deadening roar of the concussion, sharp enough to break a window more than 125 miles away. Light, heat, concussion—but first and foremost, the brilliance of the light. At the edge of the desert a blind woman was facing the explosion. She saw the light.

In the blockhouse at Alamogordo, where scientists watched, feelings of joy and relief were mixed with foreboding. The bomb had worked. Theory had been turned into practice. And devastating as the explosion appeared, the resulting fireball had not ignited the earth's atmosphere, as some scientists had predicted. But the foreboding was impossible to shake. Humankind now had in its hands unprecedented power to destroy.

General Leslie R. Groves, director of the atom bomb project, shared none of the scientists' fears. Groves could barely contain his joy when he wired the news to President Harry Truman, who was meeting allied leaders at Potsdam outside the conquered city of Berlin. "The test was successful beyond the most optimistic expectations of anyone," reported Groves. Buoyed by the message, Truman returned to the conference a changed man. British Prime Minister Winston Churchill noticed the president's sudden self-confidence. "He stood up to the Russians in a most decisive and emphatic manner," Churchill remarked. "He told the Russians just where they got on and got off and generally bossed the whole meeting." Since the British were partners on the bomb project, Churchill soon learned what had so lifted Truman's spirits.

Less than three weeks later, on August 6, 1945, a second mushroom cloud rose, this time above Hiroshima, Japan. That explosion destroyed an entire city; it left almost 100,000 people dead and thousands more dying from radiation poisoning. Three days later another bomb leveled the city of Nagasaki. Only then did World War II come to an end, the bloodiest and costliest war in history. Ever since, the world has lived with the stark prospect that in anger or in error, some person, group, or government might again unleash the horror of atomic war.

The New Mexico test of the first atom bomb marked the successful conclusion of the Manhattan Project, the code name for one of the largest scientific and industrial efforts ever undertaken. Between 1941 and 1945 the United States spent more than $2 billion to build three atom bombs. Twenty years earlier that amount would have equaled the entire federal budget. The project required some thirty-seven factories and laboratories in nineteen states and Canada, employed more than 120,000 people, and monopolized many of the nation's top scientists and engineers during a period when their skills were considered essential to national survival. Leading universities, as well as some of the nation's largest corporations—Du Pont, Eastman Kodak, and General Electric—devoted substantial resources to the undertaking.

Even before the Manhattan Project, the trend in modern industrial society was for physicists and other scientists to conduct their work within large organizations. For much of the nineteenth century, scientists, like artists, worked alone or in small groups, using relatively simple equipment. Thomas Edison, however, led the way toward rationalized, business-oriented research and development, establishing his own "scientific" factory at Menlo Park, New Jersey, in 1876. Like a manufacturer, Edison subdivided research tasks among inventors, engineers, and toolmakers. By the first decades of the twentieth century, Westinghouse, Du Pont, U.S. Rubber, and other major corporations had set up their own industrial labs.

Then too, World War I demonstrated that organized, well-funded science could be vital to national security. During the war, scientists joined in large research projects to develop new explosives, poison gases, optical glass for lenses, airplane instruments, and submarine detection devices. In less than two years, physicists and electrical engineers had doubled the advances of radio technology over the previous ten years. The government, for the first time, funded research on a large scale. But scientists were as much committed to the notion of laissez-faire as any conservative robber baron. They were suspicious of any "scheme in which any small group of men, appointed

At 0815 hours August 6, 1945, the bomber Enola Gay and its flight crew received weather clearance and proceeded toward Hiroshima. An hour later, flying at 328 miles per hour, it dropped its bomb directly over the city, from 31,000 feet. It then turned and dove sharply in order to gain speed. The bomb detonated at about 2,000 feet above Hiroshima in order to increase the effective radius of its blast; the resulting cloud, photographed by a nearby observation plane, reached 50,000 feet into the air and was visible for 390 miles. The final statistic: approximately 100,000 people killed and thousands dying from radiation poisoning.

as a branch of the government, attempt to dominate and control the research of the country," as one scientist put it.

The end of the war halted government interference and financial support. Still, like most Americans, scientists shared in the prosperity of the 1920s. Economic boom meant increases in research budgets. Success in the laboratory attracted contributions from private foundations and wealthy individuals. American science began to produce both theoretical and applied results that rivaled the quality of science in Europe.

The Depression of the 1930s forced researchers to tighten their belts and lower their expectations. The government, though seldom an important source of funding, drastically cut the budgets for its scientific bureaus. Even when the New Deal created jobs for scientists, it did so primarily to stimulate employment, not research. But by the late 1930s private foundations had resumed earlier levels of support. One of their most prominent beneficiaries was Ernest Lawrence, a physicist with a flair for showmanship who had established himself as the most famous, most funded, and most bureaucratically organized scientist in the United States. During the 1930s Lawrence built what he called a cyclotron, a machine designed to accelerate atomic particles in a focused beam in order to penetrate the nucleus's shell and unravel its structure and dynamics. By 1939 his Radiation Lab at the University of California at Berkeley was raising the unprecedented sum of $1.5 million to build an enormous, 100-million-volt cyclotron.

The movement of science toward organization and bureaucracy reflected similar forces at work elsewhere in American society. As Lawrence expanded his laboratory at Berkeley, the New Deal was establishing new regulatory agencies, social welfare programs, and other government organizations that reached into many areas of daily life. Furthermore, much that the New Deal instituted through government and politics in the 1930s, large corporations had accomplished in the preceding era. Centralized slaughterhouses, with their elaborate distribution system involving railroads, refrigerated warehouses, and trucks, replaced the local butcher as the source of meat for many American tables. What Armour and Swift did for meatpacking, Heinz did for the pickle, Henry Ford for the automobile, and other corporations for the multitude of food, clothing, and goods used in American homes and industry. To understand the nature of the modern era, to grasp an undertaking as vast as the making of an atomic bomb or a decision as complex as how to use it, historians must understand how large organizations work.

MODELS OF DECISION MAKING

"Truman dropped the atom bomb in order to win the war as quickly as possible." Historians routinely use such convenient shorthand in their historical narratives. Yet physically, of course, Truman was nowhere near Japan or the bomb when it was dropped. He was halfway around the world, returning from the Potsdam Conference with Stalin and Churchill. The actual sequence of events was rather more complicated. President Truman did give an order. It passed through the Pentagon to an airbase on the island of Tinian in the western Pacific. The base commander ordered a specially trained crew to arm an American airplane with a single atom bomb, designed and built by scientists and technicians under the authority of the War Department. The pilot of the plane then followed an order, conveyed through the military chain of command, to proceed to a target in Japan, selected by the secretary of war in consultation with his military advisers, in order to destroy a Japanese city and thereby hasten the end of the war.

The difference in meaning between "Truman dropped the atom bomb" and what actually happened encapsulates the dilemma of a historian trying to portray the workings of a systematized, bureaucratic modern society. The first explanation is coherent, clear, and human. It accords with Harry Truman's own well-known maxim "The buck stops here"—implying that the important, truly difficult decisions were his and his alone. The second explanation is cumbersome and confusing, but more comprehensive and descriptive. It reflects the fact that the president stood at the tip of a pyramid of advisers, agencies, bureaus, offices, and committees, all going about their own business. And such organizations create their own characteristic ways of gathering information, planning, working, and acting. To a large extent, what Truman decided or did not decide depended on what he learned from those organizations. To that extent also, the shorthand "Truman dropped the atom bomb" conceals as much as it reveals.

To better analyze the workings of organizations, historians have borrowed a technique from the social sciences. They work with interpretive models. For many people the term *model* might bring to mind an object like a small plastic airplane or an electric train. For social scientists a model, not unlike the small plane, reduces the scale of reality and increases the researchers' capacity to describe the characteristics of what they observe. Models can be applied to systems as basic as individual behavior or as grand as the world's climate. If the average daily temperature goes up, will we have more or less rain? If the amount of carbon dioxide in the atmosphere increases, will temperatures rise? A computer model of weather patterns allows meteorologists to test the relationship between such variables in the climate. Even so, the number of variables is so great, meteorologists are forced to speak of probabilities, not certainties. While their model provides insights into several components of a weather system, it inevitably simplifies as well. In that sense, models too have limits.

The phrase "Truman dropped the atom bomb" typifies the application of what some social scientists have called a "rational actor" model. This interpretive framework may be what historians most often adopt without even thinking about models. Rational actor theory treats the actions of governments and large organizations as the acts of individuals. Further, it assumes that the individual actor, like Adam Smith's capitalist, behaves rationally in that he or she uses the most efficient means to pursue ends that are in his or her self-interest. When forced to choose among a range of possible actions, government leaders will select the option that achieves the best result at the lowest cost. One does not use a bat to swat a fly, nor would a government go to war to collect a small debt, unless war served some larger purpose.

The appeal of this model lies in its predictive powers. Often enough, governments do not make clear why they act. On other occasions, they announce their goals but keep their strategies for achieving them secret. By applying standards of rational behavior, an analyst can make inductive leaps about a government's unclear goals or hidden actions. If we know that a government has suddenly ordered highly mobile assault troops to the borders of its nation, but we lack evidence about its goals, we might still conclude that a rational actor would not use mobile assault troops merely to defend borders: an invasion is planned. The process works in reverse as well. If analysts know what goals a nation has at hand, they can guess with some confidence what its leaders might do in a situation, given their resources.

Franklin Roosevelt's decision to launch the Manhattan Project presents historians with an example of how rational actor analysis can help reveal motivations and goals. Roosevelt was not an easy person to read—either for his advisers or for historians. Often enough, his orders to different people seemed contradictory. Or he would encourage competing bureaucracies to implement the same policy. In setting in motion the bomb project, Roosevelt left little evidence about why he made his decision. But the rational actor model suggests that Roosevelt recognized the military potential of nuclear fission; calculated that the United States had the financial, industrial, and scientific resources needed; and concluded that the nation's security demanded full-scale research and development.

The available evidence does support that conclusion. The Manhattan Project owed its beginnings to several physicists, primarily refugees from fascist Germany and Italy who feared that recent atomic research would allow the Nazis to develop a weapon of unparalleled destructive force. In March 1939 Enrico Fermi, a Nobel prize–winning physicist who had fled from Mussolini's Italy, paid his own way to Washington to warn the military. Fermi himself had been on the verge of discovering fission reactions in 1934, but had not then recognized the meaning of his results. If he had, the fascist powers might have appropriated his results and put the process of fission to military use. Although Fermi had become an American citizen and a faculty member at Columbia University, Navy technical experts ignored his warning. Other refugee physicists, led by Leo Szilard, joined the campaign. Szilard persuaded Albert Einstein, the world's most admired scientist, to lend his name to a letter explaining their concern to President Roosevelt. Alexander Sachs, an economic adviser to the president, acted as their emissary. After Roosevelt read the letter and heard Sachs out, he remarked, "Alex, what you are after is to see they don't blow us up."

The president took immediate action, but he did not yet set in motion a massive research project. That step would have been irrational, for as Sachs had made clear, the scientists had not yet found a way to harness the power of fission for war. Instead, Roosevelt merely created a Uranium Committee to promote American research on a fission bomb. The research got under way slowly, for the committee requested only $6,000 for its first year of operations. Other, more promising experimental efforts competed for research funds that were particularly scarce since the United States was not yet at war.

In England, however, two German emigrés were making progress in understanding how a "superbomb" might work. When war had broken out in

September 1939, British security restrictions barred former German scientists such as Otto Frisch and Rudolph Peierls from being involved in sensitive projects. Thus they were free to do their own research. In June 1941 they determined that the fast neutrons needed to set off an explosive chain reaction could be produced using either plutonium or uranium 235, a fissionable isotope that could be separated from uranium 238. They also suggested ways to separate uranium 235 from uranium 238. The amount of fissionable material needed would be small enough to fit into a bomb that existing aircraft could carry. Such a bomb, Frisch and Peierls calculated, could probably be built within two years. What was more frightening, German physicists were known to have made similar discoveries. Their high-quality physics programs might have put them as much as two years ahead of Allied efforts.

The British passed this information along to the American administrators supervising war research, the National Defense Research Committee (NDRC). Its head, Vannevar Bush, wasted no time in bringing news to Roosevelt in June 1941. "If such an explosive were made," he told the president, "it would be thousands of times more powerful than existing explosives, and its use might be determining." The British research had given the rational actor—in this case President Roosevelt—cause to commit the United States to a larger project. To accelerate the research effort, Roosevelt replaced the ineffective Uranium Committee with a group called S-1. The membership of the committee reflected the new priority of the bomb project. It included Bush, now head of the Office of Scientific Research and Development; his successor at NDRC, James Conant (the president of Harvard University); Vice President Henry Wallace; Secretary of War Henry Stimson; and Chief of Staff General George Marshall. Bush and Conant assumed primary responsibility for overseeing the project and keeping the president informed. In September 1942 they were joined by General Leslie Groves, who had been appointed to command construction and operation of the rapidly expanding facilities that were named the Manhattan Project.

For three years, American, British, and emigré scientists raced against time and what they feared was an insurmountable German lead. At first, research focused on the work of scientists at the Chicago Metallurgical Laboratory (another code name). There, on a squash court under the old University of Chicago football stadium, Fermi and his associates achieved the first self-sustaining chain reaction. The next goal was the separation of enough pure uranium 235 or sufficient plutonium to build a bomb. That goal required the construction of huge plants—an expense that now seemed rational, in light of the work at Chicago. Conant authorized Groves to begin building facilities at Oak Ridge, Tennessee, and Hanford, Washington.

Actual design of the bomb took place at a remote mountain site near Los Alamos, New Mexico. Los Alamos was the choice of physicist Robert Oppenheimer. As director of the design laboratory, Oppenheimer sought a place to isolate the most outstanding collection of experimental and theoretical physicists, mathematicians, chemists, and engineers ever assembled. Free from the intrusions of the press and inquisitive colleagues, world-renowned scientists rubbed elbows with brilliant, eager young graduate students, all applying the

J. Robert Oppenheimer directed the construction, completion, and testing of the first atomic bomb at a remote desert site near Los Alamos, New Mexico. He was an intense, introspective man and a chain-smoker early in his career; he confessed he found it nearly impossible to think without a cigarette in his hand. The burden of the Manhattan Project took its toll on him: the chain-smoking commenced again, and his weight, normally only 130 pounds, dropped to 116.

abstract theories of physics to the question of how to produce an atomic weapon.

By the summer of 1944 the race with the Nazis had ended. Spies discovered that German physicists had long since given up hope of building a bomb. As Allied forces marched into Berlin in April 1945, scientists knew that peace would come to Europe before the bomb was ready to be used. Still, the war against Japan seemed far from over. As Allied troops approached the home islands, Japanese resistance grew more intense. Fearing heavy American casualties during an invasion, President Roosevelt had asked Stalin to enter the war against Japan. Yet as the tide of battle began to favor the Allies, the president became more reluctant to draw the Soviets into Japan. If the bomb could win the war for the United States, all the sacrifices of time, personnel, and materials would not have been in vain. Oppenheimer, Groves, and the Manhattan Project scientists redoubled their efforts to produce a working bomb.

Thus the rational actor model explains adequately the progression of events that brought about the bomb's development: (1) physicists saw the potential of nuclear fission and warned the president; (2) Roosevelt ordered a speedup in research; (3) scientific breakthroughs led to greater certainty of eventual success, causing the president to give bomb research top priority; (4) the race with Germany, and then Japanese resistance in the Far East, encouraged scientists to push toward success.

Although this outline of key decisions proceeds logically enough, there are troubling features to it, suggesting limits to the rational actor model. Certainly Roosevelt could be viewed as the rational actor. But we have already seen that a host of committees and subgroups were involved in the process. And the model becomes murkier when we seek answers to a number of controversial questions surrounding the decision actually to use the bomb. Did the military situation in the summer of 1945 justify launching the attacks without warning Japan? Could a nonmilitary demonstration of the bomb's power have persuaded the Japanese to surrender without immense loss of life? Why drop a second bomb on Japan so soon after the first? And finally, who did the United States really want to shock with its atomic might—Japan or the Soviet Union?

To be sure, rational actor analysis provides answers to these questions. The problem is, it provides too many. Historians have offered contradictory answers to the way a rational actor might have been expected to behave under the circumstances.

To begin with, what was the most crucial problem to be solved by a rational actor in that summer of 1945? On the one hand, convincing Japan to surrender was the primary goal of the war—something the use of atomic bombs would be expected to hasten. On the other hand, military and diplomatic planners had already begun to focus on the transition from war to peace. Increasingly, they worried about the postwar conduct of the Soviet Union. Following the surrenders of Italy and Germany, the Russians had begun consolidating control over Eastern Europe. Many British and American officials feared that Stalin saw victory as a way to extend the global reach of communism. The larger the role assumed by the Soviets in the Pacific, the greater their opportunity for expansion there too.

But what if the bomb were used to end the war before Stalin's troops could make any headway in the Far East? Wasn't it likely Stalin would become more cooperative once he saw the awesome power of such a weapon? That "rational" line of reasoning raises an unsettling possibility. Did the United States drop the bomb primarily to send a warning to the Soviet Union? So concluded historian Gar Alperovitz. Alperovitz argued that after Franklin Roosevelt's untimely death in April 1945, President Truman was more concerned with containing the Soviet Union than with defeating Japan.

Alperovitz came to that conclusion by examining the information available to Truman and his advisers in the summer of 1945. That data, he argued, should have convinced Truman (or any rational actor) that the United States had no compelling military reason to drop atomic bombs on Japan. The American navy had already established a tight blockade around Japan, cutting off delivery of raw materials and isolating Japan's army in Manchuria from the home islands. Allied land-based bombers had leveled whole sections of Tokyo without opposition from Japanese fighters. By July 1945 Japan was ready to consider capitulation, except that in 1943 Roosevelt had laid down uncompromising terms of "unconditional surrender." The Japanese feared that the United States would insist that their emperor leave his throne, a humiliation they wished at all costs to avoid. Their only hope was to negotiate terms of surrender, using the Russians as intermediaries, to obtain a guarantee that the institution of the emperor would be preserved.

Truman knew that the Japanese had made overtures to the Soviet Union. "Unconditional surrender is the only obstacle to peace," the Japanese foreign minister had cabled his emissary in Moscow, in a coded message intercepted by American intelligence. Still, Truman refused to deviate from Roosevelt's policy of unconditional surrender. At the Potsdam Conference, Allied leaders issued a vaguely worded proclamation warning the Japanese that they faced "prompt and utter destruction" if they fought on. Nowhere did the proclamation mention the existence of a new superbomb. Nor did it offer hope that the Allies might permit the Japanese to keep their emperor. When the Japanese ignored the warning, the Americans concluded that Japan had resolved to continue fanatic resistance.

In fact, the emperor himself had taken unprecedented, though cautious steps to undermine the war party. He had decided that the military extremists must accept surrender on Allied terms. But the bombing of Hiroshima, on August 6, followed two days later by a Russian declaration of war, threw the Japanese government into confusion. Before it could digest this double shock, Nagasaki was leveled on August 9. Even then, the Japanese surrendered only when the United States made an implicit commitment to retain the emperor. Despite Truman's insistence on an "unconditional" surrender, in the end it had been conditional.

Alperovitz's conclusion is sobering. If ending the war had been Truman's *only* goal, the rational response would have been to give Japan the extra few days or weeks to negotiate a surrender. There would have been no need to drop the bomb. But of course it *was* dropped. Therefore (so the logic goes) the president's primary goal must have been to intimidate the Soviets. This possibility was one that Alperovitz understandably condemned, for it would have meant that Truman had wantonly incinerated hundreds of thousands of Japanese for reasons that had nothing to do with the war itself. Furthermore, if Truman had hoped to intimidate the Russians into cooperating, he seriously erred—for the Soviet Union became, if anything, more intractable after Japan's surrender. Failure to achieve a nuclear arms control agreement with Stalin while the United States and Britain had a monopoly on atomic weapons led to a postwar arms race. Possession of the atom bomb resulted finally in a decrease in American security and a loss of moral stature. Those consequences are not the desired results of rational decision making.

Alperovitz's reconstruction of Truman's choices placed most emphasis on the diplomatic effects of dropping the bomb. But were these effects the factors that weighed most heavily in the minds of Truman and his advisers? Other historians have placed more emphasis on the military factors behind the development of the bomb—not only in 1945 but in the years preceding it. In doing so, they have constructed an alternate set of motivations that might have influenced a rational actor.

Franklin Roosevelt was the first president who had to consider whether the bomb would actually be used. And merely by approving the massive effort to build a weapon, there was an implicit assumption on the president's part that it would be used. "At no time," recalled former Secretary of War Stimson, "did I ever hear it suggested by the President, or by any other responsible member of the government, that atomic energy should not be used in the war." Robert Oppenheimer, whose leadership at Los Alamos played a critical role in the success of the project, confirmed Stimson's point about the bombs: "we always assumed if they were needed, they would be used."

In fact, Roosevelt was proceeding a bit more cautiously. He discussed the delicate subject with British Prime Minister Winston Churchill when the two men met at Roosevelt's home in Hyde Park in September 1944. At the end of their private interview, with only the two of them present, they signed a memorandum summarizing their attitudes. Both men agreed that the bomb would be kept a secret from the Russians, an action that made it clear (as Alperovitz contended) that the leaders recognized how valuable a lever the weapon might be in postwar negotiations. As for the war itself, Roosevelt and Churchill agreed that the bomb might be used against Japan after "mature consideration," while warning the Japanese "that this bombardment will be repeated until they surrender."

If Roosevelt had lived, conceivably he might have proved more cautious than Truman. But if he had any serious doubts about using the bomb, they died with him. None of his military and diplomatic advisers were aware of the Hyde Park memorandum. After Roosevelt's death, responsibility for atomic policy shifted largely to Secretary of War Stimson, the cabinet officer in charge of the Manhattan Project. The new president, Truman, knew nothing about the bomb or, for that matter, most other critical diplomatic and military matters. Roosevelt had seldom consulted the vice president or even met with him. Once, while acting as chair of a Senate committee, Truman had stumbled onto information about the vast sums being spent on some unknown project, only to be persuaded by Stimson that secrecy should prevail. As the war approached its end and the new president faced a host of critical decisions, Stimson cautiously introduced him to the bomb. "I mentioned it to you shortly after you took office," the secretary prompted him on April 23, 1945, "but have not urged it since on account of the pressure you have been under. It, however, has such bearing on our present foreign relations . . . I think you ought to know about it without further delay."

To present his case, Stimson prepared a memorandum setting out his two most pressing concerns. He wanted Truman to recognize the monumental importance of the bomb for postwar relations, particularly with the Soviet Union. And he wanted to emphasize the bomb's capacity to shorten the war. Stimson displayed no qualms about using it against Japan and considered no steps to avert a postwar nuclear arms race. But the two men did agree that Stimson should form a committee to formulate further policy options. It would seem that the rational actor was at work: if Truman wanted to weigh all his options, the committee would provide him with a full range from which to choose.

The Interim Committee, as the group was known, met three times. It also created a scientific panel that included Oppenheimer, Fermi, Lawrence, and Arthur Compton (head of the Chicago lab) to advise the committee. During its meetings, it scarcely touched the question of whether to drop the bomb on Japan. "It seemed to be a foregone conclusion that the bomb would be used," Arthur Compton recalled. "It was regarding only the details of strategy and tactics that differing views were expressed." When those issues were debated, some members briefly considered a nonmilitary demonstration in place of a surprise military attack. They asked Oppenheimer how such a demonstration might be prepared. Since the bomb had yet to be tested, Oppenheimer could only estimate its power. He replied that he could not conceive of any demonstration that would have the impact of an attack on a real target of factories and buildings. Furthermore, the committee had to consider what might happen if Japanese representatives were taken to a test site and the mighty atomic "demonstration" fizzled. And if the Japanese were given advance warning about a superbomb, wouldn't that allow them to prepare their defenses or move American prisoners of war to likely bombing targets?

For all those reasons the Interim Committee decided against giving any advance warning. In addition, it made several assumptions about Japan that predetermined its recommendations to the president. First, committee members considered the military leadership of Japan so fanatic that only a profound shock such as an atomic attack would persuade them to surrender. Kamikaze attacks by Japanese pilots, as well as other resistance, continued to claim a heavy toll in American lives. General Douglas MacArthur, who had led the Western Pacific campaign against Japan, discounted the effectiveness of either a naval blockade of the home islands or continued air raids with conventional bombs. Only a full-scale invasion, MacArthur argued, would compel surrender. The army continued to organize an invasion for November 1, anticipating as many as a half million American casualties.[1]

In any case, by 1945 committee members had become somewhat hardened to the idea of killing enemy soldiers or civilians. Conventional firebombing had already proved as horrifying as the atom bomb promised to be. In one incen-

1. This casualty figure has become quite controversial. Historian Martin Sherwin has discovered that a number of prominent military figures offered a much lower estimate, which would have made an invasion a more reasonable option.

diary raid, American bombers leveled one-quarter of Tokyo, left 83,000 people dead, and wounded another 40,000. Having lived with the fear that the Germans might use an atom bomb against the United States, committee members had ample reason to see it as a potential weapon against the Japanese. Since it promised to save American lives, the committee sensed that the public would want, even demand, combat use. And finally, though the members were far from agreement, the committee decided that a combat demonstration would facilitate negotiations with the Russians. From those assumptions they reached three conclusions: (1) the bomb should be used as quickly as possible against Japan; (2) to maximize the shock value, the target should be a war plant surrounded by workers' homes; (3) no warning should be given. When Stimson communicated those views to Truman, he included a recommendation that both bombs scheduled for completion by August should be dropped in separate raids, in order to maximize the shock and convince Japanese leaders that further resistance meant certain destruction.

In only one small but vital way did Truman deviate from the committee's determination of how and why to use the bomb. A group of scientists at the Chicago laboratory, led by Leo Szilard, had become persuaded that combat use of the bomb without warning would lead to a postwar arms race between the Soviets and the Americans. They urged Truman and his advisers to tell the Russians about the bomb and to plan a demonstration before using it in combat. In a concession to Szilard and his colleagues, the Interim Committee recommended that Truman disclose the bomb to Stalin in order to help gain his cooperation after the war. At Potsdam, Truman chose not to discuss the bomb or atomic energy. But he did make an oblique reference to Stalin "that we had a weapon of unusual destructive force." Stalin was equally cryptic in his reply. "He was glad to hear it and hoped we would make 'good use of it' against the Japanese," the president recalled. And so Truman acted.

By retracing the series of decisions made over the entire year preceding the attack on Hiroshima, it becomes clearer that, for Truman, military considerations about how to end the war with a minimum number of casualties remained paramount. Resolution of Soviet-American differences was a secondary goal, though rapidly becoming the administration's chief concern. Using the bomb would also forestall any criticism in Congress for having spent $2 billion on the secret Manhattan Project. Thus the bombing of Hiroshima and Nagasaki appeared to be the optimum way to reach the administration's primary objective, with the additional virtue of promoting secondary goals as well. When applied at the level of presidential decision making, rational actor analysis suggests that the decision to drop the bomb was consistent with perceived American goals.

A MODEL OF ORGANIZATIONAL PROCESS

Despite those results, the rational actor model exhibits definite limitations. It leads us to focus attention on the policy-making debates of key actors like Roosevelt and Truman, or even on scientists like Szilard and Oppenheimer.

But in truth, our narrative of events has involved numerous committees far from the top of the organizational pyramid: the Uranium Committee, S-1, the National Defense Research Council, and the Interim Committee. Roosevelt and Truman relied on the recommendations of those groups in making decisions. Should their reliance make any difference to our explanations?

Imagine, for a moment, the government as a kind of giant clock. Rational actor analysis would define the telling of time as the visible movements of the hands controlled by a closed box. Inside are the gears, springs, and levers that move the clock's hands: the bureaucracy supporting decision makers at the top. In the rational actor model, these gears are seen as neutral cogs in the machine, passing along the energy (or in government, the information) that allows the hands to do their highly visible work. But suppose we look at the decision-making process using a model that focuses on the organizational processes themselves. Is there something about their structure or behavior that influences the outcome of decisions made by supposedly rational actors?

Of course, the actions of bureaucracies and agencies are usually less regimented than the movements of a clock. Often enough, the subgroups that make up a government end up working at cross-purposes or pursuing conflicting objectives. While the Surgeon General's office has warned that cigarette smoking is "hazardous to your health," the Department of Agriculture has produced films on the virtues of American tobacco. Perhaps, then, it would be better to envision not a clock but a football team. If we observe a game from the stands, the players can be seen moving in coordinated patterns, in an effort to control the movement of the ball. Rational actor analysis suggests that the coach, or another centralized decision maker like the quarterback, has selected the strategies best suited to winning the game. That larger strategy, in turn, determines the plays that the offense and defense use.

After closer observation, we begin to sense that the play is not as centrally coordinated as we anticipated. Different groups of players move in patterns determined by their positions as well as by the team strategy. We come to understand that the team is made up of subgroups that execute regularly assigned tasks. Linemen block, ends run pass patterns. On each down, the players do not try to think anew of the best imaginable play. Rather, they repeat actions they have been trained to perform. A halfback will generally advance the ball by running and leave the passing to the quarterback. On some plays, we observe that a few players' actions seem inappropriate. A halfback runs when he should be blocking. Whereas the rational actor model might interpret such a move as a purposeful attempt to deceive the opposing team, a model focusing on organizational processes might recognize it as a breakdown of coordination among subgroups. What one model treats as planned, the other treats as a mistake.

Thus the organizational process model leads the historian to treat government behavior not as centralized acts and choices, but as the actions of bureaucracies functioning in relatively predictable patterns. Organizations begin by breaking problems into parts, which are assigned to the appropriate subgroup to solve. The subgroups do not have to understand the larger problem, only the piece assigned to them. They follow what the military refers to as SOP—standard operating procedure. If the quarterback decides on a sweep to the right, the lineman's SOP is to block left. On a sweep to the left, he blocks right; for a pass, straight ahead. SOPs allow organizations to coordinate the independent activities of many groups and individuals.

While SOPs make coordination possible, they also limit the actions of organizations. The more specialized a subgroup, the fewer tasks it is able to perform. Its training is more narrowly focused, its equipment is more specialized, and the information available to it is more limited. All those factors make it difficult for the group to deviate from regular routines. The weather bureau, for example, would find it impossible to apply its computer programs and specialized knowledge to predicting changes in the economy rather than the weather. Furthermore, the rational actor is presumed to weigh all available choices to select the best one, but in the real lives of organizations, SOPs determine the range and pattern of choices that are considered. Specialized groups are generally content to choose standardized and previously determined policies rather than searching for the optimum one.

Since organizations are generally more concerned with avoiding failure than with gambling on success, they also tend to be more conservative. Although the rational actor might weigh the potential benefits against possible consequences and then make a bold new departure, organizations tend to change in small, incremental steps. Corporations, for example, like to test-market a product before investing in expensive new plants, distribution networks, and advertising. And we have already seen that the American government moved relatively slowly in producing an atomic bomb. In authorizing the quest for a bomb, Roosevelt was ordering the government to do something it had never done before: conduct nuclear research. He soon discovered that the military and scientific bureaus could not readily execute such an unprecedented decision. They lacked the scientific personnel, equipment, and research routines that made the Manhattan Project possible. In the end, Roosevelt and project managers such as Groves, Conant, Bush, and Oppenheimer had to create new organizations and routines.

Reward structures in organizations reinforce their conservatism. Workers who do their jobs properly day after day continue to work. Those who make errors lose their jobs or fail to win promotions. Critical decisions are generally made in committees so that no individual assumes sole responsibility if a venture fails. But committees take much longer to act and often adopt unwieldy compromises. (An old adage defines a camel as a horse designed by a committee.) As a further hedge against failure, goals and responsibilities are set well within the individual or group performance capabilities. Such practices stifle individual initiative and encourage inefficiency. Mountains of paperwork and miles of red tape are the ultimate symbol of organizational caution and conservatism.

By treating the decision to drop the bomb not as a single act but as the outcome of many organizational routines, historians can see more clearly why progress on the bomb came slowly. In fact, the project could not have gotten under way in the first place if emigré scientists had not broken through the bureaucratic chain of command. When Fermi first approached navy officials, none of them could even comprehend the concept of nuclear power. Only by writing the president directly did scientists attract the support they needed. To get the project under way, Roosevelt was forced to create an ad hoc committee to investigate the military potential of nuclear fission. His decision to appoint Lyman Briggs, a government physicist, as head of the Uranium Committee may have delayed the project by at least a year. As the director of the Bureau of Standards, Briggs knew little about nuclear physics. He was by temperament "slow, conservative, methodical"—ideal bureaucratic qualities totally unsuited to the bold departure Roosevelt sought. Not until the president created the National Defense Research Committee did nuclear physics gain adequate support.

As chairman of NDRC, Vannevar Bush made the farsighted decision to keep his organization independent of the military bureaucracies. He knew generals and admirals would fight against civilian interference and that scientists would balk at military regulation of their research. Under Bush, scientists remained free to pursue the research that they and not the military thought was important. Traditional definitions of missions and military needs would not cut off funds for new research projects. Furthermore, Bush wisely chose to operate under the jurisdiction of the War Department rather than the United States Navy.[2] The navy had repeatedly shown either indifference or hostility to advice from civilian scientists. The army and particularly its air corps branch proved far more receptive to new research. Consequently, the atom bomb was developed with the army's mission and routines in mind. Bush's skillful negotiation of organizational bottlenecks was a crucial factor in shifting the Manhattan Project into high gear.

In other areas, organizational conflicts resulted in delays. President Roosevelt had established two incompatible priorities for Bush: speed and security. The scientists felt speed should come before security; military administrators like Groves opted for security over speed. Military SOP had well-established ways to safeguard classified material. Officers were required to operate strictly within the chain of command and were provided information only on a "need-to-know" basis. Thus each soldier performed only a portion of a task without knowledge of the larger mission and without talking with anyone beyond his or her immediate circle. In that way, information was "compartmentalized"— securely protected so that only a few people at the top of the chain of command saw the entire picture.

To maximize security, Groves proposed placing the laboratory at Los Alamos under military control. All scientists would don uniforms and receive ranks based on their importance. As a group, however, scientists were

2. At that time the army and navy had separate organizations. The head of each held a cabinet post. The marines were a branch of the navy; the air corps, a branch of the army. Congress created a unified defense structure under a single secretary in 1947.

In 1942 General Leslie Groves was placed in charge of the construction and operation of the Manhattan Project. He got the job in part because he was a good organizer, having supervised the construction of the Pentagon, still unfinished in this 1942 photo. The building became the largest office facility in the world, containing 16 miles of corridors, 600,000 square feet of office space, and a capacity to house 32,000 workers. As historian Warren Susman recognized, it also became a symbol of its era: "For the age it climaxed indeed the triumph of order, science, reason. . . . And yet, for the age being born it was the home of the atom bomb and a frightening bureaucratic structure, the beginning of a brave new world of anxiety."

among the least likely candidates for military regimentation. Their dress was more informal than most working professionals (*sloppy* might have been the adjective that jumped to the military mind). In their laboratories, they operated with a great deal of autonomy to pursue research as they saw fit. Oppenheimer could not recruit many scientists to come to Los Alamos until he assured them the project would not be militarized.

Compartmentalization, also promoted by Groves, seriously inhibited research. Physicists insisted that their work required access to all relevant information. They thought best when they understood the wider implications of their work. Groves disdained their habit of engaging in creative, freewheeling discussions that regularly drifted far afield of the topic at hand. Scientists should stick to their jobs and receive information only on a need-to-know basis. "Just as outfielders should not think about the manager's job of changing pitchers," Groves said to justify his system, "each scientist had to be made to do his own work." While compartmentalization promoted security, it denied researchers vital information from other areas of the project. Some scientists, like Szilard, simply violated security procedures whenever they chose to. Oppenheimer eased the problem at Los Alamos by conducting seminars during which his staff could exchange ideas and information. But information never flowed freely among the many research and production sites.

Security procedures indicate, too, that long before the war ended many policymakers saw the Soviet Union as their chief enemy. Few precautions were designed against Japanese or even German agents. Military intelligence concentrated its counterespionage against Soviet and communist spies. Known communists or scientists with communist associations were kept under constant surveillance. Had intelligence officers prevailed, they would have barred Oppenheimer from the project because of his previous involvement with communist-front organizations. To his credit, Groves overruled the nearsighted sleuths in army intelligence and saved the project's most valuable member. In the meantime, security precautions against a wartime ally continued to work to the advantage of the Nazis by delaying the project.

The military was not solely responsible for project bottlenecks. The procedures of organized science caused delays as well. Scientists recruited from private industry did not share their academic colleagues' preoccupation with speed. Work in industry had conditioned them to move cautiously, with an eye toward efficiency, permanence, and low risk. Academic scientists felt such industrial values "led to a considerable retardation of the program." But the traditions of academic science also created problems. The bulk of research money had most often been directed to the celebrities in each field. Ernest Lawrence's reputation made him a magnet for grants and contributions. Manhattan Project administrators automatically turned to him as they sought methods to refine the pure uranium 235 needed for the bomb. Much of the money spent at Oak Ridge, Tennessee, went into Lawrence's electromagnetic process based on the Berkeley cyclotron.

In the end, Lawrence's program proved to be a conspicuous failure. By 1944, Oppenheimer had the design for a uranium bomb, but scarcely any uranium 235. In desperation he looked toward a process of gas diffusion developed four years earlier by Harold Urey and a young, relatively unknown physicist named John Dunning. Lawrence had been so persuaded of the superiority of his own method that Groves gave it priority over the process developed by Urey and Dunning. And compartmentalization prevented other physicists from learning more about gas diffusion. As Dunning recalled, "compartmentalization and security kept news of our program from filtering in to Ernest and his Laboratory [the Radiation Lab at Berkeley]." Physicists soon acknowledged that electromagnetic separation was obsolete, but in the meantime, the completion of the uranium bomb, "Little Boy," was delayed until July 1945.

A MODEL OF BUREAUCRATIC POLITICS

Clearly, bureaucratic structures and SOPs played major roles in determining how the bomb was developed. Yet the example of an energetic and forceful Vannevar Bush makes clear that within that organizational framework, not all bureaucrats were created equal. Powerful individuals or groups can often override the standard procedures of organizations as well as the carefully thought-out choices of rational actors. It makes sense, then, for historians to be alert to decisions shaped by the politics within government institutions.

If we return to our vantage point in the football stadium, we see linebackers blocking and receivers going short or long—all SOPs being executed as parts of a complex organization. The team's coach—the rational actor—remains prominent, pacing the sidelines, deploying forces. But we notice now that often an assistant sends in a play or the quarterback makes a decision at the line of scrimmage. The field has not just one decision maker, but many. And the play finally chosen may not reflect rational choice, but bargaining and compromise among the players and coaches. Although final authority may rest with a coach or the quarterback, other players, such as a star halfback, gain influence and prestige from the skill with which they play their position.

A historian applying those insights, in what might be called a model of bureaucratic politics, recognizes that a person's official position as defined by the organization does not alone determine his or her bargaining power. According to an organizational flowchart, the most influential members of the executive branch, after the president, would be the secretaries of state, defense (war and navy), and treasury. Yet American history abounds with examples in which power has moved outside normal bureaucratic channels. Sometimes a political actor, through astute jockeying, may convert a relatively less influential office into an important command post, as Henry Kissinger did when he was Richard Nixon's national security adviser. Kissinger, through forceful advocacy, shaped foreign policy far more than Secretary of State William Rogers. Colonel Edward M. House, the most influential adviser to Woodrow Wilson, held no formal position at all. House achieved his power by maintaining a low profile and offering the president seemingly objective counsel. For Attorney General Robert Kennedy, it was family ties and political savvy, not the office, that made him a powerful figure in his brother's administration.

In the case of the atom bomb, the lines of political influence were shifted by President Roosevelt's untimely death. When Harry Truman assumed the presidency, all the old institutional and informal arrangements of decision making had to be readjusted. Truman had had little access to the Roosevelt administration's information and decision-making channels. Ignorance of Roosevelt's policies forced Truman to rely far more heavily on a wider circle of advisers. Stimson, for one, suddenly found that for several months the need to initiate the president into the secrets of S-1 or the Manhattan Project greatly enhanced his influence.

Thus during the same months that Truman was trying to set up his own routines for decision making, individuals within various bureaucracies were jockeying for influence within the new order. And amid all this organizational turmoil, key decisions about the bomb had to be made—decisions that were neither clear-cut nor easy. Would a Soviet entry into the war force

Japan to surrender? Would conventional bombing raids and a blockade prove sufficient to end the war? Did Japan's peace initiatives indicate victory was at hand? Would a compromise on unconditional surrender, specifically a guarantee for the emperor, end the war? Would a demonstration of the bomb shock the Japanese into suing for peace?

As critics of Truman's decision have pointed out, each of those options had significant advocates within government circles. And each presented policy makers with reasons to avoid dropping the bomb—something that, as historian Barton Bernstein pointed out, was "precisely what they were not trying to do." But why not? Why did the decision makers who counseled use of the bomb outweigh those who championed these various alternatives? By applying the bureaucratic politics model, historians can better explain why the alternatives were never seriously considered.

The chief advocates for continued conventional warfare came from the navy. From the beginning, navy leaders had been skeptical of nuclear fission's military potential. Admiral William Leahy, the senior navy representative on the Joint Chiefs of Staff and also an expert on explosives, always doubted the bomb would have anywhere near the force scientists predicted. The Alamogordo test laid his argument to rest. Chief of Naval Operations Admiral Ernest King believed a naval blockade would successfully end the war. King had no qualms about developing the bomb, but as a loyal navy officer, he hated to see the air force end a war that his service had dominated for four years. He knew, too, that the bomb might undermine the navy's defense role after the war. Among military brass, Admirals Leahy and King had somewhat less influence than General George Marshall, army chief of staff. Marshall, along with General Douglas MacArthur, felt that further delay would necessitate an invasion and an unacceptable loss of American lives. Since they favored using the bomb instead, the navy lost that round.

Some members of the State Department, led by Acting Secretary of State Joseph Grew, believed that diplomacy should end the war. As early as April 1945 Grew had urged administration officials to extend some guarantee that the imperial throne would not be abolished. Without that assurance, he felt, the peace party could never overcome the military's determination to fight on. As former ambassador to Japan, Grew knew more about Japanese politics and culture than any major figure in the Truman administration. On the other hand, he had spent much of his career as a foreign service officer far from Washington. Thus he could exert little personal influence over Truman or key advisers. Even within the State Department, Assistant Secretaries Dean Acheson and Archibald MacLeish, both more influential than Grew, opposed his position. They considered the emperor as the symbol of the feudal military tradition they hoped to see destroyed. By the time of the Potsdam Conference, Grew had made just one convert for negotiations— Secretary Stimson—and a partial convert—Harry Truman. "There was [sic] pretty strong feelings," Stimson recalled, "that it would be deplorable if we have to go through the military program with all its stubborn fighting to the finish." Truman showed sufficient interest to arrange talks between Grew and the military chiefs, but he did not feel he could bring congressional and public opinion in line with Grew's position on the emperor.

The ghost of Franklin Roosevelt proved to be Grew's major opponent. Lacking Roosevelt's prestige, popularity, and mastery of government, Truman felt bound to pursue many of FDR's policies. Any move away from "unconditional surrender" posed political risks at home and military risks abroad that Truman did not feel strong enough to take. Acheson and MacLeish reminded their colleagues that Americans despised Emperor Hirohito as much as they did Hitler. The Joint Chiefs of Staff argued that premature compromise might reduce the emperor's incentive to subdue military extremists after the armistice.

James Byrnes emerged as the leading defender of unconditional surrender. In contrast to Grew, Byrnes had little training in foreign affairs. His importance in the government reflected his consummate skill at domestic politics. During the war, many people considered him second in power only to Roosevelt. In fact, Truman himself had risen to prominence as Byrnes's protégé and had repaid his debt by making Byrnes secretary of state. Deep down, Byrnes could not help feeling that he, not Truman, was the man best qualified to be president. He never got over thinking of himself as Truman's mentor.

Byrnes was exceptionally sensitive to the political risks of modifying unconditional surrender. More important, among Truman's advisers he was the most preoccupied with the growing Soviet threat. Using the bomb quickly would minimize Russian demands for territorial and political concessions in Asia, he believed, as well as strengthen the United States in any postwar negotiations. Since Byrnes's chief opponents, Grew and Stimson, were old and near retirement, and since he had strong support in both the military and State Department, his position carried the day. If the Japanese "peace feelers" to Moscow had been followed by more substantive proposals, either to the Russians or the Americans directly, perhaps some compromise might have been reached. But no other proposals were forthcoming. Thus at Potsdam, Byrnes and Truman remained convinced that the peace party in Japan would never marshal enough support against the military unless American attacks made further resistance seem futile. And it was again Byrnes who persuaded Truman to delete a provision in the Allied declaration that would have guaranteed the institution of the emperor.

By now it must be obvious why none of Truman's advisers wanted to rely on Soviet entry into the war as an alternative to dropping the bomb. By the time of the Potsdam Conference, Japan's military position had become hopeless. Why encourage Stalin's imperial ambitions, especially when the bomb was available for use?

Some Americans proposed that the bomb be demonstrated before a group of international observers instead of being dropped on Japan without warning. But advocates of this alternative were found largely among scientists working at the Chicago Metallurgical Laboratory. This group had been the first to finish its work on the bomb. While the Los Alamos lab rushed to

Fat Man, also familiarly known to scientists working on the project as Fat Boy. The graffiti on the tail included the notation, "Chicago is represented in here more than once."

complete the designs for Little Boy and Fat Man, the Chicago lab began discussing the postwar implications of nuclear weapons and the threat of an international arms race. The eminent scientist Niels Bohr had already raised those issues with Roosevelt and Churchill. Yet as we have seen, Churchill and Roosevelt agreed at their 1944 Hyde Park meeting to keep the bomb secret from Stalin, hoping to use it to advantage in any postwar rivalry with the Russians.

Unaware of the Hyde Park agreement, scientists continued to press their case. Ironically it was Leo Szilard, the physicist who marshaled support for creating the bomb, who six years later led the opposition to its use against Japan. The chain of command required Szilard to make any appeal outside the Chicago lab through its director, Arthur Compton. Instead, Szilard violated security rules and tried to reach Truman through his newly appointed secretary of state. After all, it had been an earlier unorthodox appeal that first persuaded Roosevelt of the bomb's importance. But this time, James Byrnes acted as the gatekeeper. A man of shallow mind and deep prejudices, he had little patience with an intellectual like Szilard and almost no understanding of the scientists' concerns about a nuclear arms race. To Byrnes, the bomb was a weapon that would cripple Japan and shock the Russians. He refused to take up Szilard's concerns with Truman. The internal politics of the situation proved determinative.

Nonetheless, scientists at the Chicago lab continued to speak out on bomb policy. Arthur Compton had organized a series of committees to make further recommendations, the most important of which was headed by emigré James Franck. The Franck Committee concluded that a surprise attack against Japan would destroy the trust and goodwill of other nations for the United States, as well as "precipitate the race for armaments, and prejudice the possibility of reaching an international agreement on the future control of such weapons." When Franck went to present the report to Stimson, the secretary avoided a meeting. The Interim Committee then steered the report to their scientific panel, whose members were Karl Compton, Fermi, Lawrence, and Oppenheimer. Those scientists, all of whom had greater prestige and influence, concluded that they could "propose no technical demonstration likely to bring an end to the war . . . and no acceptable alternative to direct military use."

That conclusion came before the first test of the bomb, and Oppenheimer later regretted the panel's shortsightedness. The explosion over the New Mexico desert so profoundly moved him that its eerie glow recalled an image from the Bhagavad Gita: "I am become death, the shatterer of worlds." Perhaps after Alamogordo, the scientific panel might have concluded that a demonstration would be worthwhile, but by then the time for deciding had passed. The momentum of the bureaucrary proceeded inexorably toward launching the missions over Japan. Scientists lacked the political influence to alter the assumptions of leading policy makers.

The only decisions remaining, then, were where specifically to drop the bombs and when to use them. Here, too, our models reveal both organizational processes and bureaucratic politics at work. To select the targets, Groves appointed a target committee composed of scientists and ordnance specialists. Their priorities reflected both the military's desire to end the war quickly and the scientists' hope to transmit a dramatic warning to the world. They sought cities that included military installations, but they also wanted a site with a large concentration of structures subject to the blast, in case the bomb missed its primary target. Kyoto, the ancient cultural and political center of Japan, topped their list.

Secretary of War Stimson vetoed that choice. As a former secretary of state and a person of broad cultural and political experience, he believed that the destruction of Kyoto would engender in the Japanese an undying bitterness toward the United States. Any hopes of integrating a revitalized and reformed Japan into a healthy postwar Asia might die with Kyoto. Stimson's position near the top of the organizational hierarchy gave him a different perspective from lower-level planners who weighed other issues. On the final target list Hiroshima ranked first, Nagasaki ranked fourth, and Kyoto not at all.

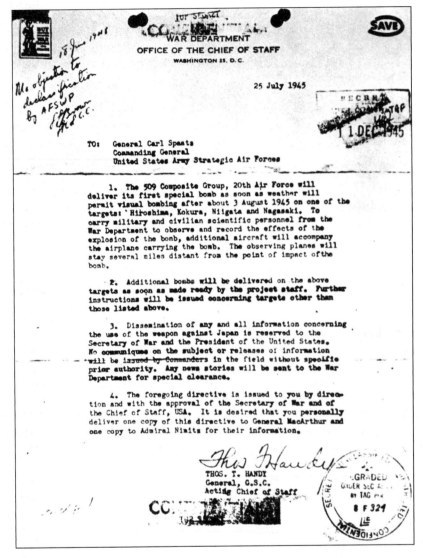

The letter outlining SOP for dropping the bomb. It authorized the "509 Composite Group, 20th Air Force" to "deliver its first special bomb as soon as weather will permit visual bombing after about 3 August 1945 on one of the targets: Hiroshima, Kokura, Niigata and Nagasaki." In a reflection of protocol, as well as a hint of the rivalry between the army and navy, the letter instructs General Spaatz, in paragraph four, to inform General MacArthur and Admiral Nimitz of the decision personally.

It was the weather and the routines of organization, not diplomatic or military strategy, that sealed Nagasaki's fate. After the bombing of Hiroshima and the Russian declaration of war, Japanese leaders decided to sue for peace. Advocates of surrender needed only enough time to work out acceptable terms and to reconcile military officers to the inevitable. As the Japanese discussed policy, the Americans followed standard military procedure. Control shifted from the commander in Washington, President Truman, to the commander of the bomber squadron on the island of Tinian in the Pacific. Plans called for Fat Man, a plutonium bomb, to be ready by August 11. Since work went faster than expected, the bomb crew advanced the date to August 9. The forecast called for clear skies on the ninth, followed by five days of bad weather. Urged on by the squadron commander, the crew had Fat Man armed and loaded on the morning of the ninth. And again following military SOP, the pilot shifted his attack to Nagasaki when clouds obscured his primary target.

Had the original plan been followed, Japan might well have surrendered before the weather cleared. Nagasaki would have been spared. But the officer who ordered the attack had little appreciation of the larger military picture that made Nagasaki a target or that made the Soviet Union a diplomatic problem connected with the atom bomb. He weighed factors important to a bomb squadron commander, not to diplomats or political leaders. The bombing of Nagasaki slipped from the hands of policy makers not because of some rogue computer or any power-mad, maniacal general, but simply because of military SOPs.

And so two bombs were dropped and the world entered the atomic age.

If historians based their interpretations on a single model, they would never satisfy their desire to understand the sequence of events leading to Nagasaki. Each model provides its own particular perspective, both clarifying and at the same time limiting. The use of several models allows the historian the same advantage enjoyed by writers of fiction who employ more than one narrator. Each narrator, like each model, affords the writer a new vantage point from which to tell the story. The facts may not change, but the reader sees them in another light. As organizations grow more complex, models afford historians multiple perspectives from which to interpret the same reality.

And yet we must remind ourselves that models do not work miracles, for their potential to reveal new insights depends on the skills of the people who build and apply them. If poorly applied, their seeming precision, like reams of computer printout, conveys a false sense of empirical legitimacy. Data specialists have coined the acronym GIGO to suggest the limits of such mechanical devices—"garbage in, garbage out." In the end historians must remember that organizations are open systems existing within a broader historical and cultural context. Even when our models have accounted for goals, strategies, SOPs, and political influence, there remain those pieces of the picture that are still irreducible: from Robert Oppenheimer's uneasy, almost mystical vision out of the Bhagavad Gita to the inanimate, complex meteorological forces that combined to dissipate the clouds over Nagasaki in August 1945.

Some elements of history will always remain stubbornly intractable, beyond the reach of the model builders. The mushroom clouds over Japan did

The reaction of scientists watching the detonation of the first atomic bomb in New Mexico was recalled by Robert Oppenheimer: "A few people laughed, a few people cried, more people were silent. There floated through my mind a line from the Bhagavad Gita in which Krishna is trying to persuade the Prince that he should do his duty: 'I am become death, the shatterer of worlds.' I think we all had this feeling, more or less." The photograph is of an atomic blast detonated at Bikini Island in July 1946.

not merely serve as a dramatic close to World War II. The afterglow of their blasts destroyed a sense of security that Americans had enjoyed for almost 150 years. After the war, the nuclear arms race turned the United States into an armed camp. Given the limits of human understanding, who in 1945 could have appreciated all the consequences that would result from the decision to drop the atom bomb?

Additional Reading

The easing of cold war tensions only emphasized the nuclear terror that much of the world had felt during the previous half century. That profound unease has informed the debate over the decision to drop the first atomic bombs on Japan. Indeed, the creation and uses of nuclear energy must rank with slavery, democratic reform, civil liberties, and economic justice as issues critical to the study of the American past, a point made in Jack Holl and Sheila Convis, eds., "Teaching Nuclear History," available from the Department of Energy (Washington, DC, 1990). Holl and Convis provide comprehensive bibliographies from courses taught on the scientific, military, diplomatic, and political aspects of nuclear energy and weapons.

Many people who lived with the bomb, however, did not initially see it as quite so threatening, as Paul Boyer reveals in *By the Bomb's Early Light: American Thought and Culture at the Dawn of the Atomic Age* (New York, 1985). The same point is made with wry irreverence in the film documentary *The Atomic Cafe* (1982). During the early cold war, most Americans willingly accepted the rationale for dropping the bombs offered in official accounts such as Harry S. Truman, *Memoirs, 1945: Year of Decisions* (New York, 1955); Henry Stimson (with McGeorge Bundy), *On Active Service in Peace and War* (New York, 1947); Leslie Groves, *Now It Can Be Told* (New York, 1962); and Richard Hewlett and Oscar Anderson, *The New World: 1939–1946*, vol. 1 of a *History of the United States Atomic Energy Commission* (University Park, PA, 1962).

Then in 1965 came Gar Alperovitz's bombshell, *Atomic Diplomacy* (New York, 1965; rev. ed., 1985). Suddenly the rationale for building and using the bomb seemed much less obvious. Alperovitz raised difficult questions about the decision to drop the bomb at a time when the Vietnam War led many Americans to doubt the explanations of their government. Herbert Feis defended the official view in *The Atomic Bomb and the End of World War II* (Princeton, NJ, 1966). The debate was continued with critical studies by Martin Sherwin, *A World Destroyed*, rev. ed. (New York, 1985), and Barton Bernstein, "Roosevelt, Truman, and the Atomic Bomb: A Reinterpretation," *Political Science Quarterly* 90 (spring 1975): 23–69. McGeorge Bundy reviewed the moral and political debates about the bomb in *Danger and Survival* (New York, 1988). George Kennan, the father of the cold war policy of containment, became more cautionary of nuclear diplomacy in later years, as reflected in his *The Nuclear Delusion* (New York, 1982).

An excellent collection of primary documents on the bomb's development can be found in Michael Stoff, Jonathan Fanton, and R. Hal Williams, eds., *The Manhattan Project: A Documentary Introduction to the Atomic Age* (New York, 1990). Many of the diaries, letters, and top-secret memoranda are reproduced in facsimile form. A brief history of the bomb project is offered by the Department of Energy: F. G. Gosling, *The Manhattan Project: Science in the Second World War* (Washington, DC, 1990). The decision-making models we discuss are more fully developed in another context in Graham Allison, *The Essence of Decision: Explaining the Cuban Missile Crisis* (Boston, MA, 1971). Richard Rhodes, *The Making of the Atomic Bomb* (New York, 1986) has written the most comprehensive and readable account of the bomb project. Daniel Kevles, *The Physicists* (New York, 1977) and Nuel Pharr Davis, *Lawrence and Oppenheimer* (New York, 1986 reprint) provide background on members of the science community who helped create the bomb. Many went on to raise profound questions about what they had done and how their work was put to use. Gregg Herken, *Brotherhood of the Bomb: The Tangled Lives and Loyalties of Robert Oppenheimer, Ernest Lawrence and Edward Teller* (New York, 2003) traces the relationship of the three key physicists and the issues over which they divided. Issues of nuclear policy have attracted a rich variety of films, videos, and documentaries. The most comprehensive, taking the Soviet as well as the American side, is *War and Peace in the Nuclear Age* (PBS, 1988). *The Day after Trinity* (1980) focuses on Robert Oppenheimer, the Manhattan Project, and the scientists' views on the bomb.

The military context of the bomb's development is important for understanding the implications of atomic weaponry. The evolution of military weapons and strategy is traced broadly in William H. McNeill, *The Pursuit of Power* (Chicago, 1982), and Robert O'Connell, *Of Arms and Men: A History of War, Weapons, and Aggression* (New York, 1989). Russell Weigley discusses the *American Way of War* (Bloomington, IN, 1977), while Ronald Spector, in *The Eagle against the Sun* (New York, 1985), examines the Pacific campaigns of World War II. Some critics have suggested that racism made it easier for American leaders to use the bomb against Japan than against Germany. John Dower, *War without Mercy: Race and Power in the Pacific War* (New York, 1986) demonstrates that both Japan and the United States allowed racist misperceptions to inform key decisions. The bombing of Hiroshima and Nagasaki was an outgrowth of the rise of air power and doctrines of strategic bombing, discussed in Michael Sherry, *The Rise of American Air Power* (New Haven, CT, 1987) and *In the Shadow of War: The United States since the 1930s* (New Haven, CT, 1995), and Ronald Schaffer, *Wings of Judgment: American Bombing in World War II* (New York, 1985). The impact of the bombing on the Japanese is movingly explored in John Hersey, *Hiroshima* (New York, 1946) and in the French film *Hiroshima Mon Amour* (1960).

After years of contested debate, controversy over atomic diplomacy erupted with new fervor in the 1990s. It was, after all, fifty years since the dawn of the nuclear age. The most politicized controversy involved the nature of a proposed commemorative exhibition at the Smithsonian's Air and Space Museum in Washington, DC. That story is well told in Philip Nobile, ed., *Judgment at the Smithsonian: The Bombing of Hiroshima and Nagasaki* (New York, 1995). A more scholarly, but equally engaged debate reraised the question of whether dropping the bombs saved lives. Barton Bernstein had raised the issue in "A Postwar Myth: 500,000 Lives Saved," *Bulletin of the Atomic Scientists* 42 (June/July 1986), as had Rufus Miles, "Hiroshima: The Strange Myth of Half a Million Lives Saved," *International Security* 10 (fall

1985). Bernstein later subjected Henry Stimson's 1947 *Harper's* article defending the bomb decision to a close analysis in "Seizing the Contested Terrain of Nuclear History," *Diplomatic History* 19 (winter 1993). A useful and full-length study of the numbers question is John Ray Skates, *Invasion of Japan: Alternative to the Bomb* (Columbia, SC, 1994). Once again, Gar Alperovitz and a team of research assistants responded to critics of his *Atomic Diplomacy* in a thoroughly researched new book, *The Decision to Use the Atomic Bomb* (New York, 1996). Another student of the bomb controversy, J. Samuel Walker, has summarized much of the evidence in *Prompt and Utter Destruction: Truman and the Use of the Atomic Bombs Against Japan* (Chapel Hill, NC, 1997).

Interactive Learning

The *Primary Source Investigator* supplies additional materials that explore the decision to drop the atomic bomb on Hiroshima and Nagasaki at the end of World War II. Included are images and videos of atomic weapons and their signature mushroom clouds. This selection also contains a number of letters between Albert Einstein and President Roosevelt, letters from Roosevelt to Congress concerning Japan and to J. Robert Oppenheimer, and various military reports and memoranda that complicate any simple account of how the decision to drop the bomb was made.

CHAPTER 14
From Rosie to Lucy

It was 1957. Betty Friedan was not just complaining; she was angry for herself and uncounted other women like her. For some time, she had sensed that discontent she felt as a suburban housewife and mother was not peculiar to her alone. Now she was certain, as she read the results of a questionnaire she had circulated to about 200 postwar graduates of Smith College. The women who answered were not frustrated simply because their educations had not properly prepared them for the lives they were leading. Rather, these women resented the wide disparity between the idealized image society held of them as housewives and mothers and the realities of their daily routines.

True, most were materially well off. The majority had families, a house in the suburbs, and the amenities of an affluent society. But amid that good fortune they felt fragmented, almost as if they had no identity of their own. And it was not only college graduates. "I've tried everything women are supposed to do," one woman confessed to Friedan.

> Hobbies, gardening, pickling, canning, being very social with my neighbors, joining committees, running PTA teas. I can do it all, and I like it, but it doesn't leave you anything to think about—any feeling of who you are. . . . I love the kids and Bob and my home. There's no problem you can even put a name to. But I'm desperate. I begin to feel I have no personality. I'm a server of food and putter-on of pants and a bedmaker, somebody who can be called on when you want something. But who am I?

A similar sense of incompleteness haunted Friedan. "I, like other women, thought there was something wrong with me because I didn't have an orgasm waxing the kitchen floor," she recalled with some bitterness.

This growing unease led her to raise some disturbing questions. Why, she wondered, had she chosen fifteen years earlier to give up a promising career in psychology for marriage and motherhood? What was it that kept women from using the rights and prerogatives that were theirs? What made them feel guilty for anything they did in their own right rather than as their hus-

346

bands' wives or children's mothers? Women in the 1950s, it seemed to Friedan, were not behaving quite the way they had a decade earlier. During World War II the popular press extolled the virtues of women like "Rosie the Riveter"—those who left homes and families to join the workforce. Now, Rosie was no longer a heroine. The media lavished their praise on women who devoted themselves to family and home. In the closing scene of one 1957 *Redbook* article, the heroine, "Junior" (a "little freckle-faced brunette" who had chosen to give up her job), nurses her baby at two in the morning sighing, "I'm so glad, glad, glad I'm just a housewife." What had happened? "When did women decide to give up the world and go back home?" Friedan asked herself.

Questions like those have engaged historians since the 1970s, but they were not ones housewives of the 1950s were encouraged to ask. For a red-blooded American to doubt something as sacred as the role of housewife and mother was to show symptoms of mental disorder rather than a skeptical or inquiring mind. Whatever the label attached to such feelings—neurosis, anxiety, or depression—most people assumed that unhappy women needed an analyst, not a historian, to explain their discontent. Such malaise was a problem for individuals, not society, to cure. Those women needed only to become better adjusted to who and what they were.

Friedan, however, was no ordinary housewife. Before starting her family, she had worked as a newspaper reporter; even after her children came, she wrote regularly for the major women's magazines. By 1957 she was fed up with the endless stories about breast-feeding, the preparation of gourmet chip dips, and similar domestic fare that was the staple of *Redbook*, *McCall's*, and *Ladies' Home Journal*. She had noticed many women like herself who worked outside the home and felt guilty because their jobs threatened their husbands' roles as providers or took time away from their children. Thus Friedan began to wonder not only about herself as a woman, a wife, and a mother, but also about the role society had shaped women to play.

The results of the Smith questionnaire engaged Friedan's reportorial instincts. She sensed she was onto a story bigger than anything she had ever written. But when she circulated an article describing the plight so many women were experiencing, the male editors at the women's magazines turned it down flat. It couldn't be true, they insisted; women could not possibly feel as guilty or discontented as Friedan claimed. The problem must be hers. "Betty has gone off her rocker," an editor at *Redbook* told her agent. "She has always done a good job for us, but this time only the most neurotic housewife could identify."

Friedan was not deterred. If the magazines would not print her story, she would do it as a book. For five years, she researched and wrote, exploring what she called the "feminine mystique," a phenomenon she saw embedded in American culture:

> The new mystique makes the housewife-mother, who never had a chance to be anything else, the model for all women . . . it simply makes certain concrete,

A happy housewife with a week's work. By 1947 many women laborers were back in the home full-time and the baby boom was under way. *Life* magazine celebrated the labors of a typical housewife by laying out a week's worth of bed making, ironing, washing, grocery shopping, and dish washing for a family of four. An incomplete tally shows more than 250 plates being washed and thirty-five quarts of milk consumed a week. Did the wife drink the majority of the six cups of coffee that seem to have been consumed per day?

finite, domestic aspects of feminine existence—as it was lived by women whose lives were confined by necessity to cooking, cleaning, washing, bearing children—into a religion, a pattern by which all women must now live or deny their femininity.

By the time Friedan was finished, the book had become a crusade. "I have never experienced anything as powerful, truly mystical, as the forces that seemed to overtake me as I wrote *The Feminine Mystique*," she later admitted. Published in 1963, the book soon joined the ranks of truly consequential books in American history. What Harriet Beecher Stowe did for slaves in *Uncle Tom's Cabin*, Jacob Riis for the urban poor in *How the Other Half Lives*, Upton Sinclair for public health in *The Jungle*, or Rachel Carson for the environment in *Silent Spring*, Friedan did for women. No longer would they bear their dissatisfaction in silence as they confronted the gap between their personal aspirations and the limited avenues society had left open to them. Friedan helped inspire a generation of women to demand the equal rights and opportunities that men routinely claimed. Together with other activists, she founded the National Organization for Women (NOW) in 1965 to press for reforms on an institutional level, donating royalties from her book to support it.

RETREAT FROM REVOLUTION: A DEMOGRAPHIC PROFILE

The feminist movement that blossomed in the wake of the civil rights movement of the 1960s had a profound impact on the study of history as well. After all, many of the questions Friedan raised were the sort that historians are trained to explore. Why hadn't women followed up on the gains in employment they experienced during World War II? What caused society in postwar America to place so much emphasis on home and family? What was the image of women that the mass media, scholars, and other opinion makers presented? Friedan, however, was a journalist, not a historian. True, historians and journalists share many methods in common. Both rely on varied sources for their evidence. Both write more confidently when they can confirm their story from multiple sources. Like many historians Friedan turned to the social sciences for theory and methods. She canvassed articles in popular women's magazines, studied the recent scholarship, and talked to psychologists, sociologists, and marriage counselors who regularly treated women. She conducted in-depth interviews with women of varying ages, backgrounds, and social classes.

It was not her methods, however, that influenced the study of history. Rather it was the subject she chose to probe. Prior to the 1970s, history as a discipline gave slight attention to the experience of women, even though they constituted more than half the world's population. The vast majority of studies (most of which were written by men anyway) concentrated on topics in the public arena. Politics, business, intellectual life, diplomacy, war—all were areas in which males defined the terms of action. The few women who did enter the history books were there most often because, like Eleanor Roosevelt, they had lived a public life; like Jane Addams, they initiated social reform; like Margaret Mead, they contributed in major ways to the social sciences; or like Willa Cather, they stood among the nation's leading writers and artists. Those women were exceptional, and it was the exceptional, not the commonplace, that historians generally preferred to study.

Still, history has by no means been confined to the rich, powerful, famous, and male—as we have seen in earlier chapters. And particularly for the twentieth century, documentary materials like the census made it possible to study ordinary people in a macrocosmic sense, looking at the actions of millions of people in the aggregate. Along with the new statistical census procedures adopted in 1940 came sophisticated opinion polling. Advertisers in the 1930s sought to discover more about consumer preferences so they could pitch their products more effectively. George Gallup developed survey techniques that allowed pollsters to determine mass opinions on a multitude of issues. Polling had been done before Gallup began his work, but he and his rivals undertook it much more systematically, devising better ways of recording opinions, more sophisticated techniques for minimizing margins of error, and more scientific means of asking questions.

In the academic world, the expansion of social science theory enlarged the kinds of information people thought worth having as well as the means for interpreting such data. As we saw in Chapter 12, social scientists were able to learn much about the causes for mass migrations in the 1930s. Thus when historians began investigating women's status in the mid-twentieth century, they could draw on a good deal of statistical information. The data they found in some ways challenged Friedan's picture of women being pushed out of the workforce, but in other ways her view was strikingly confirmed.

Census data and other governmental records indeed show that many women entered higher-paying and more-skilled jobs as early as World War I. But those gains were short-lived. With the return of peace, women faced layoffs, renewed wage discrimination, and segregation into female-only jobs such as teaching and nursing. Women made little headway over the next decade, despite the hoopla about the emancipated "new woman" of the twenties. Behind the stereotype of the smart-talking flapper with her cigarette, bobbed hair, and boyish clothes, traditional ideas about women and their proper roles prevailed in the labor marketplace. In 1920, 23 percent of women worked; by 1930, the figure was only 24 percent. Access to the professions increased but remained heavily restricted. For example, women earned more than 30 percent of all graduate degrees but accounted for only 4 percent of full professors on college faculties. Most women workers were young, single, and without children, and they toiled at unskilled jobs. Between 1920 and 1930, the percentage of women in manufacturing fell from 22.6 (the same as 1910) to 17.5, while percentages of women in both domestic service and clerical work—the lowest paying jobs—rose.

Real gains for women came during World War II. A rapidly expanding war economy absorbed most of the reserve labor force of underemployed or unemployed male workers. The military alone siphoned off some 15 million men and women. That left married women as the single largest untapped labor reserve. Suddenly, the propaganda machinery that had once discouraged women from competing with men for jobs urged them to enlist in the workforce. The patriotic appeal had the desired effect. What faithful wife could sit at home when the media warned that her husband in the service might die from the lack of ammunition? Commando Mary and Rosie the Riveter became symbols of women who heeded their country's call to join the production line.

Women of the *Saturday Evening Post*, Part One. In the midst of the war, the *Post*'s "cover girl" was this confident Rosie, patriotic buttons across her chest, goggles over her eyes, macho watchband around her wrist, and biceps calculated to make Charles Atlas envious. As one real-life Rosie commented about welding, "We were happy to be doing it. We felt terrific. Lunch hour would find us spread out on the sidewalk. Women welders with our outfits on, and usually a quart of milk in one hand and a salami sandwich in another. It was an experience that none of us had ever had before."

Patriotism by itself did not explain the willingness of married women to take jobs. Many found higher war wages an attractive inducement. Indeed, with so many husbands earning low military pay, families needed additional income to survive. Absent husbands also meant that domestic life was less central. Women had more time and opportunity for work outside the home. And wartime restrictions on leisure activities made jobs a more attractive outlet for women's energies. Whether stated as raw numbers or percentages, the statistical gains for women were impressive. From 1940 to 1945 some 6.5 million women entered the workforce, more than half of them for the first time. Women accounted for just 25 percent of workers in 1940 but 36 percent in

1945. Perhaps more significant were the kinds of women who now found employment outside the home. Young, single women no longer dominated. By 1950 married women were a majority of the female workforce, compared with only a third in 1940. Similarly, older women between ages fifty-five and sixty-four became a major working group, rising from 17 percent in 1940 to 35 percent by 1960.

It was not only the numbers of working women that soared but also the quality of their jobs. Women had an opportunity to work in skilled areas of manufacturing and to earn much higher wages. Black women in particular, who had been stuck in low-paying farm and domestic jobs, rushed to the factories that offered higher pay and better hours. Women on the assembly lines shaped sheet metal, built airplanes, and performed a host of skilled tasks. Suddenly, stereotypes about traditional male and female roles had shattered.

Yet for all these undeniable gains, the situation brought about by a world at war was a special case, and most Americans perceived it that way. The men returning home intended to pick up their jobs, and most men assumed that women would return to their traditional household duties. As a result, the war led to few structural changes affecting women's economic roles. For example, working mothers needed some form of day care for their young children. The government was slow to provide it, and even where it existed, many mothers were reluctant to use it. They or other family members continued to have primary responsibility for children. One result was a much higher absentee rate for working mothers. In addition, those mothers worked shorter hours. For them, the responsibilities of the job were secondary to those of the home.

Most professions continued to maintain barriers against women. Among the female workers who flooded government bureaucracies and factories, few received managerial status. And many employers found ways to avoid government regulations requiring equal pay for men and women. General Motors, for example, simply changed its job classifications. Jobs once designated as male or female became "heavy" or "light." Women generally were assigned to the light, lower-paying categories. Fearful that rapidly rising wages would spur inflation, the government was slow to enforce its own rules protecting women from discrimination.

Certain social trends seemed to underscore the traditional resistance to working mothers. Men did not easily reconcile themselves to women in once-masculine jobs. One newspaper columnist grumbled in print about what he called the "new Amazon," a woman who could "outdrink, outswear, and outswagger men." More worrisome to public officials were statistics indicating that wartime stresses threatened to undermine the family. Americans have always seen the family as the foundation of the social order, and wartime did nothing to change that view. The increase in alcohol abuse, divorce, and juvenile delinquency all suggested a weakening in family structure. Apparently, so did emotional problems among children such as bed wetting, thumb sucking, and truancy.

Observers were quick to blame those problems on one cause—maternal neglect. In fact, there was no clear evidence that the families of working women had any disadvantage over those whose mothers stayed home. Extraordinary wartime mobility, not the fact that the mothers worked, seems to have accounted for many of those problems. The sudden rush of workers, both male and female, to industrial centers overtaxed all manner of public services, including housing and schools, which were of particular importance to families with young children. The war disrupted families whether mothers worked or not.

What is striking is that by 1945, despite all the gains women had made, most attitudes about women and work had not changed substantially. Surveys showed that Americans, whether male or female, continued to believe that child rearing was a woman's primary job. Thus the marked demographic shift of women into the workforce was revolutionary in import, but it brought no revolution in cultural attitudes toward gender roles. As historian William Chafe commented, "The events of the war years suggested that most Americans would accept a significant shift in women's economic activities as long as the shift was viewed as 'temporary' and did not entail a conscious commitment to approve the goals of a sexual revolution."

Despite the general expectation that women would return to the home after the war, female laborers did not simply drop their wrenches and pick up frying pans. Many continued to work outside the home, although mostly to support their families, not to find career alternatives. As peace came in 1945, polls indicated that more than 75 percent of all working women wanted to continue at their jobs. About 88 percent of high school girls surveyed said they hoped for a career as well as the role of homemaker. Although employment for women did shrink slightly, a significantly higher percentage of women were working in 1950 than in 1940 (28 percent versus 24 percent). Even more striking, that figure continued to rise, reaching 36 percent by 1960. Those numbers included older women, married women with children, and women of all social classes.

Such statistics would seem at first to undercut Friedan's notion that the vast majority of American women accepted the ideal of total fulfillment through housework and child rearing. Some 2.25 million women did voluntarily return home after the war, and another million were laid off by 1946. At the same time, 2.75 million women entered the job market by 1947, leaving a net loss of only half a million.

But even if Friedan was mistaken in seeing a mass female exodus from the workforce, a significant shift did take place in the types of work performed. When women who had been laid off managed to return to work, they often lost their seniority and had to accept reduced pay in lower job categories. Employment in almost all the professions had decreased by 1960. Despite gains in some areas, women were concentrated in jobs that were primarily extensions of their traditional responsibility for managing the family's physical and emotional well-being: they were nurses, not doctors; teachers, not principals; tellers, not bankers. Far more worked in service jobs (as maids or waitresses, for example) than in manufacturing. Overwhelmingly, job opportunities were segregated by gender. About 75 percent of all women workers held female-only jobs. In fact, gender segregation in the workplace was worse in 1960 than in 1900—and even worse than segregation by race. Thus, even though women's participation in the workforce remained comparatively high, it did not inspire a corresponding revolution in attitudes about women's roles in society.

RETREAT FROM REVOLUTION: THE ROLE OF MASS MEDIA

Attitudes, of course, were at the center of Friedan's concerns in *The Feminine Mystique*, and the demographic profile we have sketched underlines the reason for her focus. If the percentage of women holding jobs continued to increase during the 1950s and if young women, when polled, said they hoped to combine work in some way with motherhood, how did the cult of the "feminine mystique" become so firmly enshrined? If wartime laboring conditions produced a kind of revolution in fact but not in spirit, what elements of American culture reined in that revolution and kept it from running its course?

As Friedan was well aware, economic and demographic factors played a crucial role in renewing the concern with home and family living. The hard times of the depression had discouraged couples from starting large families. But as war production renewed prosperity and soldiers headed off to war, the birthrate began to climb. With the return of peace in 1945, GIs were eager to do more than kiss their wives hello. For the next fifteen years the United States had one of the highest birthrates in the world, rising from an average of 1.9 to 2.3 children for each woman of childbearing age. Large families became the norm. The number of parents with three children tripled, while those with four quadrupled. Women also married younger. The average age of marriage dropped from 22 in 1900 to 20.3 in 1962. With the highest rate of marriage of any nation in the world, American men and women chose to organize their lives around family.[1]

Clearly, material conditions not only pushed women out of the workplace as GIs rejoined the peacetime economy but also pulled women back into the home as the birthrate rose. Friedan acknowledged these changes but noted that the birthrates of other economically developed nations—such as France, Norway, and Sweden—had begun to decline by 1955. Even more striking, the sharpest rise in the United States came among women aged fifteen to nineteen. In Great Britain, Canada, and Germany, on the other hand, the rise was more equally distributed among age groups. What was it that made so many American teen brides give up the chance of college and a career for early marriage and homemaking?

---

1. At the same time, the United States had the world's highest divorce rate. Enthusiasm for marriage was apparently no guarantee of success.

Friedan's answer was to look more closely at the mass media. Magazines, radio, movies, television had all come to play a predominant role in the modern era. They exposed Americans by the millions to powerfully presented messages conveying the standards and ideals of the culture. The media, observed sociologist Harold Lasswell in 1948, had come to perform many of the tasks that in medieval Europe were assumed by the Catholic Church. Like the church, the media possessed the capacity to send the same message to all classes at the same time, with confidence in their authority to speak and to be heard universally. Friedan, for her part, found it significant that in the postwar era the media's message about women—what they could dream of, set their sights on, and accomplish—underwent a marked shift. The purveyors of popular culture suddenly seemed determined to persuade women that they should not just accept but actually embrace the idealized image of women as wives and mothers.

Having written for the mass-circulation women's magazines, Friedan already knew the part they played in promoting the feminine mystique. What surprised her was how much the image of women had changed. In the 1930s, the woman most likely to appear in a magazine story had a career and was as much concerned with a goal of her own as with getting her man. The heroine of a typical *Ladies' Home Journal* story in 1939 is a nurse who has "strength in her hands, pride in her carriage and nobility in the lift of her chin . . . she left training, nine years ago. She had been on her own ever since. She had earned her way, she need consider nothing but her heart." And unlike the heroines of the 1950s, these women did not have to choose invariably between marriage and career. If they held strongly to their dreams, they could have both. Beginning in the 1950s, however, new heroines appeared. These, Friedan noted, were most often "young and frivolous, almost childlike; fluffy and feminine; passive; gaily content in a world of bedroom and kitchen, sex, babies, and home." The new women did not work "except housework and work to keep their bodies beautiful and to get and keep a man." "Where," Friedan asked rhetorically, "is the world of thought and ideas, the life of the mind and the spirit?"

Talking with some of the few remaining editors from the 1930s, Friedan discovered one reason for the change. "Most of the material used to come from women writers," one explained. "As the young men returned from the war, a great many women writers stopped writing. The new writers were all men, back from the war, who had been dreaming about home, and a cozy domestic life." Male editors, when queried, defended themselves by contending that their readers no longer identified with career women, no longer read serious fiction, and had lost almost all interest in public issues except perhaps those that affected the price of groceries. "You just can't write about ideas or broad issues of the day for women," one remarked.

Just as the image of women changed in mass magazines, so too did women's fashions follow Rosie the Riveter out of the factory. As historian Lois Banner has observed, in the 1930s only a movie star like Katharine Hepburn could get away with wearing slacks. During the 1940s, however, a boyish or mannish look for women became popular. Narrow skirts, padded shoulders, and suits all had a vogue. That ended in 1947, when Parisian designer Christian Dior introduced the "new look." Dior-inspired fashion emphasized femininity. Narrow waistlines drew attention to shapely hips and a fully defined bosom. Most women had to wear foundation garments to achieve the necessary look. The new styles reached their extreme in the baby-doll fashions, with cinched-in waists that set off full bosoms and bouffant skirts held out by crinoline petticoats. Women's shoes ushered in a bonanza for podiatrists. Toes became pointier and heels rose ever higher, until it became dangerous for women to walk. Banner concluded that "not since the Victorian era had women's fashions been so confining." That fashion was a male image of the ideal feminine look.

In the 1930s, magazines and movies had set the fashion. By the 1950s, both those media had begun to lose their audience to television. Women who had once gone to the matinee stayed home to watch the latest episode of *As the World Turns*. In 1951, cities with television networks reported a 20 percent to 40 percent decline in movie attendance. Almost overnight, television became the preeminent mass medium, carrying images—feminine or otherwise—of American culture into the home. By 1949, there were about a million sets and 108 licensed stations, most in large urban markets. By 1952, 15 million Americans had bought sets; by 1955, the figure had jumped to 30 million; by 1960, television had entered 46 million homes. In fact, more American homes had television sets than had bathrooms! Obviously, if we are to understand how the mass media of the 1950s shaped the image of women, television must be at the center of our focus.[2]

And indeed, television portrayed women of the fifties in predictable ways. Most often they were seen in domestic dramas or comedies in which Mom and Dad were found living happily with their two or three cute children and possibly a live-in maid or relative to provide additional comic situations. The homes in which they lived, even that of blue-collar airplane riveter Chester Riley (*The Life of Riley*, 1949–1950, 1953–1958), were cheerfully middle class, with the antiseptic look of a furniture showroom. As for Mom herself, she never worked outside the home and seldom seemed to do much more than wave a dust cloth or whip up a three-course meal at a moment's notice. Sometimes, as in *The Adventures of Ozzie and Harriet* (1955–1966), she is competent, cool, and collected. Ozzie, in fact, often seems rather a lost soul when turned loose in his own castle and has to be guided gently through the current week's predicament by Harriet. In other series, such as *The George Burns and Gracie Allen Show* (1950–1958), women like Gracie Allen and her friend Blanche play the role of "dizzy dames," unable to balance checkbooks

---

2. The technology of broadcasting had been available in the 1920s, but only after World War II did commercial application begin in earnest. As secretary of commerce, Herbert Hoover had his image transmitted in 1927, making him the first president to have appeared on television, although this appearance occurred before his election in 1928. Franklin Roosevelt was, in 1939, the first president in office to appear on television.

Women of the *Saturday Evening Post*, Part Two. Biceps and riveting guns had deserted Post covers by 1956. Instead, these two women—like Margaret in *Father Knows Best*—can barely get their cars out the driveway, let alone down the street. No doubt, however, they could stir up a mean Jell-O salad.

and sublimely oblivious to the realities of the business world. When Harry Morton announces to his wife, Blanche, "I've got great news for you!" (he's been offered a new job), Blanche replies, "When can I wear it?"

Perhaps the domestic comedy that best portrayed the archetypal family woman was *Father Knows Best* (1954–1962). The title says it all: Robert Young, playing Jim Anderson, never lacks a sane head, while his wife, Margaret, is devoted though something of a cipher. She lacks Gracie Allen's originality yet still can be counted on as a source of genial humor as she tries vainly, for instance, to learn to drive the family car. Warmhearted, attractive, submissive, competent only within the sphere of her limited domain, she is the fifties housewife personified.

In one sense, then, Friedan does have a case. The mass media of the 1950s, television prime among them, saturated the American public with the image of the new feminine mystique. But to establish that finding merely raises a much thornier issue: what sort of relationship is there between the media and reality? Friedan is arguing not merely that the institutions of mass communication promoted the feminine mystique; she is suggesting that, through their influence and pervasiveness, the media seduced women into the cult of domesticity. In that light, we can understand why women's gains during the war were not translated into a revolution of the spirit.

REFLECTION VERSUS MANIPULATION

What effect do the mass media have on real life? Obviously, that question is a complex one. Most Americans resist the idea that the images they see on television, in advertising, or in films have any purpose beyond plain and simple entertainment. But surely the reality is more complicated. Every day Americans are bombarded by images that in ways both subtle and overt exert a powerful, though far from clearly understood, influence.

In sorting out possible answers, we can see two sharply contrasting hypotheses for gauging the media's impact. On the one hand is the argument that, in fact, the media have very little effect on the real world, since they merely reflect tastes and opinions that mass audiences already hold. Confronted with a need to attract the largest number of consumers, media executives select programs that have the broadest appeal. Advertisers seek less to alter values than to channel existing ones toward a specific choice. Americans already value romantic love; once Calvin Klein has his way, they wear his jeans to achieve it. In the most extreme form, this reflection hypothesis would see the media as essentially passive—a simple mirror to society. And with that argument, a good deal of Friedan's examination of female imagery might be instructive but beside the point. Women of the fifties were portrayed the way they were because, for whatever reasons, they had been transformed by the conditions of postwar culture.

But that extreme form of the reflection hypothesis breaks down for several reasons. First, if we argue that the mass media are merely reflections, then what are they reflecting? Surely not "real life" pure and simple. Only in commercials do the people who wear Calvin Klein jeans make their mates swoon. The parents on *Father Knows Best* are happily married with two children, hardly the statistical norm in America even then. Divorced, single-parent mothers were unknown in sitcom land. African American, Latino, or Asian families were virtually nonexistent. Obviously, while the media reflect certain aspects of real life, the reflection hypothesis must be modified to admit that a good deal of what is reflected comprises idealized values—what people would like to be rather than what they really are.

But if mass communications reflect ideals as much as reality, whose ideals are these? African American scholar bell hooks (she purposely uses the lowercase in her name) argued that "many audiences in the United States resist the idea that images have an ideological intent . . . Image making is political—that politics of domination informs the way the vast majority of images are constructed and marketed." That domination was precisely the problem Friedan addressed. As she pointed out, most of the editors, producers, directors, and writers of the 1950s were men. If male rather than female ideals and aspirations were being communicated (or, for that matter, white rather than Latino, middle-class rather than lower-class, or the ideals of any limited group), then it again becomes legitimate to ask how much the ideals of one segment of America are shaping those of a far wider audience.

Of course, many of the people involved in producing mass culture would argue that in the matter of dreams and ideals, they are not selling their own, they are merely giving the audience what it wants. But do audiences know what they really want? Surely they do sometimes. But they may also be influenced, cajoled, and swayed. Persuasion, after all, is at the heart of modern advertising. A fifties marketing executive made the point quite freely, noting that

> in a free enterprise economy, we have to develop the need for new products. And to do that we have to liberate women to desire these new products. We help them rediscover that homemaking is more creative than to compete with men. This can be manipulated. We sell them what they ought to want, speed up the unconscious, move it along.

A better case for domination or manipulation would be hard to make. Perhaps the most obvious case of an audience susceptible to persuasion is children. Psychological research has indicated that among children, a process called modeling occurs,

> simply by watching others, without any direct reinforcement for learning and without any overt practice. The child imitates the model without being induced or compelled to do so. That learning can occur in the absence of direct reinforcement is a radical departure from earlier theories that regarded reward or punishment as indispensable to learning. There is now considerable evidence that children do learn by watching and listening to others even in the absence of reinforcement and overt practice.

Obviously, if young girls learn week in and week out that father does indeed know best and that a woman's place is in the home, the potential for asserting an ideology of male dominance is strong.

The hypothesis that the media may be manipulative contrasts sharply with the theory that they are only reflective. More realistically, though, the two alternatives are best seen as the poles of a continuum. In its extreme form, the reflection hypothesis sees the media as entirely passive, with no influence whatever. The manipulative hypothesis, in its extreme form, treats the media as highly controlling, brainwashing viewers (to use a term popular in the anticommunist fifties) into believing and acting in ways they never would have on their own. But a young girl, no matter how long she watches television, is also shaped by what she learns from her parents, schoolteachers, religious instructors, and a host of other influences. Given those contending factors, how decisive a role can the media play?

Ironically, the more extreme forms of the manipulative hypothesis have been supported by both left and right wings of the political spectrum. During the 1950s, for example, with worries of foreign subversion running high, conservative ideologues warned that communists had come to rely "more on radio and TV than on the press and motion pictures as 'belts' to transmit pro-Sovietism to the American public." On the other hand, liberal intellectuals charged that mass culture, at its worst, threatened "not merely to cretinize our taste, but to brutalize our senses by paving the way to totalitarianism."

Historians have stepped only gingerly into the debate over media influence. In part their hesitation may be because, like most scholars, they tend not to be heavy consumers of mass culture themselves. Preferring a symphony by Brahms to rap, Federico Fellini's *8½* to *The Matrix Reloaded*, or *Masterpiece Theater* to *American Idol*, their instinctive reaction is to deem popular fare "worthy of attention only if it is created by unpaid folk and 'serious' artists who do not appear to think about making a living," as sociologist Herbert Gans has tartly remarked.

By temperament and training, most historians are also more comfortable with the traditional print media. When they seek to explicate a document, book, or diary, they can readily find the text and use common critical strategies to identify thematic, symbolic, or cultural content. Insofar as the author of the document is sensitive to issues that concern some significant sector of society, the text can be said to reflect on social reality.

But what if the "text" is a series of commercials plugging the virtues of Crest toothpaste or a year's worth of the soap opera *General Hospital?* In that case, historians confront two difficulties. A vast amount of broadcast material is ephemeral—not permanently recorded at the time it was broadcast and no longer recoverable. The actual content of many broadcasts can be reconstructed, if at all, only from file scripts or memories of viewers or participants. Even in situations in which television material has been saved and can be analyzed for its cultural content, a knowledge of how the audience received a program or commercial is crucial. As Gans has insisted, "cultural values cannot be determined from cultural content, until we know why people chose it." Do viewers watch a program intensely or for background noise or because it is the best of a bad lot? Historians seldom have the means to answer those questions satisfactorily.

Sociologists and cultural anthropologists are the allies most likely to help historians determine the influence of the media—particularly television—in modern life. But while sociologists have run a number of interesting studies involving the effect of television violence and racial stereotypes on viewers, much less systematic evidence has been gathered on television's effect on women. The most promising work has centered on what is known as content analysis. A content-analysis researcher examines a body of evidence, scanning it systematically in order to answer a few objective questions. How often are sex and violence linked in network crime shows? The researcher picks a sample group of shows, views them on a regular basis, and counts the number of incidents involving sex and violence. The results, of course, are descriptive within fairly limited bounds. They can tell us, for example, how often women appear in certain roles, but not how the audience perceives or values those roles. Nor can we know, except indirectly, what the shows' producers actually intended. If women are always portrayed in inferior positions, we can infer that the producers saw women as inferior; but the inference remains unproved.

Content analysis of early programming has led sociologist Gaye Tuchman to conclude that television practiced the "symbolic annihilation of women." By that she meant that women were "demeaned, trivialized, or simply ignored." Surveys of television programs revealed that women, who constituted more than half the population, accounted for just 32 percent of the characters in prime-time dramas. Most of the women who did appear in prime time were concentrated in comedy series. Children's cartoons had even fewer female characters. In the shows in which women appeared most often—daytime soap operas—they still held inferior positions. A 1963 survey showed, in fact, that men held 80 percent of all jobs in prime-time shows.

Women were demeaned in other ways. They were most often the victims of violence, not the perpetrators. Single women were attacked more frequently than married women. The women most favorably portrayed were those who were courting or had a family role. In the 1950s two-thirds of all the women characters on television shows were married, had been married, or were engaged. Even in soap operas, usually set in homes in which women might presumably be allowed to act as leaders, women's roles were trivialized, for it was usually men who found the solutions to emotional problems.

Much early content-analysis research was not designed to focus specifically on women. But studies analyzing the settings of shows and the psychological characteristics of heroes, villains, and supporting characters indirectly support Tuchman's conclusion, because they show that the world of television drama was overwhelmingly white, middle class, suburban, family centered, and male dominated. In eighty-six prime-time dramas aired during 1953, men outnumbered women 2 to 1. The very young (under twenty) and the old (over sixty) were underrepresented. The characters were largely of childbearing age and were employed or employable. High white-collar or professional positions were overrepresented at the expense of routine white-collar or blue-collar jobs. Most characters were sane, law abiding, healthy, and white (more than 80 percent). Blacks, who accounted for 12 percent of the population, appeared in only 2 percent of the roles. Heroes outnumbered heroines 2 to 1; and since heroic foreigners were more likely to be women, that left three American heroes for each American heroine.

In these same eighty-six shows, male villains outnumbered female villains. Feminists might take this fact to heart as a more positive presentation of women. Villains, however, had many traits that Americans admired. Although they were unattractive, dishonest, disloyal, dirty, stingy, and unkind, villians were also brave, strong, sharper, or harder than most heroes, and had inner strength. Thus they were imposing, if undesirable, characters. In minimizing women as villains, television preserved a male-comforting stereotype while depriving women of yet another set of roles in which they could be effective. Similarly, television dramas presented the most favorable stereotypes of professions in which men dominated. Journalists, doctors, and entertainers all had positive images, while teachers—a large majority of whom were women—were treated as the slowest, weakest, and softest professionals (though clean and fair).

So far as content analysis is able to go, then, it confirms that television did systematically reinforce the feminine mystique that Betty Friedan found so prevalent elsewhere. But along with the advantages of content analysis come limits. To be rigorous, the method of measuring must be standardized and the questions asked must be fairly limited and objective. For example, one content analyst described her approach in this way:

> Between March 18 and March 31, 1975, I watched and coded the shows, according to pretested categories. Using a specially prepared timer, I examined the first verbal or nonverbal interaction clearly between two people in thirty seconds of one-minute segments of the programs. I recorded who was dominant, dominated, or equal in each interaction and noted the relevant occupation status, sex, race, and family role of each participant.

This approach is admirably systematic, but it leaves little room for more qualitative judgments—for evaluating the nuances of an image as well as its overt content. Sociologists, of course, would say that such subjective analysis is precisely what they are trying to avoid, because any nuances are likely to incorporate the prejudices of the researcher. As we know by now, historians have traditionally felt that this possible bias was a risk worth taking. They are inclined to examine documents for what they hint at or even do not say as much as for what they do. Because we are not in a position to undertake field research on how audiences of the fifties were affected by programs involving women, let us instead resort to a subjective analysis of television's product itself and see what its leading characters and dramatic themes reveal.

MALE FRAMES AND FEMALE ENERGIES

The most promising programs for exploring gender issues are the sitcoms of the 1950s. As we have seen, other genres popular in the 1950s—crime shows, westerns, quiz programs, and network news—tended to ignore women or place them in secondary roles. A majority of the sitcoms, however, take place in a domestic setting in which women are central figures. The plots regularly turn on misunderstandings between men and women over their relationships or the proper definition of gender roles. As a consequence, of all television programs, sitcoms had the most formative influence on the image of women.

As a genre, sitcoms had their roots in radio shows like *The Jack Benny Program*, *The Burns and Allen Show*, and *Amos 'n' Andy*.[3] That origin helps ex-

---

3. *Amos 'n' Andy*, a show about a taxicab company operated by blacks, presented a special crossover problem. The white actors who starred in the show on radio were hardly appropriate for a visual medium.

plain why comedy in television shows came to be more verbal than comedy in film, which blended physical and verbal humor. Sitcoms derived most of their laughs from puns, repartee, or irony. What the camera added were close-ups and reaction shots, since the small television screen limited the detail that could be shown. Tight focus revealed the visual delivery comedians often achieved through subtle gestures: a raised eyebrow, a curled lip, or a frown. "You know what your mother said the day we were married, Alice?" grumps the obese Ralph Kramden on *The Honeymooners*. [A close-up, here, for emphasis; the double-chin juts in disdain.] "You know what she said? I'm not losing a daughter; I'm gaining a ton." Or another time, when Ralph's vanity gets the better of him, he brags, "Alice, when I was younger, the girls crowded around me at the beach." "Of course, Ralph," replies Alice. "That's because they wanted to sit in the shade." [Cut to Ralph's bulging eyes.]

From the historian's point of view, the more intriguing sitcoms are not the predictable ones, such as *The Adventures of Ozzie and Harriet* or *Father Knows Best*, but those that do not seem to fit the standard mold. It is here—where the familiar conventions come closest to being broken—that the tensions and contradictions of the genre appear most clearly. In different ways, *Our Miss Brooks*, *I Love Lucy*, and *The Honeymooners* all feature unconventional characters and unusual plot situations. *Our Miss Brooks* stars Eve Arden as an aging, unmarried schoolteacher whose biting humor makes her a threat to the bumbling men around her. *I Love Lucy*, with Lucille Ball, follows the zany attempts of Lucy Ricardo to break out of her narrow domesticity into the larger world of show business or into some moneymaking venture. Although the Ricardos had a child midway through the series, he was not often featured in the show. *The Honeymooners* was perhaps the most offbeat sitcom of the fifties. It featured the blue-collar world of the Kramdens, a childless couple, who lived in a dreary Brooklyn flat with their neighbors Ed and Trixie Norton, also childless. Ralph, a bus driver, and Ed, a sewer worker, seem unlikely subjects to reinforce the middle-class values of Friedan's feminine mystique.

Despite their unusual formats, all three sitcoms were among the most popular shows of the fifties, and *Lucy* stayed at the top of the ratings for almost the entire decade. By looking at these sitcoms, we can better understand on what basis a show could deviate from traditional forms and still remain successful.

As it happens, none of these shows is as exceptional as it might first seem. All incorporate elements of the traditional family show structure, with male authority remaining dominant, middle-class values applauded, and the proper order of society prevailing by the end of each episode. Still, there is more to them than the simple triumph of the feminine mystique. The three leading female characters—Connie Brooks, Lucy Ricardo, and Alice Kramden—reveal through the force of their comic personas certain tensions that slick production styles and pat plot resolutions cannot hide. Each series offered glimpses of women's discontent as well as women able to cope with adversity.

The comic tensions in *Our Miss Brooks* arise from two primary sources: Miss Brooks constantly clashes with her authoritarian principal, Osgood Conklin, and at the same time has her amorous eye on the biology teacher, Mr. Boynton. Boynton seems oblivious to her sexual overtures yet is the best prospect to save her from spinsterhood. In one show she walks in with her arms full of packages. "Can I hold something?" he asks. "Sure, as soon as I put these packages down," she cracks. He ignores the sexual innuendo that she employs in her attempt to stir his interest.

Miss Brooks is oppressed on several levels. She recognizes that society places little value on her role as a teacher. There is no future in her job, where she is bullied, exploited, and underpaid. Marriage offers the only way out, but since she is superior in intellect and personality to the men and no longer young and fresh, her prospects for marriage are dim. Thus she faces a future in which she cannot fulfill the feminine mystique. Her only hope is to use her wiles to trick Mr. Boynton into marriage. She must be passive-aggressive, because convention prevents her from taking overt initiatives. At the same time, she must accept a career situation that is beneath her talents. Rather than challenge the system that demeans her, she survives by treating it as comical and transcending it through the force of her superior character.

The first episode of the series establishes many of those themes as well as its somewhat irreverent style. Miss Brooks gets an idea that she can arouse Mr. Boynton's interest by starting a fight. That leads to a number of laughs as Mr. Boynton ducks each provocation. Before she makes headway, she is called on the carpet by Mr. Conklin, the principal. From behind his desk, Conklin radiates authority, glowering at her and treating her with disdain. But Miss Brooks hardly folds before the onslaught. She tricks him into reminiscing about his youth, and as he becomes more mellow (and human), she assumes greater familiarity, until she is sitting casually on the corner of his desk. By the end of the meeting, Connie has sent Mr. Conklin on a wild-goose chase that leads to his arrest by the police. In his absence, she becomes acting principal, clearly relishing the sense of authority she gains from sitting in the seat of power. The duly constituted authority has been effectively subverted. Of course, male hierarchy is reestablished in the end, but before order returns, we have had a glimpse of a world in which women have power.

The liberties taken in the show, however, amount to scarcely more than shore leave. A traditional sense of domestic order underlies the surface mayhem. Even though the central characters are unmarried, the show does have a surrogate family structure. Despite her relatively advanced age, Miss Brooks's real role is that of a smart-talking teenage daughter. She lives in an apartment with a remarkably maternal housekeeper. One of the students at school, Walter (who these days would be classified as an eminent nerd), serves as a surrogate son, while Mr. Conklin, of course, is the father figure. That leaves Mr. Boynton to be paired off as Miss Brooks's reticent steady. Her challenges to Mr. Conklin's male authority are allowed only because the principal is pompous, arbitrary, and occasionally abusive of his position. And Mr. Boynton is scarcely as dumb as he acts; indeed, at the end of the first episode, as Miss

Lucy (Lucille Ball), Ethel Mertz (Vivian Vance), and Ricky Ricardo (Desi Arnaz) look on anxiously as French film star Charles Boyer straightens his pocket handkerchief in an episode of *I Love Lucy*. Lucy, who could not confront a celebrity without causing trouble, had torn Boyer's raincoat and crushed his hat. For all her zaniness Lucy generally appeared dressed in the latest fashions, and her apartment reflected tasteful middle-class decor.

Brooks waits eagerly for a kiss that will demonstrate his interest, he holds back and winks at the audience—indicating that he can dish it out too. With Mr. Conklin back in charge and Mr. Boynton clearly in control, the male frame is reestablished. Miss Brooks has been chastened for her presumption, and the normal, male-dominated order has been restored.

Similar tensions operate in the *I Love Lucy Show*. Lucy's efforts to escape the confines of domesticity threaten her husband, Ricky, and the well-being of the family. The plot generally thickens as Lucy cons her neighbor Ethel Mertz into joining her escapades. Ethel and Lucy then become rivals of their husbands. In an episode that could have generated biting commentary, Lucy and Ethel challenge Fred Mertz and Ricky to exchange roles. The women will be the breadwinners, the men the housekeepers. Both, of course, prove equally inept in the others' domain. Ethel and Lucy discover they have no significant job skills. After much frustration, they end up working in a chocolate factory. Their boss is a woman who is far more domineering and arbitrary than Mr. Conklin ever was. In a parody of Charlie Chaplin's *Modern Times,* Lucy and Ethel fall hopelessly behind as they pack candies that run relentlessly along a conveyor belt. They stuff their pockets and their mouths until they are sick and the floor is heaped with fallen candies. By the end of the day they return home emotionally drained, humbled, and thwarted.

In the meantime, Ricky and Fred have virtually destroyed the apartment. How much rice do they need for dinner? They decide on several pounds, so that the kitchen is soon awash. Just as Ethel and Lucy are relieved to return home, Fred and Ricky are overjoyed to escape the toils of domestic life. Each side learns to respect the difficulties facing the other.

Despite the schmaltzy ending, there is a real tension in the structure of this episode and the series as a whole. Within the orthodox framework (Lucy and Ricky are firmly middle class, worrying about money, friends, schools, and a house in the suburbs), the energy and spark of the show comes precisely because Lucy, like Miss Brooks, consistently refuses to recognize the male limits prescribed for her. Although Ricky manages to rein her in by the end of each episode, the audience realizes full well that she is too restless, too much restricted by four walls and a broom, and far too vivacious to accept the cult of domesticity. She will be off and running again the following week in another attempt to break loose.[4]

More than any other sitcom of the fifties, *The Honeymooners* seems to deviate from middle-American stereotypes. As lower-class, childless couples living in stark apartments, the Nortons and Kramdens would scarcely seem ideal reflections of an affluent, family-centered society. Ralph and Alice struggle to get by on his $67.50-a-week salary as a bus driver. Sewer worker Ed Norton and his wife, Trixie, live off credit. Whenever their appliances or furniture are repossessed, Ed replaces them with merchandise from another store. The show's main set was the Kramden's living room-cum-kitchen, which had the look of the depression era, not the 1950s. Ralph and Alice have no television set, telephone, vacuum cleaner, or other modern appliances. They have only a bureau, a table and chairs, a standing sink, an icebox (literally), and a stove.

The show turns on Ralph's obsession with money and status. He is forever trying to get rich quick, earn respect, and move up in the world. All that saves him from himself and disaster is Alice's stoic forbearance. She has had

4. The show's most successful moment might also serve as a model of 1950s family life. In its early years, television honored all the middle-class sexual mores. Even married couples slept in separate beds, and the word *pregnant* was taboo (since it implied that a couple had been sexually active—at least once). The producers of *Lucy* thus faced a terrible dilemma when they learned that their star was indeed with child. What to do? They made the bold decision to incorporate Lucille Ball's pregnancy into the show. For months, television audiences watched Lucy become bigger and more uncomfortable. On January 19, 1952, the big day arrived. The episode "Lucy Has Her Baby" (filmed earlier in anticipation of the blessed event) scored the highest rating (68.8 percent) of any show of the decade. In newspaper headlines, news of the birth of Desi Arnaz Jr. rivaled the inauguration of Dwight D. Eisenhower, which occurred the following morning.

In a typical scene from *The Honeymooners*, Ralph Kramden (Jackie Gleason) adopts a pompous pose before his skeptical wife, Alice (Audrey Meadows), and her anxious friend Trixie Norton (Joyce Randolph), while his friend Ed Norton (Art Carney) looks on with bug-eyed disbelief. Inevitably, Ralph's confidence shattered in the face of his bungling attempts to get rich quick, leaving Alice to pick up the pieces and put him back together again.

to live through all his efforts to assert his authority—"I'm the boss, Alice, and don't you ever forget it!"—and to resist his harebrained schemes (diet pizza parlors, wallpaper that glows in the dark to save electricity). And it is Alice who cushions his fall when each new dream turns to ashes. Like most middle-class American couples, Ralph and Alice bicker over money. Ralph is a cheapskate, not by nature but to mask his failure as a breadwinner. Alice must use her feminine wiles to persuade him to buy anything, even a television or a telephone. To protect his pride, Ralph accuses her of being a spend-thrift. Their battles have far more bite than those seen in any other sitcom of that era. In no other show do the characters so regularly lay marriage, ego, or livelihood on the line.

Why, then, did the audience like this show? For one thing, it is very funny. Ed Norton's deadpan is a perfect foil to Ralph's manic intensity. It is a delight to watch Norton take forever to shuffle the cards while Ralph does a slow burn. And Alice's alternately tolerant and spirited rejoinders complete the chemistry. In addition, there is a quality to the Kramdens' apartment that separates it in time and space from the world in which middle-class viewers live. The mass audience is more willing to confront serious questions if such issues are raised in distant times or places. Death on a western does not have the same implications as a death on *Lassie*. Divorce for Henry VIII is one thing; even a hint of it for Ozzie and Harriet would be too shocking to contemplate. Thus the depression look of the Kramdens' apartment gives the audience the spatial and temporal distance it needs to separate itself from the sources of conflict that regularly trouble Ralph and Alice. The audience can look on with a sense of its material and social superiority as Alice and Ralph go at it:

> RALPH: You want this place to be Disneyland.
> ALICE: This place is a regular Disneyland. You see out there, Ralph? The back of the Chinese restaurant, old man Grogan's long underwear on the line, the alley? That's my Fantasyland. You see that sink over there? That's my Adventureland. The stove and the icebox, Ralph, that's Frontierland. The only thing that's missing is the World of Tomorrow.
> RALPH (doing his slow burn): You want Tomorrowland, Alice? You want Tomorrowland? Well, pack your bags, because you're going to the moon! [Menaces her with his raised fist.][5]

Underneath its blue-collar veneer, *The Honeymooners* is still a middle-class family sitcom. Alice and Trixie don't have children; they have Ralph and Ed. In one episode Trixie says to Alice, "You know those men we're married to? You have to treat them like children." Reversal of social class roles makes this arrangement work without threatening the ideal of male authority. Because the middle classes have always equated the behavior of the poor with that of children—and Ralph and Ed are poor—no one is surprised by their childish antics. Trixie and Alice, both having married beneath their social status, maintain middle-class standards. At the end of almost every episode, Alice brings Ralph back into the fold after one of his schemes fails. Surrounding her in an embrace, he rewards her with his puppy dog devotion: "Baby, you're the greatest."

One episode in particular reveals the price Alice paid to preserve her man/child, marriage, and selfhood. A telegram arrives announcing, "I'm coming to visit. Love, Mom." Ralph explodes at the idea of sharing his apartment with his dreaded mother-in-law. Whenever she visits, she showers him with criticisms and insults that wound his brittle pride. After numerous jokes at Ralph's expense, along with some cutting commentary on mothers-in-law, Ralph moves in upstairs with the Nortons. There he provokes a similar fight between Ed and Trixie. But just as this upheaval threatens the domestic order, marriage and family prevail over wounded pride. Kicked out by the Nortons, Ralph returns home, only to discover that

---

5. Similarly, a show like M*A*S*H could more easily explore topical issues such as racism because it was set in Korea, not the United States, and in the 1950s, not the present, even though the issues were contemporary.

"Mom" is Mother Kramden. Alice, of course, has welcomed her with the very warmth Ralph denies Alice's mother. Alice's generosity of spirit once again reduces him to a shamefaced puppy.

This victory is so complete that it threatens to destroy Alice's relationship with Ralph. Any pretense of masculine authority has been laid to ruin. As if to soften the blow to Ralph's pride, Alice sits down to deliver her victory speech. She lowers her eyes, drops her shoulders, and speaks in tones of resignation rather than triumph. The episode ends as she reads a letter that describes mothers-in-laws as having the "hardest job in the world." Ironically, the letter is one Ralph wrote fifteen years earlier to Alice's mother. The sentiments expressed are so sappy that they virtually undercut the comedy. Like Ralph, the producers must have thought it better to eat crow than leave a residue of social criticism. Their material had been so extreme, the humor so sharp, and the mother-in-law jokes so cruel that they threatened middle-American values.

Even after its apology, the show ends with a disturbing image. Mother Kramden has gone off to "freshen up." A penitent Ralph admits his defeat, then announces he is going out for some air—in essence, to pull himself back together. But what of Alice? She is left alone in her kitchen holding nothing more than she had before—dominion over her dreary world. While Ralph can escape, if only briefly, Alice's domestic role requires her to stay with Ralph's mother. For Alice, there is no escape. When the show ends, she is no better off than before the battle began. Her slumped posture suggests that she understands all too well the hollowness of her triumph. We must believe that many women in videoland identified with Alice.

The Honeymooners, I Love Lucy, and *Our Miss Brooks* all suggest that while the male characters in the series maintain their ultimate authority, the "symbolic annihilation" of women that Gaye Tuchman spoke of is, in these comedies at least, not total. A battle between the sexes would not be funny unless the two sides were evenly matched; and setting sitcoms in the domestic sphere placed women in a better position to spar. Further, although men had an advantage through social position, rank, and authority, women like Miss Brooks, Lucy, and Alice vied on equal terms. The authority that men assumed through male hierarchy, these women radiated through the sheer strength of their comedic personalities. The producers, of course, were not closet feminists in permitting this female assertiveness to occur; they simply recognized that the female characters accounted for much of their shows' popularity. And the shows' ratings were high, we would argue, partly because they hinted at the discontent many women felt, whether or not they recognized the strength of their feelings.

If that conclusion is correct, it suggests that neither the reflective hypothesis nor the manipulative hypothesis explains how the mass media affect history. At bottom, the extreme forms of each explanation slight one of the constants in historical explanation: change over time. If the mass communications industries simply reflected public taste and never influenced it, they would become nonentities—multibillion-dollar ciphers with no causal agency. All change would be the consequence of other historical factors. On the other hand, if we assign a role to the media that's too manipulative, we find it difficult to explain any change at all. As agencies of cultural hegemony, the media could stifle any attempt to change the status quo. How was it, then, that millions of girls who watched themselves being symbolically annihilated during the fifties supplied so many converts to the women's movement of the sixties?

In other words, the mass media, although influential in modern society, are perhaps not as monolithic in outlook as they sometimes seem. A comparison to the medieval church is apt, so long as we remember that the church, too, was hardly able to impose its will universally. Even where orthodoxy reigned, schismatic movements were always springing up. Today's heretics may be feminists rather than Anabaptists, but they are nonetheless responding to growing pressures within society. From a feminist point of view, we have not automatically achieved utopia merely because television since the 1980s has regularly presented sitcoms and dramas with women as their central characters. All the same, there has been change. Lucy is not Ellen DeGeneres, any more than Rosie the Riveter was Gracie Allen. We should remember that the same mass culture industry that threatened women with symbolic annihilation also published *The Feminine Mystique*.

Additional Reading

This chapter draws on material from three different fields—women's history, social history and popular culture, and the history of television. Among broad surveys of the fifties we suggest John Patrick Diggins, *The Proud Decades* (New York, 1988); Ronald Oakley, *God's Country: America in the 1950s* (New York, 1986); and David Halberstam, *The Fifties* (New York, 1993). James Gilbert, *A Cycle of Outrage* (New York, 1986) has provided a look at juvenile delinquency that also offers insights into family life and popular culture. For overviews of the image of women in our culture, see Lois Banner, *American Beauty* (New York, 1983); Ann Douglas, *The Feminization of American Culture* (New York, 1977); and Molly Haskell, *From Reverence to Rape* (New York, 1974). Haskell's study of the image of women in movies confirms what we learn from examining other areas of popular culture. A most intriguing strategy for decoding gender signs in the mass media is Erving Goffman, *Gender Advertisements* (New York, 1976).

For readers more concerned with the feminist movement and women's history, Betty Friedan, *The Feminine Mystique* (New York, 1963) is one place to start. Her book retains the vitality that spurred its wide popularity and remains an interesting social history of the 1950s. Ruth Rosen, *The World Split Open: How the Modern Women's Movement Changed America* (New York: 2000) covers the roots of feminism in the 1950s. Kate Millett's *Sexual Politics* (New York, 1970) is another important feminist essay. More general is Lauri Umansky, *Motherhood Reconceived: Feminism and the Legacy of the 1960s* (New York, 1996). For another take on women and media we suggest Joan Jacobs Brumberg, *The Body Project: An Intimate History of American Girls* (New York, 1997). For an overview of women in twentieth-century America, see Lois Banner, *Women in Modern America* (New York, 1974). In this brief history, Banner resists the argument of two leading male historians writing on women—Carl Degler, *At Odds* (New York, 1980), and William Chafe, *The American Woman* (New York, 1972)—who both stress demographic and economic patterns to explain changing roles for women. Banner gives more credit to the political efforts women have exerted. Nancy Woloch, *Women and the American Experience* (New York, 1994) is a good survey.

The explosion of thinking and writing in women's history makes it impossible to mention more than a few valuable studies. The historian who looks at both television and Feminism is Susan Douglas, *Where the Girls Are: Growing Up Female with the Mass Media, 1995*. Carroll Smith-Rosenberg has been a leader among women historians; her article "The New Woman and New History," *Feminist Studies* 3 (1975–1976): 185–198, offers useful perspectives. Similarly, Rosalind Rosenberg, *Beyond Separate Spheres: The Roots of Modern Feminism* (New Haven, CT, 1982) and *Divided Lives: American Women in the Twentieth Century* (New York, 1992) are worthwhile. In addition to Chafe and Degler on women, work, and politics, we found useful Ruth Schwartz Cowan, *More Work for Mother: The Ironies of Household*

Technologies from Open Hearth to Microwave (New York, 1983); Susan Es-
tabrook Kennedy, *If All We Did Was to Weep at Home: A History of White
Working-Class Women in America* (Bloomington, IN, 1981); and Barbara M.
Wertheimer, *We Were There: The Story of Working Women in America* (New
York, 1977). The female side of adolescence is told in Wini Breines, *Young,
White, and Miserable: Growing Up Female in the Fifties* (New York, 1992).
Carol Warren, *Madwives: Schizophrenic Women in the 1950s* (New York, 1987)
treats a dark chapter in women's experience. Most recently, Gail Collins
America's Women: 400 Years of Dolls, Drudges, Helpmates, and Heroines (New
York, 2003) places the fifties in a much broader context.

As we mentioned, historians have not written extensively about television.
Clearly, the best place to begin is Eric Barnouw, *Tube of Plenty* (New York,
1975), which is a condensed version of his three-volume history of television
and broadcasting. His study, *The Sponsor* (New York, 1978), takes a highly
critical look at television advertising. More recently, Karal Ann Marling, *As
Seen on TV: The Visual Culture of Everyday Life in the 1950s* (Cambridge, MA,
1994) has taken up the topic of this chapter. Several collections of essays are
quite interesting: John O'Connor, ed., *American History, American Television*
(New York, 1983); Horace Newcomb, ed., *Television: The Critical View* (New
York, 1976); E. Ann Kaplan, ed., *Regarding Television* (Los Angeles, 1983);
and Alan Wells, ed., *Mass Media and Society* (Palo Alto, CA, 1972) all contain
useful historical and critical materials. Raymond Williams, *Television: Technology and Cultural Form* (New York, 1975) has some of the most interesting
insights into the evolution of television and its impact on society. David
Marc, *Demographic Vistas: Television in American Culture* (Philadelphia, PA,
1984), and Robert Sklar, *Prime Time America* (New York, 1980) are two critical essays on television.

When we turned to sociology and the fields of popular culture, we found
a rich, though uneven, literature. Gaye Tuchman, Arlene Kaplan Daniels,
and James Benet, eds., *Hearth and Home: Images of Women in the Mass Media*
(New York, 1978) is an invaluable source of statistics and ideas. The often
sharp debate over popular culture in the 1950s still makes lively reading in
the essay collection edited by Bernard Rosenberg and David White, *Mass
Culture* (New York, 1957). Herbert Gans, *High Culture and Popular Culture*
(New York, 1974) may have gotten in the final and most persuasive word for
the functional school of sociological thought. Charles Wright, *Mass Communications* (New York, 1959) provides a sociological approach to the mass media in the 1950s, while Klaus Krippendorff, *Content Analysis* (London, 1980)
covers the topic named.

In an earlier edition of this book, we invited readers to do their own
sleuthing into 1950s television programs, using the collections of the Museum of Broadcasting in New York City. Karen McHale, a student from
Michigan, did not visit the museum but did write to inform us that the figure at far left in the photograph on page 365 was not Fred Mertz of *I Love
Lucy*, as we had claimed, but Charles Boyer. We were skeptical: after all, we
knew what Mertz looked like, even if the hat in the photo blocked some of

his face. And both CBS and a photo supply house had identified the man as William Frawley. When we wrote McHale, sticking to our guns, she did us one better: she wrote to Lucy. Lucille Ball was kind enough to set us straight—it was Boyer. As we sheepishly wrote to McHale, some of the fun of doing history is catching the "experts" in errors.

Interactive Learning

The *Primary Source Investigator* supplies a variety of resources that explore the evolution of the role of women from World War II to the economic boom of the 1950s. Included are war posters asking women to go to work and join the fight at home, popular magazine advertisements geared toward keeping women feminine after they entered the workforce, and speeches given by politicians on the role of women in society. Also included are images and video clips from popular television shows in the late 1940s and early 1950s depicting many of the problems that went along with the newfound role of women in postwar American society.

CHAPTER 15
Breaking into Watergate

When the reports first came over the news wires, Ron Ziegler, press secretary to President Richard Nixon, called the break-in "a third-rate burglary attempt" and warned, "certain elements may try to stretch this beyond what it is."

Ziegler was referring to the arrest of an unusual group of burglars who on June 7, 1972, had forced their way into Democratic Party headquarters in the plush Watergate apartment complex in Washington, DC. Despite Ziegler's disclaimer, the story would not go away. In the months that followed, reporters for the *Washington Post* linked the five intruders to officials on President Nixon's White House staff. In March 1973 a jury convicted not only the five burglars but also two former presidential aides. When the aides refused to say who had ordered the burglary, trial judge John Sirica angrily threatened prison terms of twenty to forty years. The threat seemed to have its effect, for one of the officials confessed that they had been under "political pressure to plead guilty and remain silent." Suddenly, high White House officials were hiring criminal attorneys. By the summer of 1973 the "third-rate" Watergate burglary had blossomed into a full-fledged scandal that threatened to force Richard Nixon from office.

Americans got a close-up look at the events when a special Senate committee, convened by Senator Sam Ervin of North Carolina, televised hearings on what the entire country called "Watergate." Viewers saw a parade of witnesses testify that former Attorney General John Mitchell, the highest law enforcement officer in the land, had been present at meetings in which one of the convicted officials outlined proposals for the Watergate burglary and other espionage attempts. Testimony confirmed that burglar G. Gordon Liddy had reported directly to John Ehrlichman, the president's chief domestic advisor, as part of a security group called "the Plumbers," which investigated leaks to the press. The Plumbers, it was revealed, were no strangers to burglary. In 1971 they had broken into the office of a psychiatrist in search of damaging information about a former defense department official named Daniel Ellsberg.

Former White House Counsel John Dean consults a portion of his testimony as Senator Sam Ervin (left) speaks with Dean's lawyers. Dean's low-key manner, meticulous testimony, and remarkable memory impressed many listeners, but until the existence of the tapes became known, it was Dean's word against the president's.

The Ervin committee's most astonishing witness was John Dean. Dean, until recently White House legal counsel, looked like a cross between a boy scout and a choirboy. Testifying in a soft, precise monotone, he charged that the president had been actively involved in efforts to cover up White House connections to Watergate. When one of the convicted burglars threatened to tell prosecutors what he knew, Dean had met with the president and his aides on March 21, 1973, and approved hush money of up to a million dollars to buy the Watergate burglars' silence.

Of all the witnesses, only Dean claimed that Richard Nixon had participated in the cover-up. It was his word against the president's. Bearing down on Dean, Senator Howard Baker, the Republican Senate minority leader, subjected him to a vigorous cross-examination. Baker asked Dean to begin with the "central question" of the investigation: "What did the President know and when did he know it?" Dean remained unshaken in his testimony but his account was widely questioned. Then came the most stunning revelation of all.

For months, investigators had noticed that certain White House figures, especially Nixon and his White House Chief of Staff H. R. (Bob) Haldeman, showed a remarkable grasp of details when recalling past meetings at the

White House. On occasion the two had even provided direct quotes. Still, no one had thought to ask any witness whether the White House had a taping system of some kind. Ironically, it was an investigator for the Republican minority who popped the question.

Donald Sanders was a ten-year veteran of the FBI (Federal Bureau of Investigation) before he became a congressional staffer. Listening to the responses of several former presidential advisers, Sanders "felt a growing certainty that the summaries had to have been made from verbatim recordings." He further assumed that the president "would never have said anything incriminating on the record." Since Nixon's conversations would be "self-serving," Sanders concluded that the tapes "would prove the President's innocence." He had but one reservation. If there were recordings that cleared Nixon, "why hadn't the President revealed the system and used it to advantage?"

Hence Sanders approached his questioning of Alexander Butterfield, an aide to Haldeman, with some trepidation. Why, he asked the witness, might the president have taken Dean to one corner of the room and spoken to him in a whisper, as Dean testified? "I was hoping you fellows wouldn't ask me that," Butterfield replied. Reminded that the proceedings were official and that he was under oath, Butterfield then admitted that, "Well, yes, there's a recording system in the White House." When he gave televised testimony to that effect, his revelation stunned virtually everyone, from millions of television viewers to members of Congress and even the president himself, who had assumed that the secret of the tapes was safe. John Dean welcomed the news as "absolutely fantastic" and said he was "ecstatic" at the promise of vindication. If the committee could listen to those tapes, it would no longer be Dean's word against the president's. The tapes could tell all.

But obtaining the evidence did not prove easy. Archibald Cox, who in May had been appointed as special prosecutor to investigate the new Watergate disclosures, subpoenaed relevant tapes. The White House refused to provide them. When the courts backed Cox, the president fired him on Saturday, October 20, 1973. Reaction was swift and vehement. Nixon's own attorney general and his immediate subordinate resigned in protest. Reporters dubbed the firing and resignations the "Saturday Night Massacre." In Congress, twenty-two separate bills were introduced calling for possible impeachment of the president, and the House Judiciary Committee began deliberations on the matter.

Under immense pressure, President Nixon named a new special prosecutor, Leon Jaworski of Texas, and released the subpoenaed tapes to Judge Sirica. Then came yet another jolt. The new White House counsel told the court that some sections of the requested tapes were missing. One contained a crucial eighteen-and-a-half-minute "gap." When asked if the erasure might have been caused by human error, one expert replied "it would have to be an accident that was repeated at least five times." Alexander Haig, the president's new chief of staff, could only suggest lamely that "some sinister force" was at work. By April 1974, Special Prosecutor Jaworski and the

House Judiciary Committee had requested additional tapes. At first the president refused; then grudgingly agreed to supply edited transcripts. White House secretaries typed up more than 1,200 pages, which the president with a show of virtue made public.

The transcripts were damaging. They revealed a president who was often vindictive, vulgar, and small-minded. The pivotal meeting with John Dean on March 21, 1973, showed Nixon discussing in detail how his aides might, as he put it, "take care of the jackasses who are in jail." "How much money do you need?" Nixon asked Dean. "I would say these people are going to cost a million dollars," Dean estimated. "We could get that," replied the president. "You could get a million dollars. And you could get it in cash. I know where it could be gotten. I mean it's not easy, but it could be done."

In the following months, events moved swiftly. Neither the Judiciary Committee nor Jaworski was satisfied with edited transcripts, and Jaworski appealed directly to the Supreme Court to obtain the originals. In July, the court voted unanimously to order the president to produce the tapes. The same month, the Judiciary Committee passed three articles of impeachment, accusing the president of obstructing justice, misusing his presidential powers, and refusing to comply with the committee's requests for evidence. In August, even the president's own lawyers insisted that he release transcripts of three conversations with Chief of Staff Haldeman recorded on June 23, 1972, only a few days after the Watergate burglary.

This tape soon became known as the smoking gun, for it demonstrated beyond all doubt that the president had been involved in a cover-up from the beginning. Haldeman had warned Nixon that the "FBI is not under control" and that agents had "been able to trace the money" found on the burglars. The two planned to frustrate the investigation by playing the CIA (Central Intelligence Agency) off against the FBI. "The FBI agents who are working the case, at this point, feel that's what it is. This is CIA," explained Haldeman. Nixon hoped that because four of the burglars were Cubans, the FBI would assume the break-in was a "Cuban thing" carried out as a part of a covert CIA operation. He suggested that the FBI be told, "'[D]on't go any further into this case,' period." With the release of these transcripts, all but the president's staunchest congressional supporters deserted him. Facing certain impeachment, Richard Nixon announced his resignation on August 9, 1974.

PRESIDENTIAL TAPES

In the end, the president had been done in by reel upon reel of audiotape recordings he himself had ordered to be made. For more than two decades, however, the National Archives allowed access to only sixty hours that had been available to the special prosecutor. In 1974 Congress legislated that all the Nixon presidential recordings be released "at the earliest possible date," but Nixon was equally determined the tapes would remain unheard. Until his death in 1994 he worked energetically to rehabilitate his reputation, assuming the role of elder statesman, advising presidents, writing articles and books about foreign policy—and fighting against the release of the tapes in court.

Yet for historians the tapes promised a remarkable portrait of the Nixon presidency, providing details of crucial meetings that no recollection or memoir could match. They offered, in effect, the audio equivalent of the camera's "mirror with a memory": a snapshot of the words, inflections, laughs, stutters, and even coughs, exactly as they had been uttered.

Although such documentation was unparalleled, it was not without precedent. A week after his election in 1968 Nixon toured the White House with President Lyndon Johnson. Johnson proudly showed his successor the elaborate secret taping system he had in place. Such a system, he advised Nixon, would be vital for writing memoirs and keeping on top of events. "You've got to know what's happening, and the only way you can do that is to have a record of it," he explained. Nixon was less than impressed. Upon entering the White House he ordered Johnson's system torn out. Two years into his presidency, however, for reasons that remain unclear, he had a change of heart and ordered a new system installed.

No doubt Nixon said little about the tapes because he understood that bugging the conversations of his staff, diplomats, and other visitors was difficult to justify. Indeed, once Alexander Butterfield acknowledged the existence of the tapes, many in the press and Congress condemned the practice. Nixon and his defenders responded that he was hardly the first president to make secret recordings. In fact, presidents had been doing so on and off for thirty years. In 1940 Franklin Roosevelt had a microphone hidden in a desk lamp so that he could secretly record his press conferences. The machine also caught Roosevelt promoting a whispering campaign to discredit his presidential opponent, Wendell Willkie. Willkie, it seems, had a mistress and Roosevelt wanted the nation to know about her without being identified as a source of the rumor. That episode ended FDR's flirtation with bugging. Harry Truman was so offended at the idea of secret recordings that he had the equipment dismantled. President Dwight Eisenhower shared Truman's misgivings, but he mistrusted Washington politicians enough that he had a crude Dictaphone device installed. Eisenhower explained, "I want to have myself protected so they can't later report that I had said something else." All the same, he used the system little.

John F. Kennedy was the first president to make extensive audio recordings, though not until eighteen months after he assumed office. Like Nixon, Kennedy never revealed his motives for doing so. He had certainly showed no compunction about authorizing secret FBI bugging and wiretaps, which he agreed to more than once during his term. All the same, the system Kennedy installed was primitive. Secret Service agents placed microphones in light fixtures in the Cabinet Room and in the president's Oval Office desk. When Kennedy wanted the system turned on, he flipped several switches. He could also signal his secretary to start a separate machine for recording phone calls. Thus he had to make a conscious decision that he wanted a conversation recorded.

After Kennedy's assassination several people made an effort to transcribe the tapes he had made, and Robert Kennedy consulted them in writing his memoir of the Cuban missile crisis of 1962. Otherwise, until the Watergate investigation, they remained a well-kept secret. When Nixon suggested that other presidents had similarly recorded conversations, Senator Ted Kennedy confirmed the existence of some 248 hours of taped meetings and 12 hours of telephone conversations from the Kennedy White House. The tapes primarily recorded meetings of ExCom, the high-level group of officials Kennedy convened during the Cuban missile crisis.

Efforts to decipher the tapes were frustrated, not by Kennedy family obstruction, but by poor sound quality. Two historians, Ernest May and Philip Zelikow, later attempted to transcribe them. They reported that "the large majority of the tapes crackle, rumble, and hiss. Conversation is as hard to make out as on a factory floor or in a football stadium." But once May and Zelikow cleared away the static and verbal debris, the tapes told a riveting story. They showed the president and his advisers striving to respond, under intense pressure, to the secret placement of Soviet offensive nuclear missiles at launching sites in Cuba only ninety miles from American shores. With the world as close to all-out nuclear war as it has ever come, the tapes recorded what May and Zelikow suggested "may be the most harrowing episode in all of human experience."

Lyndon Johnson's tapes possessed their own distinct flavor. Unlike earlier presidents, Johnson began recording as soon as he moved into the Oval Office. In fact, as Senate majority leader, he had secretaries and aides eavesdrop on telephone conversations and take shorthand notes. As president, Johnson replaced Kennedy's system with better microphones installed in the Cabinet Room and Oval Office, in the kneeholes of his secretaries' desks, in the Situation Room, at the LBJ Ranch in Johnson City, Texas, and even in his White House bedroom. Johnson talked incessantly on the phone, whether in his office, his bedroom, or his bathroom. If he wanted a conversation recorded in his office, he twirled his finger in the air to let his secretary know that she should turn on the system.

Johnson did leave a clue about why he had made his recordings. In mid-January 1973 the former president called his long-time assistant, Mildred Steagall, to his office. Steagall could tell from his blotchy skin and gaunt appearance that Johnson was not well. Indeed, he informed her that he did not have long to live and, hence, wanted her assurance that the tapes, in her custody, would not be opened for at least fifty years. In fact, he told her, as far as he was concerned most of them should remain secret forever. Johnson had clearly wanted the tapes for his private use alone. A week later, the former president was dead from a massive heart attack. Steagall then transferred the sealed boxes to the Johnson Library under the conditions Johnson had set: the library director and chief archivist of the United States could not listen to them until 2023. At that point the two would determine whether to reseal them or make them public. Six months later Nixon exposed the existence of the Johnson tapes as part of his own defense, but the significance of that announcement was lost in the swirl of Watergate revelations.

Lyndon Johnson talked incessantly on the phone. When sculptor Jimilu Mason went to have Johnson pose, he tired of the constant phone interruptions. In that spirit Mason finally decided to cast Johnson dashing around with a phone to his ear. That anecdote may help explain why the large majority of Johnson tapes preserve telephone conversations, while most of the tapes from John Kennedy and Richard Nixon are of face-to-face meetings.

Given these precedents, Nixon could legitimately claim that in bugging his offices he was merely following a well-established practice. Yet, as in many of his actions, Nixon did not simply mirror his predecessors. Once he decided to record private conversations, he went at it with a vengeance. Unlike earlier systems, his was voice-activated, starting up whenever someone spoke. Why he went to such lengths is not clear, though Alexander Butterfield commented to investigators that "the President is very history-oriented and history-conscious about the role he is going to play, and is not at all subtle about it, or about admitting it." Nixon reinforced this notion in an offhand remark recorded on the tapes themselves, when Chief of Staff Bob Haldeman commented that the Secret Service had told him the recording system was "extremely good. I haven't listened to the tapes." "They're for future purposes," the president assured him. In his memoirs Nixon offered a hint at what "future purposes" might be served by the tapes. They "were my best insurance against the unforeseeable future. I was prepared to believe that others, even people close to me, would turn against me just as Dean had done, and in that case the tapes would give me some protection."

While Nixon argued that the tapes were his private property, historian Stanley Kutler believed with equal fervor that the public had a right to know their contents. In 1991 Kutler and the group Public Citizen sued Nixon (and later the Nixon estate) and the National Archives to release the tapes. About the same time, a public uproar erupted following the release of Oliver Stone's film *JFK.* The film suggested that the CIA and other government officials had been involved in Kennedy's assassination. To satisfy public interest, Congress passed the John F. Kennedy Assassination Records Act. All government archives were required to release any documents bearing on the assassination.

The Johnson Library faced a quandary. On the one hand, Johnson had ordered his tapes kept under lock and key. On the other hand, the library director and LBJ's widow, Lady Bird Johnson, had together already determined that they could overrule Johnson's order sealing the tapes. Further, they worried that the tapes might deteriorate if left unattended. Finally, they wanted to avoid the kind of controversy that arose when Kutler sued the Nixon estate. Showing great regard for history and for the public's right to know about its government, they ordered the opening not only of the assassination records, but of the entire collection. And finally, in 1996, some two years after Nixon had died, Kutler reached an agreement in which the National Archives promised to release all 3,700 hours of Nixon's tapes within four years. The first batch included 201 hours of conversations that related specifically to Watergate, including some dealing with other illegal operations of Nixon's secret security unit, the Plumbers. Kutler published transcripts of excerpts from these tapes. At almost the same time, Ernest May and Philip Zelikow published transcripts of the Kennedy tapes, and Michael Beschloss, those of the early Johnson presidency.

What, then, would the public learn from this sudden exposure of presidential secrets? The historians who had worked with the tapes believed they were like no evidence available before. "The material in this book offers the most complete set of data available on how a modern government actually made a set of important decisions," concluded May and Zelikow about the Kennedy tapes. Michael Beschloss observed that "LBJ was famous for concealing himself"; hence, the Johnson tapes were important because they "allow us to listen in on an American presidency from beginning to end." Compared with other records of the same events, the tapes have a "towering advantage," Beschloss observed. "Meaning is conveyed through not just language but tone, intensity, pronunciation, pauses, and other aspects of sound." And as Stanley Kutler commented, "The tapes of Richard Nixon's conversations with political intimates compel our attention as do few other presidential documents."

Popular reaction to the presidential tapes was even more enthusiastic. They became the subjects of newspaper stories, magazine articles, and television news programs. As historian Bruce Shulman wryly noted, "Seldom do historical documents receive such lavish attention from the national media." Most commentators were thrilled that the tapes allowed Americans the rare opportunity to become "flies on the wall" inside the Oval Office. On the face of it, the tapes seemed less prone to the kinds of selective bias operative in the creation of photographic images or written accounts. Set the tape reels going, and they would record any sound within reach of the microphone. Observers in the media seemed persuaded that the public could now have history pure and simple without the interfering hand of the historian. The tapes *would* tell all.

THE TAPES AS EVIDENCE

Readers who have followed us this far will hardly be surprised to discover that historians have been more skeptical—even those who transcribed the tapes. Michael Beschloss, for example, warned his readers that "a President who knows he is taping a conversation can manipulate or entrap an interlocutor who does not. He can also try to present the best face for history."

Then there is the problem of setting down on paper what the tapes actually contain. Only with repeated listening and extensive research can the conversations be transcribed with any degree of accuracy. Kutler, for example, traveled to the National Archives in Washington to listen to the original Nixon recordings. (They could not be removed from the archives.) Because no transcriptions were available for most tapes, he had professional court reporters and transcribers prepare a first draft. Then he and his research assistant listened to the tapes, trying to check for accuracy and fill in the many "unintelligibles" marked in the transcripts. "The process of deciphering the tapes is endless," Kutler admitted. "Different ears pick up a once unintelligible comment, or correct a previous understanding." Kutler also eliminated "what I believe insignificant, trivial, or repetitious"—comments like "right," "yeah," and "okay." Government archivists removed other materials that they considered sensitive for reasons of either personal privacy or national security. So from the beginning we must recognize that the transcripts as presented include omissions, deletions, and "unintelligibles."

Beschloss offered one striking example of how audiotapes can be misunderstood. Background noise, heavy accents, and scratchy voices all distorted the content of the more primitive Dictaphone recordings. On one occasion a White House secretary transcribed Lyndon Johnson as complaining in his Texas twang that he had a "pack them bastards" waiting to meet him. Only after Beschloss listened repeatedly and checked Johnson's daily diary did he realize that Johnson actually said he had the "Pakistan ambassador" waiting.

Such pitfalls aside, let us assume that the Nixon tapes are transcribed accurately enough that we can use them with reasonable confidence. What story do the tapes have to tell? Here is the transcription of the very first excerpt in Stanley Kutler's book *Abuse of Power* (1997). The conversation takes place almost a year before the Watergate break-in.

JUNE 17, 1971: THE PRESIDENT, HALDEMAN, EHRLICHMAN, AND
 KISSINGER, 5:17–6:13 P.M., OVAL OFFICE
HALDEMAN: You maybe can blackmail Johnson on this stuff.
PRESIDENT NIXON: What?
HALDEMAN: You can blackmail Johnson on this stuff and it might be worth
 doing. . . . The bombing halt stuff is all in that same file or in some of
 the same hands. . . .

Richard Nixon sits on his desk while conferring with his key aides (*from left to right*): National Security Adviser Henry Kissinger, General Counsel John Erlichman, and White House Chief of Staff Bob Haldeman. Few people ever saw the President in the Oval Office without prior approval from Haldeman.

PRESIDENT NIXON: Do we have it? I've asked for it. You said you didn't
    have it.
HALDEMAN: We can't find it.
KISSINGER: We have nothing here, Mr. President.
PRESIDENT NIXON: Well, damn it, I asked for that because I need it.
KISSINGER: But Bob and I have been trying to put the damn thing together.
HALDEMAN: We have a basic history in constructing our own, but there is a
    file on it.
PRESIDENT NIXON: Where?
HALDEMAN: Huston swears to God there's a file on it and it's at Brookings.
PRESIDENT NIXON: Bob? Bob? Now do you remember Huston's plan?
    Implement it.
KISSINGER: Now Brookings has no right to have classified documents.
PRESIDENT NIXON: I want it implemented. . . . Goddamn it, get in and get
    those files. Blow the safe and get it.
HALDEMAN: They may very well have cleaned them by now, but this thing,
    you need to—
KISSINGER: I wouldn't be surprised if Brookings had the files.
HALDEMAN: My point is Johnson knows that those files are around. He
    doesn't know for sure that we don't have them around.

Taken by itself, this conversation is rather mysterious and more than a little unnerving. What is going on here? Perhaps we should begin with what we
know for sure. The four participants are easy to identify, for they are the major figures in the administration: in addition to Richard Nixon, there are
Chief of Staff Bob Haldeman, General Counsel John Ehrlichman, and National Security Adviser Henry Kissinger. As for the subjects of the conversation, "Johnson" was no doubt former President Lyndon Johnson. The
reference to a "bombing halt" gives us a clue that "the stuff" they have on
Johnson has something to do with the war in Vietnam. Johnson used the halts
in American bombing raids to encourage the North Vietnamese to negotiate.
But why does Nixon need "the stuff," and why is he trying to blackmail Johnson? Isn't blackmail illegal? There is no mention of the Watergate complex
or Democratic headquarters, but there seems clearly to be some sort of burglary involved. "Blow the safe," suggests the president.
    Whose safe? "Brookings" is easy enough to identify as the Brookings In-
stitution, a Washington policy center not especially sympathetic to Nixon or
his administration. But who is Huston? What was his plan? Has the president really just given an order for an illegal break-in and safe-robbery? Was
the order carried out? Even though we have the raw evidence of history before us, we are left with more questions than answers.
    In fact, however, Stanley Kutler does not reprint the transcript in quite
the form we have presented above. As we have come to appreciate, historians are not simply messengers bringing us materials from the past. Even
when selecting and printing documentary evidence, they usually have a case
to make, based on their research. Kutler's research into Watergate has per-

suaded him that he knows the answer to Senator Howard Baker's question: What did the President know and when did he know it? "The President knew everything about Watergate and the imposition of a cover-up, from the beginning," Kutler informed his readers. As a consequence, his annotations help to make the evidence clearer:

> JUNE 17, 1971: THE PRESIDENT, HALDEMAN, EHRLICHMAN, AND KISSINGER, 5:17–6:13 P.M., OVAL OFFICE
>
> A few days after the publication of the Pentagon Papers, Nixon discusses how to exploit the situation for his advantage. He is interested in embarrassing the Johnson Administration on the bombing halt, for example. Here, he wants a break-in at the Brookings Institution, a centrist Washington think tank, to find classified documents that might be in the Brookings safe.
>
> HALDEMAN: You maybe can blackmail [Lyndon B.] Johnson on this stuff [Pentagon Papers].
>
> PRESIDENT NIXON: What?
>
> HALDEMAN: You can blackmail Johnson on this stuff and it might be worth doing. The bombing halt stuff is all in that same file or in some of the same hands. . . .
>
> PRESIDENT NIXON: Do we have it? I've asked for it. You said you didn't have it.
>
> HALDEMAN: We can't find it.
>
> KISSINGER: We have nothing here, Mr. President.
>
> PRESIDENT NIXON: Well, damn it, I asked for that because I need it.
>
> KISSINGER: But Bob and I have been trying to put the damn thing together.
>
> HALDEMAN: We have a basic history in constructing our own, but there is a file on it.
>
> PRESIDENT NIXON: Where?
>
> HALDEMAN: [Presidential aide Tom Charles] Huston swears to God there's a file on it and it's at Brookings.
>
> PRESIDENT NIXON: Bob? Bob? Now do you remember Huston's plan [for White House-sponsored break-ins as part of domestic counterintelligence operations]? Implement it.
>
> HALDEMAN: Now Brookings has no right to have classified documents.
>
> PRESIDENT NIXON: I want it implemented Goddamn it, get in and get those files. Blow the safe and get it.
>
> HALDEMAN: They may very well have cleaned them by now, but this thing, you need to—
>
> KISSINGER: I wouldn't be surprised if Brookings had the files.
>
> HALDEMAN: My point is Johnson knows that those files are around. He doesn't know for sure that we don't have them around.

The situation now is a little clearer. Nixon was angered by the publication of the Pentagon Papers, a classified 7,000-page report that analyzed the conduct of the Vietnam War under Presidents Kennedy and Johnson. The Pentagon Papers proved especially embarrassing for Johnson, because they provided evidence that LBJ had deceived the American public when he obtained permission from Congress to escalate the war. Nixon did not mind seeing Johnson embarrassed, but he worried that if the Pentagon Papers were allowed to be published, other disgruntled officials might come forward exposing other government secrets. Hence the administration went to court to block the *New York Times* from publishing. That effort failed. At the same time, Nixon and his advisers saw a possibility that they could use similar classified files at the Brookings Institution to damage Johnson and, through Huston's domestic counterintelligence operations, other enemies as well.

Why does Kutler begin his book with this transcript about Brookings? This conversation suggests that Richard Nixon clearly had few compunctions about breaking the law to advance his own political agenda. Even if he did not specifically order the Watergate break-in in June 1972, he had previously approved and encouraged illegal operations like this break-in at Brookings—and those who worked for him knew it. But there is an irony here. Even though we can come to these conclusions by reading the tape transcripts, historians have been able to piece together not only the story of Watergate but also the Brookings episode by using other sources. Here is the way Stanley Kutler reconstructed Brookings in 1990, before he had access to the tapes:

> One of the more bizarre by-products of the Pentagon Papers affair was a plan either to raid or to firebomb the Brookings Institution and to pilfer papers there belonging to Leslie Gelb and Morton Halperin, former National Security Council aides. These papers allegedly represented a Pentagon Papers analogue for the Nixon years. The Brookings plan has been described by three people: Ehrlichman, Dean, and Caulfield. All agreed that Charles Colson pushed the idea, but all asserted that Nixon inspired it. . . . Dean claimed that Nixon had demanded he obtain the Gelb-Halperin papers, and he also learned from Egil Krogh that White House people thought Dean had "some little old lady" in him because of his reluctance to go along with the plan. Dean claimed credit for thwarting the plan, but his rival John Ehrlichman insisted that he had blocked it. Only later, Ehrlichman wrote, did he learn that Nixon knew about the plan. . . . Meanwhile, John Dean was not so passive. He gave Krogh copies of the Brookings tax returns and proposed to "turn the spigot off" by revoking some of the institution's government contracts.

This account is more informed and informative than the versions from the tapes. We learn, for example, that the mysterious files belong to Leslie Gelb and Morton Halperin, a former Kissinger assistant. New players appear—Charles Colson, Egil Krogh, and John Dean—all central Watergate figures. And two new crimes have been added. While Nixon had ordered his aides "to blow the safe," someone else apparently introduced a plan to destroy the documents by firebombing Brookings Institution. So to plotting blackmail we can add a charge of plotting arson. As if that were not enough, John Dean, the president's White House counsel and a supposed "little old lady," illegally passed along tax information to Egil Krogh with the idea of undermining the Brookings Institution. Finally, we have reasonable evidence that, beyond Dean's abuse of the tax records, the plot against Brookings was never carried out. John Ehrlichman claims to have blocked it.

The historian's version does something the tapes alone could not do—it places the conversation in context. As Kutler's footnotes reveal, he consulted a host of other sources—in this instance John Ehrlichman's memoirs, records of the Select Senate Committee staff that investigated Watergate, and the papers of John Dean. From this perspective, the tapes seem hardly the crucial source that will tell all but rather a sometimes vivid, sometimes cryptic record that cannot be fully understood without a great deal of additional digging. Far from being the key to the story, the tapes seem to be the proverbial icing on a cake that journalists and historians baked years earlier.

THE TAPES AS A WINDOW INTO RICHARD NIXON

The reality that the tapes are only peripheral to the story would seem to dampen our enthusiasm about them. If the recordings tell us only part of the truth and much that they contain merely confirms what we already know, why get so excited? What is left for the tapes to tell? Kutler seemed to sense that problem when he published the transcripts. On the one hand, he had to admit that tapes "are far from the whole of the record of the Nixon presidency." The National Archives, the private and public papers of Nixon and his aides, the records of the news media—all have materials essential to understanding the subject. On the other hand, Kutler argued that the tapes still had great significance; they "are the bedrock in laying bare the mind and thoughts of Richard Nixon. They constitute a record of unassailable historical documentation he cannot escape." In other words, even if the outlines of Watergate are clear enough without the tapes, the transcripts remain invaluable in helping us understand Richard Nixon the man. The possibility is tantalizing, for Nixon has long been an enigma to historians.

In part this is because he was essentially a loner. Uncomfortable around most people, Richard Nixon had few close friends. In times of crisis he turned inward, often spending long solitary hours brooding and planning his own course of action. Yet this loner chose to go into politics, the most public of careers and one that requires a facility for dealing with people. The Nixon who distrusted the media devoted much of his career to convincing them that he should be portrayed as a tough, competent, resilient, and honest politician. In a private memorandum at the end of 1970, the president sat one night in the Lincoln Room of the White House, compiling a list of traits he wished to project in terms of "visible presidential leadership":

> compassionate, humane, fatherly, warmth, confidence in future, optimistic, upbeat, candor, honesty, openness, trustworthy, boldness, fights for what he believes, vitality, youth, enjoyment, zest, vision, dignity, respect, a man people

Richard Nixon spent long hours alone in his office pondering problems or planning political strategy. This photo of the Oval Office in 1971 shows Nixon in a characteristic contemplative pose.

can be proud of, hard work, dedication, openmindedness, listens to opposing views, unifier, fairness to opponents, end bombast, hatred, division, moral leader, nation's conscience, intelligent, reasonable, serenity, calm, brevity, avoid familiarity, excitement, novelty, glamour, strength, spiritual, concern for the problems of the poor, youth, minorities, and average persons.

This public persona—and the earnest, often awkward way Richard Nixon went about establishing it—was projected most strikingly early in Nixon's career, when his position as Eisenhower's vice presidential candidate in the election of 1952 was threatened by a scandal over a secret campaign slush fund that came to light. Facing calls to step down from the ticket, Nixon gave what became known as the "Checkers speech," in which he used his wife, the family's modest finances, their two little girls, and even their cocker spaniel, Checkers (a gift from supporters), to win public sympathy. "And you know the kids, like all kids, love the dog," Nixon told the 55 million people watching and listening, "and I just want to say this right now, that regardless of what they say about it, we're going to keep it." Critics thought the presentation both saccharine and hypocritical (one condemned the speech, hyperbolically, as "the most demeaning experience my country has ever had to bear"). Even Nixon's wife, Pat, asked plaintively why her husband had "to

In 1952 a young Richard Nixon appeared on a television studio set to give what would become known as his "Checkers speech." His wife, Patricia Ryan Nixon, looked on with a supportive smile. In private Pat Nixon had doubts about Nixon's exposure of his family's financial circumstances to arouse public sympathy. The speech, however, won widespread public support for the beleaguered Nixon and secured his position on the 1952 Republican presidential ticket. (Corbis/Bettmann/UPI)

tell people how little we have and how much we owe?" The general public, however, swamped national Republican headquarters with messages supporting Nixon. He remained on the ticket.

In 1962, two years after his loss to John Kennedy in the 1960 presidential election, Nixon lost a race to become governor of California. At his concession speech he showed a different face: bitter, sarcastic, and self-pitying. "You won't have Nixon to kick around anymore," the dejected candidate told reporters. "Just think how much you're going to be missing." The press quickly wrote his political obituary. Six years later a "new Nixon" arose from the ashes of political defeat to become president. The respected liberal commentator Walter Lippmann applauded this version of Nixon as "a maturer, mellower man who is no longer clawing his way to the top. . . . who has outlived and outgrown the ruthless politics of his early days." By 1972 Nixon had become a much-admired statesman who traveled triumphantly to Beijing and Moscow in a dramatic effort to ease cold war tensions with Communist China and the Soviet Union. Despite his successes, Nixon remained angry with anti–Vietnam war protestors, student radicals, and a list of personal political "enemies" both real and imagined. After winning a landslide reelection in 1972, a bitter Nixon plotted to settle old grudges by using, as he put it, "the available federal machinery to screw our political enemies."

Which of these images, then, was the real Richard Nixon? The humble man of modest means? The whiner who quit politics in 1962? The "new," maturer candidate of 1968? The world leader who redirected the cold war? The vindictive winner of the 1972 election? Precisely because there seems to be such a gap between the public and private Nixon, the tapes offer a chance to tell all in the sense of providing a window into the "real" Nixon—"uninhibited," in Kutler's words, "by the restraints of public appearance, [capturing] him in moments alone with trusted confidants."

This view of the real Nixon, of course, was one reason the earliest tape transcripts, released in April 1974, had such shock value; the private Nixon often departed radically from his public persona. Kutler's new transcripts reinforce that disjunction between the public and private image. Here, for example, is a meeting between Nixon and Haldeman:

SEPTEMBER 13, 1971: THE PRESIDENT AND HALDEMAN, 4:36–5:05 P.M.,
   OVAL OFFICE
PRESIDENT NIXON: . . . But [the Reverend] Billy Graham tells an
   astonishing thing. The IRS is battering the shit out of him. Some
   sonofabitch came to him and gave him a three-hour grilling about how
   much he, you know, how much his contribution is worth and he told it
   to [John] Connally [the former governor of Texas and a Nixon
   supporter]. Well, Connally took the name of the guy. I just got to get
   that nailed down to Connally when you get back. He didn't know it.
   Now here's the point. Bob, please get me the names of the Jews, you
   know, the big Jewish contributors of the Democrats. . . . All right. Could
   we please investigate some of the cocksuckers? That's all.
      Now look at here. Here IRS is going after Billy Graham tooth and
   nail. Are they going after Eugene Carson Blake [President of the
   National Council of Churches, a liberal group]? I asked—you know,
   what I mean is, God damn. I don't believe—I just know whether we are
   being as rough about it. That's all. . . .
HALDEMAN: Yeah.
PRESIDENT NIXON: You call [Attorney General John] Mitchell. Mitchell
   could get—stick his nose in the thing. . . . Say, now, God damn it, are we
   going after some of these Democrats or not? They've gone after
   Abplanalp. They've gone after Rebozo. They've gone after John Wayne.
   They're going after, you know, every one of our people. God damn it,
   they were after me. . . .

The comparison between the Richard Nixon in this conversation and the man who gave the Checkers speech is astonishing. Where the younger, public Nixon appeared modest and upright, this private Nixon is angry, vulgar, and vindictive. He is clearly persuaded that enemies in the Internal Revenue Service are out to attack supporters such as Robert Abplanalp and Bebe Rebozo, businessmen and social companions with whom Nixon liked to relax, and John Wayne, the actor, also noted for his conservative politics. Like Nixon himself, all three had faced Internal Revenue Service audits. The focus of this tape, however, is the Reverend Billy Graham, one of the most widely admired religious figures in America. Having developed a huge following as an evangelical preacher, Graham became a spiritual adviser to many presidents. He had been part of Nixon's political circle since the 1950s.

Given the volume of donations to Graham's ministry and the range of his related business dealings, the IRS may well have had some cause to examine Nixon's tax returns. Nixon, however, saw the audit not as a reasonable inquiry, but as an indirect effort to discredit the White House and its allies. Rather than make inquiries about the audit through proper channels, Nixon preferred to bring the wrath of the White House down on the unlucky agent and to suggest that, in return, the IRS be used illegally to harass political enemies. Billy Graham, for his part, later deplored "the moral tone implied in these papers" and regretted that Nixon had "used" him to promote his own moral image.

The tactic of using the tapes as a window onto a hidden—and therefore somehow more real—Nixon does carry risks. In replaying private conversations, we experience an almost unavoidable illicit pleasure of being privy to information not meant for our ears, and being privy, to magnify that information precisely because it is hidden and forbidden and therefore more fascinating. Yet it would be misleading simply to replace the "public" with the "private" Nixon or to assume that the value of these audiotapes lies solely in the candor with which they catch their subjects. Candor is a tricky concept, and historians need to be just as cautious in assessing the tapes as they are in assessing any evidence.

One way to impose a measure of prudence is to search for patterns in the tapes rather than picking out isolated events. Nixon's reference in the previous transcript to "big Jewish contributors" as "cocksuckers" is truly shocking, but it might be put down as an aberration—except that Kutler's transcripts include more than fifteen similar slighting or stereotypical allusions. None are quite so extreme, but the president makes offhand comments about "Jews with the Mafia," worries that a loyal aide investigating Nixon's political enemies might "be soft on the Jews" because he is Jewish himself, and expresses disbelief that someone Jewish might be considered to run the FBI. ("Christ, put a Jew in there?") Equally striking, it is Nixon himself who always injects the reference into the conversation. He is not reacting to the comments of others. The pattern here reinforces the impression that Nixon's anti-Semitism was a part of his personality.

Similarly, transcripts covering the weeks after Nixon's suggestion of undertaking a Brookings burglary reveal a highly significant pattern. Nixon's tirade about blowing the safe is no momentary rage. Two weeks later, on

June 30, the president again is telling Haldeman, "I want Brookings, I want them just to break in and take it out. Do you understand?" The following day, July 1, the demands continue: "Did they get the Brookings Institute raided last night? No. Get it done. I want it done. I want the Brookings Institute's safe *cleaned out* in a way that makes somebody else [responsible?]." Later in the day, at yet another meeting, the president complains to Ehrlichman that Henry Kissinger isn't pushing hard enough on the Brookings documents: "Henry welshed on these, you know. He's a little afraid. . . . John, you mop up. You're in charge of that. And I want it done today and I'd like a report." And in case his aides have somehow missed the point, again on July 2: "Also, I really meant it when—I want to go in and crack that safe. Walk in and get it. I want Brookings cut. They've got to do it."

More than Kutler's succinct summary, the tapes' repetitive, insistent, unremitting demands make clear how much Watergate was Nixon's own undoing. Indeed, the transcripts are full of laments by the president that he can find no one as ruthless as he. Kissinger, we have seen, is "a little afraid." Attorney General John Mitchell, known to the public as a stern-faced man, is not tough enough. "John is just too damn good a lawyer, you know," comments Nixon. "It just repels him to do these horrible things, but they've got to be done." Should John Ehrlichman and John Dean be anointed as hatchet men? Alas, they're good lawyers too, "always saying, well, we've got to win the court case [over the Pentagon Papers] through the court. . . . I don't want that fellow Ellsberg [who leaked the Pentagon Papers] to be brought up until after the election. I mean, just let—convict the son of a bitch *in the press. That's the way it's done*. . . . Nobody ever reads any of this in my biographies. Go back and read the chapter on the Hiss case [in which Nixon accused Alger Hiss in 1948 of being a communist spy] in *Six Crises* and you'll see how it was done. It wasn't done waiting for the Goddamn courts or the attorney general or the FBI."

Conversations such as this one are convincing instances of candor: Nixon speaking unguardedly, off the record, venting strong feelings. Although he knew—at one level—he was being recorded in the Oval Office, it was impossible to carry on the press of business, day in, day out, with half an ear constantly cocked for the long view of history. Furthermore, Nixon never suspected he might one day lose control of the tapes. Still, there were times when an awareness of the recorder must have put the president on his guard. Consider the following exchange in the midst of the Watergate crisis:

MAY 16, 1973: THE PRESIDENT AND KISSINGER, 9:07–9:25 A.M., OVAL OFFICE

PRESIDENT NIXON: Yeah. Christ, there's something new every day, you know. Now it's the CIA wanting to do this shit.

KISSINGER: And then they—Haig and I went on the offensive yesterday on these—

PRESIDENT NIXON: Which you should.

KISSINGER:—National Security wiretaps.

PRESIDENT NIXON: Those are totally legal.

KISSINGER: We said they were legal. We had the duty to do it. What is wrong with the National Security?

PRESIDENT NIXON: Well, the point is—I think—the next thing you can say we had—I mean, the leaks the least as it was, seriously impaired some of our negotiations and that they be allowed to continue, the great initiatives might not have come up.

KISSINGER: That's what I am saying.

[Withdrawn item. National security.]

PRESIDENT NIXON: Let's not worry about it. We didn't—the idea that it was ever used. Some jackass Senator said that perhaps—what he was saying is that it was used politically.

KISSINGER: Never.

PRESIDENT NIXON: Those taps never saw the light of—I never saw them, you know. I didn't even know what the Christ was in those damn things. The only one I ever saw was the first one on [journalist Henry] Brandon and it was certainly much of nothing. Do you know what I mean? Hell, they didn't have anything on Brandon.

KISSINGER: They have none. But Brandon wasn't ours anyway. It was J. Edgar Hoover's.

PRESIDENT NIXON: I know. Well, nevertheless, he did a lot of taps.

[Withdrawn item. National security.]

PRESIDENT NIXON: They were legal, but Henry, it's a rough time, I know. A rough time for all of us around here. . . .

Several potentially key elements have been removed by archivists for reasons of national security. As a result, the information about whose phones were being tapped and why remains tantalizingly vague. But a more puzzling problem remains. The tone of this conversation is more stilted than the previous conversation with Haldeman. Why are Nixon and Kissinger going to such lengths to justify to each other their reasons for ordering phone taps on reporters? They seem, almost, to be pleading their case to some unknown audience. Nixon assures Kissinger that the taps were legal, and both agree they were used for national security reasons. Leaks, Nixon claims, had "seriously impaired some of our negotiations," and had they not sought to close the leaks, "the great initiatives might not have come up." Notice also the attempt to shift some responsibility to J. Edgar Hoover and his FBI.

We must suspect the possibility that Nixon (and perhaps Kissinger as well) was speaking to the tapes. If so, the two men held this conversation less to persuade each other than to influence the way history would judge their actions. In writing his memoirs or answering hostile critics, Nixon could cite this conversation to demonstrate that he had always acted from within the law and with the nation's security interests in mind. Historians should thus treat this piece of evidence with caution.

On the other hand, no matter what Nixon intended, the conversation provides useful clues about his behavior. Nixon regularly blamed others for those actions that history was likely to condemn. In this instance, he asserts that he was forced to tap phones because other people leaked sensitive information. Nor was he alone in doing such bugging, he insists; J. Edgar Hoover had also tapped reporters' phones. Rather than conclude that Nixon was acting out of principle or to protect national security, historians may deduce from the perceived *lack* of candor that Nixon is rationalizing his breaking of the law.

So the tapes are not valuable merely because they show unguarded moments. Candor is not that simple. In fact, even if we assume that *all* the people being recorded are oblivious of the tape recorder, it remains unavoidable that whenever two or more people talk with one another, they present different public selves, depending on who is in the room. It is too simple to contrast a public versus a private Nixon. Almost unconsciously Nixon will behave one way when Henry Kissinger is with him and another way when only Bob Haldeman is in the room. In this regard Nixon is no different from any of us. We fine-tune the presentation of our outward selves depending on whether we are in the company of a mentor, a parent, a pastor, or a lover.

But the dynamic of Watergate, as it unfolded, ensured that conversations recorded by the tapes became increasingly strained and less candid. As more lower-level officials began cooperating with prosecutors and implicating those closer to the White House, higher officials such as Mitchell, Dean, Haldeman, and Ehrlichman saw their own peril increasing. For this reason John Dean, the president's lawyer, steeled himself on March 21, 1973, to tell the president that the cover-up was unraveling and that Nixon needed to act to contain the crisis. "We have a cancer—within, close to the president, that's growing," he began, and laid out in his lawyerly way the perils they faced in order "to figure out how this [growing scandal] can be carved away from you, so it does not damage you or the Presidency. 'Cause it just can't. It's . . . not something you are involved in."

"That's true," replied the president.

"I know, sir, it is," replied Dean. "Well, I can just tell from our conversations that, you know, these are things that you have no knowledge of." Yet in truth, there is little candor in this exchange on the part of either man. Far from having no knowledge of the Watergate burglary, Nixon consistently attempted to cover it up over the previous nine months. And Dean relates in his memoirs that during this very conversation, he was constantly being surprised at how much the president knew about the burglars and the hush money they were demanding. With everyone exposed increasingly to the threat of criminal prosecution, it was difficult to be frank. Nixon himself confided to his diary that night: "It will be each man for himself, and one will not be afraid to rat on the other."

By the end of April, Nixon was certainly following his own advice. After forcing Haldeman to resign, he was protesting his own innocence to Alexander Haig, Haldeman's replacement as chief of staff: "Let me say this, Al. I am not concerned myself about anything incriminating in anything that I've done. I mean, I know what I've done. I mean, I've told you everything I did. You know what I mean. I frankly—I was not informed and I don't blame people for not informing me." Haldeman, who from the very start had conspired with Nixon to limit the FBI's investigation, departed the administration declaring to the president, within range of the microphones, "I did not know, and you did not know, and I don't know today, and I don't believe you do really, *what happened* in the Watergate case." Yet as Haldeman and Ehrlichman left the White House, they worried with the president whether Dean might convict them with his own evidence. "I just wonder if the son-of-a-bitch had a recorder on him," Nixon speculated.

It is the ultimate irony. Far from being "candid" records of unvarnished feelings, the White House tapes ended up bearing witness to a hall of mirrors in which conspirators told lies to one another that neither the listeners nor the speaker sometimes believed, and microphones recorded the anguished speculation that someone *else* might be taping. "One of the challenges of reading the Watergate transcripts," noted Nixon biographer Stephen Ambrose, "is trying to keep up with the daily reconstruction of history. These guys could move the pea under the walnut far faster than the human eye could follow. They invented motives for themselves, or presented the most self-serving rationalizations for what they had done and could not escape, or when they could get away with it simply lied."

Novelist E. M. Forster once discussed the difference between characters in a novel and people in real life. A character in a novel is different from the rest of us, Forster proposed, because he or she "belongs to a world where the secret life is visible, to a world that is not and cannot be ours, to a world where the narrator and the creator are one." Real life, on the other hand, is quite different, haunted as it is "by a spectre. We cannot understand each other, except in a rough and ready way; we cannot reveal ourselves, even when we want to; what we call intimacy is only a makeshift; perfect knowledge is only an illusion."

Following the auditory trail of Richard Nixon, we have come somewhat to the same conclusion. It would be misleading to portray Nixon as a man neatly divided between private and public selves, just as it would be a mistake to assume that the audiotapes reveal only his secret, therefore "true" self. The tapes are only another piece of raw material against which historians must deploy all their considerable skills in order to place the conversations in context. Although the tapes do provide a window into the lives of the people whose voices they captured, they do not supply us with a clearly unobstructed view. Even now, many aspects of Nixon remain puzzling. Henry Kissinger, who knew Nixon well and who was an accomplished student of history, once confessed himself at a loss to explain his former employer. Ironically, these off-the-record comments were picked up by a microphone left on by accident in a pressroom where Kissinger had been speaking. Nixon "was very good at foreign policy," Kissinger told his hosts and—unwittingly—the world, but

he was a very odd man. . . . He is a very unpleasant man. He was so nervous. It was such an effort for him to be on television. He was an artificial man in the sense that when he met someone he thought it out carefully so that nothing was spontaneous, and that meant he didn't enjoy people.

People sensed that. What I never understood is why he became a politician. He hated to meet new people. Most politicians like crowds. He didn't.

Kissinger's praise of Nixon's skill at foreign policy suggests one final caution. Neither the excerpts of the tape-recordings quoted here nor the 600 pages of transcripts released by Kutler can convey anywhere near the whole complexity of the Nixon presidency. Whereas the tapes of the Cuban missile crisis show Kennedy at his best, Watergate captures Nixon at his worst. Think what a different image we might have if, as with Kennedy and the Cuban missile crisis, the only surviving recordings covered Nixon during his triumphant trips to China and the Soviet Union. As more tapes are released, we will learn much of interest about Nixon's diplomatic achievements and about his controversial, often iconoclastic domestic policies. Viewing the man through the lens of Watergate inevitably injects a certain distortion.

Yet it must be said: this focus on presidential crimes was Richard Nixon's doing. The pattern of behavior established early on—demonstrated by the president's reaction toward Brookings—leaves no doubt that Nixon himself was the navigator who steered his administration full speed onto the shoals of Watergate. It was not unruly subordinates but the man at the top who kept repeating, "We're up against an enemy, a conspiracy. They're using any means. *We are going to use any means.* Is that clear?" And it was Nixon, in the final hours of the conspiracy, who could not resist making one last effort to retain the allegiance of Haldeman and Ehrlichman before they went to talk to the prosecutors. "Let me ask you this, to be quite candid. Is there any way you can use *cash?*"

Despite the worst of his inner demons, Nixon will be remembered for more than Watergate. But abuses of power this corrosive have only once in American history precipitated what would surely have been an unequivocal and bipartisan conviction on impeachment. For that reason alone, Nixon will never escape Watergate. Like a can tied to the tail of an offending dog, it will rattle and bang through the corridors of power for all of—one must excuse the phrase—recorded history. Historians may have tied on the can, but Nixon supplied the tail. And the tapes.

Additional Reading

Stanley Kutler, *Abuse of Power: The New Nixon Tapes* (New York, 1997) is the place to begin. Readers who want to listen for themselves should go to the National Archives in Washington, though Dove Audio has produced a version of the tapes read by professional actors. Such a rendition raises some interesting questions about authenticity, since the actors provide their own interpretations of the evidence. Some of the first transcripts on Nixon foreign policy are available from a different archive, collected by a former aide of Henry Kissinger. See William Burr, ed., *The Kissinger Transcripts: The Top-Secret Talks with Beijing and Moscow* (New York, 1998). Over the past few years the National Archives has released most of the Watergate tapes as well as additional Nixon materials. To hear them online go to http://www.archives. gov/nixon/tapes/tapes.html. Kutler's take on the "White House horrors" is laid out in *The Wars of Watergate* (New York, 1990). Walter Isaacson, *Kissinger* (New York, 1992) draws a portrait in which Kissinger provided much of the damning evidence about himself.

More recently the Miller Center at the University of Virginia has transcribed tapes from John Kennedy and Lyndon Johnson that offer new insights into the politics of civil rights. For discussion of those materials see Jonathan Rosenberg and Zachary Karabell, *Kennedy, Johnson, and the Quest for Justice: The Civil Rights Tapes* (New York, 2003). Ernest R. May and Philip D. Zelikow, eds., *The Kennedy Tapes: Inside the White House during the Cuban Missile Crisis* (Cambridge, MA, 1997) includes excellent analysis and commentary. Michael R. Beschloss, ed., *Taking Charge: The Johnson White House Tapes* (New York, 1997) provides an invaluable running commentary on the Johnson tapes. The tapes are available in an audio version, which makes for riveting listening. Originals of the Kennedy tapes and transcripts are available from the John F. Kennedy Library in Boston, and the Johnson tapes are also available through the Lyndon B. Johnson Library in Austin, Texas.

To help place the Kennedy tapes in context, consult Alexander Fursenko and Timothy Naftali, *"One Hell of a Gamble": The Secret History of the Cuban Missile Crisis* (New York, 1997) written with the advantage of access to previously secret Soviet archives. On Lyndon Johnson, Robert Dallek, *Flawed Giant: Lyndon Johnson and His Times, 1961–1973* (New York, 1998) is the most balanced biography. For an incisive commentary on the presidential tapes see Bruce Shulman, "Taping History," *The Journal of American History* 85, 2 (September 1998): 571–578. A much fuller discussion of presidents and taping is William Doyle, *Inside the Oval Office: White House Tapes from FDR to Clinton* (New York, 1999).

Bob Woodward and Carl Bernstein describe their pursuit of the Watergate break-in and cover-up stories in *All the President's Men* (New York, 1974), which focuses primarily on events through April 1973. *The Final Days* (New York, 1976) picks up chronologically where the first book left off. One comprehensive history of Watergate is J. Anthony Lukas, *Nightmare: The*

Underside of the Nixon Years (New York, 1976; rev. ed. 1988). Stephen Ambrose, in writing *Nixon: The Triumph of a Politician, 1962–1972* (New York, 1989) and *Nixon: Ruin and Recovery, 1973–1990* (New York, 1991), had less access to tape materials than Kutler did; Ambrose takes a more charitable view, but still lays the blame for Watergate squarely with Nixon.

Memoirs of the participants also supply useful information. From the ranks of the coconspirators have come the following books, listed roughly in diminishing order of administrative rank: Richard Nixon, *The Memoirs of Richard Nixon* (New York, 1978), in which Nixon, after many pages, still seems puzzled over what the fuss was about; Henry Kissinger, *White House Years* (Boston, 1979) and *Years of Upheaval* (Boston, 1982), in which Kissinger minimizes his own culpability; H. R. Haldeman, *The Ends of Power* (New York, 1978); John Ehrlichman, *Witness to Power: The Nixon Years* (New York, 1982); John Dean, *Blind Ambition: The White House Years* (New York, 1976), one of the more perceptive accounts; Charles Colson, *Born Again* (Old Tappan, NJ, 1976); Jeb Magruder, *An American Life* (New York, 1974); E. Howard Hunt, *Undercover: Memoirs of an American Secret Agent* (New York, 1974); James McCord, *A Piece of the Tape* (Rockville, MD, 1974); and G. Gordon Liddy, *Will* (New York, 1980).

Other areas of the Watergate story have been recounted by those who brought the malfeasants to justice. "Maximum John" Sirica, as he was known in legal circles, gives the bench's perspective in *To Set the Record Straight* (New York, 1979). The story from the Ervin Committee includes Senator Sam's version itself, perhaps somewhat ambitiously titled *The Whole Truth* (New York, 1981), as well as Samuel Dash, *Chief Counsel: Inside the Ervin Committee* (New York, 1976), and Minority Counsel Fred D. Thompson, *At That Point in Time* (New York, 1975). For the story from the special prosecutor's office, see Leon Jaworski, *The Right and the Power* (New York, 1976); Richard Ben-Veniste and George Frampton Jr., *Stonewall* (New York, 1977); and James Doyle, *Not above the Law* (New York, 1977). Howard Fields, *High Crimes and Misdemeanors* (New York, 1978) covers the impeachment proceedings, as does a large part of Elizabeth Drew's perceptive *Washington Journal: The Events of 1973–1974* (New York, 1975).

Several sourcebooks lay out the primary documents of Watergate. For excerpts from the Ervin Committee hearings, consult *The Watergate Hearings* (New York, 1973), assembled by the *New York Times*, or else the full version issued by the *Senate Select Committee on Presidential Campaign Activities, Hearings, Watergate and Related Activities* (Washington, DC, 1973). For the impeachment proceedings, see the House Committee on the Judiciary's *Impeachment of Richard Nixon, President of the United States* (Washington, DC, 1974). And transcripts of the original White House tapes, prepared by the Nixon White House staff, are available either in *The Presidential Transcripts* (New York, 1974), as issued by the *Washington Post*, or in *The White House Transcripts* (New York, 1974), by the *New York Times*.

Interactive Learning

The *Primary Source Investigator* provides materials that illuminate the psychology and political motives behind the presidential involvement in the break-in at the Watergate apartment complex. Images of President Nixon conferring with his aides, early campaign speeches, and testimony from prominent White House officials are included. Also on the CD-ROM are images of the microphones and address book that were crucial to advancing the case for impeachment of the president.

CHAPTER 16
Where Trouble Comes

P OV: the abbreviation sounds military. It could be part of the shorthand used so often in the Vietnam War, either to label geographic areas (LZs are landing zones), to name armies (VC stands for Viet Cong), or even to list the status of soldiers (KIAs—killed in action, WHAs—wounded in hostile action). POV, however, is not military jargon. It is a screenwriter's abbreviation for *point of view*. In films, a "POV shot" records a scene as if it were being viewed through the eyes of one of the actors. Where the director chooses to place the camera, to establish POV, determines to a large degree how the story is told.

Where should one place a camera in the Vietnamese village of Son My on March 16, 1968? When the artillery shells begin falling early Saturday morning, any camera angle would probably seem arbitrary. But for a moment, consider the question in terms of altitude: camera positions measured in feet above sea level.

POV, ground level: A dirt road, running past rice paddies not far from the South China Sea. Nguyen Chi, a farmer's wife, is already on her way to the market when she hears a series of explosions. She turns to see billowing smoke rising about a mile back, in the cluster of houses where she lives. Frantically she runs toward a hut by the road whose occupants have just rushed outside, and follows them to a small underground bunker built for such occasions. After several minutes the boom of the artillery fades. Helicopters advance across the sky. As Nguyen Chi peers from the earthen shelter, she sees one of the choppers land in a rice paddy not far down the road.

POV, altitude 500 feet: Nine large army assault helicopters sweep over the countryside. At 7:30 in the morning the sun is already heating up their gleaming black bodies. Inside, men from the 11th Brigade's Charlie Company sit nervously. They are launching a surprise attack on the Viet Cong's crack 48th Battalion, said to be holed up in the village below. Expecting heavy resistance, the men carry twice the normal load of rifle and machine-gun ammunition as well as grenades and other ordnance. As the choppers descend, their blades change pitch for the landing, making a sharp, crackling *pop-pop-pop*. It sounds almost like rifle fire. The nervous door gunners spray the surrounding fields with rockets and machine-gun fire. These last few moments of descent are the most vulnerable: with no troops on the ground and the choppers settling like clumsy ducks on the water, the men will be easy prey for an ambush. Scrambling, soldiers drop into the paddy and fan out, securing the landing zone.

POV, altitude 1,000 feet: Lieutenant Colonel Frank Barker hovers in a smaller chopper. Charlie Company is part of his task force, assembled to root out the Viet Cong in the area. Barker watches the operation from his assigned air lane at 1,000 feet. After about twenty minutes, he sees the second wave of helicopters flying in below, unloading another fifty men. Charlie Company regroups and heads into the hamlet, where the vegetation is denser than in the open fields. At 1,000 feet, it is difficult to see what's going on. But there is smoke and, over the crackling static of the radio, the sound of small-arms fire. At 8:28 Barker radios Captain Ernest Medina, the commander on the ground. "Have you had any contact down there yet?" he asks. When Medina replies that they have killed 84 Viet Cong ("Eight-four KIAs"), Barker's chopper banks and heads home for the unit's operations center.

The POVs could continue their upward spiral. The air corridor at 2,000 feet is reserved for the American Division's commander, Major General Samuel Koster, who flies over Son My several times that morning, well above reach of ground fire. At 2,500 feet the operations commander also monitors the action. Stacked in layers of airspace, looking on from higher and higher perches, these POVs provide increasingly wider views of the terrain. Yet the perspective also becomes more remote with the increase in altitude. Because these observers see more, they also see less.

The report of the morning's action becomes distorted not only by height but by distance, as it is relayed to the world at large. At the operations center, Press Officer Arthur Dunn telephones a two-page "after action" report into division headquarters. Dunn uses the statistics compiled by Colonel Barker's staff. The totals have risen since Medina's earlier report, to a final count of "128 enemy killed, 13 suspects detained and three weapons captured." The body count is the largest recorded for the task force since it began operations two months earlier. But one number makes Dunn uneasy: the three weapons captured. Could the Viet Cong retreat from a fierce fight taking along virtually all their dead comrades' firearms? Unlikely. To Dunn, something seems fishy.

In Saigon, more distant from the field of battle, the press officer has no time for such questions. He merely provides reporters with their story, which makes no mention of the number of weapons captured. Based on the briefing, the *New York Times* front page reports that "about 150 men of the Americal Division encountered the enemy force early yesterday. . . . The operation is another American offensive to clear enemy pockets still threatening the cities."

Another offensive to clear enemy pockets: As the *Times* recognized, this operation was neither the first nor the last of such sweeps. It amounted to one more confusing day in a war that, by 1968, was being waged with more than half a million American troops. How important, really, was Charlie Company's assault? For journalists scrambling for a story, the picture remained unclear, and there was little time to follow up on yet another skirmish in a distant hamlet. None of the dispatches coming out of Vietnam gave any hint that the events at Son My, if told from the perspective of the men who entered the village that morning, might send tremors across America that would change how the nation thought about the war. For the time being, their POVs went unreported.

CINEMATIC MYTHS AND VIETNAM

During the same months that Charlie Company was conducting its search-and-destroy operations, Warner Brothers completed final work on *The Green Berets*, Hollywood's first dramatization of the war. The film's star and coproducer, John Wayne, had made a career of climbing into the boots of outsized heroes. For more than thirty years "the Duke" had been the featured player in countless westerns, including *Stage Coach*, *Fort Apache*, and *The Alamo*. He had assaulted enemy-held islands in World War II dramas such as *The Sands of Iwo Jima*, *Back to Bataan*, and *They Were Expendable*. In the midst of this new war, Wayne watched with dismay the growing domestic protest against American involvement in Southeast Asia. As a conservative patriot, he decided to fight back by directing and starring in a combat epic designed to show why Americans were at war.

The turbulent events of 1968, however, made patriotism a harder sell, even for an old hand like Wayne. In January, the Viet Cong had launched a series of surprise attacks during the Vietnamese celebration of Tet, the lunar new year. The strength of the Tet assault shocked many Americans, who began more and more to doubt the government's rosy progress reports. By the end of March (several weeks after Charlie Company's operation at Son My), the war had so divided the nation that President Johnson chose not to seek reelection. Events at home as well as abroad seemed increasingly violent and chaotic. In April, Martin Luther King Jr. was gunned down by an assassin; in June, so was Robert Kennedy, the candidate who seemed most likely to replace Johnson on the Democratic ticket. Both King and Kennedy had become outspoken opponents of the war.

In such tumultuous times, Warner Brothers became edgy about the prospects of its new film. Newspaper ads touting *The Green Berets* were almost defensive: "So you don't believe in glory. And heroes are out of style. And they don't blow bugles anymore. So take another look—at the Special Forces in a special kind of hell." Although antiwar demonstrators picketed the film's premiere ("John Wayne profits off G.I.'s blood," read one sign), an eager theater audience cheered as their hero, a tad paunchy at 61, led his Green Berets to a newly erected outpost "in the heart of VC country." At the end of more than two hours of action, U.S. Special Forces had tangled with mortar fire, nighttime raids, and poison punjee sticks, emerging triumphant in a fight for their embattled outpost. If newspaper stories like the one about Charlie Company seemed a bit distant from reality, *The Green Berets* presented instant history that was just the opposite. Its POVs were bold, colorful, larger than life.

The Green Berets was easy for the critics to dismiss. ("A film best handled from a distance and with a pair of tongs," sniffed the *New Yorker.*) But enough of Wayne's fans rallied round to make it a solid financial success. And while *The Green Berets* was the first feature film to use the war as its setting, it was hardly the last. Over the past thirty years, at least twenty-five films have portrayed aspects of the conflict. For better or worse, with more accuracy or less, far more Americans have come by their understanding of the war by viewing dramatic films than by reading scholarly histories. In that sense historians and filmmakers have become rivals: revisiting the same battlefields, reconstructing similar dramas in rice paddies or small villages, delving for significance in an ambiguous past.

How should we approach films that purport to portray history, especially a subject as controversial as the Vietnam War? There are, of course, a number of straightforward ways to evaluate historical dramas. We can give each film a scrupulous fact-checking to determine which parts are true and which false. Are the costumes right? Did a historical figure do the things he or she is said to have done on screen? If the characters are fictional, are they representative of historical figures in similar situations? This approach—administering a kind of historical lie-detector test—can reveal a great deal. But as we have seen, historians routinely use more imaginative ways to examine the past. If we can ferret out unspoken biases in the photographs of Jacob Riis, why not probe the cultural assumptions of *The Green Berets*? If the audiotapes of Richard Nixon can reveal nuances of personal character, why not explore the camera's points of view in a film like *Apocalypse Now?*

Still, a good deal of caution is needed when examining historical films for information about the past. The historical "reality" presented by dramatic films is radically different from that of a letter or diary, or even from a secondary account like *The Jungle.* At their best, movies have a visual and emotional immediacy more vivid than any reality evoked by the printed page. Movies about Vietnam confront viewers with the *feel* of war—the oppressive heat of a jungle trail, the explosive chaos of a firefight. Yet even the best filmic realism is false or misleading. To begin with the obvious: the soldiers tramping across a rice paddy, machine guns in hand, are actors, not the original combatants. The location in which they appear is almost never that of the historical event. In other words, any dramatic film sequence is an artful *construction of reality* rather than reality itself. Just as historians re-create their own versions of the past in prose narratives, so also do directors and their production crews on film.

But filmmakers and historians part company on their principles of reconstruction. A historian's first commitment is to remain faithful to the historical record. Of course, that commitment can be difficult to keep. As we have seen, any knowledge of what "really" happened in the past is conditioned by the primary sources available and the way we analyze them. We are not simply messengers between past and present, but active agents, doing our best to reconstruct an ambiguous past. Still, no matter how ingeniously historians tease meaning from the evidence, the source material remains our starting point.

For filmmakers, far different principles of construction are paramount. They involve questions of drama, not fidelity to the evidence. Does the screenplay move along quickly enough? Do the characters "develop" sufficiently? Does the plot provide enough suspense? These matters dominate the making of a film, even when that oft-repeated claim flashes across the screen: "Based on a True Story." If historical sources cannot supply enough material to round out a tale, directors and screenwriters will tinker with the plot and characters until the story provides them with what they need.

The kinds of changes that are routinely made can be seen in Oliver Stone's *Born on the Fourth of July* (1989). Stone based his film on the memoir of a Vietnam veteran, Ron Kovic, who became involved in the antiwar movement. Kovic's faith in the war had been shaken by two traumatic events that overtook him in Vietnam: a nighttime firefight in which he accidentally killed one of his own men, and another night patrol during which his unit killed and wounded some Vietnamese women and children. According to Kovic's book, the two events took place several months apart, but the film combines them into a single incident. Similarly, Kovic describes a trip to Washington for an antiwar rally; in the film, he attends a protest at Syracuse University instead, where his high school sweetheart attends college. In fact, Syracuse had no violent demonstration and Kovic's book made no mention of a high school sweetheart. And the film contains many other similar alterations of detail.

Do these alterations disqualify the film as history? In one sense, yes. By deliberately changing the historical record or inventing it out of whole cloth, Stone has done what no historian would do. No doubt he would defend the changes for dramatic reasons. Consider, for example, the most crassly commercial alteration: giving Kovic a girlfriend. To justify a budget of millions, a film must make money, and over the years box-office receipts have proved that audiences are attracted to plots with an element of romance. For dramatic reasons, too, the idea makes sense. Young, innocent Kovic goes off to Vietnam a patriotic marine, while his sweetheart goes off to college and becomes an antiwar demonstrator. Now Kovic's struggle to come to terms with the war is intertwined with his search for a romantic relationship. Similarly, it makes dramatic sense to distill Kovic's traumatic war experiences into one vivid sequence, to leave time for the rest of the film to focus on his growing involvement with the antiwar movement. As for the decision to invent a protest at Syracuse rather than re-create the one in Washington, one suspects that Stone simply wanted to save on production costs. Recreating a full-scale march around the monuments of the nation's capital would have been much more expensive.

Even with these changes, Stone could argue that he has remained faithful to the essence of Kovic's story. If the goal of the film is to show the long, painful road from patriotic innocence to disillusionment and finally to a new commitment to political change, do the smaller details of the plot really matter? This piece is a dramatic film, not a scholarly monograph. Like novels or plays, films strive for an artistic standard of "truth" that resides less in the particulars of the historical record than in rendering situations and characters in authentic, human ways. In aesthetic terms, Stone could argue that he respected the integrity of Kovic's story and that *Born on the Fourth of July* reveals a great deal about many Americans who fought in Vietnam.

But the point remains. No matter how "true" a feature film tries to be to the emotions of its characters, its makers will always place dramatic considerations above strict fidelity to the historical record. And this recognition leads the historian to ask a more interesting series of questions. Instead of simply trying to discover which details of a film are based on historical facts and which are not, why not analyze the dramatic construction of the film itself? Accept, for the moment, that producers and directors are concerned with a different kind of artistic "truth" than historians are. Grant that the search for profits often pushes Hollywood to distort the past in hopes of making films that its audiences need or want to see. Dramatic films about history do not portray what actually happened in the past so much as what *ought* to have happened—at least in the minds of the audience or the film's creators. In short, we are leaving behind the reconstruction of a nation's history for an exploration of its myths.

A myth, to quote one dictionary definition, is "any real or fictional story, recurring theme, or character type that appeals to the consciousness of a people by embodying its cultural ideals or by giving expression to deep, commonly felt emotions." Most often, we think of myths as traditions that have survived from preliterate societies: tales of gods such as Thor and Zeus, or hazy historical figures such as Helen of Troy or Hiawatha. But the myths of modern culture are not simply derived from older traditions. Novelists and playwrights routinely create new narratives that speak to more recent hopes or anxieties. And Hollywood, an industry that markets the fantasies and fears of popular culture, inescapably finds itself in the myth business, creating stories, themes, and character types that embody the cultural ideals of its audiences and give expression to their deepest feelings.

What sorts of myths? Consider the story and characters in *The Green Berets*. Audiences already knew John Wayne as the star of films that embodied two well-established mythic traditions of American cinema. The first was the western, whose central tale is a saga of white settlers crossing the prairie in order to subdue the wilderness and supplant it with a new, more vibrant civilization. Wayne, whether playing a rangy cowpoke or a dashing cavalry officer, embodied the highest ideals of that new America. He was strong, independent, honest, and fair, at once tender and tough. Equality and liberty were the watchwords of the West, contrasting sharply with the inequality of aristocratic Europe or even with the decadent, overcrowded cities of the East.

From John Wayne the hero of the West, it was only a short step to Wayne the Green Beret of Vietnam. Instead of hunting coppery-skinned Indians who menaced defenseless settlers, the Duke would now chase Asian guerrillas who lurked in the jungle. Rather than commanding a fort in Apache country, he would defend an outpost near the Laotian border—this one conveniently nicknamed Dodge City. Once again, the heroes of the West would have a chance to uproot the corruptions of the East, this time the infection of communism that had spread across Eurasia.

Wayne's previous roles reflected a second mythic tradition of American cinema: the combat epic that came of age during World War II. In the standard-issue World War II melodrama, an ethnically mixed assortment of recruits is thrown together in a frontline platoon, each soldier finding himself tested in the heat of battle. As the platoon shares the agonies and triumphs of a common experience, they are forged into a dedicated fighting unit. In effect, the story retells the classic myth of the American melting pot, in which immigrants from a multitude of ethnic backgrounds learn to live in a single nation. As the platoon unites to work for victory, it embodies the very democratic ideals that set America apart from other nations. Repeatedly, Wayne played the hero who made this myth so powerful. Like many others of his generation, Ron Kovic remembered viewing as a boy one of Wayne's classic Pacific combat films:

> Castiglia and I saw *The Sands of Iwo Jima* together. The Marine Corps hymn was playing in the background as we sat glued to our seats . . . watching Sergeant Stryker, played by John Wayne, charge up the hill and get killed before he reached the top. And then they showed the men raising the flag on Iwo Jima with the marines' hymn playing, and Castiglia and I cried in our seats. I loved the song so much, and every time I heard it I would think of John Wayne and the brave men who raised the flag on Iwo Jima that day.

Combat films like *The Sands of Iwo Jima* and westerns like *The Alamo* and *Fort Apache* worked because the tales they told reinforced Americans' ideas about themselves as a people. Indeed, the mythic traditions of both the western and the World War II epic assumed that Americans were in many ways an exceptional people, set apart by their experience with democracy and liberty. This tradition of American exceptionalism could be traced back as far as John Winthrop's sermon to his fellow Puritans in 1630, that their new colony in Massachusetts would stand as "a city on a hill" and a shining example to the rest of the world. Winthrop's pride was motivated by a religious vision of the Puritans as a chosen people, but over the years that vision gained a political dimension as well, from the heritage of the American Revolution. The vision became overtly nationalistic during the nineteenth century as the "manifest destiny" of western expansion transformed the United States into a continental nation. Wayne's films were among the many dramas that drew upon such themes.

In making *The Green Berets*, Wayne was well aware of the myths and messages he was constructing. In late 1965, knowing he would need army cooperation to help film battle scenes, he wrote President Johnson, making a successful pitch for the picture:

Colonel Kirby (John Wayne) brings medical assistance to a young Laotian girl while the skeptical liberal journalist (David Janssen) looks on. In this scene from *The Green Berets*, the visual message reinforces the film's mythic themes: that Americans are bringing order and democracy to a land threatened by an enemy as ruthless as the stereotypical Indians portrayed in Wayne's westerns.

> Some day soon a motion picture will be made about Vietnam. Let's make sure it is the kind of motion picture that will help our cause throughout the world. I believe my organization can do just that and still accomplish our purpose for being in existence—making money. We want to tell the story of our fighting men in Vietnam with reason, emotion, characterization and action. We want to do it in a manner that inspires a patriotic attitude on the part of our fellow Americans—a feeling which we have always had in this country in the past during times of stress and trouble.

Wayne also recognized his own near-mythic stature in the American cinema. "Thirty-seven years a star, I must have some small spot in more than a few million people's lives," he told the president. "You cannot stay up there that long without having identification with a great number of people."

How does *The Green Berets* establish its myths? Since film is above all a visual medium, we should perhaps examine first the images conjured up by the characters in Wayne's drama. Wayne himself plays Colonel Mike Kirby, a tanned, tall, laconic officer who hates the bureaucratic hassles of his high rank and insists on joining his Green Berets in the field. Kirby's dramatic foil is George Beckworth (David Janssen), a liberal newspaper columnist who attacks American involvement in Vietnam. The visual images confirm his status as antagonist: Beckworth is a nervous chain-smoker, generally unwilling to look anyone in the eye.

At Dodge City, Colonel Kirby meets his South Vietnamese ally, Captain Nim, an able sort, but distinctly more bloodthirsty than the Green Berets are. He has "personally greased" fifty-two Viet Cong that year, one of the men informs Kirby, and Nim hopes to double the number before another year goes by. (He keeps score on the wall of his "hootch," or thatched hut.) Like all the film's Vietnamese characters, Nim speaks a Hollywood pigeon English. "My home is Hanoi," he tells Kirby. "I go home too, someday . . . you see! . . . first kill all those stinking Cong . . . then go home."[1]

Beckworth is upset to find Captain Nim slapping around a captured VC spy. Indeed, Nim shakes the man so violently that Kirby feels called upon to restrain him. When Beckworth demands an explanation, Kirby reveals that the spy had killed an American medic on a mission of mercy in a nearby Montagnard village. The doctor was found in the jungle "beheaded, mutilated," says Kirby. "His wife wouldn'ta recognized him." Such contrasts of brutality and innocence defiled become the central stuff of Wayne's mythical Vietnam. While the Green Berets provide villagers with humanitarian aid, the VC assume the role of savages, raping young girls and torturing wives in front of their husbands.

To provide viewers with a heartrending visual reminder of the war's horrors, the fort at Dodge City is also furnished with a lovable Vietnamese orphan whose parents have been killed during a VC raid. Named (of all things) Hamchunk, the orphan is followed about by a little puppy, apparently because the film's producers felt that an Asian orphan alone was not quite enough to melt the hearts of American viewers. In the climactic assault on Dodge City, the VC commit the ultimate atrocity: they kill poor Hamchunk's pooch, and the tearful orphan buries it as the bombs fall helter skelter around him. The valiant Captain Nim perishes too. "He bought the farm, sir," one of the men informs Wayne, but adds reassuringly, "he took a lot of 'em with him."

As so often happens when questions of drama are paramount, complex issues of geopolitics are reduced to intensely personal relationships and bold visual images. The can-do American colonel, the stalwart South Vietnamese ally, the hapless orphan—all reinforce the myths embraced by *The Green Berets*. Here is a war much like World War II (the so-called good war), in

---

1. Like the other Vietnamese characters, Nim is not played by a Vietnamese. The role was filled by a Japanese American, George Takei, known to many as Mr. Sulu of *Star Trek* fame. In 1968, allowing Asian Americans of any sort to take principal speaking roles was a measure of progress compared with the days of World War II, when a WASP-like Katharine Hepburn played one of the noble Chinese peasants in *Dragon Seed* (1944). The mythic image Takei projects in *Star Trek* stands rather humorously at odds with his character in *The Green Berets:* Sulu the navigator, ever the cool head in an interstellar crisis, versus the bloodthirsty, inarticulate Nim.

which decent Americans prevail over an unscrupulous enemy. The film ends with Hamchunck once again at loose ends, walking with Wayne along the beaches of the South China Sea. "What will happen to me now?" he asks plaintively. Wayne sets a Green Beret atop the boy's head and then (as in so many earlier westerns) walks into the sunset with his pal. "You let me worry about that, Green Beret," he says. "You're what this war is all about." No matter that Vietnam's beaches face *east* (this sun would have to be rising); the message of these visual images is strong and clear. Americans have come to Vietnam to protect innocents and promote democracy just as they had in Hollywood's previous wars.

While visual images help establish mythic themes, the structure of a film's narrative can be equally revealing. As we have seen, filmmakers are constantly constructing their versions of history with dramatic considerations uppermost. When a soldier is wounded fatally in a firefight, we must ask ourselves, why at that point in the screenplay and not earlier? When a woman discovers something unsettling about the personal background of her lover, we must wonder, why now? Or why at all? For historians, questions about why events happened in a particular order can be resolved only by analyzing the primary sources. In the case of films, characters are killed off or lovers are jilted because the screenwriters, the director, or the producers wish these events to happen. Thinking about the way a story is put together, in other words, can expose the intentions and the values of the film's creators.

In this light, the plot of *The Green Berets* is tantalizingly odd. Its various parts don't quite fit together. Most of the film focuses on Colonel Kirby's defense of his border outpost. But tacked onto this tale is a second, unrelated story. As he prepares the defenses of Dodge City, Kirby is suddenly flown from his outpost to attend dinner at "Le Club Sport," a fancy nightspot in the port city of Da Nang. There, he sees an Asian beauty dining with a Vietnamese companion. Before we can learn more, a couple of Green Berets appear and yank Wayne from his dinner: the VC attack has begun.

Only after Dodge City is safely retaken do we discover that the mysterious lady in Da Nang is a double agent ready to lure the Viet Cong's highest-ranking general into a trap. The film then embarks on a plot in which Wayne leads a commando team armed with drug-tipped arrows and crossbows deep into enemy territory. Sneaking into the general's bedroom, the Green Berets drug him and pack him off in a body bag to a rendezvous where he is lofted on high by a helium balloon and whisked away by an American airplane dragging a hook. The whole concoction is sheer, implausible fantasy, with no relation to the rest of the film. Even worse, the extra length makes *The Green Berets* drag interminably.

Why tack on the extra plot? Any Hollywood script doctor could have seen that the obvious way to shorten an overly long film was simply to eliminate it. But if the producers considered that option, they never carried it out. Why not?

Put yourself in the place of the screenwriter. Try eliminating the second plot and walk with John Wayne through what has now become the final scene of your new, shorter epic. Everything remains as before—the same dialogue, same camera angles. See how the new ending plays.

The Green Berets stand victorious outside Dodge City, thanks to an air attack that has strafed and killed nearly every VC in the fort. "We can probably move in there tomorrow," says Wayne, "God willin' and the river don't rise." Sounding like he's back in sagebrush country, Wayne does move in. The VC flag, fluttering over the outpost, is cut loose and blows away. As Wayne surveys the territory, one of his sergeants walks up hesitantly:

SERGEANT: What do we do now, sir?
KIRBY: First we get some sack time . . . [Pause. Looks grimly around.] And then we start all over again.

And then we start all over again? Can this be the climax to all the tragic bloodshed, the anguished deaths, the carnage? We start all over again? When the flag went up at Iwo Jima, it stayed up. But in 1968 the course of fighting in Vietnam was different—as even Wayne and his coproducers recognized. American armed forces did not try to capture territory; instead they attempted to kill as many enemy as possible in a war of attrition. When American search-and-destroy missions cleared an area, they usually either moved on in another sweep or returned to their base, leaving the territory once again to the enemy. In Vietnam, the victories never quite stayed won.

Suddenly, the reason for the awkward second plot becomes clearer. In 1968 the real war in Vietnam could provide no prospect of a definitive victory. Yet unlike history, an action-adventure film demands a climax that will satisfy audiences that the hardships and deaths of its heros have not been in vain. The only finale Wayne's writers could devise was a second, wholly implausible victory. *The Green Berets* clings valiantly to the cinematic myths of World War II and the Wild West, but only by abandoning even tenuous links with reality.

SON MY: AT GROUND LEVEL

The realities of the war, however, were becoming harder to evade. John Wayne's film demonstrated that although myths might distort history, they could not ignore it entirely if they hoped to speak to audiences in lasting and satisfying ways. The tension between the ideal and the real, between "what should have been" and "what was," made *The Green Berets* an unconvincing film for many Americans. And already in the summer of 1968, the seemingly routine search-and-destroy mission at Son My was beginning to catch up with the myths in which Wayne sought to clothe American involvement in Vietnam.

Several days after Charlie Company returned from Son My in March, another helicopter from the 11th Brigade swept low over the area. Ronald Ridenhour, a door gunner, was struck by the desolation. Nobody seemed to be around. When Ridenhour spotted a body, pilot Gilbert Honda dropped down to investigate. It was a dead woman, spread-eagled on the ground. As Ridenhour recalled later, she had an 11th Brigade patch between her legs, as if it were some type of display, some badge of honor. We just looked; it was obviously there so people would know the 11th Brigade had been there. We just thought, "What in the hell's wrong with these guys? What's going on?"

As the chopper continued its sweep, several Vietnamese caught sight of it and ran to a bunker. Ridenhour wanted to flush the men out with a phosphorus grenade, but the pilot refused to come in low enough. Ridenhour was angry. Why hadn't Honda pursued? The pilot was evasive; all he would say was, "These people around here have had a pretty rough time the last few days."

At first Ridenhour forgot the incident. Then a friend mentioned Charlie Company's operation. According to the word going around, Charlie Company had eliminated the entire village. Astonished, Ridenhour talked throughout the next few months with a number of soldiers who had been at Son My. The more he heard, the more outraged he became.

When he returned home to Phoenix, Arizona, Ridenhour could not let the matter rest. In March 1969 he summarized what he had learned in a letter and sent copies to the White House, the Pentagon, the State Department, and members of Congress. Prodded by several members of Congress, the army began an inquiry. By the end of August 1969 the Criminal Investigation Division had interviewed more than seventy-five witnesses. Many of Charlie Company's members had already finished their tours of duty and were technically beyond reach of army discipline. But the investigators' attention centered increasingly on the leader of the first platoon, Second Lieutenant William Calley. On September 5 the army charged Calley with the premeditated murder of 109 "Oriental human beings . . . whose names and sexes are unknown, by means of shooting them with a rifle." Because of regulations, the charges had to be filed by the commanding officer where Calley was currently stationed. That was Fort Benning, Georgia, a location used two years earlier by John Wayne to film much of *The Green Berets.*

To the surprise of some Pentagon officials, newspapers did not feature the story. But one or two reporters became interested. Following a tip, journalist Seymour Hersh interviewed first Calley and then other Charlie Company veterans in Utah, California, New Jersey, and Indiana. One, Paul Meadlo, agreed to tell his story to *CBS Evening News* on November 21. His revelation sent reporters scrambling. Both *Time* and *Newsweek* ran cover stories. These new accounts referred less often to Son My, the name of the village used in the newspaper accounts of 1968. Instead they used the name of the smaller hamlet within the boundaries of Son My. On the army's map, that village was labeled My Lai.

Inevitably, the memories that surfaced were fragmentary, imperfect. Some members of Charlie Company preferred not to talk with anyone. Others felt an aching need to speak out. In the end, there were only partial points of view: wrenching, disjointed perspectives from which to piece together what happened that March morning as the men disembarked from their helicopters.

POV, on the ground, at hamlet's edge: The soldiers, high-strung, advance nervously. They expect return fire at any minute—or the concussion of a booby trap exploding underfoot. A sergeant turns, sees a man near a well. "The gook was standing up shaking and waving his arms and then he was shot," recalls Paul Meadlo. Another soldier: "There was a VC. We thought it was a VC." As the platoons reach the first houses, they split up and begin pulling people out of the hamlet's red brick houses and its hootches.

Below ground, in a bunker: Pham Phon hears the artillery stop. When he pokes his head out, several American soldiers are about 200 feet away. Telling his wife and three children to follow, he crawls out. Phon knows how to act when the Americans come. Above all, one must never make a sudden movement, running away from the soldiers or toward them—they will become suspicious and shoot. One must walk slowly, gather in small groups, and wait quietly. As Phon approaches the Americans, his children smile and call out a few words of English; "Hello! Hello! Okay! Okay!"

The Americans are not smiling. The soldiers point their rifles and order the five to walk toward a canal ditch just outside the hamlet.

A group of infantry: There is noise, suddenly, from behind. One of the men whirls, fires. It's only a water buffalo. But something in the group seems to snap, and everyone begins firing, round after round, until the buffalo collapses in a hail of bullets. One of the soldiers: "Once the shooting started, I guess it affected everyone. From then on it was like nobody could stop. Everyone was just shooting at everything and anything, like the ammo wouldn't ever give out."

Soldiers began dynamiting the brick houses and setting fire to the thatched hootches. Private Michael Bernhardt: "I saw these guys doing strange things. . . . They were setting fire to the hootches and huts and waiting for the people to come out and then shooting them. They were going into the hootches and shooting them up. They were gathering people in groups and shooting them."

At the center of the hamlet, about forty-five Vietnamese are herded together. It's about 8:15 A.M. Lieutenant Calley appears and walks over to Paul Meadlo. "You know what to do with them, don't you?" Meadlo says yes. He assumes Calley wants the prisoners guarded. About fifteen minutes later Calley returns. "How come you ain't killed them yet?" he asks. "I want them dead." He steps back about fifteen feet and begins shooting. Meadlo is surprised, but follows orders. "I used more than a whole clip—used four or five clips."

Ronald Haeberle follows the operation into the hamlet. Haeberle is a photographer from the Public Information Detachment. Because the army anticipates that this mission will be a major action, he is there to cover the engagement. He comes upon some infantry surrounding a group of women, children, and a young teenage girl. Two of the soldiers are trying to pull off the top of the girl's black pajamas, the traditional Vietnamese peasant garb. "Let's see what she's made of," says one. "Jesus, I'm horny," says another. An old woman throws herself on the men, trying to protect the girl. The men punch and kick her aside. One hits her with his rifle butt.

Army photographer Ron Haeberle's searing photographs of the events at My Lai, published in *Life* magazine in December 1969, provided shocking counterimages to those in *The Green Berets.* The older woman is being restrained by other villagers after she attacked soldiers who had been molesting a younger woman (*right rear,* buttoning her blouse). "Guys were about to shoot these people," Haeberle recalled. "I yelled, 'Hold it,' and shot my picture. As I walked away, I heard M16s open up. From the corner of my eye I saw bodies falling but I didn't turn to look."

Suddenly they look up: Haeberle is standing there with his camera. They stop bothering the girl and continue about their business. "What should we do with 'em?" one soldier asks. "Kill 'em," says another. Haeberle turns away as an M16, a light machine gun, is fired. The women and children collapse on the ground, dead.

As he makes his way through the hamlet, Ronald Grzesik comes upon Paul Meadlo, crouched on the ground, head in his hands. Meadlo is sobbing like a child. Grzesik stoops and asks what's the matter. Calley made me shoot some people, Meadlo replies.

Pham Phon and his family wait nervously at the top of the canal ditch. By now perhaps a hundred villagers have been herded together. At first they stand, but soon the Americans make them sit, to prevent them from running away. Phon hears gunfire in the distance and has a horrible premonition. He tells his wife and children to slip down the bank into the ditch when the soldiers are not looking.

Lieutenant Calley orders some of the men to "push all those people in the ditch." Calley begins shooting and orders Meadlo to follow his lead. Meadlo: "And so I began shooting them all. . . . I guess I shot maybe twenty-five or

twenty people in the ditch . . . men, women, and children. And babies." Another GI, Robert Maples, refuses to use his machine gun on the crowd. But
other soldiers fire, reload, and fire again, until the villagers in the ditch lay
still.

Underneath the mass of bodies, Phon and his family lie terrified. They
are unhurt, except for one daughter, wounded in the shoulder. As the hours
pass, Phon says nothing, praying his daughter will not moan too loudly from
the pain; praying the soldiers will move on.

By 11:00 the guns have fallen quiet. At his command post west of the
hamlet, Captain Medina has lunch with his crew and several platoon leaders,
including Lieutenant Calley. Two girls, about ten and eleven, appear from
out of nowhere. Apparently they have waited out the siege in one of the rice
paddies. The men give the girls cookies and crackers. After lunch, Charlie
Company blows up a few underground tunnels they have discovered, demol-
ish the remaining houses, and move out of My Lai.

Or more precisely, they move out of what on army maps is labeled "My
Lai (4)." Actually, the map gives the name My Lai to six different locations
in the area. To outsiders, Vietnamese place names can be confusing. "Villages" such as Son My are really more like American counties or townships.
Many hamlets exist within each village, and even these are divided into sub-
hamlets, each with its own name. The Army has not successfully transferred
all the names onto their maps. Thus when friendly Vietnamese informants
tell Army Intelligence that the Viet Cong's 48th Battalion is based, say, at
"My Lai," they do not realize that the army shows six My Lais on their maps.
On this morning of March 16, Americans have attacked the wrong hamlet,
one approximately two miles away from the reported stronghold of the 48th
Battalion.

The people who live in this settlement do not call it My Lai. Its official
name is Xom Lang—merely, the *hamlet.* For years, though, residents have
also referred to their home by a more poetic name, Thuan Yen; a rough
English translation is *peace,* or *the place where trouble does not come.*

DENIAL

By the time the facts about My Lai became known, the wider debate over
the war had forced Lyndon Johnson from office. Richard Nixon began a
lurching, four-year course of scaling back the conflict. Antiwar protests
flared when Nixon sent American troops into neighboring Cambodia, but
they tapered off again as the president carried out his policy of "Vietnamiza-
tion," steadily withdrawing American troops, leaving South Vietnamese
forces to absorb the brunt of the fighting. By 1973 American and North
Vietnamese negotiators had hammered out a treaty that allowed Nixon to
claim "peace with honor." But this treaty was largely a face-saving gesture.
Despite all pretenses, the war's outcome was a defeat for the United States.
Few knowledgeable observers were surprised to see the North Vietnamese
complete their conquest of South Vietnam two years later.

As the war wound down by fits and starts, so did the controversy over My Lai. The details of the attack had been so repellent, many Americans at first found them hard to accept. A poll taken by the *Minneapolis Tribune* revealed that nearly half of the 600 persons interviewed believed that the reports of mass murder were false. Other citizens angrily defended the accused. "It sounds terrible to say we ought to kill kids," said a woman in Cleveland, "but many of our boys being killed over there are just kids, too." At the end of a lengthy military trial, Lieutenant Calley was found guilty of "at least twenty-two murders" and sentenced in 1971 to life imprisonment. Following appeals and a forty-month stay in federal custody, Calley was paroled in 1976. Four other soldiers were court-martialed, but none convicted.

Supporters of the war resented the publicity given My Lai. They pointed out that only months before, communist forces had massacred several thousand civilians at the provincial capital of Hue. They noted too that since the late 1950s, the Viet Cong had engaged in a campaign of political terror, assassinating village officials appointed by the American-backed South Vietnamese regimes. In contrast, they portrayed My Lai as an aberration in American policy: "the actions of a pitiful few," in the words of General William Westmoreland. President Nixon admitted that there "was certainly a massacre" but believed it to be "an isolated incident."

In one sense, historians have confirmed that judgment. The available records for the war reveal no other mass executions of similar magnitude. At the same time, congressional hearings as well as conferences sponsored by Vietnam Veterans Against the War produced testimony of other GIs who had on many occasions subjected civilians or suspected Viet Cong to harsh treatment, torture to extract information, or indiscriminate killing. Those opposing the war pointed out that even in the case of My Lai, where misconduct had occurred on a large scale, the story had not come to light until a soldier entirely outside the army's chain of command had prodded high officials to push for an investigation. How many other, lesser incidents went routinely unreported? Historians themselves have not yet undertaken any systematic investigation of such incidents, in part because the task would be so daunting.

Although the ultimate significance of My Lai remains unclear, one thing was certain. The encounter became a defining moment in the public's perception of the war. It did so, a historian might suggest, because it left shaken the long-cherished myth of American exceptionalism. As defenders of a democratic culture, Americans were supposed to behave differently from the rest of the corrupt world. They were not the sort, *The Green Berets* suggested, who would rape young girls or execute innocent civilians. Furthermore, My Lai attracted so much attention because it made the issue concrete and personal, in just the way that film dramas strived to do. John Wayne had reduced complex political and economic issues to visual, intensely personal images ("You're what this war's all about," Kirby tells little Hamchunk). Similarly, Ron Haeberle's searing photographs, reproduced in *Life* magazine, served as counterimages that shattered the mythic stereotypes of *The Green Berets*. Henceforth it would be impossible to take the plot and themes of a western or a World War II epic and merely recreate them in Vietnam. The old myths could no longer be used unchanged.

For nearly a decade, Vietnam remained a subject too hot to handle in feature films. Hollywood dared approach the war only indirectly, as in the irreverent comedy *M*A*S*H* (1970), set during the Korean War. By 1978, however, attitudes were changing. A new wave of Vietnam movies were scheduled for release, encouraged by reports of Francis Ford Coppola's epic under way, *Apocalypse Now.* "When I started," Coppola recalled, "basically people said, 'Are you crazy? You can't make a movie on Vietnam, the American public does not want it.' " Coppola was prudent enough to hire two presidential pollsters to undertake a survey before he committed to the project. The results indicated that the public would indeed buy a "nondidactic" film. "The movie doesn't make you feel guilty," Coppola explained about his work in progress, "but it attempts to be cathartic."

Before Coppola could fulfill his lofty ambitions, however, Michael Cimino beat him in the race to capture Vietnam's mythic high ground. "Ready for Vietnam?" asked the *New York Times,* as *The Deer Hunter* opened in December 1978. Cimino told the *Times* that he had joined the army about the time of the Tet offensive. "For me, it's a very personal film. I was attached to a Green Beret medical unit. My characters are portraits of people whom I knew." Judging from the first reviews, Americans were indeed ready to confront Vietnam head-on. "The film dares to say that things have come down to life versus death, and it's time someone said this big and strong without fear," enthused *Newsweek.* "What really counts is authenticity, which this movie has by the ton," raved *New York* magazine.

But what was meant by "authentic"? To a historian viewing the film, the characters do seem less stereotyped than those in *The Green Berets.* The dialogue is more natural, less stilted. Yet the film's story and images seem just as mythic. The first third of the drama takes place not in Vietnam but in Clairton, a steel town nestled in the foothills of the Alleghenies. Michael (Robert De Niro), Nick (Christopher Walken), and Steven (John Savage) are leaving their mill jobs in this Russian American community, off to serve in Vietnam. Steven is married after his last day at work; then he and his buddies head into the mountains for one last deer hunt together. Michael, the obvious leader of the group, regards the hunt as a defining, purifying moment. One must do the job right, he tells Nick: bring down a buck with only one shot. Like Natty Bumppo, James Fenimore Cooper's nineteenth-century hero of *The Deerslayer,* Michael embodies America's noble ideals. The film's visual images emphasize the deep, almost ritualistic ties binding these men: at work, the fiery flames of the blast furnace; after hours, the enveloping dark of the neighborhood bar; at the wedding, the glittering icons of the Russian Orthodox church; out hunting, the misty, otherworldly peaks where Michael seeks his buck.

Moving and bold—yes. But authentic? The answer to that question is less clear. Cimino went to extreme lengths shooting these sequences, not so much to re-create historical reality as to obtain the proper "look" for his

Images of the "one-shot kill" are central to *The Deer Hunter.* Michael (Robert De Niro, *left*) embodies the frontier ideals of America. For him, the encounter with a buck on the mountainside is a defining, purifying moment. In contrast, the Viet Cong are depicted as inhuman torturers who pervert the idea of a "one-shot kill" into Russian roulette, which Michael and Steven (John Savage, *right*) are forced to play.

myths. Clairton is an imaginary town, created by shooting in eight different locations spread over four states. Its imposing Russian Orthodox church is from Cleveland and is twice the size of anything a town like Clairton might afford. The hunting scenes were shot not in the Alleghenies but on the other side of the continent, in the Cascades of Washington. When the deer proved too small for Cimino's taste, he airlifted in larger animals from a New Jersey preserve. "We needed big deer," he said. "I told them there would be a revolution in the theaters if we killed Bambi." Audiences *expect* big deer and overwhelming mountain peaks. And because myth deals with expectations rather than reality, Cimino obliged.

The first third of the film ends with the men sitting quietly in an empty bar, one of them rather implausibly playing a melancholy bit of Chopin on a piano. Still in semidarkness, we hear the first faint *whump whump whump* of helicopter blades. In a flash we are in Vietnam—the lush vegetation, the smoke, choppers bearing down on a hamlet. Things now happen quickly, confusingly. A Viet Cong guerilla throws a grenade down a bunker, wounding the peasant inside. We see Michael lying, perhaps stunned, in the grass nearby. Suddenly he springs up and incinerates the VC soldier with a flamethrower. Reinforcements appear, among them Steven and Nick.

After a firefight, the scene shifts abruptly to a Viet Cong camp where Steven, Nick, and Michael are being held with other prisoners. Sadistic guards force them to join a hideous game of Russian roulette, in which a prisoner places against his temple a pistol loaded with a single bullet, spins the cylinder, and fires. The losers die; the winners play the next challenger. Nick is nearly unmanned by the experience but survives. Michael one-ups his tormentors by daring to play with not one bullet but three. When he wins, he uses the bullets to kill the guards and then escapes with Nick and Steven.

The three men manage to reach American lines, but Steven loses both legs, while Nick, his sanity shaken, disappears into the underworld of Saigon, where casinos offer the same ghastly game of roulette. The final third of the film follows Michael back to Clairton, where he attempts to reconstruct the lost world of loyalty and community that the war has shattered. Finally he returns to Vietnam in a last attempt to rescue Nick, now a dazed, drug-addicted professional on the roulette circuit. The two face each other over the table—Michael, hoping that one final game will jolt Nick into returning home. But in his haze Nick plays on, and this time loses. Back in Clairton, his friends gather after the funeral. As the film ends, they sing "God Bless America"—tentatively at first, then with feeling.

The roulette scenes "act as a central metaphor of this film," noted Jean Vallely, a writer who interviewed Cimino for *Esquire* magazine. Certainly, the scenes are emotionally wrenching, impressively acted, and vividly shot—far more powerful than anything in *The Green Berets*. "I wanted people to feel what it was like to be there, to be in jeopardy every moment," Cimino explained. "How do you get people to pay attention, to sustain twenty minutes of war without doing a whole story about the war?" For Cimino, authenticity seems to revolve around dramatic *feelings*, constructing an emotionally arresting moment rather than a re-creation of the war's historical context. ("How do you get people to pay attention?") When Vallely probed for more information about the roulette scenes, Cimino seemed reluctant to talk, admitting only that he had read about such games "in a newspaper report."

Journalists who covered the war were less reticent. None of them had read any reports of Viet Cong forcing prisoners to play roulette, to say nothing of Saigon casinos practicing the sport. The best *Times* magazine could dig up was one or two unnamed "old hands" who were said to have recalled "a few episodes" from the 1920s and 1930s. Peter Arnett, a journalist awarded a Pulitzer for his reporting from Vietnam, complained, "I am now discovering that increasing numbers of Americans believe the last act of the war took place in a sinister back room somewhere in Saigon, where greedy Oriental gamblers were exhorting a glazed-eyed American G.I. to blow his head off." Seymour Hersh, who had helped bring the crimes at My Lai to light, walked out of a screening of *The Deer Hunter* in disgust.[2]

---

2. Apparently, Cimino's mythmaking was not limited to the movies. Reporter Tom Buckley discovered that the filmmaker had fudged his age in the *Times* interview, claiming he was thirty-five instead of forty. He had never been a Green Beret, had spent most of his six months of active duty at Fort Lee, New Jersey, with about a month thrown in for medical training in Texas, where he might have met a few of the Special Forces. This active duty occurred not in 1968, but 1962—well before the heaviest American involvement in Vietnam.

But if *The Deer Hunter* is not authentic in terms of historical details, do the film's myths in some way reflect a kind of emotional truth about the war? To answer that question, we need to consider what emotions are being called forth by the plot of *The Deer Hunter.* Just as we did with *The Green Berets*, we may want to ask what meanings can be deduced from the way that the film is constructed.

The Deer Hunter is an even longer film than *The Green Berets:* three hours and four minutes, to be exact. Yet how much of it concerns the actual experiences of American GIs in Vietnam? If we eliminate the scenes about the games of roulette—events that bear no relation to the real Vietnam—the answer is, *less than four minutes.* In that brief interval we see a Viet Cong guerilla drop a grenade into a bunker; we see Michael retaliate; and we see Michael, Nick, and Steven become prisoners. The structure of the film, in other words, suggests that very little of *The Deer Hunter* had *anything* to do with Vietnam. Yet of course it does. We need only imagine our Hollywood script doctor rewriting the plot to eliminate the war entirely. In the new version, Michael, Nick, and Steven are leaving Clairton to dig for gold in the jungles of Venezuela. Once there, they are captured (in about four minutes) by rival prospectors, who force them to play roulette . . . and so on, until Nick tragically blows his brains out in a backroom bar in Caracas. The structure of this new plot is precisely the same as the old one. The dramatic tension should be every bit as gripping. Yet would such a film receive the attention lavished on *The Deer Hunter?* Probably not.

Clearly, Cimino intended that audiences come away believing they had experienced something of the war's agonies: the haunting trauma of shattered communities, friendships, and lives. But in suggesting how that trauma came about, the film's plot amounts to a comforting, even racist fantasy. By spending only four minutes considering American actions in Vietnam, *The Deer Hunter* deflects attention away from the real traumatic events of the war and onto stereotyped villains. *They* did it to us, the film suggests: we were shattered by swarthy, inhuman tormentors. In their evil hands, the holiest myth of the West—the ritual of the one-shot kill—was perverted into an evil game of torture. This message was tailored perfectly for those filmgoers who, as Coppola said, didn't want to "feel guilty" and who could now leave the theater singing "God Bless America," believing that the myths at the center of Michael's world (and theirs) remained intact. Not surprisingly, *The Deer Hunter* received the Academy Award for Best Picture in April 1979. As Michael Cimino bounded to the podium to collect his Oscar, the man who handed it to him, now gaunt from a bout with cancer, was none other than John Wayne.

And in one final irony, the realities of Vietnam once more stood cinematic myth on its head. For there *was* at least one documented case of roulette that remained unnoticed by *The Deer Hunter*'s critics. The day after My Lai, Captain Ernest Medina flushed out another Viet Cong suspect as Charlie Company continued south. When the man refused to talk, Medina took his thirty-eight caliber revolver, placed it at the man's temple, and spun the barrel. Median later insisted that the gun was empty, but several of his men disagreed. When the villager still refused to talk, Medina "grabbed him by the hair and threw him up against a tree," said one eyewitness. "He fired two shots with a rifle, closer and closer to the guy's head, and then aimed straight at him." The suspect broke down and began babbling; he was indeed a communist province chief. Pleased, Medina posed for a picture. Drinking from a coconut held in one hand, he held in his other hand a large knife at the prisoner's throat.

THE SEARCH FOR NEW MYTHS

By using the same techniques of analysis that we brought to bear on *The Green Berets*, it becomes clear that the anguished experiences of Vietnam made it impossible for *The Deer Hunter* to follow the older, patriotic myths of the western or the combat dramas of World War II. Cimino's film won critical acclaim because it acknowledged the pain of Vietnam. Yet for all that, it refused to come to grips with the actual circumstances of the war. In 1979 director Francis Ford Coppola's *Apocalypse Now* provided a rival portrait that faced the realities of Vietnam more squarely.

Although the central plot of *Apocalypse Now* was as fictional and almost as far-fetched as *The Deer Hunter*'s, it did portray the kind of stresses laid bare at My Lai. Coppola's audience could never confuse his soldiers with the fresh-faced GIs who followed John Wayne or with Cimino's injured innocents abroad. In a sequence some critics hailed as the most thrilling battle scene ever filmed, Colonel Kilgore (whose name reflects his temperament) leads a helicopter assault nearly as ruthless as the one at My Lai. Although immensely harrowing, the assault seems almost surreal because the choppers descend on their target hamlet blasting Wagnerian opera from huge loudspeakers. (This move is to "scare the shit out of the slopes," Kilgore explains, reflecting the casual racism so often a part of the war.)

Just as the troops at My Lai left an 11th Brigade patch between the legs of a prominently displayed corpse, so Kilgore deals out playing cards of death on the bodies of his slain villagers, to serve both as boast and warning to the VC. Just as Charlie Company set up camp after the massacre and went swimming along the beaches of the South China Sea, Kilgore eagerly unpacks a surfboard to ride the waves offshore. The resonances with My Lai are unmistakable. Yet audiences may have been so swept away by the sheer bravado of the chopper assault that they failed to realize how much the scene undermined the cherished myth that Americans invariably preserved their humanity in the heat of battle. Often enough, viewers embraced the scene's affirmation of America's technological supremacy. In a chilling example of life imitating art, some American assault helicopters in the Gulf War of 1991 attacked Iraqi positions as loudspeakers aboard boomed out recordings of Wagner.

Colonel Kilgore's excesses, however, are only a prelude to a more metaphysical confrontation with the realities of My Lai. Captain Willard (Mar-

Mythical images of the West are twisted in Francis Ford Coppola's *Apocalypse Now*. In place of the can-do Colonel Kirby of *The Green Berets*, Colonel Kilgore, played by Robert Duvall, conducts a harrowing raid on a Vietnamese village. Duvall's cavalry hat and spurs draw the connection with the cinematic genre of the western, but the tragedy at My Lai has given this gleeful colonel a grim undertone: "I love the smell of napalm in the morning," says Kilgore after his conquest is complete.

tin Sheen) has been sent on a mission to eliminate a Green Beret colonel named Kurtz, who has deserted and is operating independently just across the Laotian border. As Willard journeys farther into the jungle, he himself becomes more ruthless, more like Kurtz. When the boat taking him upriver is sidetracked by a needless attack on a peasant sampan (the jittery crew opens fire prematurely), Willard shocks the other soldiers by cold-bloodedly killing a wounded woman so that his mission will not be delayed while they take her downriver for medical attention.[3] Willard recognizes the hypocrisy of the situation: "It was a way we had over here of living with ourselves. We'd cut 'em in half with a machine gun and give 'em a bandaid. It was a lie; and the more I saw of them, the more I hated lies." But instead of disavowing the war, Willard pushes deeper into the jungle toward the amoral Kurtz. He is descending, it seems, toward the same elemental savagery that characterized My Lai.

But in the end, *Apocalypse Now* is defeated by its own literary pretensions. In trying to make the film more than just another war picture, Coppola modeled his story on Joseph Conrad's literary classic *Heart of Darkness* (1902). Set along Africa's Congo River at the height of European imperialism, Conrad's tale concerns a man sent to investigate a colonial ruler gone "native"—also named Kurtz. Coppola's implication—that Vietnam is America's own imperialist nightmare—was an intriguing notion. But as played by an overweight, eccentric Marlon Brando, Kurtz only distracts from the grittier horrors of the real war. His lunacy is so otherworldly that it has no connection to the experiences of ordinary American GIs in Vietnam or to the earlier scenes in *Apocalypse Now* that gave the film its mythic power.

Meanwhile, many Americans remained reluctant to examine the causes or context of the brutality demonstrated at My Lai. It was simpler to embrace again the traditional myths of American valor, honor, and decency. The most prominent advocate of this approach was Ronald Reagan, a Hollywood actor turned politician who understood well how cinematic myths were made. As a presidential candidate in 1980, a year after the release of *Apocalypse Now*, Reagan called on Americans to "stand tall" and praised the war in Vietnam as a "noble cause." Reagan's views were in tune with a number of studies appearing in defense of the American role in Vietnam.

Hollywood too revised and burnished its views of the war. Two of the most popular films of the Reagan years starred Sylvester Stallone as the smoldering, half-Indian, half-German, entirely muscle-bound John Rambo. In *First Blood* (1982), Rambo seems to resemble yet another damaged and deranged vet from films of the 1970s. But times have changed: underneath the antisocial shell of this misunderstood ex–Green Beret lurks a noble savage. When Rambo is challenged by the sadistic sheriff of a corrupt town in the Pacific Northwest, he undertakes a private war against the establishment, leaving the town in ruins. In terms of Hollywood myths, this film is a revenge fantasy in which the innocent warrior, in tune with the land, vents his rage against the weak-kneed politicians and bureaucrats who refused to let him fight to win in Vietnam.

The relation of this revenge myth to the war was made clearer in a sequel, *First Blood, Part 2* (1985). A "Special Operations" unit from Washington wants

---

3. In a no-doubt unintended parallel with *The Green Berets*, the sampan firefight is triggered by a woman moving toward a crate that the Americans suspect contains weapons. In fact, the crate holds yet another puppy—a rather unlikely pet for this Vietnamese family. This time, of course, the irony is reversed: it's the *Americans* who are the wanton killers.

to send Rambo back into Vietnam to discover whether Americans listed during the war as MIAs (missing in action) are still being held as prisoners. In the film's entirely fictional plot, Rambo locates an MIA prison camp with the help of an Asian beauty he encounters deep in enemy territory. ("Too much death—death everywhere—maybe go America—live the quiet life," she remarks hopefully to the one American who has proved himself utterly incapable of settling down peacefully anywhere.) But treachery is afoot: when Rambo radios in the camp's location, the "stinking bureaucrat" from Special Operations calls back the rescue helicopter. He had assumed Rambo would fail, thus allowing the controversy over MIAs to disappear. Needless to say, Rambo manages to fight off entire detachments of Vietnamese and their Russian allies, rescuing the American prisoners and piloting them safely home.

Once again, consider the film's dramatic structure. How does the film's plot reflect a mythic rather than a historic reality about Vietnam? To begin with, although the producers clearly supported the notion that Vietnam was a "noble cause," the plot is not about the war itself. Why? In an escapist adventure, Rambo must be allowed to win. And even from Hollywood, where producers rewrite history to their taste, audiences would not accept a rewritten war in which the United States won. By focusing instead on the issue of MIAs, "victory" was defined in terms of the far simpler task of rescuing a dozen prisoners. And like *The Deer Hunter*, the film's motivation centers on what *they* did to *us*, rather than on the more ambiguous question of American involvement in Vietnam.

Furthermore, the mythical Green Beret of the 1960s has been transformed. In 1968, when real lives were being lost and real atrocities committed, *The Green Berets* was careful to show John Wayne restraining his bloodthirsty South Vietnamese allies. By the 1980s, however—a generation away from the real horrors of the war—Rambo's new version of valor is a muscular superman whose body becomes a well-oiled, finely tuned killing machine. (During the years when the war was actually fought, Stallone himself was spending his draft-age years teaching at a private girl's school in Switzerland, studying acting in Miami, and acting in a soft-core porn film titled *A Party at Kitty and Stud's*.)

The villains of the eighties have changed too. The Vietnamese still conform to the Hollywood stereotypes of Asian soldiers (they shout a lot and run around ineffectively), but Stallone's real opponent becomes a blond Russian sadist named Colonel Petrovsky. Vietnam had faded from the front pages, after all, while President Reagan was still referring to the Soviet Union as an "evil empire." Perhaps most revealing, the climax of the film occurs not when Stallone rescues the MIAs, but when he stomps into the American intelligence operations center and, in righteous wrath, machine-guns the files, computers, and radio equipment of the quaking traitor from Washington. "Do we get to win this time?" Rambo asks at the beginning of the film. By the time the last credits roll, he *has* won, not only defeating the Vietnamese and the Russians, but also the greatest villain of Ronald Reagan's domestic evil empire—the government bureaucrat.

In part, the passage of time and fading memories made it possible for a wide audience to accept Rambo's fantastic myths. Americans no longer had to face the war every night on the news. But greater distance had also drained the political debate of some of its old divisiveness. That opened the door, by 1986, to a very different film about Vietnam. The director of *Platoon*, Oliver Stone, had served in Vietnam for fifteen months and had been wounded twice. Returning home, he wrote a screenplay about the war, but in 1976 no one would produce it; memories were too fresh. A decade later, producers were willing to take the risk.

Platoon became one of the first commercially successful films to look at the war itself; to see Vietnam as history. As the opening credits roll, Chris Taylor (Charlie Sheen) steps out of the giant maw of a cargo plane into the oppressive heat of Vietnam. But the raw sounds of jet engines, jeeps, and airport clatter are muted. Over them, a serenely sad melody fills the soundtrack, a technique that distances us from what we are seeing. The music is Samuel Barber's *Adagio for Strings*, a composition that first received widespread attention in 1945, when it was broadcast following the announcement of Franklin Roosevelt's death. In *Platoon*, its elegiac melody mourns men and times past, a feeling reinforced by an epigraph on the screen: "Rejoice, O young men in thy youth." Taken from the Bible's book of Ecclesiastes, the words are not those of celebration but of warning, spoken by one whose youth has long vanished. ("I have seen everything that is done under the sun, and behold, all is vanity and a striving after wind.") As Taylor and other GIs cross the runway, they see the body bags of dead servicemen being loaded into the plane, heading home—those who have striven, perhaps, in vain.

At the outset, *Platoon's* format seems much like the old World War II dramas, with their ethnically balanced mix of soldiers learning the hard lessons of war. But this is Vietnam, and *Platoon* recognizes the differences. We meet Bunny, the violent redneck who takes bites out of beer cans; Rhah, the tough-minded Puerto Rican; King, a black draftee from the rural hills of Tennessee; Lerner, a naive white recruit; Junior, a street-smart black soldier from the urban north; and Chris Taylor—the observer, newcomer, and college-educated odd man out who has volunteered for service. Because of the war's duty rotation system, recruits stayed in Vietnam for only one year. Thus the composition of fighting units was constantly changing, as each "grunt" in the field served out his 365 days and departed. Under such a system, morale was more difficult to maintain, since newcomers were treated suspiciously as greenhorns whose mistakes were likely to get the old hands killed. And the old hands had every incentive to duck tough assignments that might send them home in a body bag.

Platoon also dramatizes the anguish of fighting in Vietnam. Sheen is tormented by ants that crawl over him; he faints from the heat and humidity of a hard march; he stares anxiously into a rainy, impenetrable dark, trying to spot the invisible enemy. Then on New Year's Day 1968, the platoon comes upon an enemy bunker complex. At the center of the jungle camp a fire still burns—evidently the VC have fled only moments earlier. Sergeant Elias (Willem Dafoe) probes a tunnel complex, inching along in the dark, hoping not to be blown away by a waiting guerilla. Others in the platoon are spread out along the camp's perimeter, each nervous about being isolated. Suddenly a booby trap explodes, killing a soldier.

From out of the jungle the men march to a nearby village. The VC have retreated here, haven't they? Along the way, another soldier is found brutally murdered, leaving the platoon in a dangerous mood. The villagers go placidly about their farmwork; yet the Americans realize that at the very least the hamlet's residents have been helping the guerrillas, and perhaps are VC themselves. The scar-faced Sergeant Barnes (Tom Berenger) stalks angrily through the settlement, finding concealed ammunition, herding some of the women into a pigpen. Taylor flushes one man from a bunker and, temporarily enraged, shoots at the feet of a peasant, making him dance in fear. Then Bunny crushes the man's skull with his rifle butt. Outside, other women and children are crying as Barnes questions the village's headman. The hysteria, the fear, and the rage clearly upset many of the men, who are on the verge of opening fire indiscriminately. Sergeant Barnes shoots one woman who has been yelling at him; then points his rifle at the headman's daughter and is about to execute her when Elias physically attacks him and tells him to stop. Barnes backs off, but fixes Elias with a steely eye. "You're dead," he says. The platoon's lieutenant gives the order to torch the village, and then the soldiers move out.

What makes this sequence remarkable is that unlike *The Green Berets, The Deer Hunter,* or Rambo's fantasies—even unlike *Apocalypse Now*—it provides an answer to a question that is at bottom historical rather than mythical. What we see unfolding before us is My Lai—or rather, a My Lai in the making, averted only because Sergeant Elias steps in. But because the film has followed the platoon's mission over the course of several months, we are seeing the incident *in context*—a context that closely mirrored the Vietnam experience of many American GIs. The trauma of Vietnam becomes not merely a question of what they did to *us*. Nor is it even a question of what we did to *them*, which is the equally distorted reverse-angle perspective. *Platoon* makes it easier to see that in a civil war, where the civilian population is divided, war becomes an ambiguous, dangerous occupation, especially for foreigners who understand little of Vietnamese culture. The women who protest "No VC! No VC!" may be cooking enough rice to feed an entire unit hiding nearby; and the children who accept candy from GIs and call out "Okay! Okay!" may turn around and lob a grenade. "I used to like kids," said Herbert Carter, one of the soldiers at My Lai, "but I can't stand them any more."

In a war in which territory was never gained permanently, how could victory be measured? Body counts were one way. "Anything that's dead and isn't white is a VC," went one Army joke making the rounds. A member of Charlie Company recalled being shocked, shortly after he arrived in Vietnam, to see a troop carrier drive by with "about twenty human ears tied to

The amoral Sergeant Barnes (Tom Berenger) threatens to kill a young villager in *Platoon*. Contrast this scene with the one of John Wayne in *The Green Berets* on page 407. The events at My Lai have obviously altered dramatically the cinematic images of Americans at war in an ambiguous conflict.

the antenna." Even Lyndon Johnson could not resist exhorting troops in Vietnam to "come home with the coonskin on the wall." When GIs began to measure victory in terms of bodies counted, when friend and foe looked alike, and when more than a half dozen men in Charlie Company had been killed by exploding booby traps, the ingredients for trouble were present. "It just started building," recalled Ronald Grzesik. "I don't know why. Everybody reached the point where they were frustrated. . . . I remember writing a letter home saying that I once had sympathy for these people, but now I didn't care." Two days before My Lai, Gregory Olsen, a devout Mormon in Charlie Company, wrote his father about what happened after another booby trap incident:

> It all turned out a bad day made even worse. On their way back to "Dotti" [other members of the company] saw a woman working in the fields. They shot and wounded her. Then they kicked her to death and emptied their magazines in her head. They slugged every little kid they came across.
>
> Why in God's name does this have to happen? These are all seemingly normal guys; some were friends of mine. For a while they were like wild animals.

It was murder, and I'm ashamed of myself for not trying to do anything about it.

This isn't the first time, Dad. I've seen it many times before. I don't know why I'm telling you all this; I guess I just want to get it off my chest.

To its credit, *Platoon* reflects these realities. Yet it reaches no hard conclusions about the issues it raises. Having made reference to My Lai, the scene in the hamlet ends with an image of American innocence. Against the backdrop of burning huts, the platoon escorts frightened villagers to safety. GIs who moments earlier were ready to murder and rape now cradle children in their arms—just as, at the real My Lai, Colonel Medina and Lieutenant Calley shared cookies and crackers with two girls from the village. Repeatedly, *Platoon* returns to this tension between good and evil. During another mission, the violent Barnes makes good his threat to kill the saintly Elias. The mythical overtones are strong: with a church in the background, Elias dies like Christ, his arms stretched out as if in crucifixion. But here, good and evil do not boil down to *us* versus *them*. The good Elias is every bit as much a soldier as the evil Barnes. The experience of My Lai has forced *Platoon* to give up the myth of American exceptionalism—that Americans are more virtuous, thanks to their special circumstances. Americans must wrestle with the evil within themselves as all people do.

Elias as a Christ figure, Barnes as an amoral realist . . . These are mythological and dramatic—rather than historical—concepts. But they reflect the circumstances of the war in far different ways than do the myths of *The Green Berets* or *The Sands of Iwo Jima*. *Platoon*'s ambiguities reveal the difficulty of imposing traditional myths on Vietnam, a war that demanded myths of its own.

In the end, it will not do to say that *Platoon* is better history than *The Green Berets*—although most historians might conclude that it more accurately portrays the conditions of the war. Myths of the cinema will always reflect the needs of drama more than the requirements of historical evidence. For their part, historians must remain faithful to their own creed: to examine the images of the silver screen rationally and with the same skepticism they bring to any primary or secondary source.

But is a rational, skeptical approach enough? If truth be told, people do not often make love or die for their country on rational grounds alone. The best history recognizes those deep-seated emotions that myths address. For that reason we have examined not only the facts of My Lai but the more intangible effects the event has had on our self-image as a nation. In their eagerness to become mythmakers for the millions, the magicians of Hollywood have offered us not one but many myths with which to shape our lives. The power of history to undertake a reasoned analysis of the past offers hope—and perhaps a method by which we may come to appreciate the authentic truths that the best myths reveal.

So let us return one last time to Son My. As historians, we cannot expunge the painful record of what took place, but it may be worth reiterating that

My Lai stood as an extreme of the American experience in Vietnam. If the booby traps, the ambushes, the frustrations of an unseen enemy worked on all soldiers, not all chose to behave in the same way, even at My Lai.

POV, above the hamlet in an observation helicopter: Chief Warrant Officer Hugh Thompson, of Decatur, Georgia, is sweeping the area. He spots a wounded girl by the side of a rice paddy and decides to mark her location with a smoke grenade so that the men on the ground can provide medical help. Thompson is astonished to see a captain walk over to the girl and shoot her. Turning north, Thompson sees a small boy bleeding along a trench and marks *his* location with smoke. Casually, a lieutenant walks up and empties a clip into the child.

Beside himself with anger, Thompson tries to contact ground forces. When he cannot get through, he radios a loud protest to brigade headquarters. Then, circling over the hamlet's outskirts, he sees a canal ditch with "a bunch of bodies in it." A pilot nearby is reminded of "the old Biblical story of Jesus turning water into wine. The trench had a grey color to it, with the red blood of the individuals." Thompson spots some children still alive among the mass of bodies. Nearly frantic, he lands his small chopper and picks up a child about two years old, dazed with shock. He calls in another gunship for a dozen more youngsters. In the air once again, he sights the same lieutenant who shot the child he had marked earlier. The lieutenant—Thompson later identifies him as Calley—is in the process of destroying a bunker in which women and children are huddled.

This time Thompson lands, gets out of the chopper, stalks over to Calley, and tells him to remove the civilians. The only way to get them out, responds Calley, is to use hand grenades. "You just hold your men right here," Thompson retorts angrily, "and I will get the women and kids out." Thompson orders one of the waist gunners in his chopper to aim his machine gun "at that officer" and shoot if he tries to interfere. Then Thompson walks back and places himself physically between Calley's troops and the women and children, until a chopper arrives to evacuate them.

For his actions, Thompson was belatedly awarded the Distinguished Flying Cross. The curious historian may consult the citation in Army records; it is less than direct in describing the conditions under which Thompson had been "disregarding his own safety." It notes only that he found the children "between Viet Cong positions and advancing friendly forces." As usual, the raw material of the past is neither as clear-cut nor as comforting as the larger-than-life deeds of the cinema. It remains for historians, sifting through such telltales, to fashion narratives that are worth not only dying for, but living with.

Additional Reading

Rather than provide a comprehensive survey of the many films of the Vietnam War, we chose to explore a few films in depth. We strongly recommend that students view for themselves at least some of those films. All are available on videocassette and DVD. For broader coverage of the films of Vietnam, see Albert Auster and Leonard Quart, *How the War Was Remembered: Hollywood and Vietnam* (New York, 1988); Linda Dittmar and Gene Michaud, eds., *From Hanoi to Hollywood: The Vietnam War in American Film* (New Brunswick, NJ, 1990); and Pat Aufflerheide, "Vietnam: Good Soldiers," in Mark Crispin Miller, ed., *Seeing through Movies* (New York, 1990). Nor did we discuss documentary films about Vietnam. *Hearts and Minds* (1974) illustrates how the format can convey a highly interpretive message; *Vietnam: A Television History* (1983) is a thorough thirteen-part series originally aired on the Public Broadcasting System (PBS). Both pay far more attention to the Vietnamese side of the war than most American accounts. Another PBS series, *Frontline*, has examined the My Lai incident in *Remember My Lai* (WGBH Television, 1989). Michael Lee Lanning, *Vietnam at the Movies* (New York, 1994) reviews some 380 films with Vietnam War themes and characters.

Over the past decade historians have begun to take a much more serious view of media, both for historical content and for the treatment of historical subjects. *The Journal of American History* regularly reviews commercial films and documentaries, and the *American Historical Review* has published film forums. Mark Carnes, ed., *Past Imperfect: History According to the Movies* (New York, 1995) gathered more than sixty scholars to discuss films covering history. Two recent studies take up this interest: Robert Brent Toplin, *History by Hollywood: The Use and Abuse of the American Past* (Urbana, IL, 1996), and Robert Burgoyne, *Film Nation: Hollywood Looks at U.S. History* (Minneapolis, 1997). See also a collection of essays sponsored by the American Historical Association: John E. O'Connor, ed., *Image as Artifact: The Historical Analysis of Film and Television* (Malabar, FL, 1990). For those unfamiliar with filmmaking, James Monaco provides an excellent introduction to understanding how the medium shapes its message in *How to Read a Film*, 3d ed. (New York, 2000).

Two journalists have provided detailed reconstructions of the events at My Lai: Richard Hammer, *One Morning in War: The Tragedy of Son My* (New York, 1970), and Seymour Hersh, *My Lai 4: A Report on the Massacre and Its Aftermath* (New York, 1970). Both authors also examined aspects of the military investigations and trials: Hersh in *Cover-up: The Army's Secret Investigation of the Massacre at My Lai 4* (New York, 1972) and Hammer in *The Court Martial of Lieutenant Calley* (New York, 1971). Ronald Spector, *After Tet: The Bloodiest Year of the War* (New York, 1994) puts the massacre into wider perspective. Psychiatrist Robert Jay Lifton uses psychological theory to explain the soldiers' experience in *Home from the War: Vietnam Veterans—Neither Victims nor Executioners* (New York, 1973), while Peter Goldman and Tony

Fuller profile a single company (not the one at My Lai) in *Charlie Company: What Vietnam Did to Us* (New York, 1983). One of the most controversial studies on combat trauma is Jonathan Shay, *Achilles in Vietnam: Combat Trauma and the Undoing of Character* (New York, 1995). On the issue of war crimes, see *The Winter Soldiers Investigation: An Inquiry into American War Crimes* (New York, 1972), issued by Vietnam Veterans Against the War.

The number of books on the war itself is vast. Robert Schulzinger, *A Time for War: The United States in Vietnam, 1941–1975* (New York, 1997) covers the America side, while Marilyn B. Young, *The Vietnam Wars, 1945–1990* (New York, 1991) pays more attention to the Vietnamese context. A judicious introduction is George Herring, *America's Longest War: The United States in Vietnam, 1950–1975*, 2d ed. (New York, 1986). Two other useful jumping-off points are Stanley Karnow, *Vietnam: A History* (New York, 1983), and George Kahin, *Intervention: How America Became Involved in Vietnam* (New York, 1986). Two recent books, Fred Logevall, *Choosing War: The Last Chance for Peace and the Escalation of the War in Vietnam* (Berkeley, 2001), and David Kaiser, *American Tragedy: Kennedy, Johnson, and the Origins of the Vietnam War* (Cambridge, MA, 2000) explore the political decisions leading to American involvement. Michael Lind, *Vietnam: The Necessary War: A Reinterpretation of America's Most Disastrous Military Conflict* (New York, 2002) rejects both liberal and conservative interpretations of the war, placing it in a wider cold war context.

Among the many memoirs and accounts of those who fought the war, we can recommend Christian Appy, *Patriots: The Vietnam War Remembered from All Sides* (New York, 2002); Tim O'Brien, *If I Die in a Combat Zone* (New York, 1989); Philip Caputo, *A Rumor of War* (New York, 1977); and Ron Kovic, *Born on the Fourth of July* (New York, 1977). Kovic's book, of course, invites comparison with Oliver Stone's film of the same title and provides an interesting example of how filmmakers change stories for dramatic reasons. Three oral histories survey a range of GIs' experiences: Al Santoli, *Everything We Had* (New York, 1981); Mark Baker, *Nam: The Vietnam War in the Words of the Men and Women Who Fought* (New York, 1983); and Wallace Terry, *Bloods: An Oral History of the Vietnam War by Black Veterans* (New York, 1984). Finally, Michael Herr's *Dispatches* (New York, 1978) is a personal history of the war that captures its extremes almost better than anything else. A comprehensive account of reporting on the war is found in the Library of America's two volumes, *Reporting Vietnam: American Journalism, 1959–1969* (New York, 1998) and *1969–1975* (New York, 1999). William Hammond, *Reporting Vietnam: Media and the Military at War* (Lawrence, KS, 1998) is also informing.

Among other films worth seeing but not discussed in this chapter are *Coming Home* (1978), an early attempt to explore the struggle of returning vets, and *Go Tell the Spartans*, based on a novel by Daniel Ford (*Incident at Muc Wa*). This low-budget film was eclipsed in 1978 by *Coming Home* and *The Deer Hunter*, but it portrayed the war's gritty ambiguities far more accurately. A more recent pair worth comparing are *Casualties of War* and *Born on the Fourth of July*. Both were released in 1990, both featured well-known stars, both dealt with painful experiences of the war. Yet one film succeeded at the box office, while the other did badly. Based on the principles set forth in this chapter, readers should be able to explain why in terms of myths and audience expectations. Stanley Kubrick's *Full Metal Jacket* explores the dehumanizing experiences of basic training and war (1987). *We Were Soldiers* (2002) re-creates the first major battle of the war in the Ia Drang Valley in 1965. The movie's success suggests a continued interest in Vietnam. In charting the effects of the Vietnam War on American cinematic myths, John Wayne's earlier westerns and war epics are worth viewing. Lifton's book (cited above) notes how many eager recruits went off to war with images of John Wayne in their heads. To better understand Wayne's popular image, look at Gary Wills, *John Wayne's America: The Politics of Celebrity* (New York, 1997).

Two edited collections allow readers to engage for themselves the issues raised by My Lai and the Vietnam War. David Anderson, ed., *Facing My Lai: Moving Beyond the Massacre* (Lawrence, KS, 1998) gathered a distinguished group of historians, military people, veterans, and journalists for a conference on My Lai; this book contains their perspectives on the massacre and its meaning. James S. Olson and Randy Roberts, eds., *My Lai: A Brief History with Documents* (New York, 1999) gathered primary materials about this tragic event.

Interactive Learning

The *Primary Source Investigator* provides materials that explore the media portrayal of the Vietnam War. This section contains images of cinematic legends such as John Wayne in *The Green Berets*, as well as reviews of popular films depicting the Vietnam War. Also included are documentary images and written accounts of Vietnamese and Americans, which can be contrasted with the Hollywood portrayals.

CHAPTER 17
The Body in Question

In the early 1980s Richard Gordon was a young psychology professor at Bard, a small liberal arts college north of New York City in the Hudson Valley. He had also established a part-time clinical practice in nearby Red Hook, a village so middle-American that some locals called it "a meatloaf and gravy town." Gordon soon discovered a curious link among some of his patients. One young woman who came to see him confessed she "was making herself sick." Obsessed about being fat, she had locked herself into a cycle of overeating and vomiting. Yet Gordon observed that she was at most only slightly overweight. Soon, more patients with eating disorders came to seek treatment, though Gordon was not known as a specialist. All these patients were women, and most were young, college-aged, and from middle- or upper-middle-class backgrounds. Local counseling centers confirmed his sense that two disorders were on the rise among college students: bulimia nervosa, which involves repeated cycles of binging on food and then purging; and anorexia nervosa, which is characterized by severe undereating.

In 1983, shortly after Gordon began noticing an increase in the number of these cases, popular singer Karen Carpenter died suddenly of cardiac arrest, brought on by acute anorexia. News media ran photos of her gaunt face and cadaverous body. Obsessed with making herself thin, Carpenter had been regularly dosing herself with ipecac, an over-the-counter emetic. Whereas doctors recommended ipecac to induce vomiting in cases of accidental poisoning, Carpenter used it to purge her food. The notion of a beautiful young celebrity starving herself to death aroused both popular curiosity and horror about anorexia.

Although Carpenter's anorexia attracted widespread attention, bulimia was the more commonly diagnosed disorder. One clinical text offered a particularly graphic description of a food obsession triggering a bulimic episode. The account begins with a young woman's trip to the supermarket to buy ice cream and a brownie mix. On her way home, unable to contain her urge, she

The death of singer Karen Carpenter in 1983 brought the spreading epidemic of anorexia and bulimia to the attention of the wider public. Carpenter had been wrestling with the problem for years, having begun a "water diet" in 1967 that brought her weight down from 140 pounds to 120. By the autumn of 1975 she was severely underweight at 80 pounds, and at one Las Vegas singing appearance she collapsed on stage while singing "Top of the World." Here Carpenter (right) accepted a trophy at the American Music Awards in 1977.

buys and consumes a dozen doughnuts. And then the binging begins in earnest:

> I'd hastily mix up the brownie mix and get the brownies in the oven, usually managing to eat a fair amount of the mix as I was going along. Then, while they were cooking, I ate the ice cream. Only by eating the ice cream could I bear the delay until the brownies came out of the oven. Sometimes I'd finish the whole gallon even before the brownies were done, and I'd take the brownies out of the oven while they were still baking. At any rate, I'd start eating brownies, even though by this time I was feeling sick, intending to stop after two or three. Then it would be five or six. Pretty soon, I'd have put away fifteen or twenty brownies, and then I would be overcome with embarrassment. What if one of my roommates were to come home and see that I'd eaten

twenty brownies! The only way to disguise it obviously was to finish the other fifty-two brownies myself, wash the pan and clean everything up. . . .

Seventy-two brownies later the depression hit. I'd go to the bathroom, stick my finger down my throat, and make myself throw-up. I was so good at it that it was almost automatic . . . instant vomiting, over and over until there was nothing coming out of my stomach except clear pale-green fluid.

Richard Gordon puzzled over the increase in eating-related disorders. He first encountered a case of anorexia when working as an intern in New York some ten years earlier. His supervisor at the Payne Whitney Psychiatric Clinic remarked that such a case was rare and that Gordon would probably see few such patients in his entire career. Yet now they were coming to him regularly. Looking for guidance, he attended a workshop sponsored by the recently founded Center for the Study of Bulimia and Anorexia in New York. He expected to be one of a handful of professionals. The center's director had planned for an audience of fifty to a hundred, yet several hundred people registered. At the lectures and seminars Gordon learned what he had come to suspect: that his own cases of anorexia and bulimia were part of a growing national epidemic.

By the mid-1980s health professionals were counting eating disorders as the third most common health problem—after obesity and asthma—for adolescent females. New cases of anorexia were increasing some 35 percent every five years from 1950 to 1984, after which the rate appeared to slow. The total number of anorexics in the United States by the mid-1980s hovered somewhere around 300,000. The figure for bulimia was likely closer to a million, but since many bulimics kept their affliction secret, the number may have been significantly higher. Given that adolescent females are normally one of the healthiest population cohorts, what made these totals disturbing was the high percentage of fatal cases (5 to 20 percent in diagnosed cases, depending on how the cause of death is interpreted). Anorexia and bulimia had become so widespread that Gordon decided to become a specialist in the field, publishing a widely read study on eating disorders in 1990.

In the 1980s clinicians regularly referred to both the anorexic and the bulimic as "her" because over 90 percent of the patients suffering from the diseases were women. Indeed, until recently most researchers assumed that the excessive preoccupation with body image and appearance was an almost exclusively female phenomenon. American culture taught boys and men that it was inappropriate, indeed feminine, to be overly concerned with their appearance. But by the 1990s clinicians began to realize that obsessive worries about body shape and body image were spreading among men too—though with a difference. Whereas women worried they could never be too thin, men feared they could never be big enough. Researchers established that men's dissatisfaction with their body appearance had "tripled in less than thirty years—from 15 percent in 1972 to 34 percent in 1985 to 43 percent in 1997." Indeed, they were surprised to learn "that men were catching up to women." What clinicians came to call muscle dysmorphic disorder among men—

known more popularly as "bigorexia"—paralleled the increase in anorexia and bulimia among women.

Public awareness of that disorder was slow in coming, despite the growing popularity in the 1980s of muscle-bound film stars such as Arnold Schwarzenegger and Sylvester Stallone. In 1998 when slugger Mark McGuire broke Babe Ruth's home-run record, he admitted using a food supplement containing androstenedione, a steroidal compound that promoted muscle growth by increasing testosterone. Several years later, bereaved families of a 28-year-old bodybuilder in Las Vegas and a 27-year-old Marine Corps officer in Florida sued a nutritional supplement manufacturer, Twin Laboratories, blaming the men's deaths on an ephedra supplement called "Ripped Fuel."

These and other cases served as a warning that disorders centered on body image were hardly limited to women. Researchers described a condition among boys, some even in grade school, who suffered from low self-esteem and depression because of dissatisfaction with their body image. And the potential medical and social consequences were serious. When men used anabolic steroids in an effort to bulk up, they faced an increased risk of heart disease, stroke, and prostate cancer. Worse, some men taking steroids became aggressive to the point of committing violent crimes—most commonly, the abuse of women. Steroids also proved addictive. Those who attempted to withdraw often suffered severe depression.

The obvious lesson—that there is a certain rough equality to the fact that both men and women are subject to such ills—is not the most interesting conclusion to be drawn. More tantalizing is the *differing* anxieties of men and women, for these differences seem rooted in gender identity. *Gender* is defined as "sexual identity, especially in relation to society or culture," and in some way, gender's link to society or culture seems central to the creation of body dysmorphias. If so, then an attempt to understand anorexia, bulimia, and bigorexia may require more than just a narrowly medical approach. Historians may use these abnormal behaviors as a lens to analyze how sexual differences are shaped by larger forces in American society.

DISEASE AS CULTURE-BOUND

Research done on body image and eating disorders generally falls into three categories—genetic/organic, psychological, and cultural. The first category sees the root of body dysmorphia as essentially organic: genetics or somatic and biological factors are the primary causal agents. Accordingly, treatment calls for medical intervention such as hospitalization and drug therapy.

Scientific research does suggest that genes play a role in determining body shape and in influencing what percentage of any population is thin or fat. In addition, genetic factors seem to make some people biologically prone to depression or, as one researcher put it, to "a predisposition to developing obsessive-compulsive symptoms" that can be expressed as anorexia, bulimia, or muscle dysmorphia. Studies of identical twins separated at birth are often used to assess the influence of genetic factors in shaping behavior. If twins develop similar behaviors, even when raised in different environments, then a genetic explanation seems in order. In a study of identical twins and anorexia nervosa, when one sibling developed the disorder, the separately raised twin developed anorexia about 55 percent of the time.

As that percentage also suggests, genes cannot be the only factor. (Why, after all, didn't the other 45 percent develop anorexia?) So scientists have studied a second set of causal factors: psychological dynamics. For example, during therapy, anorexics often reveal that they were emotionally or sexually abused as children, or that at least one parent was preoccupied with weight issues. Other patients speak of parents who place an extremely high value on achievement, or of a male parent or grandparent who has failed in some competitive aspect of his life. Many men with muscle dysmorphia recall being teased as boys or even humiliated about the inadequacy of their bodies. It makes sense, then, that the psychological contours of an individual's life contribute to the development of behavioral disorders.

Yet to focus on *individual* circumstances—looking at cause and effect on a case-by-case basis—misses a larger point. As Richard Gordon realized, anorexic and bulimic patients were appearing in significantly larger numbers during the 1980s, compared with only a decade or two earlier. Presumably, social or cultural forces were behind that upswing, shaping the psychological conditions experienced by so many individuals. To the historian, for whom change over time is a central concern, it is highly suggestive that the epidemic of body dysmorphias began in the late 1970s and early 1980s and not, for example, in the 1950s. What changes in American society might have created the conditions for not just a few cases of body dysmorphia but an epidemic?

In looking at the three causal categories sketched here—genetic/organic, psychological, and cultural—the genetic explanation lies on one end of the spectrum. If we could explain anorexia, bulimia, and muscle dysmorphia in terms of genetic or organic factors alone, then the disease's cultural context would not matter in the slightest. Someone with a certain biological makeup would develop body dysmorphia whether he or she grew up in Boise, Bombay, or Mexico City. On the other hand, if cultural conditions alone produced the disorder, we might expect an epidemic of even greater size than what social scientists have recorded. A million cases of anorexia or bulimia is surely a large number. Yet millions more adolescents were exposed to broadly similar cultural conditions but were not similarly affected. Presumably, the middle category—the psychological explanation—serves to mediate between cultural and genetic/organic theories of causation. Perhaps the influence of both genetic factors and cultural conditions is heightened by individual psychological circumstances arising out of family relations, childhood histories, and so on.

For the psychologist seeing one patient at a time, individual psychology remains paramount. For the historian studying the behaviors of larger groups, however, cultural explanations come to the fore. If cultural conditions determine whether some disorders become common, that is another way of saying that the disorder is culturally constructed, at least in part. Body dysmorphia spreads among large numbers of people because the conditions promoting it are widespread at a certain place and time.

As Richard Gordon studied body dysmorphias, he came to believe that the epidemic was generated by specific aspects of American culture. In order to understand how such disorders could depend on cultural factors, he looked for other illnesses or disorders closely associated with a single culture but uncommon elsewhere. He discovered that such "culture-bound" illnesses had been explored by George Devereux, a social psychologist active during the 1950s. Devereux studied a variety of illnesses not seen in western societies. They included *amok*, violent homicidal rampages among men in Indonesia, Malaysia, and New Guinea; *latah*, a trancelike "fright syndrome" experienced by women in the South Pacific; and *koro*, a delusion among men in southern China that their penises were receding into their bodies.[1]

Each of these disorders was widespread only within a single culture; clearly, conditions within those societies promoted the outbreaks. But what interested Devereux—and Gordon—was that these culture-bound disorders expressed "crucial contradictions and core anxieties of a society," that is, although the disorders were not viewed as normal, the behaviors associated with them were in fact exaggerations of values that were approved and even prized by the culture.

This dynamic could be seen in the case of *amok*, whose name has found its way into the English language in the phrase *running amuck*. The Southeast Asian cultures in which *amok* most commonly occurred exercised strict control over aggressive behavior and demanded deference to authority. If an individual perceived that he had been insulted, there was often no socially acceptable way to vent deeply felt resentment. In extreme cases, an offended man fell to brooding and withdrew for a time, before "running *amok*"— exploding in a murderous fury and literally dashing through the streets or countryside killing anyone who crossed his path. Malaysians so feared such outbursts that most villages kept a weapon at hand with which to stop an "*amok* runner."

Not surprisingly, the society in general condemned such behavior and severely punished it. Yet the term *amok* was a traditional ritual war cry, something called out by Malaysian medieval warriors as they went into battle. Such warriors were highly valued, and those who became *amok* runners were appropriating to their own behavior a role model exalted by the culture. As Devereux perceived, the deviant behavior of running *amok* reflected conduct that, under other circumstances, was sanctioned and even lauded.

These dynamics revealed by Devereux's analysis help illuminate the American outbreak of body dysmorphias. Like the culture-bound disorders

1. Devereux, and Gordon following him, use the term "ethnic disorders" to describe syndromes such as *amok*, *latah*, and *koro*. Other scholars refer to these disorders as "culture-bound," and we prefer that term, given this chapter's concern with cultural history, and given the potential confusion caused by the more traditional way that historians use the term *ethnic*.

found in Southeast Asia and China, anorexia, bulimia, and muscle dysmorphia have become widespread only in certain regions and under certain conditions. As in the case of *amok*, body dysmorphias involve behaviors valued
by society but taken to extremes. There is a connection, then, between the
way the body is perceived and the broader social and economic forces at
work in American society.

Recognizing this link, cultural historians have made increasing efforts to
study the cultural context of the body: verbal and visual images of it, popular discourse about it, and fantasies created around it. In doing so, they have
insisted that the body should be considered in a double light—one focusing
on the physical, corporeal, and material; and the other on the symbolic.

In its symbolic form, the body is a text of culture. The shapes that it takes,
the fashions with which it is adorned, and the uses to which it is put all reveal
the values of the culture or place in which a body exists. Personal grooming
habits, the way people stand or sit, and table manners are all ways in which
the values of a certain culture become physical. Think of the difference in
meaning between eating with a fork or eating with one's fingers, of shaving
or not shaving, of sitting sprawled in a chair or sitting erect, of wearing one's
hair long or short, of piercing one's body or having one's nose "fixed" through
plastic surgery. Indeed, color as a body attribute can have great social significance; recall the images once conjured up by referring to Indians as "red
men." Over the past decade, a school of analysis known as "whiteness studies" has considered similar implications for Anglo-American culture, in which
body color has been a key marker in framing the nebulous concept of race. In
hundreds of different ways, over hundreds of centuries, the male and female
human form has been used to *embody*—the term is appropriate here—the attributes and values of a culture.

Anthropologists have noted that societies prone to famine tend to place a
high value on large or fat bodies. In such cultures, full or rounded figures
serve as tangible symbols of success. As anthropologist Margaret MacKen-
zie wrote, "In a context where only a King can control enough food resources and labor supply to eat enough and do no physical labor so that he
becomes fat," high status is conferred on those who are heavy. By contrast,
a thin person appears to be too poor to afford sufficient food, or someone
who works too hard to put on weight. In modern societies, where famine is
rare and manual labor less common, thinness in women often confers higher
status. The body, then, is not simply a physical thing; it is also a cultural symbol laden with values. Through diet, exercise, fashion, and plastic surgery
people can shape their bodies to make a cultural statement.

GENDER AS HISTORICALLY BOUND

In searching for cross-cultural parallels, Richard Gordon was behaving as a
historian might. Convinced that this epidemic of body dysmorphias was
rooted in evolving cultural conditions, he was, in effect, looking for historical context.

To readers of this book, the need for context may seem obvious. Yet Gordon's notion that the epidemic was culturally constructed has not always been evident, especially when dealing with gender. Because men and women possess clear biological differences, more than a few social scientists have supposed that many aspects of male and female gender are biologically determined. Men, they have assumed, possess certain masculine qualities, just as women are born with their own innate feminine characteristics. Yet the historian's constant refrain—"Observe change over time!"—suggests caution about concluding that all gender characteristics are innate. As historians, we can put to good use the notion that the body can be studied as a cultural symbol. Why not investigate whether society's notions of the "essential" male or female changes from one era to the next? If gender is primarily biological, notions of what is masculine or feminine should not vary much over time. But in truth, even a brief examination of body images suggests that many aspects of gender are cultural constructions that constantly shift and evolve in response to social influences. Gender roles and gender identity are psychological and sociological, as well as biological, expressions.

Look, for example, at the way masculinity and femininity are embodied in the rapidly changing world of fashion. In seventeenth-century Europe, men made themselves sexually attractive by wearing wigs and sporting tight knee stockings to show "a bit of calf." They also doused themselves with powder and perfume. In the American backcountry of the 1830s, on the other hand, men's cologne was mocked as "skunkwater," and tight stockings were derided as effeminate. Yet in both eras the clothed male body became a symbol of historically generated values. Men wore wigs in seventeenth-century France because King Louis XIV was bald and adopted them to conceal his self-perceived infirmity. In the rude equality of the frontier, colognes and stockings were viewed as aristocratic luxuries because most men had neither the money to afford them nor the time to use them.

In terms of making comparisons across time, the latter half of the nineteenth century is particularly illuminating. During those decades tensions over gender identity were clearly reflected in the cultural ideals of men's and women's bodies.

In mid-nineteenth-century America, a visual ideal of what it meant to be a woman had been articulated in paintings, illustrations, and theatrical performances. A characteristic example appears in the drawing from 1829 on page 440. When it came to beauty, one American observed, "You must dismiss all ideas of voluptuousness, commanding figure" and instead "summon up such associations as you have been accustomed to connect with the words sylph and fairy." Often women were portrayed with their heads tilted modestly, suggesting a proper submissiveness. Hands and feet were tiny and delicate, as were waists. Yet a stiff rectitude clung to the paintings and engravings of the era—so much so that one fashion critic at the dawn of the twentieth century archly referred to the type as the "steel-engraved lady."

Historian Lois Banner, who studied the changing ideals of beauty, has pointed out that the physical attributes of these steel-engraved beauties were

Hourglass figures and waspish waists were part of the feminine ideal of beauty in the mid-nineteenth century. The lips display the proper "bee-stung cupid bow" to finish off the appearance of these "steel-engraved ladies."

no more "natural" than the high-cheekboned, full-lipped look of present-day models. Women had to *work* to embody the desired qualities. Note the women's mouths in the illustration: they resemble rosebuds or, in the words of observers of the time, the "bee-stung cupid bow." To attain the look, women learned to pucker their mouths by pronouncing a series of words beginning with the letter *p: peas, prunes, prisms* . . . The proper way to enter a room, according to one etiquette manual, was with the word *prisms* fading from one's lips. The hourglass waist was a similarly artificial creation, accomplished through the use of a corset. The lacing had to be pulled so tight that for any woman too poor to afford a servant's assistance, a bedpost had to be used—wedged up under the strings—to provide leverage. The "steel-engraved" ideal reigned for decades.

In the years following the Civil War, however, the ideal of womanhood began to change. Prominent doctors in the 1870s commended plumpness as a sign of health and urged both men and women to gain weight. One New York socialite reported that her physician had advised her to eat for two and to "part with her figure" after she bore her first child. In 1868 Harriet Beecher Stowe could still complain that "Our willowy girls are afraid of nothing so much as growing stout." But by 1875 an English visitor to the United States was reporting that American women were "constantly having

"There was nothing wraith-like about Lillian Russell," wrote one male admirer, who had worked with her briefly during the 1880s. "She was a voluptuous beauty, and there was plenty of her to see. . . . Our tastes were not thin or ethereal." Russell's padded dress and corseted waist epitomized the height of fashion during the late nineteenth century, when fuller figures were in vogue.

themselves weighed, and every ounce of increase is hailed with delight. . . . When I asked a beautiful Connecticut girl how she liked the change, 'Oh! immensely,' she said, 'I have gained eighteen pounds in flesh since last April.'"

The new ideal was communicated in a variety of ways. Increasingly, middle- and upper-class Americans were exposed to European painters such as Adolphe Bouguereau, whose nude representations of nymphs and satyrs were buxom and voluptuous—hardly the sylphlike fairies envisioned earlier in the century. Many Americans flocked to the theater, where Lydia Thompson, an English actress, led a popular troupe of scantily clad but quite full-figured women known as the "British Blondes." Later in the century, the actress Lillian Russell embodied the ideal of a full-figured beauty.

Despite the marked contrast with the "steel-engraved lady," women still had to work to achieve the new look. The corset remained indispensable, this time using the cinched waist to emphasize a buxom chest and rounded hips. Dresses exaggerated the full appearance by gathering fabric and padding into a bustle that rode on the buttocks to fill out a dress. As a final touch, heels became ever higher, forcing women to thrust forward their breasts and push out their derrieres into a newly fashionable S shape. Such practices so tortured the female anatomy that many women suffered medically from the constrictive wear.

Why the change in gender ideals, from "slender" to "voluptuous"? We have already seen one avenue of evolution: Americans were exposed to a mix of high-art paintings from Europe, theater troupes, and fashion magazines. Feminist Margaret Sanger recalled that as a young woman in the 1890s, she and her high school classmates compared their body proportions with the full-figured actresses pictured on cigarette cards. But beyond such cultural influences, the American population was changing socially. In an urbanizing and industrializing world, many newly well-to-do Americans of lower-class or immigrant backgrounds preserved a preference for full-figured women and stout men. In addition, an urban subculture flourished among prostitutes, in the theatrical world, and in the upper and working classes, in which a voluptuous female body was associated with sensuality.

As gender images for women evolved, masculine ideals changed as well. Men in the 1870s and 1880s also began to prize weight as a symbol of solidity and wealth. Gaining that heft proved no problem for the affluent, who had come to delight in large meals with many courses. But as with women, the ideal of a heavier man also reflected the values of working-class immigrants. During his heydey in the 1880s, prizefighter John L. Sullivan was celebrated as "the finest specimen of physical development in the world." Sullivan showed off his physique in theaters, where he would stride onstage and challenge all comers, announcing, "My name's John L. Sullivan and I can lick any son-of-a-bitch alive." To present-day sensibilities, the fighter's appearance seems hardly overwhelming. His frame is large and his weight ample, but his physique is not particularly well defined. Yet he reflected the ideals of the day: heavy, yet well built.

Only a year after the photograph on page 443 was taken of Sullivan, the definition of what constituted "the finest specimen of physical development" changed radically with the arrival from Europe of strongman Eugen Sandow. Sandow's physique made Sullivan's appear flabby by comparison, and in his cross-country theater tours, Sandow not only lifted huge barbells but supported a wooden platform on his shoulders, onto which multiple people balanced.

Sandow's public appearances were distinguished from Sullivan's by an aura of middle- and upper-class refinement, which the newcomer projected whether wearing tights or adorned in classic Roman sandals and fig leaf. Even so, when Sandow appeared at public receptions in mixed company, the atmosphere was charged. "I want you to feel how hard these muscles are,"

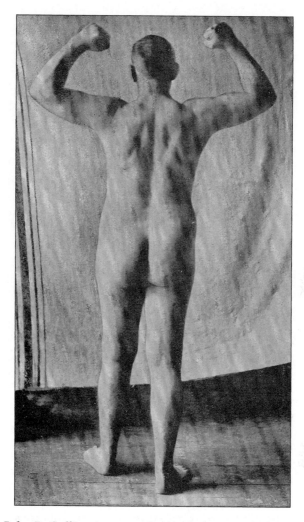

Prizefighter John L. Sullivan was examined and photographed in 1892 by Dudley Sargent, a scientist who championed physical fitness and was director of Harvard University's Hemenway Gymnasium. Sargent praised Sullivan's "large trunk" as "a reservoir of vital action" and his "powerful . . . thighs as a basis of support."

he encouraged a group of women. "As I stop before you, I want each of you to pass the palm of your hand across my chest." The conclusion by observers was painfully self-evident. Once New Yorkers had witnessed Eugen Sandow, wrote one reporter, they "will realize what a wretched, scrawny creature the usual well-built young gentleman is compared with the perfect man."

"Wretched, scrawny creature"—there was a hint, in the commentary, that American men had much to worry about. Indeed, by 1893 many influential citizens had become anxious about the social consequences of an increasingly

Wearing tights and Roman sandals, to provide a classical touch, Eugen Sandow awes a reception of American gentlemen and ladies. When asked by Sandow to "pass the palm of your hand across my chest," one woman demurred. "Oh, please—never mind." "Ah, but you must," Sandow rejoined. "These muscles, madam, are hard as iron itself, I want you to convince yourself of the fact." According to one reporter, she gasped, "It's unbelievable!" and staggered back.

industrial nation. As American cities swelled, once-vigorous farmers were turning into effete urban residents. The new corporate economy had created a class of managers and clerks whose daily routines involved the exercise of brain rather than brawn. As one observer commented, "The middle class is becoming a salaried class, and rapidly losing the economic independence of former days." Then, too, the new wave of immigrants from southern and eastern Europe provoked concern among native-born Americans, both as a competing source of cheap labor and a harmful cultural influence. One observer wondered whether industrial cities were filling up with "beaten men from beaten races, representing the worst failures in the struggle for existence." Prophets of gloom warned that the nation's Anglo-Saxon population faced potential "race suicide."

Historian John Kasson suggests that the celebrity status of Eugen Sandow reflected many Americans' anxieties. When Sandow arrived for his first tour, in the summer of 1893, the nation had begun a downward plunge into the worst economic depression the nation had yet experienced. Banks and small businesses were failing across the country, and thousands of citizens found themselves unemployed. If Americans were to survive both the short-term crisis of economic depression and the long-term threats of a new industrial world, men would need the kind of strength Sandow so confidently radiated. And this quest for masculinity was spread in many ways, not least through a Protestant movement known as "Muscular Christianity." That movement offered a doctrine of manly physical health that walked hand in hand with spiritual morality. Muscular Christianity gave birth to the YMCA—Young Men's Christian Association—whose branches in cities across the country offered exercise and sports programs intended to control destructive physical urges and thereby ensure public order.

On the political stage, the new ideal of an aggressive, even belligerent masculinity was embodied in the person of Theodore Roosevelt, who, as we saw in the fight over meatpacking reform, popularized the ideal of the strenuous life. As a young man, doctors had warned Roosevelt that he had a weak heart and should limit himself to a sedentary existence. He chose, unsurprisingly, to defy the doctors. Through exercise he imposed a powerful body on his formerly thin frame. Whether as a collegiate boxer, western cowboy, Rough Rider, or big-game hunter, Roosevelt flaunted his masculine vigor.

Thus the 1890s were a time in which men were especially receptive to gender redefinitions. Several historians have noted how much the rhetoric of masculinity framed the debate as the United States went to war with Spain in 1898. When a mysterious explosion sank the U.S. battleship *Maine* in Havana harbor, Senator Richard R. Kenny of Delaware exploded over the insult. "American manhood and American chivalry give back the answer that innocent blood shall be avenged," he declaimed. The country should take up arms, insisted Illinois Representative James R. Mann, not because of some "fancied slight" or "commercial wrong," but "because it has become necessary to fight if we would uphold our manhood." Newspaper cartoons, historian Kristin Hoganson has pointed out, were full of masculine imagery. In one drawing, a determined Uncle Sam spoils for a fight as he rips his jacket from his chest. Those skeptical of war, including President William McKinley, were portrayed as timid women.

Perhaps significantly, some women were not at all timid in condemning the war. In their view Congress was too eager—and too male—to do anything but fight. Alice Stone Blackwell, editor of the prosuffrage *Woman's Journal*, put it bluntly: "Assuming for the sake of argument that this war is . . . utterly inexcusable . . . it is a Congress of men that has declared it."

One reason men may have been so anxious about their masculinity was that women like Blackwell were challenging their dominance of the public sphere. Indeed, Blackwell was only one of many female reformers who rejected the notion that women belonged at home and that men alone were fit to manage government. Activists, proclaiming the arrival of the "New Woman," looked to feminine virtue to temper the corrupt male domination of the political system. Reformers such as Jane Addams pushed for opportunities to enter into a

Off comes his coat—now look out!—*Minneapolis Journal.*

"Off comes his jacket—now look out!" reads the caption for this political cartoon (*left*) appearing at the time of the Spanish American War. Theodore Roosevelt (*right*), who risked his life and won fame at the Battle of San Juan Hill, is shown with his jacket off too—in a photo taken when he was younger and a member of Harvard's rowing team. Masculinity was a virtue much prized in the 1890s.

"larger life" beyond the domestic sphere. For some, that meant going to an academically rigorous women's college, such as Vassar or Bryn Mawr, or to coeducational schools. Graduates could embark on professional careers as teachers, librarians, nurses, or even, occasionally, as physicians. Other women found employment in factories and offices. Addams inspired a movement to clean cities of disease, filth, and corrupt politicians.

The assertiveness of such confident women was reflected in yet another change in body ideals. The New Woman championed physical exercise as well as a slender figure—all part of a larger redefinition of attitudes not only about sexuality and marriage, but also, as Lois Banner noted, "what it meant to be female in general, and about female achievement in particular." Actress Lillie Langtry set the new standard. Many critics noted that with her long nose, full lips, and a trim, firmly toned body, Langtry, like Eugen Sandow, resembled a classical statue. The press revealed that she maintained her figure through diet and exercise.

Langtry's look did not please all American audiences. Yet many young women of the 1880s and 1890s followed her athletic example. In the 1870s women played a sedate form of tennis; by the late 1880s they had adopted the more aggressive male style of using an overhand serve and rushing the net. Women's colleges began to include more vigorous sports and calisthenics. And nothing did more to promote exercise and physical activity for

The clothing of these female bicyclists makes a strong statement of independence in this photo taken in Denver around 1900. Note that knickerbockers—divided skirts—are needed, since the bicycle frames include crossbars. The women's shirtwaists reflect a style popularized around the turn of the century in the drawings of Charles Dana Gibson. His stylish "Gibson girls" were widely admired as being "symbolic of a wholesome, healthy, utterly American girl," Gibson's sister once explained. The typical Gibson girl "liked sports, was a little ahead of her time, definitely athletic. . . . Importantly, she carved a new kind of femininity suggestive of emancipation."

women than the newfound popularity of the bicycle. By 1893 almost a million Americans, a good number of whom were women, were riding bicycles.

While other athletic activities took place out of the public eye, women on bicycles put themselves on display. In effect, they made a feminist statement. On their bikes they left the domestic sphere behind to enter a public world of work and recreation. In the process they gained greater mobility and modeled a new independence. Riding astride, as men did, they broke an old taboo that had restricted most female horseback riders to the sidesaddle. The new riding and exercise fads required looser clothing such as split skirts, popularly referred to as "knickerbockers."

If, then, gender is "embodied" in a variety of ways for both men and women, it becomes easier to understand culture-bound diseases as the extremes of those embodiments. In the late nineteenth century, increasing numbers of men and women suffered from what doctors of the time referred to as neurasthenia, an ailment whose symptoms were both physical and spiritual.

Sufferers complained of nervous exhaustion, dyspepsia (chronic indigestion), depressed moods, insomnia, headaches, asthma, and loss of weight. Among men, Anglo-Saxons from the social elite seemed most susceptible to the onset of lassitude and nervous anxiety. Among women, symptoms of neurasthenia included the self-starvation and emaciation characteristic of anorexia. Indeed, around 1870 the first modern cases of anorexia nervosa were reported in London and Paris.

The spread of another disorder, hysteria, suggests that women especially found themselves "in conflict with the times." How would they choose between the incompatible demands of a voluptuous fullness and a slender athleticism? Between the Victorian ideal of a submissive, home-centered women and the professional independence of the New Woman? While neurasthenia troubled both men and women, hysteria afflicted women almost exclusively, again largely from the upper and middle classes. Sufferers exhibited a baffling array of symptoms that included fainting spells, seizures, sensory disturbances such as loss of hearing or blindness, and even paralysis. Examination of hysterics seldom provided any physical cause. But historian Carroll Smith-Rosenberg has suggested that like neurasthenia, hysteria offered women a socially sanctioned "loophole" through which they could express anger and frustration with their culture's conflicting pressures. As Richard Gordon observed, the symptoms of hysteria "exaggerated the stereotypes of femininity: they were dramatic, emotional, and conformed to the ideal of female vulnerability and weakness." They allowed women to express their sense of powerlessness in a male-dominated culture yet also assert some control over their lives by denying unwanted sexual demands or isolating themselves from an abusive husband.

GENDER IN THE LATE TWENTIETH CENTURY

Having seen how supposedly innate gender ideals shifted during the late nineteenth century, we can now return to the late twentieth century—to look at a remarkably similar evolution.

For women, the changing social context can be readily sketched. By the mid-1950s the independent women of the prewar era had been constrained by a cult of suburban domesticity, as we saw in Chapter 14. Clothes reinforced that feminine ideal. Gone were the loose outfits and tight bodies championed by the bicycle-riding New Woman or working Rosie the Riveter. French fashion designer Christian Dior introduced the "new look," with narrow waistlines emphasizing shapely hips and a full bosom. Like their late-nineteenth-century grandmothers, women of the 1950s were encouraged to wear constricting foundation garments to achieve the desired shapeliness. Shoe heels became higher and toes pointier. Once again women had to walk with shoulders and buttocks back and breasts thrust forward. The young starlet Marilyn Monroe exemplified the new image.

The new look of the 1950s, launched by French designer Christian Dior, marked a return to the fashion styles and attitudes of the 1880s. Girdles had replaced corsets as a means of cinching the waistline, and while the skirts had no bustle, they were usually long and stylishly flared. The jackets were fitted, narrow in the shoulders, and snug in the bodice. Gone was the casual, comfortable fit of the New Woman; now high, spiked heels were in fashion along with ornamental hats.

The postwar world also provided a new social context for the male body. The return to peace inaugurated a quarter century of economic expansion, with the growth of suburban housing and a full-blown consumer culture that had been dampened for two decades by depression and war. Businesses were increasingly yoked in conglomerates, uniting multitudes of sedentary white-collar workers within large bureaucracies. By 1950 the number of office workers bound to desk jobs had jumped to 37 percent of the workforce.

With a more prosperous life within reach thanks to the postwar boom, the establishment ideal of masculinity centered less on a man's looks and more on the work he did and the money and power he wielded. The ideal male was not particularly young, muscular, or virile, but rather a "symbolic father" with a touch of gray in his sideburns and wrinkles that suggested wisdom. Indeed, men who worried too much about their appearance were considered vain or effeminate. "A woman carries a vanity case and a man carries a briefcase," opined the *Saturday Evening Post* smugly in 1954. If men lost

"A woman carries a vanity case and a man carries a briefcase," opined the *Saturday Evening Post* smugly in 1954. In a booming economy where men's status came from their role as family provider, an image of solid prosperity was paramount. Although comic books carried bodybuilding advertisements, the family breadwinner was permitted a double chin and a loose-fitting suit.

their hair, they were expected to simply ignore their baldness. Ill-fitting toupees were a staple of comedy routines. On the other hand, hair that was *too* long was rejected as unmanly. The crew cut, used in the army during World War II, went mainstream in the civilian culture of the fifties. Given the social dynamics, historian Lynne Luciano concluded, success came to those who were "clean cut and [looked] like the fellow next door—who was assumed to be white, Anglo-Saxon, and altogether average."

Being average also meant putting on pounds. For most of the twentieth century, few men worried about excess weight. An ample girth often accompanied financial success. And since earnings mattered more than physical appearance, men had little incentive to slim down—until research began to demonstrate a connection between obesity and heart disease. By the 1950s heart attacks had become the number one cause of death for middle-aged men. "We are digging our graves with our teeth," one researcher warned. Overweight employees developed more health problems than their thinner counterparts. Popular prejudice against fat hardened to the point that one national magazine described a beer belly as "the kiss of death to any man who seriously wants to get ahead in his career."

A historian might hypothesize that the increase in obesity and its connection to heart disease would spur a craze for dieting and exercise—a craze that might lead to an epidemic of body dysmorphias. Many companies did introduce programs to help their executives take off excess weight. Presidents Dwight Eisenhower and John F. Kennedy shared a concern that unfit citizens could not compete successfully in the cold war struggle between the

United States and the Soviet Union. Yet this particular concern did not spread to the general population—for the simple reason that Americans seemed to pay little attention to the call for fitness. According to a 1959 Gallup poll, fully a quarter of American men remained entirely sedentary, not even participating in less physically demanding sports like golf and bowling. If Americans were feeling stress over their physique during the 1950s and early 1960s, they did not show it by developing culture-bound disorders such as neurasthenia, hysteria, anorexia, bulimia, or muscle dysmorphia. One key factor missing from the social context was tension over gender roles. Ideals of masculinity and femininity remained relatively fixed during the two decades following World War II.

What happened after the mid-1960s to undermine masculine and feminine stereotypes? The years following proved to be exceptionally turbulent. Not since the Civil War had the United States been so divided, as Americans disputed almost every facet of their society, whether in civil rights, politics, music, or the lifestyles of a youthful counterculture. Gender roles were especially contested. The assault began, as we saw in Chapter 14, when Betty Friedan attacked the cult of domesticity in *The Feminine Mystique*. By decade's end, feminism had emerged as major force in American politics. Gender relations, feminists argued, needed to be reconstituted. No longer would women accept male assertions that differences between men and women were inevitable reflections of biological destiny.

Addressing the growing number of single workingwomen, Helen Gurley Brown published *Sex and the Single Girl* in 1962. Her book championed both economic and sexual independence. "A job gives a single woman something to be," Brown wrote. Even if the Single Girl intended some day to marry, Brown urged her to enjoy her sexual freedom and to play the field—much as men did. The advice became more practical with the introduction of the birth control pill in the early 1960s. Fear of unwanted pregnancy had long inhibited women from casual or recreational sex. But now, Brown argued, the paradigm had shifted: it no longer required that boys chase girls, when girls possessed the power to chase boys.

In 1970 a coalition of feminist groups organized the Women's Strike for Equality to commemorate the fiftieth anniversary of the women's suffrage amendment. The strike offered women an opportunity to step out of their ordinary roles and protest against sexism, whether in the workplace or at home. Strike organizers from a variety of groups agreed on three demands that would become the core feminist agenda: equal opportunity in work and in education, the right to child care, and the right to abortion. Most feminists also supported an equal rights amendment to the Constitution.

The strike mobilized the largest number of women since the marches on behalf of suffrage. In New York City, between 20,000 and 50,000 women left work to parade up Fifth Avenue. Signs such as "Don't Cook Dinner—Starve a Rat Today" and "Don't Iron While the Strike is Hot" caught the attention of the news media. Most commentary, almost always from male reporters and newscasters, was condescending. The three television networks each

"Equal Pay for Equal Work" was a core demand of the feminist movement in the 1960s and 1970s. At this women's liberation demonstration held in August 1970, fashions had changed markedly since the Progressive Era marches for woman suffrage. Instead of long dresses of the purest white, common in protests of the early 1900s, women of the 1970s appeared in short skirts, slacks, and jeans. Hair styles included Afros (*center left*). Fashions of the time thus allowed women to represent their bodies to reflect their cultural and political values.

featured a story about West Virginia Senator Jennings Randolph, who had labeled feminists "bra-less bubbleheads." In part as a response to such coverage, feminist Gloria Steinem launched *Ms.* magazine to address issues and ideas from a female point of view. Despite predictions that it would fail, *Ms.* developed a wide audience.

While feminists pursued the politics of gender, other social trends were accelerating the liberation of women. Between 1960 and 1980 the percentage of women in the labor force jumped from 35 to over 50 percent—the largest increase in any twenty-year period. By 1980, over 50 percent of all college undergraduates were women, with female enrollments in graduate professional schools also rising rapidly. The increased education and employment translated into greater independence.

Men too felt pressure as gender roles and masculine images were redefined. Early skirmishes began in the 1950s with long-haired cultural icons such as James Dean, star of *Rebel Without a Cause*, and, of course, Elvis Presley. Both evoked a hairstyle popularly associated with lower-class bikers and hoods. But male hair became a veritable cultural battleground with the ascent of the Beatles as a rock-and-roll phenomenon. The Fab Four's longish hair, mod clothes, and zaniness defined a new masculine style that was youthful rather than macho, irreverent without being overtly rebellious. By the end of the 1960s rock stars had displaced movie stars as the public figures defining the male image. Mick Jagger of the Rolling Stones rejected the idea that "being masculine means looking clean, close-cropped, and ugly." Men too could be beautiful, even if they had to give up their barbers for hairstylists in order to achieve the new look. African American men and women found an alternative way to make long hair into a cultural statement. To express racial pride they gave up the wavy processing or short cuts that mirrored Anglo styles and let their hair grow into bushy Afros. Many whites with naturally kinky or curly hair imitated the look.

Already contested by the youthful rebels of the sixties, the predominant masculine ideals of the 1950s suffered a double blow in the 1970s. The first came from a downturn in the economy. Real wages, which had risen steadily after World War II, dropped sharply as recession crippled the nation. The American defeat in Vietnam also challenged the ideal of masculine domination. Popular culture frequently portrayed veterans of the war as the tortured victims of combat fatigue struggling with drug addiction, unemployment, and chronic nightmares.

The new sexual freedom of the 1960s did not make men and women more secure about what it meant to be masculine or feminine. Some men felt threatened by women who took the lead in sexual affairs. Women in turn discovered that sexual liberation and women's liberation were not the same thing. More often than not, "free sex" meant sex without any emotional commitments, and it was all too easy for "liberated" men to treat women as objects of desire rather than as potential partners. Historian Barbara Ehrenreich called such attitudes a "flight from commitment." *Ms.* magazine agreed: "The Sexual Revolution and the Women's Movement are at Polar Opposites. Women have been liberated only from the right to say 'no.'"

Was it mere coincidence that an epidemic of body dysmorphia emerged after Americans had entered a period of uncertainty about what it meant to be male or female? The evidence offered by clinicians and social scientists suggests that cultural conflict over gender did contribute to the rise of body dysmorphias.

Once again, examine how gender ideals "embodied" social trends. The rise in feminist consciousness coincided with the return of the thin ideal for women. Symbolically, the changeover could be charted in the making of the 1961 film *Breakfast at Tiffany's*, in which the character Holly Golightly, an independent young social butterfly, proves willing to sacrifice her freedom—but only when she finds the right (meaning "rich") man. Holly had a good deal in common with Helen Gurley Brown's Single Girl. Truman Capote, the author of *Breakfast at Tiffany's*, imagined the full-figured Marilyn Monroe in the role. In the end, however, Audrey Hepburn was cast: an elegant, slender actress whose waiflike vulnerability, as much as her thinness, appealed to audiences. Yet beneath Holly's cheerful veneer was a troubled woman with low self-esteem, a potential poster girl for anorexia. The trend

Audrey Hepburn's slender, almost waiflike appearance was applauded by a culture of prosperity, in which thinness contributed to social status. Ironically, as a child Hepburn had suffered from malnourishment. Her interest as an adult in the charitable causes of famine relief and aid to refugees was not coincidental.

toward thinness reached its apogee in the popularity of a new generation of super-thin media icons personified by Twiggy, the aptly named fashion model who weighed a mere 92 pounds.

Thus the late 1960s offered the same confusing signals encountered by Victorian women. On the one hand, feminists claimed a new power and greater equality. At the same time, American culture devalued the traditional female careers in which nurturing played a central role. Nursing, teaching, and social work—which the New Woman of the 1890s had embraced—remained low-paying professions with little status. That reality pushed ambitious women toward what were previously male-dominated fields such as law, medicine, and business. Yet to succeed in a male domain, many women believed they had to adopt the masculine values of toughness, authority, and control—all the while remembering to appear pleasingly feminine, attractive, and submissive, as many of their male office mates expected.

How to reconcile such contradictory demands? The pop culture of the 1980s offered up the "superwoman" ideal, a term coined by journalist Ellen Goodman and embraced in another Helen Gurley Brown manifesto, *Having It All* (1982). The superwoman was ambitious, capable, and successful, yet nurturing, caring and sexually attractive.[2] Above all, the superwoman was thin. Two research studies charted the importance of thinness by comparing a woman's average weight, based on government health and nutrition surveys, against the average weight of Miss America contestants and *Playboy* centerfolds. As the 1960s gave way to the 1970s and 1980s, the two trend lines headed in opposite directions. While the average weight of most American women (and men) was gradually rising, the average weight of Miss America contestants and *Playboy* centerfolds was dropping. In short, the real and the ideal were diverging.

An extreme example of the pressures arising out of such conflicts could be seen by following the careers of ballet dancers, whose world was intensely competitive *and* required maintaining an extremely slender shape—the superwoman's dilemma in a nutshell. At one ballet school, where "weigh-ins" occurred every Monday, a student commented, "You should have seen this place on Sunday nights. . . . Nobody would eat anything past twelve noon, and the whole second floor bathroom would smell so bad [from the purging] that you couldn't use it." Several studies indicated that the incidence of anorexia among ballet students and performers was much higher than among the general population. But that is what Gordon's and Devereux's model of culture-bound disease would have predicted, since the world of ballet took the cultural ideals of the superwoman to their extremes.

If women during these years felt at a competitive disadvantage, it might seem surprising that males too began experiencing body disorders. Yet men faced a crisis of masculinity similar to the one a hundred years earlier. More and more occupations had become sedentary, as a growing service economy eliminated high-salary jobs while "outsourcing" other employment to low-wage countries abroad. Competition for work also increased as immigration spiked in the 1980s and 1990s. At the same time, more women entered the workforce. By the year 2000 many more women claimed jobs in the once-predominantly male domains of law, medicine, the military, as well as professional sports and politics. Thirty percent of working women earned more than their husbands. Women comprised 57 percent of all college graduates; 49 percent of PhD's; and 43 percent, 46 percent, and 69 percent of all graduating physicians, lawyers, and veterinarians, respectively. Experience and seniority no longer guaranteed a man the same secure future as in the 1950s.

---

2. The times seem not to have changed much. A study by Duke University released in 2003 conjured up a similarly daunting ideal: women students there reported feeling under pressure "to be 'effortlessly perfect': smart, accomplished, fit, beautiful and popular, all without visible effort," according to the *New York Times*.

Sports fans ranked bodybuilding thirty-fifth in popularity in one survey taken in the mid-1970s; even tractor-pulling ranked higher. The 1977 documentary *Pumping Iron*, about Arnold Schwarzenegger, changed that. Schwarzenegger stressed the health benefits to the sport. And he was not only fast on his feet but humorous and quick with his tongue. But for those serious about the sport, bodybuilding required a ten-year commitment of four hours a day and at least three hundred days a year in order to develop one's physique fully.

As women gained economic clout, they began to attach less importance to a man's ability as a provider. A female journalist remarked, "with women growing ever more financially independent, aspiring suitors are discovering that they must bring more to the table than a well-endowed wallet if they expect to win (and keep) the fair maiden." "What is new," added another social scientist, "is that women are more likely to leave a marriage when they fail to get what they want." A survey of personal ads placed by women "in search of men" revealed that nearly one third emphasized particular physical traits such as "muscular," "vgl" (very good looking), "no beer bellies," and "must have hair." Or as a poster at a health club bluntly proclaimed, "No Pecs, No Sex."

By the end of the 1970s men began to respond to the new female expectations. One example was a surge in the popularity of bodybuilding, given impetus by the 1977 documentary *Pumping Iron*, starring Arnold Schwarzenegger.

Over time, G.I. Joe dolls and other military action figures underwent a striking metamorphosis in terms of body images. The toy on the left, issued in 1982, still appears relatively normal in its musculature. By 1992 (*center*) the figure had begun to bulk up, but it seems diminutive when set side by side with the figure on the right, produced in 1995.

Schwarzenegger brought charisma to an activity once derided as a subculture of narcissists and muscle-bound dolts. And in his wake came other models of the new hypermasculine ideal, including the brawlers of the Worldwide Wrestling Federation, professional football players, and the actor Sylvester Stallone, whose *Rambo* films about Vietnam we examined in Chapter 16.

For millions of adherents, bodybuilding was both a competitive sport and an approach to health and fitness. But for some the sport morphed (the term is appropriate, given its toy-warrior associations) into a preoccupation leading to muscle dysmorphia. As with other culture-bound disorders, the symptoms appeared at the sport's extremes. Bodybuilding reflected values American culture had celebrated through a whole generation of action movie heroes and toys such as G.I. Joe, a doll whose appearance progressed from being modestly fit (upon the toy's introduction in the 1960s) to Joe's hugely muscled physique of the 1990s. But men consumed with attaining hypermasculinity might easily spend four hours a day working out, leaving that much less time to spare for work and friendship outside the gym. Physical injury was common, and the fat-free, protein rich diet caused a variety of disorders, including kidney failure. Many bodybuilders employed steroids to achieve a "cut" or "ripped" look, but like anorexics, those men suffering from muscle dysmorphia found it difficult to maintain an objective sense of themselves. They remained convinced that no matter how "pumped up" they became, their physique was too small.

CONSUMPTION AND RESTRAINT IN AMERICAN SOCIETY

Interestingly, bigorexics shared with both anorexics and bulimics a phobia of becoming fat. This fear had a broader social context, for in a society that increasingly valued a body that was either slender or well muscled, statistical surveys indicated that Americans were becoming the fattest people on earth. By 2000, over 20 percent of the population could be classified as obese and a majority of Americans were at least slightly overweight.

Was there a broader social context connecting the epidemic of obesity to the spread of body dysmorphias? During the 1990s Richard Gordon became increasingly uncomfortable with the term "eating disorders"; it seemed to him too narrow a diagnosis. While abnormal eating patterns were certainly one part of the mix, most patients seemed far more concerned with body shape than with food or eating. Patients tended to view fat as almost morally repulsive. As the patient of another researcher noted, "if you are thin they don't think that you are rich and that your life is too easy."

Given the *moral* tone of this condemnation—that fat is not just ugly but somehow self-indulgent or slothful—we may legitimately wonder whether body dysmorphia was a reaction in part against a broader culture of consumption and excess, for which obesity was only a powerful symbol. In that light, historian Hillel Schwartz has linked the stigma imposed on fat people to concerns with overproduction, excessive materialism, and waste. The families of those with body dysmorphia take special pride in their ability to restrain their consumption amidst so much abundance. As they engage in a puritanical ethic of work and self-control, they believe that fat people, in contrast, have given way to lazy excess.

That tension has been present across centuries of American history, with a Protestant ethic of self-restraint at war with the all-American pursuit of material gain. Puritans condemned a love of luxury; prohibitionists fought against the excessive use of alcohol; conservationists condemned the wasteful exploitation of natural resources; and the counterculture of the 1960s, harking back to Henry David Thoreau, rejected society's excessive materialism. Yet historians have traced, across these same centuries, the rise of consumer-driven societies powering the economies of the industrialized West and, increasingly, the entire globe. Consumption is deeply embedded in the American dream, and the tensions arising out of it may help us understand the extremes of culture-bound disorders of the body.

For Richard Gordon, as for us, establishing historical context has been crucial in illuminating how gender differences operate in society. Those who live only in the present tend to universalize their circumstances. They assume that the way things *are* must be the way they always have been, especially when matters of biology are involved, as with gender. Women "want first and foremost to be womanly companions of men and to be mothers," insisted Harvard social scientist Joseph Rheingold in 1964, in a decade when women would take to the streets to prove him wrong. Our own comparison of body imagery indicates that neurasthenia, hysteria, anorexia, bulimia, and muscle dysmorphia cannot be understood without taking into account the multiple interrelations of society, economy, and culture.

This chapter has traveled a long road: from a single therapist in a "meat-loaf and gravy town" to a view of American history, contrasting the trends of consumption versus self-control and restraint. It has also reinforced a theme echoing through these pages: that history involves seeking out connections and contexts that are *not* obvious at first glance. When anorexic young women came to his office in the early 1980s, Richard Gordon had no idea where their concerns with body image might lead him. He sought out clues to their disorders not only in their personal case histories, but also in the broader cultural landscape.

So it has been for the authors of this book. Whether exploring why the oral histories of freedpeople were shaped by a society still segregated in the 1930s, how the meatpacking scandals of Chicago illuminated the political tactics of Theodore Roosevelt, or how a payroll robbery in South Braintree, Massachusetts, uncovered deep questions about the rule of law in American society, our topics have all linked individuals to their wider world and the larger forces that shape our destinies. We believe people need the sense of connectedness that history provides. Without it we would find ourselves adrift in a landscape where the events of our time seem random, and lacking a coherent path to the future.

Additional Reading

The issue of body image breaks down into a number of subtopics that include eating disorders, weight and diet, masculinity and femininity, popular culture, and the politics of gender. Psychologists, anthropologists, doctors, physiologists, and historians have all contributed to our understanding of this complex topic. Because the inspiration for this essay came in large part from conversations with Richard Gordon, Professor of Psychology at Bard College, we suggest that anyone interested in anorexia, bulimia, and the cultural context of eating disorders should turn to his pioneering book *Eating Disorders: Anatomy of a Social Epidemic*, 2d ed. (Malden, MA, 2000). Gordon has contributed, along with fellow editors Melanie Katzman and Mervat Nasser, to a collection of essays, *Eating Disorders and Cultures in Transition* (New York, 2001), that explores the problem in a transnational context. Harrison G. Pope Jr., Katherine Phillips, and Roberto Olivardia's *The Adonis Complex: The Secret Crisis of Male Body Obsession* (New York, 2000) addresses body-image pathologies in men; in many ways this book supports Gordon's analysis of cultural factors in anorexia and bulimia.

Susan Bordo, *Unbearable Weight: Feminism, Western Culture, and the Body* (Berkeley, CA, 1993) explores in depth the ways in which the female body has been represented and understood in aesthetic, political, and philosophical terms. Bordo's essays have the virtue of being both insightful and a pleasure to read. More recently in *The Male Body: A New Look at Men in Public and Private* (New York, 1999) she has given to maleness—including essays on the penis, male beauty standards, and sexual harassment—the same critical and engaging reading she did to the female body. Like Bordo, Joan Jacobs Brumberg, *Fasting Girls: The Emergence of Anorexia Nervosa as a Modern Disease* (New York, 1988) sees the cultural origins of the disorder but insists that ultimately the problem is medical and must be treated as such. In *The Body Project: An Intimate History of American Girls* (New York, 1997), Brumberg places contemporary societal and psychological pressures on adolescent girls and their body images in a historical context. She identifies an evolving notion of bodily perfection nurtured by marketers of products that deal with such problems as pimples, menstruation, and nascent sexuality.

Historians have long been interested in race, ethnicity, social class, and gender; more recently they have begun to focus on how body image is refracted through those categories. Our essay obviously gained much of its understanding of the shifting standards of female beauty from Lois Banner, *American Beauty* (Chicago, 1983), a sweeping study that is particularly rich on the Victorian era and the emergence of the "Culture of Beauty" in the early twentieth century. Nancy Etcoff, *The Survival of the Prettiest: The Science of Beauty* (New York, 1999) argues provocatively that beauty has a biological function and plays a critical role in the Darwinian struggle. Joan Wallach Scott, *Gender and the Politics of History*, rev. ed. (New York, 1999) offers insight into feminist theory and the uses of gender as a category for doing history. John Kasson, *Houdini, Tarzan, and the Perfect Man: The White Male Body and the Challenge of Modernity* (New York, 2001) identifies the crisis in racial consciousness at the end of the nineteenth century that created a preoccupation with the "white male body." Kasson has some interesting insights into neurasthenia. Lynne Luciano, *Looking Good: Male Body Image in Modern America* (New York, 2001), while breezy in style, offers a compelling explanation of why contemporary men have become more preoccupied with their looks. E. Anthony Rotundo, *American Manhood: Transformations in Masculinity from the Revolution to the Modern Era* (New York, 1993) examines the many historical contexts from which masculine values have emerged. In a similar vein, Milette Shamir and Jennifer Travis, eds., *Boys Don't Cry: Rethinking Narratives of Masculinity and Emotion in the U.S.* (New York, 2002) is a collection of essays that explore the stereotype of the emotionally stifled American male. To gain a better understanding of hysteria we relied on Carroll Smith-Rosenberg, "The Hysterical Woman: Sex Roles in 19th Century America," *Social Research*, 39 (1972), pp. 652–678. Brett Silverstein and Deborah Perlick, *The Cost of Competence: Why Inequality Causes Depression, Eating Disorders, and Illness in Women* (New York, 1995) provides insight into a range of disorders including hysteria, neurasthenia, and anxiety.

Diet and eating habits form another dimension of body-image pathologies. These are largely the province of anthropologists and social historians. Sidney Mintz has done much to explain "why we eat what we eat and what it means" in *Tasting Food, Tasting Freedom: Excursions into Eating, Culture, and the Past* (Boston, 1996) and *Sweetness and Power: The Place of Sugar in Modern History* (New York, 1985). Carole M. Counihan, *The Anthropology of Food and the Body: Gender, Meaning, and Power* (New York, 1999) takes a global approach to the gender politics of food. Anyone who is curious why Americans tend toward fat and the French remain thin and still eat *foie gras* and butter should read Peter Stearns, *Fat History: Bodies and Beauty in the Modern West* (New York, 1997). Harvey Levenstein, *Paradox of Plenty: A Social History of Eating* (New York, 1993) looks at the evolution of the American diet since the 1930s. Hillel Schwartz's *Never Satisfied: A Cultural History of Diets, Fantasies, and Fat* (New York, 1986) is sometimes anecdotal and funny about how bodies and food are central to our national culture. Finally, Greg Critser, *Fat Land: How Americans Became the Fattest People in the World* (New York, 2003) provides some intriguing explanations for the obesity crisis that threatens to become the nation's number one health problem.

Interactive Learning

The *Primary Source Investigator* provides materials that illustrate the changing physical ideals embodied by famous Americans such as Theodore Roosevelt, Harry Houdini, Arnold Schwarzenegger, and current athletes and performers. Several documents reveal the passion and the intensity of many advocates of physical culture, as well as the connections they made between such mundane activities as exercise and the very health and future of the American nation.

Credits

Chapter 1
Page 4: Library of Congress; p. 13:
Neimeyer Tabaksmuseum,
Groningen, The Netherlands; p. 18:
Library of Congress

Chapter 2
p. 34: Yale University, Sterling
Memorial Library; p. 44: By
Permission of The British Library
(Add. 32496 f. 51)

Chapter 3
p. 50: Jonathan Wallen Photography;
p. 53: John Trumbull, "The
Declaration of Independence." United
States Capitol Historical Society.
Photo: National Archives; p. 068:
Virginia Historical Society

Chapter 4
p. 73: © Pocumtuck Valley Memorial
Association, Deerfield MA. All rights
reserved. (Acc. no. 1960.17); p. 74L:
The New York Public Library; p.
74R: The New York Public Library;
p. 75: © Pocumtuck Valley Memorial
Association, Deerfield MA. All rights
reserved. (Acc. no. 1897.09); p. 77:
© Pocumtuck Valley Memorial
Association, Deerfield MA. All rights
reserved. (Acc. no. 1999.13.507); p.
78: John Lewis Krimmel, "Quilting
Frolic," 1813. Courtesy, Winterthur

Museum, DE. (Acc. No.
1953.0178.002); p. 79: Old Sturbridge
Village, MA (Acc. No. B29098); p. 80:
John Lewis Krimmel, "Quilting
Frolic" (detail), 1813. Courtesy,
Winterthur Museum, DE. (Acc. No.
1953.0178.002); p. 81: Courtesy of
Historic Deerfield. Photograph by
Amanda Merullo. (Acc. no. 1998.35);
p. 82: Hannah Barnard. Press
Cupboard, c.1710. The Henry Ford
Museum, Dearborn MI. (36.178.1);
p. 84: Courtesy of Historic Deerfield.
Photograph by Amanda Merullo.
(Acc. no. 56.140); p. 90: Old
Sturbridge Village, MA; p. 91: Old
Sturbridge Village, MA; p. 92: "There
Is No School Like the Family
School," from The Mother's Assistant
and Young Lady's Friend

Chapter 5
p. 101L: Collection of The University
of Wisconsin-Madison Archives;
p. 101R: The Huntington Library,
San Marico, California. (Box 58 #16);
p. 107: Library of Congress; p. 110:
Thomas Scully, "Andrew Jackson,"
c.1857. Library of Congress; p. 114:
Library of Congress; p. 118: Photo
Courtesy of Edward E. Ayer
Collection, The Newberry Library,
Chicago

Chapter 6

p. 125: Photo by D. F. Barry. The Denver Public Library, Western History Collection. (No. B-937); p. 130: Alfred Jacob Miller, "Prairie Fire," c.1847. Walters Art Gallery, Baltimore, Maryland. (Acc. no. 37.1940.198); p. 139: The National Library of Medicine/Visual Image Presentations; p. 141: Alfred Jacob Miller, "An Indian Girl (Sioux) on Horseback," 1837. Walters Art Gallery, Baltimore, Maryland. (Acc. no. 37.1940.198); p. 143: John Carbutt, "Wagon trains crossing the plains to Montana with Captain Fisk's expedition," 1866. © Collection of The New York Historical Society (Neg. no. 67962)

Chapter 7

p. 151: Library of Congress; p. 153: Library of Congress; p. 155: Library of Congress; p. 156: Library of Congress; p. 169: Library of Congress; p. 171L: Library of Congress; p. 171R: Library of Congress

Chapter 8

p. 178: Library of Congress; p. 179: John Jacob Omenhausser, "Guard Challenging Prisoner," 1864. © Collection of The New York Historical Society. (ae00045); p. 182: Library of Congress; p. 188: National Archives; p. 198: National Archives

Chapter 9

p. 214: Library of Congress; p. 216: Library of Congress; p. 219: Library of Congress; p. 220: William Henry Jackson, "Teton Range," 1872. National Archives; p. 223: Library of Congress; p. 225: Museum of the City of New York, The Jacob A. Riis Collection; p. 226: Museum of the City of New York, The Jacob A. Riis Collection; p. 227: Museum of the City of New York, The Jacob A. Riis

Collection; p. 228: Museum of the City of New York, The Jacob A. Riis Collection; p. 229: Museum of the City of New York, The Jacob A. Riis Collection

Chapter 10

p. 235: Library of Congress; p. 236: Library of Congress; p. 238L: Library of Congress; p. 238R: Library of Congress; p. 240: Library of Congress; p. 242: Library of Congress; p. 244: Library of Congress; p. 246: Scientific American, November 7, 1891/ Yale University, Sterling Memorial Library; p. 250: Library of Congress

Chapter 11

p. 263: Library of Congress; p. 270: Library of Congress; p. 271: National Archives; p. 273: Library of Congress; p. 283: Ben Shahn, "Bartolomeo Vanzetti and Nicola Sacco," from the Sacco-Vanzetti series. 1931–32. Gift of Abby Aldrich Rockefeller. The Museum of Modern Art, New York, NY. (144.1935) Photo: Digital Image © The Museum of Modern Art/Licensed by SCALA/Art Resource, NY. © Estate of Ben Shahn/ Licensed by VAGA, New York, NY

Chapter 12

p. 290: Kansas State Historical Society; p. 291: Library of Congress; p. 294L: Library of Congress; p. 294R: Library of Congress; p. 310: Courtesy of The Bancroft Library, University of California, Berkeley. (1945.007:4); p. 311: Copyright the Dorothea Lange collection, Oakland Museum of California, City of Oakland. Gift of Paul S. Taylor. (Acc. no. A67.137.7876); p. 313: Library of Congress

Chapter 13

p. 319: National Archives; p. 324: Library of Congress; p. 333L:

National Archives; p. 333R: National Archives; p. 338: National Archives; p. 340: National Archives; p. 342: National Archives

Chapter 14
p. 348: Time Life; p. 351: Printed by permission of the Norman Rockwell Family Agency. Copyright c. 1943 the Norman Rockwell Family Entities; p. 357: © 1956 SEPS: Licensed by Curtis Publishing, Indianapolis, IN. All rights reserved. www.curtispublishing.com; p. 365: CBS Photo Archive; p. 367: CBS Photo Archive

Chapter 15
p. 375: AP/Wide World Photos; p. 380: Jimilu Mason, "On the Run." LBJ Library Collection. Photograph by Frank Wolfe. © Jamilu Mason. All rights reserved; p. 383: National Archives; p. 388: © Bettmann/ CORBIS; p. 389: © Bettmann/ CORBIS

Chapter 16
p. 407: Film Still Archives/Museum of Modern Art, New York; p. 413: Life Magazine, © Time Warner; p. 417: Film Still Archives/Museum of

Modern Art, New York; p. 421: Film Still Archives/ Museum of Modern Art, New York; p. 426: Film Still Archives/Museum of Modern Art, New York

Chapter 17
p. 433: The Micheal Ochs Archives; p. 440: Smithsonian Institution, Division of Costumes; p. 441: © CORBIS; p. 443: The New York Public Library, Rare Book Collection; p. 444: The Newberry Library, Chicago; p. 446L: Houghton Library, Harvard University, The Theodore Roosevelt Collection; p. 446R: Houghton Library, Harvard University, The Theodore Roosevelt Collection; p. 447: Courtesy of the Colorado Historical Society, from the Lillybridge Collection. Gift of John Wernes; p. 449: Hulton Archive/ Getty Images; p. 450: © 1952 SEPS: Licensed by Curtis Publishing, Indianapolis, IN. All Rights Reserved. www.curtispublishing.com; p. 452: Stockphoto.com; p. 454: © Bettmann/CORBIS; p. 456: White Mountain Productions/The Kobal Collection; p. 457: Harrisson G. Pope; p. XV: Library of Congress

Index

Note: Page numbers followed by *n* indicate notes.